Effective Legal Negotiation and Settlement
SIXTH EDITION

Effective Legal Negotiation and Settlement

SIXTH EDITION

2009

CHARLES B. CRAVER
Freda H. Alverson Professor of Law
George Washington University

Matthew Bender & Company, Inc.

978-1-4224-2953-2

Library of Congress Cataloging-in-Publication Data

Craver, Charles B.
Effective legal negotiation and settlement / [Charles B. Craver]. -- 6th ed.
p. cm.
Includes index.
ISBN 978-1-4224-2953-2 (perfect bound) 1. Compromise (Law)--United States. 2. Negotiation. I.
Title.
KF9084.C7 2009
347.73'9--dc22
2008054388

Editorial Offices
744 Broad Street, Newark, NJ 07102 (973) 820-2000
201 Mission St., San Francisco, CA 94105-1831 (415) 908-3200
www.lexisnexis.com

MATTHEW◆BENDER

(2009–Pub.3038)

ACKNOWLEDGMENTS

It would be impossible to prepare a book on the negotiation process without relying substantially upon the theories and concepts articulated by many diverse scholars. During the years I have been a negotiator and a legal negotiating teacher, I have benefited greatly from the literature cited in the bibliography listed at the end of this book. I wish to express my appreciation to those writers and to acknowledge the fact that many of their ideas have influenced my understanding of the negotiation process. I must especially cite Professors Cornelius Peck and Robert Fletcher of the University of Washington (Peck & Fletcher, 1968) and Professor James J. White of the University of Michigan (White, 1967), who initially conceived and developed the concept of clinical negotiating courses. I must thank the hundreds of law students who have taken my Legal Negotiating course and the thousands of practicing lawyers who have participated in my Effective Legal Negotiation and Settlement programs who have provided me with new insights and interesting examples. Many of their thoughts have found expression in this book. I am also indebted to Professor Robert Condlin of the University of Maryland who has generously shared his cogent thoughts with me both in a joint teaching setting and through his writings (Condlin, 1992; Condlin, 1985). My former colleague Nancy Schultz and my ADR book coauthor Edward Brunet have provided both encouragement and valuable insights. I must finally thank Thomas Colosi, James Freund, Joseph Harbaugh, Laurence Sweeney, and Gerald Williams who have greatly enhanced my understanding of the negotiation process during jointly conducted continuing legal education programs. I would finally like to note the work of Mary Parker Follett whose work during the first half of the last century recognized the importance of integrative bargaining designed to generate mutually beneficial agreements — long before academics began to explore these concepts (Tone, 2003).

I would also like to thank Martin Latz of the Latz Negotiation Institute who developed ExpertNegotiator to assist professionals with their pre-negotiation preparation and their post-negotiation assessment. He has kindly made this site [www.ExpertNegotiator.com] available to law students on a no-fee basis to assist them with the learning process. I would encourage students to visit this site to see how they can use it to help them when they work on negotiation exercises.

ABOUT THE AUTHOR

Charles B. Craver is the Freda H. Alverson Professsor of Law at the George Washington University Law School where he regularly teaches a course on Legal Negotiating. He previously taught at the University of Illinois, the University of California at Davis, the University of Virginia, and the University of Florida. He has taught continuing legal education courses on the negotiation process and on alternative dispute resolutions procedures to over eighty thousand practitioners throughout the United States and in Canada, Mexico, England, Puerto Rico, Austria, Germany, Turkey, and the People's Republic of China. He has frequently lectured to judicial organizations on the mediation function. He was formerly associated with the law firm of Morrison & Foerster in San Francisco, where he specialized in employment law and litigation practice. Professor Craver is a member of the American Law Institute, the National Academy of Arbitrators, Association for Conflict Resolution, the Dispute Resolution, Criminal Law, and Labor and Employment Law Sections of the American Bar Association, the International Society for Labor and Social Security Law, and the American Arbitration Association. He has published numerous law review articles pertaining to dispute resolution and labor and employment law. He is the author of *Skills & Values: Legal Negotiating* (Lexis 2009), *The Intelligent Negotiator* (Prima/Crown 2002) and *Can Unions Survive? The Rejuvenation of the American Labor Movement* (N.Y.U. Press, 1993), and he is co-author of *Alternative Dispute Resolution: The Advocate's Perspective* (Lexis, 3d ed. 2006), *Legal Negotiating* (West 2007), *Employment Law Treatise* (2 vol.)(West, 4th ed. 2009), *Employment Law Hornbook* (West. 4th ed. 2009), *Labor Relations Law* (Lexis, 11 th ed. 2005), *Employment Discrimination Law* (Michie, 4th ed. 1994), *Human Resources and the Law* (B.N.A. 1994), *Labor Relations Law in the Public Sector* (Michie, 4th ed. 1991), and *Collective Bargaining and Labor Arbitration* (Michie, 3rd ed. 1988). He received his B.S. from Cornell University in 1967, his Master's Degree in Labor Law and Collective Bargaining from the Cornell University School of Industrial and Labor Relations in 1968, and his J.D. from the University of Michigan in 1971.

PREFACE

Most legal practitioners use their negotiating skills more frequently than their other lawyering talents. They negotiate when they don't even realize they are negotiating. They do so when they interact with their partners, associates, legal assistants, secretaries, prospective clients, and current clients, yet they only think they are negotiating when they deal with other lawyers on behalf of current clients. Despite the critical nature of bargaining skills, few attorneys have received formal education pertaining to the negotiation process. Most law schools now include limited-enrollment legal negotiating courses in their curricula, and many states provide continuing legal education programs on this important subject. Nonetheless, the vast majority of practicing attorneys must regularly employ talents that have not been explored or developed in any organized manner.

During law school, students focus primarily on substantive and theoretical legal doctrines. Once they enter the legal profession, attorneys tend to continue this focus. They spend hours each week reading advance sheets and related materials pertaining to the substantive areas they practice. When they prepare for bargaining encounters, they spend substantial amounts of time on the legal, factual, economic, and political issues involved, but no more than ten to fifteen minutes formulating their negotiating strategies. In fact, when most attorneys begin a negotiation, they have only three things in mind that directly relate to their bargaining strategy: (1) their bottom line; (2) their ultimate objectives; and (3) their planned opening offer. After they articulate their opening offer, they "wing it" — viewing each bargaining encounter as a wholly unstructured event. Few take the time to read books and articles concerning the negotiation process. When I teach courses to practitioners, I tell them that the results of most legal interactions are determined more by negotiating skill than by pure substantive knowledge. While proficient negotiators must become thoroughly familiar with the operative legal principles to be effective advocates, they do not have to learn the entire field. Carefully prepared negotiation experts generally prevail over substantive experts who lack negotiating expertise. It thus behooves lawyers to continually enhance their knowledge of both substantive law *and* dispute resolution skills if they wish to maximize their professional effectiveness.

The legal negotiating process is only indirectly affected by traditional legal doctrines. Even though the general parameters of particular interactions are loosely defined by the operative factual circumstances and the relevant legal principles, the process itself is more directly determined by reference to other disciplines. This is due to the fact that negotiations involve interpersonal, rather than abstract, transactions. As a result, psychological, sociological, communicational, and game theories are the primary phenomena that influence the bargaining process (Bazerman, Curhans & Moore, 2001). This book examines these pertinent fields and provides a conceptual negotiating frame-work that is both theoretical and practical.

My previous practice experience and current work as a mediator and adjudicator of labor and employment disputes have convinced me that most lawyers are not interested in purely academic formulations that bear little resemblance to the real world. While esoteric models may stimulate interesting scholarly debate, they are frequently based upon assumptions that are unrelated to real-world situations. Nonetheless, it must be emphasized that many psychological and sociological phenomena that regularly affect the negotiation process are ignored by practitioners who doubt the applicability of those seemingly arcane concepts.

Most legal practitioners are inherently suspicious of social science theories regarding the factors that influence human behavior. These abstract concepts do not appear to have discernible bases. This phenomenon is typified by an example from my first-year Criminal

PREFACE

Law class at the University of Michigan. Dr. Andrew Watson, a psychiatrist on the law faculty, was asked by Professor Yale Kamisar to visit our class. During his discussion of various mens rea doctrines, Dr. Watson interjected his view that most criminals are in prison because they consciously or subconsciously want to be there. Professor Kamisar excitedly challenged this assertion: "Come on, Andy. Three people rob a bank. One is overweight and unable to run as fast as his partners, and is apprehended." The students were generally sympathetic to this perspective, and Dr. Watson did not pursue the matter. Pandemonium would undoubtedly have reigned had Dr. Watson replied: "But Yale, the perpetrator in question most likely overate intentionally to become obsese and develop diminished mobility so that he would be captured and incarcerated." As a first year law student, I would probably have questioned such a Freudian suggestion. Nonetheless, my practice experiences, my teaching observations, and my review of the pertinent psychological literature over the past thirty years have made me realize that such seemingly farfetched theories should not be rejected too hastily. I continue to be amazed by how frequently inadvertent "verbal leaks" and unintended nonverbal signals disclose critical information during bargaining interactions. While various psychological and sociological concepts discussed in this book should not automatically be accepted as universal truths, these theories should not be summarily dismissed. They should be mentally indexed for future reference in recognition of the fact they may actually influence the negotiation process.

During the years I have taught Legal Negotiating courses, I have frequently wondered whether there was any correlation between overall law school performance — measured by final student GPAs — and the results obtained on my simulation exercises. In 1986,1 performed a rank- order correlation on the data I had for the previous eight years at the University of Illinois and the University of California at Davis (Craver, 1986).* In 1999, I replicated this study for the thirteen years of data I had amassed at George Washington University (Craver, 2000). In both studies, I found the complete absence of any statistically significant correlation between overall law school achievement and negotiation exercise performance. This would certainly suggest that the skills imparted in traditional law school courses have little impact upon a student's capacity to obtain favorable results on negotiation exercises.

I was initially surprised by the lack of any significant correlation between overall student performance and negotiation exercise results, because I had thought that the qualities likely to make one a good student (intelligence, hard work, etc.) would contribute to negotiation success. As I sought an explanation for the unexpected results, I realized that I was comparing unrelated skills. Individuals who do well on law school exams have high abstract reasoning capabilities, measured by SAT, LSAT, and IQ scores. They possess the ability to learn rules, to discern issues, and to apply abstract legal principles to hypothetical fact patterns. People who are successful on negotiation exercises, however, possess the interpersonal skills (*i.e.,* "emotional intelligence") necessary to interact well with other persons (Goleman, 1995). They are good readers of other people, and they know what arguments are most likely to influence different opponents.

At George Washington University, my Legal Negotiating students can take my course for a traditional letter grade or on a pass/fail basis. In 1998, I compared the negotiation exercise results achieved by graded students with the outcomes attained by pass/fail students (Craver, 1998). Although my students had often suggested that the pass/fail students had an inherent bargaining advantage since they could be more risk-taking when deciding whether to risk nonsettlements, I found that the graded students had achieved significantly higher results. This

---

* To avoid the use of distracting footnotes, abbreviated citations appear in parentheses. Complete citations are provided in the Bibliography at the end of the book.

reflects the fact that successful negotiators generally work harder than their less successful cohorts. If students have to decide whether to spend an additional thirty minutes preparing for bargaining encounters or spend an extra hour trying to induce their opponent to give them what they want, the students receiving a letter grade is more likely to make this commitment than the students guaranteed a "pass" if they do the required work. Practitioners who wish to obtain optimal results for their clients must be willing to make the extra effort it takes to generate consistently beneficial outcomes.

In 1986, I also sought to determine whether the abilities developed in legal negotiating courses are transferrable to future settings. During 1983 and 1984, most of the students who had taken my fall semester Legal Negotiating course participated in a spring term negotiation simulation conducted in a colleague's Trial Advocacy class. My research established the presence of a statistically significant positive correlation between the negotiation results achieved by the individuals who had previously received legal negotiating training vis-a-vis those Trial Advocacy participants who had not received such prior instruction (Craver, 1986). This finding strongly suggests that negotiating skills can be effectively taught and improved through the discussion of applicable concepts and the use of simulation exercises.

Some individuals might question the ethical and/or moral propriety of several of the tactics explored in this book. These approaches are not included because of their general acceptance, but because of their occasional use by at least some negotiators. Even if most people were to decide not to employ these tactics as part of their own strategies, they would be likely to encounter them in some circumstances. If they are familiar with these techniques and understand their strengths and weaknesses, they will be in a better position to counter their use than they would if they ignored their existence.

It has become fashionable for some academics to suggest that all negotiations should be conducted on a "win-win" basis designed to generate "fair" results that provide both sides with relatively equal returns. It should be obvious that certain negotiations must be undertaken on a "win-win" basis if they are to achieve their desired objectives. For example, on-going negotiations between family members, close friends, business partners, and others in symbiotic relationships must be designed to produce results that satisfy the basic needs of both participants if they are to be truly successful for either. Both parties must feel that they "won" something from their interaction, or their relationship would be jeopardized. Even in these settings, however, attorneys should not ignore the fact that their clients expect them to obtain better terms than they give to their opponents if this can be achieved amicably (Shapiro & Jankowski, 2001, at 5; Mnookin, Peppet & Tulumello, 2000, at 9).

Legal practitioners frequently encounter highly competitive situations that do not involve on-going relationships. In these circumstances, a few negotiators may only believe that they have "won" if they think the other party has "lost." No negotiator should enter a negotiation with a "win-lose" desire to defeat or injure the opposing party, because no rational benefit would be achieved from this approach. All other factors being equal, negotiators should strive to maximize *opponent* returns if this does not diminish the value obtained for their own clients. This practice increases the likelihood of agreements and the ultimate honoring of those accords. On the other hand, it must be recognized that in most bargaining transactions, the parties rarely possess equal bargaining power and equal negotiation skill. One party may be more risk-averse than the other, and the overly anxious participant may be willing to accept less generous terms. As a result, one side usually obtains more favorable terms than the other (Karrass, 1970, at 144).

In these "distributive" settings in which both sides wish to obtain many of the same items, some degree of competitive bargaining is inevitable (Korobkin, 2000, at 1791; Kennedy, 1998, at 16–18; Wetlaufer, 1996). I believe that advocates have an ethical obligation to seek the

PREFACE

most beneficial agreements for their clients they can obtain without resorting to unconscionable or unethical tactics (Kramer, 2001, at 342; Bastress & Harbaugh, 1990, at 345). I would be reluctant to suggest that advocates contemplate the rejection of offers that seem overly generous to their own clients based upon their initial assessments of the underlying circumstances. It is quite possible in these situations that their adversaries possess important information they have not discovered. When opponents evaluate client situations more generously than their own attorneys anticipated, I believe that their legal representatives are obliged to defer to the assessments of opposing counsel. These lawyers might otherwise place themselves in the awkward position of having to explain to their clients that they could have obtained better settlements had they not concluded that it was more important to ensure a greater degree of success for their opponents. Until we adopt a system that requires adjudicators to issue decisions guaranteeing "win-win" results in all cases ("we feel strongly both ways!"), I believe that negotiators should amicably and ethically seek to attain bargaining results with the same commitment they would exhibit if the matter were being litigated — what Ron Shapiro and Mark Jankowski have characterized as "W1N-win" results, with the "WIN" share on their own client's side (Shapiro & Jankowski, 2001, at 45) (see also Watkins, 2006, at 8–9).

When people suggest that only "fair" deals should be accepted, they usually intimate that outcomes near the mid-point between the parties' respective positions would be proper. If one spouse is physically abusing the other four times per week, would two times per week be "fair"? If a thief were to demand all of the money in our pockets, should we feel obliged to offer that person half of what we possess? While it is clear that ethical practitioners should avoid unconscionably one-sided arrangements that would not be legally enforceable, we should not expect advocates to fully protect the interests of less proficient opponents. If negotiators are able to obtain highly beneficial results through the use of entirely appropriate tactics, they should be respected, not criticized.

Some academics believe that the outcomes of most bargaining encounters can be accurately predicted through the application of economic theory. They suggest detailed formulas including such factors as participant preference curves and degree of risk aversion to determine the "rational" outcomes. They fail to appreciate the highly subjective nature of bargaining interactions (Kennedy, 1998, at 23). How much does one party wish to resolve the current dispute? How much does someone want to buy or sell a particular firm or license new technology? How fair do they think the bargaining process was (Hollander-Blumoff & Tyler 2008)? It is difficult to believe that one could combine an inexact science — law — with another inexact science — human behavior — and quantify the resulting aggregation. So much of what influences negotiation outcomes is based upon subjective considerations. This explains why experienced attorneys negotiating the identical exercises in my continuing legal education courses achieve results that vary widely — by factors of five or even ten fold. Even students who have been trained in law and economic analysis allow subjective factors to influence their decision-making (Houston & Sunstein, 1998).

This book provides readers with a thorough understanding of the psychological, sociological, and communicational factors that meaningfully influence bargaining interactions. The various negotiation stages are explained, and the different bargaining techniques that practitioners are likely to encounter are discussed. Certain specific bargaining issues are covered, and the impact of ethnic or gender differences on negotiation encounters is explored. Public and private international bargaining transactions are discussed, in recognition of the increased relevance of such transnational interactions. The use of neutral mediators to assist negotiating parties is reviewed, and the ethical aspects of the negotiation process are examined. This comprehensive approach provides readers with a greater appreciation of the negotiation process and is designed to enhance their bargaining confidence. They will understand the different stages and the objectives to be achieved in each. They will recognize the various tactics they observe and feel more capable of responding effectively to diverse approaches. Since the negotiation process involves interpersonal transactions in which more confident advocates generally achieve more favorable results than their less certain cohorts, such a psychological advantage is likely to produce tangible rewards.

The First Edition of this book provided a basic framework pertaining to the negotiation process. The Second Edition greatly expanded upon the topics covered in every chapter. The Third Edition constituted a refinement of the prior editions. I added new concepts — particularly with respect to nonverbal communication and negotiating techniques. Because of the growth of transnational interactions, I included a new chapter on international negotiating. At the urging of several book users, I replaced the previous chapter on judicial mediation with a broader chapter covering general mediation concepts and other voluntary dispute resolution techniques used to assist negotiating parties. In the Fourth and Fifth Editions, I retained the existing organizational structure, as I have in the Sixth Edition. Every chapter has been refined to reflect recent scholarly developments, with the most significant changes occurring in the chapters on international negotiating, mediation, and negotiation ethics.

TABLE OF CONTENTS

TABLE OF CONTENTS

TABLE OF CONTENTS

TABLE OF CONTENTS

TABLE OF CONTENTS

TABLE OF CONTENTS

TABLE OF CONTENTS

TABLE OF CONTENTS

TABLE OF CONTENTS

TABLE OF CONTENTS

TABLE OF CONTENTS

TABLE OF CONTENTS

TABLE OF CONTENTS

TABLE OF CONTENTS

TABLE OF CONTENTS

TABLE OF CONTENTS

TABLE OF CONTENTS

TABLE OF CONTENTS

TABLE OF CONTENTS

TABLE OF CONTENTS

TABLE OF CONTENTS

TABLE OF CONTENTS

TABLE OF CONTENTS

TABLE OF CONTENTS

TABLE OF CONTENTS

Chapter 1

INTRODUCTION

§ 1.01 VALUE OF NEGOTIATING SKILLS

The art of legal negotiating includes skills rarely taught in traditional law school curricula. Since practicing attorneys constantly encounter situations that require various forms of negotiation, the lack of formal education in these skills is unfortunate. Negotiation is clearly applicable to lawsuit settlements, contractual undertakings, real estate and corporate transactions, dealings with federal, state, and local regulatory agencies, and so forth. However, it is also applicable to other, equally important, areas of law practice. For example, most clients employ legal counsel either to resolve problems or to prevent their occurrence. They generally need professional assistance with respect to established relationships or with the creation of new relationships. In these situations, the retained attorneys can usually advance the interests of their respective clients most effectively through the bargaining process. Lawyers must recognize that two professional practitioners who are intimately familiar with the fundamental interests of their respective clients can usually formulate a more efficient resolution of the underlying client problem than can an external decision-maker who will rarely possess the same degree of knowledge or understanding. This would explain why over 95 percent of law suits are resolved without adjudications (Brazil, 2006, at 243–44; Galanter, 2006, at 7–10; Samborn, 2002), and why a similar percentage of criminal cases are disposed of through negotiated plea bargains (see generally Herman, 2004, at 1). In federal courts today, less than two percent of civil cases are resolved through adjudications (Galanter, 2006, at 7–8).

Both litigators and transactional specialists should recognize that the negotiation process may provide beneficial results even when no final agreements are achieved. Litigation discussions that do not culminate in case settlements may be used to narrow and define the issues to be presented for adjudication, and to generate factual and/or legal stipulations that will expedite trial proceedings. Inter-party talks may also be employed during discovery procedures to enable the participants to agree upon the information to be exchanged. This is why litigators who conclude that no overall settlement agreements are possible should not eschew further case discussions. They must simply shift their focus from final resolutions to interim accords that may streamline the litigation process.

Transactional negotiators should similarly realize the future benefits they can derive from current interactions that fail to produce immediate deals. These discussions may lay the foundation for future negotiations between the instant parties that will ultimately result in mutual accords. Furthermore, even if the present parties are unlikely to have future dealings once the current talks are terminated, the participating attorneys may themselves engage in future negotiations involving other clients. If these advocates can establish beneficial relationships during the present discussions, they will greatly enhance the likelihood of success when they have future business encounters (Greenhalgh, 1987).

Even when they are not involved in negotiations on behalf of existing clients, practitioners must regularly employ their negotiating skills (Ryan, 2005, at 235, 263–64). The establishment and maintenance of client relationships are determined through attorney-client negotiations. Financial arrangements and strategic decisions must be mutually resolved. The bargaining process similarly affects the manner in which lawyers deal with associates and partners within their own firms. Attorneys must also structure their relationships with legal assistants, secretaries, and other firm personnel. It should thus be obvious that practitioners must expend a substantial amount of their professional lives utilizing their bargaining talents.

Many individuals discount the importance of negotiating skill by naively suggesting that bargaining outcomes are primarily determined through the application of objective criteria. They think that amorphous legal doctrines can be objectified, and that subjective human needs and interests can be quantified. Unfortunately, when inexact legal concepts are combined with subjective personal judgments, the results are anything but objective (Rachlinski, 2003, at 1165). Relatively objective factors are used by negotiating parties to calculate their respective *bottom lines*. Nevertheless, a subjective battle of wills is likely to determine the final outcome within the *settlement range* that is bounded by their respective bottom lines. Dr. Chester Karrass, in advertisements for his "Effective Negotiating" course, aptly notes that "In business, you don't get what you deserve, you get what you negotiate." The same truism governs bargaining interactions between lawyers. When groups of law students or practicing attorneys negotiate the identical exercises, they are surprised how diverse the settlement agreements are. It is only in such circumstances that participants truly appreciate the impact of negotiating ability on the final outcomes of bargaining interactions.

It is important to recognize that the negotiation process has little to do with traditional legal doctrines, except perhaps those of basic contract law. It is instead governed by the same psychological, sociological, and communicational principles that influence other interpersonal relations. As a result, lawyers who rely primarily upon narrow legal frameworks to guide their negotiations may ignore the most relevant factors that affect the negotiation process. They may have a thorough understanding of the applicable legal concepts, but overlook the crucial factors that are likely to determine the outcome of their interactions (Ryan, 2005).

§ 1.02 NEGOTIATION AS A PROCESS

As we explore various factors of negotiation and settlement, it is important to recognize that we are concerned with the *negotiation process*. It takes time for the *process* to evolve. Certain ritualistic behavior and identifiable stages must develop in almost all bargaining situations. Many individuals hate to waste time at the outset of negotiations with small talk pertaining to sports, politics, weather, and other seemingly irrelevant considerations. They prefer to begin their transactions with discussions regarding the issues of immediate interest. They fail to recognize that the preliminary exchanges put anxious participants at ease and establish a beneficial tone for the more salient talks to come. Less proficient bargainers are often frustrated by the inordinate time it takes for some opponents to move from an initially adversarial mode to a more conciliatory posture. Impatient participants occasionally attempt to accelerate the process by moving directly to the Closing Stage in an effort to conclude their transactions expeditiously. They are bewildered when the process breaks down. They fail to appreciate the fundamental rule that parties who hasten the negotiation process generally take longer than those who patiently allow the process to develop more naturally. The bargaining stages break down and have to be repeated. Impatient negotiators also tend to generate less efficient agreements than their more patient cohorts because of the absence of effective cooperative bargaining.

People unfamiliar with the process often dislike the need to discuss ancillary legal and factual topics not directly related to the particular issues at hand. To demonstrate the difficulty encountered when negotiators confine themselves to communication pertaining to the specific items in dispute, I generally have students and continuing legal education participants engage in a short silent negotiation. They are given a simple personal injury hypothetical and instructed to determine the amount of money to be paid by the defendant to the plaintiff. They must communicate entirely on paper, and may only write down monetary sums reflecting offers and demands. By the time they complete this exercise, they begin to realize that they cannot limit negotiations in such a narrow manner. The ancillary discussions are a lubricant that enable the talks to continue on a relatively even keel between position changes.

It is also crucial to understand the fact that the negotiation process begins to unfold at the time of first contact between the participants. I always cringe when students prepare papers for my Legal Negotiating course that describe the commencement of their negotiation in the following fashion:

> Our opponents suggested that we meet on Wednesday evening at 8:00, and we agreed. They then proposed that we get together at their apartment, and we concurred. After we arrived at about 8:00 p.m., they generously provided us with wine and cheese. We discussed the basketball game that had taken place the night before. After approximately thirty minutes of irrelevant conversation, the negotiations began.

These students are shocked when I point out how they initially conceded the day, the time, and the location for the bargaining sessions. They then permitted their opponents to create feelings of obligation, through their offer of food and drink, that may have subtly influenced the negotiation outcome. They thus placed themselves at a potential disadvantage before they even realized the process had begun. While it is possible that these factors may not actually affect the final results of particular exchanges, it is important to understand that they could.

§ 1.03 CULTURAL DISLIKE OF NEGOTIATION

Most Americans are not comfortable negotiators. We have not been raised in a society in which we regularly barter with merchants over fruits, vegetables, breads, meats, clothing, and other necessities. When we visit supermarkets and department stores, we normally pay the listed prices or forego the items in question. In many other societies, however, people constantly bargain with merchants over these goods, and they view the asking prices as merely the beginning of the auction process. They feel comfortable with this approach and look forward to negotiating opportunities. They do not view compromise as a sign of weakness, but rather as a mutually beneficial exercise.

United States lawyers must begin to appreciate the professional and personal *opportunities* represented by negotiation encounters. Each bargaining exchange provides the participants with the chance to improve their respective circumstances. If the parties could not improve their situations, they would not be communicating with each other. Parties should thus welcome bargaining interactions as challenging and potentially beneficial endeavors, and attorneys should work diligently to advance the underlying interests of their respective clients.

Another factor that causes many lawyers to feel uncomfortable during bargaining interactions concerns the deliberate deception associated with most legal negotiations. Side A begins the transaction by stating that it cannot pay more than X when it is perfectly willing to pay 2X, while Side B initially states that it must obtain at least 3X when it would be satisfied with 1 1/2 X. The participants are pleased that they have begun the process successfully, even though both have begun with overt misrepresentations! As we shall see in Chapter 17, *infra*, dealing with ethical considerations, misrepresentations regarding one's settlement intentions and/or values are excluded from the scope of Model Rule 4.1 which proscribes deliberate lawyer misstatements. While it is clear that attorneys may never lie about *material fact* or *material law*, it is ethically permissible for negotiators to use deceptive tactics in an effort to generate more favorable terms in their settlement. Negotiating attorneys must learn to distinguish between acceptable "puffing"/"embellishment" and impermissible mendacity.

§ 1.04   IMPACT OF NEGOTIATOR PERSONALITIES

A person's negotiating ability is directly affected by his or her personal strengths and weaknesses. The pertinent personal factors vary greatly from individual to individual. A few effective negotiators employ a style that is aggressive and/or even abrasive, while others are successful using a calm and even deferential approach. For example, I briefly worked with a negotiator who was derisive and sarcastic. He treated everyone with utter contempt, yet he could be a proficient bargainer. His adversaries felt so uncomfortable when dealing with him that they sought to terminate their interactions expeditiously. Opponents who were anxious to achieve final resolutions of the matters in dispute often agreed to his one-sided entreaties. Other opponents, however, severed their talks and accepted their nonsettlement options. Furthermore, his own partners found him impossible to deal with, causing the dissolution of a successful law firm!

It is discomforting to negotiate for prolonged periods with nasty individuals, and most persons do not have the ability or the desire to match such people's sarcasm on a quid pro quo basis. As a result, those confronted by these adversaries should act to diminish their effectiveness. Short sessions, frequently conducted on the telephone, significantly restrict the capacity of abrasive negotiators to gain momentum and to cause the intended anxiety through their usual tactics. If one suspects they are a target for this type of negotiator, the use of telephonic exchanges provides an added element of control. It's easy to announce that one has another call or other engagement and terminate the current interaction. Further, by exercising this degree of control, one increases their self-esteem and confidence. This enables them to enhance their respective bargaining situations.

At the opposite extreme are the seemingly inept and pathetic characters who evoke such sympathy that they induce their opponents to concede everything necessary to satisfy the needs of these poor souls. A good example of this type of negotiator was artfully created by actor Peter Falk in his Lieutenant Columbo character. He bumbles along during criminal investigations without any apparent direction or competence until he adroitly extracts confessions from the guilty parties. Highly skilled "belly-up" negotiators, who will be discussed more fully in Chapter 10, *infra*, are able to use these tactics to fleece unsuspecting opponents. The most amazing aspect of these interactions concerns the ability of "belly-up" negotiators to induce cleaned-out adversaries to feel wonderful about their results! Practitioners must learn to recognize "belly-up" tactics and be careful not to modify their own behavior in a manner that favors their manipulative opponents.

This book does not attempt to define a specific negotiating style intended to guarantee optimal results for everyone. Given the diverse personalities possessed by lawyers, it would be impossible to prescribe a generally-applicable approach. The book instead identifies the important considerations and seeks to assist individual readers to appreciate their own personal attributes. It is hoped that they will obtain a better understanding of the way in which they interact with other people in stressful situations, and, conversely, how others interact with them. This should permit them to learn to employ their strengths more effectively in future negotiations, while minimizing the impact of their possible weaknesses. Aggressive individuals must adopt styles that suit their personalities, and calm and deferential persons must do the same. Negotiators must also select styles they think will optimally work with the particular opponents with whom they are interacting — and will suit the unique bargaining circumstances involved.

Summary

1. Even though most attorneys regularly negotiate, few have had formal training with respect to this important lawyering skill.

2. Even when negotiators fail to resolve on-going disputes or do not achieve business accords, they may use their bargaining skills to streamline the litigation process or to lay the foundation for future deals.

3. Negotiators must recognize that they are participating in a process consisting of specific stages that take time to develop. Impatient parties who endeavor to artificially hasten their transactions usually prolong their interactions and generate less efficient agreements.

4. The negotiation process is influenced by the same psychological, sociological, and communicational factors that affect all interpersonal transactions.

5. The negotiation process begins at the time of first contact. In many cases, the initial contact sets the tone of the negotiation and can affect the settlement terms.

6. Since Americans do not regularly barter with merchants, most of us are not comfortable with the negotiation process. We feel uncomfortable with the deceptive behavior that is indigenous to most bargaining interactions.

7. Different negotiation approaches may be equally effective. Individuals must develop styles that are consistent with their own personalities, the personalities of their opponents, and the particular bargaining circumstances involved.

8. Bargainers rarely possess equal power and skill. Advocates who possess greater power or skill should seek superior results from their less powerful or skillful opponents.

Chapter 2

BASIC FACTORS AFFECTING NEGOTIATION

§ 2.01 PERSONAL NEEDS OF PARTICIPANTS

Negotiators must recognize that the personal needs of the different participants must be minimally satisfied before successful results can be achieved. Many attorneys make the mistake of focusing their attention exclusively on the stated needs of their own clients and those expressed on behalf of opposing clients. This practice frequently causes bargainers to ignore other highly relevant information. Lawyers must initially endeavor to ascertain the true underlying needs of their own clients, and then seek to determine the less visible needs of opposing clients and of opposing counsel (Riskin, 2002, at 613).

[1] Unspoken Client Needs

Individuals who seek legal advice often disguise their ulterior motivations when conversing with their own attorneys. They express their apparent objectives in terms that are likely to generate appropriate legal action. For example, a defamed individual may express a desire for financial recompense. If the underlying motivations are probed, the patient attorney may discover that this person would prefer an expeditious retraction and a public apology over a delayed monetary judgment. This information would undoubtedly make it easier for the lawyer to achieve an acceptable pretrial resolution.

Clients involved in marital dissolutions may similarly conceal their true feelings. Seemingly objective discussions of alimony, child custody and visitation privileges, and property rights may mask a strong urge for emotional retribution. If council can manage to adroitly expose and sympathetically handle hidden agendas, they will enhance the likelihood of a mutual accord. Legal representatives must acknowledge the presence of such disguised feelings in opposing clients and try to understand their nature and strength.

[2]   Needs of Counsel

Lawyers frequently expend so much energy concentrating on the underlying needs of their own clients and of opposing clients that they fail to sufficiently consider their own personal needs or those of their legal adversaries. I have seen skilled practitioners decline simulation exercise settlement offers that would have provided them with results far more favorable than nonsettlements, simply because they feared the possibility of appearing weak or foolish. These situations graphically demonstrate the need negotiators have to gratify their own egos and competitive desires. Since client interests are expected to take precedence over the personal drives of their advocates, such results should never occur. Undoubtedly, these results happen on a frequent basis.

[3]   Needs of Opposing Counsel

Opposing counsel have their own personal needs that must similarly be satisfied if settlements are to be obtained. A savvy lawyer can manipulate these motivational factors and precipitate favorably disposed states of mind. Through employment of the opponent's apparent desire for professional respect counsel may generate greater concessions with disingenuous appeals to the opposition's reputation for reasonableness and fair dealing. One can also rely on most people's distaste for the internal stress associated with unresolved disputes in order to move negotiators inexorably toward beneficial agreements.

Other factors may also influence the willingness of opposing attorneys to accept offers. If their law offices are experiencing cash flow difficulties, as many newer firms do, and if they are operating on contingent fee bases, they may be more inclined to settle cases near the first of each month as their major bills become due. Other litigators may succumb to a different kind of pressure. If they are handling an expansive number of cases, they may not be in a position to devote a substantial amount of their time to any one dispute. By noticing all pertinent depositions and filing thorough interrogatories and motions to produce, aggressive attorneys can frequently cause these opponents to look more favorably upon settlement proposals in an effort to alleviate the inordinate time pressure associated with the particular case. If the information being sought is relevant to the pending action and is being sought in preparation for trial, this practice would not contravene applicable ethical standards.

Some lawyers who are being compensated on an hourly basis feel little incentive to resolve matters expeditiously. When negotiating with attorneys retained on an hourly rate, it may occasionally be necessary to permit the process to develop in a sufficiently deliberate fashion to enable them to generate exalted fees. If reasonable offers are made prematurely, these practitioners will strongly encourage their clients to reject the proposals. Negotiators must patiently allow these opponents to take the time they require to enhance their fees before they present their real offers. While one may question the ethics of attorneys who delay settlement opportunities for the purpose of increasing their fees, advocates who ignore this consideration either have to provide these adversaries with unnecessarily enhanced offers or risk the possibility of avoidable nonsettlements.

[4]   Unlikelihood of Equal Satisfaction

Even when the operative value systems affecting the persons involved in a specific negotiation have been disclosed, this does not automatically dictate the final outcome. While each side must acquire some degree of personal satisfaction before any mutual accord can be achieved, nothing requires that both sides be equally satisfied. Risk-averse participants are not willing to endure the possibility of a nonsettlement. Therefor, they may be willing to accept less than other similarly situated individuals who are willing to accept the risk of a nonsettlement. Furthermore, since different individuals may obtain diverse levels of satisfaction from the identical transaction, it must be remembered that parties being offered objectively less beneficial results may derive more gratification from this exchange than their opponents. When one side thinks it is getting the better deal, it should try to induce the other party to believe the items have been fairly divided (Guthrie, 2004, at 833–834; Welsh, 2004). People who think they have been treated fairly are more likely to accept the final terms and to carry out their contractual obligations.

§ 2.02   NEGOTIATING STYLES OF PARTICIPANTS

Most negotiators tend to exhibit a relatively "*cooperative*" or a relatively "*competitive*" style (Williams & Craver, 2007, at 12–73; Thompson, 2005, at 114–119; Craver, 2003; Schneider, 2002; Shell, 1999, at 9–11; Gifford, 2007, at 18–25; Gifford, 1985, at 48–59; Williams, 1983, at 18–39). "Cooperative" advocates usually employ a "problem-solving" approach (Mnookin, Peppet & Tulumello, 2002; Fisher & Ury, 1981), while "competitive" individuals use a more "adversarial" methodology (Dawson, 2001; Ringer, 1973). Certain traits may be employed to distinguish between these two diverse styles. (See also Kennedy, 1998, at 177–198).

[1]   Different Negotiating Styles

Cooperative/Problem-Solving	*Competitive/Adversarial*
Move Psychologically *Toward* Opponents	Move Psychologically *Against* Opponents
Try to Maximize *Joint* Return	Try to Maximize *Own* Return
Seek Reasonable Results	Seek Extreme Results
Courteous and Sincere	Adversarial and Disingenuous
Begin with Realistic Opening Positions	Begin with Unrealistic Opening Positions
Rely on Objective Standards	Focus on Own Positions Rather Than Neutral Standards
Rarely Use Threats	Frequently Use Threats
Maximize Information Disclosure	Minimize Information Disclosure
Open and Trusting	Closed and Untrusting
Work to Satisfy Underlying Interests of Opponents	Work to Satisfy Underlying Interests of Own Client
Willing to Make Unilateral Concessions	Attempt to Make Minimal Concessions
Reason with Opponents	Manipulate Opponents

Cooperative/problem-solving negotiators tend to begin their interactions with realistic positions that are designed to create positive bargaining environments (Boulle,

Colatrella & Picchioni, 2008, at 158–59; Lewicki & Hiam, 2006, at 127–156). They work to maintain harmonious relationships through courteous and professional discussions. They readily disclose their critical information, and try to explore the underlying interests of the parties in an effort to expand the overall pie to be divided up. This enables them to seek efficient agreements that maximize the joint gains achieved by the parties. They invoke objective norms to lead the participants toward fair, win-win results. They rarely resort to threats or other disruptive tactics designed to intimidate opponents, preferring cooperative techniques intended to generate reciprocal movement.

Competitive/adversarial negotiators begin with more extreme opening positions that are used to intimidate opponents (Boulle, Colatrella & Picchioni, 2008, at 152–53; Lewicki & Hiam, 2006, at 73–91). They hope to achieve one-sided agreements that favor their own side. They frequently employ threats and other disruptive tactics to keep their opponents on the defensive. They withhold their negative information, and use the disclosure of beneficial information to induce adversaries to think they possess superior strength. They try to induce opponents to bid against themselves by making unreciprocated concessions. When competitive/adversarial bargainers think it will advance their situations, many employ insulting or demeaning behavior.

[2]   Relative Effectiveness of Negotiating Styles

[a]   Competitive/Adversarial Negotiator Results

Many attorneys think that competitive/adversarial negotiators (see above) who use aggressive and even abrasive tactics are more likely to achieve beneficial results for their clients than cooperative/ problem-solving negotiators. This notion was contradicted by an empirical study of legal practitioners in Phoenix conducted in 1976 by Professor Gerald Williams. He found that lawyers considered 65 percent of their colleagues to be cooperative/problem-solvers, 24 percent to be competitive/adversarial, and 11 percent to be unclassifiable (Williams, 1983, at 19; Williams, 1992, at 2). Lawyers indicated that the results achieved by effective cooperative/problem-solving negotiators were as beneficial for their clients as the results obtained by effective competitive/adversarial bargainers (Williams, 1983, at 41). On the other hand, while responding attorneys in Professor Williams' study indicated that 59 percent of cooperative/problem-solving negotiators were "effective" and 38 percent were "average," they suggested that only 25 percent of competitive/adversarial bargainers were "effective" and 42 percent were "average" (Williams, 1983, at 19). Furthermore, while a mere 3 percent of cooperative/problem-solving negotiators were considered "ineffective," 33 percent of competitive/adversarial bargainers fell into the same category.

A more recent study of attorneys in Chicago and Milwaukee, conducted by Professor Andrea Kupfer Schneider, employed Professor Williams' basic methodology (Schneider, 2000, at 24; Schneider, 2002). Although the percentage of effective cooperative/problem-solving negotiators declined slightly from 59 percent to 54 percent, the percentage of effective competitive/adversarial bargainers dropped from 25 percent to 9 percent (Schneider, 2002, at 167). In addition, while the percentage of ineffective cooperative/problem-solvers also remained the same, the percentage of ineffective competitive/adversarials rose from 33 percent to 53 percent. It is also interesting to note that Professor Schneider found competitive/adversarial bargainers in the late 1990s to be less pleasant and more uncivil than the competitive/adversarial negotiators described in Professor Williams' earlier study (Schneider, 2002, at 172). This behavioral change may explain why she found fewer competitive/adversarial negotiators to be considered effective, and more characterized as ineffective.

Competitive/adversarial negotiators are more likely to employ adversarial bargaining strategies designed to intimidate their opponents than cooperative/problem-solvers. In law suit negotiations, they are more inclined to make "zero offers" (*i.e.*, they offer absolutely nothing) intended to induce less confident plaintiffs either to not file actual law suits or to withdraw the suits they have already filed. Studies of actual law suits, however, indicate that this tactic is likely to *increase* the percentage of cases taken to trial by plaintiffs who are angered by such offensive bargaining behavior and see no possible gain through non-adjudication alternatives (Gross & Syverud, 1991, at 342–45). If defense counsel offer even modest amounts to plaintiffs, they significantly increase the likelihood of settlements, since plaintiffs facing sure gains and the possibility of greater gains or no gains tend to be risk averse and they appreciate the fact that trial costs will decrease the value of judgements obtained through litigation.

[b]   Cooperative/Problem-Solving Negotiator Results

In the many years I have practiced and taught Legal Negotiating, I have not found cooperative/problem-solving negotiators less effective than competitive/adversarial bargainers. The notion that one must be uncooperative, selfish, manipulative, and even abrasive to be successful is erroneous. One must simply possess the capacity to say "no" forcefully and credibly in order to achieve beneficial negotiation results. They can do so courteously and quietly — and be as effective as those who do so more demonstrably. I have only noticed three significant differences with respect to the outcomes achieved by different style negotiators. First, if a truly extreme agreement is reached, the prevailing party is usually a competitive/adversarial negotiator. Since cooperative/problem-solving bargainers tend to be more fair minded, they generally refuse to take unconscionable advantage of inept or weak opponents. Second, competitive/adversarial advocates generate far more nonsettlements than their cooperative/problem-solving cohorts. The extreme positions taken by competitive/adversarial bargainers and their frequent use of manipulative and disruptive tactics make it easy for their opponents to accept the consequences associated with nonsettlements.

The third factor concerns the fact that cooperative/problem-solving negotiators tend to achieve more efficient *combined results* than their competitive/adversarial colleagues — *i.e.*, they tend to maximize joint return to the parties. Cooperative/problem-solvers are usually open and trusting individuals who seek to enhance the disclosure of information and maximize the overall return to the participants. They are thus more likely to attain higher joint values than are more closed and untrusting competitive/adversarial bargainers who are primarily interested in the maximization of their own side's results (Mnookin & Ross, 1995, at 8–9). Advocates who hope to achieve Pareto efficient agreements that benefit both sides must be willing to cooperate sufficiently to permit the participants to explore areas of possible joint gain. While these people may simultaneously seek to maximize their own client's returns, their attempt to enhance opponent interests increases the likelihood of agreement *and* the probability of mutually efficient terms.

[c]   Different Negotiating Style Interactions

When cooperative/problem-solving bargainers interact with other cooperative/problem-solving individuals, the transactions are usually cooperative (Raiffa, 2003, at 288–291), while interactions between competitive/ adversarial negotiators are generally competitive (Raiffa, 2003, at 298–301). Nonetheless, when cooperative/problem-solving bargainers deal with competitive/adversarial opponents, their transactions tend to be more competitive than cooperative (Tinsley, O'Connor & Sullivan, 2002, at 634–35). The cooperative/problem-solving participants are forced to assume a more competitive posture to avoid the exploitation that would result if they were too open and accommodating with their manipulative and avaricious opponents. These cross-style interactions generate less efficient agreements and increase the likelihood of nonsettlements (Tinsley, O'Connor & Sullivan, 2002, at 635). This phenomenon would explain why Professors Williams and Schneider found that a greater percentage of cooperative/problem-solving negotiators are considered effective than competitive/adversarial bargainers.

When really competitive/adversarial negotiators interact with truly cooperative/problem-solving bargainers, the competitive/ adversarial participants are likely to enjoy an advantage if their cooperative/problem-solving opponents continue to behave in a naively cooperative manner (Watkins, 2006, at 78; Tepley, 2005, at 59–60). Competitive/adversarial persons feel more comfortable in an openly competitive environment than their cooperative opponents who may feel compelled to behave in an uncharacteristically competitive fashion to protect their own interests. Competitive advocates tend to have higher client goals than their cooperative adversaries, and they are less concerned about the joint return achieved. Truly cooperative negotiators are also likely to disclose more critical information than their less forthcoming competitive opponents, providing the competitive participants with the advantage of an information-imbalance (Gilson & Mnookin, 1994, at 515–17; Kritzer, 1991, at 78–79).

When cooperative/problem-solvers begin interactions with opponents they do not know well, they should be cautious regarding the critical information they initially disclose. To protect themselves against manipulative competitive/adversarial — even competitive/problem-solving adversaries — they should disclose certain pieces of information initially and see if their openness is being reciprocated. If so, they can continue to be open in an effort to jointly determine the underlying needs and interests of the negotiating parties. This will enable them to have open discussions designed to maximize the joint returns achieved by the participants. On the other hand, if they find that their preliminary openness is not being reciprocated, they should behave more strategically and disclose less of their important information. If they fail to modify their approach in this regard, they will leave themselves open to unfair exploitation by manipulative opponents who will use the information imbalance to obtain one-sided deals favoring their own sides.

In his study, Professor Williams found that certain traits are shared by both effective cooperative/problem-solving negotiators and effective competitive/adversarial bargainers (Williams, 1983, at 20–30). Successful negotiators from both groups are thoroughly prepared, behave in an honest and ethical manner, are perceptive readers of opponent cues, are analytical, realistic, and convincing, and observe the customs and courtesies of the bar. He also found that proficient negotiators from both groups endeavored to *maximize* their *own client's return.* Professor Schneider also found this client maximizing objective among both effective cooperative/problem-solving negotiators and effective competitive/adversarial negotiators (Schneider, 2002, at 188).

Since this factor is most associated with competitive/adversarial bargainers, it would suggest that a number of successful cooperative/problem-solving negotiators are actually wolves in sheepskin. They exude a cooperative style, but seek competitive objectives. (Allred, 2000, at 394-95; Movius, 2008, at 513-15).

[d]   Competitive/Problem-Solving Approach

Most successful negotiators are able to combine the most salient traits associated with the cooperative/problem-solving and the competitive/adversarial styles (Condlin, 2008, at 298–99; Neale & Fragale, 2006, at 32; Freund, 1992, at 24–27; Kritzer, 1991, at 78–79; Woolf, 1990, at 34–35). (See generally Condlin, 2007). They endeavor to maximize client returns, but attempt to accomplish this objective in a congenial and seemingly ingenuous manner (Mayer, 1996, at 7–8, 92). Unlike less proficient negotiators who view bargaining encounters as "fixed pie" endeavors in which one side's gain is the other side's corresponding loss, they realize that in multi-term interactions the parties generally value the various items differently (Mnookin, Peppet & Tulumello, 2000, at 14–15, 174; Thompson, 1998, at 113). They may attempt to claim more of the distributive items desired by both sides (Wetlaufer, 1996; Goodpaster, 1996), but they also look for shared values (Watkins, 2006, at 8–9; Shapiro & Jankowski, 2001, at 45–61). They appreciate the inherent tension between "value crestion" and "value claiming" (Hurder, 2007, at 271–79). They are fairly open with their interests to enable the interactants to look for areas of joint gain, but they work to claim more of the discovered surplus than they give up.

Cooperative/problem-solving negotiators recognize that, by maximizing the joint returns, they are more likely to obtain the best settlements for their own clients. Although they try to manipulate opponent perceptions, they rarely resort to truly deceitful tactics. They know that a loss of credibility would undermine their ability to achieve beneficial results. Despite the fact that they want as much as possible for themselves, they are not "win-lose" negotiators. They realize that the imposition of poor terms on opponents does not necessarily benefit their own clients. All other factors being equal, they want to maximize opponent satisfaction as long as it does not require significant concessions on their part. When they conclude bargaining interactions, they do not compare their results with the terms achieved by their opponents. They instead ask whether they like what they got, realizing that if they attained their objectives they had successful encounters.

Some overly-cooperative negotiators try to generate opponent appreciation through the use of unilateral concessions. During the initial stages of their interactions, they concede items without obtaining reciprocal concessions. This approach tends to embolden competitive opponents who begin to think they will do better than they anticipated, and it often induces the accommodating individuals to adopt a concessionary frame of mind that may cause them to make additional unreciprocated concessions throughout the entire interaction. To avoid this trap, competitive/problem-solvers should use the "IF . . . , THEN . . . " approach in which they suggest that IF the other side is willing to accommodate their needs in a specific way, THEN they will provide them with something they value (Kennedy, 1998, at 190–97). If the recipient of such a conditional offer is unreceptive, the offerors can stand firm and not place themselves in the position of making unilateral position changes.

Competitive/problem-solvers appreciate the importance of negotiation *process*. Individuals who feel that the bargaining process has been fair and that they have been treated respectfully, are more satisfied with less objectively beneficial terms than they are with objectively more beneficial terms achieved through a process they found to be less fair and less respectful (Hollander-Blumoff & Tyler, 2008). It is thus important for competitive/problem-solvers to always treat opponents with respect and professionalism, and to leave them with the feeling a the conclusion of their interactions that those persons obtained "fair" terms.

Proficient negotiators do not seek to maximize opponent returns for purely altruistic reasons. They understand that this approach most effectively enables them to advance their own interests. First, they have to provide adversaries with sufficiently generous terms to induce them to accept proposed agreements. Second, they want to be sure opponents honor deals agreed upon. If the other side experiences post-agreement "buyers remorse," they may try to get out of the deal. Finally, they acknowledge the likelihood they will encounter their adversaries in the future. If those people remember them as courteous and professional negotiators, their future bargaining interactions are more likely to be successful (Lax & Sebenius, 2006, at 17–18; Nelken, 2001, at 190).

Effective cooperative/problem-solving and effective competitve/adversarial negotiators realize that people tend to work most diligently to satisfy the needs of opponents they like personally (Lewicki, et al., 1994, at 219–20). Overtly competitive/ adversarial bargainers are rarely perceived as likeable. They exude competition and manipulation. Seemingly cooperative bargainers, however, appear to be seeking results that benefit both sides. Since others enjoy interacting with them, these individuals find unsuspecting opponents more willing to lower their guard and make greater concessions. They also generate more positive moods that promote cooperative behavior and the attainment of more efficient joint agreements (Tinsley, O'Connor & Sullivan, 2002; Freshman, Hayes & Feltman, 2002; Forgas, 1998).

These eclectic negotiators really employ a composite style. They may be fairly characterized as "competitive/problem-solving" advocates. They seek competitive goals (maximum client returns), but endeavor to accomplish those objectives through "problem-solving" strategies (Allred, 2000; Dawson, 2001, at 128; Kritzer, 1991, at 78–79). This may partially explain why Professors Williams and Schneider found more effective "cooperative/problem-solving" negotiators than effective "competitive/adversarial" bargainers. It is quite possible that many effective "competitive" negotiators were so successful in their use of "problem-solving" tactics, that they induced their opponents to characterize them as "cooperative," rather than "competitive." Professor Donald Gifford has sought to avoid this classification dilemma by treating "problem-solving" negotiators as an entirely separate group — distinct from "cooperative" and "competitive" bargainers (Gifford, 2007, at 18–25). Under his approach, the individuals I would include in the "competitive/ problem-solving" category would be placed in the discrete "problem-solving" group. (See also Volkema, 1999, at 60–64 (dividing people into five styles: (1) competitors; (2) accommodators; (3) collaborators; (4) avoiders; and (5) compromisers)).

Professor Kathleen Reardon likes to divide negotiator styles into four slightly different classifications: (1) the "Analyzer," who likes to focus on logic, make rational arguments, and prioritize outcomes; (2) the "Achiever," who likes detailed planning, seeks to control interactions, and focuses on outcomes; (3) the "Motivator," who likes to use creativity to foster collaboration, and encourage innovative thinking in opponents; and (4) the "Mediator," who tries to establish rapport, listens carefully to others, favors consensus, and works to generate mutual gains (Reardon, 2004, at 54–60). Analyzers, Motivators, and Mediators are similar to Cooperative/Problem-Solvers, while Achievers are more like Competitive/Adversarials. When Achievers combine that approach with styles borrowed from Analyzers, Motivators, and/or Mediators, they are analogous to Competitive/Problem-Solvers. As noted above, I believe that such hybrid approaches are optimal for negotiators who hope to advance the interests of their own clients while simultaneously maximizing the returns shared with their opponents.

Over the past several decades, Americans in general and legal practitioners in particular have become less polite toward one another. We have become more "win-lose" oriented.We seem to fear that if others get what they want, then we will not be able to obtain our own goals. These changing attitudes are adversely affecting legal practice and negatively influencing bargaining interactions. Experienced attorneys regularly bemoan the decreasing civility encountered in daily practice. Lawyers who encounter a lack of civility from opposing negotiators should recognize that such inappropriate behavior is a substitute for bargaining proficiency. Good negotiators practice civility. They realize that insulting conduct is unlikely to induce others to give them what they want.

Lawyers should not take the negotiation process personally. They must recognize that their opponents have nothing against them — they are merely endeavoring to advance the interests of their own clients. Lawyers should not view opponents as the "enemy." Those individuals are actually their best friends. Attorneys should appreciate the fact that their adversaries are the ones enabling them to earn a living. If no one was at the other end of the telephone line or sitting across the bargaining table from them, they would be unemployed!

[3]   The Collaborative Law Approach

A negotiation approach that emphasizes the problem-solving style is being employed by a number of lawyers in Canada and by American lawyers — especially family law specialists (*see generally* Mosten, 2008; Lande, 2003, and authorities cited therein) (see also Webb & Ousky, 2007; Macfarlane, 2005; Fairman, 2005; Cameron, 2004; Gutterman, 2004). Attorneys using the collaborative law approach enter into pre-dispute resolution agreements under which the clients *and* the legal representatives agree to negotiate from the outset employing the problem-solving, interest-based style. They promise to be completely open with each other, minimizing the need for formal discovery procedures, and to work to achieve mutually beneficial accords. To demonstrate their total commitment to the negotiation process, the attorneys include a disqualification clause precluding them from representing their respective clients if the case is not resolved and either party elects to proceed to trial. (*See also* Peppet, 2005; Lande, 2007; Fairman, 2007; Fairman, 2005) (suggesting changes in ethical standards that would permit lawyers to negotiate specific standards of candor, openness, and good faith that would apply to their bargaining interactions that would be enforceable through bar disciplinary procedures))

Many of the attorneys who have accepted the collaborative law approach are personally uncomfortable with the competitive aspect of traditional adversarial bargaining (Macfarlane, 2005, at 17–18). They feel more comfortable working in environments where everyone seeks to satisfy the interests of both sides. In some cases, the concern of such attorneys for the interests of the other side may induce them to strive for terms that are less beneficial to their own clients than they might otherwise have obtained (Macfarlane, 2005, at 44–48). If, in the long term, such agreements make it easier for their clients to resolve their current disputes and get on with their lives, this approach may be highly beneficial. On the other hand, collaborative lawyers willing to seek terms that are less beneficial for their own clients should be careful to explain that fact to their clients to enable those persons to decide whether they wish to agree to such arrangements.

The general commitment to the problem-solving approach is designed to avoid competitive, value-claiming tactics that might disrupt interest-based bargaining. To the extent these dispute resolution arrangements encourage cooperative interactions, they can be quite beneficial. The most controversial aspect of these undertakings concerns the promise that both lawyers will withdraw if litigation is ultimately initiated (Lande, 2003).

In 2007, the Colorado Bar Association Ethics Committee decided that the aspect of the collaborative law approach which requires the attorneys to withdraw from the representation of their respective clients if the matter is not mutually resolved contravenes Model Rule 1.7(a)(2) which forbids a lawyer from representing a client if the client's representation may be "materially limited by the lawyer's responsibilities to . . . a third person." [Colorado Ethics Op. 115 (2007) Under Rule 1.7(b), an attorney may represent a client with such a potential conflict of interest if (1) the lawyer reasonably believes they will be able to provide competent and diligent representation and (2) the client gives informed consent confirmed in writing. The Colorado Bar Committee found that the collaborative law practice presents a potential conflict under Rule 1.7, since the disqualification agreement gives the lawyer "responsibilities" to a "third person" — the opposing counsel — that may impair the attorney's representation of their own client. The Committee finally concluded that this potential conflict could not be cured by client consent, because whenever the collaborative negotiation process is unsuccessful, the attorney's obligation to the opponent will trump the lawyer's obligation to their own client to pursue, or at least consider, the alternative of litigation. The Colorado Committee recognized that both Kentucky [Ky. Ethics Op. E-425 (2005)] and New Jersey [N.J. Ethics Op. 699 (2005)] had held that attorneys may ethically enter into collaborative law agreements requiring them to withdraw if settlement agreements are not achieved, but it noted that those opinions had not focused on Rule 1.7 conflicts. The American Bar Association has similarly indicated that collaborative law agreements do not contravene ethical standards, so long as informed client consent is obtained [ABA Formal Ethics Op. 07-447 (2007).

The Colorado Committee went on to note the availability of "cooperative law" agreements that incorporate the general good faith, cooperative, and interest-based aspects of collaborative law agreements, but which do not require the negotiating attorneys to withdraw if litigation becomes necessary (see Lande, 2008; Peppet, 2008). This more limited cooperative law arrangement would not contravene the Model Rules, since under Rule 1.2, an attorney and client may agree in advance that the representation will be confined to the cooperative law approach. These arrangements would also not involve the types of potential conflicts of interest indigenous to collaborative law programs requiring the attorneys to withdraw if no settlements are attained.

Many litigators, especially in large value cases, find that serious settlement offers are only forthcoming as trial dates approach. When both the plaintiffs and the defendants — especially the defendants in most cases — are convinced that the other side is willing to try the cases if necessary *and* are fully prepared to do so, they begin to ask whether they want to risk the costs and unpredictability of adjudications.

Over the past ten to fifteen years, I have occasionally worked with plaintiff attorneys as a negotiation specialist. In almost every case, we have achieved settlement agreements within one week of trial. If defense lawyers knew from the outset that we could not represent the claimants if the cases were to be litigated, I am convinced they would not be as generous.

Whenever litigators begin settlement talks, they should assume they will achieve peaceful resolutions of their claims. Fewer than two percent of federal civil complaints culminate in adjudications today, and similar figures pertain to most state court dockets. It thus behooves lawyers to use nondisruptive, problem-solving techniques that will effectively and efficiently advance client interests. The overwhelming majority of clients want to control their own legal destinies. They rarely wish to have judges, juries, or arbitrators determine their fates. By assuming an interest-based approach, legal representatives further this client objective. On the other hand, if they promise not to represent the clients in the rare instances in which mutual accords cannot be achieved, they may undermine the litigation credibility they need to induce other parties to treat them as seriously as they would opponents who are authorized to litigate if this option becomes necessary.

§ 2.03   TYPE OF NEGOTIATION

Different kinds of negotiations involve different participants and/or unique consider-ations that may influence the negotiation process. Advocates must consider these factors when developing bargaining strategies. Some transactions are very complex in terms of legal or factual issues, such as complicated antitrust and securities law cases and corporate merger agreements. Other dealings do not raise complex legal or factual issues, such as uncomplicated personal injury disputes and rudimentary contractual arrangements. The more complicated an interaction is factually or legally, the more protracted the negotiation process is likely to be. Parties must generally obtain a basic understanding of the overall circumstances before they can achieve a mutually acceptable result. Any effort to unduly accelerate this process may only serve to create suspicion and prolong the discussions.

Business people often complain about the opportunities they have lost because of excessive legal formalism practiced by many attorneys. While these individuals may underestimate the need for appropriate circumspection by their legal representatives in some situations, there are undoubtedly times when they're correct. Unnecessary emphasis on legal irrelevancies can in some circumstances preclude beneficial transac-tions. Negotiators should try to minimize reliance on pure "legal principle," when this would either prevent agreements or lock the parties into uncompromising positions. Negotiators are more likely to succeed when they can structure an arrangement in alternative ways.

I recall one practice situation in which blind adherence to legalistic principle would probably have destroyed a client. We represented a large motor speedway that conducted several major races each year. During pre-event time trials and on actual race days, several hundred workers were employed at the track. During the remaining periods of the year, only about twenty-five people remained employed. The labor organization that represented all of the non-supervisory employees requested a collective bargaining agreement that included a "service fee" provision. This provision would require those individuals employed only in connection with the major events to pay a fifty-cent-per-day representational fee. Since the National Labor Relations Act does not authorize mandatory union security arrangements until "on or after the thirtieth day following the beginning of such employment" [29 U.S.C. § 158(a)(3)], it was apparent that the labor organization was seeking a technically impermissible provision. It, however, considered this matter a "strike issue," because it would be legally obliged to represent not only the regular employees but also those people hired to work the main races. Had the raceway relied exclusively on legal principle, it would most likely have precipitated a disastrous work stoppage. Since the union proposal was reasonable in light of the beneficial representation provided for the temporary employees, we accepted it. Nonetheless, to fully protect the interests of our client, we insisted upon, and obtained, an indemnification clause under which the labor organization agreed to hold the raceway harmless for any litigation that might result from the special "service fee" term included in the bargaining agreement. It is interesting to note that no challenge to the legality of this provision has been raised by any person during the many years of its operation.

In some negotiations, each party is in a position to deal with other persons if an agreement is not reached between the current participants. In other settings, however, the result of a nonsettlement is either an adjudication or no transaction. This factor significantly affects the need of the bargaining parties to achieve mutual accords. When present discussions prove fruitless, and alternative arrangements are likely, the parties have no reason to permit irrational anxiety to culminate in disadvantageous agreements. On the other hand, when no external options are readily available, bargainers should endeavor to maximize the likelihood of mutual accords. It should be apparent that tactics used in the former low-risk situation may be inappropriate in the latter setting.

Some transactions, such as tort suits, involve one-time interactions between clients, while others, such as labor-management dealings, marital dissolutions involving child-custody arrangements, and franchisor/franchisee undertakings, entail continuing relationships. The possibility of future dealings could influence the tactics used during the current negotiation. It is thus advisable to avoid techniques that might adversely affect subsequent interactions (Lewicki & Hiam, 2006, at 25–28). Similar considerations apply when an agreement must be satisfied over a period of time instead of immediately, such as a construction contract.

Even when the respective clients are unlikely to engage in future transactions, their legal representatives will probably interact again (Gilson & Mnookin, 1994). This should preclude resort to tactics that may produce a short-term gain for the present client at the expense of prospective clients (Johnston & Waldfogel, 2002). One may argue that because a lawyer is obliged to zealously represent the interests of the instant client, they should use whatever tactics they deem necessary regardless of any fear of negative future consequences vis-a-vis opposing counsel. I do not agree. If the adoption of such a negotiating strategy would prejudice future dealings with this or other practitioners, the behavior is beyond the bounds of propriety. No clients should have the right to expect their legal representatives to employ disreputable tactics that would likely diminish their ability to represent future clients. Lawyers can be zealous advocates while behaving in a courteous and professional manner.

When the immediate clients have complete control over the transaction, it is generally easy to obtain client consent to negotiated results. On the other hand, when one or both clients have additional constituencies that must ultimately approve any proposed agreement (*e.g.*, negotiating with a governmental entity about a matter that will necessitate political action before effectuation, or participating in a corporate transaction in which any resulting contract must receive board-of-director or shareholder approval) different considerations apply. A complete record should be carefully maintained, so that a detailed explanation can be given to the constituent body regarding the rationale underlying each agreed upon term. This approach will usually facilitate ultimate ratification.

Summary

1. Negotiators must understand the personal needs of the advocates and the clients involved in their transactions Only then, can they formulate agreements that satisfy those underlying interests.

2. Cooperative/problem-solving negotiators tend to behave in a realistic, congenial, and trusting manner. They endeavor to maximize joint returns and to accommodate the competing interests of the different participants.

3. Competitive/adversarial negotiators tend to behave in a closed and untrusting manner. They frequently use threats or other manipulative tactics to obtain extreme results that benefit their own clients.

4. The most proficient negotiators tend to be competitive/problem-solving individuals who employ congenial, problem-solving techniques to obtain highly beneficial terms for their own clients. Within this framework, they also attempt to maximize opponent returns when it can be accomplished at minimal cost to their own side.

5. Advocates should not take the negotiation process personally — viewing their opponents as the "enemy" — but should instead recognize that they would have no business if it were not for their dealings with opposing counsel.

6. The type of negotiation may influence the process, depending on whether the transaction is complex or straight-forward, and whether it involves a one-time interaction or a continuing relationship.

Chapter 3

VERBAL AND NONVERBAL COMMUNICATION

§ 3.01 VERBAL COMMUNICATION

[1] Determining Validity

All bargaining transactions involve communication. This is accomplished through verbal discourse and nonverbal signals. Because of the importance of nonverbal exchanges, this topic will be explored separately in the following section.

Verbal expressions can convey very different messages, even when they superficially appear to say the same thing. Negotiators must carefully consider the exact words chosen to determine whether speakers actually intend the message they seem to be conveying. If an unambiguous statement is involved, the speaker's assertion is clear. The recipient must decide whether the representation has been made in a credible manner. On the other hand, the speaker may through the inclusion of a "verbal leak" undermine the seemingly definitive nature of the representation (LePoole, 1991, at 34). Verbal leaks, among other aspects, afford the recipient the opportunity to recognize the equivocal message being conveyed.

21

[2]   Verbal Leaks

Why do individuals frequently use verbal leaks during bargaining encounters? They feel uncomfortable employing direct deception. They have been raised to believe that lying is reprehensible. They thus feel uneasy saying they cannot offer more when they are authorized to do so. To assuage their consciences, they include the modifiers that make their statements more truthful. They don't *want* to offer more or are *not inclined* to do so. Opponents do not care whether these speakers want or are inclined to raise their present offers. Their adversaries only care whether they will actually offer more.

Negotiators who recognize verbal leaks contained in opponent representations must be patient. The modifying phrases indicate that further progress is likely, but it may take time for concessions to develop. If the speakers are pushed too quickly, they will feel compelled to preserve their credibility through temporary intransigence. They must be given sufficient time to formulate face-saving explanations for their seemingly inconsistent position changes.

Negotiators must also monitor their own language. During the critical stages of transactions, they should employ more definitive terms that do not include verbal leaks. This technique makes their representations more effective and forces their opponents to speculate about the veracity of the messages. If unequivocal speakers subsequently discover that they need to make additional concessions to reach an agreement, they can always take a break "to consult" their clients. They can thereafter modify their previous positions without undermining their credibility. Consider the following examples:

1. "I cannot offer you any more!"

In this statement, the speaker is unequivocally indicating that no additional concessions can now be made. If their nonverbal clues evidence congruent signals (*e.g.*, open, sincere posture with palms extended toward the listener to indicate that nothing is being deceptively hidden), it is likely that the declarant means exactly what they say.

2. "I am *not authorized* to offer you any more."

This is a more equivocal communication on its face, because it uses limited client authority as the basis for the representation being made. The reliance upon client authority may be used to provide verisimilitude for a significant misrepresentation. It may alternatively be included for the purpose of indicating that no further concessions will be forthcoming from the speaker prior to a subsequent recess during which the absent client may be consulted. This "limited authority" technique, which will be discussed further in Chapter 10, may enable this negotiator to obtain more generous offers from his or her opponent under circumstances in which no reciprocal concessions can be immediately expected.

3. "I am not able to offer you any more *at this time*."

In this type of statement, the speaker is indicating that his or her expressed recalcitrance is most likely a temporary condition, as evidenced by the qualifying term "at this time." This type of language is frequently used to convey the message that reciprocal concessions will be made if only the other party will indicate that they are amenable to compromise. This supposition can easily be tested through a slight change of position intended to precipitate an appropriate counteroffer.

4. *"I do not believe* **that I can offer you any more."**

The inclusion of the "do not believe" phrase should induce a careful listener to suspect that the statement is somewhat disingenuous. A simple, unambiguous declaration, such as Statement 1, could easily have been used had the speaker intended to convey a definitive message. Since most people have been taught that mendacity is morally reprehensible, they frequently use qualifying words to soften the degree of dishonesty involved. If this person were subsequently induced to make a seemingly contradictory concession, he or she could always suggest that the additional information and/or entreaties of the responding party generated the change of mind.

5. *"My client is not inclined/does not wish* **to offer any more."**

Phrases like "is not inclined" and "does not wish" constitute classic verbal leaks. Since these speakers do not want to lock themselves into unalterable positions or make deliberate misrepresentations, they include modifying language that leaves room for further movement. The critical question is not whether the opponent "is inclined" or "wants" to make additional concessions. The question is merely whether that party will actually do so.

6. **"That's** *about as far* **as I can go"/"I don't have** *much more* **room."**

Statements like these indicate that the speakers have not reached their true bottom lines. They still have room to move. With patience, they can be induced to make additional concessions.

7. **"I** *must have* **Item 1, I** *really want* **Item 2, and I** *would like to have* **Item 3."**

This statement includes verbal leaks indicating the degree to which the speaker values the items in question. Item 1 is critical to the deal because the speaker *must have* it. Item 2 is important, but not a deal-breaker. Item 3 would be nice, but it is not that important to the demanding party. A careful listener should be aware of these semantic distinctions and appreciate the prioritizing information.

[3] Signal Words

"Signal words" may similarly influence the communication process. They may be used by speakers to create disingenuous impressions in the minds of opponents. They may also be employed by listeners to induce speakers to disclose more information than they intended to divulge. Examples of this phenomenon can be observed in the following statements:

1. *"To be perfectly candid,* **this is the most I can offer you."**

Assuming that the declarant has not used phrases such as "to be perfectly candid," "to be candid," "to be honest," etc., throughout the negotiation when making obviously correct assertions, the recipient of this type of message should be suspicious of its veracity. Such a term frequently accompanies a misrepresentation to enhance its credibility. Negotiators should carefully note the manner in which such signal words have been used by the speaker throughout the bargaining session. When they appear in a context suggesting a lack of candor, listeners should be particularly vigilant.

2. *"In my humble opinion,* **I think that my proposal would satisfy the needs of both of our clients."**

Many negotiators effectively use false humility to induce their adversaries to lower their guard in anticipation of an easy interaction. Phrases such as "in my humble opinion," "far be it for me to say," "if I might suggest," and "if you can accept the view of a woman" are often used to soften the competitive nature of the declarants, thereby disguising their hidden desire for bargaining "victories" (Nierenberg & Calero, 1981, at 31). Opponents should recognize the manipulative nature of these phrases.

3. "Do you mind if I suggest . . . "; "How about . . . "; "Have you ever considered . . . "

Passive-aggressive negotiators who lack the ability to display their aggression often use softening terms such as these. Their purpose to mask the negtiator's desire to dictate the terms they really want. This approach may subtly undermine negotiations, because they involve "parent" to "child" transactions that fail to accord listeners appropriate "adult" respect (Berne, 1964). More overt examples of such *downers* include "don't be ridiculous" and "don't make me laugh" when rejecting proposals (Nierenberg & Calero, 1981, at 38–39).

4. "You probably lack the authority to accept the generous offer I am proposing."

Even though this apparently objective statement seems to entail an "adult" to "adult" exchange rationally indicating that the listener is not authorized to make a final commitment regarding this proposal on behalf of his or her client, it simultaneously involves an ulterior transaction. The speaker conveys a hidden message of a "parent" to "child" relationship suggesting that the "child" may not accept the tendered offer. If the recipient of the message irrationally responds in a child-like manner, he or she may well accept the proposed agreement to spitefully demonstrate his or her capacity to do so (Berne, 1964, at 33).

5. "I understand how you feel."; "I see."

Good bargainers are active listeners (Ordover & Doneff, 2002, at 18–20). While they do not accept all of the representations being made by their opponents, they interject terms such as these to let speakers know that they are being heard. Patient listening communicates a supportive environment, frequently inducing less skilled adversaries to disclose more information than they intend. It also demonstrates respect for the declarants and helps to create an atmosphere that is conducive to open and collaborative discussions.

[4]   Body Posture, Speech Pattern Mirroring, and Sensory Preference Reflection

[a]   Body Posture and Speech Pattern Mirroring

When individuals interact with others, they tend to respond more favorably to persons who exhibit body postures and speech patterns similar to their own (Goleman, 2006, at 30–31; Pease & Pease, 2006, at 250–64, Anderson, 2004, at 203; Madonik, 2001, at 59, 158–59; Ury, 1991, at 46–47). Negotiators who wish to take advantage of this factor can try to mirror the body postures of those with whom they are interacting. If their opponent leans back in her chair, they lean back in their own chair. If that person decides to cross one leg over the other, they cross the same leg over their other leg to reflect that individual's posture. If their adversary leans forward in her chair, they lean forward in a similar manner. If the other party leans to one side, they adopt a similar position.

They may similarly mirror the speech patterns of their adversary by speaking more slowly when he does so and speaking more rapidly when he picks up the pace. They may similarly work to reflect the other person's speech tone and inflection. If the other party elevates his voice pitch, they may do the same with their voice.

Negotiators mirroring the postures and speech patterns of their opponents must be careful to do so inconspicuously to avoid detection. If they accomplish the desired objective, they will make themselves more likeable to their opponents. On the other hand, if their actions become obvious, their conduct may be perceived as disingenuous and even mocking. Their behavior would have a negative impact and undermine their interaction.

[b]   Sensory Preference Reflection

When people think and speak, they tend to employ one of three sensory preferences (Madonik, 2001, at 24–31, 128–29, 160–61; Hogan, 1966, at 144–45). Some individuals have a *visual* orientation. The eyes of such persons either move upward or stare in an unfocused manner. Their words describe visual images of what they are discussing. For example, they may ask if you can *picture* what they are proposing, or they may say that they can *see* what you are requesting. Such visual persons respond most favorably to people who reply in a similar fashion. For example, opponents might describe their position graphically. They might alternatively indicate that they can *see* what is bothering the other side.

Other persons have an *auditory* orientation. When they talk, their eyes tend to move from side to side or move downward and to their left. Their words describe auditory messages. They may ask opponents to *listen to* what they are proposing, or indicate that their proposal has *rung a bell* with them. They might alternatively suggest that adversaries *voice* their opinion about something. These persons are likely to be receptive to opponents who respond with similar auditory references. They might suggest that they *hear* their concerns. Adversaries might indicate that their proposed joint venture would *explode* across the business world or would be received with a *bang* on Wall Street.

The third group of people tend to have a *kinesthetic/feeling* framework. They are individuals who *feel* or *sense* things. When they speak, their eyes tend to move down and to their right. They are likely to say that something *smells bad* or has left a *bad taste* in their mouth. They may rely on a *gut feeling*. To maximize the receptiveness of such persons to opponent communications, others should reflect their kinesthetic/feeling orientation. They might respond that their proposal *feels good*. Adversaries might indicate that they understand why the other side is *not comfortable* with the proposal on the table.

Negotiators who listen carefully for the sensory orientations of opponents should be able to determine whether they are visual, auditory, or kinesthetic/feeling persons. By responding in the same framework, they can increase the likelihood their ideas will be favorably received. Such an approach can greatly enhance communication between the bargaining parties.

[5]   Gain-Loss Issue Framing

[a]   Impact

Negotiators must recognize that they can increase the likelihood that opponents will select choices by the way in which they frame problems. Most people are risk averse when choosing between a *sure gain* and an uncertain alternative that *may result* in a greater gain or nothing. On the other hand, when one option entails a *definite loss* and the alternative *involves greater loss or the possibility of no loss,* most people become risk takers (Korobkin, 2006 at 308–12; Guthrie, 2003, at 1117–27; Korobkin, 2002, at 14–15; Guthrie, Rachlinski & Wistrich, 2001, at 794–99; Kahneman & Tversky, 1979; Tversky & Kahneman, 1981).

This gain-loss framing phenomenon explains why most law suit settlement discussions favor defendants. Both plaintiffs and their lawyers, who are usually compensated on a contingent fee basis, view defense offers as sure gains, while the defendants appear to be facing sure losses. The sure-gain plaintiffs tend to be more risk-averse than the sure-loss defendants (*see generally* Rachlinski, 1996).

Negotiators confronting negative frames tend to obtain more favorable outcomes for themselves than negotiators facing positive frames (Thompson, Neale & Sinaceur, 2004, at 12). This is caused by the fact that people dealing with negative frames work harder to avoid negative consequences than individuals dealing with positive frames do to enhance their positive results. Negotiators who can induce their opponents to view bargaining interactions in terms of positive frames are thus more likely to obtain better results for themselves than persons dealing with opponents facing negative frames.

[b]   Sure Gain vs. Possible Greater Gain or No Gain Decision Making

Assume that you must choose between the following two options:

If you select Option A, you will receive $20,000.

If you select Option B, there is a 20 percent probability that you will receive $100,000 and a 80 percent probability that you will receive nothing.

Most individuals would accept the certain $20,000 gain offered by Option A, rather than the risk of receiving nothing associated with Option B — even though Option B provides them with a 20 percent possibility of obtaining $100,000 (Guthrie, 1999, at 54–59; Pratkanis & Aronson, 1991, at 61–63; Bazerman & Neale, 1992, at 33–39).

[c]   Sure Loss vs. Possible Greater Loss or No Loss Decision Making

If the options were framed in the following manner, which would you choose?

If you select Option A, you will lose $20,000.

If you select Option B, there is a 20 percent probability that you will lose $100,000 and a 80 percent probability that you will lose nothing.

When confronted with the second set of alternatives, most individuals choose Option B. They are unwilling to accept the certain loss of $20,000 and prefer the alternative *that may avoid any loss* despite the fact it involves a 20 percent possibility of losing $100,000. This framing concept explains why typical law suit settlement discussions favor defendants. Plaintiffs (and plaintiff counsel) offered a *sure gain* and the possibility of a greater gain or no gain at trial, tend to opt for the certain gain, while defendants (and defendant counsel) facing a *sure loss* and the possibility of a greater loss or no loss at trial tend to select the trial option that may provide them with no loss (Guthrie, 2003, at 1122–23). This factor may explain why defendants who reject plaintiff settlement offers and go to trial substantially underestimate their likely trial losses compared to plaintiffs who reject defendant offers in favor of trial proceedings (Kiser, Asher & McShane, 2008, at 566–67).

[d]   Framing Methods that Maximize Appeal

When individuals negotiate, they should present their proposals in a manner that maximizes the likelihood their opponents will accept their preferred choice. They may usually accomplish this objective by providing opponents with options that appear to provide *certain gain* and force them to choose between these proposals and alternatives that merely involve possible gain. If their opponents are concerned about probable losses, bargainers should propose alternatives that make it appear that they are offering their opponents a *sure gain*. For example, a plaintiff demanding money to resolve a lawsuit can indicate that for this amount of money, the defendant's legal problem will be solved. If they can induce their adversary to view their proposed settlement as a *gain*, they will be more likely to persuade the other side to accept their proposal.

These framing tendencies are only reversed when the probabilities are significantly altered so that Option B provides a much greater possibility of gain or loss. For example, if Option A guaranteed someone $5,000 and Option B gave them a 5 percent probability of receiving $100,000 and a 95 percent probability of receiving nothing, most people would become risk taking and select Option B because of the much greater gain they could achieve. On the other hand, if Option A guaranteed someone a $5,000 loss and Option B gave them a 5 percent chance of losing $100,000 and a 95 percent chance of losing nothing, most individuals would become risk averse and choose Option A in an effort to limit their potential loss (Guthrie, 2003, at 1124–25; Guthrie, 2000, at 166–67, 176–81; Korobkin & Guthrie, 1997, at 95–101; Tversky & Kahneman, 1981, at 454).

This explains why law suit settlement discussions pertaining to seemingly frivolous law suits favor plaintiffs. When plaintiffs are offered $5000 to settle these "nuisance" suits but have a 5 percent possibility of obtaining $100,000 and a 95 percent probability of receiving nothing at trial, they tend to accept the trial option. On the other hand, defendants who have the opportunity to resolve such suits for $5,000 and have a 95 percent probability of prevailing at trial but a 5 percent probability of losing $100,000, tend to select the $5000 settlement option to limit their possible loss. It thus behooves plaintiffs in such high risk cases to hold out for greater offers from defendants who are afraid of the small risk of losing substantial sums at trial.

[6]   Impact of Endowment Effect

Transactional parties trying to negotiate an exchange of different items they possess should appreciate the possible impact of the "endowment effect" on their interaction. Under this theory, people tend to value more highly the items they possess than the items they are thinking of purchasing, even if those commodities are objectively of equal value (Korobkin, 2003, at 1227–35; Kahneman, Knetsch & Thaler, 1990). For example, if half of the persons in a group possess coffee mugs and the other half possess large Swiss chocolate bars of a similar value and people are asked whether they would like to trade the item they possess for the item possessed by the other group members, respondents generally prefer to keep what they have (Knetsch, 1989). This "endowment effect" induces sellers of business firms to value their companies more highly than perspective purchasers, just as prospective buyers tend to undervalue those enterprises vis-a-vis whatever they are thinking of exchanging for them. As a result, negotiators should not be surprised when initial offers and demands are some distance apart. This does not mean that a seller's demand is excessive or that the prospective buyer's offer is insufficient. It merely reflects the tendency for each party to overvalue the items they presently possess, and to undervalue what they are thinking of obtaining in exchange for those items. Through an objective evaluation of the different assets of the business enterprise — perhaps with the assistance of a neutral facilitator — the parties should be able to generate more realistic assessments.

[7]   Loss Aversion

Suppose you are a homeowner deciding whether to add more insulation to your home. You might be told that if you add the new insulation, you will save x cents per day. You might alternatively be informed that if you fail to add the new insulation, you will lose x cents per day. Are you more likely to add the insulation to *save* x cents per day or to avoid losing x cents per day? Studies indicate that we are more likely to make the insulation change to avoid the loss of x cents per day rather than to save x cents – despite the fact that both statements effectively convey the identical information (Malhotra & Bazerman, 2007, at 160-61). What does this mean to negotiators? When they are trying to induce another party to take certain action, they will be more likely to obtain compliance with their request if they indicate how much the other side will *lose* if it fails to act, rather than by stating how much the other side will *gain* if they do so!

[8]   Regret Aversion

Another factor that can influence the negotiating behavior of parties concerns "regret aversion" (Guthrie, 1999). Most people do not like to make decisions that may be shown by subsequent developments to have been incorrect, because such developments cause them to suffer sincere regret. For example, litigants tend to prefer settlements that avoid the possibility of trials that could culminate in final terms worse than those rejected during settlement discussions. Corporate buyers and sellers similarly prefer current deals that avoid subsequent developments indicating that rejected offers were preferable to the final deals achieved. To effectively use "regret aversion" theory to influence opponent behavior, negotiators should subtly suggest to those individuals that their nonsettlement alternatives may turn out to be worse than what they are presently being offered. To avoid the possibility of discovering that they should not have rejected the sure offers placed before them now, the offerees are likely to accept those terms and get on with their lives.

[9]   Optimistic Overconfidence

Various empirical studies indicate that individuals tend to be overconfident regarding their predictions pertaining to the outcomes of future events (Korobkin, 2006, at 284-88). For example, if different people are given identical information with respect to a hypothetical law suit and are asked to evaluate the probability the plaintiff or the defendant will prevail if the case is adjudicated, individuals designated the "plaintiff" tend to overestimate the likelihood the plaintiff will prevail while individuals designated the "defendant" tend to overestimate the likelihood the defendant will prevail. How does this psychological phenomenon influence negotiating parties? It tends to widen the gap between the two sides, due to the fact the plaintiffs are overconfident of their likelihood of trial success, while the defendants have similar overconfidence with respect to their probability of success. Legal representatives should appreciate the impact of this factor both upon their clients *and* themselves, and they should try to evaluate the true probability of success as objectively as possible. In larger cases, they can use focus groups to determine how neutral parties evaluate their situations. In smaller cases, they can ask non-involved colleagues or friends to assess the operative circumstances.

[10]   Attribution Bias

When beneficial things occur, people tend to overestimate the degree to which their own personal efforts ("dispositional characteristics") contributed to those results, but when negative things take place, individuals tend to underestimate their personal responsibility for those events attributing them to "situational characteristics" beyond their control (Malhotra & Bazerman, 2007, at 135-36; Korobkin, 2006, at 298-302). For example, if defendants are involved in accidents or business disputes, they are likely to attribute the negative consequences to factors beyond their control. This phenomenon can anger the adversely affected parties who think the responsible persons are unfairly refusing to accept the blame for their actions. If individuals think their own actions have meaningfully contributed to negative results, they should at least minimally acknowledge their responsibility and offer sincere apologies to the persons adversely affected. This approach can diminish the emotional baggage that would otherwise exist in the harmed parties.

This "self-serving attribution bias" also becomes apparent in negotiation courses as students work on a series of negotiation exercises. As the term progresses, students who have performed well on the exercises attribute their success to personal characteristics such as intelligence, perseverance, and careful planning (Malhotra & Bazerman, 2007, at 135). On the other hand, students who have not achieved good results tend to criticize the "unrealistic" exercises or blame their "uncooperative" or "unethical" opponents. This phenomenon makes it difficult for instructors to work with students who have not performed well to modify their behavior in ways that might improve their results. Since they blame external factors for their lack of success, it is not easy for them to accept the fact that some of their own attributes may be undermining their performance.

[11]   Paradox of Choice and Influence of the Impact Bias

When people negotiate, they must make many decisions. They must initially decide whether to negotiate at all. They must then plan their strategies, their objectives, and their opening positions. As the bargaining interactions develop, they must decide whether to accept particular offers being tendered. Several interesting psychological factors influence how individuals deal with these choices. It is often assumed that the more options persons have the easier it will be for them to determine the optimal one. Studies indicate that the opposite may be true (*see generally* Schwartz, 2004). When we compare various alternatives, we often fail to explore them together. We compare Option A with Option B, then Option C with Option D, and Option E with Option F. Even though Option B may best suit our overall needs, we may select Option F because when we evaluate it, we only compare it to Option E. Since it is clearly preferable to E, we accept Option F. Had we compared it closely with Options A through D, we would have appreciated the fact that Option B is the best of the four.

To minimize the likelihood decision-makers will be adversely affected by the *Paradox of Choice*, they should initially work to eliminate the inferior options from their final assessment group. They should also list the pros and cons of each alternative that will be finally considered. If they can reduce their ultimate number of options to a finite number and develop relatively objective assessments of each, they should find it easier to select the one that is actually optimal for them.

Another phenomenon also influences the decision-making process. People have a tendency "to overestimate the impact of future events on their emotional lives" (Wilson & Gilbert, 2003, at 349). They often over-estimate what they think will make them happy and the long-term impact of their choices (Kahneman, 1997, at 107-16). For example, this "impact bias" may cause clients to believe that certain negotiation outcomes will greatly please them for many years to come, when their degree of euphoria may be both less significant and shorter in duration than they anticipate (Guthrie & Sally, 2004, at 618-27). If they allow their visceral feelings to dictate their decision-making, they may opt for negotiated terms that will bring them far less pleasure than they anticipate. Although their legal representatives have an ethical obligation to allow them to decide what terms to accept or reject under Model Rule 1.2, it would not be improper for their attorneys to ask some questions designed to induce them to consider two critical factors. First, will the proffered terms be as satisfying as they presently think they will be? Second, will the long-range impact of those terms be as on-going as they believe they will?

I observe the impact of the "impact bias" on employment discrimination cases I mediate. Discriminatorily discharged claimants often initially hope to obtain large monetary amounts that may enable them either to retire early or to accept lower paying positions elsewhere. The amount of money involved seems substantial, and they expect it will bring them eternal happiness. When they consider their alternatives more carefully, however, they realize that the money would be exhausted more rapidly than they initially thought, and they would actually prefer to return to their challenging former positions than move to less demanding jobs elsewhere. They then decide to take a closer look at the alternative of less compensation with reinstatement to their prior positions or to equally stimulating ones with their former employer.

[12]   Influence of Attorney Perspectives on Client Choices

Studies indicate that lawyers are less influenced by such factors as anchoring, gain-loss framing, regret aversion, and similar psychological phenomena than are the litigants they represent (Korobkin & Guthrie, 1997, at 95-112). This is attributed to the fact that lawyers are trained to be detached, objective, and analytical, causing them to evaluate settlement offers based more on their true value than on subjective considerations. When attorneys describe to clients the impact on their decision-making of such factors as anchoring, gain-loss framing, and regret aversion, the studies indicate that the clients tend to assess outstanding opponent offers in a more objective manner (Korobkin & Guthrie, 1997, at 113-121). Although lawyers must be careful to recognize that the final decision to accept or reject offers rests with their clients under Model Rule 1.2(a), it is entirely appropriate for legal representatives to educate their clients about the possible impact of these psychological influences when they are evaluating opponent offers to enable them to make more objective and less emotional determinations.

§ 3.02 NONVERBAL COMMUNICATION

[1] Reading and Interpreting Nonverbal Communication

Nonverbal communication, one of the most important sources of information available to negotiators, is frequently overlooked, even though it constitutes a majority of the communication being conveyed (Pease & Pease, 2006, at 10; Stark & Flaherty, 2003, at 45). Participants generally concentrate on what is being verbally communicated by their opponents. Bargainers who ignore nonverbal stimuli are only cognizant of the most controlled communication being sent by opposing parties (Quilliam, 2004, at 9; Ekman & Friesen, 1975, at 135–136). They also miss nonverbal messages that are being conveyed while adversaries are not speaking. Unless they can train themselves to appreciate the subtle nonverbal signs that significantly influence the negotiation process, advocates will rarely have a comprehensive understanding of the transaction. In fact, through oversight of nonverbal communication, they may miss the most trustworthy messages that their adversaries convey. They may also fail to appreciate the nonverbal messages they are conveying to the other side (Quilliam, 2004, at 11–13).

Should negotiators try to fake their nonverbal signals to confuse their opponents? Rarely can persons manipulate their own signals in a credible manner (Anderson, 2004, at 5). Although most people can tell credible lies verbally, few individuals who have not studied acting and become proficient performers are able to convey disingenuous nonverbal messages in a believable way.

During their formal law school education, students are forced to think in a logical and abstract fashion. They are instructed to disregard emotional considerations that do not have an empirically verifiable foundation (Ryan, 2005). The truly personal aspect of relationships is viewed as irrelevant to the lawyering function. Mere intuitive "feelings" are to be accorded little or no respect.

People with negotiating experience can all recall circumstances in which they sensed that their adversaries were being disingenuous. Numerous "last offers" have been rejected, along with "final last offers" and even "absolutely final last offers" as preludes to more generous proposals that were subsequently accepted. What induced these persons to sense that the allegedly "final" position statements were merely intermediate steps in the overall process? These suppositions are generally based upon the reading of nonverbal signals which are not congruent with the verbal messages being conveyed (Calero, 2005, at 89–90).

True final offers are not casually transmitted from persons who are sitting back in their chair with their arms folded across their chest. The speakers are likely to be leaning slightly forward in the chair with their arms extended and their palms facing outward to demonstrate the openness and sincerity of their positions. It is only when the nonverbal signals are consistent with the words being expressed that the verbal representations become credible.

[2]   Barriers to Effective Reading and Interpreting

Negotiators must learn to seriously consider the tentative "feelings" they experience (Ryan, 2005, at 275–76). When they have the sense that their opponent is making a misrepresentation or is receptive to their most recent offer despite oral protestations to the contrary, they should endeavor to understand the reasons for their suspicions. They may well be based upon their subconscious interpretation of nonverbal messages that provide an accurate impression of the opponent's true situation. These interpretive "feelings" should not be rejected until it can be established that they are not premised on rational considerations.

Most bargainers fail to observe many of the nonverbal signs emanating from their opponents. Some naively believe that there is no need to look for these messages, because no competent negotiator would be so careless as to divulge important information in such an inadvertent manner. Anyone who harbors this opinion should consider theatrical performances by well known actors. Rarely can actors eliminate all of their own involuntary gestures and mannerisms and portray only those attributable to their characters. If these professionals are unable to avoid unintended nonverbal disclosures, surely untrained negotiators will experience less success in this regard.

Other negotiation participants focus so intently upon the responses they are formulating that they miss direct verbal as well as nonverbal messages sent by opponents. This problem is compounded by the fact that negotiations involve stressful settings that tend to decrease the cognitive abilities of the participants (Hopmann & Walcott in Drukman, 1977, at 306). Bargainers must force themselves to observe their adversaries more diligently, even while planning their own internal strategy. People who find such a bifurcated approach too difficult may wish to have other persons participate on their negotiation teams as observers. These assistants could carefully listen to and observe opposing counsel. They could also determine if any unintended information is being inadvertently disclosed by their own spokespersons.

[3]   Advantages in Training and Background

Some individuals tend to be more adroit readers of nonverbal communication than others. People trained in psychology, counseling, and theatrics are usually more cognizant of nonverbal stimuli. A number of empirical studies have found that women are typically more sensitive to nonverbal messages than their male cohorts (Pease & Pease, 2006, at 13–14; Ford, 1996, at 208–09; Hall, 1984, at 16–17, 27; Mayo & Henley, 1981, at 7; Henley, 1977, at 13–15). Studies have also found that African-Americans are more attuned to nonverbal signals than Caucasians (Hall, 1984, at 41–42; Henley, 1977, at 14).These gender and racial differences may reflect the fact that members of groups that have historically had less societal empowerment have learned to be more perceptive with respect to nonverbal clues as a means of counterbalancing their power imbalance (Henley, 1977, at 14–15).

Persons who are not especially sensitive to nonverbal stimuli can easily enhance their ability in this regard. Various books have thoughtfully explored the nonverbal communication area in a manner that is comprehensible to people who have not formally studied this important topic (Pease & Pease 2006; Calero, 2005; Anderson, 2004; Dimitrius & Mazzarella, 1998; Morris, 1994; Hall, 1984; Druckman, Rozelle & Baxter, 1982; Henley, 1977; Beir & Valens, 1975; Nierenberg & Calero, 1971; Fast, 1970). By reading several of these books and concentrating more intently on the nonverbal behavior of others in social as well as business settings, less skilled nonverbal readers can significantly improve their capabilities. They should carefully observe the facial expressions, hand movements, and body postures of those with whom they interact, and they should ask themselves what these movements say about the individuals being watched.

[4] Common Nonverbal Signals

One of the most obvious forms of nonverbal communication involves facial expressions. A derisive smile may be employed to demonstrate disdain for a wholly unacceptable proposal. Conversely, a subtle smile or other sign of relief in response to a person's fourth or fifth proposal may indicate that this offer is almost acceptable. Such a supposition may be reinforced by the fact that the responding negotiator did not reject this offer with the same alacrity with which previous submissions were declined. It may also have been renounced through the use of a "signal" phrase such as "to be candid" or "to be honest." On the other hand, if a few proposals have been exchanged and a bargainer's effort to make a suggestion believed to be quite reasonable is received with a pained expression (*e.g.*, taut lips and/or the gnashing of teeth evidenced by the visible expansion and contraction of the jaw muscles on both sides of the face), it should be apparent that either or both participants have incorrectly assessed the true value of this transaction.

Negotiators should always look for "double messages" that emanate from clients or adversaries. For example, individuals may, while stating how disappointed they are regarding some unfortunate developments, accompany their sad words with inappropriate signs of pleasure (*e.g.*, smiles). These contradictory facial expressions would strongly suggest that these speakers are not really as disconsolate as their unembellished statements might otherwise indicate. These persons most likely enjoy their current plight and do not want to have their problem alleviated too expeditiously.

Attorneys who negotiate in teams need to establish specified means to communicate with one another during bargaining sessions without inadvertently divulging confidential information. If they fail to resolve this problem beforehand, they may disclose their thoughts through a casual sideways glance or a slight nod toward a partner following a particular offer. They may communicate a similar message when they decide to caucus over an offer under circumstances in which the five prior proposals had been summarily rejected without the need for any conference. When several individuals plan to represent the same party it is frequently advantageous to designate a single speaker to make the immediate decisions necessary during the bargaining meetings. This member would be authorized to do so without consulting the other team members first. In order to avoid letting their opponents know how interested they are in particular offers, this speaker can initially announce an intention to caucus every hour or two to discuss developments.

Negotiators must remember that facial expressions are generally controlled more readily than are less voluntary body movements. Contrived smiles or frowns may be carefully orchestrated to convey deceptive messages, while less voluntary arm, leg, and upper body movements are more likely to communicate true feelings. It is thus imperative for bargaining participants to observe as many informative body movements as possible. They should not merely focus on facial signals. Furthermore, no isolated signal should be given a definitive interpretation. People must look for *changes in the behavior of others* and predictable *patterns of conduct* (Pease & Pease, 2006, at 21; Calero, 2005, at 73; Stark & Flaherty, 2003, at 47). The following examples illustrate various forms of nonverbal communication:

1. Facial Expressions

Even though facial expressions are generally the most easily manipulated form of nonverbal communication, subtle clues may frequently be perceived by careful observers. Taut lips may indicate anxiety or frustration. A subtle smile (usually hidden by a bowed head) or brief signs of relief around the corners of an opponent's mouth when a new offer is being conveyed may indicate that the offer is approaching or has entered that person's settlement range. The nonverbal indication of relief evidences that individual's belief that a final settlement is likely.

2. Flinch — Pained Facial Expression

This may be an uncontrolled response to a surprisingly inadequate opening offer. An uncontrolled flinch sincerely indicates to the offeror the wholly unacceptable nature of his or her initial position. Adroit negotiators may employ a contrived "flinch" to silently challenge opposing party opening offers without having to engage in verbal discourse (Dawson, 1995, at 18–21). Skilled use of the "flinch" may subtly undermine opponent confidence in their position, and it may induce careless adversaries to modify their initial offers before they obtain opening position statements from their flinching adversaries.

3. Raising of One Eyebrow

The involuntary raising of a single eyebrow generally connotes skepticism (Morris, 1994, at 51). This signal may sincerely indicate that the actor is suspicious of opponent overtures. It may be disingenuously employed by manipulative negotiators to suggest their disappointment with opponent offers or concessions.

4. Raising Both Eyebrows/Widening of Eyes

This is a clear indication of surprise. It is often visible when a negotiator's opening offer or subsequent position change is more generous than the recipient anticipated. It may similarly follow the disclosure of wholly unanticipated information. When negotiators observe such signs, they should suspect potentially serious tactical errors on their part. They should quickly reassess their present situations and try to determine whether they have made inadvertent tactical mistakes.

5. Scratching Head/Brushing Cheek with Hand

These are usually indications of puzzlement (Morris, 1994, at 16, 143). Such behavior may suggest that the actor is having difficulty comprehending the opponent's negotiating behavior. The actor is likely to believe that the bargaining process is not moving in the right direction.

6. Wringing of Hands

This is frequently an indication of frustration or tension. Particularly distraught people are likely to twist their hands and fingers into seemingly painful contortions. This message usually emanates from people who are unhappy with substantive developments or anxious about the aggressive tactics being employed by their opponents.

7. Tightly Gripping Arm Rests/Drumming on the Table

People who are impatient or frustrated often tightly grip the arm rests of their chair or drum their fingers on the table in front of them. Negotiators who are displeased by a perceived lack of progress may engage in this kind of conduct.

8. Biting Lower Lip/Biting Fingernails/Running Fingers Through Hair/Rubbing Forehead

These signs usually indicate stress or frustration. They tend to emanate from individuals who are disappointed by the lack of negotiation progress or by perceived opponent intransigence. As they feel greater frustration, these signals tend to become more intense.

9. Eyes Wandering/Looking at Watch/Crossing & Uncrossing Legs/Doodling/Head Resting in Hand/Sighing

These are signs of boredom and/or disinterest (Dimitrius & Mazzarella, 1998, at 62). These signals would indicate that you're your opponent is not interested in your presentation. You may wish to ask some questions that are designed to get your adversary more actively involved in the discussions and to elicit their real concerns.

10. Shifting Back and Forth in Chair/Tilting Head from Side to Side/Opening and Closing Mouth Without Speaking

These are indications of indecision (Dimitrius & Mazzerella, 1998, at 67–68). The message sender is not sure how to proceed and is contemplating his or her options. You should patiently and silently wait to give this person the time they need to formulate an opinion they can express.

11. Hands Neatly Folded in Lap

This often denotes contrite penitence and possibly even submissiveness (Folberg & Taylor, 1984, at 122). This posture tends to be exhibited more by females than by males. If this information appears to be consistent with other signals emanating from the negotiator, the opposing party should certainly endeavor to encourage this attitude and take advantage of it. However, some people who have been carefully raised to be "good little boys and girls" might sit in this fashion merely because of their prior upbringing. Negotiators should normally avoid such a seemingly submissive posture — unless they are deliberately attempting to induce over-confident opponents to take them lightly.

12. Sitting on the Edge of One's Chair

When this action appears to occur involuntarily following a recent proposal and the posture did not accompany the receipt of previous offers, this may suggest increased interest on the part of the actor. If this interpretation is correct, it may indicate that the offeror is approaching the offeree's zone of expectation. Most persons do not sit literally on the front of their chair. They only move slightly forward in their seat. A few individuals, however, are more demonstrative. They lean so far forward that they place their elbows on the table in front of themselves. This gesture is often made by individuals who are preparing to disclose important information or to make concessions (Calero, 2005, at 84–85).

13. Hands Touching Face/Stroking Chin/Playing with Glasses/Playing with Papers or Notes

These acts are often indications of meditative contemplation. Since people feel awkward regarding the prolonged silence while they are considering proposals and formulating appropriate responses, they frequently resort to these artifices to camouflage their thinking. This conduct may suggest that their opponent's most recent proposal has finally forced them to think seriously about the proper reply. They plan to reject the new offer, but do so in a more positive manner. It may take twenty or thirty seconds for them to formulate their revised rejection statement. To disguise the resulting silent pause, they play with their glasses, stroke their cheeks, or look at their notes. If they did not employ these diversionary actions when they considered prior offers, this probably demonstrates that they perceive the instant proposal to be quite reasonable.

14. Steepling Gesture (Hands Pressed Together with Fingers Uplifted or Hands Together with Interlocked Fingers also Uplifted, with Elbows Out in Expansive Manner)

This conduct often indicates that the actor feels confident (Pease & Pease, 2006, at 132–35; Calero, 2005, at 78–82). Negotiators who observe this behavior should be certain that they are not conceding more than is necessary, since their opponents appear to be pleased with developments. Individuals being interviewed on television frequently display steepling signs when they think they are doing well.

15. Leaning Back in Chair with Hands on Back of Head

This posture is adopted more by males than by females. It is usually an indication of confidence and contentedness (Pease & Pease, 2006, at 245–46). When men who are interacting with women adopt this posture, it is not only a sign of confidence but an indication of perceived domination. Female negotiators who observe this behavior in male opponents should be especially cautious, because those people may think that things are going their way. This action is also an indication of power and authority, and is frequently employed by superiors when they interact with subordinates.

16. Placing One Hand Behind Head

When someone uses one hand to clasp the neck behind their ear, this is usually an indication of distress (Morris, 1994, at 168). It is as if the person is psychologically giving himself or herself a consoling hug to offset the negative consequences being experienced. During bargaining interactions, such a posture is likely to indicate that the actor sees negative developments ahead.

17. Extending Hands Toward Opponent with Fingers Pointed Upward and Palms Facing Out

This is common behavior by individuals who are being verbally assaulted by aggressive bargainers. It is a defensive posture used to symbolically (but ineffectively) protect the actors against the oral onslaught emanating from their opponents (Ilich, 1992, at 161–62).

18. Rubbing Hands Together in Anticipatory Manner

This behavior is often exhibited by anxious negotiators who anticipate beneficial offers from their opponents (Pease & Pease, 2006, at 128–130; Morris, 1994, at 197). This conduct usually suggests an over-eagerness that may be satisfied with a minimal position change.

19. Placing Palm of Right Hand over Heart

Some people voluntarily or involuntarily place the palm of their right hand over their heart when attempting to appear sincere or credible. If this behavior seems inadvertent, it may be a sign of true sincerity. If this action occurs in a deliberate manner, however, it is likely to be a disingenuous effort to mislead the opponent.

20. Open or Uplifted Hands with Palms Facing Out

This technique is generally used to demonstrate openness and sincerity. It is a posture one normally expects when being given true final offers. The posture may be very open — with the hands far apart — or more subtle — with the hands closer together. If the gesture appears stilted, it is probably a deliberate attempt to deceive the observer.

21. Crossed Arms/Crossed Legs

This may constitute an aggressive, adversarial posture or a defensive position, depending on the particular position involved. If the arms are folded high on the chest and the legs are crossed in a "figure-four" position (with the ankle of one leg placed on the knee of the other leg in a typically masculine fashion), this represents a competitive or combative posture. This is especially true if the arm-crosser's fists are also in a closed position (Pease & Pease, 2006, at 95–96), if the arms are folded low on the chest and one leg is draped across the other, this tends to be a defensive position. The intimidated actor is likely to be leaning back in their chair in a subconscious effort to escape the verbal onslaught of the opponent. Both of these crossed arms/crossed legs postures constitute unreceptive poses (Pease & Pease, 2006, at 91–94; Calero, 2005, at 84–85).

If an opponent commences negotiations with arms folded and legs crossed, it is beneficial to try to establish sufficient rapport with this person to soften his or her stance prior to the commencement of formal discussions. Serious final offers should never be made when one's arms are folded and one's legs are crossed, because this does not present a credible appearance.

22. Standing with Hands on Hips

This is a rather aggressive posture that tells others to stay away from the actor (Pease & Pease, 2006, at 237–39; Morris, 1994, at 4). It is often exhibited by angry individuals who do not wish to interact with those around them. People who do not like to negotiate may greet new opponents in this position.

23. Gnashing of Teeth

This is a frequent indication of anxiety or anger, and is evidenced by the contracting and relaxing of the jaw muscles on both sides of the face. Aggressive negotiators should carefully watch for the gnashing of teeth, the wringing of hands, and other reactions that may suggest the opponent is experiencing substantial stress, in recognition of the fact that continued combative conduct may precipitate a cessation of the talks.

24. Covering and Rubbing One Eye

It is not uncommon for individuals to casually cover and rub one eye when they find it difficult to accept something being expressed to them (Morris, 1994, at 49; Scheflen, 1972, at 79). This is the nonverbal equivalent of the expression "my eye" that may be uttered by someone who doubts the veracity of a speaker's comments. Negotiators who encounter this signal when they are making crucial representations should recognize the substantial possibility that their statements are not being accorded much respect. They may wish to rephrase their communication in a more credible manner.

25. Rubbing Chin in Inquisitive Manner

This is another nonverbal sign of disbelief (Morris, 1994, at 31). While the actor may be unwilling to express his or her disbelief verbally, this nonverbal conduct conveys a similar message.

26. Picking Imaginary Lint from One's Clothing

People who disapprove of or are made particularly uncomfortable by shocking or outrageous statements being made by others may begin to pick imaginary lint from their clothing "especially when they are hesitant to express their disapproval or discomfort directly" (Pease & Pease, 2006, at 236; Scheflen, 1972, at 109). This behavior is common in response to graphic descriptions of severe injuries or gory medical procedures.

27. Casual Touching (*e.g.*, Prolonged Hand Shake; Hand or Arm on Opponent's Shoulder or Forearm)

This device can be effectively used to indicate one's sincerity and to establish some rapport (Pease & Pease, 2006, at 104–106). A warm handshake at the commencement of a bargaining interaction can often reduce the likelihood of needless interpersonal conflict. Even during negotiation sessions, casual touching of the other participant's hand or forearm can be used as a "personal touch" to maintain harmonious relations. Even though Americans are not as touching as some cultures, we tend to touch each other during interactions more frequently than most of us realize, even when talking with relative strangers. This is true whether we communicate with persons of the same or the opposite gender.

On rare occasions, a negotiator may try to place an arm over the shoulder of the opposing party in a condescending fashion to denote a superior-subordinate relationship. This tactic may be used by a larger individual toward a smaller person or by a male toward a female. Since the speculative benefits that might be derived from such patronizing conduct would be minimal and this behavior could easily offend the recipient, the use of this approach is definitely not recommended.

People who doubt the value to be obtained through casual touching should study the behavior of airport or train station solicitors. These adroit "negotiators," who possess no real power, commence their brief encounters with the creation of obligation through the provision of a small gift in the form of a flower or booklet. They rapidly enhance their position through the use of touching. I have noticed that when these solicitors are able to touch prospective donors four or five times on the hand, arm, or shoulder in a wholly inoffensive fashion, the likelihood of a contribution increases substantially. Readers who question the general validity of nonverbal signals should ask themselves why some people who respond negatively to these solicitors are immediately left alone, while other persons who provide identical verbal replies are often followed and induced to make contributions. Individuals in the latter category quite obviously emit nonverbal signals indicating that their negative responses are really tentative.

28. Direct Eye Contact

People who make regular eye contact with others are often perceived as being more personable and forthright than those who lack this trait. Negotiators who can maintain nonthreatening eye contact with opponents, can frequently enhance their apparent credibility. They are also likely to be more cognizant of the nonverbal messages emanating from their adversaries. On the other hand, intensive staring is usually perceived as intimidating and combative.

29. Head Nodding

Casual head nodding is generally employed by active listeners to indicate their comprehension of what is being said. Head nodding by listeners is occasionally misinterpreted by speakers as a sign of agreement. Rapid nods, however, may indicate a lack of interest or may be employed by impatient individuals to encourage speakers to get to the point more expeditiously.

30. Turning Around in Chair and Looking Away from Opponent After Making New Offer

This behavior is often expressed by individuals who hate to compromise. They cannot stand to look at opponents after they make concessions. People interacting with these bargainers should not be personally offended by this seemingly disrespectful conduct, but should expect to see it after other position changes.

[5]   Nonverbal Indications of Deception

The preceding part of this section covered various nonverbal clues that do not pertain specifically to the discovery of deliberate deception. This section explores those inadvertent signals that often indicate the employment of intentional misrepresentations. Readers should not, however, be induced to think that they can discern all or even most of the dishonest statements uttered during their negotiations. Few can hope to be so perceptive.

In his book *Telling Lies*, Psychologist Paul Ekman noted that people are surprisingly inept at discovering when they are being told lies (Ekman, 1992, at 86–87; *see also* Sternlight & Robbennolt, 2008, at 486–87; Frank & Ekman, 1997; Ekman, O'Sullivan & Frank, 1999; Vrij, 2000, at 2–4). This phenomenon may be partially due to the fact that mendacity occurs in different forms ranging from mere "puffing" to unabashed prevarication. It must be acknowledged that many of the stereotypically accepted indicia of deceit have little empirical support. This fact was eloquently recognized by a prominent and experienced labor arbitrator:

> Anyone driven by the necessity of adjudging credibility, who has listened over a number of years to sworn testimony, knows that as much truth must have been uttered by shifty-eyed, perspiring, lip-licking, nail-biting, guilty-looking, ill at ease, fidgety witnesses as have lies issued from calm, collected, imperturbable, urbane, straight-in-the-eye perjurers (Jones, 1966, at 1286).

Bargainers who endeavor to rely upon the traditionally cited indicators of deception will undoubtedly reject many generous offers from seemingly untrustworthy fidgetors and accept many disingenuously parsimonious proposals made by seemingly reliable Machiavellian negotiators.

Despite the empirically demonstrated unreliability of the conventionally enumerated indicia of dishonesty, there are clues that can meaningfully assist people to evaluate the veracity of opposing negotiators (Krivis & Zadeh, 2006; Lieberman, 1998; Ford, 1996, at 201–03, 213; Ekman, 1992; Ekman, O'Sullivan, Friesen & Scherer, 1991; Morris, 1994; Druckman, Rozelle & Baxter, 1982). Individuals who plan to make deliberate misrepresentations often emit nonverbal signals that should caution alert observers. Some of these nonverbal messages reflect the stress associated with lying — generated by fear of the truth combined with anxiety regarding the possibility of being caught lying (Ekman, 1992, at 49–64). Other nonverbal behavior is designed to enhance the credibility of the misrepresentations being made. If people are going to engage in mendacious conduct, they want to increase the likelihood they will be believed!

No one signal should be accepted as a definitive indication of deception. Observers must look for *changes* in the speaker's usual behavior and *patterns of behavior* that are consistent with dishonesty. The general anxiety associated with most bargaining encounters may cause someone to exhibit signs of stress, but these should be apparent throughout the critical stages of the interaction. On the other hand, if obvious signs of stress become apparent just before the utterance of a questionable statement, the listener should be suspicious. To further complicate matters, individuals who are afraid that their truthful representations are not going to be believed may exhibit similar signs of stress (Ekman, 1992, at 94).Listeners should also be aware of verbal leaks or signal words (e.g. "To be candid", "to be truthful"), which often indicate the presence of deception. Signal phrases, like "to be candid," are used to induce others to listen more intently to the misrepresentations that follow.

1. Decrease or Increase in Specificity of Statements

When people tell the truth, they fill in the little details as they recall them, adding a substantial amount of incidental information. When individuals fabricate, however, there are no details to remember. As a result, they tend to omit the usual amplifying information, providing the bare details of their lie (Vrij, 2000, at 105; Ekman, 1992, at 106). On the other hand, persons who have prepared elaborate lies may provide an excessive amount of information in an effort to make their fabrication more credible (Lieberman, 1998, at 31). When they get no response to their misrepresentation, they nervously restate the lie. Specific questions about particular facts can often help to deter or discover whether explicit stories are credible (Schweitzer & Croson, 1999). Individuals find it more reprehensible to lie in response to direct questions, and they find it more difficult to provide believable fabrications in response to inquiries that seek specific information.

2. Partial Shrug

People who shrug their shoulders usually indicate that they are ignorant or indifferent. However, if they are being deceptive, they often exhibit a partial shrug of one shoulder that is only briefly visible (Lieberman, 1998, at 16; Ekman, 1992, at 102–03.)

3. Increased or Reduced Gross Body Movement

When people interact, they move their arms, legs, and torso on a fairly regular basis. Rarely do individuals sit or stand perfectly still. Under stressful circumstances, some persons become more fidgety and move their arms and legs at an increased rate (Krivis & Zadeh, 2006, at 123). Some openly fidget or shake. Deceitful people tend to exhibit this behavior as well. However, people may also exhibit contrary behavior when they resort to deceitful tactics. They know that fidgety speakers appear less credible. They attempt to counteract this phenomenon by making a discernible effort to decrease their gross body movement for the purpose of enhancing the trustworthiness of their mendacious comments. Deceitful persons may also exhibit reduced gross body movement as they concentrate on the story they are fabricating (Vrij, 2000, at 38). Negotiators should be especially cautious when they evaluate the veracity of statements made by individuals who have obviously increased *or* decreased their gross body movement.

4. Casual Placing of Hand Over Mouth

Most people have been raised to believe that prevarication is morally wrong. They suffer from a guilty conscience when they engage in deliberate deception. Psychologists have noticed that liars often place their hand over their mouth when they speak, in a subconscious effort to hold in their morally reprehensible falsehoods (Pease & Pease, 2006, at 148–49; Lieberman, 1998, at 15). I have frequently observed this behavior when watching negotiators misstate their client values or settlement intentions.

5. Unconscious Touching of Nose with Finger Tip or Back of Finger; Rubbing One Eye

These gestures are often considered a more subtle equivalent to the "covering of one's mouth" as someone prepares to prevaricate (Pease & Pease, 2006, at 150–51; Morris, 1994, at 182). While these signals may appear in isolation, it is common for deceivers to initially cover their mouth and then quickly touch the side of their nose. Deceitful people may alternatively rub one eye with one or two fingers (Pease & Pease, 2006, at 151–52; Morris, 1994, at 49).

6. Inconsistent Nodding or Shaking of Head

When individuals verbally lie, their heads occasionally give them away (Ford, 1996, at 204). For example, people who say that they are unable to do something may casually nod their heads in an affirmative manner, or persons who state that they want to do something may casually shake their heads in a negative fashion. Their subconscious head movements contradict their misrepresentations and truthfully indicate their intentions.

7. Eyes Looking Up to Wrong Side

When people try to *recall* past events from memory, right handed individuals tend to look up and to the left and left handed persons tend to look up and to the right. On the other hand, when individuals try to *create an image or fact*, right-handed persons tend to look up and to the right and left handed people look up and to the left (Quilliam, 2004, at 28–29; Lieberman, 1998, at 162). When a right handed individual looks up and to the right or a left handed person looks up and to the left, it often means that they are not trying to recall actual circumstances but rather to create a false story.

8. Dilated Pupils and More Frequent Blinking

When people experience stress, the pupils of their eyes become dilated and their rate of blinking usually increases (Krivis & Zadeh, 2006, at 122; Thompson, 2005, at 346, Calero, 2005, at 69–70; Andersen, 2004, at 147; Ekman, 1992, at 114, 142). Even though legal negotiators rarely interact in such close environments that they can observe pupil enlargement, increased blinking should be readily discernible.

9. Involuntary Raising of Inner Portions of Eyebrows

Most individuals are unable to control the muscles that control the movement of their inner eyebrows. Under stressful conditions, however, many people experience an involuntary lifting of their *inner eyebrows or the raising and pulling together of both eyebrows* (Ekman, 1992, at 134–36). These movements tend to be transient and are frequently overlooked, but may be noted by discerning observers.

10. Narrowing and Tightening of Red Margin of Lips

Stress is frequently manifested just before persons speak by the brief narrowing and tightening of the red margin of their lips (Ekman, 1992, at 136). Careful viewers can see the lips of prospective speakers tighten into a narrow line across their lower face prior to their utterance of planned misrepresentations.

11. Licking Lips or Running Tongue Over Teeth

These are signs of stress and discomfort, and are often associated with deceptive behavior (Dimitrius & Mazzarella, 1998, at 60).

12. Heightened Vocal Pitch

People experiencing anxiety often raise their vocal pitch when they speak (Krivis & Zadeh, 2006, at 122–23; Thompson, 2005, at 345; Ford, 1996, at 213; Ekman, 1992, at 93). Even though intentional prevaricators attempt to control their voice when they talk, listeners can frequently discern this heightened pitch.

13. More Deliberate or More Rapid Speech

Individuals who resort to intentional misrepresentations want to ensure a receptive audience. To accomplish this objective, they often utter their misstatements in a more deliberate manner to be certain that their message is completely received. On the other hand, people experiencing greater stress may speak more rapidly (Dimitrius & Mazzarella, 1998, at 60; Ekman, 1992, at 93, 122).

14. Increased Number of Speech Errors

Studies have found that people who are attempting to deceive others tend to have a greater number of speech errors. These may manifest themselves as stuttering, the repeating of phrases, the increased presence of broken phrases, the failure to finish sentences, or the inclusion of nonsubstantive modifiers ("It is clear that . . . "; "you know") (Krivis & Zadeh, 2006, at 123; Andersen, 2004, at 146; Vrij, 2000, at 26; Ekamn, 1992, at 121–22; Gifford, 1989, at 129). It is as if their conscience disrupts the communication between the brain and the mouth to prevent issuance of their morally wrongful prevarications.

15. More Frequent Clearing of Throat

The tension associated with deceptive behavior often manifests itself in more frequent throat clearing (Gifford, 1989, at 130). As speakers prepare to utter knowingly false statements, they nervously clear their throats in a relatively apparent manner.

16. Change in Frequency of Looking at Listener

As some speakers experience stress associated with their deliberate deception, they become more nervous and look less frequently at their listeners ("gaze aversion") (Vrij, 2000, at 38; Lieberman, 1998, at 13). However, other deceivers exhibit the opposite behavior. They realize that people who look others in the eye are perceived as being more credible. To enhance the likelihood that their misrepresentations will be believed, they make an obvious effort to look at their listeners more intently while they are lying (Andersen, 2004, at 148).

17. Duping Delight

Some individuals enjoy the challenge of successful deception. When they mislead their listeners, they exhibit a smug contempt toward their targets (Andersen, 2004, at 150; Ekman, 1992, at 76–79). These deceivers may also exude signs of pleasure (*e.g.*, self-satisfied smile). These signals are especially likely when these persons are misleading people they think are difficult to fool.

Negotiators should carefully monitor the nonverbal signals emanating from their opponents. They should be especially alert to signs of stress or increased behavior designed to enhance the credibility of questionable representations. While no single sign should be considered conclusive evidence of deception, observable changes in behavior and the presence of suspicious patterns of conduct should cause listeners to become more circumspect.

If one suspects someone of deceit, they can use silence to enhance the speaker's stress level. If the speaker prattles on nervously and reiterates their story, this may indicate deception. One may also ask specific questions that force the individual to fill in details that would be part of any normal story. Difficulty providing these pieces of information is grounds for suspicion (Lieberman, 1998, at 119; Ekman, 1992, at 44–46, 106–07).

Since it is difficult to remember and consider all of the different indicators of deception mentioned here, it might be helpful to picture the following absurd scenario. After reviewing this section, readers should ask their spouse or "significant other": "Do you love me?" If their partners increase or stop their fidgeting, look them in the eye, lift their inner eyebrows, place one hand over their mouth, blink more frequently, preface their affirmative response with "to be truthful," and shake their head negatively while answering in a deliberate and higher pitched manner, the relationship is probably in big trouble!

Two other indicators of deception should also be mentioned. People who lie regularly tend to exude a mistrust of others (Lieberman, 1998, at 40; Lewicki, et al., 1994, at 35–36). They think that most people are dishonest and expect others to use the same deceptive tactics they employ. As a result, negotiators who encounter adversaries exhibiting a distrustful predisposition should be circumspect regarding representations made by those participants. They should try to verify critical representations. Verbal leaks may similarly disclose deceptive statements. Since most people feel uncomfortable making direct misstatements, they frequently use modifiers to mask the extent of their dissembling. For example, negotiators who would hesitate to state directly "and untruthfully" that they cannot go above or below a particular figure may indicate that they are "*not inclined*" to do so. If that figure represented their actual limit, they would be unlikely to use the "not inclined" modifier. Opponents hearing such modifiers should recognize the verbal leak those words represent and be distrustful of the message the speakers appear to be conveying.

Summary

1. Verbal communication constitutes a critical aspect of the bargaining process. Negotiators should carefully listen for verbal leaks that indicate the true intentions of their opponents.

2. During the important stages of negotiations, the participants should use definitive language that more forcefully advances the points they are making.

3. Bargainers who mirror the body postures of opponents, emulate their speech patterns, and reflect their sensory orientations are likely to generate more favorable responses from these people.

4. Nonverbal signals provide significant clues regarding the true intentions of participants during bargaining interactions. Less controlled nonverbal signs tend to be more trustworthy than more contrived verbal representations.

5. Bargainers should not ignore their "feelings" regarding opponent intentions. These feelings may be based on an accurate subconscious perception of valid nonverbal signals emanating from their adversaries.

6. Negotiators should look for signs of confidence, sincerity, disingenuity, or anxiety, and decide whether these are consistent with or contrary to the verbal messages being conveyed.

7. Bargainers should be particularly alert for nonverbal indications of stress and nonverbal efforts to enhance the credibility of questionable statements. These factors may indicate the presence of deceptive behavior.

8. Negotiators should be suspicious of the integrity of people who indicate a general mistrust of others, recognizing that dishonest persons tend to expect others to be similarly untrustworthy. They should listen carefully for verbal leaks that undermine the veracity of what speakers appear to be saying.

Chapter 4

PREPARING TO NEGOTIATE (ESTABLISHING LIMITS AND GOALS)

[2]   — Own Office

[3]   — At Office of Opposing Counsel

[4]   — Chairs and Tables

§ 4.01 CLIENT AND LAWYER PREPARATION

[1]   Benefits

If you know the enemy and know yourself, you need not fear the result of a hundred battles. If you know yourself but not the enemy, for every victory gained you will also suffer a defeat. If you know neither the enemy nor yourself, you will succumb in every battle. (Sun Tzu, 1983, at 18) (*See also* LePoole, 1991, at 43).

People who carefully prepare for a negotiation generally achieve more beneficial results than those who do not (Lewicki & Hiam, 2006, at 41–70; Adler & Silverstein, 2000, at 61–67; Reardon, 2004, at 32–60; Latz, 2004, at 42). While this assertion may seem obvious, it is amazing how many individuals enter negotiations either unprepared or only partially prepared (Ross, 2006, at 132–33; Kennedy, 1998, at 47). When the items in dispute are relatively insignificant and the negotiator has already established a firm bottom line — *e.g.*, a nuisance value case where the insurance company representative is willing to offer up to a set amount without going higher — pre-negotiation preparation may not be critical. The person's previous experience with this type of case coupled with their establishment of a definite limit usually provides the needed guidelines. In more complex and more substantial situations, however, there is rarely any substitute for prudent forethought (see generally Fisher & Shapiro, 2005, at 169–177; Zwier & Guernsey, 2005, at 45–75; Kolb & Williams, 2003, at 40–69).

The direct correlation between the degree of preparation and negotiation outcome is based upon the fact that knowledge constitutes power in the bargaining context (Ross, 2006, at 130–133; Volkema, 1999, at 28–35; Young, 1975, at 10–11). Thoroughly prepared negotiators tend to exude greater confidence in their positions than less prepared advocates (Donaldson, 2007, at 68–69). The confidence possessed by well prepared negotiators undermines the self-assurance of their less prepared opponents. In turn,under-prepared individuals commonly begin to question the certitude of their positions. As they subconsciously defer to the greater certainty exhibited by their more knowledgeable adversaries, they generally make more frequent and more substantial concessions.

[2]   Client Preparation

[a]   Ascertaining Needs and Interests

When it becomes clear that legal representatives must negotiate on behalf of clients, they should take several preliminary steps. They should elicit all of the pertinent factual information possessed by the clients (see generally Gifford, 1987). They must also determine what their clients really hope to achieve through legal representation (see Chapter 2). Clients frequently do not disclose their true underlying interests and objectives when they are merely asked what they expect to obtain. Often failing to contemplate better alternatives that may be available, they only consider options they think attorneys are capable of attaining for them. It is thus necessary to thoroughly probe client objectives, and listen carefully to their responses (Shapiro, 2008, at 47–51;

Hurder, 2007, at 285–87; Riskin, 2002, at 649–50; Ordover & Doneff, 2002, at 32–33).

Persons who indicate a desire to purchase or lease particular commercial property may suggest that they are only interested in that specific location. When these individuals are asked probing questions regarding their intended use, it often becomes apparent that alternative locations may be equally acceptable. Knowledge of the alternatives that a client will accept significantly enhances bargaining power. It is beneficial to provide other options if the negotiations pertaining to their initially preferred property do not progress satisfactorily. Business clients who are contemplating the investment of resources in other firms must be asked about their ultimate objectives. Are they willing to invest their assets in a single venture, or would they prefer to diversify their holdings? Are they willing to risk their principal in an effort to achieve a higher return, or would they prefer a less generous return on an investment that would be likely to retain its overall value?

Clients who initially appear to be interested in obtaining only monetary relief through the legal process may have similarly failed to consider alternative solutions to their underlying difficulties. For example, defamed persons may really prefer retractions and public apologies to monetary awards. Individuals contemplating legal action against relatives or neighbors may be happier with apologies and preserved relationships. Permanently injured personal injury clients may concentrate on mere dollar amounts, when they would be equally, or even more, satisfied with structured settlements that would guarantee them lifetime care. A business seller may accept future cash payments, shares of stock in the purchasing firm, or in-kind payments in the form of goods or services provided by the buying party.

Failing to ascertain the underlying interests and needs of their clients, attorneys may ignore options that could enhance their bargaining strength (Fisher & Ury, 1981, at 101–11). As a result, they may not fully appreciate the external options available to their clients if no mutual accords are achieved. They may thus fail to represent the interests of their respective clients as effectively as they could if they possessed all of the relevant information. When clients indicate what they want to obtain, attorneys should ask them why they desire those items. The answers to these "why" questions are likely to disclose the underlying interests that actually motivate the clients (Kennedy, 1998, at 50–51).

As lawyers explore client needs and interests, they must attempt to ascertain the degree to which their clients want any given item. Most legal representatives either formally or informally divide client goals into three basic categories: (1) essential; (2) important; and (3) desirable (Reardon, 2004, at 61–64; Cohen, 2003, at 127–28; Kennedy, 1998, at 54–59). "Essential" items include objectives the clients must obtain if agreements are to be successfully achieved. "Important" goals concern things the clients would very much like to acquire, but which they would forego if the "essential" terms were resolved in a satisfactory manner. "Desirable" needs involve items of secondary value that the clients would be pleased to obtain, but would be willing to exchange for more important terms.

Attorneys should try to determine how much clients value different levels of attainment for *each* relevant item to be negotiated (Raiffa, 2003, at 129–47). For example, money may be an "essential" issue for a person who has sustained serious injuries in an automobile accident. The client may consider the first $200,000 critical, both to make up for lost earnings and to pay off unpaid medical bills and increased credit card debt. While the client would like to obtain more than $200,000, she may only consider amounts above $200,000 "important," rather than "essential" (Brown, 1997, at 1664, 1669–70). If the client had to choose between a firm offer of $215,000 and a possible loss at trial, she would accept the definitive amount. On the other hand, she would most likely reject an offer of $175,000, since this figure would not satisfy her minimal needs. A firm purchasing land for a new facility may require a minimum of ten acres, but would like to get fifteen or twenty to allow for future expansion. If attorneys representing these parties can appreciate the degree to which each client values different amounts of particular commodities, they can understand how much of the different items they must obtain and the degree to which greater amounts of those items may be traded for other "essential" terms.

Lawyers must also ascertain the relative values of the different items to be negotiated within each broad category (Lewicki & Hiam, 2006, at 51–52; Watkins, 2006, at 22–23). Does the client value Item A twice as much as Item B, or two-thirds as much? How does Item C compare to items A and B? It helps to mentally assign point values for the various items to enable legal representatives to understand how they can maximize overall client satisfaction (Malhotra & Bazerman, 2007, at 72–73). Different software programs have been developed to induce parties preparing to negotiate to explore the various issues involved and to evaluate the degree of personal interest associated with each (Lodder & Zeleznikow, 2005, at 310–312). Advocates must use these relative client preferences to appreciate the items they must try to achieve and the ones that may be traded for other more highly valued terms.

When determining client needs and interests, attorneys should avoid substituting their own values for those of their clients (Gifford, 1987, at 819–21). If clients are more or less risk-averse than their lawyers, the client preferences should be respected. Legal representatives should be hesitant to tell clients they are wrong when they articulate preferences their attorneys find strange. While it is entirely appropriate for lawyers to probe stated client objectives to be certain the clients comprehend the available alternatives and truly desire what they have requested, it is inappropriate for practitioners to disregard client interests with which they do not agree.

Lawyers should not be constrained by judicial authority or "usual" business practices. Negotiating parties can agree to any terms they find beneficial that are not illegal. Litigators may thus agree to conditions a court could not impose (*e.g.*, an apology) and business parties may agree to unconventional arrangements that satisfy client needs. When they prepare for bargaining interactions, lawyers and their clients should not hesitate to brainstorm. They must appreciate underlying client interests and try to formulate innovative packages that would satisfy those needs. They should not hesitate to think outside the box (Kelley, 2001). They must look beyond conventional practices and look for alternatives that would most effectively advance client interests.

[b]   Setting Expectations

Once attorneys obtain a basic understanding of particular client problems, they should educate their respective clients concerning the manner in which the representational process is likely to unfold. Attorneys should tell their clients what they hope to achieve, but with appropriate circumspection. Since all of the operative factual circumstances may not yet be known, there is the risk of elevating client expectations unnecessarily. When negotiators raise client expectations unduly during the preliminary portion of the bargaining process, the clients may be dissatisfied with ultimate agreements they would have initially been pleased to achieve. (I can recall one sad situation in practice when a negotiator — not once but twice — raised client expectations unduly during the early discussions, causing the client to be wholly dissatisfied with the final terms. Although the results were really quite beneficial, they were below the client's artificially raised expectation!) Plaintiff attorneys who prepare exorbitant demand letters for insurance adjusters and send copies to their clients should specifically advise those individuals about the exaggerated nature of their demands to avoid subsequent difficulties with unrealistic client expectations.

Clients should be acquainted with the procedural stages that are likely to develop. Even when clients appear to desire litigation to vindicate their rights, their legal advocates should at least briefly mention the likelihood of settlement discussions. While angry clients may initially reject the possibility of compromise, it is beneficial to suggest it to them at an early date. As they begin to appreciate the financial and emotional costs of litigation, and move from the retributive stage to the healing stage, they are likely to become more receptive to negotiated solutions.

Attorneys should take the time to explain the negotiation process to their clients. This way, clients will understand the anticipated time-frame and the usual need for numerous preliminary and substantive contacts with opposing counsel before the consummation of final accords. As the process evolves, clients should be regularly informed of bargaining developments, even if they are not immediately significant, to apprise them of the fact that their lawyers are continuing to be concerned with their circumstances. This information practice makes it easier for clients to understand and appreciate the legal services being provided, enhances their comprehension of the value of ultimately recommended agreements, and substantially decreases the likelihood they will question final fee statements submitted to them.

Some clients may express a desire to participate personally in the negotiations pertaining to their respective situations. It is generally advisable to preclude their participatory role. During preliminary discussions with the opposing party, it may be cathartic for that party to cast some aspersions upon the other lawyer's client regarding the unfortunate circumstances that have precipitated the need for the current settlement talks. This is especially likely with respect to conflicts of an emotional nature — *e.g.*, marital or partnership dissolutions, neighborhood disputes, or wrongful termination claims. So long as the comments being expressed are not intemperate, it may be beneficial to permit the other party to use this technique to vent penned-up animosity that might otherwise disrupt subsequent negotiations. In addition, clients who are present during negotiating sessions frequently divulge — either verbally or through nonverbal signals — information their counsel did not intend to disclose. Their presence may also hinder the use of negotiating techniques — such as "limited authority" — that their counsel may wish to employ (Ilich, 1973, at 26–27).

[3]   Lawyer Preparation

[a]   Knowledge of Relevant Legal and Theoretical Doctrines

Once lawyers have ascertained the pertinent factual circumstances and underlying interests of their own clients, they must become thoroughly acquainted with the applicable legal doctrines. They must develop cogent theories that support their positions and anticipate the counter-arguments that are likely to be made by opposing counsel. This latter exercise is especially important, because negotiators who are confronted by anticipated contentions are unlikely to have their confidence undermined by those claims. On the other hand, if unexpected concepts are advanced, these may cause unprepared negotiators to lose confidence in their positions and induce them to make unintended concessions.

[b]   Determining the Expected Value of Transaction

After attorneys have become familiar with the relevant factual and legal matters affecting their own side, they must determine what Roger Fisher and William Ury call their BATNA — their Best Alternative to a Negotiated Agreement (Fisher & Ury, 1981, at 101–11). What is the best situation they could achieve through external channels? (Donaldson, 2007, at 53–74; Dietmeyer & Kaplan, 2004, at 43–53). Some litigators use the term WATNA, symbolizing their Worst Alternative to a Negotiated Agreement. The answer to this question should establish their *bottom line*. Lawyers should not enter into agreements that are worse than what would happen if no accords were attained, because poor settlements are worse than nonsettlements (Korobkin, 2000, at 1797; LePoole, 1991, at 60–61).

Negotiators who are initially unable to evaluate the results of nonsettlements must take the time to develop alternative options (Shapiro, 2008, at 91–96). They need to be imaginative and bold. When they believe that only one specific commercial property would satisfy the needs of their client, they must reassess the situation. They have to probe their client's underlying needs and interests to determine what is really required. They must endeavor to locate other properties that may provide the client with what is needed. During this process, they may even discover a better property or a reasonably acceptable location that can be acquired or leased for less money. Even if no equivalent alternatives are discerned, the information gathered through this process directly defines the parameters for the primary negotiation. They may even decide to create a Decision Tree to graphically depict the strengths and weaknesses associated with each option (Kaplow & Shavell, 2004; Hammond, Keeney & Raiffa, 1999; Prestia, 1994). Each limb represents a different alternative, with the advantages and disadvantages of each option being listed. This makes it easier for many individuals to appreciate the comparative values of the different alternatives. Through the judicious disclosure of this information to opposing counsel, these bargainers can more effectively strive to obtain optimal terms for their client.

[c]   Understanding and Communicating Real Costs of Non-Settlement to Clients

When the alternative to a negotiated resolution is an administrative or a judicial proceeding, lawyers must carefully assess the likely outcome of the adjudication process. Not only must they review the pertinent factual circumstances and legal doctrines, but also evaluate such subjective factors as witness credibility and the tribunal sympathy that may be accorded the different parties involved. Even when it appears that their client should theoretically prevail they must consider the possibility that the adjudicator may endeavor to provide their sympathetic opponent with something.

When they attempt to assess the likely trial result, they must not only predict which party is likely to prevail with what degree of probability (*e.g.*, 60% or 70% likelihood), but also the expected result of such an award (Senger, 2004; Thompson, 1998, at 84–85).

Table 4–1 provides a decision tree pertaining to a medical malpractice case.

TABLE 4-1 PLAINTIFF DECISION TREE
MEDICAL MALPRACTICE CASE

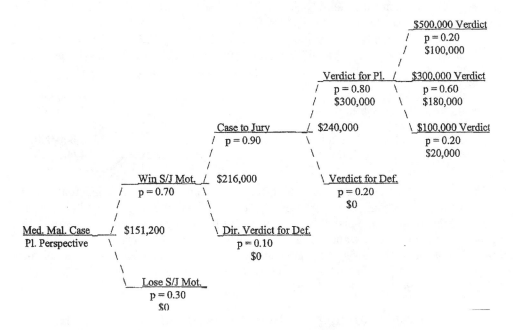

The projected value for this case from the Plaintiff's perspective would be $151,200 — the sum of the various branches of the decision tree. Due to an "egocentric bias," claimant attorneys tend to over-estimate likely jury outcomes, while defense lawyers tend to under-estimate such outcomes (Kaplow & Shavell, 2004, at 1–34; Raiffa, 2003, at 146–47). Two critical factors bring the two sides closer together. First, the fact that plaintiffs usually focus on their *downside risks* (losing or obtaining lower verdicts), while defendants focus on their *upside risks* (losing large awards). The second factor concerns the impact of *transaction costs*.

The monetary and nonmonetary transactional costs associated with settlement and nonsettlement must be considered. It is obvious that a negotiated agreement avoids many of the costs of trial. Such a result also avoids the psychological trauma of litigation and provides a definitive result at a specific time. These factors are particularly important to risk-averse clients. Negotiators must also recognize that these factors affect their opponents. They must not ignore these considerations when they estimate the nonsettlement alternatives available to the other side.

Litigants must appreciate the fact that projected transaction costs should be *subtracted* from the anticipated plaintiff's trial result, since these costs would diminish the value of any plaintiff verdict. Furhter, since the defendant would incur these expenses no matter who prevails at trial, the costs should be *added* to the defendant's expected result. This seemingly contradictory impact of transaction costs greatly encourages both sides to settle disputes. Once the plaintiff realizes the degree to which transaction costs will decrease any award obtained and the defendant recognizes how much transaction costs will enlarge its ultimate liability, the distance between their overall positions narrows substantially.

This same expected value analysis should be performed by persons preparing for transactional encounters. What is the value of the item(s) they are seeking to exchange? For example, suppose the owner of a corporation is deciding how much they should expect to obtain from the sale of their firm. Let's assume the owner believes there is a 10 percent chance the business will sell for $60 million, a 30 percent chance it will sell for at least $55 million, a 60 percent chance it will sell for at least $50 million, a 90 percent chance it will sell for at least $45 million, and a 100 percent chance it will sell for at least $40 million. What should be the expected value of the corporation?

0.10 (10%) x $60 million	....	$6,000,000
0.20 (30%-10%) x $55 million	....	$11,000,000
0.30 (60%-30%) x $50 million	....	$15,000,000
0.30 (90%-60%) x $45 million	....	$13,500,000
0.10 (100%-90%) x $40 million	....	$4,000,000
	Expected Value:	$49,500,000

The attorney for the seller must understand how much money the seller really needs to satisfy her underlying financial interests (Raiffa, 2003, at 129–47), and her personal degree of risk tolerance. A risk taking client might be willing to hold out for a sales price in the $55 million range, while a risk averse seller may focus more on the $50 million area. In any event, the lawyer and the client must also estimate the transactional costs — monetary and psychological — of holding out for a higher sales price and factor this consideration into their deliberations.

[d]   Understanding the Real Costs of Nonsettlement to Opposing Counsel and Clients

Once attorneys have determined their own side's expected value, they often think they have completed this part of the evaluative process. If so, they will ignore a critical piece of information. They must attempt to calculate their *opponent's* expected value (Hurder, 2007, at 269–270; Zwier & Guernsey, 2005, at 65–68; Thompson, 2005, at 28–29; Dietmeyer & Kaplan, 2004, at 53–60; Harvard Bus. Essentials, 2003, at 18–19; Reardon, 2002, at 46–51; Korobkin, 2000, at 1797–99). They should employ formal and informal discovery techniques to obtain the relevant information possessed by opposing parties. They must endeavor to understand the underlying needs and interests of their adversaries, since this may enable them to formulate proposals that would be beneficial to both sides (Malhotra & Bazerman, 2007, at 19–23; Schoonmaker, 1989, at 33–43). They must also attempt to determine the options available to *opposing* clients if no mutual accords are achieved through the present negotiations. What is their BATNA? (Kolb & Williams, 2003, at 62–64). These opponent alternatives directly affect the likelihood of an agreement. If the other side's nonsettlement alternatives are worse than this party's external options, this side possesses greater bargaining power. The cost of disagreement to this side is less onerous than the cost of nonconcurrence to the other participant. Furthermore, if legal representatives do not ultimately offer their adversaries terms that are preferable to those parties' nonsettlement options, they will probably be unable to produce mutually beneficial results.

[e]   Accurate Assessment of Strengths and Weaknesses Affecting Own Side and Opposing Side

When negotiators attempt to understand their clients' strengths and weaknesses and those of their adversaries, they must avoid the tendency to over-estimate their own weaknesses and to under-estimate the weaknesses of their opponents (Cohen, 2003, at

167–68; Adler & Silverstein, 2000, at 14–16; Kahneman & Tversky, 1995, at 46–47.) Since lawyers are intimately familiar with their own client situations, they tend to recognize and amplify their areas of vulnerability. They simultaneously assume — usually incorrectly — that opposing counsel possess the same information regarding these matters as they do. They ignore the fact that they have successfully concealed many of their weaknesses from their opponents. They must ask themselves what their adversaries probably do know about their particular circumstances.

Negotiators must then review the limited information they have been able to elicit from their opponents. Many negotiators overlook the negative factors affecting their adversaries, because those pieces of information have been carefully camouflaged. They thus assume the presence of unwarranted adversarial strength, causing them to over-estimate how little the claimant is willing to accept or to under-estimate how much the defendant is willing to pay (Larrick & Wu, 2007). To counter this tendency, negotiators must ask themselves what negative factors may influence their opponents that have not been disclosed during bargaining discussions.

A classic example of this phenomenon is provided by litigators whose clients are deposed by opposing counsel. A day or two before the scheduled depositions, they invite their clients to their office to prepare them for the up-coming interrogation. As they run through the anticipated questions, their clients do not limit their responses to the specific questions asked, they frequently provide unsolicited information, and they are not very articulate. Their legal representatives instruct them to listen carefully and to answer only the exact inquiries propounded. They are told to avoid unrequested disclosures, and they are encouraged to formulate more eloquent replies. As a result of this preparation, their clients perform admirably during their depositions. Nonetheless, while opposing counsel consider their clients solid witnesses, based upon their deposition behavior, these advocates still remember their clients' pre-deposition difficulties and discount the value of their testimony. They ignore the fact that opposing counsel are unaware of their performance during the preparatory sessions.

[f]   Assessment of Opposition Value Systems

Negotiators frequently make unrealistic assumptions regarding opponent value systems that affect their assessment of opponent resolve. For example, counsel for large law firms often fear opponents represented by legal aid attorneys, since those clients do not have to pay for the legal services they receive. On the other hand, many legal aid lawyers are afraid of large law firms, because they allegedly possess both greater financial resources and lower per-attorney workloads. If either the large firm lawyers or the legal aid attorneys were to understand the actual strengths they possess and recognize the trepidations affecting their opponents, they could significantly enhance their bargaining power!

Other lawyers who represent wealthy corporate clients may indicate their apprehension with respect to opponents on the verge of bankruptcy, thinking that such parties have nothing to lose by not settling on-going litigation. When such lawyers are asked what would happen to the owners of the financially moribund firms if they actually went out of business, these initially fearful attorneys begin to recognize that their opponents' fear of failure and concomitant loss of employment does indeed exert pressure on those individuals. Counsel representing parties on the verge of bankruptcy must similarly change their focus from the powerful economic position of their corporate adversaries to the advantage they may derive from even casual reference to their client's possible resort to bankruptcy. They should also realize the fear those entities usually exhibit may result from the instant transaction. (Recipients of publicity threats should remember that only the most extraordinary controversies tend to generate any real public notice.)

Before negotiators accord their opponents greater respect than deserved, they should carefully reassess their own strengths and reconsider the actual pressures affecting their adversaries (Lax & Sebenius, 2006, at 70–72). They should also recognize that even the most professional negotiators find it difficult to really place themselves in the shoes of their opponents. It is impossible for them to disregard their own personal value systems and to actually substitute those of their opponents. This phenomenon is obvious when plaintiff attorneys try to understand the view of defense lawyers, and when defense specialists attempt to appreciate the perspective of plaintiff representatives. In the corporate world, takeover advisors often find it difficult to comprehend the viewpoint of target firms, and vice versa.

It can be especially beneficial to estimate the issues the opposing side values most highly. When these items are the same ones this side hopes to obtain, they are distributive terms the two parties will vie for. On the other hand, when the other side wants items of little or no value to this side, these terms may be used as bargaining chips to advance other interests. This side may list several of these issues in its set of initial demands, hoping to convince the other side the importance of these items to this side. If this approach is effective, the other party may trade items of importance to this side in exchange for the terms this side is willing to give up.

[g] Importance of Establishing High Aspirations, Inner Confidence, and Elevated Opening Offers

[i] *Elevated Aspirations and Inner Confidence Generate Better Outcomes*

It is vital for people preparing for bargaining transactions to understand that negotiators obtain higher and more satisfactory outcomes when they begin their interactions with elevated rather than moderate goals (Orr & Guthrie, 2006, at 624–25; Thompson, 2005, at 47–48; Korobkin, 2002, at 4, 20–30; Schneider, 2004; Dawson, 2001, at 16–17; Bazerman & Neale, 1992, at 28; Rubin & Brown, 1975, at 267). These goals should always be more beneficial than their bottom lines if the negotiators hope to obtain optimal deals (Dietmeyer & Kaplan, 2004, at 27–35; LePoole, 1991, at 62–63). Bargainers should never create modest objectives merely to avoid the possibility they might not obtain everything they want (Shell, 1998, at 32–33; Latz, 2004, at 27–28). I have seen this postulate confirmed many times by the more proficient students in my Legal Negotiating course and by successful participants in my continuing legal education programs.

The consistently successful negotiators initially take the time to establish elevated aspiration levels before commencing negotiations with their opponents (Lax & Sebenius, 2006, at 186–87; Kramer, 2001, at 37; Shell, 1999, at 31–33; Brown, 1997; White & Neale, 1994, at 305–07; Schoonmaker, 1989, at 30–32; Karrass, 1970, at 17–18). If they are involved in multi-item exchanges, they carefully establish goals for *each* term, recognizing that if they fail to do so for every issue, they may readily forfeit the items for which they have no set aspirations (LePoole, 1991, at 59). They ascertain the pertinent factual circumstances and applicable legal principles. They also review their estimate of *opponent* nonsettlement options and try to visualize final offers that reasonably risk averse opponents would be unlikely to reject when facing the possibility of bargaining stalemates (Brown, 1997, at 1668–69). Then, having determined the most generous results they could reasonably hope to obtain, they *increase* their goals slightly and work diligently to formulate arguments that make their seemingly excessive new objectives appear reasonable! They do not begin to interact with their adversaries until they have established specific goals for the issues to be negotiated and feel entirely comfortable with the beneficial positions they have developed (Cohen, 2003, at 128). They are thus able to develop rest *confidence* in their positions, and their inner confidence is likely to induce less certain opponents to think these thoroughly prepared persons may be right (see generally Sullivan, O'Connor & Burris, 2006).

Proficient bargainers use their *aspiration levels* as their goals when they negotiate, and they work diligently to achieve those elevated objectives (Malhotra & Bazerman, 2007, at 48; Neale & Fragale, 2006, at 29–30; Shell, 1999, at 28–29). They only focus on their bottom lines when they have to decide whether to continue interactions that appear to be going nowhere. On the other hand, less skilled negotiators tend to focus excessively on their *bottom lines* from the beginning of their interactions. Once they attain these minimal objectives, they relax, knowing that some agreement will be achieved and they no longer work as hard to surpass their bottom-line goals (Babcock & Laschever, 2008, at 268–69; Schoonmaker, 1989, at 152–53). Observant opponents can discern their relaxed states and become less generous with respect to substantive concessions. These bottom-line oriented negotiators thus settle for less generous final terms than their cohorts who continue to focus on their aspiration levels throughout their bargaining encounters (Thompson, Neale & Sinaceur, 2004, at 14; Shell, 1999, at 24–32).

When the previous opponents of successful negotiators are asked why they ultimately acquiesced to the substantial demands of those persons, the most common response indicates that they were persuaded by the *overt confidence* exhibited by those bargainers. The carefully prepared individuals seemed so certain that their positions were appropriate that their less successful adversaries decided that they had to re-evaluate their own circumstances. Since it is difficult to quantify the objective reasonableness of the positions being taken in most isolated negotiations and one's exuded confidence level can significantly influence the final outcome of these subjective interpersonal transactions, negotiators who can bolster their confidence through diligent aspiration-level preparation usually prevail over their less prepared adversaries (Kahneman & Tversky, 1995, at 49).

When individuals prepare for bargaining encounters, they must establish generous — but realistically attainable — objectives (Harvard Bus. Essentials, 2003, at 48–49). If their goals are entirely unreasonable, they may discourage their opponents and induce those persons to think that mutually acceptable agreements are not achievable. Their effective narrowing of the settlement range available to the bargaining parties may thus increase the probability of nonsettlements (Korobkin, 2002, at 62–63). People who begin discussions with unduly elevated goals may encounter an additional problem. Once they get into the negotiations and realize that their objectives are unattainable, they lose this important touchstone and may move quickly toward their bottom lines. When bargainers realize that their preliminary aspirations are unrealistic, they need to take a short break to establish new goals they believe may be achieved. This gives them another benchmark well above their reservation points.

I occasionally have students or attorneys tell me that they must be effective bargainers since they always get what they want when they negotiate. These individuals are usually ineffective negotiators. There is only one way to repeatedly obtain everything one wants when one negotiates — don't want anything! Such persons regularly get when they want and are the happiest of bargainers, until they work on identical exercises with other groups of negotiators and discover how modest their own returns are compared to other individuals representing the same side. Individuals with appropriately elevated bargaining objectives frequently come up short. They are disappointed by their inability to achieve everything they sought and think they did poorly. Effective negotiators must recognize the fact that they will often fail to achieve all of their lofty targets. This indicates that they began with beneficial aspirations. On the other hand, persons who always attain their modest goals must *raise their objectives*. They need to do so in ten to fifteen percent increments, because if they try to double or triple their goals, they will fail and return to their old habits. If they continue to attain their elevated goals, they should raise them again by ten to fifteen percent. They should continue this incremental process until they begin to come up short. Only then can the be confident that they are setting appropriately elevated objectives.

[ii]   High Initial Proposals Keep Options Open

Advocates who commence bargaining discussions with elevated opening positions recognize that it is impossible for even highly proficient negotiators to accurately calculate the value of impending interactions solely from their own side's perspective. Until they begin to interact with their opponents, they have no idea how much those individuals want or need the prospective deal. They must determine how risk-averse or risk-taking their adversaries may be. If their opponents feel compelled to achieve accords, they may be willing to accept less beneficial terms to ensure the desired result. On the other hand, if their adversaries are willing to accept the consequences of nonsettlements when beneficial arrangements cannot be achieved, these participants may have to moderate their goals. By beginning the process with heightened position statements, bargainers can preserve their options until they are able to ascertain whether their preliminary assumptions pertaining to opponent needs and desires are accurate.

[iii]   Against Forming Modest Initial Proposals

Many individuals are hesitant to formulate excessive opening offers for fear of offending their opponents. Proficient negotiators generally attempt to develop the most extreme positions *they can rationally defend* (Orr & Guthrie, 2006, at 624–25; Shell, 1999, at 160–61; Bazerman & Neale, 1992, at 29; Schoonmaker, 1989, at 141–42). If their initial demands are truly excessive, they feel awkward when they attempt to justify their positions and undermine their credibility. On the other hand, if they begin with inappropriately deflated demands, they immediately place themselves at a distinct disadvantage. When in doubt, negotiators should select more, rather than less, extreme opening offers (Korobkin & Guthrie, 1994; Dawson, 2001, at 13–18; Kritzer, 1991, at 54–55). It is far easier to retreat from excessive positions, than it is to counteract the negative impact of unrealistically low demands, and the offeror's subsequent concessions are likely to induce opponents to think they are getting better deals even when they are actually receiving less generous final terms (Blount, 2000, at 239–240; Cialdini, 1993, at 49–50).

[iv]   Impact of Anchoring

Some individuals prefer to commence bargaining interactions with the articulation of modest proposals hoping to generate reciprocal behavior by their opponents. Opening offers that are overly generous to adversaries are likely to have the opposite effect due to "anchoring" (Orr & Guthrie, 2006, at 599–611; Lax & Sebenius, 2006, at 187–89; Dietmeyer & Kaplan, 2004, at 112–18; Korobkin, 2002, at 30–36; Shell, 1999, at 161–62; Birke & Fox, 1999, at 40–41; Korobkin & Guthrie, 1994, at 138–42). When people receive better offers than they anticipated, they generally question their own preliminary assessments and *increase* their aspiration levels. The unexpected opponent generosity convinces them that they will be able to obtain better terms than they initially anticipated. This anchoring impact significantly disadvantages advocates who make excessively generous opening offers (Korobkin & Guthrie, 1997, at 101–107). Because of increased opponent aspirations, the likelihood of nonsettlements goes up. Furthermore, if mutual terms are finally achieved, the overly modest opening parties are likely to give up far more than they would have if they had begun with less generous initial proposals.

Bargainers who begin with parsimonious preliminary offers have the opposite anchoring effect. They immediately begin to reduce opponent expectations (Orr & Guthrie, 2006, at 611; Pratkanis & Aronson, 1991, at 182). As adversaries decrease their preliminary aspiration levels, they expand the parties' settlement range and increase the probability of settlement. The lowering of opponent goals simultaneously enhances the likelihood of obtaining final terms that are more favorable to their own clients.

I have demonstrated this phenomenon with attorneys by giving them identical fact patterns involving a car accident. Half of the participants are told the plaintiff has demanded $100,000, while the other half are told the plaintiff has demanded $50,000. I tell the lawyers to assume they represent the defendant and ask them how much they think they will have to pay to settle the case. The persons facing a $100,000 demand respond with significantly higher figures than the people facing a $50,000 demand. (*See* Guthrie, Rachlinski & Wistrich, 2001, at 787–94).

[v] A Method for Achieving Expectations

Skilled bargainers recognize the importance of opening offers, and they carefully formulate their initial proposals (Neale & Bazerman, 1991, at 48–50; Bartos in Zartman, 1978, at 20). Having established appropriately elevated aspiration levels, they try to plan negotiating sequences likely to culminate in optimal results. To accomplish this task, they must necessarily make some predictions regarding the expected behavior of their opponents. They endeavor to place themselves in the shoes of their adversaries to determine what their opening positions and target areas are likely to be. Since bargainers tend to move inexorably toward the mid-point between their respective opening positions, proficient negotiators attempt to establish initial offers that, when averaged with the anticipated opening offers of their opponents, approximate their desired objectives (Dawson, 2001, at 18–20). This "bracketing" phenomenon explains why most negotiators prefer to have opposing counsel articulate their opening positions first. Once their adversaries have taken their firm positions, these individuals carefully adjust their initial proposals to keep their target points near the center of the opening offers.

On some occasions, preliminary opponent offers are more favorable than anticipated. When this occurs, adroit negotiators should immediately reassess their initial positions *and* target areas in recognition of the fact that opposing counsel may be cognizant of circumstances which they are not. Bargainers who fail to modify their behavior and goals in response to unexpectedly generous opponent offers may inappropriately deprive their own clients of beneficial terms.

[h] Use of "Principled" Opening Offers

[i] Explicable Rationales

When negotiators formulate their initial offers, they should simultaneously develop *principled* rationales they can employ to explain the exact manner in which they arrived at their positions (Malhotra & Bazerman, 2007, at 34–35; Thompson, 2005, at 51–52; Ilich, 1992, at 112; Freund, 1992, at 122–23). For example, if attorneys representing a plaintiff in a personal injury case wish to initially demand $500,000, they should carefully substantiate, both factually and legally, the liability of the defendant. They must next calculate the medical expenses, likely future rehabilitation costs, prior and anticipated lost earnings, property loss, etc. and add an appropriate amount for pain and suffering. They should not merely request a lump sum (*e.g.*, $350,000) for the pain and suffering, because such a general figure can be easily discounted. They should instead calculate the overall number of months or years for which pain and suffering relief would be appropriate, compute the number of days or even hours involved, and determine the amount per day or hour required to attain their target figure. The development of a specific figure supported by logical assertions demonstrates a firm commitment to that position, and enhances the offeror's credibility (Lax & Sebenius, 2006, at 190–191; Krieger, et al., 1999, at 282–83). It also makes it harder for opponents to dismiss such positions without careful consideration of the supporting rationales (Pratkanis & Aronson, 1991, at 26–27).

When plaintiff advocates present their detailed computations to opposing counsel, their comprehensive approach allows them to accomplish several objectives. It provides a highly principled rationale that carefully documents the various elements of their overall figure, and it gives their position the aura of objective legitimacy. If their adversary asks how they could expect such a large amount, they can reiterate the detailed foundation for their demand. If they are fortunate, the opposing party may suggest that their estimates for future rehabilitation and/or pain and suffering are excessive. The other side is implicitly conceding liability and the need to compensate the plaintiff for the property loss, medical expenses, and lost earnings. It is also acknowledging the need to provide monetary relief for both of the controverted items. The disagreement merely involves the *amount* the defendant must pay for these components. This approach effectively allows plaintiff-attorneys to seize control of the negotiation agenda and to dictate the way in which the discussions proceed.

Similar strategic planning must be undertaken by attorneys participating in transactional negotiations. For example, the offeror and the offeree in a corporate buy out should evaluate each component of the target firm's assets as they prepare their principled opening offers from the perspective of their respective clients. They must value the real property, the building and equipment, the inventory, the accounts receivable, patents and copyrights, good will, and other pertinent factors. The prospective buyer devalues these items as much as realistically defensible. The seller values the real property as well, though in the opposite direction. This approach enables buyer and seller representatives to begin with specific opening offers that are rationally supportable and more persuasive than the use of round numbers. Individuals who commence bargaining interactions with such principled positions will find that their opponents treat their initial offers more seriously than they do unexplained opening proposals.

[ii]   Solicitation of Sympathy

Plaintiff lawyers should try to induce defendant attorneys to view the case from the plaintiff's perspective. They should develop a presentation that effectively asks their opponents how much *they* would expect if *they* were afflicted with injuries as extensive as those experienced by the plaintiff. To demonstrate the potential impact of this technique, I frequently ask groups of students or practitioners how much they would demand in exchange for my right to tear off their right arm. This question is usually greeted with incredulity. After giving them a brief period to contemplate monetary sums, I inform the audience that they are now members of a jury that must decide the amount to be awarded to my client — a person whose right arm was severed because of the clear negligence of the defendant. This inquiry is treated with complete respect, and the monetary figures they envision in response to this query are substantially lower than the figures they contemplated in response to my initial question.

[iii]   Defence Against the Solicitation of Sympathy

The lawyers representing the defendants in this scenario should be prepared to respond to the initial plaintiff demand in a similarly "principled" manner. Instead of succumbing to the blandishments of plaintiff attorneys, they should begin their own presentations with their own analysis of the liability issue. They need to indicate why their client has limited or nonexistent exposure. When they address the damage question, they must do so from a more realistic perspective reflecting their client's situation. They should not permit their feelings of sympathy for the plaintiff to distort their judgment (Birke & Fox, 1999, at 11). They must point out the typical awards for cases of this nature reported in recent issues of *Jury Verdict Reports* pertaining to their jurisdiction. They need to change the focus of discussion from the amount they would accept for the plaintiff's injuries to the amount conservative jurors would be likely to award if the case were to be tried. They should then discount this figure to take into account the monetary and psychological costs of trial and to reflect the limited nature of defendant liability.

[i]   The Importance of Foresight and Flexibility

Plaintiff and defendant advocates should plan their respective negotiation strategies as if they were choreographing a ballet. They should create a visual image of a successful bargaining interaction in their mind (Hogan, 1996, at 31). How do they plan to move from their opening position to their ultimate goal? (Latz, 2004, at 146–48; Schoonmaker, 1989, at 43–48). Since they do not know the exact manner in which opposing counsel will respond to their initial entreaties, they must, of course, retain substantial flexibility. They should formulate primary and alternate plans that will enable them to effectively counter unexpected opponent gambits. As will be discussed more thoroughly in Chapter 7, they must devise anticipated concession patterns, and prepare principled reasons to indicate why each particular concession is being made. They must be ready to modify their behavior and objectives as they receive new information from their opponents (Balachandra, Bordone, Menkel-Meadow, Ringstrom & Sarath, 2005; Gulliver, 1979, at 100). They must be prepared to make "final offers" that will be sufficiently tempting to their opponents vis-a-vis the external options available to them that they will be hesitant to accept the risks associated with nonsettlements.

[j]   Negotiation Preparation Form

Table 1 sets forth a *Negotiation Preparation Form* that may be used by individuals getting ready for negotiations. It asks advocates to consider the issues that will determine the value of their impending transactions and the bargaining leverage possessed by the respective participants. It is applicable to both litigation settings and transactional encounters.

TABLE 1

Negotiation Preparation Form

1. Your "*resistance point*"(*i.e.*, "*Bottom Line*") — minimum terms you would accept given your Best Alternative to a Negotiated Agreement (BATNA) — Do not forget to include the monetary and nonmonetary transaction costs associated with both settlement and nonsettlement:

2. Your "*target point*" — best result you hope to achieve — Be certain that your target point is sufficiently high. Never commence a negotiation until you

have mentally solidified your ultimate objective with respect to *each item* to be negotiated:

3. Your estimate of *opponent's* "resistance point" — Be certain to include monetary and nonmonetary transaction costs when estimating the nonsettlement options that appear to be available to your opponent:

4. Your estimate of *opponent's* "target point" — Try to use your opponent's value system when estimating his/her target point:

5. Your factual and legal leverage with respect to *each* issue (strengths and weaknesses) — Prepare logical explanations supporting each strength and anticipate the ways you might minimize your weaknesses. What is the best alternative result you could achieve through other channels if no agreement can be attained through the negotiation process? What are the monetary, psychological, tax-related, temporal, etc. costs associated with settlement and nonsettlement:

6. Your *opponent's* factual and legal leverage with respect to each issue — What counter-arguments can you use to challenge the claims you expect your opponent to make:

7. Your *planned* initial position — Prepare rational explanations to support each component of your "principled" opening offer:

8. What *information* do you *plan* to elicit during the Information Stage to determine the opponent's underlying needs, interests, and objectives? What information-seeking questions do you anticipate using:

9. What *information* are *you* willing to disclose and how do you plan to divulge it? (Best to disclose important information in response to opponent questions) How do you plan to prevent the disclosure of your sensitive information ("*Blocking Techniques*"):

10. Your *negotiation strategy* (agenda and tactics) — How do you envision moving from where you begin to where you hope to end up? Plan your anticipated concession pattern carefully to disclose only the information you intend to divulge and prepare principled explanations to support each planned concession:

11. Your prediction of *opponent's* negotiation strategy and your planned counter-measures — How may you neutralize your opponent's strengths and exploit his/her weaknesses:

12. What *negotiating techniques* do you plan to use to advance your interests? (Be prepared to vary them and to combine them for optimal impact):

13. What *negotiating techniques* do you expect your *opponent* to use, and how do you plan to counter those tactics.

[k]   Importance of Establishing Good Reputations

Neophyte litigators should recognize that they can greatly enhance their on-going bargaining power if they initially establish reputations both as outstanding trial lawyers and as individuals who are not afraid to employ the adjudication option if beneficial settlements cannot be negotiated. Attorneys who are not respected litigators are not accorded the same deference at the bargaining table as those who have demonstrated their litigation skills. This is based on the fact that other lawyers assume less onerous nonsettlement options for less proficient litigation opponents than they do for highly skilled litigation opponents. Furthermore, even talented litigators are not likely to be granted well- deserved respect during negotiations when they exude a reluctance to go to trial. Once young attorneys establish reputations as outstanding litigators who enjoy the trial process, they can settle far more cases and achieve better results than they ever contemplated.

[1]   Multi-Party Negotiating Teams

[i]   Coordinating Strategy

Attorneys involved in multi-party litigation or large corporate or governmental transactions may occasionally be required to participate in negotiations that include a large number of persons. If the interaction is to be successfully concluded, it is imperative that the individuals on the same side develop unified goals and a coordinated strategy. A large intra-group preparatory phase is crucial. Each interest group must be included and be encouraged to express their basic objectives and the appropriate means they visualize to achieve those objectives. If the inter-organizational discussions begin before a common team plan has been formulated, proficient opponents will discern and exploit intra-group weaknesses. Substantive disagreements will undermine bargaining effectiveness, and strategic conflicts will preclude the presentation of a united front.

One risk associated with multiple person negotiation teams concerns the tendency for individuals negotiating in front of observers to exhibit greater advocacy for their own side (Neale & Bazerman, 1991, at 6). This phenomenon may generate a more competitive negotiating environment. Negotiators should appreciate the possible impact of this factor and work to minimize unintended, overtly competitive behavior.

[ii]   Appointing a Spokesperson and Controlling Interparty Communication

When expansive bargaining teams are involved, organizational leaders must decide which persons will speak during the inter-party discussions. It is unwise and risky to allow more than two or three representatives to participate actively, since opponents will attempt to benefit from internal group discord. Passive team members must be careful to avoid the disclosure of information through inadvertent nonverbal signals. The individuals who are to do the major speaking must ensure that they work together in a unified manner. When the expertise of other team members is required, the designated representatives can elicit the requisite facts in an appropriate fashion.

Each team member should be assigned a function that suits his or her personal capabilities (Shapiro, 2008, at 181–200). One person may be a good planner, another a persuasive speaker, and a third and active listener. If they are assigned roles that suit their areas of expertise, they will enhance team cohesiveness. On the other hand, if they are assigned roles that do not suit their strengths, serious problems may develop.

§ 4.02   SETTING THE STAGE

[1]   Importance

One final issue that is usually ignored by negotiators should be briefly mentioned. Most people preparing for a negotiation are so concerned with the anticipated substantive and procedural aspects of the process that they fail to consider the importance of the location and the setting for the bargaining discussions — the "contextual" factors (Schoonmaker, 1989, at 48–49). Most individuals feel more comfortable in familiar surroundings. Thus they prefer, if possible, to negotiate in their own environment. Of course, those persons who like to storm out of bargaining sessions to demonstrate how determined they are may wish to negotiate at the office of their opponents, since it is embarrassing to walk out of one's own office!

[2]   Own Office

When negotiations are scheduled for an attorney's own office, he or she should decide ahead of time upon the manner in which he or she wants to control the basic environment (Latz, 2004, at 228). Combative negotiators frequently establish adversarial settings in which the participants directly face each other across square or rectangular bargaining tables (see Figure 1). They may even provide themselves with chairs that are higher than those given to their adversaries. A few negotiators may even cut off a small piece from each of the front legs of the chairs to be used by their opponents to make them feel uncomfortable during the bargaining interactions. Manipulative individuals may also place their own seats near the middle of the room and locate those to be used by their adversaries with their backs literally against the office wall. This type of seating arrangement tends to make the participants with their chairs against the wall behave in a defensive manner. Some lawyers who must deal with chain-smoking opponents may remove the ashtrays to make their adversaries feel less comfortable. A few individuals may even set up their offices so that their opponents have bright sunlight in their eyes. This makes it more difficult for them to observe the nonverbal signals being emitted by those who created the Machiavellian environment. Even though these tactics may seem absurd to many, it must be remembered that if they give the users a psychological advantage, they may actually influence the ultimate outcome of the negotiations.

[3]   At Office of Opposing Counsel

When lawyers enter the office of an opposing party and feel uncomfortable, they should immediately survey the setting to ascertain if deceptive techniques are being employed. If they discover the existence of bargaining artifices, they should suspect that other similarly opprobrious tactics may be used against them by their apparently competitive opponents (Ilich, 1973, at 31). To counter such techniques as lowered chairs or poorly positioned seats, negotiators might elect to remain standing during the discussions so they can look down at their adversaries, rearrange the furniture in a more cooperative configuration, or look for another more neutral setting in the office and suggest that the discussions occur in that area. They may alternatively wait until their opponents leave the room, to get coffee or to caucus, and exchange places with them! As soon as their adversaries return to the room, they will realize that their unbalanced environment has been discovered. Their resulting embarrassment may soften their subsequent behavior.

[4]   Chairs and Tables

Individuals who wish to encourage cooperative "win-win" bargaining sessions should use a round table where the seats are not located directly opposite each other, or have the negotiators sit next to each other in an L-shaped configuration (see Figure 1). They should similarly ensure the development of a hospitable, nonthreatening environment. (Excellent descriptions of these setting-related phenomena may be found in Korda, 1975.)

FIGURE 1

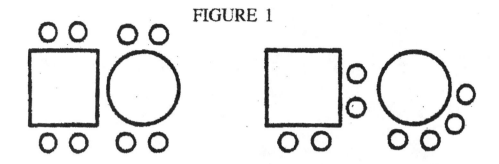

Adversarial Settings   Cooperative Settings

Summary

1. Practitioners should prepare their clients for bargaining transactions by educating them about the process and the likelihood of negotiated results.

2. Legal representatives must be thoroughly prepared regarding the relevant facts and operative legal doctrines, and they must fully comprehend the underlying needs and interests of their clients.

3. Negotiators should try not to over-estimate their own side's weaknesses or to under-estimate the weaknesses affecting their opponents, and they must remember that both sides are working to disguise their underlying vulnerabilities.

4. Attorneys must determine their own BATNA (Bottom Line) and the BATNA of their opponents, to ascertain which side possesses greater bargaining power.

5. Proficient bargainers develop high aspiration levels for each item to be exchanged and an inner confidence in the positions they plan to assert, and they formulate "principled" opening positions that can be rationally explained to their opponents.

6. In order to provide themselves with expansive bargaining room and to undermine opponent aspiration levels, successful negotiators tend to begin discussions with positions that are as far from their ultimate objectives as they can rationally defend.

7. Successful negotiators carefully choreograph their interactions and thoughtfully plan their tactics and intended concession patterns to enable them to move effectively from their opening positions to their ultimate objectives.

Chapter 5

THE PRELIMINARY STAGE (ESTABLISHING NEGOTIATOR IDENTITIES AND TONE FOR INTERACTION)

§ 5.01   ASSESSING NEGOTIATOR PERSONALITIES

[1]   Prior Familiarity with Opponent

Lawyers who have previously opposed one another at the bargaining table are usually familiar with each other's basic negotiating style. They are generally able to commence new negotiations without having to formally establish preliminary ground rules. Nonetheless, they should still take the time to initially reestablish cordial environments that will contribute positively to their impending substantive discussions. Individuals who have not had extensive prior dealings with one another should normally expect to spend the initial period of their interaction establishing their personal and professional identities and the intended tone for their substantive negotiations (Sternlight & Robbennolt, 2008, at 502–04). Both formal and informal guidelines must usually be developed (Gifford, 2007, at 77–97; Schoonmaker, 1989, at 52–62).

During the initial portion of bargaining interactions, lawyers should look for common interests they share with opponents (Goleman, 2006, at 29–30; Fisher & Shapiro, 2005, at 55–56). They may be from the same city or state, they attended the same college or law school, their children attend the same schools, they enjoy the same music or sports, etc. Person who can identify and share such common interests enhance the likelihood they will like each other and will develop mutually beneficial relationships (Guthrie, 2004, at 831; Moore, 2003, at 184–85). Such circumstances contribute to the establishment of rapport and increase the probability of cooperative behavior during the subsequent stages of the bargaining process (Mayer, 2006, at 19–23; Nadler, 2004; Kray, Thompson & Galinsky, 2001, at 953–55).

[2]   Unknown Negotiators

[a]   Consulting Outside Sources

Attorneys who are unfamiliar with the negotiating philosophy and approach of opposing counsel should initially endeavor to obtain pre-negotiation information about their adversaries from people in their own firm and from other lawyers they know. It is particularly important to ascertain whether they can expect candor or dissembling — cooperation or pretense. Are their opponents likely to begin the process with realistic offers or extreme positions? What types of bargaining techniques do they like to employ? It is generally beneficial to try to establish an atmosphere that is conducive to cooperative, "win-win" interactions.

[b]   Initial Assessment of Opponents' Disposition towards Cooperation

Having gathered any available information from other sources, we move on to the initial personal impressions. Individuals who encounter seemingly cooperative opponents should expeditiously seek to determine whether those people's apparent predisposition toward cooperative transactions is consistent with their actual behavior. Until they verify this fact, they should not disclose excessive amounts of critical information regarding their strengths and weaknesses without obtaining reciprocal responses from their opponents. They may otherwise permit Machiavellian adversaries to create false impressions of cooperation so they can take unfair advantage of the situation (Lowenthal, 1982, at 82). The need for circumspection was recently reinforced by two experienced lawyers from different areas of the country who gleefully informed me that they regularly send copies of *Getting to Yes* (Fisher & Ury, 1981) to their younger opponents to induce them to anticipate open and cooperative negotiations. When their unsuspecting adversaries divulge an excessive amount of information, they deceptively employ competitive tactics to obtain a significant bargaining advantage!

§ 5.02   ESTABLISHING NEGOTIATION TONE

[1]   Understanding Negotiators' World Views

Empirical studies indicate that competitive individuals generally behave competitively regardless of the behavior of their opponents, while cooperative persons tend to behave like those with whom they interact — cooperatively with other cooperative parties and competitively with competitive adversaries (Rubin & Brown, 1975, at 185). This phenomenon results from the fact that cooperative persons see the world as being composed of both cooperative and competitive individuals, while competitive people believe that others behave in a uniformly competitive manner (Rubin & Brown, 1975, at 185; Zartman & Berman, 1982, at 25). Cooperative negotiators feel more comfortable interacting with other cooperative persons, because this permits them to employ the cooperative style they prefer to use. Nonetheless, when they confront competitive opponents, they appropriately recognize the need to behave more competitively to prevent exploitation by less open and more adversarial opponents. Since competitive negotiators consider all opponents adversarial, they think that an adversarial approach is required to best advance the interests of their own clients.

Some lawyers exhibit overtly competitive tendencies at the outset of negotiations. They deliberately create competitive office environments that are designed to make their opponents feel uncomfortable. When they are forced to negotiate in the offices of other people, they select seats directly across from — instead of adjacent to — their opponents. They are likely to sit initially with their arms folded across their chest and with their legs crossed. They exude little personal warmth. Some continue to address opposing counsel as "Mr. or Ms. _____" instead of by their first names, even when they are themselves being addressed by their own first names. This permits them to depersonalize their interactions with persons they psychologically view as their enemy. This device also allows them to employ tactics they would not be likely to use against someone they knew more personally.

[2]   Congenial Relations Generate Better Results

As lawyers begin the negotiation process, they should take the time to develop positive rapport with opposing counsel. Through warm eye contact and a pleasant demeanor, they can establish a mutually supportive environment. This enhances future communication, and reduces the unproductive anxiety and anger created by overtly adversarial conduct. Each person must acknowledge that the other participants are merely doing their jobs. They are appropriately attempting to obtain beneficial terms for their clients. Negotiators must recognize that they can be forceful advocates without resorting to disagreeable tactics (Woolf, 1990, at 34–35). Individuals who equate offensive behavior with effective negotiating strategy are likely to be doubly disappointed — their professional interactions will be increasingly unpleasant and they will find it more difficult to obtain optimal results for their clients.

The initial part of a negotiation is crucial, because the participants generally create an atmosphere that affects their entire transaction. If the interaction begins on an unpleasant or distrusting note, subsequent discussions are likely to be less open and more adversarial than if the process had begun in a congenial and cooperative manner (Woolf, 1990, at 34–35; Scott, 1981, at 6–10). Even inherently competitive legal negotiations — such as those pertaining solely to money — do not have to be conducted in a hostile fashion. In fact, negotiators who can induce their opponents to like them and their clients and who treat their opponents respectfully and courteously (Hollander-Blumoff & Tyler, 2008, at 484) are usually able to obtain better results than bargainers who do not generate sympathetic feelings (Latz, 2004, at 52–54; Birke & Fox, 1999, at 54).

Studies have found that persons who commence bargaining interactions in positive moods negotiate more cooperatively, reach more agreements, and are more likely to employ problem-solving efforts designed to maximize the joint returns achieved by the parties (Sullivan, O'Connor & Burris, 2006, at 578; Ryan, 2005, at 269–270; Freshman, Hayes & Feldman, 2002, at 15, 19; Riskin, 2002, at 657–58; Thompson, Nadler & Kim, 1999, at 142–44; Forgas, 1998, at 566–74). On the other hand, people who begin their encounters in negative moods negotiate more adversarially, reach fewer agreements, and tend to generate less efficient overall results (see generally, Van Kleef, De Dreu & Manstead, 2004). In addition, negative mood participants are more likely to resort to deceptive tactics than others, while positive mood actors are more likely to honor the agreements reached than their negative mood cohorts (Freshman, Hayes & Feldman, 2002, at 22–24; Thompson, Nadler & Kim, 1999, at 143). It is thus beneficial for individuals beginning bargaining encounters to take a few minutes to create supportive environments designed to generate positive moods that should make their interactions more pleasant and enhance the probability they will maximize the joint returns achieved (Fisher & Shapiro, 2005, at 7–9).

As a result of "emotional contagion," persons who begin bargaining encounters in positive moods tend to generate positive moods in their opponents (Barry, Fulmer & Van Kleef, 2004, at 74). It is thus beneficial for negotiators to work to establish positive moods in themselves before they begin to interact with people on the other side. Individuals who are experiencing negative feelings should try to modify those feelings prior to personal sessions with others.

§ 5.03 ESTABLISHING EFFECTIVE ONGOING NEGOTIATOR RELATIONS

[1]   Expectations for Approaching Various Personalities

Lawyers who have learned, either from previous personal experience or from other reliable sources, that particular adversaries approach negotiations in a competitive manner should initially attempt to demonstrate their willingness to engage in mutually cooperative behavior. Although they should be careful not to disclose too much significant information without receiving some reciprocal cooperation, evidence suggests that cooperative conduct promotes the development of trust and contributes to the establishment of mutually supportive relationships (Nadler, 2004b, at 237–47; Ury, 1991; Rubin & Brown, 1975, at 263). If these tactics do not produce the desired behavioral results, the unsuccessful initiators of cooperative behavior can still adopt a more circumspect approach. On the other hand, if they initially respond to the competitive overtures of opposing counsel with competitive conduct of their own, it is likely that unpleasant, combative negotiations will result.

[2]   Games of One-Upmanship

Attorneys who meet professionally for the first time frequently engage in games of one-upmanship. Individuals from prestigious firms hand opposing counsel gilded business cards indicating that they are with "Sullivan, Weiss, Wasp & Wealth" or similarly impressive entities. Persons with prominent government agencies (*e.g.*, U.S. Justice Department or State Attorney General's Office) make equally grand gestures. Some lawyers even ask prospective adversaries where they went to law school, whether they were on the law review, and where they finished academically in their graduating classes. If the persons being questioned in this manner have truly distinguished academic backgrounds, they may wish to seize the opportunity to gain a psychological advantage through their disclosures. Others may prefer to ignore these inquiries or respond with appropriately humorous answers (*e.g.*, "I attended Our Lady of the Divine Forest Law School in Poughkeepsie!"). Individuals who do not have distinguished academic backgrounds should remember the results of my Legal Negotiating course studies that found absolutely no statistically significant correlation between the negotiation exercise results achieved by students and their overall law school grade point averages (Craver, 2000; Craver, 1986).

When lawyers initially feel the need to disclose their academic backgrounds, the names of the important attorneys and jurists they know, the identities of their more impressive clients, etc., their opponents should recognize the lack of professional confidence evidenced by this behavior. If these people are truly insecure, it may be important to take the time to make them feel more comfortable and less threatened by the impending negotiation. Without these preliminary amenities, the fears being entertained by these individuals may have a deleterious impact upon the basic interaction to the detriment of both counsel and their respective clients. Furthermore, negotiators who can induce insecure opponents to feel less threatened by the present interaction can more easily obtain the beneficial terms they want for their own clients.

[3]   Knowing the Opposition

Attorneys who encounter openly competitive "win-lose" opponents should recognize that while they may not be able to convert those individuals into cooperative "win-win" negotiators, they may be able to take action that should diminish the competitive aspects of their forthcoming interactions. Through the use of friendly introductions, sincere smiles, and warm, prolonged handshakes, they can attempt to establish more personal relationships. They can also use an extended Preliminary Stage to further enhance their negotiation environments. They should emit nonthreatening nonverbal signals and attempt to sit in cooperative positions. They may ask such opponents about their families and their colleagues, while making similar disclosures about themselves. They may thus be able to establish first-name relationships that accentuate the personal nature of their transactions. Even when these efforts do not substantially counteract the competitiveness being exuded by opposing counsel, lawyers must always remember that client legal problems — not opponent behavior — constitute the real "enemy" that must be overcome (Zartman & Berman, 1982, at 144). They should never allow summary rejection of their cooperative overtures by adversaries to cause them to lose sight of this crucial fact.

It is beneficial to depersonalize the conflict, but to personalize the bargaining interaction. In order to minimize the impact of negative emotional feelings, negotiators should try to separate the people from the problem. On the other hand, they should try to personalize their encounter by establishing mutual rapport. No matter how large the clients being represented by the attorneys on both sides, it is John and Mary interacting — not the XYZ Corporation or the U.S. Department of Justice (Shapiro & Jankowski, 2005, at 7–12).

[4]   The Benefits of Attitudinal Bargaining

Attitudinal bargaining is an approach to the negotiation process that encourages an atmosphere of cooperative bargaining while mitigating the potentially damaging effects of adversarial bargaining. Attitudinal bargaining may often be used to induce competitive opponents to tone down their inappropriate conduct (Ury, 2007; Raiffa, 2003, at 300–01; Ury, 1991). This process enables the participants to develop more hospitable negotiating environments.

Attorneys who encounter opponents initially exhibiting cooperative tendencies should make every effort to reinforce that behavior. It will make their professional interactions far more harmonious, and minimize the likelihood of opposing counsel's resort to inappropriate tactics. Manipulative negotiators may even wish to encourage cooperative attitudes so they can employ disguised competitive techniques to advance their own objectives. If they are adroit negotiators, these competitive/problem-solving bargainers may be able to maintain pleasant bargaining environments, while they disingenuously seek more favorable results for their own clients. Sincerely cooperative participants in the bargaining process should always be prepared for the possibility of such occurrences so they may defend themselves accordingly.

When opposing negotiators exhibit overtly competitive or even abrasive behavior at the commencement of the negotiation process, their adversaries should recognize their right to initiate "*attitudinal bargaining*." They may appropriately indicate their unwillingness to view the bargaining process as a combative exercise, and suggest their desire to establish some preliminary ground rules (Kramer, 2001, at 264–65; Adler & Silverstein, 2000, at 90–92; Steinberg, 1998, at 144–49). Litigators may suggest that if the other side prefers open hostility, a trial setting would be the appropriate forum due to the presence of a presiding official. Transactional negotiators may indicate that their clients are seeking mutually beneficial, on-going relationships that cannot be created through untrusting adversarial behavior. They can suggest that their clients do not wish to enter into business partnerships with parties that treat them disrespectfully (Donaldson, 2007, at 146–48).

I can recall my initial interaction with an aggressive National Labor Relations Board attorney. We were preparing for the trial of an unfair labor practice case. He asked if I would stipulate to certain factual circumstances that he could clearly establish. I replied that this would be acceptable if he would stipulate to several factual matters raised by me. Although he admitted that the facts encompassed by my proposed stipulation were uncontroverted, he refused to accept my proposal, claiming that my facts would be irrelevant to the proceeding. Following further unfruitful discussions, I indicated that I could not understand why he was behaving in such an uncooperative manner. His reply amazed me: "This is war! I see no need to cooperate unnecessarily with the enemy!" At this point, I appealed to his patriotism and suggested that it was improper for a government attorney who represented the public interest to require two or three days of needless trial merely because he thought that certain uncontrovertible factual circumstances were irrelevant. He finally became embarrassed and sheepishly agreed to enter into a joint stipulation covering the items we both wanted. I later learned that his initially belligerent attitude was caused by the fact that his prior dealings with one of the senior attorneys in my firm had been highly competitive and most unpleasant. Had I not challenged his preconception of the negotiation process we were commencing, we would certainly have encountered continuing problems. Our subsequent dealings were always conducted on a congenial and wholly cooperative basis.

When attitudinal bargaining fails to generate appropriate behavior, individuals who know they must interact with a nasty opponent should try to control their encounter in a way that diminishes the ability of the other side to adversely affect them. For example, against a sarcastic and belittling opponent, they could use the telephone to conduct their talks. When the other side's conduct begins to bother them, they can indicate that they have another call or another matter to take care of and break off discussions. They can call back their adversary after they have calmed down. If a particularly aggressive opponent tries to intimidate people by invading their space during in-person encounters, they could meet in a conference room containing a large table and place their adversary on the opposite side. This would make it difficult for that person to try to invade their space, since such behavior would be pathetically obvious and ineffective.

[5]   The Benefits of an Apology

Legal practitioners should recognize the benefits that may be derived at the outset of a conflict-resolution interaction from an acknowledgment of the other party's plight and the issuance of a simple apology (Folberg & Golann, 2006, at 171–77; Brown, 2004b; Fuchs-Burnett, 2002; O'Hara & Yarn, 2002; Cohen, 1999). Most individuals only resort to litigation after all other efforts to achieve mutual resolutions of their underlying controversies have failed. The aggrieved persons are frustrated and angry regarding the perceived unwillingness of the responsible parties to acknowledge their contribution to the problem. So often, if the seemingly responsible individuals indicate an understanding of the injured party's situation and state that they are sorry for what has befallen the adversely affected persons — without admitting any legally cognizable wrongdoing — the aggrieved persons accept their expressions of sympathy and either endure their fate alone or work constructively to generate mutually acceptable resolutions.

Some might suggest that an effective apology must include an admission of responsibility for the injuries suffered (Robbennolt, 2003, at 486–491; Pavlick, 2003, at 835–36; Taft, 2000), but I have not found this to be true. If someone sincerely sympathizes with the loss suffered by the other side or acknowledges the basis for that side's negative feelings, this can significantly diminish the impact of those negative emotions, even if the sympathizing party does not unequivocally acknowledging personal responsibility. Negotiators should remember that many highly controverted legal disputes are expeditiously settled following the expression of appropriate contrition by the responsible parties.

A lawyer once shared an interesting story with me. A police officer has shot and killed a fleeing teenage burglary suspect late at night. Although the officer thought the suspect possessed a weapon, he did not. The parents of the deceased boy brought a wrongful death action against the police department which dragged on for a couple of years. The parents and the police officer never talked to one another, because the police department attorney had instructed the police officer to avoid such contacts. At a meeting involving all of the participants, the father asked the officer if he ever thought of their son. He tearfully replied that he did so every single day. He indicated that he had children of his own and couldn't imagine the pain they had been experiencing. He profusely apologized to them and expressed great sadness at what had occurred. The parties settled their law suit that afternoon. The father said that they had buried their son two years earlier, but could not have the funeral until that morning when they appreciated the officer's sympathetic understanding of their plight.

People from group-oriented cultures that especially value relationships (*e.g.*, Japan) are generally more willing to apologize for transgressions than persons from individually-oriented cultures like the United States (Pavlick, 2003, at 840). Perhaps because of their greater respect for relationships, women are more likely to apologize than men (Pavlick, 2003, at 851). Individualistic males who find it difficult to apologize must accept responsibility for the greater likelihood of divisive adjudications instead of mutually beneficial settlements.

Should evidence of apologies be admissible in subsequent trials — to bolster plaintiff claims of defendant liability or to reduce the amount of damages to be awarded — to prevent opportunistic behavior by insincere apologists who use their seeming contrition to obtain strategic benefits during case settlement discussions? (O'Hara & Yarn, 2002) If apologies are admitted solely for the purpose of establishing liability against the apologists, this will discourage contrite conduct by rational actors and encourage opportunistic behavior by claimants. On the other hand, if apologies are admissible by defendants to demonstrate — sincerely or insincerely — their contrition, this would tend to reduce damage awards against the apologists. To counteract these phenomena, Professors O'Hara and Yarn suggest that apologies either be admissible both to establish liability and to mitigate damages or for neither purpose. This approach would decrease the risk to sincere apologists, and diminish opportunistic behavior by claimants who only wish to elicit apologies they can use to establish defendant liability at trial (O'Hara & Yarn, 2002, at 1191).

I should finally reiterate the important fact that the negotiation process commences with the first direct or even indirect contact with opposing counsel. Lawyers should strive from the outset to establish the negotiation atmosphere they desire. If adversaries display unwelcome competitive gamesmanship at the beginning of the process, they should not be accorded excessive trust thereafter. For example, attorneys who reject several proposed meeting times due to their "extremely busy schedules" may be trying to demonstrate how much more valuable their time is than that of their opponents. When I suspected such tactics in practice, I usually responded by rejecting their initially suggested meeting times. They usually got the hint that I would not tolerate such tactics, and we quickly settled upon mutually acceptable times to meet. Our subsequent interactions were generally conducted on a positive basis.

Summary

1. At the outset of a negotiation, the participants establish their identities and the tone for the interaction.

2. Individuals should not be overly impressed by the educational backgrounds and firm associations of opponents. These factors do not determine bargaining proficiency.

3. People who project cooperative attitudes and attempt to create positive negotiating environments at the commencement of their interactions are likely to minimize competitive/adversarial behavior and maximize cooperative exchanges.

4. Negotiators who do not like the way in which bargaining interactions commence should use "attitudinal bargaining" to modify inappropriate opponent behavior and to develop more positive environments.

5. If attitudinal bargaining does not curtail offensive opponent conduct, people should try to control the interaction in a way that minimizes the ability of the obstreperous person to disrupt the bargaining process.

6. Defense lawyers should recognize the benefits that may be derived from their acknowledgment of opponent plights and sincere apologies by seemingly responsible parties. The apologies should indicate remorse for the difficulties suffered by the prospective plaintiffs without admitting liability for those difficulties.

Chapter 6

THE INFORMATION STAGE (VALUE CREATION)

§ 6.01   QUESTIONING

[1]   Where Information Stage Begins

Following the preliminary establishment of negotiator identities and the creation of a mutually acceptable atmosphere for the impending interaction, the first truly formal stage of the negotiation process begins. Lawyers can usually recognize the commencement of the "Information Stage," because this point coincides with a shift from seemingly innocuous "small talk" to questions regarding the other party's needs and objectives. During this part of the process, the participants attempt to determine what items are available for their joint distribution. They try to look for ways in which they may expand the areas of mutual interest — *i.e.*, engage in *"value creation."* The more effectively they can accomplish this objective, the more efficiently they should be able to conclude their interaction successfully (Mnookin, Peppet & Tulumello, 2000, at 11–43). The optimal way to elicit information from opponents is to *ask questions* (Shapiro, 2008, at 113–20–; Malhotra &Bazerman, 2007, at 40–41; Salacuse, 2003, at 48–52; Stone, Patton & Heen, 1999, at 172–73; Thompson, 1998, at 60–61; Barkai, 1996, at 735–36). People who continue to use declarative sentences give away information. They don't obtain it. This is why proficient negotiators spend twice as much time asking opponents question compared with less capable negotiators (Movius, 2008, at 513–14) (*see also* Volkema, 1999, at 37; Kennedy, 1998, at 143).

[2]   Nature of Question

[a]   Obtaining information about Skills, Resources and Experience of Adversary

The focus of the Information Stage is always upon the knowledge and desires of the *opposing party*. Each participant asks the other side which items it wants and why it wants them. For example: "What do you want/need?" "What does your client hope to obtain?" "Why do you and your client wish to obtain that?" Each side endeavors to obtain as much relevant information about their adversary's situation as possible, without disclosing too much of the confidential circumstances influencing their own situation.

[b]   Starting with Open-Ended, Information-Seeking Questions

Since opposing counsel's knowledge or lack of knowledge may significantly influence negotiation developments, it is initially beneficial to ascertain their expertise with respect to the type of legal transaction involved. Questions should also be asked regarding the resources available to the other side. Is the opposing client represented by a large law firm with many experienced specialists and with substantial resources, or by a relatively small firm with a limited financial capacity? What resources are available to the client involved?

How much authority does opposing counsel possess? Can they make final decisions that will bind their clients, or must they obtain the approval of absent principals? If they represent a larger organization, will different individuals have to approve any agreement achieved? Are there ways key decision makers can join the current discussions? If not, are there ways you may be able to communicate directly with those principals later if you think that would be beneficial? The answers to these questions may make it easier to understand what you will have to go through once a tentative accord is reached with current counsel to make those terms final.

Attorneys should not consider negotiations to be wholly bilateral interactions, because they are usually more complicated. The complexity of even a relatively simple bargaining interaction is depicted in Figure 2.

FIGURE 2

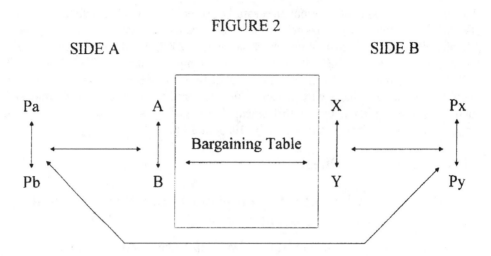

SIDE A

SIDE B

While A and B may appear to be negotiating with X and Y, A and B are also bargaining with each other and with their principals Pa and Pb. X and Y are doing the same thing with each other and with their own principals Px and Py (Colosi, 2001, at 22–29). Each side's principals are communicating with each other, and, in some instances, (*e.g.*, transactional encounters), they are directly negotiating with the principals on the other side. It is critical that A and B and X and Y appreciate these dynamics, so they can try to control the flow of information from one side to the other in ways that maximizes their bargaining effectiveness.

Which of these bargaining participants are *stabilizers* who work to keep their teams moving toward agreements, *destabilizers* who work to create discord among their own team members, and *quasi-mediators* who work to resolve conflicts between the stabilizers and the destabilizers? (Colosi, 2001, at 22–25). Such stabilizers, destabilizers, and quasi-mediators are frequently operating on both sides of the bargaining table, making it necessary for each participant to appreciate the roles of the different actors. Effective negotiators are able to use quasi-mediators to minimize the disruptive actions of destabilizers, to enable the stabilizers to move toward mutual accords.

During the preliminary portion of the Information Stage, many parties make the mistake of asking narrow, highly-focused questions that can be answered with brief responses. As a result, they merely confirm what they already suspect. It is far more effective to ask broad, open-ended information seeking questions (Lax & Sebenius, 2006, at 208–09; Volkema, 2006, at 46–47; Latz, 2004, at 54–55; Korobkin, 2002, at 12; Ordover & Doneff, 2002, at 20–22; Ilich, 1992, at 68; Stone, Patton & Heen, 1999, at 174–75; Goldman, 1991, at 134; Bastress & Harbaugh, 1990, at 413; Gifford, 1989, at 124–25). Negotiators want to induce their opponents to talk. The more people speak, the more information they directly and indirectly disclose (Cohen, 2003, at 226–29; Schoonmaker, 1989, at 113–14). If participants suspect something about a particular issue, they should formulate an expansive inquiry covering that area. The persons being interrogated have no way of knowing exactly what their questioners already comprehend. They often erroneously assume the questioners know more about their situations than those opponents actually know (Van Boven, Gilovich & Medvec, 2003, at 118–24). When they respond to the broad inquiry, they are likely to divulge new leads and additional pieces of information. No matter how carefully they plan their responses, they are likely to include informative verbal leaks regarding particular items or their bargaining priorities.

When opponents appear to have answered particular questions, additional information can often be elicited through silence (Miller & Miller, 2002, at 70). The persons who
asked the inquiries simply say nothing for ten or twenty seconds after the other parties
have responded. Such silent pauses may induce careless negotiators to fill the void with
further comments. As they do so, they usually provide new pieces of information and
new leads that can be explored through different questions. On the other hand, once
negotiators have given intended answers, they should become quiet and patiently await
new questions or statements from their opponents. They should not allow questioner
silence to induce them to say more.

[c]   Narrowing Queries

Once questioners think they have elicited a sufficient amount of general information,
they may use more specific queries to confirm their understandings (Zwier & Guernsey,
2005, at 98–106; Latz, 2004, at 55–56; Guernsey, 1996, at 62–63). Opponents may
attempt to avoid direct responses to these inquiries, in an effort to prevent the
disclosure of particular information. They may ignore the questions or provide
ambiguous answers. When this occurs, the questioners should rephrase their inquiries
in a manner that compels the other parties to provide more definitive replies (Gifford,
1989, at 123). They should not permit opponents to employ evasive tactics to avoid the
disclosure of pertinent information.

[d]   Questioning Process as Powerplay

The questioning process not only enables interrogators to elicit beneficial responses,
but may also permit them to seize control over the preliminary stages of the interaction
(Ilich, 1973, at 142). Effective questioners can steer the discussions in the direction they
wish to proceed, and they may be able to avoid the exploration of issues they prefer to
ignore. This permits them to obtain more crucial knowledge during the early part of
their interaction than their opponents, and they may use their cognitive advantage to
enhance their confidence and their bargaining power.

[e]   Value of Active Listening

Negotiators must listen intently and observe carefully during the Information Stage
(Latz, 2004, at 58–59; Ordover & Doneff, 2002, at 23–26; Shapiro & Jankowski, 2001, at
76–77; Goleman, 1998, at 178–80; Steinberg, 1998, at 166–68; Barkai, 1996, at 728,
737–42). They should try to maintain supportive eye contact to encourage further
opponent disclosures and to discern verbal leaks and nonverbal signals (Harvard Bus.
Essentials, 2003, at 58–60). Smiles and occasional head nods are likely to generate more
open responses from people who feel they are being heard (Cohen, 2003, at 226–27).
Occasional "mm-hms" or "I can see" can be used to encourage further disclosures, as
can silent periods following opponent responses (Zwier & Guernsey, 2005, at 113–15).
Questioners should take minimal notes. When people write, they miss much of what is
being said, and they are oblivious to the nonverbal cues emanating from the
respondents. Active listeners who concentrate on the answers their queries elicit are
often surprised by how much they remember about the replies they receive (Brach,
2008, at 31). They usually recall far more than others who asked the same questions but
attempted to write down as much as they could during the exchanges. Negotiators must
not only listen carefully to what is being said by opponents, but also what is not being

covered, since omitted areas may suggest weaknesses adversaries do not wish to address (Kramer, 2001, at 234).

It is amazing how much verbal and nonverbal communication is missed by parties during bargaining interactions. When we videotape students or practitioners and replay the tapes, the participants are shocked at two things: (1) how much *their opponents* said that they never heard and (2) how much *they* said that they do not recall having stated. They are so busy thinking about what was just said, what is being presently stated, and what they plan to say next, what negotiating techniques are being employed by their adversaries and which tactics they plan to use next, and who made the last concession and who should make the next concession, that they fail to perceive many obvious verbal and nonverbal signals.

[f]   Value of Patience

Participants must proceed slowly during the Information Stage. Patience is generally rewarded with the attainment of greater knowledge. Too many negotiators are anxious to solidify the deal they hope to consummate through the negotiation process, and they hurry through the Information Stage. They can hardly wait to begin and conclude the substantive discussions (McCormack, 1984, at 152). This conduct is frequently counterproductive. When advocate anxiety generates an abbreviated Information Stage, the impatient negotiators may ignore crucial verbal and nonverbal signals emanating from opposing counsel. Important pieces of information may not be ascertained and considered. The shortened interaction may thus culminate in a final agreement that is less beneficial than if the questioning process had been permitted to unfold more deliberately. It thus behooves negotiators to be conscious of the developmental stages of a negotiation. When they sense that participant anxiety is causing the process to evolve in an unduly accelerated manner that may inure to the detriment of themselves or the interests of their clients, they should adopt a more deliberate approach. They can ask more detailed questions or provide more leisurely answers and comments. They should be careful, however, not to let the situation cause them to disclose more of their confidential information than they ever intended.

[g]   Identifying Issues that Lend Themselves to Mutually Beneficial Resolution

Negotiating parties must initially identify the issues to be resolved (Schoonmaker, 1989, at 14–15). Since bargaining is a problem-solving process, all of the participants should understand the underlying matters that must be addressed if they want the results to be fruitful. It is only at this point that the negotiators can begin to recognize and explore the relevant options and their consequences. Advocates who ignore this crucial consideration — and who fail to at least minimally disclose their own underlying needs and interests — are likely to obtain inefficient accords.

Once the negotiators have identified the different issues to be exchanged, they should begin to determine the relative value of each of those items to the opposing side. They should ask whether Item 1 is more or less important than Item 2 or Item 3. How much more does the other side value Item 1 versus Item 2 — twice as much or only fifty percent more? How do Items 1 and 2 compare to Item 3? Questioners should listen carefully for verbal leaks that may disclose the relative interests of the opponents. Which items do they *have* to obtain (*i.e.,* "essential" terms); do they really *want* to get (*i.e.,* "important" terms); and would they *like* to get (*i.e.,* "desirable" terms). Rational opponents should be willing to trade "imprtant" terms for "essential" items or other "important" terms, and they should be willing to trade "desirable" items for "essential" or "important" terms.

Negotiators should not assume that the parties are dealing with a "fixed pie" that cannot be expanded, based upon the erroneous belief that both sides want to obtain the identical terms (Bazerman & Shonk, 2005, at 54–55). Questioners should compare their own rankings of different issues with those of the other side. This enables them to begin to look for possible exchanges that will allow the bargaining parties to expand the overrall pie to be divided and enable them to maximize the joint returns generated (Hurder, 2007, at 270–71). Each side should be willing to trade items they value less for terms they prefer more. When both sides value the items equally, they will compete for those terms. On the other hand, when they value items differently, they should look for trades that will simultaneously enhance their respective positions.

[h]   Obtaining Information

[i]   Opponent Strategies, Strengths and Weaknesses

Since negotiators cannot unilaterally impose their expectations on opposing parties, they must become aware of the needs and interests of their adversaries, and seek to at least partially satisfy the underlying goals of those participants. Without this consideration, they cannot hope to achieve mutual accords. Negotiators on one side cannot obtain the requisite insights into these factors in isolation, but must endeavor to learn as much as possible about opponent potential and actual choices, their preferences and their intensity, their planned strategy, and their operative strengths and weaknesses (Gulliver, 1979, at 107). Bargainers must always be cognizant of the fact that opponent perceptions of particular situations may be more favorable to their own positions than they anticipated. Only through careful and patient probing may they successfully discern these beneficial circumstances.

Negotiators should ask a number of *"what"* and *"why"* questions (Malhotra & Bazerman, 2007, at 85–86). *What* items does the other side wish to obtain, and *why* does it want those items? The *what* questions are designed to determine the terms the other side wants, while the *why* questions are designed to ascertain the interests underlying those demands. Although one side may not be willing to provide the other side with exactly what it is requesting, it may be able to satisfy the other side's underlying interests in a manner that is less costly to itself.

[ii]   Opponent Pressures

Each side needs to comprehend the external and internal pressures influencing the opposing party, since such factors directly affect that party's assessment of the situation. Do they have a constituency that has established some irrational constraints? Are they using an unanticipated value system to assess their perception of bargaining proposals? Have their previously articulated positions truly reflected their underlying needs and interests? Have they restricted their offers to legalistic options when they would really prefer some nonlegal alternative? Too many negotiators limit their discussions to those items that could be achieved through formal legal channels, without recognizing that bargainers generally possess the capacity to formulate other resolutions of their differences. While administrative and judicial tribunals are constrained by conventional remedial doctrines, negotiators may agree to any mutually advantageous terms as long those terms do not contravene applicable legal prohibitions.

[i]   Need for Continuing Attorney-Client Interactions

Throughout the Information Stage — and the subsequent stages of the negotiation process — attorneys should communicate regularly with their own clients (see generally Gifford, 1987). As critical information is exchanged concerning opponent needs and interests, lawyers should share that information with their own clients who must continuously reassess their own hopes and aspirations. Clients with unrealistic expectations have to be counseled about the final terms they are likely to achieve. Lawyers who keep their clients well informed about negotiation developments with the other side are likely to find their clients more receptive to the terms ultimately obtained.

§ 6.02   OFFERS

[1]   Who Goes First

[a]   Initiating vs. Responding

Negotiators frequently wonder whether they should state their positions first or attempt to induce their opponents to do so. Since there is no statistical correlation between who makes the initial offer and the outcome of most interactions (Thompson, 2005, at 49; Bastress & Harbaugh, 1990, at 493), many people believe that this factor is irrelevant. Some bargaining experts even indicate a preference for going first, because they think that this tactic enables them to define the basic negotiation range, anchor the impending discussions, and discourage opponent offers that are wholly unacceptable (Malhotra & Bazerman, 2007, at 27–30; Thompson, 2005, at 49–50; Latz, 2004, at 151–52, 166–67; Birke & Fox, 1999, at 40; Steinberg, 1998, at 52–53; Freund, 1992, at 114–15). Even individuals who frequently employ this technique, however, recognize the need to be cautious in some circumstances. "Don't go first unless you know value (or are well advised on that score) and have formulated a realistic expectation to guide your negotiating strategy." (Freund, 1992, at 115)

Individuals who announce firm, beneficial, and well-supported opening offers can gain a significant advantage over less-prepared opponents who are not sure where they should begin (Thompson, 2005, at 49). Such preemptive offers can anchor the talks and induce less confident adversaries to begin with their own opening positions closer to where the initial offerors hope to end up. Against thoroughly prepared adversaries who have established their own firm aspiration levels and set opening offers during their own preparation, however, preemptive opening offers are unlikely to have such a beneficial anchoring impact.

[b]   Benefit of Obtaining First Offer

The use of preemptive first offers can be an especially effective bargaining technique when both sides have a realistic understanding of the actual value of the items to be discussed. In situations in which no common value system can be relied upon to guide the participants, I prefer to have opponents make the initial offers (Shapiro & Jankowski, 2001, at 148; Schoonmaker, 1989, at 74–75). There are three reasons for this view.

[i] Revealing Miscalculated Values

First, if one or both sides have miscalculated the value of the transaction, the individuals who go first disclose the misunderstanding and place themselves at a distinct disadvantage. Even though skilled negotiators are frequently able to predict the opening positions that their opponents are likely to present, they can never be certain. The opponents may know more about their own weaknesses than was unilaterally surmised by this side, or they may have overestimated the strength possessed by this party. For example, plaintiff attorneys may hope to obtain $75,000 for their client. If defense counsel initially offer more than plaintiff lawyers anticipated — *e.g.*, $50,000, $75,000, or more — the plaintiff representatives can immediately reassess their circumstances and adjust their opening demand upward to provide them with the flexibility they need to test their increased value hypothesis. Instead of beginning in the $150,000 to $200,000 range, they might start with a demand of $400,000 or $500,000. This approach may enable them to achieve settlements in the $200,000 to $250,000 range, despite the fact they never comprehend why the other side is willing to provide such generous terms.

[ii] Bracketing

A second factor involves a phenomenon known as *"bracketing."* If negotiators can induce their opponents to make the initial offers, they can *bracket* their objectives by adjusting their own opening offers to place their goals near the mid-point between their respective opening positions (Latz, 2004, at 156–57; Birke & Fox, 1999, at 41; Dawson, 2001, at 18–20). For example, if plaintiff attorneys hope to get $300,000 and defense counsel initially offer them $100,000, they can begin with a demand in the $500,000 range to keep their $300,000 target in the middle. Since parties tend to move inexorably toward the center of their opening positions, due to the generally accepted obligation of bargaining parties to make reciprocal concessions, the people who go second can manipulate the central point and place their adversaries at a psychological disadvantage.

As the bargaining encounter unfolds and further offers and counter-offers are exchanged, it is psychologically beneficial to use bracketing to keep one's aspiration near the mid-point between the current positions of the parties. If the defendant moves from $100,000 to $150,000, the defendant can come down from $500,000 to $450,000. If the defendant subsequently moves to $200,000, the plaintiff can move to $400,000. Since bargaining parties tend to move toward the center of their existing positions, bracketing can be employed to keep one's goal in that central location.

[iii] Inducing First Concession

The third reason for inducing opponents to make the first offers concerns the fact that while opening *offers* do not significantly influence negotiation outcomes, initial *concessions* do. There is a slight, but statistically significant, inverse correlation between opening concessions and final results, with persons who make the initial concessions tending to do less well than their opponents (Bastress & Harbaugh, 1990, at 493; Kritzer, 1991, at 68). People who make the first concessions tend to be anxious negotiators who make more and larger concessions than their opponents (Schoonmaker, 1989, at 101). Individuals who can induce their opponents to issue the first offers have a good chance of persuading them to make the initial concessions. After their opponents make the first offer, this side's opening position looks like a counter-offer. It is thus easy for this side to look to their opponents for the next position statement — *i.e.*, the first concession.

[c]   Never Accept Opponent's Opening Offer

When negotiators articulate their initial offers, they do not expect them to be accepted. They start some distance from where they think the parties will end up to give themselves some bargaining room. They anticipate similar conduct by their opponents that will generate reciprocal concessions until the parties reach mutually acceptable agreements somewhere between their opening positions. If the recipient of a surprisingly generous opponent opening offer immediately accepts the proposed terms, the offeror is likely to experience "buyer's remorse" and try to get out of what they now think is a poor deal.

Negotiators should be careful not to accept opening offers articulated by opposing parties. They should instead respond with offers of their own and allow the usual give-and-take to unfold. Even when they think opponent offers are great, they should try to talk the offerors up or down a little before they accept their proposed terms. This allows their adversaries to think that their bargaining efforts influenced the outcome, and it leaves them with the feeling they obtained good deals.

[2]   Inducing the Initial Offer

If anxious negotiators can be induced to make the first offers, adroit opponents may be able to induce them to "bid against themselves" by getting them to make consecutive and unreciprocated opening offers. If the recipients of an initial offer can flinch and appear shocked by what they have heard, they may cause an uncertain party to provide them with a more generous position statement (Dawson, 2001, at 29–31). Other recipients of first offers try to accomplish the same result verbally. They look disappointed and inform the offeror that "you'll have to do better than that." (Dawson, 2001, at 42–45) This approach frequently generates additional offeror movement.

It is certainly not easy to persuade all opponents to make the initial offers. In some negotiations, the circumstances dictate the persons who are expected to go first. This obligation often falls upon the ones who initiate the discussions. Nonetheless, adroit bargainers may be able to avoid having to make the first real offer even when they originate the interaction. For example, individuals who have indicated a desire to sell certain property may respond to inquiries regarding the amount they want to obtain by asking the prospective purchasers how much they are willing to pay (Ilich, 1973, at 169). If the respondents are careless, they may be induced to disclose important information through initial offers that should not have been made first. The seller may alternatively announce a wholly unreasonable asking price, hoping to impel prospective buyers to articulate the first real offers. Plaintiff lawyers may write demand letters that detail the injuries sustained by their clients, but omit specific dollar amounts for the items listed. This approach may induce defendants to make the first definitive offers.

There are occasions when both parties are being so coy that neither is willing to initiate the substantive discussions. The participants continue to ask each other questions and talk around the actual issues to be addressed, but neither side is willing to place a firm offer on the table. If this situation continues, the negotiators may give up or simply reach an impasse. If someone has sought to induce the other party to articulate the first offer by asking what they hope to achieve and they have received no substantive response, they may have to begin the real discussions with an offer of their own. They should be careful to leave themselves sufficient bargaining room. Although they should not start with a wholly unrealistic position that could undermine the interaction, they should begin with a position that allows them flexibility once the other side states its position.

What should a party do if they finally place their position on the table and receive no meaningful response from the other side? They must be especially careful not to bid against themselves by making consecutive and unreciprocated opening offers. They should be patient and use silence to induce the other side to respond in a substantive way. If no counteroffer is forthcoming, they should expressly ask the other party to indicate what it hopes to achieve. If this approach fails to generate a meaningful response, they should indicate their willingness to terminate the present discussions to give the other side the time it may need to formulate its opening position. If a recess in talks becomes necessary, it can be beneficial to agree upon a future meeting time to avoid the possibility that neither negotiator will feel comfortable assuming the responsibility to initiate the subsequent talks.

[3]   Ascertaining Validity of Offer

[a]   Initial Offer

It is important to recognize that the opponents-go-first technique is only of assistance when it generates the first *real* offer. For example, plaintiff lawyers who hope to achieve a $100,000 settlement may have been contemplating a $250,000 initial demand. If they instead decide to open the negotiation process with a $1,000,000 figure, it should be apparent that no *real* offer has yet been made. Defendant attorneys who planned not to disclose their own opening position until they received the first demand from their adversaries should not be induced to divulge their own figure in response to this outrageous initiating statement. They must acknowledge the wholly disingenuous nature of the $1,000,000 proposal and patiently continue the preliminary discussions. Lawyers should not focus so intently on the first offer issue that they fail to understand how easily they can be deceived by false opening offers or demands.

Negotiators who are presented with wholly unreasonable opening offers should not react to those terms in a nonchalant manner (Lax & Sebenius, 2006, at 194–95). If they casually reject these offers, they may lead opponents to believe that their positions are not that extreme. It will become increasingly difficult to subsequently disabuse them of this erroneous notion. It is incumbent upon individuals who receive truly unrealistic offers to reject them swiftly and unambiguously (Freund, 1992, at 125–26). They must immediately convey their disbelief in the terms being stated. This action should preclude subsequent misunderstandings that could adversely affect future negotiation progress.

Negotiators who are not thoroughly prepared may allow an opponent's opening offer to anchor their thinking toward the other side's initial position (Galinsky & Mussweiler, 2001). If the recipients of an opponent's offer either focus on their adversary's aspiration level or their own bottom line, they are likely to accord the other side's opening offer more respect than it deserves. This phenomenon is caused by the fact the anchoring impact of the opening offer is reinforced by a comparison with the offeror's goal or this side's bottom line. When this occurs, the party making the initial offer tends to achieve better results than the recipient of that offer. On the other hand, when offer recipients focus on the offeror's bottom line or their own side's aspiration level, the anchoring effect is negated. This is because the other side's bottom line and this party's goal are inconsistent with the opening offer being considered. It is thus imperative for negotiators who receive opening offers from opponents to have a firm belief in their own side's aspiration level and a good estimate of the bottom line of the offerors. A good way to prevent opponent opening offers from anchoring the subsequent discussions is for the person eliciting the first offer to have an opening response planned before the serious talks commence.

[b]   Demands and Offers in General

[i]   Considering Reputation and Contextual, Factual, and Legal Circumstances

Negotiators must recognize that opponents frequently employ disingenuous tactics to obtain a bargaining advantage. Some engage in outright mendacity, while others resort to mere "puffing." (Most negotiators seem to always categorize their own exaggerations as "puffing," while classifying similar deception by their adversaries as unconscionable prevarication!) In an effort to determine the actual substance of questionable representations, lawyers must initially consider the speaker's reputation for truth and veracity. They should simultaneously assess the credibility of the information being received by comparing it to the factual and legal circumstances they have already confirmed independently and by evaluating the context in which it appears.

[ii]   Gauging Congruence of Verbal and Nonverbal Signals

Listeners must evaluate the congruency of the verbal and nonverbal signals emanating from their opponents. If their intuitive feelings suggest the presence of verbal deception, they should try to understand the reasons for their suspicions. They may well determine that the nonverbal stimuli being emitted by their adversary suggest the presence of mendacity. (See Chapter 3, *supra*.) When they do not wholly believe the statements being made by opposing counsel, but find that the verbal and nonverbal messages appear to be congruent, negotiators should recognize that their apprehension may not be well founded. They may thus wish to tentatively accept the representations in question. Individuals should alternatively consider the possibility that they are attributing unfounded meaning to what is actually being conveyed. They may be reading more into their opponent's representations than is warranted — or intended — and this phenomenon may be the basis for their resulting confusion. When this type of interpretative problem is suspected, it may be beneficial to ask some probing questions that may clarify the actual meaning intended by the other party. If the original speaker discovers that a misunderstanding has inadvertently occurred, he or she can more carefully elucidate the matter.

[4]   Assessing Target and Resistance Points

[a]   Definition

Parties to a negotiation normally begin the process with the establishment of *"target points"* they hope to achieve (*i.e.*, their aspiration level) and *"resistance points"* they do not plan to go above or below, preferring to accept the consequences of no agreement if terms at least as favorable as these bottom lines cannot be achieved (Menkel-Meadow, 1984, at 769; Bellow & Moulton, 1981, at 58–63). This phenomenon is graphically depicted in Figure 2.

[b]   Example

FIGURE 2

Plaintiff Hopes to Get $100,000   Plaintiff Will Accept No Less Than $50,000

(P_t = Plaintiff's Target Point)   (P_r = Plaintiff's Resistance Point)

Plaintiff's Settlement Range

Defendant's Settlement Range

Defendant Hopes to Pay $35,000   Defendant Will Pay Up to $80,000

(D_t = Defendant's Target Point)   (D_r = Defendant's Resistance Point)

The HIGHLIGHTED AREA in Figure 2 between P^r ($50,000) and D^r ($80,000) represents the parties' "Zone of Possible Agreement" (ZOPA) (Mnookin, Peppet & Tulumello, 2000, at 18–22), or "Settlement Range." (Lax & Sebenius, 2006, at 89–90). The plaintiff will accept the trial alternative, rather than agree to less than $50,000, while the defendant would choose to litigate if more than $80,000 continues to be demanded. The negotiation process will determine whether any final agreement will be closer to the $50,000 or the $80,000 figure (Korobkin, 2000).

[c]   Adjusting to Noncoinciding Ranges

In some situations, the parties initially establish settlement ranges that do not overlap or that coincide only minimally.

In the former setting, no negotiated settlement can be achieved, unless one or both parties realize the need to reassess their original positions. In the latter situation, it will be difficult for adversaries to locate the narrow zone of agreement. Nonetheless, when proficient negotiators begin to recognize the minimal or nonexistent zones of agreement, they are often able to convince each other during the Information Stage of their need to reassess their preconceived settlement ranges. They are thus able to create or expand their zones of agreement and enhance the likelihood of mutual accords. When ample zones of agreement initially exist, negotiators should have little difficulty reaching a mutually acceptable agreement. The only issue to be resolved concerns which party is to achieve the more favorable result (i.e., a final settlement on its side of the zone of agreement midpoint).

[5]   Awareness of Opponent Flexibility

Professional negotiators always try to learn as much as possible about the personal skill and experience of their adversaries. During the pre-negotiation stage, they gather pertinent input from other lawyers who have previously confronted opposing counsel. They try to ascertain what tactics their adversaries prefer to use and how they normally respond to various techniques. Are opposing counsel "true believers" who are blind to the merits of the positions espoused by others or are they pragmatists who recognize that negotiators are merely advocates for the positions of their respective clients? Once the actual negotiation commences, adroit bargainers attempt to verify the information they have amassed about their adversaries. When they discern reactions that differ from what they initially expected, they adjust their planned strategy accordingly.

[6]   Various Methods of Presenting Demands and the Information They Convey

[a]   Most or Least Important First

The manner in which adversaries present their initial demands is frequently revealing with respect to multiple item transactions. Bargainers normally focus on finite groups of topics once serious negotiations commence. Discerning negotiators can often obtain crucial information from the groups of items initially emphasized by opponents when serious discussions commence. Most bargainers begin with a cluster of their most important or their least important topics. They rarely mix significant and insignificant items.

[b]   Advantages of Understanding Relative Values

If opponents initiate the auction process with a group of five items, four of which are insignificant to the offeree and one of which is relatively important, it is likely that all five topics are unimportant to the offeror. An adroit offeree can casually claim the beneficial term during the early discussions and obtain a significant benefit in exchange for almost nothing. The opponent may conversely begin with five items, four of which are critical to the offeree and one of which is relatively unimportant. It is likely that all five terms are significant to the offeror. This knowledge permits the offeree to use this topic as a bargaining chip that may be exchanged for a substantial item. While some might suggest that it is improper to trade an insignificant topic for a substantial term, they must remember that the value of an item is in the eye of the beholder. If one side wants something the other side possesses, they may reasonably be expected to offer something of value to obtain that term, even when the other side does not really value the topic being exchanged.

[c]   Beneficial to Plan to Discuss Several Different Items Together

When advocates prepare for the serious discussions, it can be helpful to plan to address groups of different items together (Malhotra & Bazerman, 2007, at 75–78). If the parties tackle items one at a time, each side's gain is usually a loss for the other side. On the other hand, if they focus on several items simultaneously, they can efficiently trade one or two items of their own for one or two items from the other side. Once they discern which of these terms are more valued by Side A and which by Side B, each side can decide to concede the items it values less in exchange for the items it prefers and the other side values less. This will enable the negotiators to effectively expand the overall pie to be divided between them, and enable them to generate more efficient overall agreements.

[d]   Opening Substantive Discussions

[i]   Key Topics

Anxious negotiators frequently begin the substantive talks with several of their most important topics in an effort to produce an expeditious, albeit tentative, resolution of those issues. They are nervous, risk-averse advocates who wish to diminish the tension associated with the uncertainty of the bargaining process. They believe they can significantly decrease their concern regarding a nonsettlement by achieving accelerated progress on their primary topics. They unfortunately fail to realize that this approach enhances the possibility of a counterproductive stalemate (Schoonmaker, 1989, at 68). If their principal objectives correspond with the primary goals of their adversaries, this presentation sequence is likely to cause an immediate clash of wills. The distance between their opening positions on these key items seems insurmountable. Opposing counsel may rapidly decide that irreconcilable differences exist, and conclude that little progress is presently attainable. This result can only exacerbate the anxiety being of the party endeavoring to achieve an expeditious resolution.

[ii]   Ancillary Topics

Other negotiators prefer to begin the bargaining process with their less significant subjects, hoping to make rapid progress on these less controverted items. This approach is likely to develop a cooperative atmosphere that should facilitate compromise when the more controverted subjects are subsequently explored (Cohen, 2003, at 132–33; Watkins & Rosegrant, 2001, at 21–22; Rubin & Brown, 1975, at 148). The advantage of this approach is that it develops in both parties a *psychological* commitment to the negotiation process (Harvard Bus. Essentials, 2003, at 73). If there are twenty-five basic items in dispute and the parties are able to achieve tentative agreement on nineteen or twenty with minimal difficulty, they begin to sense a successful interaction. They do not wish to negate this progress with an impasse on the remaining issues. They are thus more likely to work diligently to avoid unproductive stalemates with respect to the last five or six topics (Karrass, 1970, at 72–73).

On rare occasions, a particular issue must be resolved in a definite manner if any satisfactory deal is to be achieved. When this is true, many negotiators prefer to raise this issue at the outset and directly indicate how it must be handled (Schoonmaker, 1989, at 66). The other side may agree to this approach, so long as a critical topic for them is resolved in a manner they find acceptable. Once these key terms have been exchanged, the negotiators return to the less significant issues and work their way up toward the other important terms. If the parties are unwilling to agree preliminarily upon a mutually acceptable resolution of these essential items, they usually terminate the interaction, since they do not believe that further discussions would be beneficial.

Individuals who decide to present their less significant items first can employ either of two approaches to enhance their probability of prevailing when the more important issues are subsequently discussed. Some believe that it is appropriate to make tentative, but seemingly magnanimous, concessions on the preliminary subjects, to create feelings of guilt and obligation in their opponents. They hope that this pattern will induce reciprocal concessions from their adversaries when the primary topics are being resolved. If this technique does not produce the desired results, they can always reopen talks pertaining to the previously settled matters. Other negotiators think that they should strive to obtain favorable concessions on the early items, to establish concessionary mind-sets in their opponents. If they can generate bargaining momentum in their favor, they may be able to induce opposing counsel to continue their concession-oriented attitude with respect to the primary topics. If they are successful in this regard, they may end up with everything they want!

[7]   Difficulties in Conveying Credible Representations

When negotiators realize that opponents are not treating their truthful representations with appropriate respect, they should endeavor to determine the communication problem involved. They must consider three fundamental communication barriers:

> What is spoken may not be heard.
> What is heard may not be understood.
> What is understood may not be accepted.
> (Scott, 1981, at 65)

They should carefully reiterate their position and be certain that their opponents have received and comprehended their message. If they continue to experience opponent skepticism, they most likely have a credibility problem. Their nonverbal signals may not be congruent with their verbal representations, or the substance of their message may contradict information currently believed by their opponents. They should ask their opponents to explain the basis for their skepticism. This approach may enable them to understand and correct the erroneous preconceptions influencing their opponents. If the misunderstanding concerns an important issue, they should work diligently to enhance the veracity of their representations, recognizing that continuing credibility questions may seriously undermine future discussions.

[8]   Controlling Disclosure of Own Side's Information

[a]   Importance of Information Control

As individuals prepare for a negotiation, they must decide several things regarding their own side's information. What information are they willing to disclose, and how do they plan to divulge it? What sensitive information do they wish to withhold, and how do they plan to avoid the disclosure of those facts? People who resolve these critical issues *before* they begin to interact with their opponents tend to have more successful Information Stages than those who do not think about them until forced to do so in the midst of actual negotiations.

[b]   Formulating Principled Positions

When negotiators disclose their critical information, they should frame their presentations in a manner that enables them to simultaneously advance their underlying interests. They can accomplish this objective by formulating "principled" positions that are accompanied by succinct rationales explaining the reasons they deserve those terms. This approach forces opponents to treat their position statements seriously, and it makes it more difficult for their adversaries to summarily reject their offers (Freund, 1992, at 122–23). This is based upon the fact that most people find it easier to decline unexplained requests than to rebuff substantiated entreaties (Pratkanis & Aronson, 1991, at 26–27).

It is beneficial for negotiators to explain their initial positions in terms of objective criteria that appear to be "fair and reasonable" (Latz, 2004, at 105–130). If opponents can be induced to think that neutral standards are being employed, they will treat the opening offers more seriously. They will also find it harder to challenge the underlying bases for the positions being articulated. It thus behooves bargainers to formulate principled opening positions they can justify based upon generally accepted standards.

They may rely upon market values, precedential values, expert opinions, or similar factors.

[c] Framing Offers with Certain Benefits for Opponents and Subtle Advantages for Own Position

Bargainers should also endeavor to present opponents with options that subtly favor the positions the offerors would like to obtain (Campbell & Docherty, 2004). People offered a *certain gain* and the possibility of a greater benefit tend to accept the sure gain, while individuals who must choose between a *certain loss* and the possibility of no loss tend to opt for the chance to experience no loss (Guthrie, 2000, at 166–67, 176–81; Watkins, 2001, at 123–24; Mnookin & Ross, 1995, at 16–17; Bazerman & Neale, 1992, at 33–39; Pratkanis & Aronson, 1991, at 61–63). Whenever possible, negotiators should frame their offers in terms that would provide their opponents with *certain* benefits. If those persons are forced to choose between the definitive gains and the possibility of more advantageous external alternatives, most are likely to select the certainty of a negotiated gain. On the other hand, if opponents are compelled to choose between the sure loss associated with a bargained agreement or the possibility of avoiding any loss through an external option, they are more likely to accept the nonsettlement alternative.

[d] Against Excessive Candor at Information Stage

[i] Benefit of Forcing Opponents to Ask Questions

Negotiators should not readily volunteer their most significant information. They should instead make their opponents work to extract it. The most pertinent facts should be slowly divulged in response to opponent inquiries. When adversaries ask questions, they generally listen intently to the replies they elicit. After all, they want to hear the answers to their own inquiries. They thus perceive more of what the responder is saying. Furthermore, since they attribute the speaker's revelations to their questioning skills, they accord them more credibility than they would if the same facts were voluntarily divulged. The more opponents believe they have elicited the disclosures being made, the greater the probative value given to those revelations (Cohen, 2003, at 150–153).

Should bargainers withhold critical information that would advance their interests in case they fail to achieve agreements? Litigators may plan to use concealed evidence to surprise opposing witnesses at trial if cases are not settled, and transactional experts may fear that the disclosure of information to one party may adversely affect contemporaneous or future negotiations with competing firms. Negotiators rarely gain from the withholding of information supporting their positions. If they believe that this information would further their current bargaining objectives, they should usually share it with their opponents to apprise them of the true power they possess (Ilich, 1992, at 46–47). Since the vast majority of cases are resolved without adjudications, such information would be unlikely to be used in subsequent judicial proceedings. Only in the rarest of circumstances would the disclosure of important information have an adverse impact on future trials or transactional negotiations being conducted with other parties.

[ii]   Problems with Excessive Candor

If the negotiation process is to develop in an efficacious manner, both sides have to engage in an information exchange. A number of participants consider this a straight-forward part of the transaction and see no need to employ manipulative disclosure techniques. They abhor the disingenuous devices used by many bargainers to advance their interests, and they prefer the direct approach. Once the Information Stage begins, they directly tell their opponents what they wish to obtain and why they believe they deserve the terms they are seeking (Kritzer, 1991, at 48). They naively think that their voluntary disclosures will be well received by their opponents. In most legal transactions, however, they are incorrect, because competitive adversaries can take advantage of their candor to obtain more favorable terms (Watkins, 2006, at 78–79; Kritzer, 1991, at 78–79).

Sincerely open negotiators may encounter additional problems. As straight-forward representatives honestly disclose their fundamental information, their opponents tend to become suspicious. Bargainers are not used to such candor, and they begin to think that they are being manipulated. They suspect that pertinent facts are being withheld, and that the knowledge being shared is being embellished in a disingenuous fashion. Because of these suppositions, they do not listen as carefully as they should to what the speaker is telling them. Furthermore — as a result of *"reactive devaluation"* — they discount much of what they do hear as self-serving disclosures (Mnookin, Peppet & Tulumello, 2000, at 165; Mnookin & Ross, 1995, at 22–23). They thus miss important revelations and give diminished credence to the facts they do comprehend.

§ 6.03   CONTROLLING RESPONSES

[1]   Use of Blocking Techniques

It is much easier to avoid the unintended disclosure of critical information if the opponents are unaware of the fact that knowledge is being withheld. The most effective way to accomplish this objective is through the use of *"blocking techniques"* (Tepley, 2005, at 195–98; Latz, 2004, at 64–66; Bastress & Harbaugh, 1990, at 422–28; Freund, 1992, at 64–65). Blocking Techniques enable adroit negotiators to protect their crucial information without arousing the suspicions of their adversaries.

Negotiators are frequently concerned about sensitive information they do not wish to share with their opponents. They are understandably hesitant to directly inform their adversaries of their reluctance to address these areas, because it would likely generate distrust and heighten opponent interest. When they are specifically asked about these areas, they become embarrassed and disconcerted. Even though they had planned to avoid the disclosure of this information, they find themselves divulging their secret thoughts. Individuals who want to perfect these avoidance skills should watch politicians being interviewed on talk shows. If they listen carefully, they will be amazed at the number of probing questions that go unanswered. Following are some frequently used examples of Blocking Techniques.

1. Ignore the Intrusive Question.

People who do not like inquiries posed by their opponents should simply ignore them. They should continue the current conversation or change the focus to other topics they prefer to explore. If they are effective, their opponents will not even realize that their queries have not been addressed, and they will direct their attention to the areas being discussed.

2. Answer the Beneficial Part of Compound Questions.

Persons frequently ask complex questions that contain several parts. For example, a reporter may ask political candidates whether they would be willing to raise taxes to lower the deficit. Cautious politicians are hesitant to discuss the possibility of tax increases, so they focus entirely on the deficit reduction aspect of the query. Negotiators can use the same approach when opponents formulate compound questions. They can answer the part(s) they like and ignore the other portion(s).

3. Over- or Under- Answer the Question.

When negotiators are asked specific questions regarding delicate areas, they can often prevent meaningful disclosures through the use of general responses. When they are asked expansive inquiries, they can respond with narrow answers. By over-answering narrow questions and under-answering general inquiries, they can usually protect their sensitive information.

4. Misconstrue the Question and Answer the Reframed Inquiry.

Politicians are regularly asked whether they would be willing to increase taxes. Although these specific inquiries do not seem easy to ignore, most proficient candidates are able to redirect the focus of what is being asked. "I can tell by your question that you are concerned about the deficit, and let me address that important topic . . . " Negotiators can use the same technique. They can reframe touchy questions and then answer the queries they have formulated. This permits them to steer the conversation in the direction they wish it to go.

5. Answer the Opponent's Question With Own Question.

Negotiators can often avoid the need to answer delicate inquiries by responding with questions of their own. If they do this adroitly, they can change the focus from themselves back to the original interrogators.

> OPPONENT: Is your client willing to compensate my client for the loss of consortium caused by the injuries inflicted by his/her negligence?

> YOU: Isn't it true that your client's marriage was in disarray prior to the accident?

> OPPONENT: I agree that they did not have a perfect relationship, but don't you think they deserve compensation for the impact the serious injuries have had on their marriage?

> YOU: What kind of difficulties were they experiencing?

Individuals may respond in a similar manner when they are asked about their bargaining authority. For example, if plaintiff counsel who are presently demanding $115,000 ask defense counsel who are currently offering $90,000 if they are authorized to pay $100,000, they can refocus the discussion by asking plaintiff counsel if they are authorized to accept that amount. They may alternatively treat this type of question as a new offer, praise the other party for its movement, but indicate why the new $100,000 figure is still unacceptable. Opponents who did not intend their inquiry to constitute a new offer will retreat quickly in an effort to avoid further embarrassment.

6. Rule the Question Out of Bounds.

Negotiators who are asked about such matters as their authorized limits or special research they have conducted should not hesitate to indicate that they do not respond to inquiries that inappropriately seek confidential information protected by the attorney-client privilege or nondiscoverable matters covered by the work-product doctrine. They should be careful to be sufficiently consistent with respect to this approach that they do not disclose critical information inadvertently. For example, if they like to respond that they are not authorized to agree to particular terms when they actually lack that prerogative, they should not rule questions regarding their authorized limits out of bounds when they do possess the requisite authority. People who deal with them regularly will quickly discern the different treatment being given to these inquiries, and will realize that they only refuse to respond to these queries when they are authorized to do what is being asked.

Negotiators should plan their blocking techniques in advance and vary them during their discussions. They may ignore one question, under-answer another, misconstrue a third, and respond to a fourth with an inquiry of their own. If they are proficient, they will be able to evade a number of questions without their opponents recognizing the degree to which they are withholding information.

[2]   Nonadversarial Probing of Underlying Interests and Objectives

[a]   Benefits

Although most legal practitioners appropriately view the negotiation process as an inherently adversarial interaction, they should recognize the substantial benefits that may be derived during the Information Stage through the use of relatively nonadversarial questioning techniques (Kennedy, 1998, at 118–119). Negotiators who want to create a mediative/cooperative atmosphere need to replace leading questions that are intended implicitly or overtly to challenge the positions being taken by opposing counsel with less threatening, seemingly neutral inquiries. Both parties must develop sufficient trust to enable them to explore their respective underlying assumptions, values, and goals in a relatively candid manner. Objective questions can carefully review each side's understanding of the relevant factual circumstances and applicable legal doctrines. If both sides can agree upon these basic factors in a noncompetitive fashion, the probability that they will achieve mutually beneficial results can be significantly increased (Fisher & Ury, 1981, at 41–57).

When a wide zone of possible agreement (see Figure 2, *supra*) exists with respect to a particular negotiation, the parties should encounter minimal difficulty achieving agreement. Their resulting accord will probably not, however, be a Pareto superior solution — where neither party could enhance its position without simultaneously worsening the condition of the other side. If the participants develop an open information exchange, they would likely discover a more efficient overall result. In many other bargaining situations, the zone of possible agreement tentatively ascertained by the parties during their preliminary Information Stage may be quite limited or nonexistent. If they were to accept this situation at face value, they might well conclude — usually erroneously — that no mutual resolution is possible. Such a predicament may often be avoided through a more expansive exploration of the parties' respective underlying needs and interests (*see generally* Mnookin, Peppet & Tulumello, 2000; Fisher & Ury, 1981).

On some occasions, negotiators do not achieve optimal agreements due to their failure to consider unstated alternatives. They focus entirely on the positions that have been enunciated by the participants and ignore the possibility that other formulations may more effectively satisfy the underlying interests of the parties. Brainstorming negotiators who explore their respective interests and objectives in a nonthreatening and neutral manner can usually discover options not previously contemplated by them or their clients. This is particularly true when they are not afraid to be innovative (Kelley, 2001; Menkel-Meadow, 2001; Mnookin, Peppet & Tulumello, 2000, at 37–39). Each party can then indicate candidly which of the newly discovered alternatives are better or worse for them compared to their previously articulated position statements. Their areas of mutual gain should be emphasized, with their areas of direct conflict being minimized.

[b]   Drawbacks of Adversarial Questioning

Advocates who approach bargaining sessions in a combative, trial-like manner are usually unable to obtain all of the information they need to achieve optimal results. Their opponents generally sense their "win-lose" style and endeavor to protect themselves through the judicious release of pertinent information. They withhold important information they might otherwise divulge. They may even be induced by such competitive tactics to respond in kind. Adversarial negotiators also tend to lock themselves into set positions they defend with strident arguments. They seem to believe that they can intimidate opposing counsel into submission. They frequently ignore or fail to comprehend protestations regarding their interpretation of the applicable facts and legal doctrines. They thus fail to acknowledge new information that might induce them to consider alternative proposals that may prove to be mutually advantageous.

[c]   Mediation Assistance

When advocates reach a tentative impasse during an important negotiation, they often ask a respected neutral party to assist them with the negotiation process. It is hoped that this mediator will be able to reopen communication channels and induce the disputants to consider alternatives they may not have contemplated during their own increasingly combative discussions (see Chapter 16, *infra*). Adroit negotiators do not always have to employ an outside person to perform this function. If they can decrease their adversarial behavior and effectively activate their own mediative capabilities, they can enhance the likelihood of achieving optimal results.

[d]   Discovery of Mutually-Beneficial Options

[i]   Different Valuations of Various Terms

The key to finding solutions to difficult negotiations does not merely involve compromise, but also the ability of the participants to expand the available resources that may be distributed (Brown, 2004a; Kolb & Williams, 2003, at 234–74; Raiffa, 2002, at 198–201; Mnookin, Peppet & Tulumello, 2000, at 11–43; Menkel-Meadow, 1984, at 813). Too many negotiators assume that both sides have similar value systems and analogous utility functions generating a "fixed pie" (Bazerman & Shonk, 2005, at 54–55; Birke & Fox, 1999, at 30–31; Gillespie, et al., 1999, at 367). They thus believe that their opponents want the same terms they desire. This erroneous assumption causes them to view their interactions as entirely distributive, zero-sum transactions in which one side cannot gain without the other side experiencing an equal loss. Extremely competitive/adversarial bargainers tend to think in this fashion. As a result, they frequently achieve inefficient settlement terms or end up with needless nonsettlements. These people fail to realize that in multi-term negotiations, the parties tend to value the various items quite differently (Abramson, 2004, at 37–39; Dawson, 2001, at 305). This allows them to look for trade-offs that can simultaneously benefit both sides. Through the use of brainstorming techniques, negotiators can usually discover new options that can effectively enlarge the overall pie being divided (Watkins, 2001, at 124; Shapiro & Jankowski; 2001, at 201–03; Lewicki, Saunders & Minton, 1999, at 343). For example, parties involved in a marital dissolution may both be fighting for sole custody of the children, when only one spouse really wants this responsibility. If the spouse who does not strongly desire sole custody is provided with adequate visitation rights, and perhaps some other terms that would not be very onerous from the other spouse's perspective, an amicable arrangement may be achievable. It may alternatively be possible to work out some joint custody agreement that would be acceptable to the two disputants — and good for the children involved.

Negotiators should not hesitate to explore unconventional options that may go beyond what courts might have the power to impose or that may transcend established business practices. They can agree to any lawful terms that satisfy underlying client needs. If they try to think "outside the box" and explore innovative alternatives (Kelley, 2001), they may be able to achieve terms that simultaneously improve the results obtained by both sides.

When attorneys generate innovative bargaining options, they may create client confusion. Studies indicate that when individuals are presented with multiple alternatives, they may not evaluate the different formulations rationally (see generally Schwartz, 2004). For example, a person considering Options A, B, and C, where A is preferable to B and B is preferable to C, may ignore A and compare B with C and decide to accept the "preferable" B even though A would more effectively satisfy their underlying interests (Guthrie, 2003, at 608–621). To avoid these anomalous results, lawyers should carefully work with clients to develop rational option assessment procedures that will lead to optimal results (Guthrie, 2003, at 638–645).

[ii]   Discovery of Priority Compatibilities

If negotiators hope to expand the overall pie and look for mutually beneficial exchanges, they must initially classify the goals sought by their respective sides as "essential," "important," or "desirable." They must then endeavor to determine the degree to which their own side's aims conflict with the goals of their adversary (Thompson, 2005, at 76–81; Raiffa, 2003, at 199–201; Menkel-Meadow, 2001, at 109–111; Watkins & Rosegrant, 2001, at 22–23; Goldman, 1991, at 8–11; Young, 1975, at 10–12). In some instances, both parties may actually desire the identical distribution of the items in question, allowing them to enhance their interests simultaneously. In other situations, each may wish to attain independent objectives that do not conflict with the interests of their opponent. In only some areas do both parties want to claim the identical items for themselves. The ramifications of this phenomenon are graphically represented in Table 2 (taken from Bastress & Harbaugh, 1990, at 483; see also Latz, 2004, at 38–40).

TABLE 2

	Shared Needs	Independent Needs		Conflicting Needs	
		Side A	Side B	Side A	Side B
Essential Needs					
Important Needs					
Desirable Needs					

[iii]   Greater Likelihood of Resolution of Shared Needs Through Understanding of Independent Needs

Proficient negotiators should be able to ascertain the areas of shared needs and independent needs and ensure the appropriate distribution of these non-conflicting items (Latz, 2004, at 60–70). To determine opponent needs and interests, negotiators should ask "why" and "what" questions. Why do they want a particular item? What are they trying to achieve through their request for certain terms? To the extent they accomplish this goal, they can effectively expand the pie to be divided and significantly enhance the likelihood of an overall accord. As both sides recognize the mutual gains they can achieve, the areas of conflict tend to seem less significant. Since they realize that many of their other objectives can be attained, they are more willing to consider realistic compromises with respect to the controverted issues.

[iv]   Exchanging Terms Based on Respective Prioritization

When negotiators attempt to resolve disputes over the conflicting terms, they must remember the degree of interest their respective clients have expressed regarding these items. If one side considers a disputed matter "essential" while the other side views it as "important" or "desirable," the participants should be able to generate a mutual accommodation by assigning that item to the side that values it more in exchange for something the other side considers more significant.

Competitive/adversarial bargainers, particularly those with win-lose mentalities, may be hesitant to accept this approach. They think that their aggressive tactics should enable them to seize the "essential" and "important" items for their own side, regardless of the other side's value system. While they may occasionally be able to achieve this type of skewed result against incompetent or careless opponents, they can rarely hope to do so against skilled adversaries. It thus behooves them to explore the areas that may generate joint gains. To the extent they may satisfy opponent interests at little or no cost to their own client, they greatly increase the likelihood of a beneficial agreement from their own side's perspective (Kramer, 2001, at 126). So long as they are able to obtain what their own client desires, they should not be displeased by the fact that their opponent's interests have also been satisfied.

[v]   Using Contingent Agreements to Deal with Future Uncertainties

Negotiators occasionally encounter difficulties when they discuss arrangements that must address future circumstances the parties view quite differently. For example, a personal injury claimant may think that future medical difficulties may arise, where the defendant considers that possibility unlikely. The plaintiff demands a substantial sum to cover this contingency, while the defendant only offers a minimal amount. Someone contemplating the purchase of a business may not think future sales will be as robust as those envisioned by the seller. The prospective buyer thus offers far less than the seller thinks appropriate. If the bargaining parties cannot agree upon the probability of such future possibilities, their interactions may fail. To circumvent such issues, they could employ contingent agreements (Moffitt, 2004). The personal injury defendant could offer the claimant a certain amount of money to cover existing conditions, and promise to assume responsibility for all future medical problems that arise from the underlying injuries. The prospective corporate buyer could agree to a set purchase price and agree to increase that amount in relation to future sales. Such contingent contracts allow the parties to achieve flexible agreements that will reflect actual future developments. When they draft contingent agreements, parties should specifically define the contingencies involved and the precise way in which future payments will be calculated.

[vi]   De-emphasizing Conflicts

As more beneficial alternatives are ascertained and divided, areas that previously appeared to create insurmountable barriers may no longer seem so important. This is why negotiators should not focus merely on their stated positions, but should instead explore the underlying motivational factors of their respective clients. They should not permit themselves to become locked into unyielding positions, because this situation usually generates counterproductive results (Fisher & Ury, 1981, at 5). Even though the parties may not ultimately receive what they initially demanded, if both can finally obtain terms that satisfy their true needs, the negotiation process will have functioned effectively. Such a result would generally be impossible, however, without a carefully developed and thoroughly explored Information Stage. Those individuals who ignore this critical reality and endeavor to curtail the Information Stage to permit a more rapid movement into the Competitive/Distributive Stage normally pay dearly for their tactical oversight.

Summary

1. During the Information Stage, negotiators focus on the needs and interests of their opponents. This allows them to ascertain opponent objectives and to determine the items that are available for joint distribution.

2. It is beneficial to ask open — ended, information — seeking questions that are likely to elicit expansive responses. Narrow inquiries tend to generate few new insights. "What" and "why" questions should be used to determine the items sought by the other side and the interests underlying those items.

3. Participants tend to begin the serious discussions by focusing on a group of their most or their least important topics. Knowledge of this tendency allows negotiators to obtain beneficial information from the manner in which opponents present their initial demands.

4. Individuals who begin the negotiation exchange with their less important items are likely to develop a mutual psychological commitment to settlement. This commitment benefits both sides.

5. When participants divulge their critical information slowly in response to opponent inquiries, the information they provide is accorded greater credence by their adversaries. Readily volunteering information results in reactive devaluation.

6. Negotiators who are asked about sensitive areas they do not wish to discuss may use blocking techniques to avoid answering the propounded inquiries.

7. Advocates can frequently break temporary impasses by going behind the stated positions and exploring, in an open and non-adversarial manner, the parties' underlying interests. In this way, they can discover alternative formulations that may be mutually beneficial.

Chapter 7

THE COMPETITIVE/DISTRIBUTIVE STAGE (VALUE CLAIMING)

[n] — **Raising Voice for Emphasis**

[o] — **Intense Language**

§ 7.05 ALWAYS REMEMBER CURRENT NONSETTLEMENT ALTERNATIVES

§ 7.01 "VALUE CLAIMING"

[1] Discerning Transition from Information to Competitive/ Distributive Stage

The Competitive/Distributive, or "Value-Claiming" Stage is recognized by a change of the focus of discussion. During the Information Stage, negotiators focus primarily upon the needs, interests, and objectives of their *opponents*. They attempt to determine the different alternatives that may satisfy the underlying goals of both parties. Through this process, effective participants are able to determine most, if not all, of the basic economic and noneconomic items that may be divided between them. Once this basic informational objective is achieved, the focus of the discussions usually changes from what the opposing parties hope to achieve to what the negotiators must obtain for their *own* clients. The demarcation between the Information Stage and the Competitive/Distributive Stage may be readily discerned by observant participants. The bargainers are no longer asking questions regarding each other's circumstances. They are instead articulating their own side's specific demands. Interrogatory sentences are replaced by declaratory statements, as may be seen in the following examples:

INFORMATION STAGE EXCHANGES

(1) What does your client want to obtain from this transaction?

(2) Why does your client hope to achieve that?

(3) What other items might alternatively satisfy the underlying needs and interests of your client?

(4) Do you think that ____ might provide your client with what he/she really has to have?

(5) What does your client plan to do if he/she is unable to reach a deal with us?

COMPETITIVE/DISTRIBUTIVE STAGE EXCHANGES

(1) If these discussions are going to be mutually beneficial, my client must obtain at least ____.

(2) If your client is not willing to provide us with at least ____, this situation cannot be resolved.

(3) If your client plans to demand more than ____, no settlement can possibly be achieved.

(4) I am not in a position to offer you more than ____.

(5) As I understand this case, your client is not entitled to more than ____.

[2] "Competitive" Nature of the Stage

[a] Claiming of Values

Although the Information Stage is an important part of the negotiation process, as the parties work to *"create value,"* it is the Competitive/Distributive Stage that primarily determines what each party ultimately receives. Some people prefer to regard this part of the bargaining process as the "Distributive" Stage, because it is during this portion of their interaction that the participants actually divide between them the items they think are available for distribution. I prefer to use the term "Competitive" Stage, to emphasize the inherent competition indigenous to this *"value claiming"* part of the transaction. The negotiators should diligently seek to advance the interests of their own clients, preferring to obtain as much as possible within the bounds of propriety.

[b] Focus on Outcomes

The parties are not endeavoring to divide up the available bargaining items in a wholly equitable manner, because there are seldom objective standards that can be employed to determine what each side "deserves" to receive. Negotiators rarely possess equal bargaining power and identical proficiency, and the participants with greater strength and skill should be able to obtain more beneficial results than their weaker opponents. Furthermore, the parties are likely to value the various items quite differently, thus preventing any truly detached comparison of the terms received by each (Karrass, 1970, at 144–145). The critical question at the conclusion of a negotiation is not whether a party obtained all of what it initially wanted or whether it did better or worse than the other side, but whether, given its situation, the party is pleased with what it received.

[c] Importance of Conviction

If one negotiator truly believes — correctly or erroneously — that his or her client deserves more than opposing counsel has tentatively concluded should be granted, the bargainer with the firmer belief is likely to be more successful than their more tentative adversary. The negotiation process is a psychological interaction in which reality is defined more by the perceptions of the participants than by external criteria. Negotiators who ignore this fact and attempt to obtain only "fair" results for their clients tend to achieve less beneficial agreements than they may otherwise have attained. If they fail to recognize the competitive aspect of their exchange, they may not exercise the degree of circumspection warranted in such adversarial circumstances.

[d] Testing and Applying Pre-Negotiation Evaluations

Although negotiators should never try to injure or destroy their opponents because of an irrational "win-lose" mentality, they should realize that their own preliminary assessments may have either overemphasized their own weaknesses or overestimated the strengths of their adversary. It is only through a rigorous Competitive/Distributive Stage that they can test their tentative, pre-negotiation evaluations. If their opponent has suggested that they should receive more than they anticipated, it would normally be improper for them to ignore that side's generosity. I have always believed it to be appropriate in such circumstances to defer to the greater sagacity of opposing counsel! I would also find it difficult to explain to a client that I could have achieved a better settlement based upon the opponent's assessment of the situation, but decided to accept less due to my own less generous view of the matter.

§ 7.02   CONCESSIONS

[1]   Making Principled Concessions

Persuasive bargainers begin the Competitive/Distributive Stage with the articulation of "principled" positions that rationally explain how they were developed (Latz, 2004, at 183–87). This bolsters the confidence these negotiators have in their own positions, and it provides them with reasons to indicate why they have begun at those points. Good bargainers tend to start with carefully developed concession patterns (Freund, 1992, at 130–41). They know how they plan to move from their opening offers to their final objectives. They may intend to make several deliberate, but expansive, concessions, or prefer to employ a series of incremental position changes. Effective negotiators know that this aspect of their strategy must be thoughtfully choreographed to maximize their bargaining effectiveness. They recognize the need to make only "principled" concessions that they can rationally explain to their opponents (Zwier & Guernsey, 2005, at 132–33; Schoonmaker, 1989, at 88–89). This lets others know why the precise position change is occurring, and it indicates why a greater modification is not presently warranted. This approach also helps keep them at their new position until they obtain a reciprocal concession from the other side. Their concession strategy should be based upon their pre-negotiation planning and the new insights developed during the Information Stage.

[2]   Timing

The anticipated timing of concessions is critical. Many risk-averse individuals find it difficult to cope with the uncertainty that is an inherent part of the negotiation process. They often make rapid concessions in a desperate effort to generate mutual accords. They ignore the fact that 70–80 percent of position changes tend to occur during the last 20–30 percent of the interaction (Dawson, 2001, at 171; Dawson, 1985, at 103). Those who attempt to expedite the transaction in an artificial manner usually pay a high price for their impatience (Williams & Williams, 2002, at 92–93; LePoole, 1991, at 72). Proficient opponents have little difficulty inducing these persons to close most of the distance between their opening offers. In addition, people who generate position changes easily tend to devalue them, while individuals who have to work diligently to obtain concessions tend to really appreciate them (Cohen, 2003, at 150–51; Cialdini, 1993, at 85). Negotiators should thus take their time when making concessions, to induce opponents to invest sufficient time in the process to value the new offers received.

[3]   Delivery

Concessions must be carefully formulated and tactically made. If properly used, a concession can signal a cooperative attitude. It can also communicate the need for a counteroffer if the opponent intends to continue the negotiation process. If carelessly issued, however, a concession can conversely signal anxiety and a loss of control. This type of crisis may arise, for example, when a concession is made in a tentative and relatively unprincipled manner by an individual who continues to talk nervously and defensively after the concession has been made. Such behavior indicates that the speaker does not expect immediate reciprocity from opposing counsel. When adroit bargainers encounter these individuals, they should subtly encourage them to keep talking, since this approach frequently precipitates additional, unanswered concessions (Harsanyi, 1975, at 80–81). To avoid this problem, skilled negotiators make their concessions with appropriate explanations (*i.e.*, "principled" concessions), and they then shift the focus to their opponents. They accomplish this shift with appropriate silence following their concession. By exuding patient silence at this point, they indicate that reciprocal behavior must be forthcoming if the interaction is to continue.

Hartje has insightfully recognized that a concession should emerge in four parts:

(1) A well reasoned, carefully justified relinquishment of a previous position.

(2) The arrival at a new bargaining point to which the negotiator is committed for reasons of principle, fairness, cost, precedent, logic, client direction, lack of authority, and so forth.

(3) An extraction, on the basis of the spirit of compromise and good faith bargaining, of a counter concession with a willingness to entertain further discussion.

(4) Any concession and a new commitment point should be articulated in the language of the parties' needs or interests rather than some mechanical position or posture. (Hartje, 1984, at 167)

The amount and timing of each position change are crucial. Each successive concession should be smaller than the preceding one, and each should normally be made in response to an appropriate counteroffer from the opponent (Thompson, 2005, at 70–80). Consider, for example, a plaintiff personal injury lawyer who hopes to achieve a settlement in the $40,000 to $50,000 range for an automobile accident victim who suffered a severe whiplash injury, including cracked vertebrae, that necessitated painful treatment and the wearing of a cervical collar for the past eight months. The plaintiff continues to experience pain that is expected to abate within the next four months. Plaintiff attorney might employ the following approach:

PLAINTIFF: I'm willing to start the bargaining process with a demand for $97,000. The plaintiff has had $10,000 in medical bills, lost a $5,000 automobile, and lost $8,000 in earnings. He/she will require some additional rehabilitative treatment that should cost about $2,000. He/she experienced excruciating pain for the past eight months and is expected to have less severe discomfort over the next four months. An appropriate amount for the first eight months of extreme pain might reasonably be calculated at $10 per hour for 5760 hours (8 mos. x 30 days per mo. x 24 hrs. per day) or $57,600. For the next four months of pain, a rate of $5 per hour covering 2880 hours (4 mos. x 30 days per mo. x 24 hrs. per day) would properly amount to $14,400.

DEFENDANT: [Responds with an opening offer of $15,000 covering the medical expenses and the cost of the destroyed automobile. Defendant suggests that it is not clear that the defendant was at fault.]

PLAINTIFF: I'm glad that you have at least indicated a willingness to approach this matter seriously, instead of with an unreasonably low offer. But, you have clearly failed to consider lost earnings, the expected cost of future rehabilitative treatment, and plaintiff's substantial pain and suffering. On the other hand, it is possible that a jury might find that the defendant was not negligent. My review of the facts, however, suggests that this is not too likely. We have found an independent witness who will testify that the defendant was driving carelessly. Nonetheless, recognizing the 20% possibility of a verdict for the defendant, I would be willing to reduce our demand to $77,600 (80% of $97,000).

DEFENDANT: [Responds with an offer of $25,000 covering all of the expenses except those pertaining to pain and suffering. Suggests that plaintiff was probably partially responsible for the accident in dispute, which is relevant in our assumed comparative negligence jurisdiction.]

PLAINTIFF: I'm glad to see that we are making some real progress. But once you acknowledge that the plaintiff is entitled to something, you have to recognize his/her right to relief for his/her severe pain and suffering. I realize that the plaintiff may have contributed somewhat to the accident, and if we assume for the sake of argument that he/she was 15% responsible, we would be willing to accept $65,960 (85% of prior demand of $77,600).

DEFENDANT: [Counters with an offer of $34,000, admitting that plaintiff is entitled to some compensation for his/her pain and suffering, but suggesting that plaintiff's demand regarding this item is excessive.]

PLAINTIFF: I appreciate your good faith and am confident that we can resolve this matter amicably. However, your suggested award of $9,000 for plaintiff's pain and suffering is wholly inadequate. Even if we reduced the amount for the first eight months of extreme pain to $8 per hour and that for the next four months to $4 per hour, he/she would still be entitled to $57,600 (8 mos. x 30 days per mo. x 24 hrs. per day x $8 per hr. = $46,080, plus 4 mos. x 30 days per mo. x 24 hrs. per day x $4 per hr. = $11,520). When this is reduced by the 20% possibility of a verdict for the defendant and by a possible 15% degree of plaintiff's own negligence, the total for pain and suffering becomes $39,168. When this is added to the $17,000 in other expenses ($25,000 reduced by 20% and by 15%), the total due becomes $56,168.

DEFENDANT: [Admits the partial forcefulness of plaintiff's arguments, but still claims that the amount being sought for pain and suffering is somewhat elevated, particularly with respect to that pertaining to the next four months. Counters with an offer of $42,000.]

PLAINTIFF: I'll admit that the plaintiff's discomfort is much less now than it was during the past eight months, but he/she still continues to experience some real pain. If we were to use a $2 per hour figure for the pain and suffering over the next four months, instead of the $4 figure, we could reduce our demand by $3,917 (4 mos. x 30 days per mo. x 24 hrs. per day x $2 per hr. = $5,760, which must be reduced by the 20% and 15% factors previously cited to equal $3,917). We would thus be willing to accept $52,251.

DEFENDANT: [Admits that the plaintiff is entitled to some monetary relief for the remaining four months of pain and suffering and offers $45,600.]

[From these positions, the plaintiff attorney should use similarly principled explanations to reduce his/her demand to the $50,000–$51,000 range, while the defendant lawyer increases his/her offer to the $48,000–$49,000 range. The parties would be likely to arrive at a final settlement figure near the midpoint of these last offers. The plaintiff attorney should thus achieve a result near the upper end of his/her initial target range.]

It is important to emphasize the highly "principled" rationale given by the plaintiff lawyer to explain each particular position modification. Following each new demand, he/she immediately shifted the focus to defendant counsel to generate an appropriate counter offer from that party. It should also be noted how each party's successive concessions diminished in size, as would generally be expected during a negotiation.

Successful negotiators tend to make both fewer and smaller concessions than their less successful adversaries (Karrass, 1970, at 18–19).

[4]   Preempting "Reactive Devaluation"

The use of principled concessions can also preempt a phenomenon known as "reactive devaluation" (Korobkin, 2006, at 316–318; Ross, 1995, at 27 ff.). When individuals receive concessions from opponents, they tend to devalue those position changes. They assume that if their adversaries are willing to concede the items in question, those terms must not be of significance to those participants. When explanations are provided to indicate why particular concessions are being made, the speakers can indicate how much their own side values the items being discussed and the specific reasons they are willing to modify those topics. This reduces the likelihood that concession recipients will ignore their true value.

[5]   Importance of Planning, Flexibility, and Patience

As is graphically demonstrated by the above exchange, it is crucial for negotiators to plan their anticipated concession pattern prior to the commencement of the Competitive/Distributive Stage. Nevertheless, they must recognize that opponents will not always react as they initially expected. They must thus be prepared to modify their planned behavior as new information regarding adversary strengths, weaknesses, and preferences is ascertained (Gulliver, 1979, at 100). Not only should they be prepared to adjust their aspiration level when appropriate, they must also be ready to alter their concession strategy accordingly based on mutually acknowledged objective criteria (Fisher & Ury, 1981, at 88–89). They must be patient, realizing that a particular transaction may take more time to complete than they originally anticipated. When concessions are small and the issues are numerous and/or complex, negotiators must permit the process to unfold deliberately. If they attempt to unduly accelerate the transaction, they may place themselves at a tactical disadvantage (Rubin & Brown, 1975, at 145). They would exude a fear of nonsettlement that could be exploited by an alert opponent.

[6]   Risks Associated with Poorly Planned Concessions

[a]   Unintended Consecutive Concessions

Bargainers who do not carefully monitor their concession patterns frequently encounter unexpected difficulty. Some may find themselves making unintended consecutive concessions that are not matched by reciprocal counter offers (Schoonmaker, 1989, at 86–87). When bargainers "bid against themselves" in this manner, they give up far more than they planned to concede. They should rely upon the generally recognized "norm of reciprocity" (Pratkanis & Aronson, 1991, at 180–81) to extract corresponding position changes from recalcitrant adversaries.

[b]   Irrational Concessions

Irrational concession patterns may cause similar problems. For example, if a negotiator's first concession is $10,000, his or her second concession is $8,000, and his or her third concession is $6,000, it would normally make no sense to make a fourth concession of $9,000. Such a pattern would probably indicate either that the bargainer does not know what he or she is doing or that he or she unsuccessfully attempted to establish a false position that could not be sustained after the first three concessions had been made. Either circumstance would be likely to confuse opponents and undermine the negotiation process (Hartje, 1984, at 166; Hamner & Yukl in Drukman, 1977, at 139). If the person fruitlessly sought to establish a false resistance point, he or she should not disclose this failure during the present discussions. It would be preferable for the individual to suspend the talks to enable them to confer with the absent client. The bargainer could then restart the interaction at a later date with an appropriately modified concession pattern.

[7]   Adequacy

Another consideration regarding concession strategy should be noted. When negotiators establish their anticipated opening positions and target areas, they must recognize the need to ultimately reach a settlement range that is sufficiently generous to force opposing counsel to view agreement as a viable alternative to a nonsettlement. If their planned bottom line is too one-sided, this may encourage the opponent to reject it in favor of the consequences of no accord. Only when bargainers make final offers that truly tempt their adversaries vis-a-vis the results of nonsettlement can they reasonably expect their final entreaties to be seriously considered. The actual range varies in each situation, depending upon the applicable circumstances and the personal traits of the participants. While some negotiators and their risk-taking clients may be readily willing to accept the possibility of nonsettlements, more risk-averse individuals are not. When dealing with risk-averse parties, bargainers should be careful not to be needlessly generous. They should recognize the fact that even less beneficial final offers may be viewed by risk-averse negotiators as preferable to the risks associated with bargaining stalemates. This may be particularly true, for instance, for plaintiff demands that are just within the limits of defendant insurance policies, in states where "bad faith" rejections of such demands could subject defendant insurance carriers to liability for the entire amount of subsequently obtained verdicts in excess of actual policy limits.

§ 7.03 DEALING WITH ADVERSITY

[1]   Remembering Nonsettlement Options

Negotiators must always remember their nonsettlement options and their preliminarily established resistance points as they near their bottom lines during bargaining interactions. They must recognize that it would be irrational to accept proposed terms that are less beneficial than their external alternatives. As the Competitive/Distributive Stage evolves and they approach their resistance points, many advocates feel greater settlement pressure than is warranted. When the terms being offered by opponents are not meaningfully better than their nonsettlement options, participants approaching their bottom lines possess more — not less — bargaining power than the offerors. They have little to lose if no mutual accords are achieved, and they should not be afraid to reject the disadvantageous proposals that are on the table. Instead of exuding weakness, as so many negotiators do in these circumstances, they should project strength. Since their opponents are likely to lose more than they lose from nonsettlements, they can confidently demand further concessions as a prerequisite to any final agreement.

[2]   Willingness to Divulge Nonsettlement Options

As the Competitive/Distributive Stage evolves, the parties usually encounter temporary impasses. The participants are presumably endeavoring to obtain optimal terms for their respective clients, and each is hoping to induce the other to feel the need to make the next position change. Individuals who have viable external options should not hesitate to disclose — at least minimally — this critical fact. The more their adversaries know about these matters, the more likely they are to acknowledge the need for more accommodating behavior (Latz, 2004, at 93–97). It is usually preferable to convey this information in a calm and non-confrontational fashion (Freund, 1992, at 47). Advocates who refuse to divulge the parameters of their nonsettlement alternatives at critical stages frequently fail to achieve accords that would have been attainable had their opponents been fully aware of their actual circumstances.

Nevertheless, as in other stages, a cooperative/problem-solving approach is more likely to produce beneficial results than a competitive-adversarial strategy during the Competitive/Distributive Stage. The former permits the participants to explore the opportunity for mutual gain in a relatively objective and detached manner (Gifford, 1989, at 16–18). The latter style, however, is more likely to generate mistrust and an unwillingness to share sensitive information. Furthermore, cooperative/problem-solving overtures minimize inter-party conflict and help to create a positive bargaining atmosphere.

[3]   Responding to Abrasive Tactics with Professionalism

On some occasions, negotiators encounter stereotypical competitive/adversarial opponents who hope to achieve win-lose results. As these adversaries resort to offensive and disruptive tactics, it is easy to contemplate a quid-pro-quo response. When this takes place, however, the entire process tends to break down. Patient and calm participants can frequently use different techniques to disarm nasty and abrasive adversaries (Fisher & Shapiro, 2005, at 152–163). In response to loud diatribes, they can tranquilly explore the relevant circumstances in a wholly professional manner (Freund, 1992, at 87). They should attempt to ascertain and emphasize the areas of positional overlap, and minimize the focus on highly controverted items (Ury, 1991, at 106–07) (see also Ury, 2007 (using a "positive no" to get to yes)).

[4]   Eliciting Trust Through Questioning Skills

When specific offers are met with harsh, unreceptive replies, negotiators can employ their questioning skills to direct the attention of their opponents to areas that may generate mutual gains. This may enable them to elicit information from their adversaries regarding their underlying needs and interests (Bazerman & Neale, 1992, at 90–95). As they obtain helpful insights regarding the other side's value system, they should divulge facts concerning their own side's objectives. This may permit them to generate a minimal degree of trust and allow them to encourage a mutual, problem-solving effort (Putnam, 2004, at 285–86; Lewicki, et al., 1994, at 143–59).

[5] Using Directed Questions to Induce Problem-Solving Mindset

Opponents who are summarily rejecting everything being proposed by the other side need to have their negative mind-set altered. Adroit negotiators may often accomplish this objective through a series of questions that are designed to elicit affirmative responses from the uncooperative participants (Gray, 2003, at 308).

COOPERATIVE PARTY: I gather that you are dissatisfied with our proposal?

ADVERSARIAL PARTY: You're damn right I am!

COOPERATIVE PARTY: I understand that you are most concerned about the fact that our offer doesn't help you with respect to ____?

ADVERSARIAL PARTY: That is correct. If there is going to be any agreement, you are going to have to satisfy our needs regarding ____.

COOPERATIVE PARTY: I assume that if you cannot obtain ____ (the exact term being demanded), you may be able to live with an alternative such as?

ADVERSARIAL PARTY: That is something we would seriously consider.

COOPERATIVE PARTY: I think that we can alter our position to accommodate your concerns. If we were to provide ____, I gather that this would begin to satisfy your side's basic needs?

ADVERSARIAL PARTY: Yes. That would be a vast improvement over where we began this exchange. Is there some way you might be able to address our needs pertaining to ____?

Through such inquiries, cooperative parties can induce adversarial opponents to replace their unreceptive attitudes with problem-solving mind-sets (see generally Ury, 2007 (discussing how to use a "positive no" to get to yes)). These kinds of transformations significantly enhance the probability of mutual accords.

[6] Risk of Impending Impasse

No matter how effectively negotiators have been conducting their Competitive/Distributive Stage exchanges, they may find themselves moving inexorably toward an impasse. They may have found fewer areas for joint gain than they had anticipated. The issues in direct conflict may seem more significant than they had imagined. If they are careless, they may allow these difficulties to cloud their judgment. They could then incorrectly assess that further discussions would be fruitless.

[7] Changing Focus of Discussions

Before bargaining parties permit an impending stalemate to preclude additional talks, they should consider other options that may enable them to keep the process moving (Dawson, 2001, at 66–71). If the participants appear to be taking the process too seriously or even personally, it may be beneficial to temporarily change the focus of the discussions. If the participants can be induced to briefly talk about sports, hobbies, or other extraneous activities, this may relieve the existing tension. It may similarly help to recount a humorous story that will humanize the participants and remind everyone not to take the situation too seriously.

[8]   Changing Negotiation Setting

Some negotiators may wish to change the bargaining environment. They could rearrange the furniture in a more cooperative configuration. If the advocates can eliminate overtly competitive settings, they may become more receptive to opponent overtures. The parties may alternatively move to another room or to an entirely different location. If they have been meeting at one side's offices, they could either relocate to the other side's offices or select a neutral site that may be more conducive to cooperation.

[9]   Envisioning Oneself in Adversary's Position

[a]   Active Listening Invites Understanding

Disputing parties should pause and try to appreciate each other's circumstances. Through active listening, each side may gain new insights into opponent concerns. If the participants are arguing over the phrasing of particular issues, they can attempt to reframe the issues in a manner designed to reduce tensions (Lewicki, et al., 1994, at 150–52). Such issue reframing often enables disputants to view their controversy from a less contentious perspective.

[b]   Giving Contentious Topics a Rest

If particular issues have become intractable, the negotiators could agree to hold them in abeyance while they explore other topics of mutual interest. If the controverted items are substantial, the parties could appoint subcommittees to explore those proposals separately in what they hope will be a less contentious atmosphere. With fewer people participating in the discussions, it may be easier for the designated representatives to make progress on these items.

[c]   Changing Negotiation Participants

On some occasions, the parties may conclude that negotiator personalities have created communicational problems. When this occurs, they should think of changing bargaining team participants. If a particular individual appears to be the primary irritant, they may only have to replace that person. On the other hand, if several members of their team seem to be generating unproductive animosity, the substitution of two or three new bargainers may help.

[d]   Taking a Temporary Recess

If existing bargaining tension is extreme, it may be necessary to recess the talks to give the participants an opportunity to cool off and to reconsider their current positions. They may have to reassess their nonsettlement options. They could look for mutually beneficial and yet unexplored alternatives. Before discussions are terminated, the parties should try to agree upon a future meeting date to ensure a continuation of the bargaining process. If they are unable to set a future date at the present time, they should at least agree to interact on something by a certain date. One may promise to provide the other with requested information, or they may agree to exchange additional written proposals by a definitive time. This prevents the process from breaking down entirely because of each party's hesitance to contact the other once talks have broken off.

[10] Using Contingent Agreements to Deal With Future Uncertanties

Negotiating parties occasionally encounter difficulties when they differ greatly with respect to their view of likely future developments. One may have an optimistic view, while the other is more pessimistic. For example, a business seller may expect firm sales to increase, while a prospective buyer may fear a business downturn. An injured plaintiff may be concerned about unanticipated future medical problems, while a defendant insurance carrier believes the claimant's condition has stabilized. How can negotiators handle such disagreements? They can employ contingent agreements that are formulated to take care of future uncertainties (Moffitt, 2004). The corporate seller could agree to some future payments based upon actual firm sales. The insurance carrier could promise to take care of future medical developments, in exchange for a lower cash payment when the settlement agreement is executed. This type of contingent agreement satisfies the underlying beliefs of both sides, despite their different views with respect to probable future circumstances.

§ 7.04 POWER BARGAINING

[1] Strategies

[a] Inducing Reassessment

[i] Subtle Questions and Disclosures

The Competitive/Distributive Stage generally involves some degree of power bargaining as advocates try to obtain optimal results for their respective clients (Adler & Silverstein, 2006; Wetlaufer, 1996). The purpose of power bargaining is to influence opponent perceptions regarding the interaction. This may be accomplished by inducing those persons to reassess their own situations. Have operative weaknesses been ignored or inappropriately minimized? Have strengths been overestimated? Subtle questions and disclosures may be used to undermine the confidence opposing parties have in their own positions.

For example, a party trying to lease commercial space to a business firm may know that the firm is considering alternative locations. By emphasizing the parking and public transportation associated with their building that are not available at the other locations, lessor representatives can undermine opponent beliefs regarding the equivalency of the other sites.

[ii] Manipulating Images of Strength and Weakness

Adroit negotiators may similarly expand their own bargaining power by convincing opposing counsel that they possess greater strength or less vulnerability than their adversaries initially anticipated (Bacharach & Lawler, 1981, at 60–63). They may do this by mentioning the fact that other parties have approached them regarding the space in question. If they suspect that the other side thinks they are in desperate need of immediate cash to pay off a balloon note that is coming due, they can casually indicate that they recently refinanced the building and entered into a long-term financial arrangement.

[iii]   Exuding Self-Assurance

Self-assurance is one of the most important attributes of successful negotiators. They exude an inner confidence in their positions, and always appear to be in control of themselves and their bargaining interactions. They do not seem to fear the possibility of nonsettlements, suggesting to opponents that they have developed alternative options that will protect client interests should the negotiation process be unproductive. This confidence usually causes adversaries to accord these individuals more power and respect than they objectively deserve.

[iv]   Elevated Initial Aspirations

Carefully prepared negotiators commence bargaining exchanges with appropriately elevated aspiration levels. Less proficient advocates begin with deflated objectives, fearing that their initial demands may engender hostility if they are not modest and reasonable. Even though this may be true, it is clear that those who commence the negotiation process with unpretentious objectives invariably achieve moderate results (Kritzer, 1991, at 54–55; Karrass, 1970, at 17–18). Once negotiators accept this reality and begin bargaining talks with appropriately high aspirations, they find that opponents are more inclined to defer to their judgments and grant them greater concessions.

[b]   Carefully Reviewing Actual Circumstances

Since there is really no such thing as actual bargaining power — but merely the parties' perceptions of it — confident participants often obtain negotiated results far beyond what others might have achieved in identical circumstances. Their adversaries begin to assume that these seemingly invulnerable individuals can attain beneficial outcomes through external channels if the present negotiation is unsuccessful. Adversaries then begin to ignore the external options available to their own side. As a result, they tend to exaggerate their perceived need to reach settlements. They feel that everything will be lost if they are unable to achieve mutually acceptable terms. As their perceived cost of nonsettlement increases and their perception of the opponent's cost of nonsettlement decreases, the bargaining authority they accord to their adversaries expands dramatically. Negotiation participants must always remember this crucial phenomenon. In light of this tendency, advocates should regularly review their actual circumstances to determine if they have irrationally overestimated the strength of their opponent or unreasonably undervalued their own side's situation. No matter how invulnerable their opponent's position may seem, they must go behind that side's facade and ask themselves what weaknesses they would have if they were in that party's shoes.

[c]   Listening and Observing

Problems   and   misunderstandings   frequently   arise   during   the Competitive/Distributive Stage of negotiations, as in other stages. They tend to arise when one or both participants fail to listen sufficiently to the communications coming from the other party. As people negotiate, they tend to concentrate on what they are saying and what they are planning to say. As a result, they fail to discern many of the verbal leaks and nonverbal signals emanating from the other participants. They instead attribute to their opponents what they expect them to be saying. In many instances, parties do not appreciate the fact that their adversaries are discreetly or openly indicating accommodating attitudes, because they have already assumed unreceptive responses. It is crucial for negotiators to listen carefully and observe intently to ascertain the impact of their own different bargaining techniques. If they ever determine that opponent failures to "hear" their signals are undermining the bargaining process, they should wait until they can regain the full attention of their adversaries. If necessary, they should sit patiently as opposing counsel formulate their responses to what they thought was just communicated. Once the other participants perceive the silent environment, they will be more likely to concentrate on future verbal and nonverbal messages. It is important to remember that power bargaining techniques are most effective when they are received and understood by opponents.

[d] Benefit of Combining Multiple Techniques

During the Competitive/Distributive Stage of negotiations, the participants employ various techniques to advance their respective interests. Tactics may either be used in isolation or in combination with one or more other power bargaining ploys. Negotiators should learn to vary their approach to keep opponents off balance. If bargainers become too predictable, their tactics lose effectiveness. It is thus imperative that bargainers remember the sequence of their presentations and carefully monitor the verbal and nonverbal responses emanating from opponents to determine which techniques appear to function most effectively.

[2] Common Techniques and their Effectiveness

[a] Argument

[i] Variations of Argument Substance Based on Nature of Facts

The power bargaining tactic employed most frequently by lawyers involves legal and nonlegal argument (Willimas, 1983, at 79–81). When the facts support their positions, they emphasize the factual aspects of the transaction. When applicable legal doctrines favor their claim, they cite appropriate statutes, decisions, and/or scholarly authorities. Public policy considerations are invoked when they advance client interests. When large business transactions are being discussed, the participants often include economic and even political considerations.

[ii] Arguments Under Guise of Objectivity

Competitive negotiators may adopt rhetorical and psychological maneuvers that are designed, subtly or overtly, to induce opponent acquiescence, without regard to the substantive merits. Their primary objective is to prevail, not to elucidate or to promote understanding (Condlin, 1985, at 73). These individuals hope to persuade adversaries through the use of seemingly objective contentions that do not appear to be unduly slanted in the direction of their own clients.

Persuasive advocates are individuals who are able to provide opponents with compelling reasons to give them what they want. They develop rationales that fair-minded adversaries find difficult to resist. Whenever possible, they rely on objective criteria to bolster their claims, to demonstrate their "entitlement" to what they are seeking. When appropriate, they also try to frame the relevant issues in a way that allows them to claim moral support for their positions, recognizing that this approach can be especially effective (Shell, 1999, at 104–05). Individuals with greater bargaining power than their opponents tend to argue in favor of equitable distributions that reflect the relative power of the parties, while persons with less power tend to argue for egalitarian distributions (Birke & Fox, 1999, at 34–35).

[iii]   Combining Competitive and Cooperative Arguments

Adroit negotiators should be able to combine competitive and cooperative forms of argument. When they believe that they can effectively advance client interests through the use of biased assertions without disclosing adverse information previously unknown to the adversary, they may decide to make representations skewed toward their positions. On the other hand, when weaknesses have already been disclosed, such a biased approach would be unlikely to have the intended impact. In these circumstances, it would be preferable to use a more even-handed technique. They could explore the pertinent considerations in a relatively neutral fashion, hoping to induce their adversaries to agree with their assessments.

Even when negotiators resort to cooperative arguments, it should be recognized that they are endeavoring to produce conclusions favorable to their positions. While they may eschew obviously competitive tactics for strategic reasons, they are still attempting to articulate their thoughts in a manner that generates beneficial results. Individuals who ignore this fact and are seduced by seemingly candid discussions to disclose everything regarding their own aspirations and concerns frequently find themselves at a disadvantage (Lowenthal, 1982, at 85). Few successful bargainers are willing to divulge everything that adversely affects their case, even when they claim to be engaged in completely open evaluations of their situations.

[iv]   Arguments that Surprise Opposition

Persuasive argument cannot be presented in an obviously one-sided manner. Strident assertions that do not seem to have rational foundations are unlikely to influence respondents. If competitive or cooperative contentions are to have any meaningful impact, they must appear to be even-handed and relatively objective (Zwier & Guernsey, 2005, at 125–28; Bastress & Harbaugh, 1990, at 437–38; Zartman & Berman, 1982, at 115). They must be presented in a logical and orderly sequence that will have a cumulative effect upon the recipients. Negotiations usually involve repetitive communications, as each party seeks to alter the other's assessment of the operative circumstances. Cogent arguments should not merely be reiterated. They should instead be restated in different forms to enhance their persuasiveness.

Successful negotiators can generally develop innovative and unanticipated arguments that effectively contradict preconceived assumptions. Once opponents are impelled to internally question the previously developed rationales supporting their perceptions of the transaction, they are likely to suffer a significant loss of bargaining confidence. The removal of their underlying positional foundations normally induces them to more seriously consider the legal and factual interpretations being offered by their opponents. It is this process that causes them to move more inexorably toward the entreaties of their adversaries.

[v]   Comprehensive and Well-Articulated Arguments

Effective arguments should be presented in a comprehensive, rather than a conclusionary manner (Bastress & Harbaugh, 1990, at 435–37). Applicable factual and legal information must be disclosed with appropriate detail. For example, a plaintiff lawyer who merely claims that a broken leg is worth $5,000 would not be as likely to persuade an adversary as would an attorney who carefully describes the exact injury suffered and compares it with comparable situations cited in the *Jury Verdict Reports* for the relevant geographical area indicating that a $5,000 figure is reasonable with respect to such an injury. Negotiators who ignore this consideration may frequently be challenged by effective counter arguments demonstrating that underlying factual and/or legal assumptions inherent in their initial conclusionary representations are distinguishable from the present circumstances.

Persuasive arguments must be insightful and carefully articulated. If their content is not fully comprehended and their underlying logic is not understood, their degree of influence is appreciably diminished. Efficacious assertions go beyond what is expected by opponents. Contentions that do not surprise the receiving parties rarely undermine the confidence those people have in their preconceived positions. However, assertions that raise issues not previously contemplated by the recipients are likely to induce those individuals to recognize the need for a reassessment of their current perceptions.

[vi]   Emotional Appeals

Legal practitioners should not ignore the potential persuasiveness of emotional contentions (Bastress & Harbaugh, 1990, at 439–40). Attorneys are generally intelligent people. They are able to deflect cerebral arguments that are based entirely on logical analysis. On the other hand, many perspicacious individuals have a difficult time countering emotional claims that generate guilt or compassion and interfere with their ability to analyze situations in a detached manner. Advocates should not hesitate to formulate arguments that are designed to elicit emotional responses, because these may frequently produce beneficial results. Assertions based on considerations of morality can be especially effective, due to the guilt they generate in emotional opponents.

[vii]   Approaching Complex Legal and/or Factual Issues in Manageable Parts

When complex legal and/or factual issues are involved, they should be broken down into manageable subparts. This permits adroit negotiators to achieve agreement on various uncontroverted subissues, which enhances the likelihood of an overall accord (Hartje, 1984, at 156). This technique creates an atmosphere of cooperation and generates bargaining momentum toward a final settlement (Ilich, 1973, at 147). It frequently permits disputants to minimize the direct conflict indigenous to the larger issues, and it allows them to make progress in a less controversial environment.

[viii]   Maintaining Detached Objectivity

Former Supreme Court Justice and former United Nations Ambassador Arthur J. Goldberg succinctly noted the attributes of successful bargainers:

> The best negotiator is not an advocate. The best negotiator is a man who could perform the role of mediator in the negotiations if he were called upon to perform that role. In other words, while he may have to engage in advocacy to reach a common ground, he should never be overly persuaded by his own advocacy. Advocacy should be a tactic and not an end in the negotiations (Zartman & Berman, 1982, at 115).

Negotiators must always recognize the need to retain their detached objectivity, even when they seem to be making forceful arguments. They should never become so enamored with their own assertions that they either fail to remember the overstated nature of their claims or ignore valid considerations being articulated by their opponents. Those individuals who permit the exuberance generated by their own arguments to cloud their judgment often find that they have failed to achieve beneficial agreements that were otherwise attainable. These people are also unable to provide their clients with the professional objectivity that clients need and have the right to expect from legal counsel.

[b]   Threats, Warnings, and Promises

[i]   Negative Threats and Warnings

It is rare for negotiations to occur without the presence of overt or implicit threats. The stereotypical threat consists of "a communication from one party to a second indicating that, if the second party does not settle according to terms acceptable to the first party, the first party will take action unpleasant or detrimental to the second party." (Lowenthal, 1982, at 86) Threats are employed to indicate that the cost of disagreeing with proposed offers transcends the cost of acquiescence (Katz, 2008, at 151–52; Schelling, 1975, at 329–34). Credible threats can enhance the percieved bargaining power of persons employing this technique, but their use may simultaneously make the threatening parties seem less cooperative and result in less efficient overall agreements (Shapiro & Bies, 1994, at 26–31).

Some negotiators eschew the use of formal "threats," preferring to resort to less challenging "warnings." They merely caution opponents about the consequences that will naturally result from their failure to accept mutual resolutions of the underlying disputes (Freund, 1992, at 212–13; Ikle, 1964, at 62–63). These "Warnings" are not premised upon action that the declarants are planning to take against the opposing parties, but rather the events that will independently evolve if no settlements are achieved.

When adverse consequences are likely to occur, it is frequently beneficial to articulate the negative possibilities as "warnings" rather than "threats" (Elster, 1995, at 252–53). For example, instead of litigators suggesting that they will initiate a law suit if no settlement is reached, they may alternatively indicate that their client will do so — as if their client were a wholly independent and uncontrollable actor. Labor union negotiators may similarly state that bargaining unit workers will go on strike if a new collective contract is not attained, instead of suggesting that they will request a walk out. The use of the warning device softens the statement being made. Since the resulting consequences are not based directly on what the speakers will do themselves, it makes it more palatable to the listeners (Mayer, 1996, at 64–65). In addition, the warning technique enhances the credibility of the negative alternatives being discussed, because the speakers are suggesting that the adverse consequences will result from the actions of third parties over whom they exert minimal or no control.

[ii]   Affirmative Promises

Psychologists carefully distinguish between negative *"threats"* and affirmative *"promises"* (Pruitt & Rubin, 1986, at 51–55; Schelling, 1975, at 335–37). A promise does not involve the suggestion of negative consequences, but instead consists of "an expressed intention to behave in a way that appears beneficial to the interests of another." (Rubin & Brown, 1975, at 278) For example, a bargainer might promise to respond with beneficence if the opponent first takes certain action. It is hoped that this affirmative promise will induce the desired response without the need for resort to a negative threat. Furthermore, a promise is a less disruptive face-saving technique, because the opponent is told that the suggested position change will be reciprocated. On the other hand, a party that is threatened with negative consequences if specified action is not taken is never certain that any benefit will result if it agrees to do what the threatening party is demanding.

Implicit in any promise is the threat to refrain from acting positively if the other party fails to behave appropriately. In this sense, even promises may be considered subtle "threats." The one significant distinction between affirmative promises and negative threats concerns the fact that use of the former tactic tends to elicit a positive response, while use of the latter technique tends to elicit greater hostility (Rubin & Brown, 1975, at 285). It is thus easy to understand why affirmative promises are more likely to induce position changes and contribute to an atmosphere of cooperation than negative threats which tend to generate intransigence and create a more competitive environment.

Almost all negotiators have used the classic promise technique on some occasions. After extensive discussions, the parties are only $5,000 apart. So often, one of the participants reasonably suggests that they close the remaining gap by "splitting the difference." It is far more productive to propose that each party simultaneously move $2,500, than to threaten dire consequences if the other side does not unilaterally concede $2,500. Bargainers should not hesitate to employ promises earlier in their interactions to break temporary impasses. When it appears that each side is afraid to modify its position without some indication that this action will be reciprocated, one participant can propose that they agree to prepare new position statements that will be disclosed concurrently. This permits both sides to move together without fear that their movement will be ignored by the other party.

[iii] Communication of Perceived Values Through Promises and Threats/Warnings

Promises, threats, and warnings convey significant information regarding the transmitter's perception of the other party's circumstances. Positive promises clearly indicate what the promisor believes the recipient wants to obtain, and negative threats disclose what the threatener thinks the listener fears. Recipients of this information may be able to use it to their advantage. If, for example, the opponent appears to believe that they wish to obtain a particular item for their client that is not valued by their own client, an adroit negotiator may endeavor to extract some other meaningful term in exchange for this item. Conversely, if an adversary suggests through a threat that they believe one's own client would lose more from a nonsettlement than they actually would, it is normally beneficial to disabuse the opponent of this misconception so that they will not overestimate the negotiator's need to reach agreement.

[iv] Greater Success Through Affirmative Promises

It is interesting to note that negotiators tend to transmit affirmative promises more frequently than they do negative threats (Rubin & Brown, 1975, at 282). This fact frequently surprises bargainers, because most people remember more of the disruptive threats than the face-saving promises issued during bargaining discussions. It is also important to understand that "the use of promises tends to increase the likelihood of bargainers reaching a mutually favorable agreement, while the use of threats tends to reduce this likelihood." (Rubin & Brown, 1975, at 286) This demonstrates that negotiators can usually obtain consistently better results through the use of affirmative tactics that contribute to a cooperative atmosphere, than they are likely to achieve through negative techniques that detract from the bargaining process.

[v] Use of Effective and Credible Threats

Bargainers who plan to employ express or implicit threats need to understand the characteristics of *effective threats*. They must be certain that their threats are comprehended by their opponents. Some individuals transmit such vague threats that they often go unnoticed. Threats can only be influential when the other party is cognizant of their issuance. It is similarly important to formulate threats that are credible to the opponents. A credible threat is one that is reasonably proportionate to the action the declarant intends to deter — seemingly insignificant threats are usually ignored, while excessively large threats tend to be dismissed as irrational (Lebow, 1996, at 92–93; Lowenthal, 1982, at 86). The believability of threats may be further bolstered by corroborative behavior. For example, a party threatening to take certain action detrimental to the opposing client is more convincing if the party issuing the threat openly prepares for its effectuation.

[vi]   Risks and Benefits of Promises and Threats

Parties contemplating the use of affirmative promises or negative threats to advance their bargaining interests should carefully evaluate the possible risks and benefits that may be associated with such action before they act. They need to consider the manner in which their proposed challenge is likely to be perceived. They should especially remember that negative threats tend to increase the competitiveness of the individual being threatened, thereby heightening the risk of retaliation and/or intransigence (Lowenthal, 1982, at 88). It should finally be recognized that parties should never make threats they are not prepared and able to carry out, because their failure to effectuate promised action when their bluff is called substantially undermines their negotiating credibility (Lebow, 1996, at 106; Mayer, 1996, at 64).

Negotiators should always remember that a threat or warning is most influential while it is outstanding — *i.e.*, articulated but not yet effectuated. The party facing the negative consequences must decide whether it is better off acceding to the threatening side's demands or accepting the results of noncompliance. Once the threatened party decides to accept the negative consequences associated with noncompliance, the impact of the threat or warning is dissipated. It is no longer likely to influence the behavior of the party that has decided to accept the impact of its recalcitrance.

[vii]   Consideration of Options Beyond Concession to Threats

Negotiators who are threatened with negative consequences if they do not modify their current positions must always consider one crucial factor. What is likely to be the result if no agreement is reached with the instant opponent? If their external options are more beneficial than would be the result if they acceded to their opponent's threat, they should not be afraid to retain their present positions. If they wish to preserve a positive bargaining atmosphere, hoping that the other side will reassess its circumstances, they can simply ignore the threat (Malhotra & Bazerman, 2007, at 275–78; Cohen, 2003, at 273–75; Bastress & Harbaugh, 1990, at 461–62). If they behave as if no ultimatum has been issued, their adversary may be able to withdraw the threat without suffering a loss of face.

[c]   Rational and Emotional Appeals

Negotiators who are presented with objective arguments that undercut their positions frequently counter these assertions with rational or emotional appeals. Through the use of rational appeals, they endeavor to logically challenge the foundations underlying the opponent's contentions. They attempt to demonstrate the lack of any legal or factual basis for the arguments that are being articulated. If they are successful, they may be able to induce their opponent to reconsider the substantiality of the claims being conveyed.

Even when bargainers are unable to rationally undermine arguments being made, they may formulate emotional appeals that may diminish the effectiveness of those claims. This tactic is particularly potent when used against emotional opponents. While wholly cerebral challenges would be unlikely to undercut the confidence of intelligent individuals who have articulated objectively cogent contentions, emotional pleas may cause those persons to temper the forcefulness of their claims. The use of emotional appeals on highly intelligent but emotional people frequently renders them unable to rely entirely upon rational and objective factors. If it can be demonstrated that their logical arguments would inflict a seemingly unconscionable impact upon other parties, it may be possible to convince them to take a more conciliatory approach.

[d]   Ridicule and Humor

[i]   Derisive Smiles and Laughter

Ridicule and humor are frequently used by negotiators to indicate their scorn for unreasonable positions being taken by opponents. For example, in response to extremely one-sided initial offers, many bargainers exhibit derisive smiles or sarcastic laughter. This can be done in a humorous manner or in a disdainful fashion. If this technique achieves its intended objective, it will embarrass adversaries who have articulated knowingly ridiculous demands and induce them to formulate new position statements that are more reasonable than their originally disclosed offers.

[ii]   Sarcastic Retort

Some negotiators use more than a mere smile or laugh to signal their displeasure with absurd demands. They respond directly with a sarcastic retort. When confronted with obviously excessive claims, they might ask whether opposing counsel would also like to obtain the client's first born child and/or a quit claim deed to the light side of the moon! Through this device, recipients of outrageous demands can clearly indicate their dissatisfaction without having to discuss the merits involved. Many individuals prefer this type of approach, fearing that substantive challenges might mislead unrealistic opponents into believing that their initial offers are not truly unacceptable.

Humor can be employed to soften the impact of negative statements. When negotiators want to indicate their displeasure with particular proposals or with certain opponent conduct, they can do so with smiles on their faces and twinkles in their eyes. The recipients of these statements will not be sure if the speakers actually intended their devastating pronouncements. If the speakers are asked if they really intended what was communicated, they can always suggest they were only kidding! Nonetheless, their points have been made and have been comprehended by their listeners. Individuals who do not feel comfortable using humor in this manner should refrain from doing so, because they are likely to be taken seriously and be unable to defuse the anxious situation with jocularity.

[iii]   Use of Appropriate Humor

[A]   To Gain Concessions

Humor can also be employed to accomplish other bargaining objectives. Studies indicate that the use of appropriate humor tends to increase the likability of the communicator (O'Quin & Aronoff, 1981, at 349). People should not be afraid to use humor, particularly during the preliminary stages of negotiations, to develop more open and trusting relationships with opponents. Many individuals may even use humor as a means of generating concessions. Evidence suggests that subjects who receive demands accompanied by humor are more likely to acquiesce than those who merely receive unembellished demands (O'Quin & Aronoff, 1981, at 354).

[B] To Relieve Anxiety

Humor may be used during tense negotiations to relieve anxiety and to reopen blocked communication channels (Forester, 2004, at 222–23; Ilich, 1973, at 186–87). I can recall the story of an extremely tense collective bargaining situation in which the parties had reached a complete impasse. The representatives of each side stared across the table at each other with open animosity. Finally, the chief negotiator for the labor organization arose from his seat and strolled slowly around the table to the employer side. The room became silent by the time he arrived next to the chief negotiator for the employer. He then squatted along side that individual and looked at his union colleagues on the other side of the table. When he said that "from here, you guys really do look like sons of bitches," everyone laughed, and a substantial amount of the prevailing tension was eliminated. By reminding everyone involved that they were merely trying to represent their respective constituencies, this person was able to dissipate strained and unproductive circumstances. The parties were quickly able to return to substantive discussions and achieve a collective contract.

[e] Control of Agenda

[i] Complete Control of Agenda Items

Many individuals endeavor to advance their negotiating objectives through control of the agenda (Zwier & Guernsey, 2005, at 81–85; Latz, 2004, at 214–28; Reardon, 2004, at 99–106). They attempt to limit talks to those topics that are of interest to their own clients. Proficient negotiators may accomplish this objective by beginning serious discussions with "principled" opening offers that list and value the components of the deal they want to achieve. They hope to resolve these matters favorably, before they are forced to tackle other items that the opponents may wish to raise. If they are fortunate, their control of the agenda my even induce careless adversaries to overlook subjects that should have been discussed before the consummation of an overall agreement.

[ii] Control over Order of Topics

Even when negotiators cannot control the topics to be considered, they may be able to influence the order in which they are taken up. They may thus be able to resolve certain items important to their clients before other less significant subjects are encountered. When bargainers do not like the order in which opponents endeavor to present topics, they should not hesitate to indicate their dissatisfaction and attempt to negotiate the manner in which the parties should proceed. This form of "attitudinal bargaining" may permit them to seize control of the agenda. Even when they are unable to obtain complete control, they should at least be able to counteract an ordering scheme that negatively affects their bargaining interests.

[iii] Control Over Drafts

Some negotiators attempt to gain control of the bargaining agenda by inducing their opponents to rely on their proposed draft when the parties explore the relevant topics. If their adversaries provide them with their own preliminary draft, these manipulative individuals rewrite their opponents' draft. They then include the new items they wish to obtain and delete opponent topics they prefer to ignore. When this approach is used, the original drafters should not hesitate to prepare a composite document that contains all of the provisions suggested by both sides. Where only one party has proposed a particular term, that provision would appear alone. Where different language has been suggested with respect to related items, the different drafts could be set forth in pairs to indicate the pertinent variations. This technique permits the parties to discuss each set of proposals relating to a common term together, and it avoids the situation in which one party feels that it is constantly having to ask for its topics to be added or its opponent's provisions to be deleted.

[f]   Intransigence

Successful negotiators tend to be individuals who have the ability at critical points during their interactions to convince opponents that those people must make appropriate concessions if the discussions are to continue. This may be accomplished through sheer intransigence (Katz, 2008, at 131–32). They exude an uncompromising attitude that is intended to make adversaries believe that no further progress can be achieved if those persons do not modify their current positions. Such an unyielding strategy works most effectively against risk-averse individuals who fear the real or imagined consequences of nonsettlements. When opponents have options available to them outside the present negotiation arena and it appears that they would be willing to avail themselves of those alternatives if necessary, the use of an obstinate approach is unlikely to be productive.

[g]   Straightforwardness

Most people expect opponents to be circumspect during bargaining discussions. In some situations, this preconception can be used to one's advantage. If negotiators can surprise adversaries with what appears to be complete candor, they may be able to generate feelings of guilt and/or embarrassment in those persons due to their own continued use of typically disingenuous bargaining tactics. People who experience guilt or embarrassment often attempt to regain social acceptance by doing something to please those around them. When guilt or embarrassment is created at the bargaining table, it may well induce concessionary behavior that is intended to alleviate the anxiety being felt. Even if a straightforward approach does not immediately precipitate a concession, it may alternatively induce reciprocal candor that enhances the overall negotiating environment. However, bargainers should not allow these tactics to cause them to respond with so much openness that they effectively place themselves at a disadvantage vis-a-vis someone who is not being entirely candid.

[h]   Flattery

Real or feigned respect for opponents may cause them to become more accommodating at the bargaining table. The recipients of complimentary treatment may be induced to feel sympathetic toward their apparently less talented adversaries, and this may cause them to become less aggressive negotiators. If advocates are made to feel good about themselves because of the respect being accorded them by bargaining opponents, they may not feel the same need to demonstrate their negotiating skill as they would against other less discerning opponents. They may thus be persuaded to lower their guard and to behave in a more conciliatory manner. Even if flattery does not accomplish this Machiavellian objective, it is likely to create a more pleasant atmosphere and make the negotiations progress more smoothly.

[i]   Manipulation of Contextual Factors

Some individuals attempt to gain a psychological advantage at the bargaining table through their manipulation of contextual factors. They endeavor to control the day, time, location, and environment for the negotiations (Guernsey, 1996, at 38–39). When they are able to obtain concessions pertaining to these factors, this bolsters their confidence with respect to their subsequent handling of the substantive issues. This approach also permits them to establish a concessionary mentality in prospective opponents. People who begin a negotiation by conceding the date, time, and location for the impending interaction may continue this pattern when the real subjects are discussed.

The concessionary predisposition of opponents may be further heightened through feelings of obligation created when they're provided with complimentary food and drink at the outset of their transaction. While some people may question whether insignificant gratuities could possibly influence a person's bargaining behavior, I would prefer to be the provider of such generosity rather than the recipient. Those who doubt the impact of pre-negotiation offerings should take the time to observe the behavior of the proficient religious solicitors who operate in airport or train station lobbies. They initiate their interactions with small flowers or other relatively insignificant gifts. They then attempt to establish some degree of rapport through casual touching and seemingly sincere eye contact. It is amazing to see how quickly persons who decline to make contributions try to return the flower or gift they have received!

There are times when it is strategically preferable to negotiate at opponent offices. When you believe that interruptions caused by unrelated matters may disadvantage the party directly affected by those disruptions, it may be preferable to conduct discussions at your opponent's place of business (Guernsey, 1996, at 38). If the ready availability of important information would make it difficult for a party to avoid disclosure of that information, it may be better to meet at their office. This could allow you to demand information, while permitting you to retain your ability to tell opponents that you do not possess the documents they are requesting.

[j]   Silence

Silence is one of the most potent, yet frequently overlooked, power bargaining techniques (Katz, 2008, at 132–34; Steinberg, 1998, at 171).

> Only the amateur fears to be silent for a moment lest interest lag. He depends solely on words to capture attention. The artful performer knows that rhythm patterns require silence too, and nothing is more dramatic and effective than a long motionless pause after a statement. It permits absorption of the thought. It permits reflection. But more important, it compels attention to what has been said as if an italicized finger had been pointed at it (L. Nizer, *Thinking on Your Feet* (1963), at 26).

Many less competent negotiators fear silence. They are afraid that they will lose control of the interaction if they stop talking, and they remember the awkwardness they have experienced in social settings during prolonged pauses. They thus feel compelled to speak. When they do, they tend to disclose, both verbally and nonverbally, information they did not intend to divulge (McCormack, 1984, at 108–11). They often find themselves making unintended concessions. When they are confronted by further silence from their opponents, they frequently continue their verbal leakage and concomitant loss of control.

When negotiators have something important to say, they should simply convey their intended message and become quiet. There is no need to emphasize the point with unnecessary reiteration. A clear, succinct expression accentuates the crucial nature of their communication and provides their adversary with the opportunity to absorb what has been said (Mayer, 1996, at 30). This rule is particularly critical when concessions or offers are being disclosed. Bargainers should unequivocally articulate their new positions and then quietly and patiently await responses from the receiving parties. If silence makes them feel uncomfortable, they should review their papers or otherwise look busy. They may alternatively play with their glasses or stroke their cheek. This signals to opponents that they expect those persons to reply before they say anything further.

People who discern in opponents an inability or a reluctance to remain silent should use pregnant pauses to their own advantage. After loquacious adversaries explain their positions or make offers, they may become disconcerted if no response is immediately forthcoming. As their bargaining anxiety increases, periods of silence become more unbearable. If their representations are met with cold silence, they may be induced to say more. As they fill the silent void, they frequently disclose more information, and they occasionally make further unanswered concessions.

Individuals who are confronted by taciturn opponents should not accept sole responsibility to keep discussions moving. They may decide to sit quietly until their opponents respond. If they feel too uncomfortable with this approach, they may alternatively use questions to force their adversaries to participate in the interaction. They should formulate inquiries that cannot be answered with a mere "yes" or "no," but that require some elaboration.

[k]   Patience

People involved in legal transactions must recognize that the negotiation process takes time to unfold. Parties who endeavor to accelerate developments in a precipitous fashion usually obtain less favorable results than they would have attained with greater patience. Offers that would be acceptable if conveyed during the latter stages of a negotiation may not be attractive when broached prematurely. The participants have to be given sufficient time to recognize that a negotiated result is preferable to their external options. They have to accept the need to let go of the past to enable them to move forward with their lives.

Both sides to a negotiation experience anxiety associated with the uncertainty that is inherent in these interactions. Those participants who can effectively control the tension they feel and exude a quiet confidence are generally able to achieve more favorable agreements. They have the mental and physical stamina needed to withstand prolonged discussions. They lead opponents to believe that they are willing to take as much time as is required for them to attain their bargaining objectives. I am always amazed by the number of negotiators who indicate that they finally acceded to opponent demands merely because they were unwilling to continue the process further. They had become fatigued and wanted to conclude the transaction. What they failed to recognize was that an intentional and conscious tactic had been used effectively against them. They usually attributed their opponent's success to pure fortuity!

Those negotiators who like to use patience to wear down opponents should try to develop styles that are sufficiently pleasant to keep the process going when little progress is being made. When undue tension builds up, they should carefully strive to dissipate it. When silence threatens to disrupt the talks, they need to know how to reopen communication without making unintended disclosures or concessions. They must master the art of dissembling. As soon as the negotiation process has been rejuvenated sufficiently to guarantee its continuation, they can again shift the focus to their adversaries.

[l]   Guilt, Embarrassment, or Indebtedness

Studies indicate that parties who experience guilt, embarrassment, or indebtedness are particularly susceptible to requests for concessions. They try to relieve their discomfort by satisfying the needs of those around them (Katz, 2008, at 159–160). During bargaining interactions, these factors often induce disconcerted participants to make magnanimous concessions. Some negotiators attempt to establish feelings of guilt or embarrassment by suggesting that their opponent was late for a scheduled meeting or was otherwise inconsiderate. They may alternatively blame their adversary's client for their current predicament. If they are successful in this regard, they may obtain a bargaining advantage. A simple apology can usually defuse this tactic.

Feelings of indebtedness may similarly precipitate concessions. If food and drink are to be consumed, it is preferable to be the one providing them, rather than the one accepting that hospitality. Even though some people may not permit gratuities to influence their bargaining behavior, others may unconsciously alter their conduct to their host's advantage. If important negotiations are involved, the cost of gracious hospitality toward the opponents is frequently recouped in the final settlements achieved.

[m]   Constructive Ambiguity

During complex, multifaceted negotiations, parties occasionally permit disagreement over an inconsequential item to negate their consensus regarding the more significant topics. Were they to assess the actual circumstances in a detached manner, they would probably realize that the tangential area in dispute is not even likely to become relevant during the life of their proposed agreement. When neither party is willing — or politically able — to ignore the controverted subject, they might consider the drafting of a provision that appears to define the offending topic, but that does not actually resolve the matter. The use of such "constructive ambiguity" may enable parties to achieve an agreement that would otherwise have been precluded (Zartman & Berman, 1982, at 123; Ikle, 1964, at 15). If, as is often the case, that particular provision is never questioned, the parties will have accomplished their overall objective. However, even when that contractual term subsequently does become the focus of debate, the parties can resolve their previously planned ambiguity either through further negotiations in a less contentious environment or by way of an arbitral or judicial determination. Even the party that ultimately loses that proceeding would probably end up in a better position than would have been attained had the bargainers initially allowed their discord with respect to this ancillary term to defeat their entire accord.

When deciding whether to adopt constructive ambiguity pertaining to a presently irreconcilable term, parties must consider several basic factors. How important is the disputed subject? How likely is it that the parties will be affected by it during the life of their agreement? What would be the consequences of a nonsettlement caused by the lack of accord with respect to this item? If the overall costs of nonsettlement would clearly transcend both the costs of agreement *and* the risk associated with the adoption of the ambiguous contract term, the parties should seriously consider the use of this technique to produce an agreement. By providing for an expeditious and relatively inexpensive arbitration procedure to resolve disputes arising under their agreement, parties can further minimize the transaction costs that would be involved if the matter ultimately had to be adjudicated.

[n]   Raising Voice for Emphasis

It is important to acknowledge the fact that successful bargainers are usually not entirely soft-spoken individuals. Parties who wish to convince opponents of the seriousness of their stated positions should not be afraid to raise their voices for emphasis. Controlled loudness is normally a characteristic of persuasiveness. While a few people may be able to make others offers they cannot refuse — in which case they can indeed "talk softly and carry a big stick" — most persons lack such innate authority. Increased voice volume, where appropriate, is thus an important aspect of power bargaining.

[o]   Intense Language

Individuals who use more intense language during bargaining encounters may think they are being more forceful than persons who employ less intense terms. Studies show, however, that low intensity presentations are likely to be more persuasive than high intensity assertions (Lewicki, et al., 1994, at 214). This seeming anomaly is due to the negative reaction most negotiators have toward high intensity persuasive efforts. High intensity speakers seem disingenuous and manipulative, while low intensity presenters tend to induce opponents to be less suspicious of and more receptive to their entreaties.

§ 7.05   ALWAYS REMEMBER CURRENT NONSETTLEMENT ALTERNATIVES

Throughout the Distributive Stage, negotiators should focus on their *aspiration levels* as they strive to achieve agreements (Malhotra & Bazerman, 2007, at 48–49). If they fail to do so, once they pass their bottom lines they may relax and not seek the additional gains they could otherwise obtain. Nonetheless, when the discussions become difficult, they must always remember their *current* nonsettlement alternatives. It is no longer relevant what they were six months or a year ago, when these individuals began to prepare for the present interaction. The passage of time has generally affected the options that were available then. The discovery process many have strengthened or weakened the case of litigators, while changes in the business market may have influenced the value of the firm being purchased or sold or the technology being licensed. Has the market improved the situation of the firm being purchased or sold? Are the technology rights being licensed worth more or less than they were a year ago?

If bargainers fail to appreciate changes in the value of their immediate interaction, they may enter into an arrangement that is not better than what they would have with no agreement. They must always remember that a bad deal is worse than no deal. When nonsettlement alternatives are presently more beneficial than the terms being offered at the bargaining table, they should not hesitate to walk away from the current discussions. They should do this as pleasantly as possible for two reasons. First, when their opponents realize that they are really willing to end the interaction, their adversaries may reconsider their position and offer them more beneficial terms. Second, even if the present negotiations fail to regenerate and no accord is achieved, the parties may see each other in the future. If the other side remembers these talks favorably, even if no agreement was achieved, future negotiations are likely to progress more smoothly than if these talks ended on an unpleasant note.

Summary

1. During the Competitive/Distributive Stage, the participants focus on what they have to obtain for their own clients, and they use more declaratory sentences than questions.

2. Negotiators should enter the Competitive/Distributive Stage with "principled" opening offers that indicate how they reached those proposals, and they should use "principled" concessions that rationally explain the reasons underlying each position change.

3. Concession patterns should be carefully planned to culminate in beneficial agreements, and participants must avoid premature position changes that indicate an over-anxious need to settle.

4. Negotiators should focus primarily on their *aspiration levels* and not relax until they approach those objectives. They should only focus on their *bottom lines* when the discussions become difficult and they are deciding whether to terminate the interactions.

5. When negotiations appear to be on the verge of an impasse, the participants should try to depersonalize their interaction, alleviate bargaining tension, and look for ways to keep the process moving in a productive manner.

6. Effective arguments must be presented in a comprehensive, objective, and articulate manner, and they should go beyond what opponents expect to hear.

7. "Warnings" that convey the adverse consequences that will be imposed by third parties if agreements are not achieved are less disruptive and more credible than "threats" that are to be effectuated by the threatening parties themselves.

8. Affirmative promises are more likely to induce opponent position changes than negative threats. They are also less disruptive of the bargaining process due to their face-saving nature.

9. Emotional arguments and appeals — particularly those with a moralistic component — frequently influence intelligent opponents more effectively than wholly rational entreaties.

10. Humor, patience, candor, silence, guilt, embarrassment, and other similar techniques may be effectively employed to induce opponents to provide what is being sought.

Chapter 8

THE CLOSING STAGE (VALUE SOLIDIFYING)

§ 8.01 CLOSING STAGE MOOD AND TEMPTATIONS

[1] Relief

Near the end of the Competitive/Distributive Stage, one or both participants begin to realize that a mutual accord is likely to be achieved. The negotiators feel a sense of relief, as it appears that the anxiety generated by the uncertainty of the negotiation process is about to be alleviated by the attainment of an agreement. Careful observers can often see slight signs of relief around the mouths of the individuals who reach this state. The participants may also exhibit more relaxed postures. As these bargainers become psychologically committed to settlement, they want to move expeditiously toward the conclusion of the transaction. They should avoid this temptation.

The Closing Stage is a critical part of bargaining interactions. The majority of concessions tend to be made during the concluding portion of negotiations (Dawson, 2001, at 171), and overly anxious participants may forfeit much of what they obtained during the Competitive/Distributive Stage if they are not vigilant. They must remain patient and permit the final phase of the process to develop in a deliberate fashion.

[2] Anxiety

Less successful negotiators tend to make excessive and unreciprocated concessions during the Closing Stage in an effort to guarantee a final agreement. When they are later asked about this behavior, they usually indicate that they did not wish to risk the possibility of a nonsettlement at this stage of the transaction. They emphasize their belief that the accord achieved is better for their client than no pact. When I ask them how interested their opponents were in a final accord, they appear dumbfounded. They have completely ignored this crucial consideration.

By the end of the Competitive/Distributive Stage, *both sides* have become psychologically committed to a joint resolution. Neither wants their previous bargaining efforts to culminate in failure. Less proficient negotiators tend to focus entirely on their own side's desire to achieve an agreement, and they completely disregard the settlement pressure influencing their opponents. This phenomenon causes them to increase the pressure on themselves and to discount the anxiety being experienced by their adversaries. They thus assume that they must close more of the remaining gap than their opponents if they are going to ensure a final accord.

[3]   Importance of Perceived Fairness

When people decide whether to accept proposed bargaining terms, they generally ask themselves whether the final agreements would be fair (see generally Richardson, 2007; Nadler, 1999). To demonstrate this phenomenon, I often have students play the Ultimatum Game. Class members are divided into pairs and each pair is given $10,000 to divide between themselves. One person is instructed to offer a proposed division of the $10,000 between themself and the other participant. The offer recipient can either accept the proposed division, giving each the suggested amounts, or reject the offer, leaving both with nothing. When divisions of $5000/$5000 are proposed, they are readily accepted. Divisions of $5500/$4500, $6000/$4000, and even $7000/$3000 are often accepted, with the recipients of the lower amounts feeling that these sums are better than nothing. On the other hand, as offerors try to retain more of the $10,000 for themselves, more offerees reject their proposals causing both to receive nothing. The participants begin to appreciate how much the appearance of fairness affects bargaining interactions (Richardson, 2007, at 416–17; Adler, 2005, at 716–19).

After the first round is completed, I have the participants switch roles. The person who received the offer during the first exchange is instructed to suggest a proposed division to the other student. If the offeror in the first round suggested a $5000/$5000 division, their partner usually suggests the same division during the second round. On the other hand, if the initial offeror made a proposal that allowed him or her to obtain more than $5000, their partner usually suggests a similarly one-sided division during the second round. This demonstrates the degree to which persons who feel they were treated unfairly during one interaction try to get even during subsequent interactions.

§ 8.02   CLOSING STAGE TECHNIQUES

[1]   Concessions Decrease in Size and Should Not Be
Unreciprocated

As the Closing Stage begins, *both parties* want an agreement. They would not have expended the time and effort needed to get to this point if this were not true. It is thus appropriate for each side to expect the other to move with it toward the final accord. Negotiators should be certain that they do not make concessions that are not reciprocated by their opponents. They should also avoid excessive position changes that are not matched by the other side. Bargainers should only contemplate the making of greater concessions than their adversaries when their opponents have been more accommodating during the earlier stages of the transaction *and* the verbal and nonverbal messages emanating from those participants clearly indicate that they are approaching their resistance point.

At this stage, too many bargainers see the end in sight and are eager to conclude the transaction. Instead of being a time for swift action, this is a time for patient perseverance (Harvard Bus. Essentials, 2003, at 62–63). Negotiators must continue to employ the techniques that got them to this point. They should be especially cognizant of their overall and their immediate concession patterns. They should attempt to make smaller and, if possible, less frequent concessions than their opponents. If they fail to follow this admonition and endeavor to reach a mutual accord too quickly, they are likely to close most of the distance separating the parties.

[2]   Splitting the Difference of the Remaining Difference

Overly anxious adversaries occasionally attempt to conclude the bargaining process by prematurely offering to split the remaining distance between the parties. Adroit bargainers may take advantage of this proposal by emphasizing their previous concessions and suggesting that the parties split the *distance* remaining after the opponents offered to split the difference. If this technique is successful, it induces the opponents to close 75 percent of the existing gap, while requiring this party to close only 25 percent. The difference between a 50-50 division and a 75-25 split may involve thousands or even millions of dollars.

[3]   The Importance of Patience and Calculated Silence

Patience and silence are two of the most efficacious techniques during the Closing Stage. Negotiators should rely upon "principled" concessions to clarify the extent of each position change. Following the succinct explanation for each concession being made, speakers should become quiet and patiently await the other side's response. They should refrain from reiterations that serve to highlight their anxiety, and they should not contemplate further movement without appropriate reciprocity from the other side. Guilt can also be an effective factor. By reminding opponents of the numerous position changes they made during the earlier stages of the process, proficient bargainers can often generate opponent guilt and convince the other side that they are morally obliged to provide more generous concessions during the Closing Stage.

[4]   Maintain Momentum Toward Settlement

When participants enter the Closing Stage, they must realize that the time is propitious for settlement. It is imperative that they keep the process moving inexorably toward a satisfactory conclusion. They should normally eschew disruptive tactics — such as walking out or slamming down the telephone — that may impede continued progress. If someone breaks off discussions at this point, it may take days or even weeks to again achieve auspicious settlement circumstances. Instead of employing negative threats, they should resort to affirmative promises that permit their opponents to move in a face-saving way. Temporary impasses may be effectively overcome through the promise of concurrent position changes. If they fear that a bargaining hiatus may provide their opponents with the opportunity to reassess the existing circumstances in a manner that might jeopardize a mutual accord, they should subtly work to encourage a final resolution by the conclusion of the instant session.

[5]   Offering a Way Out from the "Limited Authority" Position

On some occasions, adversaries may have locked themselves into seemingly uncompromising positions by relying on their "limited authority." It would be difficult for them to retreat from their current positions without losing credibility. They should be provided with a face-saving way out of their predicament. They should be told that the suggested agreement is fair and be encouraged to telephone their client to obtain approval of the proposed terms. It is irrelevant whether they call their client or order a pizza, so long as they are given the opportunity to return to the bargaining table with the requisite authorization.

[6]   Exuding Nonchalance

Proficient negotiators are frequently able to obtain a significant advantage during the concluding portions of interactions. As they sense heightened opponent excitement, they project an insouciant attitude. They want their adversaries to think they are wholly unconcerned about the seemingly impending accord. The more they are able to accomplish this objective, the more they can induce adversaries to feel a greater need to close the remaining gap (Dawson, 2001, at 173–76). As those participants make more expansive and more frequent concessions in an effort to end the interaction, they significantly enhance the final terms attained by the persevering side. When opponents make their beneficent concessions, they should be praised for their reasonableness and encouraged to continue their admirable behavior.

The Closing Stage is a highly competitive part of a negotiation. It frequently involves a significant number of position changes and a substantial amount of participant movement. As noted earlier, the majority of concessions tend to be made during the last portion of bargaining interactions. Negotiators who think that this portion of the transaction consists primarily of cooperative behavior are likely to obtain less beneficial results than manipulative opponents who recognize the inherently competitive aspect of this stage and who are able to induce naive participants to close most of the outstanding distance between the two sides. As they formulate their closing strategies, individuals must always remember that their adversaries also want to achieve mutual accords. Their opponents may even wish to do so more earnestly than they do. Individuals should not hesitate to take advantage of this fact. If they can project a nonchalant attitude, their anxious opponents may decide that they are the ones who must give in if final deals are to be consummated.

Summary

1. As negotiators begin to recognize that a mutual accord is likely to result from their interaction, they move into the critical and highly competitive Closing Stage.

2. Parties should avoid the use of disruptive tactics that might destroy their joint psychological commitment to settlement. Instead, they should employ more cooperative techniques that will keep the process moving toward a successful conclusion.

3. Since a majority of concessions tend to be made during the final portion of bargaining interactions, negotiators should carefully monitor their concession patterns to be certain they do not make unreciprocated or excessive position changes.

4. Silence and patience are highly effective weapons during the Closing Stage. These traits often induce anxious opponents to close more of the distance separating the two

parties.

5. If opponents have locked themselves into uncompromising positions, they should be provided with a face-saving way to move in the direction necessary to conclude the transaction.

Chapter 9

THE COOPERATIVE/INTEGRATIVE STAGE (VALUE MAXIMIZING)

§ 9.01   ADVANCING INTERESTS OF ALL PARTIES

[1]   Transition to Cooperative/Integrative Stage

Once the Closing Stage of a negotiation has been successfully completed through the attainment of a mutually acceptable agreement, many parties consider the bargaining process finished. While this conclusion may be warranted with respect to zero or constant sum problems — where neither party could possibly obtain more favorable results without a corresponding loss to the other party — it is clearly not correct for multi-issue, non-zero or non-constant sum disputes. It is not always true even for seemingly zero or constant sum transactions.

In a personal injury case involving a permanently injured plaintiff who will require substantial future care, the parties may initially discuss only monetary demands and offers that are to be satisfied immediately. The plaintiff attorney wants to obtain a sufficiently large settlement to provide life-time care for the plaintiff, but the defendant insurance carrier does not wish to transfer such a substantial sum of money to the plaintiff at the present time. It may be possible to satisfy the underlying needs and interests of both parties simultaneously through a structured settlement plan that guarantees the plaintiff continued treatment and that does not require the defendant insurance company to make an enormous payout now. Through the development of this innovative alternative, the negotiating parties are able to convert a seemingly zero sum transaction into a non-zero sum transaction.

When people are involved in negotiations concerning various issues, they tend to assume a "fixed pie" that cannot be expanded (Adler, 2005, at 740–42; Dietmeyer & Kaplan, 2004, at 35–37; Birke & Fox, 1999, at 30–31). This is rarely correct. Negotiators should instead assume the presence of a non-zero or non-constant sum interaction. It would be unlikely that both parties to the transaction would value each and every item identically and oppositely (Malhotra & Bazerman, 2007, at 108–110; Mnookin, Peppet & Tulumello, 2000, at 14–16). As a result, it is usually possible for the participants to formulate proposals that may simultaneously advance the interests of everyone involved. They can best accomplish this objective through an efficacious Cooperative/Integrative Stage.

[2]   Search for Undiscovered Alternatives

[a]   Pressure to End Talks

Once a tentative accord has been achieved through the competitive process, it is generally advantageous for the negotiators to explore alternative trade-offs that might concurrently enhance the interests of both sides (Neale & Bazerman, 1991, at 32–38). The participants may be mentally, and even physically, exhausted due to the anxiety associated with the Competitive/Distributive and Closing Stages, and they may understandably wish to memorialize their agreement and terminate their interaction. They should, however, at least briefly endeavor to explore alternative formulations that may prove to be mutually more advantageous — but were ignored during the pressure indigenous to their competitive bargaining.

During the Informative Stage, the parties over- or under-state the value of various items for strategic purposes. During the Competitive/Distributive and Closing Stages of a negotiation, the participants tend to be cautious and manipulative. Complete disclosure of underlying interests and objectives rarely occurs. Both sides are likely to employ power bargaining techniques aimed at the achievement of results favorable to their own respective circumstances. Because of the tension created by these power bargaining tactics, Pareto superior arrangements — where neither party may improve its position without worsening the other side's situation — are generally not attained due to the lack of candid disclosure. The parties are more likely to only achieve "acceptable" terms. If they were to conclude the negotiation process at this point, they may leave a substantial amount of potential, yet untapped, joint satisfaction on the bargaining table.

[b]　　Assessing Points Gained by Both Sides

In simulation exercises, it is easy to determine the extent to which the negotiators have successfully employed the Cooperative/Integrative Stage. By comparing the aggregate point totals achieved by each pair of opponents, one may assess the degree to which the participants were able to maximize their joint results. This assessment is not intended to weigh one side's points against the other. It merely evaluates the degree to which the participants were able to ascertain and distribute the total available points — regardless of which participant attained more or less of them. For example, where two opponents might potentially divide a total of approximately 1000 points between them, some teams with extraordinary cooperative skills may reach an agreement giving them a combined total of 950–1000 points. Other less cooperative groups, on the other hand, may only end up with a joint total of 700–750 points. These results graphically demonstrate to the participants the benefits to be derived from cooperative bargaining. Had the latter negotiators been more cooperative, they would have been able to share an additional 250–300 points. Such an effort would certainly have enhanced the interests of their respective clients, with both sides being able to increase their final levels of satisfaction.

[c]　　Prerequisites for Cooperative/Integrative Stage

If the Cooperative/Integrative Stage is to be employed successfully, several prerequisites must be established. The parties must first achieve a tentative bargaining accord. This would usually be generated through the use of at least some competitive bargaining tactics. Negotiators who do not observe any Information, Competitive/Distributive, or Closing Stage should always be concerned about the real possibility that they have been preempted. Parties must generally ascertain the topics that are available for distribution and decide how the basic items are to be divided between them. If one party is able to convince the opponent that there is no need for the Competitive/Distributive or Closing Stage and suggests that the participants exclusively employ cooperative bargaining techniques, it is likely that the moving participant has already won the Competitive/Distributive and Closing Stages by default. They have unilaterally dictated the fundamental division of the available topics, and now wish to determine whether they can use the Cooperative/Integrative Stage to obtain a further advantage. It is for this reason that negotiators should be careful to ensure the presence of a minimal Competitive/Distributive Stage and a Closing Stage *before* they permit transition into the Cooperative/Integrative Stage.

[d]   When and How to Initiate Talks

Once the Competitive/Distributive Stage and the Closing Stage have been tentatively concluded, one party should suggest passage into the Cooperative/Integrative Stage. If they fear that their opponent may be reluctant to progress in this direction until a provisional accord has been solidified, it may be beneficial to have the parties initial each term contained in the settlement they have already negotiated. Negotiators should not consider transition to the Cooperative/Integrative Stage until they are certain they have already reached a mutually acceptable distribution of the relevant items. Any questions in this regard should be carefully resolved before they proceed further (Dawson, 2001, at 172–73). When these matters have been settled, a participant should propose that the parties explore alternative formulations to be certain that they have not — in the heat of battle — overlooked mutually advantageous options.

[e]   Both Sides Must Recognize Transition to Cooperative/ Integrative Stage

It is imperative that both parties recognize their movement from the Competitive/Distributive Stage through the Closing Stage into the Cooperative/Integrative Stage. If one side attempts to move into the Cooperative/Integrative Stage without the understanding of the other participant, problems are likely to arise. The alternative proposals suggested may be less advantageous to the other participant than previously articulated offers. If the recipient of these new proposals does not view them as incipient cooperative overtures, he or she may suspect disingenuous competitive tactics. Why else would an opponent suggest less beneficial terms during the critical portion of the Competitive/Distributive or the Closing Stage? Allegations of bad faith and improper dealing would probably be made. As a result, the bargaining process could be disrupted. It is for this reason that a party contemplating movement toward cooperative efforts should ensure that the opponent understands the intended transition. If the circumstances do not themselves suggest the achievement of a tentative agreement and the obvious commencement of cooperative techniques, this fact should be expressly communicated.

[f]   Benefit of Directness

Once parties enter the Cooperative/Integrative Stage, they should endeavor to ascertain the presence of previously unnoticed alternatives that might be mutually beneficial. They must attempt to expand the overall economic and noneconomic pie to be divided between them (Mnookin, Peppet & Tulumello, 2000, at 11–43; Fisher & Ury, 1981, at 58–83). Perhaps they have failed to consider options that would equally or even more effectively satisfy the underlying needs and interests of one side with less cost to the other party (Karrass, 1970, at 145). To accomplish this objective, the negotiators must be willing to candidly disclose the underlying interests and objectives of their respective clients. Although they have presumably explored many of these factors during the Competitive/Distributive Stage and the Closing Stage, it must be recognized that normal circumspection and the use of some disingenuous bargaining techniques probably precluded complete disclosure during the competitive discussions. Once a tentative agreement has been reached, the parties should no longer be afraid of more open deliberations. Even if they are unable to achieve a more advantageous mutual arrangement, they can at least be certain of a final resolution on their initially specified terms. It thus behooves them to be direct and unreserved.

[g] Assessing Efficiency of Initial Agreements

Both sides must exhibit substantial candor during this process if it is to function optimally. Through the use of objective and relatively neutral inquiries, the participants should explore their respective goals and needs. They should use brainstorming techniques to develop options that were not previously considered (see generally Kelley, 2001). When one side asks the other if another resolution would be as good or better for it than what has already been agreed upon, the responding participant must be forthright. If the proposed term would not be as preferable, the parties should contemplate other options. It is only where they have effectively explored all of the possible formulations that they can truly determine whether their initial agreement has optimally satisfied their fundamental needs.

An effective technique to look for ways to expand the overall pie and improve the situations of both sides involves the use of "multiple equal offers" (Dietmeyer & Kaplan, 2004, at 131–41). One side articulates two, three, or even four different offers of relatively equal value to its side and asks the other party which alternative it prefers. For example, the prospective purchaser of a corporation that has tentatively agreed to pay $50 million in cash might offer $55 million in stock, $60 million in cash to be paid out in equal installments over the next ten years, or $40 million in cash and $13 million in goods and services. If the buyer values these equally, it can see which form of payment is best for the seller. As the parties move toward mutual agreement on the exact form of payment, the buyer could suggest possible changes in other terms it would find preferable. As this process continues, both sides may be able to increase their final levels of satisfaction.

[h] Revisiting Results of Over- and Understated Values from Competitive/Distributive and Closing Stages

An inherent aspect of the Cooperative/Integrative Stage concerns the fact that certain trade-offs made during the highly contested Competitive/Distributive and Closing Stages may not have been achieved with exemplary communication. Participants have usually over- and under-stated the value of the items being exchanged for strategic purposes. As a result, one party may have ended up with items it did not value as highly as the opponent, while the other side may have obtained some terms it did not want as much as the first party. If the negotiators can identify these topics during their cooperative discussions, they would clearly benefit from an appropriate rearrangement of their earlier settlement. These terms should certainly be exchanged, with each party receiving more satisfaction than it had previously attained.

[i] Preserving Credibility

As the participants enter the Cooperative/Integrative Stage, they must be careful to preserve their basic credibility. They may have deceived their opponents during the Information, the Competitive/Distributive, and the Closing Stages regarding client values or settlement intentions. In the Cooperative/Integrative Stage, they have to correct the inefficiencies that may have been generated by their deceptive tactics. If they are too candid about their previous prevarication, however, their opponents may begin to question the truthfulness of many of their prior representations and seek to renegotiate the entire agreement (Condlin, 1992, at 44–45). This would be a disaster. It is thus imperative that bargainers not overtly undermine their credibility while they endeavor to improve their respective positions during the Cooperative/Integrative Stage.

§ 9.02   COMPETITIVE ASPECT OF COOPERATIVE BARGAINING

It is important for individuals participating in cooperative bargaining to understand the competitive undercurrent that is present even during these discussions. While participants are using cooperative techniques to expand the overall pie and improve the results achieved by both sides, some simultaneously employ competitive tactics to enable them to claim more than their share of the newly discovered areas for mutual gain (Nelken, 2001, at 188–89). For example, consider the situation in which the parties were unable during the Competitive/Distributive and Closing Stages of their interaction to discover the existence of an additional "200 points" of possible joint satisfaction. If one participant can adroitly ascertain this deficiency, he or she may take advantage of that finding. That individual could draft a new proposal that provides an extra ten to twenty "points" for the opponent while giving the remaining 180 to 190 "points" to his or her own client. The devious participant may even attempt to enhance his or her credibility by suggesting that the proposed modification would only "slightly improve" his or her client's circumstances. Since the other party would be better off under this suggested arrangement than under their initial agreement, it might readily assent to this proposal without recognizing the deliberate imbalance involved.

[1]   Exploration of all Alternatives Prior to Final Agreement

Bargainers should endeavor to protect their client interests during the Cooperative/Integrative Stage by insisting on full disclosure before they eagerly accept a more beneficial arrangement. If they have any doubts, they should suggest several alternative formulations of their own to determine whether or not they may be able to obtain more of the newly discovered "points." It is only when they reasonably conclude that an equitable distribution of the excess "points" is being achieved that they should accept a final agreement. By employing some of the techniques usually associated with low key competitive interactions, negotiators can ensure that their client's interests are not unfairly and unnecessarily sacrificed during the Cooperative/Integrative Stage.

[2]   Leave Opponent with Sense They Got Good Deal

As the overall terms are being finalized, negotiators should remember how important it is to leave their opponents with the feeling they got a good deal (Curhan, Elfenbein & Xu, 2006). If their adversaries are left with a good *subjective* impression, they will be more likely to honor the accord and more likely to behave cooperatively when the parties interact in the future than if they merely think they get a good *objective* outcome. The crucial subjective feelings that individuals have at the conclusion of bargaining interactions are directly related to their perceptions concerning the fairness of (1) the *negotiation process* and (2) the *interpersonal process* which reflect how professionally and respectfully they were treated by the other side (Hollander-Blumoff & Tyler, 2008; Curhan, Elfenbein & Xu, 2006).

Some advocates attempt to accomplish this objective by making the final concession on a matter they do not highly value (Dawson, 2001, at 102–03). Even a minimal position change at this point is likely to be appreciated by the other side (Steinberg, 1998, at

215). Others try to do it by congratulating their opponents on the mutually beneficial agreement achieved (Dawson, 2001, at 143–44). Individuals must be careful, however, not to be too effusive. When negotiators lavish praise on their opponents at the conclusion of bargaining interactions, those individuals tend to become suspicious and think they got a poor deal.

[3]   Take Time to Review Agreement

When bargaining interactions are successfully concluded, many participants are anxious to terminate their sessions and return to other client matters. As a result, they fail to ensure a clear meeting of the minds. If both sides are not in complete agreement, subsequent misunderstandings may negate their bargaining efforts. To avoid later disagreements, the participants should take the time to review the specific terms agreed upon before they adjourn their discussions (Schoonmaker, 1989, at 172). In most instances they will encounter no difficulties and will merely reaffirm the provisions they have achieved.

On occasion, negotiating parties discover misunderstandings or ambiguities. They should not permit these difficulties to destroy their previous success. At this point in the bargaining process, the parties are usually in a particularly accommodating frame of mind. They feel good about their progress and are psychologically committed to a final accord. If they address these discrepancies now, they are likely to resolve them amicably. On the other hand, if they do not discern their divergent viewpoints until someone drafts the settlement terms, the non-drafter may question the integrity of the drafting party assuming deliberate deception during the drafting process. Recriminations may result, causing the entire deal to unravel.

[4]   Endeavor to Draft Final Agreement

Once the Competitive/Distributive, Closing, and Cooperative/ Integrative Stages have been completed and a final accord has been achieved, many negotiators are readily willing to permit opposing counsel to prepare the settlement agreement. While this may save them time and effort, it is a risky practice. It is unlikely that they and the opponent would employ identical language to memorialize the specific terms agreed upon. Each would probably use slightly different terminology to represent his or her own perception of the matter. To ensure that their client's particular interests are optimally protected, bargainers should always try to be the one to draft the operative document (Dawson, 2001, at 130–31; G. Karrass, 1985, at 181–82).

No competent attorney would ever contemplate the omission of terms actually agreed upon or the inclusion of items not covered by the parties' oral understanding. Either practice would be wholly unethical and would constitute fraud. Such disreputable behavior could subject the responsible practitioner and his or her client to substantial liability and untoward legal problems. Why then should lawyers insist upon the right to prepare the final accord? It is to allow them to draft a document that unambiguously reflects their perception of the overall agreement achieved by the parties.

Each provision should be carefully prepared to state precisely what the drafting party thinks was mutually agreed upon. When the resulting contract is then presented to the other party for execution, it is quite likely that it would be reluctant to propose alternative language, unless serious questions regarding the content of particular clauses were raised. Doubts tend to be resolved in favor of the proffered document.

This approach best ensures that the final contract will most effectively protect the interests of the party who drafted it.

[5]   Review Opponent Draft Carefully

If negotiators are unable to prepare the ultimate agreement, they should be certain to review the terms of the document drafted by the other side before they permit their client to execute it. They should compare each provision with their notes and recollections of the interaction, to be positive that their understanding of the bargaining results is accurately represented.

Draft reviewers must go through a three-step process. First, is there any language in the draft they do not like? If so, they should mark up the draft and be prepared to discuss their proposed changes with the drafting party. Second, has anything been included in the draft that was not expressly agreed upon? Nothing is "boilerplate" until both sides accept it. For example, the drafter may have specified the applicability of the laws of a particular state if disagreements arise over the interpretation of their agreement, when the other party would prefer reliance upon the laws of another jurisdiction. The drafting party may have included a dispute resolution mechanism that is not favored by the other side. Finally, has anything been omitted that was agreed upon? Draft reviewers usually look carefully at the language before them, instead of contemplating terms that may have been left out. When lawyers review draft provisions, they should check off the areas of their notes covered by each provision. When they are finished, they should see if any areas of their notes remain unchecked.

[6]   Unabashed Questioning of Drafts

Agreement reviewers should not hesitate to question seemingly equivocal language that may cause future interpretive difficulties or challenge phrases that do not appear to describe precisely what they think was intended by the contracting parties. Since practitioners now use word processors to draft contractual documents, it is easy to accommodate additions, deletions, or modifications. Bargainers should never permit opponents to make them feel guilty about changes they think should be made in finally prepared agreements. It is always appropriate for non-drafting parties to be certain that the final language truly reflects what has been achieved through the negotiation process. If the other side repeatedly objects to proposed modifications because of the additional work involved, the participant suggesting the necessary alterations can quickly and effectively silence those protestations by offering to accept responsibility for the final stages of the drafting process. It is amazing how expeditiously these remonstrations cease when such an easy solution to the problem is suggested!

[7]   Tact in Questioning

When negotiators reviewing draft agreements discover apparent discrepancies, they should contact their opponents and politely question the pertinent language. They should not assume deliberate opponent deception. It is always possible that the persons challenging the prepared terminology are mistaken and that the proposed terms actually reflect what was agreed upon. The reviewers may have forgotten modifications quickly accepted near the conclusion of the negotiation process. It is also possible that the drafting parties made honest mistakes that they would be happy to correct once they have examined their notes of the bargaining interaction. Even when document reviewers suspect intentional deception by drafting parties, they should still provide their opponents with a face-saving way out of the predicament. The best way to accomplish the desired result is to assume honest mistakes and give the drafters the opportunity to "correct" the erroneous provisions. If reviewers directly challenged opponent integrity, the dispute would probably escalate and endanger the entire accord.

[8] Vigilance Against Underhanded Tactics

In recent years, a few unscrupulous practitioners in the corporate area have decided to take advantage of the drafting stage of large documents to obtain benefits not attained during the negotiation process. They include provisions that were never agreed upon, or modify or omit terms that were jointly accepted. They attempt to accomplish their deceptive objective by providing their opponents with copies of the agreement at the eleventh hour, hoping that time pressure will induce their unsuspecting adversaries to review the final draft in a cursory manner. Lawyers who encounter this tactic should examine each clause of the draft agreement with care to be certain it represents the actual accord achieved. If necessary, they should completely redraft the improper provisions. If their proposed terms are rejected by opposing counsel, they should insist upon a session with the clients present to determine which draft represents the true intentions of the parties. When this type of meeting is proposed, deceitful drafters are likely to "correct" the "inadvertent misunderstandings" before the clients ever get together. If a client session were to occur and the other side enthusiastically supported the deceptive drafting practices of their attorneys, it would be appropriate for the deceived lawyers to recommend that their client do business with another party.

[9] Writing and Signing Items as Safeguard

A few unscrupulous negotiators attempt to obtain a tactical advantage by deliberately creating "misunderstandings" as final agreements are being drafted. They hope to extract additional concessions from unsuspecting opponents as these seeming ambiguities are being resolved. Individuals who suspect that their adversaries may employ this tactic should insist on a careful review of the basic terms at the conclusion of the bargaining process. They should write out these items and have their opponents sign the draft to indicate their concurrence. This practice makes it difficult for adversaries to later create disingenuous "misunderstandings" that can be used to obtain unreciprocated benefits for their own side.

§ 9.03 USING TIT-FOR-TAT APPROACH TO ENCOURAGE COOPERATIVE BEHAVIOR

Individuals who recognize that competitive/adversarial conduct tends to produce less efficient agreements than cooperative/problem-solving behavior may follow the "tit-for-tat" approach devised by Professor Anatol Rapoport to encourage cooperative, rather than competitive, interactions (Axelrod, 1984). He realized that people who demonstrate a willingness to conduct win-win interactions are more likely to generate win-win responses from opponents than persons who exhibit a propensity for win-lose transactions. To accomplish the desired objective, Professor Rapoport developed some fundamental principles that should be followed by bargainers who wish to encourage cooperative exchanges (Axelrod, 1984, at 109–24; see also Thompson, 2005, at 277–285; Lytle, Brett & Shapiro, 1999).

[1]   Don't Be Envious of Opponent

Negotiators should not judge their own success by how well they think their opponents have done, because they are comparing dissimilar commodities. Rarely do participants on both sides possess equal power and equal skill. The party with greater strength and ability should be able to obtain more favorable results than their weaker adversaries. Nonetheless, if advocates who possess less power get beneficial results for their clients, they should be pleased with their accords. Their terms are not diminished by the fact that their opponents are pleased with what they obtained, nor are they enhanced by the fact their adversaries have done poorly (Murnighan, 1992, at 22–23). If both sides do well, they both win; if both do poorly, they both lose.

[2]   Be Nice at Onset of Interaction

People who want to promote cooperative conduct should make it clear at the outset of an interaction that they do not plan to resort to competitive/adversarial tactics unless they are forced to do so to counteract the competitive/adversarial behavior of their opponents. Since cooperative/problem-solving people tend to bargain in a cooperative fashion with other cooperative participants, this approach will usually induce cooperative/problem-solving opponents to respond in kind. Even marginally competitive/adversarial negotiators may be persuaded to reciprocate cooperative initiatives if they know that competitive/adversarial techniques will be challenged.

[3]   Be Provocable in Response to Uncooperative Conduct

Some cooperative/problem-solving negotiators do not know how to respond to competitive/adversarial styles. They continue to be open and accommodating, and place themselves at a disadvantage. More proficient cooperative/problem-solving individuals, however, realize that overtly competitive behavior must be confronted and dealt with when it occurs. For example, after a "final" agreement has been reached, manipulative opponents may use the "nibble" technique (*see* Chapter 10, *infra*) to steal an item. They may indicate that their client is dissatisfied with a particular term and insist upon a "slight modification" of the accord. Naive persons may be afraid to let the entire deal unravel and concede the requested item. Provocable negotiators would realize that both sides want the final accord and that the other party is not entitled to a unilateral concession at this stage of the interaction. They would thus insist upon a reciprocal concession as a prerequisite to any movement on their part. If the opponents are sincere bargainers, they will acknowledge the propriety of this approach and discuss an appropriate exchange. Disingenuous competitive advocates will realize that they are not going to obtain a modification for nothing, and they will normally insist upon the terms previously agreed upon.

[4]   Be Forgiving

When negotiators encounter improper behavior, they often hold grudges that adversely affect future interactions with the offending persons. Professional bargainers know that these challenges should not be taken personally. They merely respond to inappropriate tactics in a provocable manner, to discourage future repetition, and then return to a cooperative mode. So long as their opponents exhibit cooperative behavior thereafter, they are perfectly willing to forgive the previous transgressions.

[5]   Be Transparent and Establish Clear Reputation

Cooperative negotiators — and even competitive/problem-solving bargainers — who wish to encourage cooperative behavior in others should try to project a cooperative image. They should also make it clear that they will not yield to inappropriate tactics. If opponents know they are cooperative but provocable participants, those individuals will be less likely to resort to inappropriately adversarial conduct. Their opponents will understand that if they employ adversarial techniques, these persons will discover them and take retaliatory action. Their adversaries will also realize that if they behave in a cooperative manner, their problem-solving approach will be reciprocated.

Summary

1. When negotiators reach an agreement during the Closing Stage, they should recognize the possibility that they can enhance their joint gains using the Cooperative/Integrative Stage.

2. The participants should explore alternative formulations that may enable the parties to expand the overall pie and simultaneously increase the benefits obtained by each.

3. The Cooperative/Integrative Stage has a competitive edge, because an opportunistic participant may employ manipulative techniques to seize a disproportionate share of the newly discovered items.

4. Once agreements are reached, the participants should briefly review the terms agreed upon to be certain there are no misunderstandings. They should recognize that at this point — when the parties are psychologically committed to settlement — they are more likely to rectify any discrepancies than at any later point.

5. When mutual accords are achieved, legal representatives should endeavor to draft the final terms, recognizing that they can do a better job of protecting their client interests than opposing counsel.

6. When their opponents draft the final terms, negotiators should carefully review those proposals to be sure the language reflects the joint intentions of the parties, to be certain that nothing not agreed upon has been included, and to ensure that nothing agreed upon has been omitted.

7. Cooperative/problem-solving negotiators may use the "tit-for-tat" approach to encourage opponents to behave in a more cooperative manner.

Chapter 10

NEGOTIATING GAMES/TECHNIQUES

§ 10.01 GENERAL CONSIDERATIONS

[1] Benefits of Acquaintance with Various Techniques

There are a relatively finite number of games or approaches that may be adopted by bargainers. It is thus possible to categorize and explore the various techniques negotiators would be likely to encounter (*see generally* Levinson, Smith & Wilson, 1999). If advocates can acquaint themselves with the commonly used approaches, they can more readily identify the bargaining tactics being used against them and understand the strengths and weaknesses associated with those maneuvers. This facilitates their capacity to counteract them, and it enhances their bargaining confidence and thus improves their chances of achieving beneficial results. Negotiators must also appreciate the different techniques, so they can determine which tactics they should employ to advance their own interests.

It is fairly easy to keep track of the tactics being used by negotiators who either employ one approach most of the time or use different techniques one at a time in sequence. It is more difficult to identify the devices being used by negotiators who employ various maneuvers simultaneously (*e.g.*, "Mutt and Jeff," "Anger," and "Limited Authority"). Participants adopt such a diverse approach to keep their opponents off balance. Their adversaries should carefully monitor and respond to the particular tactics being employed during the various portions of their interaction, so they can most effectively counteract the bargaining games.

Negotiators should become familiar with the commonly used bargaining techniques, so they can readily recognize them when they are introduced by opponents. While some may be employed in isolation, most are used in sequence or in combination. People who become adept at identifying the tactics being used against them are more able to counter those maneuvers than are individuals who lack this important capacity. The succeeding descriptions of the different negotiating approaches should be reviewed occasionally to reacquaint readers with techniques they may have forgotten. During actual bargaining interactions, participants who can successfully identify and deal with most of the negotiation tactics they encounter develop and exude an inner confidence that substantially enhances their innate talents. Not only can perspicacious negotiators minimize or entirely negate the psychological effectiveness of the techniques being employed by opposing parties, but they may adopt effective countermeasures that will enable them to turn the circumstances to their own advantage.

On some occasions, negotiators may counteract opponent tactics by noting the fact they are aware of the techniques being employed and suggesting that these approaches are not working (Kolb & Williams, 2003, at 133–35). If a particular tactic is considered offensive, the affected party may politely indicate that this strategy is actually undermining the discussions (Kolb & Williams, 2003, at 135–141). Once the actor realizes that his or her strategic behavior is not advancing their interests, they will usually consider less disruptive alternatives.

[2]   Intuitive Nature of Negotiating Techniques

People who participate in the negotiation process employ various games and techniques to advance their interests. Some of these tactics are natural extensions of the individuals using them. For example, persons with aggressive personalities may intuitively adopt aggressive negotiating styles, while calm bargainers may use laid-back approaches. Whether negotiators embrace a cooperative/problem-solving, a competitive/adversarial, or a competitive/problem-solving style, they must employ different devices that are designed to advance their positions.

[3]   Aggrandizement of Nonsettlement Options

Seemingly ingenuous comments that disguise ulterior motives are common to almost all negotiations. For instance, advocates may attempt to convince opponents that they possess more beneficial alternatives to nonsettlement than they actually do. The purpose of this tactic is to make the adversaries think they are not under great pressure to reach immediate accords. If their representations in this regard are believed, their bargaining power is meaningfully enhanced. Other advocates may resort to false flattery to soften strong opponents or use feigned weakness or apparent ineptitude to evoke sympathy from their adversaries.

[4]   Dual Messages

Some communications contain dual messages — one seemingly objective and forthright and the other subtle and ulterior (Katz, 2008, at 158–59). For example, a real estate seller might candidly suggest to someone who would apparently like to purchase certain property that he or she could barely afford it "you probably can't afford this house." Even though this overtly "adult"-to-"adult" statement may be objectively correct, the seller does not wish to convince the prospective purchaser of this fact, because that would preclude any sale of the property in question. The ulterior message is surreptitiously conveyed in a "parent"-to-"child" fashion, with the "parent"-seller instructing the "child"-prospective buyer that they cannot do something. If the desired response is precipitated, the prospective purchaser will respond with a child-like "Yes, I can!" (Berne, 1964, at 33–34) If this device functions properly, the salesperson will be able to sell a house to someone who was not planning to select such an expensive property.

Negotiators should normally be suspicious of statements suggesting that a contemplated transaction cannot or should not be consummated. If the transmitters of these messages truly believed this fact, they would not have any reason to participate in the bargaining process. If, despite such communications, the speakers exhibit a desire to engage in further discussions, it is likely that they are endeavoring to shame or subconsciously entrap the unsuspecting respondents into accepting what are probably disadvantageous arrangements.

§ 10.02 COMMON TECHNIQUES

[1] Numerically Superior Bargaining Team

[a] Functions of Extra Bargainers

Most legal negotiations are conducted on a one-on-one basis with a single attorney interacting with a single opponent. In some instances, however, parties attempt to obtain a tactical and psychological advantage by including extra people on their bargaining team. They hope that the additional participants will intimidate their lone adversary. The added participants also make the team more capable of discerning the verbal leaks and nonverbal messages being emitted by that individual (Hodgson, Sano & Graham, 2000, at 25). These extra participants may monitor the signals while one of their partners is speaking. Parties with expanded negotiating teams also think that since a lone opponent has to observe, listen, plan, and speak simultaneously, they can confuse that opponent with excessive verbal and nonverbal stimuli. Furthermore, the additional participants provide their group leader with someone to consult during separate caucuses.

[b] Classroom Tested Advantage

Many of the exercises used in my Legal Negotiating Class are conducted on a two-on-two basis. One of the students is occasionally unable to participate due to illness or personal obligations. In almost every such instance, the lone negotiator finishes in the bottom third of the class. In a number of such cases, that person has been dead last. (See also Thompson, 2007, at 174; Perkins, 1993).

The addition of even a single negotiating partner can significantly diminish the advantage that opponents may derive from an expansive group. Even if the extra person does not speak, he or she can carefully monitor nonverbal clues and verbal messages while his or her co-counsel is more actively interacting with the various opponents. I prefer to have a partner who actively participates in the interaction, because they may see a fleeting opportunity I might miss. If they were unable to speak, this opening would be lost. In addition, when the bargaining groups conduct separate caucus sessions, this team has at least two people who can jointly evaluate recent developments.

[c]   Defense Against Numerical Advantage

When adversaries attempt to overload their bargaining teams in an unconscionable fashion, it would not be inappropriate for someone to refuse to meet with that group until it is reduced to a more manageable size. If such a reduction could not be achieved due to the various constituencies that must be represented on the opposing team, it may be necessary to bring additional people to the sessions to counterbalance the sheer size of that group. It may also be possible to counteract this technique by conducting telephone interactions that decrease the impact of multiple opponents.

[d]   Advantage of Streamlined Team

In rare instances, institutional considerations require opposing bargaining teams to include a number of representatives from diverse constituencies. This is typical of negotiations with labor unions and governmental agencies with different departments. During these interactions, one side may have only two or three representatives, while the opposing team consists of ten, fifteen, or twenty participants. On these occasions, the smaller group may actually enjoy an advantage. Unless the more expansive opposing team members have carefully coordinated their goals and planned a united approach through detailed intra-group negotiations conducted during the Preparation Stage, the members of that group may emit mixed signals that will undermine group solidarity (Brodt & Thompson, 2001, at 212; LePoole, 1991, at 98–101). Individuals dealing with enlarged bargaining groups should not hesitate to employ tactics that are designed to divide and conquer disorganized opponents.

Organizations that must conduct negotiations through expanded group participation may be disadvantaged by a lack of intragroup preparation, and the resulting lack of group cohesiveness. If they lack common objectives and a unified strategy, proficient opponents may exploit their weaknesses. On the other hand, well prepared groups may actually outperform smaller teams if they can take advantage of their capacity to look more carefully for verbal leaks and nonverbal cues emanating from the other side (Brodt & Thompson, 2001, at 211–12). Well coordinated groups can reinforce their common beliefs and their jointly developed objectives.

Larger negotiation groups often behave more competitively, and they are less likely to employ cooperative strategies due to pressure to achieve beneficial group returns (Brodt & Thompson, 2001, at 213). This approach may generate optimal results with respect to distributive interactions that involve such issues as money, but it can create problems when integrative issues are involved. If group dynamics inhibit cooperative bargaining designed to expand the overall pie and enhance joint returns, both sides may suffer from an inability to generate efficient resolutions that may have been achieved through more integrative discussions.

[2] Use of Asymmetrical Time Pressure

[a] Advantage of Knowing Opponent's Deadline for Agreement

During the preliminary stages of an interaction, negotiators occasionally discover the existence of time constraints that affect the other party more than they influence their own side. Japanese bargainers frequently employ this factor to their advantage when they are visited by foreign corporate representatives. They initially ask about the return flight schedule of their guests — ostensibly to allow them to reconfirm those flights. They then use generous hospitality to preclude the commencement of substantive discussions until a few days before their visitors are planning to return home. The Japanese negotiators recognize that their foreign agents do not want to return home without agreements. This forces those visitors to consider extra, last-minute concessions in an effort to achieve final accords while they are still in Japan. Similar tactics are often employed by insurance company representatives who determine that plaintiffs are overly eager to settle their cases to avoid the two or three year wait for trial dates and to allow them get on with their lives. By exuding unlimited patience, these insurance lawyers are often able to convince plaintiff-attorneys that they have to make greater concessions if accords are to be achieved within the time-frames that have been artificially established by the plaintiffs (LePoole, 1991, at 104–05).

[b] Maintaining Confidentiality of Internal Deadlines

Whenever possible, negotiators should try to withhold information that might suggest the existence of an asymmetrical time constraint (Dawson, 2001, at 174). For example, individuals traveling to another country to discuss a possible business venture should refrain from booking a definite return flight. When their hosts ask them when they plan to return home, they should reply that they are prepared to remain as long as it takes to fully explore the possibility of a mutually beneficial relationship. If they can exhibit a calm patience, they can increase the likelihood of achieving an expeditious and beneficial agreement. Attorneys whose clients have established artificially abbreviated time-frames should similarly attempt to keep that information confidential. They should also inform their clients how much bargaining leverage they will lose if they are unwilling to wait until an impending trial date induces parsimonious opponents to increase their offers. If they can convince their opponents that they are not being influenced by the time factor, they can substantially enhance their bargaining posture.

[c] Considering Effect of Time Pressure on Both Sides

Negotiators feeling time pressure frequently fail to appreciate the time pressure affecting the opposing side, and they thus concede the time advantage to their adversaries (Dawson, 2001, at 174–75, 190–91). They must remember that clients always impose real and artificial time constraints. Individual clients regularly telephone their attorneys for progress reports, and corporate and government agency officials make similar requests. By acknowledging the fact that time pressure affects *both* sides, negotiators can diminish the impact of this factor on themselves.

[d]   Disclosing Internal Deadlines to Preempt Issue

When transactional bargainers have certain deadlines that must be met and their opponents are not operating under a similar constraint, they may take preemptive action to neutralize the time factor. They can announce at the beginning of discussions that everything must be concluded by their deadline if a mutual accord is to be achieved (Freund, 1992, at 148–49). Through this approach, they can impose their time constraint on their adversaries and deprive them of the opportunity to use this factor to their advantage. Negotiators should only make statements of this kind when they truly have deadlines that must be satisfied if agreements are to be attained, since a misrepresentation regarding this issue could easily preclude agreement and destroy the deceitful person's future credibility.

[e]   Deadlines Generate Concessions

I am frequently asked how negotiators can induce opponents to make generous offers early in the bargaining process. In most cases, they cannot do so. It is the immediacy of deadlines that generates action (Cohen, 2003, at 75–77). Most bargainers only begin to feel pressure to compromise when they see a deadline looming in the immediate future. It thus behooves participants to be patient during the early stages, lest they concede too much during the early part of the interaction. As a deadline approaches, both parties will feel pressure, and they should move simultaneously toward closure.

[3]   Extreme Initial Demands/Offers

[a]   Inducing Opponents to Reconsider Their Own Positions

Empirical studies have demonstrated that people who enter negotiations with high aspiration levels generally obtain more beneficial results than those who begin with less generous expectations. It thus behooves bargainers to commence their interactions with high demands or low offers (Dawson, 2001, at 13–18; Kritzer, 1991, at 54, 78–79). Bargainers who can rationally defend their seemingly excessive opening demands or apparently parsimonious offers may be able to induce careless adversaries to reconsider their own preliminary assessments (Katz, 2008, at 148–150). Once those individuals begin to doubt the propriety of their own positions, they are in trouble. They may even lose touch with reality and accept the skewed representations being advanced by their avaricious opponents.

[b]   Need to Maintain Credibility

Individuals who are formulating initial demands/offers should not to make them so obviously unreasonable that they cannot be rationally defended. Clearly absurd opening demands/offers will suffer from a lack of legitimacy, and may create unintended difficulties. If the recipients of outlandish proposals conclude that the matters in dispute cannot reasonably be resolved through the negotiation process, they may terminate the present discussions. Even when interactions are not discontinued, the participants who articulated the extreme positions may find it impossible to make the necessary concessions in an orderly manner. They may thus be forced to make large, irrational position changes, causing a concomitant loss of control.

[c]   Responding Appropriately

Persons confronted by truly unreasonable initial demands/offers should not casually indicate their displeasure with those positions, because this response may lead their opponents to think that their demands/offers are not wholly unrealistic. This may induce those people to raise their aspiration levels in a way that would be likely to generate nonsettlements. Recipients of outrageous opening demands/offers should immediately and unequivocally express their displeasure with those positions, to disabuse the offerors of any thought their entreaties are not absurd. For example: "You know and I know how utterly unrealistic your position is. If that is the area you wish to explore, we have nothing to discuss." Individuals who begin with extreme positions are often unsure of their situations. To protect themselves, they start with what they suspect are unreasonable proposals. They expect their opponents to react with disapproval, and actually feel better when their adversaries do so. This confirms their preliminary view that their starting positions were excessive, and allows them to place greater faith in their preliminary assessments.

Once the recipients of extreme offers have indicated how unrealistic those positions are, they may respond in one of several ways:

(1) They may indicate that they do not plan to articulate their own initial offer until the other side sets forth a reasonable position. The primary difficulty with this approach is the fact it requires the unreasonable participants to "bid against themselves" — *i.e.*, to make consecutive concessions. Proficient negotiators are loathe to make unreciprocated position changes, and would be unlikely to make a series of opening concessions as a prerequisite to opponent participation in the process.

(2) Some individuals counter extreme demands/offers with their own outlandish initial positions. When challenged by their opponents, they indicate that their initial offer is no more unreasonable than that of the other side. They can then use the promise technique and suggest their willingness to provide a realistic offer, *if* their opponent articulates a credible position. Such "attitudinal bargaining" is always an appropriate way to induce unreasonable adversaries to contemplate more realistic opening entreaties.

(3) A few negotiators try to ignore unreasonable opening offers by opponents and articulate realistic offers of their own, hoping to embarrass their adversaries into more accommodating behavior. This approach may create unanticipated difficulties if their adversaries do not modify their initial positions. After a number of concessions have been made by both sides, the party that started with the extreme position is likely to emphasize how far it has moved compared to the side that began with a reasonable figure. In many instances, the persons who started with realistic positions are likely to pay more or accept less than they should, because of the guilt they experience when they attempt to induce their unreasonable opponents to make concessions on a ten- or twenty-to-one basis throughout the entire interaction.

[4]   Use of Probing Questions

Negotiators confronted by wholly unreasonable positions may generate a more flexible atmosphere through the use of probing questions (Katz, 2008, at 167–68; Mayer, 1996, at 68). Instead of directly challenging those positions — a tactic that would probably cause the other side to become more resolute — they separate the different items into definitive components. They then propound a series of questions —

beginning with the more finite items that do not lend themselves to excessive puffing — designed to force the opponents to reassess each aspect of their offer. For example, if a participant in a corporate buy out were to make a wholly unrealistic offer or demand, the recipient could ask that person how much he or she allotted for the real property. If the questioner receives a realistic response, he or she writes it down and goes on to the next item. If the figure mentioned is unreasonably high or low, the questioner may cite a recent appraisal and ask how the respondent calculated his or her figure. Once a realistic amount is obtained for this term, the questioner moves on to the proposed figures for the building and equipment, the inventory, the accounts receivable, the patent, trade, or copy rights, the corporate good will, and other relevant considerations.

If these inquiries are carefully formulated in a relatively neutral and nonjudgmental manner, they may induce the other side to examine the partisan bases underlying their position statement. As each component is addressed, the opponents must either articulate rational explanations or begin to recognize the lack of any sound foundation for that aspect of their offer. When adversaries do not respond thoughtfully to queries that are posed, they should be reframed and asked again. When this process is finished and the different amounts are totaled, the sum is usually four or five times what was originally offered or one-fourth or one-fifth what was initially demanded. This is due to the fact that negotiators who begin with truly unrealistic offers have made them up and have no idea how to defend them on a component-by-component basis.

[5] Boulwareism

[a] Origin

This technique derives its name from Lemuel Boulware, a former Vice President for Labor Relations at General Electric. Mr. Boulware was not enamored of traditional "auction" bargaining that involved the use of extreme initial positions, the making of time-consuming concessions, and the achievement of final collective bargaining agreements similar to those the parties initially knew they would reach. He thus decided to determine ahead of time what the company was willing to commit to wage and benefit increases. He surveyed the employees to ascertain the areas in which they wanted the increases to be granted, and formulated a complete "best-offer-first" package. This was presented to union negotiators on a "take-it-or-leave-it" basis. He informed the labor representatives that the company would only modify its initial offer if they could convince it that some miscalculation had been made or changed circumstances had occurred. This approach precipitated a costly work stoppage and resulted in protracted unfair labor practice litigation.

[b] Potential Risks

The term "Boulwareism" is now associated with *best-offer-first* (offeror's perspective) or *take-it-or-leave-it* (offeree's perspective) bargaining (Katz, 2008, at 129–131; Adler & Silverstein, 2000, at 97–98). The people who employ this approach most frequently in the legal context are insurance adjusters and defense lawyers for insurance companies. They endeavor to establish reputations as people who make one firm, fair offer. If that proposal is not accepted by plaintiff-counsel, they plan to go to trial. A few individuals are able to employ this technique effectively. They make reasonable offers in a relatively nonthreatening manner, and many of their firm offers are accepted. On the other hand, individuals using Boulwareistic tactics must recognize that this approach may actually cost their insurance clients money. Had they been willing to engage in more conventional auction bargaining, they may have been able to settle cases for less than they were initially willing to pay. In addition, they may have avoided the rejection of what might otherwise have been acceptable agreements — but were rejected because of the patronizing way in which they were presented.

Rarely can the representatives on one side definitively determine the true value of an impending bargaining transaction *before* they meet with their opponents. No matter how thoroughly they review the information preliminarily available to them, they must remember that it is impossible to ascertain the real value of a prospective deal prior to discussions with the people representing the other side. Only through these inter-party exchanges can they learn how much their adversaries desire an agreement. They must assess how risk-averse their opponents are, and the degree to which time pressure may be influencing those people. Without such critical information, it is not possible to calculate accurately what is truly required to satisfy opponent needs and interests. If insurance company attorneys willing to pay $50,000 begin the negotiation process with an offer of $20,000 or $25,000 and become difficult once they get to the $40,000 to $45,000 range, they may be able to resolve the claim for $42,000 or $43,000 — saving their client $7,000 or $8,000! Moreover, the plaintiff-representatives would probably be more satisfied with the $42,000 or $43,000 obtained through the auction process than with the $50,000 offered in a Boulwareistic fashion.

[c] Affront to Opponents

Negotiators should also be extremely hesitant to adopt a Boulwareistic approach because of the impact of this tactic on opponents. It exudes a paternalistic arrogance, with offerors effectively informing offerees, in a "parent"-to-"child" interaction, that they know what is best for both sides. Few lawyers are willing to defer so readily to the superior knowledge of opposing counsel. This technique also deprives opponents of the opportunity to participate meaningfully in the bargaining process. Even if plaintiff-attorneys would initially have been pleased to resolve their case for $50,000, they may not be satisfied with a take-it-or-leave-it first offer of $50,000. Plaintiff-counsel want to explore the case through the Information Stage and to exhibit their negotiating skill through the Competitive/Distributive and the Closing Stages. When the process has been completed, they want to think that their own personal ability influenced the final outcome. This permits them to explain to their client how the insurance carrier opened with an unacceptably low offer, but they were able to achieve a more generous final result.

[d] Be Generous With Negotiation Process

People contemplating the use of Boulwareism must realize that this approach may only be employed effectively by negotiators who possess significant power. If weak participants attempt to use this technique, their take-it-or-leave-it demands are likely to be unceremoniously rejected. When bargainers enjoy a clear strength advantage, there is no reason to use this approach — except to avoid the need to engage in any real give-and-take negotiating. The more power negotiators have, the more generous they should be with *process* — not substance. They should permit opponents to participate meaningfully in the interaction and let them think they influenced the outcome. Studies have shown that individuals who believe that the negotiation *process* has been fair are more satisfied with objectively less beneficial terms than are persons who obtain objectively better terms through a process they did not believe to be fair (Cohen, 2008, at 542; Hollander-Blumoff & Tyler, 2008, at 489–93). The use of more traditional auction bargaining techniques increases the likelihood the parties will reach mutual accords. It simultaneously provides advocates employing conventional negotiating tactics with the opportunity to achieve final terms that are better from their own side's perspective than they were initially willing to offer.

[e]   Objectively Evaluate "Take it or Leave It" Positions

Very few people can evaluate an unabashed take-it-or-leave-it offer on the merits alone. This approach is a direct affront to their right to participate in the process on an "adult"-to-"adult" level, and deprives them of the opportunity to influence the outcome. I have talked with various lawyers who admitted that they have rejected Boulwareistic offers merely to demonstrate to offensive opponents that they cannot be treated in such an arrogant fashion. Nonetheless, recipients of Boulwareistic offers should attempt to evaluate the propriety of those proposals in a detached fashion that is unaffected by the offensive manner in which they have been presented. If the offers constitute truly reasonable proposals and they are certain they are not going to obtain more beneficial proposals, they should recommend them to their clients.

[6]   Settlement Brochures

[a]   Purpose, Method, and Common Practice Areas of Usage

Some legal advocates, particularly in the personal injury field, attempt to enhance their bargaining posture through the preparation of pre-negotiation settlement brochures. These consist of written documents that specifically articulate the factual and legal bases for the claims being asserted, and describe the full extent of plaintiff injuries. Each item for which monetary relief is being sought is separately listed and explained in an attempt to establish highly "principled" opening demands (Steinberg, 1998, at 70–71). When available, photographs depicting the accident scene and/or the injuries sustained by plaintiffs are included in an effort to evoke guilt and sympathy. Video replays may be employed to recreate the relevant events or to demonstrate pre- and post- accident plaintiff capabilities.

Transactional negotiators who represent corporate clients frequently employ settlement brochures without realizing it. They formulate detailed opening positions in writing that carefully explain the way in which they have valued the various items to be exchanged. Labor and management representatives also use this technique when they bargain with each other. It can be a particularly effective approach, if it induces opponents to afford these documents more respect than they objectively warrant.

[b]   Effectiveness

Settlement brochures may subconsciously be accorded greater respect than would verbal recitations, due to the aura of legitimacy associated with printed documents. The use of this technique may bolster the confidence of plaintiff-attorneys, and may enable them to seize control of the negotiating agenda at the outset of the bargaining process. Although some lawyers do not provide opponents with copies of settlement brochures until their first formal meeting, others have them delivered several days in advance of initial sessions to enable their opponents to review these documents before they meet.

[c]   Defense

Individuals who are presented with settlement brochures should be careful not to accord them greater respect than they deserve. The recipients should treat the factual and legal representations set forth in those documents as they would identical verbal statements. While few attorneys would think of making deliberate factual or legal misrepresentations in writing, most would not hesitate to engage in "puffing" or "embellishment." If recipients are provided with these instruments before the first bargaining session, they should thoroughly review the assertions made by their opponents and prepare effective counter arguments that they can express during their negotiation discussions. They should be cautious not to allow their adversaries to use their settlement brochures to control the agenda of their interaction.

Advocates who prepare settlement brochures frequently use charts, tables, or graphs to depict likely *future* consequences for which compensation is being sought. These may include lost earnings, future medical expenses, and/or continuing pain and suffering. Individuals presented with these claims should carefully review the assumptions underlying those projections. Has plaintiff-counsel assumed that an eighth-grade dropout working part-time at a fast-food restaurant for $9.00 per hour was planning to return to school and become a brain surgeon with future annual earnings of $500,000? Have they assumed annual pay raises of 10%, when recent annual increases have been in the 3–4% range? Have they assumed an excessive inflation rate with respect to future medical expenses? Once these underlying assumptions are accepted, the brochure presentations logically follow. This is why the basic assumptions must be perused.

Some defense counsel counter plaintiff settlement brochures with brochures of their own. After they receive written position statements, they prepare their own counter arguments explaining the reasons for limited or nonexistent liability and describing the limited damages involved. They are thus able to counteract the impact of plaintiff brochures with their own equally forceful written position statements. If they are persuasive, they may even be able to induce plaintiff-lawyers to approach the verbal discussions from the perspective of their agendas.

[7]   Multiple/Equal Value Offers

[a]   Purpose and Method

When multiple issue negotiations are involved, some participants attempt to disclose their own relative item values and elicit similar information regarding their opponents through the use of multiple/equal value offers (Malhotra & Bazerman, 2007, at 100–01; Lax & Sebenius, 2006, at 209–10; Medvec & Galinsky, 2005; Dietmeyer & Kaplan, 2004, at 131–41). They formulate several different offers that vary what they are seeking and what they are willing to give the other side. These diverse offers have a common theme. Each one provides the offeror with a relatively equal level of satisfaction. People who use this technique hope to let the other side understand the different amounts of the various items they must obtain to create equal client satisfaction.

Multiple/equal value offerors hope to induce their opponents to let them know which of these diverse offers is preferable from their perspective. They want their adversaries to indicate in their counter-offers the terms they prefer to obtain and the issues they are willing to concede to the initial offerors. The parties can then work to generate efficient agreements that maximize the joint returns achieved by the bargaining parties.

[b] Effectiveness

When employed carefully with trustworthy opponents, this approach allows the offerors to let the opposing side know which term combinations they value equally. The offerors thus disclose the relative priorities associated with their underlying needs and interests. They hope their adversaries will share their underlying priorities through their critiques of the initial offers and their own counter-offers.

As the parties explore their respective bundled offers and counter-offers, they can discard less efficient formulations, and focus on the mutually beneficial packages. If the use of multiple/equal value offers is to function effectively, the negotiating participants must indicate, with some degree of candor, which items are essential, important, and desirable, and how much of each they hope to obtain. This allows each side to appreciate the other's basic interests and encourages the development of mutually beneficial accords.

[c] Potential Risks

Parties initiating the use of multiple/equal value offers are counting on reciprocal candor from the other side. The offerors have to a significant degree disclosed their relative values. If the other side counters with manipulative and disingenuous offers designed to exploit the original offerors' openness, it may be able to claim an excessive share of the joint value created.

A second risk concerns the articulation of an excessive number of package offers. Individuals who are presented with two, three, or even four options usually do a good job of determining which alternative is preferable. On the other hand, persons presented with a greater number of options often become confused. They fail to evaluate all of the options together, but instead make comparisons among finite groups (*see generally* Schwartz, 2004). As a result, even though Package 2 may be optimal, one side may only compare Packages 3, 4, and 5 and select the preferable one of these. They fail to compare the one picked with Package 2 and end up with an inferior choice. It thus behooves negotiators using multiple/equal value offers to limit the number articulated at one time to a manageable number the recipients can assess together. This is especially important when many items are involved and offer recipients must compare expansive packages with one another. Offerors who suspect that the "paradox of choice" may be affecting the assessments of offer recipients may minimize this phenomenon by asking those parties if they have compared the offer they said they preferred with all of the other packages which have been tendered.

[8] Contingent Concessions

[a] Purpose and Method

When negotiators begin to find it difficult to make additional position changes, the discussions may approach an impasse. Each side is afraid to make a concession, fearing that its position change will not be matched by the other side. One way to get past this fear is to suggest a concession that is conditioned upon an equal value position change by the other party (Malhotra & Bazerman, 2007, at 66–71). For example, one side may be demanding $27 million for its company, while the other is offering $23 million. It may have taken a number of interactions to get the parties this close together. Neither seems willing to move. The prospective buyer may indicate that it would be willing to increase its offer to $24 million if the prospective seller could come down to $26 million. If this conditional concession is accepted, the $4 million gap is reduced to $2 million.

[b]   Effectiveness

If the party receiving the contingent concession recognizes the face-saving way for the two sides to move closer together, it may accede to the offeror's suggestion. Once the parties are only $2 million apart, one may make another position change, or another contingent concession might be proposed to bring the parties even closer together. As their respective positions begin to merge, the likelihood of agreement increases dramatically.

The use of a contingent concession provides a face-saving way for temporarily recalcitrant parties to move together. If either made a concession and it was not reciprocated, that side would feel embarrassed and angry. When the two sides agree to make simultaneous position changes, neither appears weak in the eyes of the other. In addition, neither is afraid of making an unreciprocated position change.

[c]   Potential Risks

The first risk associated with contingent concession offers concerns the fact the conditional position change may be rejected. Although the offeror will then remain at her current position, this technique clearly signals to the other side the willingness of this party to change its position. A more recalcitrant opponent may use this information to get the initial offeror to ultimately make a unilateral position change. To avoid this likelihood, the party offering a contingent concession should indicate her hesitancy to make another position change. She could acknowledge the likelihood that the other side is experiencing similar feelings. She can then suggest contingent concessions as a way for both sides to move closer together.

The second risk associated with contingent concessions concerns the fact that parties making such concessions tend to move toward the mid-point between their present positions. One side may have already conceded more than it should have, and it may be completely unwilling to achieve agreement by splitting the difference. This difficulty can be addressed by this party suggesting an unwillingness to make equal contingent concessions — but a willingness to make a position change that is one-half of the position change being offered by the other side. This party should carefully indicate why he believes that it would inappropriate for him to match the offeror's suggested concession. He might point to prior concessions he has already made, and indicate that he is not in a position to match the exact size of the proposed joint concessions. This approach might enable him to move up $1/2 million in response to the offeror's willingness to come down $1 million. If this suggestion is accepted, the parties can continue to use similar position changes to move toward agreement.

[9]   Range Offers

[a]   Message Communicated

Negotiators occasionally phrase their monetary offers in terms of a range rather than as a single figure — *e.g.*, "we would expect something in the $10,000, 15,000, or 20,000 area." This approach frequently indicates uncertainty in the mind of the offeror.

A more carefully prepared individual would have determined the precise number to be mentioned. Advocates who hope to establish a conciliatory bargaining atmosphere may use range offers to evidence their receptivity to compromise. Recipients of range offers should focus on the most beneficial end of the spectrum — *i.e.*, plaintiff attorneys should discuss the $20,000 figure, while defense counsel should explore the $10,000 demand.

[b]   Drawbacks

Advocates should usually avoid range offers, since this approach tends to undermine the persuasiveness of their presentations. When they make "principled" opening offers, the figures provided should be definitive, based on the underlying rationales provided. When "principled" concessions are articulated, they should be similarly related to the precise explanations given for those particular position changes.

[10]   Limited Client Authority

[a]   Deciphering Truthfulness

Many advocates like to indicate during the preliminary stages of a negotiation that they do not possess final authority from their clients regarding the matters in dispute (Katz, 2008, at 124–26; Adler & Silverstein, 2000, at 98–100). Some people who possess real authority employ this technique to reserve the right to check with their absent clients and reassess the terms agreed upon before tentative agreements formally bind their side. Other negotiators really do have constituencies that must ultimately approve preliminary accords before they become operative. For example, labor organizations must generally have collective contracts ratified by members. Representatives of municipal, state, and federal government entities must usually obtain legislative or departmental approval before their agreements become effective.

[b]   Fundamental Advantage

The advantage of a limited authority approach — whether actual or fabricated — is that it permits the participants using this device to obtain psychological commitments from opponents who are authorized to make binding commitments on behalf of their clients. The unbound bargainers can thereafter seek beneficial modifications of negotiated contracts based upon "unexpected" client demands. Once opponents became familiar with this tactic, they begin to hold back some of the items they were initially prepared to commit. This allows them to increase their final offers after the first contracts are rejected by their opponents. As it becomes apparent to individuals who use limited authority to obtain additional concessions at the end of transactions that their adversaries are effectively countering this approach, they begin to recognize the futility of this technique.

[c]   Defense

Bargainers who encounter opponents who initially indicate that they lack the authority to bind their clients frequently find it advantageous to state that they similarly lack final client authority over the issues being discussed. This permits them to "check" with their own absent principals before they make final commitments. If they are unable to claim limited authority of their own, they may alternatively refuse to bargain with agents who do not possess a meaningful degree of final control.

An opponent's alleged lack of client authority may occasionally be an impediment to a final agreement. That person may have specifically indicated that he or she is not empowered to accept a certain offer that is really within the scope of his or her actual authorized limits. It is rarely helpful to directly challenge that person with respect to this issue, because they are unlikely to admit overt prevarication. It is far more productive to provide that individual with a face-saving escape. By suggesting that they privately contact the client and request permission to agree to the offer on the table, a final accord may be achieved without the need for unnecessary accusations or recriminations. This approach best serves client interests by maximizing the likelihood of an ultimate settlement.

[d]   Problems with Usage

Advocates who disingenuously inform opponents that they have limited authority and must obtain client approval before agreements are final may occasionally find themselves with a dilemma. They have achieved outstanding terms and fear that their adversaries may reconsider their circumstances and reopen the negotiations prior to the perfection of mutually binding commitments. To deprive their opponents of the opportunity to reflect on the provisions that have been tentatively agreed upon, these advocates can ask for a brief recess prior to the conclusion of the current talks to enable them to "consult with their absent clients." They can then return to the bargaining table with client acceptance and procure binding commitments from their adversaries.

[11]   Lack of Client Authority

Negotiators occasionally receive telephone calls from opponent agents who would like to know their thoughts on the issues at hand. The caller asks what the recipient hopes to achieve from the impending interaction. When these targets openly disclose their initial positions, they are told that the suggested terms are outrageous and wholly unacceptable. The callers even indicate that they could not possible convey those proposals to their superiors. This device is designed to make naive respondents feel guilty about their "extreme demands" and induce them to unilaterally modify their opening offers to the benefit of their adversaries.

It is impossible to bargain meaningfully with people who lack the authority to speak for their own clients. The participants who possess real client authority can only bid against themselves by articulating consecutive opening offers. When unauthorized opponents telephone, it is apparent that they do not plan to conduct serious negotiations. They hope to obtain several concessions as a prerequisite to participation by the people on their side. Negotiators should not succumb to this approach. If they are willing to do so, they should disclose their initial offers. When the unauthorized callers criticize their position statements, the call recipients should ask the callers to state their own positions. If they indicate that they lack the authority to do so, they should be told to get some authority and to state their own positions to enable the participants to discuss their respective positions. If they indicate that they cannot get such authority, they should be instructed to have someone with actual authority contact the call recipients with offers from their side. Only when the representatives of both parties possess the authority to articulate meaningful offers can real bargaining occur.

[12]   Flinch/Krunch

When negotiators receive opening offers from the other side, they can often generate consecutive opening offers through the use of the Flinch or Krunch (Thomas, 2005, at 86–100; Dawson, 2001, at 29–32). As soon as they receive the opposing party's offer, they work to generate unreciprocated opening offers. Sometimes they say nothing. They simply look disappointed in the clearly inadequate opening offer. On other occasions, they orally indicate their disappointment in such a parsimonious opening. They hope to induce the party who initiated the bargaining process to bid against himself or herself.

If their initial Flinch/Krunch is effective and they receive another opening offer, they can continue this tactic to induce additional unreciprocated position changes. They can indicate that the new offer is "a step in the right direction" but still insufficient. If they are effective, they may generate three or four opening offers from the opposing side before they have to articulate any position of their own.

The Flinch/Krunch can be an especially effective technique when employed by individuals who can appear to be sincerely shocked by the inadequacy of the other party's initial position. If the users of this tactic seem to be disingenuously attempting to take advantage of naive opponents, they may create hostility and a negative reaction.

What should someone do if their opening offer is countered by a Flinch/Krunch? They should be careful not to bid against themselves by announcing another offer. They could remain silent and look to the other side to articulate its opening position. They could also ask that party if they are contemplating an opening offer of their own or ask them what they think would be the appropriate price.

The Flinch/Krunch does not have to be confined to opening offers. When opponents make concessions, this tactic can be employed to suggest the obvious inadequacy of their concessions. The concession recipients may again remain silent hoping to induce the other side to bid against themselves, or they may orally indicate their disappointment with the small position change. If they use this technique adroitly, they may be able to generate consecutive concessions frequently during their bargaining interactions. This should enable them to achieve final results that favor their own side.

Individuals who make concessions should be certain not to permit use of the Flinch/Krunch to induce them to bid against themselves. They should not announce additional concessions until they have received reciprocity from the other side. When the opposing party shows no indication of a willingness to change their current position, they should make it expressly clear that no further position changes will be forthcoming without reciprocal movement from the other side.

[13]   "Nibble" Technique

[a]   Method

Some negotiators "agree" to final accords with apparent client authority. Their opponents are pleased with the agreements and contact their clients to give them the good news. Several days later, these bargainers contact their opponents with seeming embarrassment and explain that they did not really possess full authority to bind their clients. They sheepishly indicate that their principals are dissatisfied with what was negotiated and require several additional concessions before they will accept the other terms of the agreements (Katz, 2008, at 140–41; Thompson, 2005, at 103–109; Latz,

2004, at 207). Since the unsuspecting opponents and their clients are now psychologically committed to final settlements and do not want to permit these items to negate their previous efforts, they normally agree to the requested modifications. This "nibble" technique is frequently employed by car salespeople who induce prospective buyers to agree to pay a certain amount for a particular automobile. The salesperson thereafter checks with the "sales manager" — who may not even exist — and contritely informs the psychologically committed customers that several hundred additional dollars are required to consummate the sales transaction. It is amazing how frequently this tactic is successfully employed (G. Karrass, 1985, at 109–110).

[b]   Defense

Individuals who are challenged by "nibbler" opponents often make the mistake of focusing entirely on the desire of their *own* side to preserve the final accords previously reached. They are afraid to let their agreements fall through over the changes being sought. They fail to direct their attention to the *opposing parties*. If they were to ask themselves whether their *opponents* would be willing to forego the agreements reached over these items, they would realize that those people also want to retain the terms already agreed upon. If they did not have that similar objective, they would not have participated in the antecedent negotiations. Persons who are asked for additional concessions to cement deals must not be afraid to demand reciprocity for the requested position changes.

When negotiators suspect that they are interacting with opponents who may try to use disingenuous client disgruntlement to obtain post-agreement concessions, they should mentally select the particular terms they would like to have modified in their favor. When their adversaries request the anticipated changes, they can indicate how relieved they are to address this matter, because of the dissatisfaction of their own clients regarding other provisions agreed upon. If their opponents are acting in good faith and are sincerely upset about the topics raised, they will acknowledge the need for reciprocity and address the proposed exchanges. On the other hand, individuals who are disingenuously using the "nibble" technique to "steal" items will be reluctant to do so. They will usually reject further discussions and insist upon the terms that were initially agreed upon! When "nibblers" put their hands in your pocket in an effort to pick it, you should remember to reach into *their* pocket to extract reciprocal benefits.

[14]   Decreasing Offers/Increasing Demands and Limited Time Offers

During the preliminary stages of some law suits — particularly those of relatively modest value — a few attorneys make fairly realistic offers or demands that they say must be accepted by specified dates (Katz, 2008, at 139–140). They make it clear that if their proposed terms are not accepted in a timely manner, they will either withdraw those offers entirely or begin to reduce the amounts being offered or increase the amounts being demanded (Freund, 1992, at 79–81). This technique is usually based on the fact that the proposers will have to expend time and money preparing for trial if their initial terms are not accepted. They thus plan to revoke their earlier offers and get ready for trial or to decrease subsequent offers or increase subsequent demands in proportion to their increased litigation expenses.

Negotiators who employ this approach should establish reputations as people who carry out their stated intentions and carefully apprise opponents of their exact intentions in this regard. This maximizes the likelihood that their initial proposals will be accepted, and it minimizes the possibility of misunderstanding. Unexpected intervening developments aside, it is assumed that offers will remain on the table once they are made and that subsequent position statements will not be less generous than earlier offers. If bargainers inexplicably withdraw or reduce outstanding offers without previously informing opponents of this possibility or providing valid explanations based on new information, their action is likely to provoke hostility and claims of unethical conduct. It will also generate nonsettlements in situations in which agreements might otherwise have been achieved.

[15]   Real or Feigned Anger

[a]   Purpose

Resort to real or feigned anger during the critical stages of a negotiation may effectively convince opponents of the seriousness of one's position (Katz, 2008, at 150–151). It may also intimidate adversaries and convince them of the need to make concessions if the bargaining process is to continue (Adler & Silverstein, 2000, at 95–96). Empirical evidence indicates that negotiators facing angry opponents tend to lower their expectations and make more generous concessions (Van Kleef, De Dreu & Manstead, 2004).

Although true anger is occasionally displayed during bargaining encounters, proficient negotiators almost never lose their tempers. They use carefully orchestrated anger that is designed to intimidate anxious opponents. I have seen collective bargaining agents shout, swear, pound the table, and walk out. As soon as they enter their side's private caucus room, they calmly ask: "Wasn't I more believable than last year?"

[b]   Danger of Real Anger

The use of real anger can be dangerous, because people who permit bargaining frustration and anxiety to precipitate unplanned diatribes frequently disclose more information during their outbursts than they intended. For example, a defendant-lawyer who has offered $75,000 to a plaintiff-attorney who is steadfastly demanding $150,000 might finally explode with a statement indicating that "this case cannot be resolved for more $100,000!" This exclamation would strongly suggest to plaintiff-counsel that the defendant insurance company is presently willing to pay $100,000, but little above that figure. This is critical information, because it provides the plaintiff-lawyer with a good approximation of the defendant's resistance point. If the plaintiff-attorney was hoping to achieve a result in excess of $100,000, he or she should realize that this result is unlikely during the current negotiations. It may thus be necessary to plan subsequent discussions, with the expectation that greater time pressure may ultimately induce the defendant insurer to reconsider its current upper limit.

[c]   Care in Usage of Feigned Anger

Individuals who wish to employ feigned anger to advance their position should plan their tactic with care. They should decide which words would be most likely to influence their opponent's assessment of the transaction, and try to limit their apparent outburst to those comments. They should simultaneously watch for signs of increased frustration and anxiety on the part of their adversary (e.g., clenched teeth, wringing of hands, or placing of open hands in front of self as defensive measure against the verbal onslaught), to be certain not to provoke an unintended reaction such as the cessation of talks.

[d]   Defense

People who find themselves berated by an angry opponent may be tempted to respond with their own retaliatory diatribe to convince their adversary that they cannot be intimidated by such irrational tactics. This quid pro quo approach involves obvious risks. At a minimum, the vituperative exchange would probably have a deleterious impact upon the bargaining atmosphere. It may even cause a cessation of meaningful discussions and force the participants to resort to their nonsettlement alternatives. While this response may be appropriate to counteract the conduct of an unreasonably angry opponent or an aggressive bully, there is a more productive way to react to contrived opponent anger. The targets of these outbursts should remain silent and listen intently for inadvertent verbal leaks and watch for informative nonverbal signals. They should look at their raging opponents as if they are behaving like petulant children. Their quiet styles may disconcert manipulative adversaries who are using feigned anger to advance their cause (Shapiro & Jankowski, 2001, at 178).

Negotiators with sincere demeanors may effectively counter angry eruptions by indicating that they have been personally offended by the ad hominem attack. They should indicate that they cannot understand how their reasonable and fair approach can be subject to such an intemperate challenge. They may recite several of their most recent position changes to demonstrate their sincere efforts to accommodate opponent needs. If they are successful in this regard, they may create feelings of guilt and embarrassment in the attacking party. This technique may even shame that person into a conciliatory concession.

[16]   Aggressive Behavior

[a]   Beneficial Impact

Aggressive behavior is usually intended to have an impact similar to that associated with real or feigned anger (Katz, 2008, at 146–48). It is supposed to convince opponents of the seriousness of one's position. It can also be used by anxious individuals to maintain control of the bargaining agenda. By being overly assertive, aggressive negotiators may be able to dominate the interaction. This technique is most effectively employed by naturally aggressive individuals. Less assertive persons who try to adopt an uncharacteristically aggressive approach do not feel comfortable with this style, and they are often unable to project a credible image.

Some highly combative negotiators attempt to augment their aggressive style with gratuitous sarcasm. Their goal is to make their opponents feel so uncomfortable that they will be induced to make excessive concessions in an effort to end their unpleasant interaction. I once worked with such an individual. He was constantly insulting and belittling those around him. Although his tactics caused many adversaries to break off settlement talks in circumstances in which accords might otherwise have been achieved, there were numerous occasions when he was able to obtain beneficial results from opponents who wanted to conclude the interactions quickly to avoid further contact with this abrasive person. Individuals who use this approach risk needless nonsettlements from opponents who refuse to tolerate their offensive behavior. They also tend to generate accords that are not as efficient as the ones they may have achieved if the parties had developed more cordial and trusting relationships.

[b]   Importance of Monitoring Opponent Responses

Aggressive negotiators, particularly those who use abrasive tactics, should carefully monitor their opponents for nonverbal indications of excessive frustration and stress. They should look for clenched teeth, crossed arms and legs, increased gross body movement, and similar signals. If they are unaware of these signs, they may generate unintended bargaining breakdowns.

[c]   Defense

Well-mannered negotiators who attempt to counter offensively aggressive bargainers with quid pro quo attacks are likely to fail, due to the capacity of those individuals to out-insult almost anyone. People who encounter these adversaries should diminish the aggregate impact of their demeaning techniques through the use of short, carefully controlled interactions. Telephone discussions or e-mail exchanges may be used to limit each interaction. When telephone discussions become tense, the targets of aggressive opponents can indicate that they have to take care of other business and terminate their immediate interactions. They can thereafter re-phone their adversaries when they are more inclined to tolerate their behavior. When people receive nasty e-mail messages, they can take their time to reply. Personal meetings should, if possible, be restricted to sessions of less than one hour in duration. These abbreviated discussions can prevent abrasive advocates from building momentum with the effect of their sarcasm. It also makes it easier for the objects of such insults to retain control over their own emotions.

[d]   Gender Differences

Negotiators must unfortunately recognize that people still view aggressive and abrasive behavior by male and female advocates differently (*see* Chapter 14, *infra*). When women employ a loud voice and crude language to intimidate male opponents, those recipients are likely to find that conduct more offensive than they would if identical tactics were employed by men. This fact would certainly suggest that female bargainers who adopt aggressive styles do not need to be as offensive as their male cohorts to achieve the same impact. My classroom observations have similarly indicated that male recipients of aggressive female behavior are less likely to respond in kind than they would if similar conduct were emanating from other males. This fact may enable female negotiators to obtain a psychological advantage over male recipients who are unable to respond to agressive female adversaries as they would against male adversaries.

[17]   Walking Out/Hanging Up Telephone

This technique is frequently employed by demonstrative negotiators who want to convince their opponents that they are unwilling to make additional concessions (Katz, 2008, at 153–55). Once the parties have narrowed the distance between their respective positions, these individuals storm out or slam down the telephone receiver in an effort to induce risk-averse adversaries to close all or most of the remaining gap. This approach may induce overly anxious opponents to cave in.

Bargainers should not permit this type of bullying conduct to intimidate them into unwarranted and unreciprocated concessions. Targets of such behavior should *never* run after their departing opponents or immediately re-telephone people who have deliberately terminated their present interactions. This would be viewed as a sign of weakness to be exploited. They should instead give their demonstrative opponents time to calm down and reflect on the current positions on the table. They should also reevaluate their own nonsettlement options to be certain they do not succumb to unreasonable opponent demands. If targets of these intimidating techniques are able to maintain their resolve, their bullying adversaries are likely to resume negotiations and make new counter offers.

[18] Irrational Behavior

[a] Purpose

A few negotiators attempt to gain a bargaining advantage through seemingly irrational conduct (Katz, 2008, at 126–27). Some of these advocates attribute the irrationality to their absent clients (*see* "Mutt and Jeff" approach, *infra*), while others exhibit their own bizarre behavior. These individuals hope to convince opponents that their side cannot be dealt with logically. Adversaries must either accept their one-sided demands or face the consequences associated with an on-going dispute with an unstable party.

People who encounter aberrant opponents tend to become frightened by their unusual behavior. They fear that these irrational bargainers will destroy both sides. To avoid these dire consequences, they frequently accept the dictates of their seemingly illogical adversaries. As a result, they end up with agreements that are worse than their nonsettlement options.

[b] Defense

Few legal advocates or their corporate clients are truly irrational. If they were, they would be unable to achieve consistently successful results in a highly competitive world. In most instances in which bizarre behavior is encountered, the actors are crazy like a fox — using *feigned* irrationality to advance their bargaining objectives. The most effective way to counter contrived preposterousness is to ignore it and respond in an entirely rational manner. As soon as these manipulative opponents caucus to consider proposed terms, they cease their illogical conduct and rationally evaluate the proposals on the table. Once they realize that their strange conduct is not having its expected impact, they are likely to forego this approach.

I know a federal district judge who uses feigned irrationality to induce parties to settle complex cases he does not wish to try. Several weeks before the scheduled trial date, he has the lawyers in chambers. He asks them to summarize the applicable legal issues. When they are finished, he asks them a series of questions that are completely "off the wall." The advocates panic, thinking that this judge lacks the mental stability to handle their arcane case. They quickly leave his chambers and settle their disputes!

On rare occasions, truly irrational opponents are encountered. While these individuals may be the legal advocates themselves, they are more frequently the individual clients involved. When such people participate in negotiations, it is impossible to deal with them logically. They are incapable of evaluating bargaining proposals and nonsettlement options in a realistic manner. They continue to reiterate their unsound proposals in an unthinking fashion no matter the risks involved. Opponents must either give in to their positions or accept their nonsettlement alternatives.

When negotiators are forced to interact with truly bizarre adversaries, they must carefully reassess their own nonsettlement alternatives. They should avoid agreements that are less beneficial than their external options. They should only accept the dictates of unstable opponents when those terms are preferable to continued disagreement. Even when agreements are consummated with irrational adversaries, bargainers should recognize the subsequent difficulties that may be encountered during the performance stages of their relationship. To protect client interests, advocates who enter into contracts with unstable opponents should try to minimize the risks associated with non- or partial performance.

[19]   False Demands

[a]   Benefit

Alert negotiators occasionally discover during the Information Stage that their opponents really desire an item that is not valued by their own client. When this knowledge is obtained, many bargainers endeavor to take advantage of the situation. They try to avoid providing the other side with this topic in exchange for an insignificant term (Katz, 2008, at 119–121). They instead hope to extract a more substantial concession. To accomplish this objective, they mention how important that subject is to their client and include it with their initial demands. If they can convince their opponents that this issue is of major value to their side, they may be able to enhance their client's position with what is actually a meaningless concession on their part.

[b]   Risk

One serious risk is associated with false demands. If individuals employing this technique are too persuasive, they may find themselves the tragic beneficiaries of an unwanted bargaining chip. It would be disastrous for them to attempt to rectify this tactical error with a straightforward admission of deception, since this confession would probably impede further negotiation progress. They should tentatively accept the item in question. As the interaction evolves, they should be able to exchange this term for some other more useful topic. Even if their opponents recognize their predicament, they should generally permit them to employ this face-saving escape route. Little would be gained by an overt challenge to the manipulative individual's personal integrity, and the risk to the bargaining process would be substantial.

[20]   "If It Weren't for You (or Your Client)"

Some parties attempt to create guilt in their adversaries by suggesting during a negotiation that they would not be involved in this unfortunate situation if it were not for the improper actions of the opposing clients.

(1) "If only your client had not driven while intoxicated. . . . "

(2) "If only your client had completely satisfied their contractual obligations. . . . "

(3) "If only you had been willing to make a more reasonable offer at the outset of negotiations. . . . "

(4) "If only you had arrived at the appointed hour for our discussions,. . . . "

Lawyers should recognize that these tactics are designed to generate inappropriate guilt or embarrassment. They should not permit this type of conduct to influence their bargaining behavior (Shapiro & Jankowski, 2001, at 179–80). It is obvious that if the clients of both participants had behaved properly, there would be no need for settlement discussions. If both parties had disclosed all of the pertinent information at the outset of their interaction and had established objectives considered reasonable and appropriate by both sides, their legal advocates would probably not still be involved in settlement talks. These considerations are indigenous to almost all bargaining transactions. If it weren't for such circumstances, most attorneys would be superfluous!

Manipulative opponents may endeavor to create feelings of guilt or embarrassment by focusing upon insignificant personal transgressions. When advocates are unavoidably late for scheduled meetings or forget to bring certain documents, they should merely apologize for their oversight and thereafter ignore these matters. If their adversaries continue to refer to these petty issues, they may turn the tables against their accusers through statements questioning that side's disingenuous effort to impede substantive talks.

[21]   Alleged Expertise/Snow Job

[a]   Benefit

A few individuals attempt to overwhelm bargaining opponents with factual and/or legal details that are not particularly relevant to the basic interaction. They cite factual matters and legal doctrines that are of no meaningful concern to the negotiating parties. They can discuss how tall the plaintiff is sitting down and explore the esoteric ramifications of recent judicial decisions. They want to bolster their own bargaining confidence through demonstrations of their thorough knowledge, and hope to intimidate adversaries who have not developed such expertise.

[b]   Defense

People should not permit opponents to overwhelm them with factual or legal minutiae. When someone tries to focus upon marginally relevant details, they should be praised for their thorough preparation and be asked to concentrate on the more salient items. If necessary, they should be asked to summarize their positions without the need for repeated reference to superfluous data. Skilled opponents may even be able to make these "experts" appear silly, and induce them to become more cooperative in an effort to overcome their resulting embarrassment.

[22]   Bracketing

Some negotiators, especially in transactions pertaining primarily to money, use a technique designed to lead opponents to the figure they hope to achieve. The work to elicit opening offers from the other side, then begin with an offer or demand that is as far away from their goal as is the other side's initial offer. For example, it the defendant begins with an offer of $100,000 and the plaintiff hopes to settle for $300,000, the plaintiff attorney counters with a demand of $500,000. If the defendant moves to $150,000, the plaintiff reduces her demand to $450,000, carefully keeping her $300,000 objective between the two sides' current positions. When the defendant goes up to

$200,000, the plaintiff comes down to $400,000. As the participants move toward the center of their positions, the plaintiff counsel can steer the defense attorney toward her $300,000 goal.

When one party appears to be employing Bracketing, the other may occasionally respond with "*Double Bracketing*" (Halpern, 2003). When the plaintiff counsel reduces her demand to $400,000 in response to a defendant offer of $200,000, the defense attorney indicates that he is unable to go as high as the $300,000 midpoint between their current positions. He then suggests a settlement at $250,000 — half way between the plaintiff's apparent objective of $300,000 and the defendant's current $200,000 offer. If the defense counsel can induce the plaintiff lawyer to succumb to this entreaty, the parties will settle at $50,000 below the plaintiff's preliminary goal.

[23]   Disingenuous Consecutive Concessions

[a]   Accidental

Whenever bargainers lose track of the offers and counteroffers being made and inadvertently make consecutive concessions, they place themselves at a disadvantage. They have probably become confused due to negotiating anxiety and pressure, and they are moving aimlessly toward the position being taken by their opponents. They normally do not realize that they are making these unreciprocated position changes. Opponents of these individuals should encourage further concessions by challenging the sufficiency of their position changes or though patience and prolonged silence following each concession.

[b]   Contrived

Other negotiators endeavor to use contrived consecutive concessions to create feelings of guilt and obligation in their adversaries. For example, they may be contemplating a move from their current demand of $500,000 to a new demand of $400,000. Instead of making a "principled" $100,000 concession, they adopt a different approach. They first move to $450,000, with an appropriate explanation for their action. After a reasonable amount of discussion, they then mention $420,000, accompanied by a suitable rationale. They finally move majestically to $400,000. At this point, they indicate that they have made three unanswered concessions. They hope to induce unsuspecting opponents to respond with a greater counteroffer than would have been produced by a direct move from $500,000 to $400,000. They not only plan to accomplish this result through guilt and obligation, but also from the fact that their successive $50,000, $30,000, and $20,000 position changes suggest that they are rapidly approaching their bottom line.

[c]   Defense

Recipients of consecutive concessions should immediately become suspicious when they are specifically apprised of their occurrence by opponents who have made them. Sincerely confused concession-makers are not aware of the fact they have made consecutive concessions. If they are clearly cognizant of their behavior, the recipients of their apparent largesse should realize that this technique is probably being deliberately used as a bargaining strategy. They should not be overly impressed by the consecutive nature of the concessions, but should instead focus upon the aggregate movement involved. They should then respond as they would have if they had been given a direct $100,000 position change.

[24]   Uproar

Negotiation participants occasionally threaten dire consequences if mutual accords are not achieved. They then indicate that the predicted havoc can be avoided if the other side agrees to the terms they are offering. Careless bargainers may be influenced by this devious technique, if they focus entirely on the damage they will suffer if the extreme consequences occur. For example, a school district may attempt to enhance its bargaining power by threatening to lay off all of the untenured teachers if their representative labor organization does not moderate its demands. The pink-slipped teachers and their tenured colleagues may panic and immediately reduce their requests. When they behave in this manner, they ignore the fact that the threatened layoffs would eliminate most of the English department or create such under staffing that the local school district would no longer be eligible for state education funding.

When extreme consequences are threatened, the affected party should ask two fundamental questions. First, what is the probability that the promised havoc would occur if no accord were attained? In many instances, they would realize that no devastation is likely to result from their refusal to give in to opponent demands. Second, if there is a possibility that the promised cataclysm may take place, how would that event affect the *other side*? A detached assessment may indicate that the negative consequences would be far greater for the threatening party than they would be for the party being threatened. If this were true, the threatening party would have more to lose if no agreement were achieved, and it would be under greater pressure to avoid a nonsettlement. If the threatened participants can be patient, they should be able to benefit from this favorable power imbalance.

[25]   Brer Rabbit (Reverse Psychology)

[a]   Origin

In *Uncle Remus, His Songs and His Sayings* (1880), Joel Chandler Harris created an unforgettable character named Brer Rabbit. The story involves a rabbit who is captured by the fox. The rabbit employs reverse psychology to effectuate his escape. While the fox is contemplating his fate, Brer Rabbit says:

> I don't care what you do with me, so long as you don't fling me in that brier-patch. Roast me, but don't fling me in that brier-patch. . .. Drown me just as deep as you please, but don't fling me in that brier-patch. . .. Skin me, snatch out my eyeballs, tear out my ears by the roots, and cut off my legs, but don't fling me in that brier-patch.

Since the fox wanted to punish Brer Rabbit, he chose the one alternative the rabbit appeared to fear most. He flung him in the brier-patch, and Brer Rabbit escaped!

[b]   Purpose

Adroit negotiators frequently employ the "Brer Rabbit" approach to obtain beneficial terms from retributive, win-lose opponents who irrationally judge their "success" not by how well they have done, but by how poorly they think their adversaries have done (Katz, 2008, at 127). Brer Rabbit bargainers subtly suggest to such opponents that they or their clients would suffer greatly if certain action were either taken or withheld, when they actually hope to obtain the very results being eschewed. They then ask for other items they do not really wish to attain. Their adversaries are so intent on ensuring their complete defeat that they force on the Brer Rabbit negotiators the items they appear to want least (*i.e.*, their real first choices). They have to play the game until the end by asking if their opponents could possibly give them something else, suggesting that their clients will be so disappointed if this is all they get. Their opponents will smile and absolutely refuse to make another concession.

[c]   Risk Involved

The Brer Rabbit technique may be successfully used by bargainers to obtain favorable results from win-lose opponents. Nonetheless, this approach involves serious risks. If it is employed against win-win opponents, they may be induced to agree to terms that the manipulative participants do not really desire. When their opponents grant them their verbally preferred choices, they may be forced either to admit their devious conduct or to accept the less beneficial terms granted to them.

[26]   Downplay of Opponent Concessions

When negotiators make concessions, they want to be certain that their opponents acknowledge their generosity. This enhances the likelihood that their own movement will generate appropriate counteroffers. A few individuals attempt to avoid their obligation to take reciprocal action by downplaying the significance of concessions that have been given to them. They act as if the items that have been granted are of little or no value to their side. Bargainers should never permit opponents to discount the value of sincere concessions. If something they have just given up is really not regarded highly by their adversaries, those participants would not mind if they took it back! It is amazing how quickly disingenuous opponents protest when advocates endeavor to regain concessions that have been characterized as meaningless.

[27]   Feigned Boredom or Disinterest

A few negotiators try to appear completely disinterested or inattentive when their opponents are making their most salient arguments. This technique is intended to undermine the significance of the statements being made and the confidence of the speakers. It can be a frustrating experience to encounter such adversaries. Some people make the mistake of countering these tactics with more forceful and frequently louder assertions. These contentions are likely to be received with equal disdain. It is usually more efficacious to force these opponents to participate in the interaction. They should be asked questions that cannot be answered with a mere "yes" or "no." These people should be required to expose the specific weaknesses they perceive in the position statements they do not seem to respect. If they can be induced to participate more directly in the discussions, their previously displayed disinterest usually disappears.

[28]   Mutt and Jeff (Good Cop/Bad Cop)

[a]   Background

The Mutt and Jeff routine constitutes one of the most common — and effective — bargaining techniques (Katz, 2008, at 122–24; Adler & Silverstein, 2000, at 94–95; Kennedy, 1998, at 115). One seemingly reasonable negotiator softens opponent resistance by professing sympathy toward the "generous" concessions being made by the other side. When the opponents begin to think a final accord is on the horizon, the reasonable person's partner summarily rejects the new offer as entirely insufficient. The unreasonable participant castigates the opponents for their parsimonious concessions and insincere desire to achieve a fair accord. Just as the opponents are preparing to explode at the unreasonable participant, the reasonable partner assuages their feelings and suggests that if some additional concessions are made, he or she could probably induce his or her seemingly irrational partner to accept the new terms. It is amazing how diligently many people interacting with Mutt and Jeff bargainers strive to formulate proposals that will satisfy the critical participant.

[b]   Method

Devious negotiators occasionally employ the Mutt and Jeff approach with the truly unreasonable person assuming the role of the "reasonable" party. That individual instructs his or her partner to reject every new opponent offer in an outraged and belittling manner. The "unreasonable" participant then suggests that no settlement is possible, so long as the opponents continue to evidence such an unyielding attitude. The "unreasonable" partner is occasionally expected to get up and head toward the exit — only to be prevailed upon to reluctantly return to the bargaining table through the valiant efforts of his or her "conciliatory" partner.

[c]   Use by Single Negotiators

Mutt and Jeff tactics may even be used by single negotiators. They can claim that their absent client suffers from delusions of grandeur that must be satisfied if any agreement is to be reached. These manipulative bargainers repeatedly praise their opponents for the munificent concessions being made, but insist that greater movement is necessary to satisfy the excessive aspirations of their irrational principal. It is ironic to note that their absent client may actually be highly receptive to any fair resolution. Since the opponents have no way of knowing this, they usually accept the representations regarding extravagant client intransigence at face value. The adversaries then endeavor to satisfy the alleged needs of the missing client.

[d]   Defense

Negotiators who encounter Mutt and Jeff tactics should not directly challenge the apparently devious scheme being used against them. It is possible that their opponents are not really engaged in a disingenuous exercise. One opponent may actually disagree with his or her partner's assessment of the situation. Allegations regarding the apparently manipulative tactics being used by those individuals would probably create a tense and unproductive bargaining environment — particularly when the opponents have not deliberately adopted a Mutt and Jeff style. Such allegations may also induce truly Machiavellian adversaries to embrace some other devious approach. Since it is generally easier to counter techniques that have already been identified, there is no reason to provide deceptive opponents with the opportunity to switch to other practices that might not be so easily recognized and neutralized.

Individuals who encounter Mutt and Jeff bargainers tend to make the mistake of allowing the seemingly unreasonable participants to control the entire interaction. They direct their arguments and offers to those persons in an effort to obtain their reluctant approval. It is beneficial to include the reasonable participants in the discussions in an effort to obtain their acquiescence — before attempting to satisfy their irrational partners. In a few instances, the more conciliatory opponents may actually indicate a willingness to accept particular proposals that will be characterized as unacceptable by their associates. If the unified position of the opponents can be shattered in this fashion, it may be possible to whipsaw the reasonable individuals against their excessively demanding partners.

If the persons representing the other side are truly employing a Mutt and Jeff approach, the reasonable participants will never suggest their willingness to assent to the particular terms being offered. Those individuals will instead reiterate a desire to obtain the acquiescence of their unreasonable partners. When this occurs, the reasonable participants should again be asked — not if their partners would be likely to accept the terms being proposed — but whether *they* would be willing to accept those conditions. Proficient "reasonable" participants will never indicate their acceptance of the proffered terms, without the concurrence of their partners, and it will become clear that the opponents are using wholly manipulative tactics.

It is always important when dealing with seemingly unreasonable opponents to remember what would likely occur if no mutual accords were achieved. If the overall cost of surrendering to the one-sided demands of those adversaries would clearly exceed the costs associated with nonsettlements, the interactions should not be fruitlessly continued. The opponents should be informed that they will have to substantially modify their assessments before further bargaining can meaningfully occur.

[29]   Belly-Up ("Yes . . . , but . . . ")

[a]   Method

Some individuals use a bargaining style that is particularly difficult for opponents to counter (Katz, 2008, at 115–17). They act like wolves in sheepskin. They wear bedraggled outfits to the offices of their adversaries and indicate how commodious those environments are. They then profess their lack of negotiating ability and legal perspicuity in an effort to evoke sympathy and to lure unsuspecting adversaries into a false sense of security. They readily acknowledge the superior competence of their opponents, and shamelessly exhibit a complete lack of ability. They then ask their adversaries what those people think would constitute fair terms.

[b]   Epitome

The epitome of the Belly-Up style was artfully created by actor Peter Falk in his Lt. Columbo police detective character, (*supra* Chapter 3). That inspector seemed to bumble along during criminal investigations with no apparent plan. When he interviewed suspects, he did so in a wholly disorganized manner. By the time the suspects realized that Lt. Columbo really understood what was happening, they had already confessed and were in police custody! Another example of this type of person was provided by the late Senator Sam Ervin of North Carolina. During the Senate Watergate Hearings, the general public became well acquainted with his masterful, down-home style. This casual "country lawyer" quoted Biblical parables and recited southern homilies while adroitly obtaining confessions to High Crimes and Misdemeanors from perspicacious administration witnesses who thought they could easily outsmart this innocuous old man. One should be especially suspicious of any self-proclaimed "country lawyer" who graduated from the Harvard Law School!

[c]   Ascertaining Truthfulness and Responding Accordingly

Especially devious Belly-Up negotiators may resort to more outrageous conduct. When opponents take tough positions, they place their hand over their heart and display pained facial expressions. If their adversaries continue to push for beneficial terms, these participants may reach into their desk drawer and extract a nitroglycerin vial! I have met several attorneys who have bragged about the effectiveness of this tactic. If you are certain these opponents do not suffer from chest pains, you can continue your aggressive approach. If, however, you were to suspect real heart problems, you should recess your discussions and contact a senior partner in the opposing law firm. Explain to that person that you are engaged in a difficult interaction with X, and indicate that you are concerned about that individual's physical or emotional capacity to participate. If the partner downplays that person's condition, you can assume that he or she is using a Belly-Up style to take advantage of you. On the other hand, if the partner suggests the participation of another attorney, you should be pleased to interact with that person. Never continue negotiations with someone you think may suffer serious health consequences as a result of your legal interactions.

[d]   Defense

Belly-Up bargainers are difficult people to deal with, because they refuse to participate in the normal negotiation process. They ask their opponents to permit them to forego traditional auction bargaining due to their professed inability to negotiate competently. They merely want their respected and honorable adversaries to formulate fair and reasonable arrangements that will not unfairly disadvantage the unfortunate clients who have chosen such pathetic legal representatives. Even though their thoroughly prepared opponents have established high aspiration levels and "principled" opening positions, the Belly-Up negotiators are able to induce them to significantly modify their planned approach.

> BELLY-UP: I've never had any real experience with cases as complicated as this one, so I'm glad to be dealing with someone who is an acknowledged expert and a highly respected member of the legal community. I don't know what my client actually deserves, so I'll have to rely upon your experience and judgment. What do you think would be appropriate in a situation like this?

> OPPONENT: [Although the opposing counsel had planned to articulate a tough opening position, he/she decides that it would be unconscionable to take advantage of such an inept practitioner and his/her poor, unsuspecting client. The opponent thus formulates an eminently reasonable proposal.]

> BELLY-UP: *Yes*, that's an extremely generous offer. I can readily understand why you have such an outstanding reputation among the judges and lawyers in our community. *But*, it doesn't really satisfy the needs of my client who was hoping to obtain more in the areas of ____ and ____. I was anticipating

that you would be able to recognize my client's requirements with respect to these matters.

OPPONENT: [Instead of asking the Belly-Up negotiator to suggest a definitive counteroffer that would directly reflect his/her client's underlying needs and interests and that could be objectively explored, the acknowledged expert decides to modify his/her initial offer in an effort to demonstrate that he/she really does understand what the other party's client has to obtain.]

BELLY-UP: *Yes*, that's a vast improvement over your first proposal. I'm so relieved that you are not trying to take unfair advantage of your superior position. Thank you for so wisely recognizing the needs of my client with respect to [the areas enhanced by the new offer], *but* your proposal doesn't seem to go far enough. I would be embarrassed if I had to recommend that proposal to my client, because they were certain that you would be able to suggest more advantageous terms with respect to ____ and ____.

OPPONENT: [Feels pleased that his/her second proposal was more suited to the needs and interests of the other lawyer's client. The parties seem to be so near to a final solution, and the opponent eagerly suggests an even better package.]

BELLY-UP: Oh *yes*, that's much better. Those modifications certainly take care of my client's concerns regarding ____ and ____, *but* your new proposal doesn't adequately protect their interests with respect to ____. I wonder if there might be some way to make a slight change in this regard?

OPPONENT: [Feels gratified and continues their valiant effort to demonstrate the ability to formulate a fair arrangement that will adequately satisfy the basic needs of the other negotiator's client.]

By the conclusion of their interaction, the Belly-Up bargainer has usually achieved a magnificent accord for his or her client, while the opposing counsel has been left figuratively naked. The extraordinary aspect of this transaction is that the opposing negotiator feels truly gratified that he or she has been able to satisfy the underlying needs of the other lawyer's poor client! It requires unbelievable skill to be able to fleece an opponent and leave that person with a feeling of accomplishment and exhilaration.

Negotiators should never permit seemingly inept opponents to evoke such sympathy that they concede everything in an effort to formulate solutions that are acceptable to those pathetic souls. It is not fair for those devious individuals to force their adversaries to do all of the work. Instead of allowing Belly-Up bargainers to alter their initially planned approach, negotiators should begin with their originally formulated "principled" offers and require those people to participate actively in the process. When Belly-Up participants challenge these opening proposals, they should be forced to articulate their own proposals, so they can be evaluated and attacked. It is generally painful for Belly-Up bargainers to interact in such a traditional manner. They are not used to formulating and defending their own proposals. They are much more comfortable trying to evoke sympathy by criticizing the offers being made to them. Once these individuals are induced to participate in the usual give-and-take, they tend to lose much of their bargaining effectiveness.

[30]   Passive-Aggressive

[a]   Method

Passive-aggressive negotiators are frequently as difficult to deal with as Belly-Up bargainers. Instead of directly challenging the tactics and proposals of their opponents, they employ oblique, but aggressive, forms of passive resistance. They tend to pout when they are unable to obtain favorable offers, and they resort to obstructionism and procrastination to achieve their objectives. For example, they may show up late for scheduled bargaining sessions or appear with incorrect files or documents. They may exhibit personal ineptitude in an effort to frustrate the negotiation progress and to generate concessions from impatient opponents. They may even conveniently misplace unsatisfactory proposals that were sent to them and act as if they never arrived. When they are expected to draft final accords, they often take an inordinate amount of time to accomplish their task and may even fail to prepare any written document.

Since passive — aggressive individuals tend to react to problems and confrontations in an indirect manner, it is particularly frustrating to interact with them. Instead of expressing their actual thoughts directly, they employ passive techniques to evidence their displeasure. People who deal with them should recognize the hostility represented by their passive-aggressive behavior. They are usually individuals who are dissatisfied with the negotiation process. They may not feel comfortable engaging in the conventional give-and-take. They may dislike their immediate circumstances or current opponents. Since these factors can rarely be altered, it is more productive to take steps that will beneficially modify the actual behavior of these Passive-Aggressive participants.

[b]   Defense

Copies of important papers should be obtained through other avenues in case they claim an inability to locate their own copies. Since passive — aggressive individuals do not say no easily — an overtly aggressive act — it is beneficial to present them with seemingly realistic offers they cannot reject. When they are given these proposals, they tend to acquiesce in a predictably passive manner. Once agreements are reached, persons bargaining against them should always offer to prepare the necessary documents. Even when the Passive-Aggressive participants insist upon the opportunity to draft the accord, as they usually do, their opponents should prepare their own draft agreements in anticipation of their failure to do so. Once Passive-Aggressive negotiators are presented with faits accomplis, they usually accept their fate and execute the proffered agreements. In those infrequent cases in which Passive-Aggressive opponents do not respond, it may be necessary to have messengers personally deliver the final documents to them and wait for those papers to be duly executed.

[31]   Splitting the Difference

[a]   Method

One of the most common techniques used to achieve final agreements following detailed auction bargaining that has brought the parties close together involves splitting the remaining difference between their most recent offers. Instead of threatening opponents with nonsettlement consequences if final terms are not achieved, the moving parties use the face-saving "promise" technique to generate simultaneous movement. For instance, parties may have commenced their interaction with a plaintiff demand for $100,000 and a defendant offer of $20,000. After various concessions and counter offers have been exchanged, the plaintiff is requesting $60,000, and the defendant is offering $50,000. One of the two participants is likely to suggest that they "split the difference" and agree to $55,000. This is an expeditious method of reaching the point these negotiators would probably have attained had they continued to rely upon other traditional bargaining techniques.

[b] Negating Unfair Advantages

People who are asked to split the outstanding difference to achieve final accords should consider the previous bargaining sequence before they too readily assent to this proposal (Freund, 1992, at 158–59). They must first decide whether their opponents were able to unfairly skew the apparent settlement range in their favor through a biased opening offer. For example, plaintiffs in personal injury cases can begin with almost any initial demands, while defendant insurance carriers are more constrained. They cannot realistically ask a plaintiff to compensate their client for the psychological trauma they suffered from driving through a red light at an excessive rate of speed while under the influence of alcohol and striking the disabled plaintiff in a crosswalk! If an unreasonably skewed initial offer has been made, it is important to be certain that the negotiation process has effectively negated the unfair advantage associated with that proposal *before* the parties contemplate a splitting of the remaining difference to achieve a final settlement.

[c] Importance of Review of Prior Concessions

People who are contemplating use of the split-the-difference technique to resolve the remaining area of disagreement should similarly review the prior concessions which have been made by both parties. If one has already made six concessions while the other has only made five, it would normally be inappropriate to split the remaining difference until the second party has made one more reciprocal concession. The final result would otherwise be biased in favor of that person's client.

[d] Inducing Opponent to Split Remaining Difference

Some experts believe that it is beneficial to let opponents offer to split-the-difference first (Dawson, 2001, at 63–64). This provides the recipient of this offer with the opportunity to decide whether it is tactically advantageous to accede to this request. It also gives the recipient the chance to obtain one last bargaining edge. Once the opponent offers to split the distance remaining between the parties, the offeree can treat the midpoint between the parties' existing positions as a new opponent offer and suggest that they split the distance that *remains* between that new opponent position and his or her most recent proposal. For example, once the plaintiff in the above hypothetical suggests an agreement at $55,000, the defendant may indicate a willingness to conclude the transaction at $52,500 — half way between $55,000 and $50,000. An overly anxious plaintiff may succumb to this blandishment in an effort to end the interaction. A more careful participant would reiterate the $55,000 figure and state that no further concessions will be made. In most cases, the manipulative defense attorneys realize that their effort to obtain an unfair advantage is not going to prevail and they accept the originally proffered amount.

[32]   "Final Offer" Checks Tendered by Defense Lawyers

[a]   Method

When protracted negotiations have failed to bring plaintiffs and defendants together, defense attorneys occasionally send checks to plaintiffs through their legal representatives containing amounts somewhere between the last positions of the two sides. The defense lawyers explicitly indicate that the cashing of these checks will constitute full settlement of the underlying claims. In large value cases, defense attorneys usually include formal releases that must be signed before plaintiffs may cash the accompanying checks. In many cases, the plaintiffs accept these checks — reflecting the impact of gain-loss framing which demonstrates that individuals offered sure gains and the possibility of greater gains or no gains tend to be risk averse and accept the certain gains. This techniques is especially effective where plaintiffs recognize that liability is uncertain and they may obtain nothing at trial. Attorneys making such "final offers" must be prepared to try the cases if their offers are rejected, or they would suffer substantial credibility losses.

Defense lawyers who contemplate resort to "final offer" checks should only take such action after extended bargaining exchanges. If they make such offers prematurely, their entreaties lack credibility. Such untimely proposals would also be likely to induce plaintiffs who are not yet ready to contemplate final settlements to opt for litigation.

[b]   Defense

Plaintiff attorneys receiving "final offer" checks may — with client concurrence — try to keep the negotiation process going by ignoring the finality of the offers they have received. They can make their own counteroffers somewhere between their own former positions and the amounts specified in the defendant checks. This approach may allow "final offer" defense attorneys to continue to negotiate without suffering credibility losses. They could respond with new offers of their own and continue the bargaining process. If such plaintiff responses fail to generate further offers from defendants, the plaintiffs have to decide whether to accept the defendant checks or to move toward trial.

Summary

1. Negotiators use various games or techniques to influence opponent behavior and to advance their own client interests.

2. Although a few bargainers may rely upon a single approach, most use different techniques in sequence or in combination to keep their opponents off balance.

3. Negotiators must become thoroughly familiar with the different techniques available. This will permit them to employ those tactics that will most appropriately advance their interests and will enable them to recognize and effectively counteract opponent games.

4. Participants who thoroughly understand the bargaining process and the negotiation devices being employed by their opponents tend to enhance their own confidence and increase the likelihood of obtaining beneficial results.

Chapter 11

POST NEGOTIATION ASSESSMENT

§ 11.01   ASKING QUESTIONS ABOUT ALL STAGES

[1]   Importance

Most attorneys negotiate their way through life without ever trying to learn from their encounters. They complete one bargaining interaction and move directly to another. If they want to improve their negotiation skills, they have to learn from their prior encounters. Which techniques worked well, and which did not? What new tactics did they encounter, and how might they have countered those techniques more effectively? Whether they win or lose, each time individuals complete a significant negotiation they should briefly review the manner in which that particular interaction developed. It is only through objective post-mortems focusing on every negotiating stage that individuals can continuously enhance their negotiating capabilities (Watkins, 2006, at 153–163; Fisher & Shapiro, 2005, at 177–182).

Empirical studies show that negotiators tend to under-estimate how high or low opponents are actually willing to go before they begin their serious discussions, causing them to over-estimate how well they have performed once agreements have been achieved (Larrick & Wu, 2007). Because of this over-confidence, they often see no reason to objectively evaluate their performances. It is thus important — even when individuals think they have done well — to do post negotiation assessments with an open mind. They really need to determine the degree to which they may have erroneously estimated during their preparation how high or low the other side was really willing to go, and think about whether they could have obtained even more advantageous terms.

[2] Preparation Stage

The first analysis should focus on the Preparation Stage. Was their pre-interaction planning sufficiently thorough? Did they carefully evaluate their nonsettlement options (*i.e.*, their bottom line) and the nonsettlement alternatives available to their opponents? Did they establish an appropriate aspiration level for *each* issue to be addressed? Did they plan a beneficial and principled opening offer? Did their pre-bargaining prognostications prove to be accurate? If not, what might have been done to provide a better preliminary assessment? Which party dictated the contextual factors such as time and location? Is it likely that these seemingly ancillary considerations influenced the substantive aspects of the transaction? Could they have been handled in a more advantageous fashion?

[3] Preliminary Stage

Did the participants have a good Preliminary Stage? Did they take the time to establish rapport with each other? Did they try to personalize their relationship, and create a positive bargaining environment? If one side did not like the way their adversary began the interaction, did they employ "attitudinal bargaining" to modify their behavior?

[4] Information Stage

The Information Stage must be similarly explored. How well was the Information Stage developed? Did they ask their opponent open-ended, information-seeking questions? Were both parties relatively candid or were they unusually circumspect? Did the unreciprocated candor of one side adversely affect it's position during the subsequent discussions? Were unintended disclosures inadvertently made through verbal leaks or nonverbal signals? If so, how might they have been prevented? Were the participants able to ascertain the knowledge they needed to permit an efficient and productive Competitive/Distributive Stage? Were they able to use Blocking Techniques to avoid the disclosure of sensitive information? What other pertinent information should have been divulged, and when and how should it have been revealed?

[5] Competitive/Distributive Stage

Which party made the first *real* offer? Were appropriate explanations used to support the precise proposals articulated — *i.e.*, were *principled* opening positions stated? Could different rationales have been employed more persuasively? How did the opponents react to the preliminary offer and its accompanying elucidation? Did they appear to be genuinely surprised, or did the proffered terms seem to be close to what they had apparently anticipated? Did the participant who made the initial offer make another proposal without receiving any definitive offer from the other side first? If so, what precipitated this conduct?

[6]　　Closing Stage

How did the Closing Stage evolve? Did it develop deliberately, with the parties moving together toward the final agreement or did one participant close an excessive amount of the distance dividing the parties? Did the bargainers continue to use the techniques that got them to this stage of the interaction, or did they resort to less effective tactics? Participants should similarly ask themselves whether they exuded sufficient patience to induce over-anxious opponents to move more quickly and more carelessly toward closure than themselves? What ultimately induced the opponent to accept the terms agreed upon or to reject the final offer that was made before the discussions were terminated?

[7]　　Cooperative/Integrative Stage

Did the parties attempt to employ the Cooperative/Integrative Stage to maximize their joint gains? Had a tentative accord been achieved before the initiation of cooperative bargaining? Did the Cooperative/Integrative Stage significantly enhance the return to each party? Were the Cooperative/Integrative Stage participants relatively candid about their respective needs and interests, or did a counterproductive competitive atmosphere permeate this portion of the interaction? How might the cooperative experience have been improved?

§ 11.02　TOPICS TO CONSIDER

[1]　　Review of Concessions

It is informative to explore the concession patterns of the two sides. Which party made the first concession and how was it generated? Were subsequent concessions by each side matched by reciprocal movement from the other party, or were either excessive or consecutive concessions made by one side? If so, were they inadvertently made? Was each concession accompanied by an appropriate explanation — *i.e.*, were "principled" concessions articulated? What was the exact size of each concession? Did successive position modifications involve consistently decreasing increments? If not, did one party unsuccessfully attempt to establish a false resistance point that could not be sustained? How close to the mid-point between the opening offers was the final settlement?

[2]　　Influence of Time Pressures on Parties

How did time pressures influence the negotiation process? Did one party appear to be operating under greater time pressure than the other? If so, why? Was the party with less time pressure able to take advantage of this situation? Did the time factor generate a greater number of concessions or more sizable position changes as the impending deadline approached?

[3]　　Specific Bargaining Techniques Used

What specific bargaining techniques were employed by the opponents? How were they countered? Could they have been more effectively neutralized? Participants should ask themselves which particular tactics they used to enhance their position. Did the opponents appear to recognize the tactics? What countermeasures did the opponents adopt to undermine those tactics? What different approaches might participants have employed to advance their position more forcefully? What other tactics might opponents have used more effectively against them? How could they have minimized the impact of these opponent measures?

[4]   Deceitful Tactics

Did either side resort to deceitful tactics or deliberate misrepresentations to advance its position? Did these involve acceptable "puffing" and "embellishment," or inappropriate mendacity? If so, how were these devices discovered and how were they countered? What impact would these tactics have on future interactions involving the same participants?

[5]   Knowing Who Achieved More Beneficial Results and Why

Negotiators should always ask whether one side appeared to obtain more beneficial results than the other party. They should not merely ask whether their own side was satisfied with the final accord, since winning and losing participants tend to express equal satisfaction with the settlement achieved (Karrass, 1970, at 24). If one side seemed to fare better than the other, what did it do to produce this outcome? What might the less successful bargainer have done differently? Did client constraints contribute to an unequal result? If so, what might have been done to minimize the impact of this factor? If no settlement was ultimately attained, was client recalcitrance the primary factor? Were client expectations unduly elevated? If the client rejected a final proposal that counsel thought should have been accepted or accepted final terms counsel thought should have been rejected, how might the counsel have more effectively educated the client regarding the negotiation process and the substantive merits of their situation?

[6]   Impact of Attribution [Self-Serving] Bias

When we evaluate how we have done, we are often influenced by self-serving attributions (Malhotra & Bazerman, 2007, at 135–36). When we are successful, we tend to attribute our success to our own skill and efforts. On the other hand, when we do not do so well, we tend to attribute our results to external factors beyond our control. For example, when students achieve good grades, they usually say "I got an A." When they do not do very well, they say "Craver gave me a C." It is as if they had nothing to do with the C they earned.

Individuals analyzing bargaining interactions should be careful not to give themselves too much credit for their successes and too little responsibility for their shortfalls. When they do not achieve good results, they should really examine what they personally may have done wrong. Were they insufficiently prepared? Did they fail to put themselves in the shoes of the other side? Did they fail to establish beneficial aspiration levels and sufficiently persuasive arguments supporting those positions to generate confidence in the positions they were taking? What else could they have done to advance their side's interests? Even if the other side possessed greater bargaining power and/or skill, what could these persons have done to have had a greater beneficial impact on the interaction?

[7] Dealing With Mistakes/New Tactics Encountered

Bargainers should finally ask two critical questions. What did they do that they wish they had not done? This inquiry relates to a mistake they may have made. If it were a mere tactical error, they should realize that their opponents were probably unaware of their mistake. Negotiators should never do anything to alert unsuspecting opponents to errors they may have made, hoping to cover up these errors. On the other hand, if true mistakes are made — such as mathematical errors — the best way to deal with them is directly. It is best that the participant confess the mistake, apologize, and make the necessary modification(s) in the originally stated position.

Advocates should similarly ask themselves what they did not do that they wish they had done. This question usually relates to a new tactic they encountered that they did not think they handled well. They should ask their colleagues if they ever encountered this approach. If so, how did they deal with it? If not, how would they try to counter such behavior? The more negotiators plan effective responses to opponent tactics they may encounter during future interactions, the more effectively they should deal with those techniques when they next experience them. Individuals who fail to consider possible counter-measures to innovative tactics — hoping not to see them again — rarely handle them more effectively when they are forced to deal with them again.

[8] Use of Checklist

Through the use of the brief checklist set forth in Table 3, negotiators may readily review almost any bargaining interaction. While it is certainly true that experience can be an excellent teacher, it must be remembered that experience without the benefit of meaningful post-transaction evaluation is of limited value. The time expended during the appraisal process should be amply recouped through improved future performance.

Summary

1. At the conclusion of each successful and unsuccessful negotiation, participants should review their performance to ascertain what they did well and what they should strive to improve.

2. Even though experience can be an excellent teacher, individuals who fail to analyze their prior negotiation experiences are unlikely to learn from those transactions and tend to repeat the same mistakes in their future interactions.

3. Negotiators must consider the Preparation Stage, the Preliminary Stage, the Information Stage, the Competitive/Distributive Stage, the Closing Stage, and the Cooperative/Integrative Stage to determine whether the entire process evolved in an efficient manner.

4. Proficient bargainers are generally able to learn from previous mistakes by increasing the influence of their efficacious behavior and by decreasing the impact of their less effective conduct.

5. At the conclusion of bargaining interactions, advocates should ask themselves what they did that they wish they had not done and what they did not do that they wish they had done.

TABLE 3
Post Negotiation Evaluation Checklist

1. Was your *pre-negotiation* preparation sufficiently thorough? Were you completely familiar with the operative facts and law? Did you fully understand your client's value system and nonsettlement alternatives? Did you carefully estimate your *opponent's* nonsettlement options?

2. Was your *initial* aspiration level high enough? Did you establish a firm goal for *each issue* to be addressed? If you obtained everything you sought, was this due to the fact you did not establish sufficiently elevated objectives? Did you prepare a beneficial and principled opening offer?

3. Did your *pre-bargaining* prognostications prove to be accurate? Did your opponent begin near the point you thought he/she would begin? If not, what caused your miscalculations?

4. Which party dictated the *contextual* factors such as time, day, and location? Did these factors influence the negotiations?

5. Did you use the *Preliminary Stage* to establish rapport with your opponent and to create a positive negotiating environment? Did you employ *Attitudinal Bargaining* to modify inappropriate opponent behavior?

6. Did the *Information Stage* develop sufficiently to provide the participants with the knowledge they needed to understand their respective needs and interests and to enable them to consummate an optimal agreement? Did you use *broad, open-ended questions* to determine what the otherside wanted, and use *what* and *why* questions to ascertain their needs and interests?

7. Were any unintended *verbal leaks* or *nonverbal disclosures* made? What precipitated these revelations? Were you able to use *Blocking Techniques* to prevent the disclosure of sensitive information?

8. Who made the *first* offer? The first *"real"* offer? Was a *"principled"* initial offer articulated by you? By your opponent? How did your *opponent* react to *your* initial proposal? How did *you* react to your *opponent's* opening offer?

9. Were *consecutive* opening offers made by one party before the other side disclosed its initial position? What induced that party to engage in this conduct?

10. What specific *bargaining techniques* were employed by your *opponent* during the *Distributive/Competitive Stage* and how were these tactics countered by you? What else might you have done to counter these tactics more effectively?

11. What particular *negotiation devices* were employed by *you* to advance your position? Did your *opponent* appear to *recognize* the various techniques you used, and, if so, how did he/she endeavor to minimize their impact? What *other tactics* might you have used to advance your position more forcefully?

12. Which party made the *first concession* and how was it precipitated? Were *subsequent concessions* made on an *alternating basis*? You should keep a record of each concession made by you and by your opponent throughout the interaction.

13. Were *"principled"* concessions articulated by you? By your opponent? Did *successive position* changes involve decreasing increments and were those increments relatively reciprocal to the other side's concomitant movement?

14. How did the parties use the *Closing Stage* to achieve an agreement once they realized that they had overlapping needs and interests? Did either side appear to make greater concessions during the *Closing Stage*?

15. Did the parties resort to *Cooperative/Integrative Bargaining* to maximize their aggregate return?

16. How close to the *mid-point* between the initial *real offers* was the final settlement?

17. How did *time pressures* influence the parties and their respective concession patterns? Try not to ignore the time pressures that affected your opponent.

18. Did either party resort to *deceitful tactics* or deliberate misrepresentations to enhance its situation? Did these pertain to material law or fact, or only to the speaker's value system or settlement intentions?

19. What finally induced you *to accept the terms* agreed upon or *to reject* the final offer made by the other party?

20. Did *either* party appear to obtain *more favorable terms* than the other side, and if so, how was this result accomplished? What could the *less successful participant* have *done differently* to improve its situation?

21. If *no* settlement was achieved, what might have been done differently with respect to client preparation and/or bargaining developments to produce a different result?

22. What did you do that you *wish* you had *not done*? Do you think your opponent was aware of your error? How could you avoid such a mistake in the future?

23. What did you *not do* that you *wish you had done* to counteract unexpected opponent behavior? How could you most effectively counter this approach in the future?

Chapter 12

FREQUENTLY RAISED NEGOTIATION ISSUES

§ 12.01   CLIENT PRESENCE DURING NEGOTIATIONS

[1]   Against Client Presence During Negotiations

When lawyers represent individual clients, it is generally preferable *not to have* those persons present during negotiation sessions. If personal clients attend negotiation meetings, they will give away important information. They may unexpectedly say something regarding issues their counsel did not want addressed. Even if they do not speak, they will provide their opponents with nonverbal signals that reveal their side's private thoughts. Furthermore, it is difficult, if not impossible, to employ such effective bargaining techniques as "Limited Authority" or "Mutt and Jeff" when clients are in attendance. If the legal advocates suggest they lack authority with respect to particular matters, their opponents can directly ask the present clients whether they will accept the proffered terms. It is awkward for attorneys to instruct their clients not to answer such questions. When clients are not in attendance, their advocates can describe them as unreasonable individuals who are displeased by current progress. The legal counsel can then portray themselves as reasonable persons who hope to achieve fair terms for both sides. With clients present, this "Mutt and Jeff" tactic is unlikely to be used successfully.

In emotionally charged situations, it may be beneficial for attorneys to permit opponents to cast some aspersions on their own clients at the commencement of bargaining interactions. Adversaries may feel the need to tell you how outrageous your clients' behavior has been before they can discuss settlement possibilities in a rational manner. These cathartic expressions may help to relieve festering animosity and enhance the general bargaining atmosphere. If your clients were present when these recriminating statements were being made, you would feel compelled to interrupt and defend your clients before the cathartic process was completed. If your clients are not present and opponent statements are not too intemperate, you may permit the emotional venting that may be a prerequisite to serious discussions.

[2]   Importance of Client Preparation if Presence is Necessary

If individual clients must attend bargaining sessions, they should be carefully prepared beforehand. The negotiation process should be thoroughly explained. In order to prevent unintended verbal leaks, clients should be instructed to speak only when asked by their own counsel. They should also be cautioned about the substantial risk of inadvertent nonverbal disclosures and be encouraged to monitor their own nonverbal signals. You must plan to conduct attorney-client communication during bargaining meetings in a manner that does not unintentionally divulge secret information.

§ 12.02   INITIATING LITIGATION SETTLEMENT DISCUSSIONS

[1]   Embracing the Settlement Process

[a]   Overcoming Reluctance and Fear

It is amazing how frequently lawyers indicate their reluctance to initiate settlement discussions. They seem to feel that the party who first suggests these talks will be placed at a disadvantage. This perception may have been fostered by more senior litigators who can recall when it was considered inappropriate to directly broach the subject of settlement. Such a reluctance to be forthright is misplaced today. In most state and federal jurisdictions, from 85% to 95% of all lawsuits are resolved through the settlement process. This statistic reflects both the high emotional and monetary costs associated with judicial proceedings, and the fact that professional attorneys are usually in a better position to evaluate the true value of particular cases than are twelve laypeople who normally lack legal training or experience.

[b]   Recognition of Professional Advantage Over Jury

Competent and rational litigators should generally be able to achieve mutual accords that optimally protect the interests of their respective clients. Although juries regularly perform their assigned tasks in a conscientious manner, they lack the technical knowledge possessed by skilled practitioners. When two adversaries fully comprehend the factual and legal issues involved in a particular case, they can normally reach an accommodation of the competing client interests. Most cases that culminate in actual adjudications could probably have been amicably resolved if the legal representatives had been more objective and cooperative. Support for this assertion is provided by the innovative work of Professors Stephen Goldberg and Jeanne Brett of Northwestern University. They established an experiment using mediation as a last step for contractual grievance disputes that were destined for arbitral adjudication. They found that approximately 85% of the employment controversies that would otherwise have been taken to arbitration — since the parties had themselves been unable to settle them during the prior steps of their contractual grievance procedures — were resolved through resort to pre-arbitration mediation (Goldberg & Brett, 1983). If legal advocates are willing to participate in the settlement process in good faith they should encounter few disputes that cannot be mutually resolved. Further, if attorneys are able, when necessary, to employ cooperative bargaining techniques to induce opponents to objectively explore the pertinent legal and factual issues with them, they should experience very agreeable settlements.

[2]   Assertive Settlement Initiation

[a]   By Complainant

Since most contemporary litigators recognize that their cases are probably going to be disposed of through the negotiation process, they should not be hesitant to initiate settlement discussions. If they are representing plaintiffs, they should not be afraid to write or telephone prospective defendants and tell them what they plan to request in their complaints if mutually acceptable resolutions of the underlying disputes cannot be expeditiously achieved. They may find it beneficial to make these contacts before they actually file suit, because the formal initiation of the judicial process causes many parties to become defensive and uncompromising. In some instances they may wish to prepare their complaint and send it to the defendant — without filing it — to let that party know they are prepared to file if that side does not want to begin settlement talks (cf. Moffitt, 2005 (suggesting pre-pleading conference before complaint filed to encourage settlement discussions before parties position themselves with complaint and answer)).

[b]   By Defense

Attorneys who represent defendants can write or telephone plaintiff lawyers who have filed complaints against their clients and ask those persons what they hope to attain through the litigation process. They may even obtain a psychological advantage from this forthright style. They can openly demonstrate their willingness to approach the dispute resolution process fairly and reasonably. They may also use this technique to establish control of the contextual factors such as the time and location for their interactions. This may enhance their bargaining confidence.

[3]   Employment of Indirect Approaches

Those attorneys who are afraid that the direct instigation of settlement talks may undermine their positions should not hesitate to employ indirect approaches. They can contact opposing counsel ostensibly to discuss some specific aspect of the case, such as discovery procedures, and casually elicit that person's perception of their dispute. They can alternatively arrange an "unexpected" meeting. When they know that an associate is scheduled to make a court appearance on some other case with the same opposing lawyer, they can accompany their colleague and nonchalantly broach the topic of interest to them during this supposedly inadvertent encounter.

Some litigators employ a more disingenuous approach to initiate settlement talks. They telephone their adversaries during the lunch hour. They assume that the call recipient will be out of the office. This enables them to leave messages requesting return calls. Since the objects of this technique usually know what cases the callers want to discuss, it is common for them to return the telephone message and launch into immediate conversations pertaining to the merits of the relevant disputes. Forgetting that it was their opponents who telephoned first, they act as if they were the ones who instigated the settlement process.

When I was in practice, I was astounded by the number of phone calls I received during the lunch hour. I can even recall how surprised many of the callers were when I personally answered the telephone! People who find phone messages when they return from lunch should not provide their manipulative callers with an unintended advantage. If they prefer to force the callers to assume the initiative, they need only return their phone calls and tersely state: "I am returning your call." Through their subsequent silence, they can unequivocally indicate their expectation that the other party should commence the substantive settlement discussions.

[4]   Patience, Silence, and Preparation

While litigators should never be afraid to indicate a willingness to discuss settlement, they must recognize that such talks can only be successful if their adversaries respond meaningfully. If opposing counsel indicate a complete unwillingness to explore settlement options, equal bargaining cannot occur. Their continued efforts are unlikely to benefit their side and may even induce them to bid against themselves. In these instances, they should wait until litigation pressure or the intervention of a judicial mediator induces opposing counsel to reciprocate their settlement entreaties. In the meantime, they should continue to prepare diligently for trial to increase the settlement pressure on their adversaries.

§ 12.03 WEAKENING OPPONENT'S SUPERIOR POSITION

[1] Recognizing that Power is in Perception

Negotiators must remember that bargaining power is rarely defined by objective factors. The strength of each party is determined more by the opponent's *perception* of the interaction, than by the actual circumstances (Volkema, 2006, at 7–8; Cohen, 2003, at 167, 239; Zartman & Rubin, 2002, at 13–14; Shell, 1999, at 111; Lewicki, et al., 1994, at 296–97). If adroit negotiators can convince seemingly stronger opponents that they are unaware of the opponent's superior strength they may effectively weaken the positions of those parties. Opposing counsel would subsequently suffer a concomitant loss of negotiating confidence.

This phenomenon explains why young children become intuitively gifted negotiators despite their obvious lack of objective bargaining power. When they interact with seemingly omnipotent parents, they disarm their adversaries by ignoring the power imbalance. Since parents are obliged to prevent "child-like" conduct, children also recognize their ability to threaten irrational, self-destructive behavior if they do not achieve their ultimate objectives. Once parents begin to doubt their actual power, they lose confidence and are easy targets for their manipulative offspring!

[2] Manipulation of Apparent Options

A factor that significantly influences a party's assessment of it's objective power concerns the alternatives that side thinks are available to it should no settlement be achieved during the present negotiations. If several options appear to constitute viable substitutes for bargained results, that party should understand the elevated strength it enjoys. If an opponent can convince that party that it really does not have as many nonsettlement alternatives as it believes or that those options are not as advantageous as it thinks, the power balance can be effectively shifted in favor of the manipulative actor (Shell, 1999, at 149–53).

Bargainers who are able to use verbal and nonverbal messages to indicate that they do not accord any credence to the actual power possessed by their opponents can meaningfully undermine opponent authority. If this strength-diffusing objective is accomplished, adversaries will be rendered incapable of using their objectively superior circumstances to influence the negotiation outcome. Opposing negotiators may be so demoralized by this tactic that they readily accept less beneficial terms than they could otherwise have obtained.

§ 12.04 STRENGTHENING OWN WEAK BARGAINING POSITION

[1] Through Expressions of Inflexibility

Representatives who find themselves with apparently anemic bargaining positions should not automatically concede everything. Even when they are unable to ignore the superior power possessed by their opponents, they may be able to take action that will permit them to artificially enhance their own situations. If they can effectively convince their adversaries that they have adopted an inflexible posture that they cannot reasonably modify, they may be able to force their stronger opponents to moderate their demands (Schelling, 1956, at 283).

[2]   Tie Weak Issues to Stronger Issues

Even when weaker parties lack significant power vis-a-vis objectively powerful opponents, they can enhance their bargaining influence if they can tie weak issues to specific items the other side values (Salacuse, 2002, at 261). For example, a firm seeking to establish a business relationship with a large corporation might lack the power to demand significant concessions from that party. On the other hand, so long as the smaller firm possesses something the larger entity needs, it can use "issue specific" power to generate concessions on other issues the other party may not particularly care about. A prospective law suit plaintiff may possess confidential information that could be damaging to a large defendant if it were to become public. The claimant could exchange a confidentiality agreement for concessions it desires from the other firm.

[3]   Reliance on Limited Client Authority

[a]   Where Opposition Strongly Desires Mutual Accords

Some negotiators circumscribe their bargaining freedom through reliance on limited client authority. They have their principals provide them with narrowly prescribed discretion, and they openly convey these client constraints to their opponents. Devious bargainers may combine this Limited Authority practice with the "Mutt and Jeff" approach. They represent their absent clients as the unreasonable parties who must be satisfied before final agreements can be achieved. If they can induce their adversaries to accept the contrived limits under which they appear to be operating, they may persuade those persons to reconsider their own positions. If the other participants seriously want to achieve mutual accords, they may be compelled to reduce their demands below what might otherwise be warranted in light of their actual strength.

[b]   Defense

When powerful opponents are confronted by limited authority claims, they may attempt to neutralize the artificially curtailed parameters by suggesting — perhaps with opposing clients in attendance — that the prescribed client limits are unreasonably narrow. If the recalcitrant clients can be induced to modify their previous instructions, the use of this ploy by their agents to enhance their negotiating posture will be seriously undermined. It is difficult to employ this technique to generate expanded bargaining agent discretion when those representatives have already taken the time to convince their principals that anything less than the previously formulated and expressed minimum settlement terms should be unacceptable. However, before negotiators decide to lock their clients into uncompromising positions in a desperate effort to enlarge their bargaining power, they should understand the significant risk associated with such client indoctrination. If it turns out that legal counsel's preliminary evaluation of the interaction was incorrect, this approach may preclude agreement. Their clients would be unlikely to move much beyond the prescribed positions, and the opponents may conclude that they would be better off accepting the consequences of nonsettlements.

[4]   Public Announcements of Minimum Acceptable Settlements

Some agents try to expand their bargaining authority through the public announcement of minimum "fair" settlements that their constituents should reasonably expect them to achieve. The President occasionally employs this technique when he broadcasts his intention to veto proposed legislation if it fails to conform to certain constraints. Once this position is publicly proclaimed, the Members of Congress recognize that the President would be unlikely to accept the embarrassing loss of face that would accompany any meaningful modification of his previously announced position.

Former Vice President Spiro Agnew was able to use publicly disclosed inflexibility to further his plea bargaining efforts when he was being accused of bribery and tax evasion. Although his lawyers indicated to the prosecutors that he would be willing to resign his office in exchange for a nolo contendere plea to a tax evasion charge, they said that he was unwilling to accept any arrangement that involved either an admission of guilt or the possibility of a jail term (Lowenthal, 1982, at 76–78). To enhance the credibility of his bargaining posture, Vice President Agnew steadfastly proclaimed his innocence and unequivocally stated that he would not resign his office even if he were indicted. The prosecutors feared a constitutional crisis if they were forced to try a sitting Vice President, and they were induced to reconsider their prior demand for an open acknowledgment of wrongdoing as a condition of any plea bargain. As a result, they finally agreed to a nolo contendere plea that did not entail any formal admission of guilt.

Labor leaders occasionally employ a similar technique to persuade employers of the seriousness of the demands they are making. They openly indicate to their members — sometimes through the news media — that they would not be effectively performing their representational function if they could not achieve certain minimal objectives that are expressly enumerated. Employers then realize that it would be difficult for the union officials who have made these representations to temporize their demands without suffering substantial humiliation and the possible loss of their positions in the next union election. If the employers would prefer to continue their relationship with the present labor leadership, they may accede to more generous employment terms than they had initially contemplated, recognizing the consequences that would likely result if the publicly stated minimum goals were not attained.

[5]   Postpone Discussions Until Power Balance Shifts

Negotiators who find themselves discussing important items over which they possess minimal bargaining leverage may alternatively counteract this deficiency by postponing any final decision on those issues until other matters are explored. They may thus delay final resolution of these matters until other terms are mentioned that the opponent seriously wants to obtain. They may then be in a position to use their stronger posture with respect to the other items to enhance their less potent situation vis-a-vis the former topics.

[6]   Consideration of Continuing Relationships

If a continuing, symbiotic relationship is involved (*e.g.*, franchisor-franchisee; labor-management), a party that temporarily finds itself in disadvantageous circumstances may be able to offset the ephemeral advantage enjoyed by the other party by indicating that any short-term "win" attained by the presently stronger side may result in a mutually destructive Pyrrhic victory. This technique may effectively remind the party with the instant superiority that appropriately moderated demands are necessary to guarantee continued harmonious dealings. A party involved in an ongoing relationship may similarly avoid the consequences of a currently weakened position by postponing negotiations until a more propitious time when the balance of power has shifted more toward equilibrium.

§ 12.05   CONFRONTING OPPONENT INFLEXIBILITY

It can be a frustrating experience to be involved in a negotiation with parties who are unalterably committed to unacceptable positions. It is tempting to challenge their uncompromising stands directly. This approach entails a serious risk that the bargaining process will be irreversibly disrupted by the unwillingness of opponents to acknowledge openly the unreasonableness of their existing proposals. It is generally more productive to employ a less confrontational technique that provides the other participants with a face-saving means of modifying their obstinate dispositions (Ury, 1991, at 90–109).

[1]   Inducing Needs and Interests Analyses

Negotiators should attempt to induce seemingly inflexible opponents to focus objectively on the underlying needs and interests of their clients. It is usually easier to generate position reappraisals through needs and interests analyses than through discussions focusing exclusively on adamantly articulated positions. Once the underlying objectives have been discerned and explored, it may be possible to formulate alternative solutions that may prove to be mutually beneficial.

[2]   Emphasizing Areas of Common Interest

During interactions with intransigent opponents, it is helpful to emphasize the areas of common interest, rather than the zone of disagreement. If they can be induced to realize the advantageous results their own sides can achieve through agreement on the less controverted items, there is a substantial likelihood they will become more conciliatory with respect to the remaining issues in dispute. As they become psychologically committed to the opportunity to attain mutually beneficial accords, they will be increasingly unwilling to allow a few unresolved topics to hinder overall agreements.

[3]   Presenting Face-Saving Opportunities

Once previously uncompromising parties have begun to tacitly acknowledge the unreasonable nature of their positions, it is time to employ a face-saving approach that permits a graceful retreat. It would be unwise to expect opponents to make wholly unreciprocated concessions. This would be tantamount to unconditional surrender. It is preferable to offer some small tokens of exchange that opposing negotiators can use to explain their conciliatory movement to their clients. The significance of these tokens should be embellished, so that opposing agents and their principals will feel that they obtained something meaningful in exchange for their truly magnanimous concessions.

§ 12.06   DEALING WITH PARTICULARLY DIFFICULT OPPONENTS

[1]   Inevitability

Almost all attorneys must occasionally interact with overtly offensive opponents. These are usually win-lose, competitive/adversarial individuals who only feel successful when they completely annihilate and even humiliate the people with whom they interact. While their behavior generally undermines the interests of their own clients — generating an excessive number of nonsettlements and inefficient agreements — they must still be dealt with by opposing counsel.

Some of these individuals may be *situationally difficult* people who are behaving badly because of the unusual stress they are currently experiencing as a result of the underlying issues involved or the negotiation encounter they are facing (Shapiro & Jankowski, 2005, at 20–21, 81–94). Others may be *strategically difficult* persons who are deliberately using their offensive conduct to intimidate opponents (*id.* at 95–105), while a few may be *simply difficult* individuals who are usually unpleasant (*id.* at 106–119). It may be possible to modify the inappropriate behavior of situationally and strategically difficult people, but it is almost impossible to change the conduct of simply difficult individuals.

[2]   Attitudinal Bargaining

The first question to ask when you encounter obstreperous adversaries is whether "attitudinal bargaining" can be employed to modify their conduct. It is wise to politely, but forcefully, indicate one's unwillingness to participate in needlessly unpleasant interactions and to suggest how much more productive professional and civilized negotiations would be. Individuals who are not truly nasty bargainers — but are affected by unusual stress or have decided to experiment with such an approach — may quickly return to their more agreeable ways (Adler & Silverstein, 2000, at 90–92).

When dealing with opponents who are adversely affected by the stress surrounding the current encounter, it is best to empathize with those persons and work to diminish the negative feelings they are experiencing (Shapiro & Jankowski, 2005, at 140–44). If they are concerned about the underlying issues, tell them those difficulties can be resolved through the bargaining process. If they are afraid to negotiate, assure them that the process need not be unpleasant. If opponents are using bad behavior as a strategic weapon to advance their bargaining objectives, it can be helpful to let them know their conduct is not working (*id.* at 157–82). Let them know you recognize what they are doing. For example, if they are employing the good cop/bad cop Mutt and Jeff approach, merely smile and tell them this tactic will not work on you. If they are being particularly aggressive, indicate that this style will not induce you to make unwarranted position changes.

If attitudinal bargaining does not produce significant improvement, one should attempt to control the number,and length of these interactions in a way that diminishes the ability of simply nasty persons to bother you. Telephone and e-mail exchanges can be especially effective, since the look of pleasure on the face of an adversary who is being offensive is not visible. This also affords one the opportunity to terminate unpleasant sessions anytime they feel frustrated. It suffices to indicate that there is other more — pressing business to which one must attend. If personal meetings are necessary, they can be scheduled in a conference room with a large table — to enable you to place your opponents on the other side — a reasonable distance away. This configuration will impede their ability to invade your space in a manner designed to intimidate you.

[3]   Setting Examples, Offering Objective Analysis, and Appreciating Opponent's Perspective

It is important when dealing with difficult adversaries to try to separate the personalities of the negotiators from the problems that must be addressed (Fisher & Ury, 1981, at 17–40). One should set a good example for unpleasant opponents by being particularly courteous and respectful. Being a good listener who patiently listens to their perspective will break down the opponent's desire to offend. Placing oneself in their shoes to see if it's possible to discern their underlying concerns and motivations will enable greater understanding of their approach (Gray, 2003, at 307–08). Are they being driven by unrealistic client expectations or by adverse economic pressures affecting their law firms? Perhaps they are tacitly expressing a personal need to prove their competence. If the problem is associated with unreasonable client considerations, one may need to help them develop rationales they can use to diminish client expectations. If their firm is experiencing present difficulties, one may wish to postpone discussions until a more propitious date. If they seem to be looking for respect from their peers, one can emphasize how much one admires attorneys who are able to generate mutually beneficial deals.

Some people apparently believe that everyone else is trying to take advantage of them. If one takes the time to appreciate their perspective — even if one doesn't agree with it — it may be possible to disarm them. Their discomfort may be associated with the way in which the negotiating issues have been formulated. They may think the issues have been stated in a manner that favors the opposing side. If one takes a few minutes to jointly reframe the problem in a mutually acceptable fashion, it's often possible to negate this potential stumbling block (Ury, 2007; Ury, 1991, at 59–85).

During the critical stages of particular negotiations, previously courteous opponents may become unexpectedly belligerent. They may fear that no agreement is going to be achieved. This is a good time to review the terms that have already been tentatively agreed upon and to emphasize how much progress has been made. This may generate a mutual psychological commitment to settlement and induce both sides to become more accommodating with respect to the remaining issues. If the participants are moving too quickly in an effort to compel an agreement, it's beneficial to recess the talks. This permits the parties to reconsider their nonsettlement options and the propriety of the positions they are currently asserting.

If one makes the effort to appreciate the negative pressures affecting opponents and works to decrease the impact of those factors, one can generate more pleasant and more productive bargaining interactions (Gray, 2003, at 308–09). This makes the practice of law more enjoyable and increases one's ability to advance client interests.

§ 12.07 TELEPHONE NEGOTIATIONS

[1] Frequency of Occurrence

Since complete reliance upon personal meetings would be unduly expensive and time-consuming, the vast majority of settlement negotiations are conducted wholly or at least partially on the telephone (*see generally* Borg, 2004, at 131–59). Telephone negotiations involve the same stages and conventional bargaining techniques as in-person interactions. They usually consist of a series of shorter exchanges than in-person transactions (Ross, 2006, at 211), and they preclude visual contact except where video telephones are available. Advocates who make the mistake of treating these electronic exchanges less seriously than they would face-to-face interactions place themselves at a disadvantage.

Time urgency is exacerbated when cell phone discussions are involved in public locations. Lawyers who call or are called while among other people are often at a disadvantage for several reasons. First, individuals on cell phones in open spaces often try to keep the calls short, and this may cause negotiators to try to conclude talks too quickly. This may induce them to give up information or make concessions on an expedited basis. Second, persons may not feel capable of saying in such settings what they would say in private offices. Third, they may talk more quietly — and thus less forcefully — to avoid being overheard by strangers. It is this advisable for lawyers who must negotiate on cell phones to move to isolated areas in which they can be themselves. It they are called while in public areas, they should not hesitate to ask to return the call when they find a more suitable location to conduct negotiation discussions.

[2] Considerations When Using

[a] Less Personal

Attorneys should realize that telephone exchanges are less personal than face-to-face interactions (Fisher & Shapiro, 2005, at 61–62). This factor makes it easier for participants to employ overtly competitive or deliberately deceptive tactics. It also makes it easier for parties to reject proposals being suggested by the other side (Ross, 2006, at 214; Cohen, 1980, at 210–11). Negotiators should recognize that telephone discussions tend to be more abbreviated than in-person encounters. It is thus more difficult to create a psychological commitment to settlement through only one or two telephone exchanges.

[b] Level of Information Available

Many lawyers think that telephone conversations are less revealing than in-person talks, because they do not involve visual interactions. They act as if opposing counsel cannot perceive nonverbal signals during these transactions. This presumption is incorrect. Some psychologists have suggested to me that many individuals are more adept at reading nonverbal messages during telephone exchanges than they are during in-person interactions. I have found support for this assertion from blind students who have exhibited an uncanny ability to read the nonverbal signals being emitted by others they cannot see. This phenomenon is attributable to the fact that in-person interactions involve a myriad of simultaneous nonverbal stimuli that are often too numerous to be proficiently discerned and interpreted. When people speak on the telephone, however, they are not as likely to be overwhelmed by the various nonverbal clues emanating from the other party. They need only concentrate on the audible messages being received to ascertain the content of the nonverbal messages being communicated.

[c]   Types of Information Available

[i]   Nonverbal Clues

A substantial number of nonverbal clues are discernible during telephone interactions (Burgoon, Buller & Woodall, 1996, at 4). Careful listeners can hear changes in the pitch, pace, tone, inflection, rhythm, and volume of speaker voices (Folberg & Golann, 2006, at 202). A pregnant pause may indicate that a particular offer is being seriously considered by a recipient who did not hesitate before rejecting previous proposals. The initial pause before the most recent position statement was verbally renounced would suggest that the proposal has entered the other party's zone of acceptability. A sigh in response to a new proposal may similarly indicate that the recipient is now confident that some settlement will be achieved.

[ii]   Voice Inflection

Voice inflection may be equally informative. People who respond to communicated offers with perceptibly increased levels of excitement may nonverbally suggest that they are more pleased with the proposal than their verbal response might otherwise indicate. Since most negotiators tend to begin the discussions with either their most important or their least important subjects, the topic sequence presented by parties may inadvertently reveal the items they value most.

[iii]   Excessively Deliberate Speech and Change in Vocal Pitch

Professor Ekman's seminal book on deception noted that individuals who engage in prevarication tend to speak more deliberately and to utter their misrepresentations with higher pitched voices (Ekman, 1992, at 92–94). Attentive listeners could easily perceive these phenomena.

[iv]   Recognition of Verbal Leaks and Nonverbal Messages

Advocates engaged in telephone negotiations should listen intently for verbal leaks and nonverbal signals being emitted by their opponents. They should simultaneously recognize the ability of their adversaries to discern the various verbal leaks and nonverbal messages emanating from themselves. They should thus be as careful to control their verbal leaks and their nonverbal messages during telephone exchanges as they would during in-person encounters. They should additionally note the use of signal words such as "to be candid" or "to be truthful." Many people use them to preface misrepresentations they hope will be unquestioningly accepted. Those participants who ignore this crucial consideration and treat telephone discussions casually may unthinkingly place themselves at a disadvantage. Following each telephonic exchange, a record of negotiation developments should always be entered in the case file for future reference.

[3]   Dynamics of Who Calls Whom

[a]   Advantage of Surprise

It is usually more advantageous to be the telephone caller rather than the recipient of the call. The caller has the opportunity to prepare for the exchange (Ross, 2006, at 212–213; Dawson, 1995, at 35). Negotiators who plan to phone opponents to discuss particular cases should prepare as diligently for these interactions as they would for in-person exchanges. This preliminary effort is usually rewarded. Since they have the opportunity to surprise unsuspecting adversaries with their calls, they may subtly gain the upper hand (Woolf, 1990, at 161). The other participants are unlikely to expect their call and are probably unprepared for the conversation that is about to occur. This permits phoning parties to advance more persuasive arguments and to elicit less planned counteroffers than would have been possible during formally scheduled interactions.

[b]   Defense for Recipient

Individuals who receive unexpected telephone calls from opponents should internally assess their degree of preparedness. If they are not fully conversant regarding the pertinent factual circumstances, legal doctrines, and prior settlement discussions, they should not make the mistake of plunging ignorantly into uncharted waters. They should not hesitate to suggest that they are presently occupied with other matters and unable to talk. They can thereafter peruse the file and telephone the other party when they are completely prepared. When they reach the initial caller, they can say that they are returning that person's call. Their subsequent silence can adroitly return the focus of the interaction to the other party.

Most bargaining techniques that could be used during in-person interactions may be employed with equal efficacy during telephone negotiations. Although it is difficult to walk out during phone calls when people want to graphically demonstrate their displeasure regarding bargaining progress, individuals who are inclined toward such histrionics may accomplish the same result by hanging up on their intransigent opponents. It must be realized, however, that this tactic may be considered less acceptable than a cessation of in-person talks effectuated by way of a walkout — due to the more contemptuous and discourteous nature of this device. People who wish to terminate current phone interactions should at least inform their opponents why they are doing so to avoid unnecessary future difficulties.

Negotiators occasionally become frustrated or confused during telephone discussions and want to discontinue telephone exchanges without evidencing total disregard for the other participants. They can adopt a different approach. Instead of hanging up while *other* people are talking, they can abruptly terminate the conversations while *they* are speaking! Since no one expects people to hang up on themselves, the targets of this maneuver will reasonably assume that the participants have been inadvertently disconnected. This gives the moving parties time to regain control over their emotions. If they do not want to continue the electronic interactions at the present time, they can have their secretary explain to their opponents when they call back that they are busy with other calls.

Many negotiators prefer in-person interactions to telephone discussions (Thompson, 2005, at 305–07). They like the psychological atmosphere they can personally establish, and they believe that they are more proficient readers of nonverbal signals during face-to-face encounters than during telephone talks. They also prefer several longer in-person interactions to numerous brief telephone exchanges. These people should not hesitate to insist on in-person sessions when serious transactions are involved and they think this will provide them with a bargaining advantage.

§ 12.08 NEGOTIATING VIA LETTERS, E-MAIL, OR FAX TRANSMISSIONS

[1] Popularity of Media

A surprising number of individuals like to conduct their negotiations primarily or entirely through letters, e-mail, or fax transmissions, especially younger persons who have grown up using e-mail, text-messaging, and similar electronic means of interacting with others (Larson, 2006a, at 637–39). They do not merely transmit written versions of terms orally discussed during earlier interactions. They limit most, if not all, of their transactions to written communications. Most people who endeavor to restrict their bargaining communications to letters, e-mail, or fax exchanges are not comfortable with the traditional negotiation process. They do not like the seemingly amorphous nature of that process, and do not enjoy the split-second tactical decision-making that must occur during in-person interactions. They forget that bargaining involves uniquely *personal* encounters that are not easily conducted entirely through written communications (Barsness & Bhappu, 2004, at 354–59; Crosson, 2004; Thompson & Nadler, 2002; Nadler, 2001; Morris, Nadler, Kurtzberg & Thompson, 2002).

People contemplating bargaining interactions that will be primarily conducted through the exchange of letters, e-mail, or fax transmissions should appreciate how difficult it is to establish rapport with opponents through those written mediums. It would thus be beneficial to initially telephone their adversaries to exchange some personal information and to establish minimal relationships (Thompson, 2005, at 316–18; Nadler, 2004b, at 237–47; Thompson & Nadler, 2002; Nadler, 2001). Individuals who first create mutual relations through such oral exchanges are likely to find their subsequent negotiations more pleasant and more efficient (Thompson & Nadler, 2002, at 115; Nadler, 2001, at 341; Morris, Nadler, Kurtzberg & Thompson, 2002, at 97). They are also likely to generate more cooperative behavior and more trusting relationships, and encounter fewer impasses (Nadler, 2004b, at 237–47). If telephone exchanges would be difficult, it would be helpful during the preliminary e-mail exchanges to disclose some personal information designed to increase the rapport between the parties (Nadler & Shestowsky, 2006, at 162).

[2] Disadvantages

[a] Cumbersome and Inefficient

The use of letters, e-mail, or fax transmissions to conduct basic negotiations is generally a cumbersome and inefficient process (Thompson & Nadler, 2002, at 112). Every communication has to be drafted and thoroughly edited before being sent to the other side. The opponents must then read and digest all of the written passages, and formulate their own replies. Due to the definitive nature of written documents, written positions seem to be more intractable than those expressed vocally over the telephone or in person. When people present their proposals orally, their voice inflections and nonverbal signals may indicate a willingness to be flexible with respect to certain items.

Written communications rarely convey this critical information (Nadler & Shestowsky, 2006, at 156–57). In addition, written encounters tend to produce less efficient outcomes than in-person exchangees, because of the lack of effective cooperative bargaining (Thompson, 1998, at 281). People also tend to be less polite — and more confrontational — when communicating through e-mail (Mc Ginn & Croson, 2004, at 339–340; Barsness & Bhappu, 2004, at 356–57; Hatta, Ohbuchi & Fukuno, 2007, at 284). They similarly tend to employ more deceptive tactics.

[b]   Misinterpretation and Permanence

Letter, e-mail, and fax exchanges may often be misinterpreted. As the recipients review and evaluate the positions set forth by their opponents, they may read more or less into the stated terms than was actually intended. They may interpret seemingly innocuous language as deliberately inflammatory. As they reread the pertinent passages, they tend to reinforce their preliminary impressions. Their misinterpretations may be compounded by their escalated written responses to the terms they erroneously think their opponents intended to convey. When the original writers receive their reply, they may not comprehend their uncompromising or negative tone, and may further exacerbate the situation with antagonistic responses of their own (Thompson & Nadler, 2002, at 119; Nadler, 2001, at 337–38). This is why e-mail negotiations tend to be less cooperative than in-person interactions (Mc Ginn & Croson, 2004, at 341). If people become especially frustrated by unpleasant e-mail exchanges, they may decide to write a negative reply. It may make them feel better to prepare such a response, so long as they click on "cancel" and not "send" when they are done.

[c]   Inflexibility

When individuals negotiate in person or on the telephone, they can immediately hear the way in which their opponents perceive their articulated positions. Their adversaries can quickly ask questions to clarify seemingly ambiguous proposals. If speakers realize that their true intentions are being misunderstood, they can expeditiously correct the misperceptions. They can thus minimize problems caused by miscommunication. The participants can also indicate through verbal leaks or nonverbal messages their willingness to modify stated proposals, and this flexibility can help to keep the process moving toward a successful conclusion.

[3]   Precautions

Some complex transactions involve numerous terms that must be carefully formulated to protect the interests of the various parties. In these cases, it is entirely appropriate for the negotiators to exchange draft proposals through letters, e-mail, or fax transmissions. To avoid communication difficulties, however, each letter, e-mail, or fax transmission should be followed by a telephone call. This enables the sending party to ascertain the manner in which the written communication has been received. If it appears that the recipient has read something into the written proposals that was not intended, the misinterpretation can be quickly corrected and the bargaining process can be preserved.

[4]   Possible Access to Metadata in Electronic Documents

When parties send documents to others in electronic form, they often inadvertently include critical information that is not obvious on the face of those documents — and which they do not intend to share with the document recipients. Parties who know how to "mine" electronic files for hidden information may be able to determine exactly how documents were prepared and edited, and even uncover editorial comments made by persons who reviewed earlier drafts. Both the New York Bar [N.Y. State Ethics Op. 782 (2004)] and the Alabama Bar [Ala. State Bar Disc. Comm. Op. 2007-2 (2007)] have indicated that attorneys have an obligation under the confidentiality duty imposed by Model Rule 1.6 to use "reasonable care" when transmitting electronic documents to prevent the disclosure of metadata containing client confidences. It thus behooves lawyers sending electronic files to opposing counsel to use means designed to preclude the unintended disclosure of confidential client information. There are several ways they can preclude the unintended transmission of such metadata. They can use one of several scrubbing software programs designed to eliminate such metadata from their files before they send the cleansed files to others. They can alternatively send PDF files, or create new files and then insert the existing files into the newly created files. My computer experts indicate that this insertion option eliminates the metadata that was contained in the existing files that were inserted into newly created files.

May attorneys who receive electronic files ethically mine those files for hidden metadata that will provide them with information the file senders clearly did not intend them to find? In 2006, American Bar Association Formal Op. 06-442 (2006) indicated that lawyers have no ethical obligation to refrain from mining and using metadata embedded in electronic files received through e-mail or other modes from adverse parties. This decision should be contrasted with Model Rule 4.4(b) which provides that "[a] lawyer who receives a document relating to the representation of the lawyer's client and knows or reasonably should know that the document was inadvertently sent shall promptly notify the sender." (Morgan & Rotunda, 2008, at 96) Should lawyers be under a similar obligation when they receive electronic files containing accessible metadata they know the senders did not intend to include? A similar conclusion was reached by the Maryland Bar Ethics Committee [Op. 2007-09], but the Maryland Committee emphasized the fact that the Maryland Bar had not adopted Model Rule 4.4(b). On the other hand, both the New York Bar [N.Y. State Ethics Op. 749 (2001)] and the Alabama Bar [Ala. State Bar Disciplinary Commission Op. 2007-02 (2007)] have indicated that such mining of metadata in electronic files contravenes Model Rule 8.4, which indicates that it constitutes "professional misconduct" for a lawyer to "engage in conduct involving dishonesty, fraud, deceit or misrepresentation [or] . . . that is prejudicial to the administration of justice." The Alabama Bar stated that the "mining of metadata constitutes a knowing and deliberate attempt by the recipient attorney to acquire confidential and privileged information in order to obtain an unfair advantage against an opposing party."

§ 12.09 LACK OF EFFORT ON BEHALF OF OPPONENT TO CONVINCE THEIR CLIENT OF MERITS OF OFFER

[1] Opposing Counsel as Primary Roadblock to Settlement

There are occasions when attorneys begin to suspect that opposing lawyers are not seriously endeavoring to convince their clients of the reasonable nature of the offers that have been recently tendered. It is even possible that opposing counsel have not communicated outstanding offers to their clients, despite their obligation to do so under Model Rule 1.4 (*see* Comment 1 to Rule 1.4 in Morgan & Rotunda, 2008, at 13). They may believe that opposing counsel, and not their clients, are preventing consummation of final accords. It is possible that those lawyers are employing a "Mutt and Jeff" approach, with their absent principals being portrayed as the unyielding parties. If those clients fully understood the generous character of the proposals that have been conveyed, they may be inclined to accept them.

[2] Heightening Opposing Client Awareness

Since it is unethical for attorneys to communicate directly with opposing clients who are represented by legal counsel (*see* Model Rule 4.2 in Morgan & Rotunda, 2008, at 94), it would be inappropriate to make any settlement overtures to those clients without presenting the proposals through their legal representatives. Nevertheless, it may be possible to make presentations in the presence of those persons. Meetings can be arranged that opposing clients must attend — *e.g.*, depositions of those individuals. During those sessions, the topic of settlement may be casually raised with opposing counsel. Offers previously communicated to the other side's attorneys can be reiterated and accompanied by carefully articulated rationales that indicate the reasonable character of those proposals. Even though these exchanges would technically be directed to the opposing lawyers, it would be difficult for those practitioners to deprive their clients of the opportunity to listen to the presentations being made. If those legal representatives were to interrupt the initial settlement overtures being explained and demand that no such discussions occur in the presence of their clients, it would probably cause those principals to become suspicious. After all, why would their own attorneys be afraid to permit those conversations to be conducted with the clients in attendance unless they had something to hide?

Lawyers who would feel uncomfortable if they used such an artifice to broach settlement in the presence of opposing clients can always wait until formal settlement conferences to accomplish the same objective. Judges generally require the clients to attend these sessions. The most recent offers are usually elicited and explored. This gives attorneys the opportunity to make their most persuasive presentations in front of opposing clients. The presiding judges may even provide additional support for the positions being articulated.

§ 12.10 RESPONDING TO "IS THIS YOUR FINAL OFFER?"

[1] If True Final Offer

After negotiators articulate new offers, they are occasionally asked by opponents whether their new positions represent their "final offers." What is the appropriate response to such an inquiry? If the new position actually represents your "final offer," it is beneficial to firmly and politely inform the other side of this fact. When doing so, one should avoid any modifiers (*e.g.*, "that's about as far as I can go;" "I don't have much room left;" "we aren't inclined to go higher/lower") which contain verbal leaks indicating that this is not really their final offer. Using unequivocal language and consistent nonverbal signals (*e.g.*, open posture with palms facing other side and sincere eye contact) can ensure that the verbal and nonverbal messages are congruent.

[2]   Making Disingenuous Final Offers

What if the most recent position statement does *not* represent one's final offer? Some negotiators may feel comfortable indicating that there may be more room if the other side modifies its current position. This effectively conveys the need for the other side to make a new offer before one decides whether to make another position change. Other negotiators may prefer to use a blocking technique to avoid a direct response. They might ignore the question and continue to focus on other aspects of the bargaining interaction — hoping their opponent will forget to restate the unanswered question. They might counter the other party's question with one of their own and ask whether that side's most recent proposal represents *their* "final offer." They might alternatively indicate that this question concerns a confidential matter between them and their client that they are unwilling to discuss directly. The problem with this response concerns the fact that if when they get to their real bottom line they are willing to disclose this fact, individuals who deal with them regularly will realize that their "no comment" response indicates that they actually possess additional bargaining room.

May a negotiator disingenuously indicate that their most recent proposal constitutes their "final offer" when it actually does not? Since Model Rule 4.1, which prohibits knowing fact misrepresentations by attorneys, has an exception for statements pertaining to settlement intentions (*see* Chapter 17, *infra*), one could probably state that they have reached their "bottom line" when they have not. Even assuming no ethical violation, however, such a tactical misrepresentation may create serious practical difficulties. If the opponent believes this misrepresentation and it is not within that side's settlement range, they may give up and break off negotiations. If the other side continues the discussions and this side subsequently places a more generous position on the bargaining table, its credibility would be undermined and the opponent may begin to question the veracity of prior truthful representations. This could cause the entire interaction to deteriorate.

§ 12.11   MULTIPLE PARTY NEGOTIATIONS

[1]   Inclusion of All Parties

When attorneys represent corporations or government agencies, institutional counsel and/or firm or agency officials may have to participate in their negotiations. These individuals may do so as organizational representatives or to provide necessary business expertise. In these circumstances, it is imperative that the outside attorneys and the corporate or agency representatives conduct their own intra-group negotiations — prior to meetings with opposing parties — to enable them to develop defined objectives and a unified bargaining strategy. This preparation will enable them to function as a coordinated team during their discussions with opposing negotiators.

[2]   Increase in Complexity

Law suits often involve multiple plaintiffs and/or defendants, and business transactions occasionally involve numerous participants. This fact greatly increases the complexity of the interaction. Not only must the plaintiffs negotiate with the defendants, but plaintiffs and/or defendants must also negotiate with each other. In multi-participant business negotiations, different parties may have to negotiate separately with other parties that have similar interests and with other entities that have dissimilar interests.

[3]   Recognition of Diverse Interests and Importance of Forming Interest-Based Alliances

Parties involved with multi-party negotiations should not assume that other participants that seem to be similarly situated necessarily share their interests (Mnookin, 2003). Each party tends to have its own institutional needs, priorities, and considerations. Internal political constraints may affect party positions and deliberations. These factors must be ascertained and taken into account when representatives interact with other participants. These priority differences and the multiplicity of participants make it more difficult for negotiators to create value through cooperative bargaining, and different parties may try to claim more than their fair share of the increased value that is generated (Mnookin, 2003, at 2–3).

Each party must initially meet with its own key leaders to develop a set of common interests and goals, and a unified bargaining strategy. Even within the same organization, different constituencies must be included and satisfied. Once these intra-organizational objectives are accomplished, firm representatives should meet with other parties that appear to have analogous interests. They may be able to form inter-party alliances that can work together to achieve common goals.

[4]   Selection of Primary Spokespeople

When plenary sessions begin with the other participants, each group should select a small number of primary spokespeople to conduct the discussions. If an excessive number of individuals are allowed to participate actively, it will be difficult to maintain a united front, and adept opponents will exploit negotiation team disagreements. During plenary negotiations, allied parties must recognize that they generally possess more power together than they do individually. They should not permit disagreements on minor items to preclude joint efforts to achieve their more significant objectives.

[5]   Incorporating Opponent's Language When Drafting Proprosals

In multi-party negotiations, the leaders of each entity tend to prefer the proposals authored by themselves and to be suspicious of proposals developed by their opponents. Whenever possible, advocates should try to incorporate language provided by other participants to make those parties feel that their ideas are being respected. If authorship difficulties occur, the group can ask a neutral facilitator to use a single-text approach that permits that person to incorporate language from the different party proposals in an overall document designed to avoid authorship problems. All subsequent modifications can then be added to that one document.

§ 12.12 USING "NEGOTIATION LINKAGE" TO ENHANCE BARGAINING OPPORTUNITIES

[1] Linking Related Interactions

In both litigation and business settings, attorneys may conduct negotiations with different parties — or even the same party — that may permit the use of "negotiation linkage" to advance their bargaining interests (Crump, 2007). For example, litigators with similar claims on behalf of different clients against the same defendant might work to settle the stronger cases first hoping to establish beneficial precedents that might carry over to weaker claims addressed later. They might alternatively try a particularly strong case to generate a favorable verdict they could employ to guide subsequent case negotiations. Litigators with similar claims against different defendants may conduct preliminary discussions with the parties they think will provide them with the best terms they can cite when they negotiate with other entities.

Business firms buying or selling products or services may use similar linkage to advance their bargaining interests. They could use the terms already achieved with other parties to influence current interactions with other companies. Economic or non-economic provisions already obtained from competing entities can be employed to establish the range for the present discussions. Negotiators may similarly employ the possibility of future negotiations with others to affect current encounters. They might suggest that if they do not receive appropriate offers now, they will do business with other firms.

[2] Scheduling Bargaining Encounters for Optimal Benefit

When it appears that different bargaining interactions may have a linkage impact, negotiators should determine the optimal order in which to proceed. If one negotiation would be likely to establish the best precedent for subsequent encounters, parties should work to resolve that matter first. On the other hand, when they think that a particular negotiation might set a poor precedent for other encounters, they should postpone that matter until they have had the opportunity to conclude more propitious discussions with other parties.

§ 12.13 PRETRIAL SETTLEMENT CONFERENCES

[1] Importance of Preparation

[a] Lawyer

Most state and federal courts now require formal pretrial settlement conferences for all cases progressing toward adjudication (see generally Brazil, 2007). The clients are normally expected to attend these meetings with their respective counselors. Lawyers should never make the mistake of appearing at these sessions unprepared, since such judicial intervention constitutes a critical stage of the settlement process. Legal advocates will be required to negotiate with the presiding neutrals, through those individuals with their opponents, and directly with their adversaries. Attorneys who exhibit a lack of factual and legal knowledge at these conferences may unwittingly enhance the confidence of opposing counsel and their clients, and may seriously impede the ability of the presiding judicial officials — magistrates and volunteer attorneys increasingly perform this important function — to fully comprehend the pertinent circumstances. Lawyers who are not familiar with the mediation techniques usually employed by judicial officials scheduled to conduct pretrial settlement conferences should try to obtain the requisite information regarding those participants from other litigators. Are they active or passive mediators? Do they discuss issues in a general or a specific manner? Do they tend to ask pointed questions regarding client settlement objectives? Lawyers should be as prepared in this regard as they would be if they were required to negotiate directly with the presiding neutrals.

[b]   Client

Legal representatives must prepare their clients for settlement conferences just as they must prepare themselves. Clients need to understand the role the judicial officers are likely to perform during these sessions, so they will not be unduly surprised by conference developments. (*See* Chapter 16, *infra*, regarding the techniques generally employed by mediators) Lawyers should explain the fact that presiding officials are likely to ask pointed questions about settlement developments. Those officers may have the parties explain their most recent offers. They may propound detailed questions regarding the relevant factual circumstances and applicable legal doctrines. Some may challenge the positions articulated by counsel and suggest possible compromises. If clients are not adequately prepared for these exchanges, they may be intimidated by the process. A few may even panic.

[2]   Deemphasizing the Adversarial Nature of the Litigation Process

Attorneys who sincerely want to achieve settlements should de-emphasize the adversarial nature of the litigation process. This will enhance the capacity of judicial officials to use conciliation techniques. Both bona fide weaknesses and operative strenghts should be at least minimally acknowledged. The detached position of presiding persons frequently permits those individuals to explore the underlying needs and interests of the different parties in an objective and relatively nonthreatening manner that could not be as successfully accomplished by the legal advocates themselves. Brainstorming discussions may be conducted to facilitate the development of alternative solutions that may satisfy the fundamental objectives of both sides. Attorneys must be flexible and maintain open minds if judicial mediators are expected to perform this function with maximum efficiency. Legal representatives must actively participate in these exchanges if they are to operate optimally.

[3]   Intervention of Presiding Officials

Presiding officials may assist attorneys to educate clients with unrealistic expectations. Those principals may be suspicious of attempts by their own legal representatives to diminish their elevated expectation levels, believing that their advocates are merely trying to dispose of their cases quickly. Lawyers who have such clients can casually disclose that fact during their conversations with the judicial officers. They may candidly acknowledge the reasonableness of the opposing offers, but indicate that their clients expect to obtain more beneficial results. Attentive mediators should readily discern the problem involved. They can then explore the operative circumstances in a manner that is designed to inform misguided clients of the irrationality of their perceptions.

Pretrial settlement conferences may similarly be employed to educate intransigent opposing clients who have summarily rejected reasonable offers. The presiding officials can carefully review the pertinent circumstances and note the manner in which analogous cases have lately been resolved by other litigants and by jury verdicts. Although regular mediators are often hesitant to predict how they think particular cases would be resolved if tried, many judges are willing to predict such outcomes (Raiffa, 2002, at 314–15; Brunet, 2003). This approach can expeditiously induce unreasonable parties to recognize the reality of their situations.

As court backlogs have grown and judicial administrators have increasingly viewed settlement conferences as expeditious means of disposing of cases without protracted litigation, the presiding neutrals have often focused too much on substantive results and given insufficient attention to notions of procedural fairness (Welsh, 2001, at 796–809). Many case facilitators eschew joint sessions during which the disputants can explain their concerns and feel they have been heard by both the other side and the presiding neutral, preferring separate caucus sessions with only attorneys present. Judicial mediators frequently evaluate the merits of the disputes being discussed and predict the likely trial outcomes to encourage lawyer movement toward settlements. While this procedure may generate substantive agreements, it deprives disputants of the opportunity to vent their emotional feelings in environments that guarantee that opponents hear their concerns. It also deprives them of the sense they have been treated respectfully and fairly. Judicial mediators should take the time to provide litigants with the chance to express their feelings. The mediators should carefully listen to the emotional concerns being expressed and make sure that opponents also listen respectfully and without interruption. If clients wish to attend subsequent caucus sessions, they should normally be allowed to do so. This will increase both the likelihood of settlements and the sense of the disputants that the resulting resolutions are substantively and procedurally fair.

[4]   Persuading Presiding Officials

Legal advocates should not feel bound by the case assessments made by presiding officers. If they do not agree with those people's evaluations of the relevant facts and law, they should not hesitate to respectfully indicate their disagreement. They can then articulate their own persuasive arguments. These presentations should be have multiple purposes. They should be intended to induce the presiding individuals to reconsider their preliminary assessments. They should also be directed at opposing counsel and their clients. A forceful submission may effectively cause opponents to reassess their own positions in a favorable manner.

[5]   Value of More Diligent Mediation Techniques

An increasing number of judicial officials are beginning to realize the value of more diligent mediation techniques. A few schedule — with or without the consent of the legal advocates — separate sessions with each side. This allows them to review the needs and interests of each party in a less threatening atmosphere where opposing counsel are not present. These conciliators usually recognize the need to maintain the confidentiality of the information candidly disclosed during these separate meetings. Nonetheless, attorneys should understand that some of the confidential details conveyed to the judicial officers may be indirectly divulged to the other party when the mediators formulate overall proposals they think are consistent with the basic desires expressed by the competing parties. When advocates develop what they hope will be mutually acceptable proposals, they should thus be careful to disclose only those circumstances they would be willing to have the conciliators consider. If attorneys are concerned about the direct or indirect disclosure of sensitive information to their opponents, they should not hesitate to discuss this issue directly with the judicial mediators and agree upon mutually acceptable ground rules before they disclose highly sensitive information.

[6]   Separate Sessions With Only Clients Present

A few judges order separate settlement sessions that only clients may attend. They ask legal counsel to leave the room. Attorneys who know that particular judges like to employ this technique must decide whether to protest the propriety of meetings they cannot attend. If they are unwilling to interpose objections, for fear of offending the presiding judges, they should ensure that their clients are prepared for such meetings. They should provide their clients with a mini-course on the negotiation process and the mediation function to enable the client to effectively further their own interests during these sessions.

[7]   Control of Communicated Willingness to Compromise

Lawyers should understand that many judicial mediators do not allow the operative factual and legal circumstances of particular cases to completely constrain their discretion. They are principally interested in the attainment of mutually acceptable resolutions (Raiffa, 2002, at 314–15). If one party exudes a greater willingness to compromise, they are likely to exert more pressure against that side in an effort to produce a final accord. Attorneys should thus be careful not to appear too malleable during the critical stages of the judicial mediation process. They may otherwise find themselves the target of expediently applied judicial influence.

[8]   Avoid All Mendacity

Although it is acceptable for legal advocates to exaggerate the strength of their respective positions during pretrial settlement conferences, it is *never* proper to engage in mendacity with a judicial official. Model Rule 3.3(a) forbids lawyers from knowingly making false statements of material fact to judicial officers, and this rule has no exceptions for statements pertaining to settlement intentions as does Rule 4.1 (*see* ABA Formal Opinion 06–439 (2006)). As a result, it is unethical for lawyers to misrepresent their settlement intentions or their side's values when they are talking with judicial mediators. What if an attorney is directly asked whether his or her client would accept $75,000 when the client would do so? While it would be improper to misrepresent this fact, the lawyer might side step the inquiry by stating that he or she "is authorized to accept $85,000."

Judges talk frequently with colleagues regarding attorneys who have appeared before them. They quite reasonably believe that no practitioner should be permitted to employ prevarication to advance the interests of clients during judicial proceedings. If they determine that particular legal representatives have employed deliberately deceptive tactics when interacting with them, they disclose those transgressions to their judicial colleagues. This type of disclosure substantially undermines the ability of such disreputable lawyers to interact effectively with other judicial officials. Attorneys should never risk such future opprobrium for the slight benefit that may be achieved for current clients through resort to inappropriate behavior.

§ 12.14 NEGOTIATING WITH GOVERNMENT AGENCIES

[1]   Consideration of Cultural and Value System Differences

Due to the different value systems involved, when private-sector parties interact with government agencies, they frequently experience cultural difficulties. When private sector lawyers evaluate prospective client transactions, they carefully engage in cost-benefit analyses based on the projected legal costs, the financial benefits to be derived from the transactions in question, and the economic value of their external alternatives. With the primary exception of tax-collecting agencies, most government representatives are not concerned about these factors. They assume a better than average likelihood of prevailing in any resulting litigation, because of the judicial deference accorded to statutes, regulations, and administrative determinations. In addition, government officials tend to ignore the costs associated with litigation, since most agencies are not charged for the legal services involved.

[2]   Defense Against Unlimited Resources

Government administrators recognize the power advantage they enjoy over most private sector parties. They know that most companies do not want to become embroiled in protracted battles with federal or state departments that seem to have unlimited resources. They know they can frighten corporate officials through extensive pre-trial litigation or negotiations that will generate substantial legal fees. They do not hesitate to remind private sector firms that they receive cost-free representation by Justice Department or Attorney General lawyers. If they have the sense that private companies are afraid of possible litigation, they are usually willing to take advantage of this weakness. It is thus necessary for firms to give serious thought to litigation when that course becomes necessary. When government officials realize that they may be forced to defend their actions before judicial tribunals, they often exhibit more accommodating behavior.

[3]   Dealing With Opponent's Lack of Authority

Private sector attorneys often find it frustrating to deal with government lawyers, because those persons rarely possess significant authority. Agency officials who must assume responsibility for departmental determinations are hesitant to provide their own lawyers with the power those advocates require to conclude most interactions. Their attorneys can merely elicit offers from private parties that must be communicated to administrative decision-makers.Government legal practitioners find this as frustrating just as do their opponents. They would like to be able to resolve matters directly, but must usually function as intermediaries between outside parties and relevant agency officials. Although experienced government lawyers frequently know what they can sell to their superiors, many junior attorneys do not know. Since they do not want to be criticized for overstepping their authority, they tend to be cautious. They feel the need to clear even minor issues with agency officials before they suggest possible solutions to their opponents.

[4]   Importance of Patience and Cooperation

Agency attorneys do not like to have their recommended settlement proposals overruled by their superiors. When they enter into agreements, they work hard to get them approved. Once private sector attorneys reach deals with their government counterparts, they should give them the information they need to convince agency officials to accept the final terms. Since the approval process may take some time, private sector counsel must be patient and give the agency lawyers the time they require to accomplish their objective.

[5]   Against Challenging Agency Policies Directly

Agency officials normally consider applicable statutes and regulations sacrosanct. People who contemplate challenges to the propriety of these rules are likely to encounter stiff resistance. Most agency representatives are prepared to litigate statutory or regulation challenges to the Supreme Court. It is thus more productive to formulate positions that do not directly attack the legality of agency rules. Company attorneys should look for ways to interpret applicable statutes or regulations in a manner that will produce the desired results. Even strained statutory constructions may be beneficial. They permit agency decision-makers to accede to their demands in a face-saving fashion.

[6]   Using Opponent's Fear of Losing in Court

Unlike their private sector counterparts, most government attorneys and administrators are keenly aware of the number of litigated cases they have won and lost. They can usually provide an exact won-lose statistic on a moment's notice. They hate to lose, believing this may adversely affect their agency's reputation. If private sector representatives can convince government representatives that they may lose in court, those legal agents and their superiors are likely to be receptive to settlement discussions. Settlement discussions may generate final agreements that will preserve their win-loss records.

[7]   Tendency to Leave Matters Unresolved

A common frustration experienced by people dealing with government bureaucracies concerns the seeming unwillingness of many officials to make definitive decisions. This reluctance is based upon the fact that with hundreds or thousands of government personnel, employees rarely stand out for making exemplary determinations. They are more likely to be noticed when they make questionable decisions. To avoid possible criticism, many government officials have modified the plaque that stood on President Truman's desk — "The Buck Stops Here" — to read "Keep the Buck Moving." They recognize that they are unlikely to be chastised for decisions they did not make!

[8]   Matching Advances Toward Resolution

When private sector attorneys encounter government representatives who are afraid to make decisions, they should use two approaches. They should first try to convince their immediate opponents that it is in their interest to make the requested decisions. They must not hesitate to give the government attorneys with whom they are interacting the information they need to persuade their agency superiors to accept negotiated deals. I once presided over a labor arbitration proceeding that consumed five days. By the end of the first day, I became aware of the fact the union and agency attorneys had agreed upon an appropriate resolution of the underlying controversy. That accord had been rejected by the Regional Director. At the conclusion of the hearing, I asked to review the issues to be addressed in the litigants' post-hearing briefs in front of the Regional Director. I noted the difficult questions involved and the close nature of the case. I indicated to the Regional Director that a negative decision would have long-term consequences from his perspective. When he suggested that such a ruling would be my responsibility, I respectfully informed him that the decision would actually be his. I would only have the authority to resolve the matter if he decided to delegate his power to me. I emphasized the fact that he could either consider the compromise proposed by the agency attorney or allow me to determine what was best for his agency. When the Regional Director fully comprehended this point, he asked to consult with his lawyer. He expeditiously decided that the proposed accommodation was preferable to the submission of the dispute for an uncertain arbitral resolution.

[9]   Approaching Higher Officials

When the immediate agency representatives are unwilling to accept proposed solutions, it may be beneficial to approach higher officials who may have the courage to make the necessary decisions. Private firm lawyers should determine who has the power to grant the results they desire and figure out how to approach those individuals. In some cases, they may wish to have a third person intercede on their behalf to get the process going. Once they get the attention of someone with authority and the fortitude to exercise that power, they should present their positions in the most forceful manner possible.

[10]   Importance of Timing

Timing is a crucial consideration when dealing with government officials. They rarely make dispositive decisions until a deadline is approaching or a critical event is about to occur — on the eve of trial, at the end of the fiscal year, or when the other side's specific offer is due to expire. Private firms that ignore the timing factor may have reasonable offers rejected or be forced to litigate cases that should have been settled. Company lawyers must patiently await the approach of a deadline that will induce the appropriate officials to act.

§ 12.15   KEEPING CLIENTS INFORMED OF NEGOTIATION/ CASE DEVELOPMENTS

[1]   Lack of Information and Client Dissatisfaction

One of the most frequent complaints lodged by clients against lawyers concerns the failure of their legal representatives to keep them adequately apprised of case developments. Many attorneys arrogantly assume that there is no need to communicate with clients regarding what they consider expected occurrences. They forget that clients tend to view pending cases as significant aspects of their lives. They desperately want to know what is happening to their legal problems, yet rarely possess a realistic understanding of the judicial process. They are used to television shows in which legal problems are resolved within sixty-minute time frames.

[2]   Managing Client Expectations

When attorneys agree to represent particular clients, they should begin to perform a continuing educational role. They should thoroughly explain the way in which their cases are likely to unfold. Anticipated legal steps should be explicated. The probability of bargained resolutions should be emphasized. The negotiation process should next be explored. If clients can be prepared from the outset to expect settlement recommendations as the litigation process develops, it will be easier to convince them of the propriety of offers their legal counsel may ultimately encourage them to accept. Excessive client expectations should be expeditiously reduced, and inordinately low client hopes should be cautiously elevated to prevent hasty acceptance of disadvantageous early settlement proposals.

[3]   Ethical Duty to Inform

Model Rule 1.4(a) requires lawyers to keep clients "reasonably informed about the status of a matter and promptly comply with reasonable requests for information." (Morgan & Rotunda, 2008, at 16) Comment 1 to Rule 4.1 indicates that this ethical duty includes the obligation to apprise clients promptly of settlement offers received, "unless prior discussions with the client have left it clear that the proposal will be unacceptable." As the judicial process develops, clients should be informed of all meaningful developments and firm offers received (see generally Gifford, 1987). Short notes or brief telephone calls may be used to let them know their interests are being protected. These communications indicate that legal services are being performed on their behalf, and they help to alleviate client anxiety. Clients with conscientious attorneys have confidence that their cases are in good hands.

As the negotiation process develops and clients learn more about opponent needs and interests, they frequently reevaluate their own goals (Gifford, 1987, at 824–28). Clients who begin the process with unrealistic expectations have to be carefully counseled about the final terms they are likely to obtain. This means that while their attorneys are negotiating with opposing counsel, they should also be negotiating separately with them (Gifford, 1987, at 813). Legal representatives who fail to appreciate the need for continuing interactions with their own clients may find it difficult to induce those clients to appreciate the truly beneficial terms they are being offered.

Model Rule 1.4(b) obliges attorneys to explain matters to clients "to the extent reasonably necessary to permit the client[s] to make informed decisions regarding the representation." (Morgan & Rotunda, 2008, at 13) If clients are kept appropriately informed of case developments, it is generally easy for their legal representatives to explain why they think the clients should accept or reject specific offers that have been tendered by opposing parties. They are also likely to understand the function that has been performed by their legal representatives during this process. As a result, they should be more appreciative of the legal services they have received, and be less likely to question the fees they are being charged. Clients who challenge final fee statements sent to them have normally not been kept well informed of the efforts their lawyers have been exerting on their behalf. Since the adverse consequences of such omissions can be readily avoided through the maintenance of thoughtful client relations, there is no reason why attorneys should encounter these problems.

§ 12.16   CLIENT'S ACCEPTANCE OF SETTLEMENT OFFER OVER ADVICE OF COUNSEL

[1]   Effect of Pressures on Client's Decision

The emotional and financial pressures associated with litigation are so substantial for some clients that they occasionally decide to accept tendered settlement offers their legal representatives have encouraged them to reject. Since it is their case, they certainly possess this prerogative. (*See* Model Rule 1.2(a) in Morgan & Rotunda, 2008, at 12) Lawyers are obliged to convey bona fide offers made by the opponents to their clients. If they think that more favorable results could be achieved if the instant proposals were repudiated, they should patiently explain the reasons for their conclusions. Despite such negative advice, however, some clients may decide to terminate the process by accepting those offers.

[2]   Advising Against Hasty Acceptance of Inadequate Offers

Some clients find the litigation process so emotionally draining that they want to end this painful experience and get on with their lives. Other clients fear the possibility of devastating consequences if the controversy continues unresolved. These risk-averse people view current settlement offers more favorably than they objectively should. Individuals who succumb to either of these driving forces and accept disadvantageous offers are likely to develop subsequent regrets. As their previous trepidations subside, they begin to wonder why they surrendered so readily. Settlement terms they originally considered substantial no longer seem adequate. They need to rationalize their miscalculations. As a result, they frequently blame their legal counsel for their judgmental errors. How could their attorneys have permitted their naive acceptance of such unsatisfactory terms? They may even forget how diligently their lawyers sought to persuade them to pursue a contrary course.

[3]   Defense Against Faulty Client Decisions and Later Repercusions

Attorneys who are unable to persuade clients to reject poor settlement offers should recognize the need to protect themselves against belated recriminations. If they are not circumspect, they may even become defendants in legal malpractice actions filed by former clients alleging that they failed to adequately protect the interests of those clients. One way to minimize this possibility is to explicitly convey their contrary advice to clients who have decided to accept inadequate settlement proposals. They may effectively accomplish this objective in the letters that accompany the settlement agreements they send to clients. They can expressly indicate their disappointment with the client decisions to reject their counseling against acceptance of the proffered offers. They could briefly recite their reasons for suggesting that the clients not succumb to those disadvantageous accords. This will provide a contemporaneous record of their opposition in case clients subsequently forget how strenuously they recommended a different course of action.

[4]   Settlement Agreement Conveyance Letters vs. Tape-Recorded Final Conferences

Several practitioners have indicated to me that they employ a more direct approach in these situations. They tape record their final client conferences in those rare cases in which clients accept settlement proposals despite their contrary advice. They do this openly and with complete client knowledge. Most lawyers would probably find it awkward to employ this practice. It might easily suggest to the clients that their legal representatives are more desirous of protecting themselves than their clients. Since carefully drafted settlement agreement conveyance letters can less intrusively accomplish the same objective, it would usually be preferable to use this technique.

§ 12.17   RENEGOTIATING EXISTING CONTRACTS/RELATIONSHIPS

No matter how carefully parties negotiate and memorialize their agreements, there are times when changed circumstances or unanticipated developments require one or both parties to modify their original understandings (Freeman, 2006; Shavell, 2004, at 75–79). When the new circumstances affect both sides in a similar manner, it is usually easy for both to get together and reassess where they should be now. On the other hand, when the unusual circumstances only impact one side or impact one side far more than the other, it may be more difficult for the adversely affected party to reopen negotiations.

[1]   Parties Requesting Renegotiation Should Directly Indicate Why the Requested Changes Are Necessary

United States lawyers and business persons are so used to the notion that contractual parties must honor their existing obligations that it may not be easy for one party to induce the other to renegotiate their specified terms. Persons seeking to renegotiate existing relationships should provide the other side with explicit reasons why that side should enter into renegotiation talks (Freeman, 2006). They must explain what that side might lose if it is unwilling to explore the need for new arrangements. The motivating factors may be due to unexpected economic or political occurrences, significant financial changes, the failures of third party suppliers, or even natural disasters. Costs may have escalated, delivery dates can no longer be satisfied, periodic payments may no longer be met, leased space may no longer be needed, unexpected environmental issues may necessitate immediate action, or similar issues may have arisen.

If parties seeking renegotiation try to cover up the real reasons for their requested changes, their partners may become suspicious and refuse to explore possible changes. Only through a direct and truthful explanation for the need for relationship modifications can requesting parties hope to achieve their ultimate goals. They must also appreciate the initial inclination of many partners to decline renegotiation requests based upon their belief that contractual obligations are both morally and legally binding. It can be especially helpful to apologize for the present situation and to throw one's self on the mercy of the other side. This approach can greatly diminish the negative emotions initially emanating from the party being asked to renegotiate. The requesting side can also point out how it is virtually impossible for it to honor the existing terms. If operational difficulties are involved, they should explain what has occurred and indicate how soon they may be able to carry out their side's obligations. If financial problems have developed, the should explain how bankruptcy proceedings may be necessary if renegotiations are not successful. Such statements let the other side know that previously promised performance is no longer a possibility. The real issue now is how best to restructure their relationship to enable both to move on successfully. Patience is especially important, because it may take some time before the other side realizes that renegotiation is preferable to inaction. Instead of looking backwards to see who may be responsible for the factors necessitating modified terms, the parties should look forward to determine how best to alter their current arrangements.

If the person asked to renegotiate existing terms is unwilling to participate, it may be necessary to contact someone else in the other side's organization who may be more inclined to do so. If an organizational policy precludes contractual changes, the party seeking the modifications must look for someone who possesses the authority to override that policy. It helps to ask a lot of "who" and "why" questions. Who has the authority to renegotiate the current arrangements? Why won't the other side consider modified terms? Why would they prefer a disastrous default to less onerous changes?

[2]   Parties Should Jointly Work Toward Mutually Beneficial New Arrangements

It can be beneficial for the party seeking modified terms to explain its underlying reasons and ask the other side how it thinks the parties should proceed. If the other side can be drawn into the problem-solving process, the two sides can begin to work together to restructure their relationship. It is important for both sides to keep open minds. They should look for their respective underlying interests and seek to formulate possible solutions that would meet the basic needs of both. What modifications would enable the defaulting party to carry out its obligations in a manner that would least disadvantage the other side? It is imperative that both sides indicate openly what they have to achieve through renegotiation (*see generally* Freeman, 2006).

It is often difficult for the individuals who negotiated the original terms to renegotiate the new terms being sought, because the side being asked to change the existing obligations quite reasonably expects performance of what was previously agreed upon. This explains why it can be helpful to have other persons conduct the renegotiation discussions (Freeman, 2006, at 142–44). On the other hand, if the original negotiators have had a long-term relationship and have worked well together, they may still be in the best position to restructure the terms of their arrangement.

Parties being asked to renegotiate existing relationships must carefully weigh their options to be sure they do not end up with situations that are worse than complete default. They must determine their BATRA — their Best Alternative to Renegotiated Agreements. They need to carefully consider their current alternatives and decide what restructured arrangements would be best for them. If they truly believe that terminated relationships or bankruptcy proceedings would be preferable to any modification they would be required to make, they should decline the changes being requested and force the defaulting party into legal proceedings.

Parties willing to restructure their existing arrangements should not hesitate to insist upon provisions that will protect their interests in case the requesting persons are unable to carry out their revised promises. They might insist upon some form of insurance or money placed in escrow that will be forfeited if full compliance with the modified obligations is not met.

§ 12.18 NEGOTIATION/SETTLEMENT AS A DISTINCT AREA OF SPECIALIZATION

[1] Better Results With Settlement Specialists

Although the overwhelming majority of lawsuits are resolved through negotiated settlements, few practicing attorneys consider themselves negotiation/settlement specialists. Lawyers instead characterize themselves as "litigators," and they work in law firm "litigation" departments. It is ironic that they prefer to view themselves as "litigators," even though they are far more likely to dispose of cases through settlements than through adjudications. Law firms may find it advantageous to rectify this unbalanced emphasis on the litigation function through the employment of acknowledged negotiation/settlement specialists (Craver, 1986; Fisher, 1983).

Law firms should assign negotiation/settlement specialists to every dispute they agree to handle. It would be their responsibility to explore the possibility of beneficial non-adjudicated resolutions, while their litigation colleagues prepare the matters for trial in case no mutual accords can be achieved. While clients might initially fear that this dual-track approach would increase legal fees, the efficient operation of this system should have the opposite effect. Cases would be settled more often and more expeditiously. This would avoid the substantial emotional and monetary costs associated with protracted litigation (Mendelson, 1996, at 150–53).

Clients would receive an additional benefit from a dual-track system. They would receive input from several experienced lawyers when they are debating whether to accept tendered settlement proposals (Mendelson, 1996, at 156–57). The negotiators would explain why they believe the offers in question should be accepted, while the litigators could indicate what would probably happen if the matters were not amicably resolved. This would provide clients with more information and enable them to make more informed decisions.

In late 1982, Jenner & Block of Chicago became the first law firm to create a separate negotiation/dispute resolution department. Several other litigation-oriented practices have followed this example. Firms that do not recognize the overall benefits of using negotiation/settlement specialists will soon realize that they are not representing their clients as effectively as they could. Law offices that have adopted a dual-track approach combine the professional efforts of separate litigation and negotiation experts. As clients begin to appreciate the benefits to be derived from such dual representation, they will increasingly seek the assistance of firms that provide these comprehensive litigation/settlement services.

[2] Bifurcating Litigation and Settlement Functions

Law firms could substantially improve their negotiation/ settlement capabilities if they were willing to bifurcate the litigation and settlement functions. To accomplish this objective, they would have to recognize negotiation/settlement as a distinct area of specialization. Instead of seeking future associates and partners who appear to possess the personal traits that would make them successful litigators, they should search for some individuals with the qualities that would enable them to become effective negotiators.

[3]   Personalities and Their Effectiveness in Settlement

[a]   Settlement

Attorney personalities have a significant impact on the negotiation process, just as they affect the outcome of litigated disputes. However, the traits that enhance one's capacity to obtain mutual settlements are frequently different from those that contribute to successful adjudications. Individuals with patient, amiable styles who are tolerant of uncertainty and anxiety are usually able to keep bargaining sessions going in circumstances in which overly competitive "win-lose" participants could not. Furthermore, bargainers who can effectively handle ambiguity are more likely to behave cooperatively than those with a low tolerance levels (Rubin & Brown, 1975, at 177–78; Hermann & Kogan in Drukman, 1977, at 253–54). Since the ability of bargainers to achieve accords depends on their capacity to continue the process in an amicable manner and to encourage collaborative behavior, these characteristics are highly beneficial.

[b]   True Believer

Experienced litigators are not necessarily capable negotiators. Even though they are usually able to evaluate cases objectively at their inception, these individuals tend to become less detached as controversies proceed toward trial. Many successful litigators are individuals who exhibit what Eric Hoffer has described as "true believer" personalities (Hoffer, 1951). They feel the need to resolve internal dissonance as they prepare for scheduled adjudications. They often eliminate all of the self-doubts they experienced when they first accepted the cases. As they become prepared for trial, they no longer entertain uncertainties concerning the right of their clients to prevail (Mendelson, 1996, at 156–57; Hyman, 1987, at 873). While this phenomenon may increase their capacity to present client cases forcefully and improve the likelihood of favorable judgments — in those relatively few cases that are not ultimately settled — it usually diminishes their ability to achieve negotiated resolutions. As these individuals become more convinced of the certainty of their impending "victories," they lose all perspective regarding the objective strengths and weaknesses of their cases (Rubin & Brown, 1975, at 51; Fisher, 1983). They thus overestimate the results they are likely to obtain if no settlements are attained, and they ignore rational arguments that might undermine their confidence. As a result, they fail to listen meaningfully to opponent representations, and tend to demand excessive offers as a prerequisite to mutual accords.

Litigators generally believe that it is preferable to limit the disclosure of critical information to the issues the opposing side has the right to explore through conventional discovery procedures (Hyman, 1987, at 892–93, 898–902). They hope their adversaries will fail to ask the right questions during depositions or in interrogatories, or fail to request pertinent documents. They plan to use these omissions to their advantage during the subsequent adjudications. This tendency to restrict the disclosure of information may hamper the search for mutually beneficially resolutions, with each side hiding information that may induce opponents to contemplate non-adjudicative solutions. While it may be tactically beneficial for litigators to limit the disclosure of negative information that might weaken their cases at trial, there is rarely a reason for lawyers to withhold information that bolsters their positions (Hyman, 1987, at 911–13). If they can use such information disclosures to enhance their situations, opposing counsel would be more inclined to contemplate settlement possibilities.

Trial lawyers tend to focus almost entirely on issues relevant to adjudication success. They seek redress courts are authorized to award. As a result, they often fail to consider non-legal options that might satisfy the underlying interests of the disputants (Hyman, 1987, at 875, 886). They may thus ignore the potential benefit of a defendant apology, or the possibility of converting a win-lose patent or copyright infringement action into a win-win licensing arrangement. Individuals who can think outside the adjudication "box" can appreciate the potential relevance of such non-legal alternatives.

Practitioners who are incapable of analyzing the strengths and weaknesses of cases with meaningful objectivity usually find it difficult to achieve amicable, pretrial resolutions of those controversies. As they become increasingly persuaded of their probable success on the merits, their judgment becomes hopelessly biased. They cannot — or will not — consider their cases with an open mind.

Candidates with relatively "black-white" minds that do not permit detached reflection would normally not make good settlement specialists. They would be inclined to adopt an "all-or-nothing" approach that would produce a few spectacular agreements and a substantial number of nonsettlements. Firms should avoid persons who exhibit these "true believer" tendencies, since it is essential for negotiation specialists to be able to evaluate the merits of their situations with relative objectivity — even with trial dates looming. Those individuals who are not capable of exercising detached judgment will find it difficult to achieve mutual accords.

[c]   Gladiator

Many successful litigators have aggressive personalities. They view themselves as modern-day gladiators. They enjoy courtroom confrontations and savor the euphoria of victory. They think of compromise as the equivalent of a "tie" in an athletic event — *i.e.*, a result that is almost as dissatisfying as a loss (Hyman, 1987, at 863–64). These people see the negotiation process as a route that can only culminate in a dreaded "tie," with neither party being allowed to experience true success. As a result of this predisposition, these litigators are only pleased with settlements that provide them with everything they want. They would prefer the exhilaration of trial by judicial combat to less favorable accommodations. Since few opposing lawyers are willing to agree to complete surrender, many cases that could have been successfully resolved by less contentious individuals must be tried by these advocates.

[4]   Dealing With Risk of Unhappy Litigators

Partnerships that adopt a dual-track approach may initially experience some conflicts between the litigators and the negotiators. The former may fear that the latter will deprive them of the opportunity to try cases. Since most litigators truly relish their participation in the adjudication process, this would be an understandable concern. However, the establishment of a successful negotiation/settlement department could actually enlarge the number of cases being handled by the firm. Most clients do not really wish to become embroiled in protracted litigation. They have legal problems they want efficiently resolved. If certain law firms were to become known as entities that dispose of controversies with a minimal amount of pain and expense, they could reasonably expect an ever expanding clientele. Even if their reliance upon negotiation/settlement specialists were to increase the likelihood of bargained results in particular cases, the fact that they have been able to expand their total number of clients would enlarge the absolute number of cases to be litigated. The litigators should thus appreciate the fact that their negotiation/settlement colleagues would both provide more cases for them to work on and increase the total legal fees being generated by the firm.

The negotiation/settlement specialists would be equally beholden to their litigation associates. The professional reputation of the litigation experts assigned to each case would significantly influence the bargaining leverage available to the negotiators involved. If those trial lawyers have established enviable adjudication records, the value of their cases would increase dramatically. This fact would inure to the direct benefit of the settlement attorneys. The negotiation specialists could further enhance their bargaining situations by emphasizing to opposing counsel how anxious the litigation experts are to try the cases if no reasonable settlements can be achieved.

[5]   Career Development of Settlement Specialists

Trial lawyers often possess limited knowledge regarding verbal and nonverbal communication and the psychological factors that influence the negotiation process — even though such enlightenment would undoubtedly improve their litigation proficiency. Settlement specialists would have to become intimately familiar with these concepts (Mendelson, 1996, at 154–55). Their continuing professional development should thus include readings on speech communication and psychology. They would also need to review regularly the literature pertaining to the negotiation process itself. Negotiators should also develop their ability to devise creative solutions to client problems (Mendelson, 1996, at 158–59). They must learn how to ascertain underlying client interests, and how to formulate offers designed to satisfy these interests.

§ 12.19   NEGOTIATION COUNSEL MODEL

Jim Golden, Abigail Moy, and Adam Lyons (2008) have advocated the "Negotiation Counsel" approach to resolve large claims expeditiously and efficiently. When firms appear to be liable for significant damages, designated negotiation counsel contact the injured parties immediately to apologize for the harm that has been caused and to see what their side can do to minimize the emotional and financial traumas being experienced by the injured parties and their families. They may even ask if it would be acceptable for them to visit injured persons or to attend the funerals of individuals who died because of the accidents involved.

[1]   Early Investigation and Expeditious Assistance

Negotiation counsel immediately investigate major calamities to determine the likelihood of firm liability. They sympathize with the families of adversely affected persons, and try to do what they can to minimize their plight. They offer to provide the injured parties with temporary financial assistance with no strings attached to minimize the economic difficulties they might be facing. As soon as attorneys have been retained, negotiation counsel schedule meetings with those lawyers at which they ask the participants to quickly share their preliminary factual findings and begin settlement discussions.

[2] Avoiding Exploitation by Adversarial Opponents

Although some persons might view this approach as a sign of negotiation weakness that might be exploited by manipulative opponents, Golden, Moy, and Lyons have not found this to be a serious risk. If claimant attorneys cooperate with them, negotiation counsel work to achieve mutually beneficial resolutions. On the other hand, if opposing attorneys behave in an adversarial manner, these legal representatives make it clear that firm lawyers are fully prepared to litigate if that course becomes necessary. They thus work closely with corporate litigation counsel. They endeavor to achieve quick and efficient settlements that will avoid costly pretrial discovery, while litigation counsel begin the trial preparation process. Jim Golden has used this collaborative negotiation approach to resolve many large tort claims resulting from trucking accidents. The empathetic work of negotiation counselors has saved transportation firms millions of dollars, while providing the families of adversely affected persons with swift and fair economic redress.

Summary

1. Lawyers should generally not have personal clients present during negotiating sessions, since their verbal leaks or nonverbal signals may inadvertently disclose important information and their attendance may constrain attorney bargaining tactics.

2. Bargaining power is defined more by participant perceptions than objective reality. Parties may thus undermine opponent strength by ignoring it and enhance their own weak positions through limited authority and public pronouncements restricting their negotiating freedom.

3. Since the bargaining process involves uniquely personal interactions, attorneys should not conduct their negotiation exchanges entirely through written communications.

4. When negotiators encounter particularly difficult opponents, they should employ "attitudinal bargaining" to modify their unacceptable behavior. Negotiators can then work to separate the people from the problems that must be solved and start looking for ways to create more cooperative environments.

5. Telephone negotiations involve the same stages and factors as in-person interactions, with participants being capable in this medium of reading the nonverbal clues associated with voice pitch, pace, tone, and volume. Prepared callers tend to have an advantage over less prepared call recipients. Recognizing the increased use of cell phones, negotiators should be careful to arrange telephone discussions when they will have the other party's undivided attention and there is no risk of being heard by third parties.

6. Lawyers who conduct e-mail negotiations should use preliminary telephone calls to establish rapport with opponents, and should phone opposing counsel shortly after they have sent e-mail proposals to *hear* the responses of those recipients. Attorneys should also be careful to eliminate the metadata contained in electronic files to be sure their opponents cannot discern all of the changes they have made in those files.

7. Attorneys should carefully prepare themselves and their clients for pretrial settlement conferences, because this increases their own effectiveness and enables them to obtain a bargaining advantage over less prepared opponents.

8. Private sector attorneys who negotiate with government lawyers must recognize the inter-cultural aspects of their transaction and key differences between the private

and government cultures. There are different value systems involved in these transactions, and agency counsel rarely possess final settlement authority over the matters being discussed.

9. Lawyers should keep their clients apprised of case developments and protect themselves against possible malpractice suits by clients who accept poor offers they strongly encourage them to reject. Attorneys may reiterate their opposition in the letters accompanying final settlement documents.

10. Law firms should recognize that the personal traits possessed by proficient litigators frequently differ from the personal characteristics possessed by successful negotiators. For this reason, firms should view negotiation as a distinct area of specialization.

Chapter 13

PSYCHOLOGICAL ENTRAPMENT

§ 13.01 WINNING AT ANY COST — A BIDDING GAME

[1] Background

Whenever I teach my Legal Negotiating course or make a continuing legal education presentation to lawyers, I auction off a $1 bill. I employ an approach that is different from traditional auctions. I announce that the $1 bill will be given to the highest bidder in exchange for his or her high bid. I then emphasize that the *second* highest bidder will *not* receive anything from me *but* will be required to provide me with the amount of his or her losing bid. The opening bid cannot exceed $0.50, to begin the auction process slowly — and to prevent someone from ending the exercise with an opening bid of $1.00 — and all subsequent offers must be divisible by $0.05 to avoid time-consuming penny increments.

[2] Process

The bidding usually opens tentatively for $0.50. Thereafter, offers of $0.55, $0.60, and $0.65 are made in rapid succession. By this point, I casually indicate that I am already guaranteed a profit from the transaction. The audience becomes suspicious. Someone offers $0.70 or $0.75, and the bidding continues to the $0.85 or $0.90 level. A participant almost always bids $0.95. That person assumes that no rational participant would offer more, because they could not possibly receive any financial gain from a higher bid. What this bidder forgets is that the second highest bidder is required to pay me his or her last bid even though that individual does not get my $1 bill. As a result, when the second highest bidder is confronted with a bid of $0.95, he or she immediately offers $1 in an effort to guarantee a break-even result. People who recognize the unusual nature of my auction before any $0.90 or $0.95 bid has been entered omit the $0.95 offer and

227

move directly to the $1 figure, hoping to end the auction with no loss to themselves.

Once a $1 bid has been received, the process comes to a temporary halt. Both the participants and the observers are shocked by the developments that have occurred. I then remind the second highest bidder, who has bid $0.90 or $0.95, that he or she can reduce his or her overall loss by offering $1.05. Even though this act would force that person to pay me more than $1.00, it would permit him or her to limit the loss to a mere $0.05. I am always able to generate a $1.05 bid. The person who had offered the $1.00 bid must now reassess his or her situation. That individual felt confident about the prospect of breaking even, until the upstart bidder made a seemingly irrational offer of $1.05. The only way to outsmart that devious character is to propose a figure of $1.10 or $1.15, which is expeditiously done.

After the $1.00 barrier is broken, the bidding frequently continues to the $1.50 or $1.75 level, before one of the two remaining participants decides to terminate the auction. On several instances, I have received final bids in the $2.50 to $3.00 range. On one memorable occasion, when the bidding had already reached double figures, one party decided to end the process with an offer of $20.00. Needless to say, that exalted bid was allowed to prevail. I was amazed by the fact the $20.00 bidder actually thought he had "won"!

The idea for this exercise came from an article by Professor Jeffrey Rubin on "Psychological Traps" (Rubin, 1981). He regularly conducted his dollar auction among undergraduate psychology students at Tufts University and usually obtained final bids in excess of $3, $4, and even $5. The elevated offers he generated compared to the lower results I have achieved may suggest either that law students and legal practitioners are more parsimonious than undergraduate students or that they are less willing to continue their participation in an obviously losing venture.

The purpose of this seemingly frivolous exercise is to graphically demonstrate how easily auction participants may become *psychologically entrapped* by the process itself (Malhotra & Bazerman, 2007, at 115–18; Thompson, 2005, at 298–301; Cohen, 2003, at 250–52; Brockner & Rubin, 1985). They initially believe they will make a profit from the transaction. They quickly discover, however, that they must accept a loss. The only question concerns the amount of their ultimate deficit. Perspicacious participants tend to minimize their exposure by terminating the auction process early, while less discerning and more competitive bidders continue for a longer period of time.

§ 13.02 WINNER'S CURSE

[1]   Irrational Victory

The dollar auction provides a perfect example of a phenomenon known as "winner's curse" (Bazerman & Neale, 1992, at 152–55; Murnighan, 1992, at 186–87). Auction participants who had initially envisioned a profit ultimately accept their negative fate but hope to at least "beat" the remaining bidder(s). The individual who finally prevails only does so when no one else thinks that further bidding would be rational. The highest bidder then "wins" what others no longer value at the price level involved — experiencing the dreaded "winner's curse."

[2]   Danger of Psychological Entrapment

Practitioners must never permit themselves to become so caught up in the negotiation "game" that they find themselves compelled to achieve final settlements no matter the cost. They have to learn to recognize when they have become involved in losing endeavors and to know how to minimize their losses. Those persons who become psychologically entrapped by the process itself usually pay a high price for their continued participation. Except in rare circumstances, bargainers always have nonsettlement alternatives that they can fall back on. Individuals who do not realize this crucial fact should take the time to ascertain the results of non-agreement before they become overly enmeshed in the bargaining process. Once it becomes apparent that their nonsettlement options are less onerous than the concessions that would be required to achieve final accords, these advocates should readily accept the fact that their non-negotiated solutions constitute the preferable choice.

Bargainers should recognize how easy it is to become psychologically entrapped by the bargaining process. I have seen people who have unsuccessfully sought to purchase several desirable homes acquire dwellings they did not really want, just to enable them to achieve "victories." Persons who have been unable to obtain employment opportunities they really wanted may thereafter be induced to accept less advantageous positions to produce "wins." Those who continue their participation in the auction process merely to make up for previous "losses" should realize that the final "successes" they attain are likely to involve Pyrrhic victories.

Participants should never continue negotiations merely because they have become psychologically entrapped by the substantial amount of time and resources they have already expended in an unsuccessful effort to obtain mutually acceptable terms. This is particularly true when they are tempted to extend present interactions for the purpose of punishing their recalcitrant opponents. While they may understandably feel frustrated by their inability to achieve final resolutions through the bargaining process, it does no good to sustain additional losses in a misguided effort to impose some degree of retribution on their adversaries. Even if they were able to generate ultimate accords through stubborn persistence, the overall cost to them and their clients would exceed the cost of the nonsettlement alternatives available to them.

§ 13.03   INABILITY TO ACCEPT NONSETTLEMENT

[1]   Illusion of Wasted Effort in Nonsettlement

Individuals often become entrapped by the bargaining process because of the effort they have made to achieve agreement. They feel that these endeavors will be wasted if they do not obtain mutual accords. They must recognize that their efforts have not been for naught. They had to expend this energy to determine whether they could obtain better results through the bargaining process than through external options. They have gathered critical information regarding the benefits that are presently available through the negotiation process. Had they not employed their negotiation skills, they would never have confirmed the preferable nature of their non-agreement alternatives.

[2]   Fear of Adverse Publicity Resulting from Lawsuit

Some legal representatives regularly exhibit negotiating behavior that suggests to opponents that they are afraid of the consequences of nonsettlements. Some casually note that they do not wish to expose their clients to the psychological trauma and monetary costs associated with adjudications. They mention their fear of adverse publicity in cases that would be unlikely to generate meaningful community notice. It must be remembered that very few lawsuits involve sufficient notoriety to engender any degree of public attention. Participants who exude a fear of nonsettlement must generally accept less beneficial results than those people who evidence a willingness to accept the consequences of non-negotiated results when the latter course would produce preferable outcomes.

[3]   Assessing Nonsettlement Options

Before individuals commence negotiations, they should establish appropriate bargaining limits. They must consider the consequences of nonsettlements and recognize when mutual accords would be less advantageous than non-negotiated results. Unless they obtain information that objectively induces them to alter their preliminary assessments, they should be prepared to terminate their participation in the negotiation process as soon as it becomes apparent that they cannot obtain beneficial solutions through that means. They should do so courteously and inform their opponents that the terms currently being offered are unacceptable. Unless the other side is willing to reassess the operative circumstances, it is clear that no beneficial accord is possible. Their civilized conduct may induce their adversaries to reconsider their situations and generate further discussions. If it does not have that impact, these participants should take advantage of their external options. If they instead continue to negotiate in a desperate effort to achieve any agreement, they are almost certain to experience "winner's curse."

§ 13.04   USE INVESTMENT OF TIME AND EFFORT TO ENTRAP OPPONENTS

When negotiators understand the degree to which their own investment of time and effort may make it difficult for them to walk away from protracted bargaining interactions without agreements, they should appreciate the degree to which this same phenomenon influences their opponents (Cohen, 2003, at 250–54, 291). Results achieved easily are usually not as highly valued as results people have to work to attain. Negotiators should thus strive to entrap careless adversaries by making those persons work diligently for the results they obtain. Instead of meeting only once or twice, it may be beneficial to schedule three, four, or even five separate bargaining sessions. Concessions should not be made quickly, but should be granted begrudgingly after lengthy discussions. The more opponents have to work to move the other side in their direction, the more they want to achieve final accords — even if the terms are not as beneficial as those they initially hoped to get. In fact, if they become entirely entrapped by their investment of time and effort in the bargaining process, they may forget their own nonsettlement options and agree to terms that are worse than what they would have achieved with no agreement.

Summary

1. Individuals who participate in negotiations (and auctions) hope to obtain something for less than face value.

2. Before people enter the negotiation process, they must consider their nonsettlement options and establish appropriate bargaining limits.

3. When participants determine that their external alternatives are preferable to the terms they are likely to obtain through further negotiations, they should terminate the interactions and accept their external options.

4. People who become entrapped by the process and continue to negotiate for the purpose of salvaging some agreement or to punish recalcitrant opponents are likely to experience "winner's curse" and achieve terms that are less beneficial than the results they could have obtained through nonsettlement channels.

5. The more time and effort people put into a negotiation, the more they want to achieve some agreement — even if the results are not as good as what they initially hoped to obtain.

Chapter 14

THE IMPACT OF ETHNICITY AND GENDER

§ 14.01 THE ADDED COMPLEXITY OF ETHNIC AND GENDER DIVERSITY IN NEGOTIATIONS

[1]   The Cooperation Inherent in Ethnic and Gender Similarity

Legal representatives must recognize that negotiations involving participants from diverse backgrounds frequently develop differently than bargaining interactions involving persons from similar backgrounds. People tend to negotiate more cooperatively with opponents of the same race, gender, and culture than with adversaries of diverse cultures — due to the fact that similarity induces trust and reduces the need for the interactors to maintain a particular face — in each other's eyes (Docherty, 2004; LeBaron, 2003, at 10–11; Rubin & Brown, 1975, at 163). This may explain why African-Americans tend to perform better when competing with Caucasian-Americans and when cooperating with other African-Americans (Fry & Coe, 1980, at 166).

[2]   Disparity in Speech and Behavior Interpretation

Different meanings may be ascribed to identical speech and behavior by members of different ethnic groups because of their different acculturation experiences (Davidson & Greenhalgh, 1999, at 20–22). Certain cultural groups generally exhibit more cooperative behavior than do other groups. For example, while African-Americans tend to speak more forcefully and with greater verbal aggressiveness than Caucasian-Americans (Davidson & Greenhalgh, 1999, at 22), they tend to negotiate more cooperatively than do Caucasian-Americans or Mexican-Americans (Rubin & Brown, 1975, at 163). On the other hand, blacks tend to make less eye contact while listening to others than do whites, which may be erroneously perceived as an indication of indifference or disrespect (Harper, Wiens & Matarazzo, 1978, at 188). Female bargainers also tend to behave more cooperatively than male negotiators (Rubin & Brown, 1975, at 172). They tend to establish more cooperative seating arrangements and have a closer, more congenial interaction distance (Harper, Wiens & Matarazzo, 1978, at 255, 278).

[3]   Disparity in Bargaining Treatment

A recent study by Professor Ayres has indicated that car dealers tend to treat male and female, and Caucasian-American and African-American customers differently when they negotiate car prices (Ayres, 1991; see also Ayers, 1995). Salespeople give male buyers more favorable opening offers and more generous final offers than female customers under identical circumstances, and they favor Caucasian-American car buyers over African-American customers. It is striking to note that the final offers given to African-American females averaged almost $900 more than those given to Caucasian-American males. These differences may reflect opportunistic car salesperson behavior designed to take advantage of what are stereotypically perceived to be less proficient female/minority bargainers, or they may reflect salesperson fears of being out-negotiated by female or minority customers. If similar disparate treatment were given to women and minority negotiators in other settings, this phenomenon would make it more difficult for African-American and female bargainers to do as well as their Caucasian-American male cohorts. Since I have found no such differences with respect to the results achieved by male and female, and minority and nonminority, students on my Legal Negotiation course exercises (Craver & Barnes, 1999; Craver, 1990), I would discount this bias with respect to negotiations involving legal practitioners.

§ 14.02   ETHNICITY IN NEGOTIATION

[1]   Stereotyping

[a]   Pervasiveness

People from diverse ethnic backgrounds bring certain stereotypical baggage into new interactions (Sammataro, 1999, at 555). It is amazing how many common characteristics are attributed by numerous persons to all individuals of a particular race. Professor Rich's study of the perceptions of UCLA undergraduate students in the early 1970's graphically demonstrated how closely Anglos and Chicanos stereotyped African-Americans, Anglos and blacks stereotyped Chicanos, and blacks and Chicanos stereotyped Anglos (Rich, 1974, at 51–62).

[b]   Adverse Affects

Students I have taught at various law schools over the past thirty-five years have often allowed their stereotypical beliefs to affect their bargaining interactions. Many of my students — regardless of their ethnicity — appear to believe that Caucasian-Americans are the most Machiavellian and competitive negotiators. They expect them to use adversarial and manipulative tactics to obtain optimal results for themselves. On the other hand, students tend to expect African-American, Asian-American, and Latino-American negotiators to be more accommodating and less competitive. When opponents do not behave in the anticipated manner, the bargaining process may be adversely affected.

Even members of one race may stereotype other members of the same race. Several years ago, a group of four African-American students in my class were randomly assigned a negotiation exercise. They seemed so pleased to have the opportunity to conduct an exercise entirely with other African-American colleagues. When they had their initial meeting, both sides announced their opening offers. They never got beyond that point. Even though the two teams met for several hours over a couple of days, neither side was willing to modify its first offer. When we discussed their resulting nonsettlement in class, I asked each pair why they had been unwilling to move toward the opposing side. Neither side had been willing to move, because each team had expected their "less competitive" African-American opponents to make the first concession! (Similar stereotyping often influences bargaining interactions between pairs of female students who expect their female opponents to be more accommodating than stereotypically competitive male adversaries and are disappointed when their adversaries fail to act in the anticipated fashion.)

[c]   Working to Establish Trust and Rapport

[i]   Use of Preliminary Stage to Generate Rapport

Individuals who commence negotiations with people of different races should understand the need to establish trusting and cooperative relationships before serious substantive bargaining discussions begin. This approach should significantly enhance the likelihood of mutually beneficial transactions. The Preliminary Stage of their interaction may be used to generate a modicum of rapport (Davidson & Greenhalgh, 1999, at 19–21). Negotiators should try to minimize the counterproductive stereotypes they may consciously or subconsciously harbor toward persons of their opponent's ethnicity. If they anticipate difficult interactions as a result of such usually irrational preconceptions, they are likely to generate self-fulfilling prophecies. If they conversely expect their opponents to behave more cooperatively and less manipulatively because of their ethnicity, they may carelessly lower their guard and give those persons an inherent bargaining advantage. They must also try to understand any seemingly illogical reactions their opponents may initially exhibit toward them as a result of those individuals' stereotyping of them.

If the first contact negotiators have with opponents indicates that those persons are expecting highly competitive transactions, they should not hesitate to employ "attitudinal bargaining" to disabuse their opponents of this predilection. They should create cooperative physical and psychological environments. Warm handshakes and open postures can initially diminish combative atmospheres. Cooperative negotiators can sit adjacent to, instead of directly across from, opposing counsel. In a few instances, it may be necessary to directly broach the subject of negative stereotyping, since this may be the most efficacious way to negate the influence of these feelings (Schneider, 1994, at 112–13).

[ii]   Focus on Circumstances of Negotiation

People who participate in bargaining transactions should recognize that the specific circumstances and unique personal traits of the individual negotiators — rather than generalized beliefs regarding ethnic or cultural characteristics — determine the way in which each interaction evolves. Each opponent has to be evaluated and dealt with differently. Is that individual a cooperative/problem-solving, a competitive/adversarial, or a competitive/problem-solving bargainer? Does the other side possess greater, equal, or less bargaining power concerning the issues to be addressed? What negotiating techniques has that individual decided to employ, and what are the most effective ways to counter those tactics? As the instant transaction unfolds, strategic changes will have to be made to respond to unanticipated disclosures or to changed circumstances.

[iii]   Reflect on Opponent's Individual Character

When negotiators find themselves attributing certain characteristics to opponents, they must carefully determine whether those attributes are based on specific information pertaining to their particular opponents or to vague generalizations regarding people of their race or culture. If persons only bargained with individuals of the same race and culture, they would quickly realize how different we all are. Some opponents would behave cooperatively, while others would act in a competitive manner. Some would be congenial, while others would be less pleasant. Some would exhibit win-lose tendencies, while others would evidence win-win attitudes. Techniques that would be effective against some opponents would be ineffective against others.

[2]   Cultural Impact on Negotiating Results

I am occasionally asked by practitioners, academics, and students whether members of particular ethnic groups obtain more advantageous negotiating results than members of other groups. During the thirty-five years I have taught my Legal Negotiating course, I have observed absolutely no differences with respect to the results achieved by members of different ethnic groups. I have had proficient students from each group, average students from each group, and less capable students from each group. Several years ago, I decided to review the data for the five years

(1977–1982) I taught culturally diverse classes at the University of California, Davis. I compared the average results achieved by minority students with the average results attained by nonminority students. I had to group African-American, Asian-American, and Chicano-American students together, because I lacked sufficient numbers of particular ethnic groups to make statistically meaningful comparisons on a more discrete basis. I found no statistically significant differences between the results achieved by minority and nonminority participants (Craver, 1990, at 17 n.81). The group averages were approximately equal, as were the group standard deviations. A recent evaluation of nine years of data comparing the negotiation results achieved by Caucasian and African American students similarly found no statistically significant differences. (Craver, 2001). I am thus confident that negotiation skill is truly a reflection of individual capability that is not influenced by one's ethnic characteristics.

§ 14.03   GENDER

[1]   Impact of Stereotyping

Gender-based stereotypes cause some lawyers great difficulty when they interact with attorneys of the opposite sex (*see generally* Kolb & Williams, 2000 & 2003; *see also* Kolb, 2000). Males frequently expect females to behave like "ladies" during their interactions. Overt aggressiveness that would be viewed as vigorous advocacy if it were employed by men is likely to be characterized as offensive and threatening when used by women (Babcock & Laschever, 2008, at 256–58; Kray & Locke, 2008, at 485; Carli, 2001, at 731–33). This is particularly true when the females in question employ foul language and loud voices. Male negotiators who would immediately counter these tactics by other men with quid pro quo responses often find it hard to adopt retaliatory approaches against "ladies." When they permit such an irrelevant factor to influence and limit their use of responsive weapons, they provide their female opponents with an inherent bargaining advantage. Men who are similarly unwilling to act as competitively toward female adversaries as they would toward male adversaries give further leverage to their female opponents.

Male attorneys occasionally make the mistake of assuming that female opponents do not engage in as many negotiating "games" as male adversaries. Even many women erroneously assume that other females are unlikely to employ the Machiavellian tactics stereotypically attributed to members of the competitive male culture. Men *and* women who expect their female adversaries to behave less disingenuously and more cooperatively often ignore the reality of their interactions and accord a significant bargaining advantage to women who are in fact willing to employ manipulative bargaining tactics.

[2]   Defense

Some male negotiators attempt to obtain a psychological advantage against aggressive female bargainers by casting aspersions on the femininity of those individuals. They hope to embarrass those participants and make them feel self-conscious with respect to the approach they are using. Female negotiators should never allow adversaries to employ this tactic successfully. They have the right to use any technique they think appropriate regardless of the gender-based stereotypes they may contradict. To male attorneys who raise specious objections to their otherwise proper conduct, they should reply that they do not wish to be viewed as "ladies," but merely as legal advocates involved in transactions in which one's gender is irrelevant.

Women lawyers who find that gender-based beliefs may be negatively affecting bargaining interactions may wish to directly broach the subject of negative stereotyping, since this may be the most effective manner of dealing with the influence of these feelings (Schneider, 1994, at 112–13). They may ask opponents if they find it difficult to negotiate with women attorneys. While most male adversaries will quickly deny any such beliefs, they are likely to internally reevaluate their treatment of female opponents. Once both sides acknowledge — internally or externally — the possible impact of stereotypical beliefs, they can try to avoid group generalizations and focus on the particular individuals with whom they must currently interact.

[3]   "Real" Differences

[a]   Trust Building

Empirical studies indicate that male and female subjects do not behave identically in competitive settings. Females tend to be initially more trusting and trustworthy than their male cohorts, but they are generally less willing to forgive violations of their trust than are males (Miller & Miller, 2002, at 42–45; Rubin & Brown, 1975, at 171–73). People interacting with female negotiators who exhibit verbal and nonverbal signals consistent with these generalities should realize that they may be able to establish trusting and cooperative relationships with them so long as they do not commit unacceptable transgressions. Men tend to establish higher goals than women in identical situations, often enabling them to obtain more beneficial results (Kray & Babcock, 2006, at 205).

[b]   Orientation of Lying

When men and women do prevaricate, they often have different objectives. Males frequently lie on a self-oriented basis to enhance their own reputations ("braggadocio"), while females who dissemble are more likely to engage in other-oriented lying that is intended to make other people feel better ("I love your new outfit"; "you made a great presentation") (DePaulo, et al., 1996, at 986–87; see also Feldman, Forrest & Happ, 2002). This difference would probably cause males to feel more comfortable than their female cohorts when they engage in deceptive behavior during negotiation encounters to advance their own interests, since such conduct would be of a self-oriented nature.

[c]   Level of Comfort with Competitive Situations

One observer has suggested that "women are more likely [than men] to avoid competitive situations, less likely to acknowledge competitive wishes, and not likely to do as well in competition." (Stiver, 1983, at 5; see Greig, 2008, at 496–97; Niederle & Vesterlund, 2005, at 3, 11–14; Babcock & Laschever, 2003, at 102–03). Many women are apprehensive regarding the negative consequences that they associate with competitive achievement, fearing that competitive success will alienate them from others (Babcock & Laschever, 2008, at 32; Gilligan, 1982, at 14–15). Males in my Legal Negotiating course have occasionally indicated that they are particularly uncomfortable when women opponents obtain extremely beneficial results from them. A few have even indicated that they would prefer the consequences associated with nonsettlements to the possible embarrassment of "losing" to female opponents (see Miller & Miller, 2002, at 132). Even some female students are more critical of women who attain exceptional bargaining results than they are of men who achieve equally advantageous negotiation terms (Burton, et al., 1991, at 233).

Males tend to exude more confidence than females in performance-oriented settings (Niederle & Vesterlund, 2008, at 450–56; Volkema, 2006, at 154; Sax, 2005, at 43; Niederle & Vesterlund, 2005, at 4, 19–20). Even when minimally prepared, men think they can "wing it" and get through successfully (Goleman, 1998, at 7). On the other hand, no matter how well prepared women are, they tend to feel unprepared (Evans, 2000, at 84–85, 90–91; McIntosh, 1985). I often observe this distinction with my Legal Negotiating students. Successful males think they can achieve beneficial results in any setting, while successful females continue to express doubts about their own capabilities. I find this frustrating, because these accomplished women are as proficient as their accomplished male cohorts.

Male confidence may explain why men like to negotiate more than women (Small, Gelfand, Babcock & Gettman, 2007), and why they tend to seek more beneficial results when they negotiate than their female cohorts (Babcock & Laschever, 2008, at 146–47; Babcock & Laschever, 2003, at 130–35, 140–41). Men tend to feel more comfortable in risk-taking situations than women (Babcock & Laschever, 2008, at 32; Babcock & Laschever, 2003, at 138). When they bargain, males tend to use more forceful language and exhibit more dominant nonverbal signals (e.g., intense eye contact and louder voices) than females (Babcock & Laschever, 2003, at 105). These gender differences may help to explain why women experience greater anxiety when they have to negotiate than men (Babcock & Laschever, 2003, at 113–14). In addition, while women tend to seek less than men when they negotiate for themselves, they set higher goals and achieve higher results when they negotiate on behalf of others (Kray & Babcock, 2006, at 215; Kolb & Putnam, 2005, at 137; Bowles, Babcock & McGinn, 2005). On the other hand, while men tend to be more win-lose oriented, women tend to be more win-win oriented, making it easier for them to use cooperative bargaining to expand the overall pie and improve the results achieved by both sides (Id. at 164–72).

In my Legal Negotiating course, students may take the class for a traditional letter grade or on a pass/fail basis. During the first session, I explain how two-thirds of their final grade will be based on comparative results they achieve on negotiation exercises. I note how some people may feel uncomfortable about the overt competition they may experience, and suggest that individuals concerned about this factor should take the class on a pass/fail basis. Although a third of the students select the pass/fail option, it is interesting to note that a greater percentage of females (38.8%) select the pass/fail alternative than males (26.7%) (Craver & Barnes, 1999, at 328–33) (see also Sax, 2005, at 40–43 (indicating that males enjoy risk-taking activities more than females); Volkema, 2006, at 154 (indicating that men tend to handle stress more comfortably than women)).

As lawyers increasingly use e-mail and other electronic technologies to negotiate, this factor may favor women. Studies indicate that females spend more time than males e-mailing and text-messaging others to further their relationships, while males spend more time playing games (Larson, 2006, at 225–26). This difference would suggest that females use such technologies more effectively than males to establish and maintain relationships and when communicating generally — both critical factors associated with negotiation proficiency.

[d]   Language Usage

During interpersonal transactions, men are more likely than women to employ "highly intensive language" to persuade others, and they tend to be more effective using this approach (Burgoon, Dillard & Doran, 1983, at 284, 292; see also Pines, Gat & Tal, 2002, at 36–37). Women, on the other hand, are more likely to use less intense language during persuasive encounters, and they are inclined to be more effective behaving in that manner (Carli, 2001, at 732–36). Females tend to employ language containing more disclaimers ("I think"; "you know") than their male cohorts (Smeltzer & Watson, 1986, at 78), which may cause women to be perceived as less forceful. Since women tend to have more acute hearing than men, they often use softer voices than men when interacting with others, and they are more likely than men to view slightly raised voices as aggressive (Sax, 2005, at 18).

[e]   Formal Education as Mitigating Factor

Formal education diminishes the presence of gender-based verbal differences. When individuals receive specific training, male-female communication distinctions are largely eliminated (Burrell, Donohue & Allen, 1988, at 453). This factor would explain why male and female lawyers tend to employ similar language when endeavoring to persuade others. Nonetheless, even when women use the same language as men, they are often perceived as being less influential (Burrell, Donhoue & Allen, 1988, at 463). This gender-based factor is offset, however, by the fact that women continue to be more sensitive to verbal leaks and nonverbal signals than their male cohorts (Pease & Pease, 2006, at 13–14; Thompson, 2005, at 341; Sax, 2005, at 18–19; Miller & Miller, 2002, at 60–61; Hall, 1984, at 15–17; Henley, 1977, at 13–15).

[f]   Views of Appropriate Bargaining Outcome

There are indications that males and females differ with respect to their views of appropriate bargaining outcomes. Women tend to believe in "equal" exchanges, while men tend to expect "equitable" distributions (Eckel, de Oliveira & Grossman, 2008, at 441; Lewicki, at al., 1994, at 330). These predispositional differences may induce female negotiators to accept equal results despite their possession of greater relative bargaining strength, while male bargainers seek equitable exchanges that reflect relevant power imbalances. Their egalitarian propensity could disadvantage women who hesitate to use favorable power imbalances to obtain more beneficial results for their own sides. On the other hand, when women are put in situations in which they are asked to negotiate on behalf of others — instead of themselves — they work more diligently to obtain optimal results for the persons they are representing (Bowles, Babcock & McGinn, 2005, 658–662).

[g]   Personal Attacks

This double-standard adversely affects female students in other aspects of their law school experience. In their study of law students at the University of Pennsylvania, Lani Guinier, Michelle Fine, and Jane Balin found that students who openly demonstrate their intellectual capabilities through regular class participation are characterized differently by other students based on their gender. While male participants are given negative labels, these tend to be of a gender-neutral variety (*e.g.*, "asshole"). Their female cohorts, however, are often given labels that directly relate to their femininity — *e.g.*, "man-hating lesbian" or "feminazi dyke" (Guinier, Fine & Balin,

1994, at 51–52). This disparate treatment of women places them in an unfair position and may be deliberately designed to undermine their law school achievements.

[4]   Role of Social Conditioning

Gender-based competitive differences may be attributable to the different acculturation process for boys and girls (Menkel, Meadow, 2000, at 362–64). Parents tend to be more protective of their daughters than of their sons (Babcock & Laschever, 2003, at 30–31; Marone, 1992, at 42–45). Most boys are exposed to competitive situations at an early age (Evans, 2000, at 12–13; Tannen, 1990, at 43–47; Gilligan, 1982, at 9). They have been encouraged to participate in little league baseball, basketball, football, soccer, and other competitive athletic endeavors. These activities introduce boys to the "thrill of victory and the agony of defeat" during their formative years (Harragan, 1977, at 75–78, 282). "Traditional girls' games like jump rope and hopscotch are turn-taking games, where competition is indirect since one person's success does not necessarily signify another's failure." (Gilligan, 1982, at 10; see also Greenhalgh, 1987, at 169). While directly competitive games teach boys how to resolve the disputes that inevitable arise, girls are less likely to have the opportunity to learn those dispute resolution skills (Babcock & Laschever, 2003, at 34–35). By adulthood, men are more likely to have become accustomed to the rigors of overt competition. While it is true that little league and interscholastic sports for women have become more competitive in recent years, most continue to be less overtly competitive than corresponding male athletic endeavors (Evans, 2000, at 80).

[5]   Influence of Physical Appearance

The physical appearance of male and female bargainers may influence the manner in which they are perceived by others (Cash & Janda, 1984, at 46–52). Empirical studies have found that attractive men are likely to be considered more competent than their less attractive male cohorts with respect to their ability to think logically and analytically. Contrary results have been obtained for female subjects. Less attractive women tend to be viewed as more cerebral than their more attractive female colleagues. This stereotypical view of attractive women is frequently based on the theory that good looking females must not have received the same intellectual capacities as their less attractive cohorts. If this assumption were correct, one would expect attractive males to be similarly disadvantaged with respect to their cerebral capabilities. Women with a "less feminine" appearance ("tailored clothes with a jacket, subtle make-up, and either short hair or hair swept away from the face") are similarly more likely to be taken seriously by others and be viewed as more assertive, more logical, and less emotional in critical situations — particularly by male respondents — than are women with a "more feminine" appearance (Cash & Janda, 1984, at 46–52).

[6]   Negotiation Styles

Other gender-based stereotypes affect the way in which men and women interact in negotiation settings. Males are expected to be more rational and objective, while females are supposed to concentrate more on relationships (Kray & Babcock, 2006, at 206–07; Pines, Gat & Tal, 2002, at 25, 39; Kray, Thompson & Galinski, 2001, at 944; Gilligan, 1982). Men tend to define themselves by their achievements, while women tend to define themselves by their relationships (Kolb & Putnam, 2005, at 137; Babcock & Laschever, 2003, at 117). Male negotiators are expected to be dominant and overtly competitive, with women bargainers expected to be passive and submissive (Babcock & Laschever, 2003, at 62–63, 75; Maccoby & Jacklin, 1974, at 228, 234). In competitive bargaining situations, participants possessing stereotypically male traits might reasonably be expected to out perform participants possessing stereotypically female traits (Kray, Thompson & Galinsky, 2001, at 946). In multi-item negotiations, however, the tendency of women to interact more cooperatively should enhance the likelihood of more integrative agreements (Kray & Babcock, 2006, at 209).

When men and women interact, men tend to speak for longer periods and to interrupt more frequently than women (Deaux, 1976, at 60). If females speak half of the time, they tend to be perceived by male participants as domineering. This masculine tendency to dominate male-female interactions could provide men with an advantage during negotiations by enabling them to control the discussions.

[7]   Evidence Against Validity of Behavioral Predictions

Professor Deaux succinctly noted that behavioral predictions based on stereotypical beliefs regarding men and women are likely to be of questionable validity in most settings.

> [Despite the persistence of stereotypes, the studies of social behavior suggest that there are relatively few characteristics in which men and women consistently differ. Men and women both seem to be capable of being aggressive, helpful, and alternately cooperative and competitive. In other words, there is little evidence that the nature of women and men is so inherently different that we are justified in making stereotyped generalizations (Deaux, 1976, at 144).

In light of the fact that most law students are relatively competitive persons and receive extensive legal training, one would certainly expect the traditionally found gender-based differences to be of minimal relevance.

Several years ago, I compared the results achieved over fifteen years by male and female students in my Legal Negotiating classes. I hypothesized that there would be no meaningful differences, and the statistical results confirmed this belief. There was not a single year for which the average results achieved by men were statistically different from the results attained by women at the 0.05 level of significance (Craver, 1990, at 12–16 & Table 1). Some people suggested that while the male and female averages might be the same, the individual results would be different with stereotypically competitive males obtaining extremely good or bad results and with stereotypically cooperative females being clustered around the mean. Had the male results been more skewed, the male standard deviations would have been higher than the female standard deviations. My data negated this hypothesis, since the male and female standard deviations were approximately equal throughout the fifteen year period. In 1999, David Barnes and I made the same statistical comparison covering the thirteen years I had taught at George Washington University, and we again found no statistically meaningful differences with respect to the negotiation results attained by male and female students (Craver & Barnes, 1999, at 339–44; *see also* Stuhlmacher & Walters, 1999).

[8]   Taking Advantage of Stereotypes

Male negotiators who take female opponents less seriously than they take male adversaries based upon gender-based stereotypes provide their female adversaries with an inherent advantage. Since they do not expect highly competitive or manipulative behavior from women, they are less likely to discern and effectively counter the use of these tactics by female opponents. While women bargainers may understandably be offended by such patronizing attitudes, there is an easy way to get even with these male troglodytes. They should clean them out! I have been amazed by the number of proficient female negotiators who have been able to accomplish this objective against unsuspecting male opponents who had no idea how adroitly they were being fleeced (see generally Miller & Miller, 2002).

[9]   Over-Valuing Male Success/Under-Valuing Female Success

One other gender-based phenomenon that continues to unfairly affect women should be noted. When men are successful, their accomplishments are usually attributed to intrinsic factors such as intelligence and hard work (Deaux, 1976, at 30–32, 41). When women are successful, however, their achievements are most often attributed to extrinsic variables such as luck or the actions of others. This phenomenon enhances male self-confidence by permitting them to accept personal credit for their achievements, while it undermines female self-confidence by depriving them of personal credit for their own accomplishments. When partners are evaluating the work of associates or firm attorneys are reviewing the qualifications of students seeking associate positions, they should be cognizant of this factor and make sure they give females as much credit for their achievements as they give to equally accomplished males.

Summary

1. People tend to interact more cooperatively and more openly with persons of the same race, gender, and culture, because they assume common values and do not feel the need to maintain a particular "face."

2. When individuals of different races, genders, or cultures negotiate, they should recognize that stereotypical beliefs may initially impede their interactions and should use an expanded Preliminary Stage to establish beneficial rapport.

3. African-Americans, Asian-Americans, and Latino-Americans are stereotypically presumed to be more accommodating, less manipulative, and less competitive than Caucasian-Americans.

4. Based upon their different acculturation experiences, males are expected to be competitive, forceful, Machiavellian, and abstract, while women are expected to be cooperative, deferential, and more concerned with relationships.

5. Advanced education and specialized training tend to eliminate ethnic and gender-based dissimilarities. I have found no statistically significant differences between the negotiation results achieved by minority and nonminority students or by male and female law students.

6. Negotiators who underestimate opponents because of ethnic or gender-based stereotypes provide those individuals with opportunities. Their adversaries should take advantage of these opportunities.

Chapter 15

INTERNATIONAL NEGOTIATIONS

[f] — Focus on Specificity of Language in Accords

§ 15.01   INCREASING SIGNIFICANCE OF NEGOTIATIONS IN GLOBALIZATION OF POLITICAL AND ECONOMIC RELATIONS

[1]   Increased Frequency of International Transactions

As instant communications and efficient transportation systems have contributed to the development of a truly global political and economic world, the extent of governmental and private international negotiating has greatly increased. International political bodies — such as the United Nations and its constituent entities and the World Trade Organization (WTO) — and regional political/economic groups — such as the European Union, the Group of Eight (G-8), and the North American Free Trade Organization — have expanded the use of bilateral and multilateral governmental interactions. Non-governmental organizations (NGOs) have begun to realize the degree to which they may become involved with matters that were previously addressed solely through governmental channels. The growth of multinational business firms has similarly increased the frequency of private transnational business negotiations. National and international bargaining transactions have many similarities and certain crucial differences (*see generally* Zartman, 1994; Kremenyuk, 2002; Bendahmane & McDonald, 1984). They generally involve the same negotiation stages and many common bargaining techniques — even though identical tactics may be given different names in different nations.

[2]   Influence of Cultural Stereotyping

Government representatives are affected by stereotypical views of their political and economic systems and their national cultures — and those of the national groups with which they are interacting. They must be cognizant of the political constraints under which they operate and, in some instances, they may have to be aware of military/security considerations. Private corporate negotiators are similarly influenced by cultural stereotyping. They may also be affected by the need for governmental involvement in what may appear to be wholly private business transactions.

Verbal communication is an indispensable part of the international bargaining process, but written and oral exchanges may be subject to interpretive difficulties — even when the participants think they are using the same language (*e.g.*, United States, British, Canadian, and Australian negotiators). Similar nonverbal signals may have different meanings in diverse cultures (Morris, 1995). National and regional cultural differences also influence transnational interactions. While a distinct international bargaining culture may have developed among public and private representatives who repeatedly interact with others in European, North American, African, and Asian nations, it is rare for most individuals to entirely escape the impact of the cultures in which they were raised and in which they currently reside (Watkins & Rosegrant, 2001, at 73–79).

§ 15.02   OFFICIAL INTERGOVERNMENT (TRACK 1) DIPLOMACY

[1]   Background

When nations negotiate with one another — *"Track I Diplomacy"* — their discussions may be carried out through formal channels or through informal "back channel" communications (Wanis-St. John, 2006, at 20–29). Formal channels are generally used for conventional interactions, while back channels are employed for particularly delicate talks or when the relevant governments do not have direct diplomatic relations. The least complicated inter-nation negotiations involve bilateral interactions between two countries (*e.g.* United States-Mexico; France-Germany; Japan-China). Multilateral transactions may include three or four countries or a hundred or more nations. They may be conducted on an ad hoc basis involving various countries with common interests or through a formal organization such as the United Nations, the Organization of American States, the World Trade Organization, or the European Union (*see generally* Zartman, 1994 (using different bargaining perspectives to analyze negotiations pertaining to the Single European Act governing the European Union and the Uruguay Round of GATT)).

[2]   Bilateral Negotiations

[a]   Nature and Concern

Bilateral negotiations are generally conducted under ad hoc procedures agreed upon by the participants for the specific interactions involved. These transactions may concern economic, political, cultural, humanitarian, or military/security issues. For example, governments may be discussing trade restrictions, immigration rules, art exchanges, human rights, and/or regional or global arms limitations. Bilateral interactions may involve participants with relatively equal (*e.g.*, Britain-France; United States-Japan) or wholly disparate (*e.g.*, United States-Cuba; China-Taiwan) economic or military power.

[b]   Approval Requirements

Bilateral agreements usually require approval by the governments of the participating nations before they become operative. When *executive accords* are involved, only the consent of the President or Prime Minister may be necessary, while *treaties* are likely to require legislative ratification. Presidents who fear protracted or divisive Senate debate over controversial bilateral pacts often resort to executive agreements that do not necessitate Senate consideration.

Most bilateral accords do not require the approval of other countries before they take effect. In some instances, however, treaty obligations may necessitate the consent of trading partners before trade agreements with other nations may become operative. Bilateral security pacts may first have to be approved by regional groups such as NATO or SEATO. Even when the approval of other nations is not necessary, new bilateral arrangements may directly affect the rights of other countries. For example, nations with "most favored nation" (MFN) trading status may claim the benefit of more generous terms given to another country.

[3]   Multilateral Negotiations

[a]   Complexity of Issues and People Involved

Multilateral interactions are usually far more complex than bilateral discussions (Raiffa, 2003, at 389–406; Zartman, 1994, at 4–5). They usually involve numerous issues and many parties. It may be difficult to know which participants will support or oppose which issues. A group hierarchy often develops, with certain individuals leading the talks, certain persons acting as mediators, and certain people undermining progress. The participants playing these roles may vary from issue to issue, depending on the national interests involved.

[b]   Negotiation Ratification Requirements

While multilateral negotiations can be conducted on an ad hoc basis, they are generally carried out through existing international organizations. These interactions usually have formal agendas and specified procedures. On some occasions, a single nation or a group of countries may initiate the discussion process and request the assistance of an appropriate formal organization, while on other occasions the existing entity may itself convene the talks. The interested participants or the sponsoring organization may schedule a pre-conference meeting to define the issues to be addressed, the countries to be invited to participate, the procedural rules, and the final approval process (see, e.g., Sjöstedt, 2002). Countries may try to link issues they hope to obtain to other issues they believe other nations prefer, to enhance the likelihood of success on their particular items (Watkins & Rosegrant, 2001, at 220–21). Some resulting agreements need only be approved by the sponsoring entity to become effective, while other accords must be approved by all or a substantial portion of the participating nations before they become binding. In some instances, domestic legislation must be enacted to effectuate the principles set forth in non-binding international agreements.

[c]   Significance of Emerging Nations on Multilateral Scene and the Formation of Blocs

When multilateral sessions were previously conducted, the talks tended to be dominated by economically and militarily powerful nations such as the United States and the Soviet Union. Less powerful countries often felt ignored. Over the past several decades, a number of emerging countries have begun to recognize the increased bargaining power they can generate through formal or informal voting blocs (Watkins & Rosegrant, 2001, at 213–15; Dupont, 1994, at 148–77; Rubin & Swap, 1994, at 137–42; see also Raiffa, 2003, at 430–49). Countries with common interests attempt to align themselves in ways designed to maximize their bargaining influence. They may unite over particular topics or work together with respect to entire agendas. Whenever possible, they try to obtain voting rules that treat large and small nations equally, since this practice may give certain blocs veto power. This tactic is frequently employed at the United Nations with respect to issues addressed by the General Assembly. Weaker members try to prevent Security Council consideration, recognizing that any one of the five permanent members (China, France, Britain, Russia, and U.S.) can veto actions in that body. Bloc behavior was critical with respect to the Law of the Sea negotiations to protect the interests of nations that lacked the technology required to exploit seabed resources.

[d] Defense Against Voting Blocs

The creation of voting blocs by weaker nations is most effective with respect to deliberations carried out through formal organizations due to the established voting rules that are generally applied (*see, e.g.*, Brams, Doherty & Weidner, 1994, at 98–103 regarding use of voting blocs during negotiations for the Single European Act). When multilateral negotiations are conducted on an ad hoc basis and the rules are determined by the more powerful participants, weighted voting procedures may be adopted to diminish the capacity of weaker nations to block overall accords. Furthermore, the convening countries can limit the number of participants to reduce the likelihood of bloc formations (Raiffa, 2003, at 450–64).

[4] Negotiators as Cultural Representatives

People who represent nations in the international arena must recognize that they are always acting in an official representational capacity. No matter how much they try to develop individual identities, they continue to be viewed as spokespersons for their respective countries. This is true when they are speaking through formal and informal channels. As a result of this phenomenon, American agents tend to be burdened with the stereotypical baggage associated with United States representatives. They are likely to be perceived as arrogant, powerful, uncompromising (*i.e.*, Boulwareistic), unsympathetic, and capitalistic. United States representatives who attempt to dispel these images by disassociating themselves from official U.S. positions are likely to create additional problems. Others will be shocked that U.S. agents would undermine their own country, and will suspect that such disreputable individuals cannot be trusted. It thus behooves U.S. agents to always behave in a manner that furthers the underlying interests of their own country, even when they are working to accomplish seemingly external objectives.

[5] Extent of Negotiator Authority

As was noted previously with respect to domestic government attorneys, designated U.S. representatives generally have circumscribed authority. Strangely enough, while low level agents involved in relatively insignificant meetings may enjoy some degree of negotiating discretion, more visible advocates who are dealing with important matters usually have limited freedom. They may be required to check constantly with the State Department, the White House, the Senate Foreign Affairs Committee, and other groups that have control over the final outcome of the current negotiations. Their actions will be orchestrated by these other entities, severely limiting their ability to do anything spontaneously.

[6] Importance of Pre-Negotiation Intra-Organizational Meetings

Since bilateral and multilateral international negotiations tend to concern issues of import to different government agencies, it is crucial to engage in thorough *intra-government* planning prior to the external discussions (Salacuse, 2003, at 29–42). In order to permit the development of common goals, all interested entities must be asked about their respective interests and objectives. Further, to guarantee the projection of unified national positions negotiating strategy must also be addressed. If these preliminary planning activities are not carried out, several negative consequences are likely to result. Opponents who sense the lack of a unified approach may try to exploit internal disagreements. In addition, if final terms are agreed upon that do not satisfy the needs of the different U.S. agencies, dissatisfied officials may attempt to undermine the accord. They may contact White House, State Department, or Senate officials in an effort to obtain a renegotiation of the disfavored items. American representatives should thus realize that their *intra-governmental negotiations* may be more contentious and protracted than the subsequent *inter-government bargaining*. People who endeavor to avoid this necessary step usually encounter more difficulties in the long run than if they had engaged in thorough intra-organizational preparation.

[7]   Determining Roles of Various Participants

When large international conferences are involved, expansive national delegations may be required. When they interact with delegates from other nations, U.S. representatives must try to determine which persons possess real influence with their home governments, which are destabilizing participants who may try to hinder progress, and which are mediators who will attempt to accommodate competing interests (Moore, 2003, at 429–33; Colosi in Bendahmane & McDonald, 1984, at 17–18). Means must be found to induce the mediative officials to neutralize the destabilizers in a way that enables the influential agents to agree to the desired objectives.

[8]   Multi-Leveled Nature of Inter-Nation Negotiations

Inter-nation negotiations at regional or global conferences generally occur at various levels. Preconference discussions between and among key participants are used to define the issues to be addressed and to determine the conference procedures to be followed. Once the conference begins, plenary sessions are used for formal speeches and public debate. Smaller working groups are frequently formed to explore specific topics and to formulate proposals that will ultimately be considered by the entire conference (Kolb & Faure, 1994, at 127–28). Informal talks between representatives from critical nations are often employed to ascertain areas of mutual interest. Countries with nonexistent or limited diplomatic relations use back channel communications to exchange ideas in a manner that preserves their public images.

[9]   Conflict Resolution

[a]   Addressing the Need for Mediation

When international negotiations do not progress satisfactorily, it is often beneficial to seek the assistance of neutral intervenors. Mediators from nonaligned nations may use their good offices to move discussions in a productive direction. Some mediators may be selected because of their current positions — *e.g.*, the Secretary General of the United Nations or the Secretary of State of a neutral country (Merrills, 1998, at 27–43). On some occasions, it may be helpful to request assistance from process experts who are not associated with governmental entities (*e.g.*, businesspeople or academics). Just as with domestic negotiations, these individuals can work to reopen clogged communication channels, to get the disputants to explore their diverse underlying interests, and to look for alternatives that may simultaneously satisfy the needs of everyone. Once agreements are achieved, the responsible nations must work to ensure their effectuation.

When disputing nations wholly distrust one another because of prior violations of trust, intermediaries cannot hope to induce them to move directly toward final accords.

They often have to employ "confidence building" measures that have the parties move in small reciprocal increments until the disputants can restore the mutual trust necessary to allow movement toward final agreements (Watkins & Rosegrant, 2001, at 167, 270). In such circumstances, each side agrees to take alternative steps toward an overall resolution that will demonstrate their respective good faith. One may agree to pull back slightly from occupied areas, while the other agrees to decrease its troop levels in the region. The first party may then agree to reduce its level of weaponry, while the other recognizes the legitimacy of some of the first party's territorial claims. Once a number of such mutual steps have been taken and bargaining credibility has been restored, the parties may be able to make the overarching commitments needed to resolve the underlying controversy (see generally Savir, 1998 (describing the various steps taken by Israel and the PLO as they worked toward the Oslo Accords); see also Wittes, 2005; Enderlin, 2002 (describing more recent Israeli-PLO peace talk developments)).

Peace negotiations are frequently conducted entirely or primarily by men (Chinkin, 2003). This deprives women of the opportunity to directly influence talks that will significantly affect their interests. It also causes excessive focus on the rights of men and the ignoring of issues of particular interest to women. In October of 2000, the U.N. Security Council adopted Resolution 1325 which urges parties negotiating peace agreements to include a gender perspective that would ensure respect for the human rights of women and girls (Chinkin, 2003, at 869–870).

[b]   Using Single-Text Approach to Preempt Disputes

Mediators occasionally use a single-text approach to avoid problems caused by reactive devaluation. All relevant proposals are included in the initial draft, with no country being directly identified with particular items. The mediators continue to refine the single-draft provisions until they become generally acceptable. This technique allows the drafting intermediaries to assume responsibility for the various provisions, and it diminishes nationalistic clashes over sponsorship disputes.

[c]   Using International Tribunals

In some instances, international tribunals (e.g., the World Court) are asked to conduct inquiries into particular disputes (Merrill, 1998, at 44–61). They listen to party presentations, and try to determine the relevant facts to facilitate settlement efforts. Disputing parties may additionally or alternatively ask respected neutrals to act as conciliators (Merrill, 1998, at 62–87). These individuals conduct hearings to ascertain the pertinent facts, and — unlike traditional mediators — make non-binding settlement recommendations they hope will be acceptable to the interested parties.

§ 15.03 PRIVATE CITIZEN INVOLVEMENT IN PUBLIC MATTERS

[1]   Recent Emergence of NGOs and Track II Diplomacy

[a]   Filling the Diplomatic Void

Certain national or international conflicts may not respond favorably to formal diplomatic intervention by government representatives. The disputants may not trust the countries that are trying to help. Regional or global balances may be undermined by the involvement of external nations. To circumvent these difficulties and fill the diplomatic void, non-governmental organizations (NGOs) have increasingly become involved. For many years, groups affiliated with the Quaker Church — *e.g.*, American Friends Service Committee (Warren, 1987, at 27–34) — have worked in many areas to promote human rights and world peace. In recent years, NGOs like the Institute for Multi-Track Diplomacy and Former President Carter's Peace Institute have provided dispute resolution assistance in areas like Northern Ireland, Cyprus, the Middle East, Yugoslavia, South Africa, and Rwanda.

[b]   Advantage of Private Citizens

The involvement of NGOs or private citizens in international conflicts has been labeled *"Track II Diplomacy"* (McDonald & Bendahmane, 1987). These private entities are not constrained by political considerations affecting official governmental institutions. Unlike State Department personnel who must always speak for their government and further their own nation's interests, private organizations and private citizens can speak as individuals. They can say things and behave in ways that would be unacceptable for government spokespersons. They do not have to worry about the political ramifications of their actions back home.

[c]   Level of Interaction in Host Nations

Groups and individuals engaged in Track II Diplomacy often interact with private organizations in the host nations. They may be forced to do this because of the unwillingness of government officials to recognize their mediative status. On some occasions, however, they are permitted to meet with government officials and to become directly involved with formal diplomatic efforts. (See Savir, 1998 (describing initial contacts between Terje Larson, a Norwegian social scientist who headed a European peace institute, two Israeli academics, and PLO representatives that ultimately generated the Oslo Accords)).

[d]   Overcoming National Stereotypes

Despite their freedom from government control, NGO representatives are still subject to cultural stereotyping that may affect they way they are perceived. When United States citizens travel abroad, it is difficult for them to entirely shed their American images. This fact makes it particularly difficult for Americans to mediate disputes that directly involve United States interests. Individuals from countries with competing interests tend to fear that even private U.S. citizens cannot completely ignore the official policies of their home government. While a few groups, like the Quakers, have been able to accomplish this objective, the involvement of the U.S. in specific controversies may necessitate the intervention of private citizens from nonaligned nations such as Sweden, Norway, or Switzerland. It is frequently easier for individuals from these neutral states to earn the trust and respect of the disputing parties.

[e] Greater Latitude of Intervention

Experienced negotiators can use Track II Diplomacy to affect inter-nation controversies, such as those between Greece and Cyprus, Rwanda and Burundi, and Israel and Syria. In these areas, they may work in parallel with Track I diplomats representing the United Nations or their home countries. Track II conciliators may also intervene in internal state disputes that threaten human rights — *e.g.*, South Africa and Yugoslavia. While it may be awkward for foreign governments to become directly involved with the internal affairs of other nations, private organizations do not have to worry about this issue. They can easily interact with other private entities within the target country. They may even be able to meet privately with government officials who do not view such discussions as infringements of their national sovereignty.

[2] Stages of Track II Diplomacy

[a] Preliminary Stage

[i] Cultural or Economic Exchanges

Track II diplomatic efforts are usually carried out in stages (Montville, 1987, at 7–15). The preliminary stage involves the establishment of personal contacts with people or organizations in the target nation(s). Once the neutral intervenors have opened communication channels with appropriate persons, they attempt to induce the disputing parties to interact at a minimal level. These efforts frequently take the form of cultural or economic exchanges that are designed to demonstrate that individuals from disputing groups or countries can work together on something. These activities also begin to generate a minimal level of inter-group trust.

[ii] Problem-Solving Workshops

Once communications are established with target groups and some cooperative ventures have been attempted, the intervenors try to convene problem-solving workshops that include respected individuals from the disputing entities. The participants are encouraged to get to know each other personally. Cultural differences are explored in an effort to develop mutual respect for the diverse backgrounds involved. Conciliators hope to personalize the disputing parties in a way that humanizes the conflict. When disputants interact — during informal sessions or structured events — they tend to exhibit less hostility toward one another. These preliminary interactions may take a few days or may have to develop over several months. When the time is propitious, group leaders begin to explore the underlying reasons for their conflict and to look for solutions that might be mutually acceptable.

[iii] Joint Brainstorming Sessions

Joint brain-storming sessions can be especially conciliatory experiences, as the disputing parties are induced to work together toward common goals. On some occasions, role reversals can be used to place individuals in the shoes of their opponents. This technique can help people understand why their adversaries are unhappy and what types of solutions must be formulated to satisfy that side's underlying concerns. If this process functions effectively, the participants begin to move from the adversarial mode to the conciliatory mode, and they look for real solutions to their conflict.

[b]   Stage II — Influencing Public Opinion

The second stage of this process involves efforts to influence public opinion in ways designed to decrease inter-group tensions and humanize the conflicting factions. Conciliators and group leaders may discuss their differences on television and radio shows or at public gatherings. Written materials may be prepared and disseminated among interested parties. This educational device is especially effective with respect to young people who may not remember past wrongs as strongly as those who lived through them. If public opinion can be generated in favor of peaceful solutions, government officials may begin to participate. Politicians are usually good readers of their constituents, and they are likely to welcome constituent efforts to eliminate strife.

[c]   Stage III — Establishment of Cooperative Programs

Once tentative resolutions of ongoing conflicts are developed, Track II Diplomacy enters the third stage. This involves the establishment of cooperative educational and economic ventures to unite the prior combatants in common programs. If they can be induced to work together, instead of in conflict, they often develop mutual ties that are difficult for others to sever.

[3]   Need for Patience

Individuals who attempt Track II Diplomatic efforts must be particularly patient. Most inter-cultural conflicts have taken years to develop, and the disputants are unlikely to change their perspectives quickly. Conciliators who try to hurry the healing process are likely to generate further distrust and undermine settlement efforts. They must start with minimal goals and work slowly but steadily toward final resolutions.

[4]   Government Employment

Track II Diplomacy is occasionally employed by government officials to achieve objectives they might not be able to seek through Track I channels (*see, e.g.*, Scali, 1987, at 73–80 (describing reporter Scali's role as intermediary between the U.S. and the Soviet Union during the Cuban missile crisis)). For example, if government representatives could not directly contact outlaw organizations, they may ask private groups or individuals to establish contacts and act as back channel communicators. Once the preliminary Track II efforts become public, State Department representatives may find it safe to participate. Governments may also use Track II intervention to suggest possible settlement options that could not be officially proposed because of their controversial nature. Once these alternatives have been subject to public debate and have generated at least minimal acceptance, they may receive formal political support.

[5]   Associated Risks

Track II diplomatic efforts are not always beneficial. When inexperienced individuals insert themselves into disputes without appreciating the risks involved, they can actually exacerbate conflicts. They may say or do something that inflames feelings and generates greater inter-group distrust. They may also be manipulated by particular disputants who hope to attain their own selfish ends (Bolling, 1987, at 56–57). They must be especially wary regarding the willingness of some conflicting parties to use mediation talks as a stalling device to prolong existing combat.

§ 15.04 TRANSNATIONAL BUSINESS NEGOTIATIONS

[1]   Greater Frequency and Influence of Facilitating Organizations

As national economies have become inextricably intertwined with the economies of other nations, domestic and transnational corporate leaders have had to become more proficient international business negotiators (*see generally* Salacuse, 1991). Creation of the North American Free Trade Zone has generated purchase and sales discussions between United States companies and Canadian and Mexican firms. As other regional economic groups, such as the European Union, are established, American firms will have to negotiate with their member entities. In the coming years, U.S. business officials will regularly bargain about the buying or selling of goods and services with their foreign counterparts in Africa, Asia, Europe, North and South America, Australia, and New Zealand.

[2]   Difficulties for Visiting Negotiators

[a]   Distance

Transnational business discussions create unique difficulties for various reasons (Salacuse, 2003, at 77–84; Dupont, 1991, at 331–42; Salacuse, 1991, at 5–6). Greater distances between negotiating parties often make it necessary for participants to travel to foreign countries. The host organization usually feels comfortable bargaining on its own turf (Salacuse, 2005). Visiting negotiators may experience serious jet-lag and fear that their presence in the other firm's territory may be perceived as an indication of their over-eagerness. They may also feel pressure to consummate a deal before they return home. They should try to arrive a day or two before scheduled talks begin — to alleviate jet-lag — and be somewhat flexible regarding their planned return trip home.

[b]   Cultural and Spatial Unfamiliarity

Visiting negotiators face other problems. They are likely to stay at foreign hotels that are not as commodious as their home environment. They are away from their families and colleagues, and must adjust to unfamiliar foods. They may have to contend with different foreign cultures and feel embarrassed when they commit a faux pas. They must generally accept hospitality from their opponent-hosts, and this may create feelings of obligation on their part which may induce them to make excessive concessions.

[c]   Offsetting Opponent's Hometurf Advantage

How may visiting negotiators counteract the apparent advantage enjoyed by their foreign hosts? They can try to make their hosts feel beholden to them by reminding them of the difficulty and expense they have assumed in an effort to accommodate the needs of their opponents. By going to the other side's country, they are demonstrating respect for that party and its culture. They are also indicating their good faith desire to establish a mutually beneficial business relationship. They may try to offset the hospitality extended by their hosts through reciprocal hospitality. They may emulate Japanese bargainers and take small gifts to their hosts. They can arrange to entertain their hosts at a local club or restaurant. If neither side feels comfortable negotiating at the other party's locale, the participants can agree to meet at a neutral site that would be equally convenient for both sides.

[d]   Counterbalancing Time Pressure

To counterbalance the time pressure usually felt by visiting negotiators, they should remind themselves how much the host firm wants the deal. If that firm were not interested in a business arrangement, they would not be spending time interacting with their foreign visitors. *Both sides* hope to achieve an accord before the visitors return home. Furthermore, if it appears that no agreement can be attained by that deadline, they can always continue their negotiations after they return home via telephone calls, e-mail, or fax transmissions. Even if these efforts do not generate a current business arrangement, they may lay the groundwork for future deals.

Eastern and Western cultures have historically thought of time quite differently. Western negotiators have traditionally viewed time as a commodity that is costly and should be preserved, while Eastern negotiators have considered time as an unlimited resource. For example, when a Chinese negotiator was being urged by a Western technology sales representative to reach a quick purchase agreement, his reply was incomprehensible to the Western businessperson: "China has been able to do without your technology for five thousand years. We can wait a few years longer." (Faure, 2002, at 407).

[3]   Greater Complexity of Issues Means Prolonged Time

Transnational business negotiations frequently take longer than domestic business discussions, due to cultural differences and the greater complexity of issues that must be addressed (Acuff, 1997, at 89; Salacuse, 1991, at 25–27). Some parties try to enhance the negotiation process by breaking their interaction into discrete stages. During the prenegotiation phase, they attempt to determine whether their contemplated interaction is likely to be mutually beneficial. If circumstances appear propitious, they use the conceptualization phase to create a common agenda for their impending interaction. During the final stage, they address the necessary details of their arrangement. This trifurcated procedure reduces the likelihood of conflict that often results when diverse parties try to achieve complete business transactions through unitary talks.

§ 15.05   IMPACT OF CULTURAL DIFFERENCES

[1]   Definition of Culture

What is "culture" and how does it influence bargaining interactions? *"Culture* is an aggregate product of the processes occurring in human society. It typically consists of such social phenomena as beliefs, ideas, language, customs, rules, and family patterns." (Gold, 2005, at 292–302; Lee, 2005, at 396–400; Rubinstein, 2003, at 30–40; Alder, 2002, at 16–24; Faure & Sjstedt, 1993, at 3) These factors provide each society with a set of shared values and beliefs that support the underlying assumptions that define the way individuals envision themselves and their societal groups. Culture affects the manner in which group members interact with each other and the way in which individuals from different groups relate to one another. These are particularly relevant considerations for negotiating parties, since the behavior of the participants is likely to vary greatly depending on their respective cultural backgrounds (Salacuse, 2003, at 89–115; Cohen, 1991, at 20–22; Salacuse, 1991, at 42–71). Professional cultures also influence international negotiations, as diplomats, lawyers, and scientists apply different approaches to deal with similar problems (see generally Sjöstedt, 2003).

[2]   Influence of Stereotyping

When Americans interact with other Americans in bargaining situations, they tend to assume similar cultural rules, even when their opponents are from different geographic regions. Verbal expressions and nonverbal signals have common meanings, and the participants are likely to share common values. On the other hand, when Americans interact with individuals from foreign cultures, they have to recognize the impact of cultural differences (*see generally* Brett, 2001; Hendon, Hendon & Herbig, 1996; Faure & Rubin, 1993; Cohen, 1991). Positive and negative stereotyping may influence their bargaining transactions (Jonsson, 1991, at 232–42). Traits may be attributed to individual participants based on their cultural backgrounds that bear no relation to reality. This phenomenon may easily undermine substantive discussions.

[3]   Key Cultural Differences

[a]   Importance Given to Punctuality

Punctuality is more important to the average American than it is to people from other cultures (LeBaron, 2003, at 42; Hall, 1973, at 140–61). It would normally be considered unacceptable for an American to arrive more than five or ten minutes late for a business appointment, while a thirty or forty-five minute delay would not be uncommon in various Latin American or Middle-Eastern countries. Americans often separate business and social discussions, while their counterparts in other areas of the world feel comfortable conducting business talks during social functions (Salacuse, 2003, at 101–02). Individuals with different time frames may have to discuss this issue and try to generate a mutually acceptable concept of punctuality (Macduff, 2006, at 40–42).

[b]   Physical Distances Between Participants

Spatial and conversational distances vary greatly among persons from different cultures (Hall, 1973, at 162–85). In North America, it is normally "proper" for interactants who do not know each other well to remain approximately two feet apart, particularly during formal business conversations. While that spatial separation may shrink somewhat in social environments, Americans rarely feel comfortable with the eight- to twelve-inch distances indigenous to some other cultures (*e.g.* Middle-Eastern countries). They feel intimidated by such close interactions. Their need for more expansive social distance often causes Americans to be viewed by people from other cultures as cold, withdrawn, or disinterested (Harper, Wiens & Matarazzo, 1978, at 249).

People who do not realize the importance of spatial distance need only consider two situations that commonly arise. Two individuals are engaged in a conversation in which one requires greater physical separation than the other. As the party who prefers a close encounter steps forward, the other person experiences discomfort and moves backward. The first party again moves closer, prompting another reactive retreat. These two participants are likely to continue this seemingly offensive and defensive pattern until the individual who requires greater spatial distance ends up with his or her back literally against a wall! This phenomenon may affect bargaining interactions when one participant gets too close to his or her opponent — either by standing next to or over that person or by moving his or her chair next to that individual. Negotiators frequently place a table between themselves to avoid this problem.

Another example involves two people eating together at a restaurant. If one invades the other's spatial territory by intentionally or inadvertently moving the salt, pepper, sugar, and other condiments to the other person's side of the table, that individual is likely to exhibit nonverbal signs of discomfort. They may consciously or subconsciously try to alleviate this anxiety by moving some or all of the offending items away from their immediate environment. Similar tensions can be generated during a negotiation, when one of the participants physically invades — with their hands, documents, or briefcase — the other party's side of the bargaining table.

[c]   Individualism vs. Collectivism

Some cultures are individualistic (e.g., United States, England) (Gold, 2005, at 296; Tan & Lim, 2004, at 20–21). They value individual independence over group cohesiveness. They reward individuals who exhibit autonomous and assertive behavior to advance their own self interests. They value personal privacy and freedom. Societal status is based primarily upon individual, rather than group, accomplishments. People in these cultures work to enhance employer interests more to demonstrate their own capabilities than to contribute to the overall success of the collective business. Managers often possess the authority to make critical decisions on their own. Persons in individualistic cultures tend to enjoy bargaining interactions, because those endeavors allow them to demonstrate their negotiation skills (Tan & Lim, 2004, at 34–35).

Other cultures have a collectivistic orientation (e.g., Japan, China) (Gold, 2005, at 296–97; Tan & Lim, 2004, at 21–22). People are defined more by their family and business ties than by their own endeavors. They tend to be evaluated by the achievements of their organization rather than by their own accomplishments. Individuals are expected to work together to enhance group interests. Managers consult their colleagues when important decisions have to be made, with final determinations being made through a consensus process. People in collectivistic cultures often dislike negotiation encounters, because they prefer conflict avoidance and dislike the loss of face associated with the give-and-take of the bargaining process (Tan & Lin, 2004, at 34–35).

[d]   Orientation Toward Overt Power Displays

Many American negotiators do not hesitate to employ overt power displays to advance their bargaining interests. In other cultures (e.g., Japan), open displays of power are considered crude and unacceptable. Analogous conflicts are encountered with respect to the use of openly aggressive behavior. Since Americans have a reputation for being overly aggressive people, they should attempt to employ less threatening tactics when they interact with persons from less aggressive cultures. They must remember that one can be forceful without being pushy.

[e]   Diverse Socio-Economic Backgrounds

[i]   Difficulty With Delayed Gratification

Individuals from disparate socio-economic backgrounds may find it difficult to appreciate each other's hopes and fears. People from wealthy nations tend to accept the delayed gratification concept without question, based on the success that has been achieved by their educated ancestors, while persons from poorer countries are less likely to postpone current gratification for the nebulous hope of attaining greater future returns. United States negotiators interacting with persons from emerging nations may have to initially emphasize the short-term benefits over the long-term possibilities if they wish to achieve present agreements.

[ii]   Using Lower Socioeconomic Status as Advantage

People from lower socio-economic environments often find it traumatic and intimidating when they first interact with individuals from wealthy backgrounds — especially if they are forced to meet in the gilded offices of their wealthy opponents. To counteract this factor, individuals representing clients from economically disadvantaged nations may wish to employ a tactic perfected during the 1960s by the late activist Saul Alinsky. He realized that rich and powerful negotiators feel just as uncomfortable in the ghettos occupied by the poor as the latter group members do in upper-class neighborhoods. He thus invited the societal power brokers to bargain with the economically disadvantaged in the areas inhabited by the latter group. For the first time, many wealthy persons began to appreciate the tragic plight of less fortunate people. They felt substantial guilt and discomfort in the pathetic environments occupied by the poor, and were adroitly induced to make significant concessions. Private firm or governmental representatives from emerging countries who think they may embarrass opponents from wealthy nations by bringing them into their national settings should not hesitate to use this approach to their advantage.

[4]   Value of Learning About Opponent's Culture

Before U.S. advocates enter into negotiations with people from different countries, they should try to learn about the cultural background of their opponents (Salacuse, 2003, at 110–15). They should study the national history and cultural practices of those people. Foreigners often criticize Americans for ignoring these factors. They assume that we arrogantly think these influences are irrelevant. When Americans demonstrate both an understanding of and a respect for the historical developments associated with other nations and for the diverse cultures indigenous to those countries, foreign negotiators appreciate the efforts and feel more comfortable interacting with their American adversaries.

[5]   Important Cultural Questions to Consider

[a]   Opponent Government History and Current Position in Global Political Landscape

Most individuals are significantly influenced by historical developments in their own countries (Salacuse, 2003, at 117–25; Salacuse, 1991, at 72–83). Do they have a history of unregulated capitalism, limited capitalism, socialism, communism, or another system? Has their economic system been subject to minimal or extensive governmental intervention? (Salacuse, 2003, at 127–33). Is their government democratic, autocratic, plutocratic, or monarchical? Has their government been relatively stable or unstable? Has their country been invaded by people from other areas and have they been occupied by foreign powers? Persons from nations that have been invaded by major powers — especially those that have been occupied by foreign armies — are likely to be suspicious of what may be perceived as economic invaders. It is thus imperative for American corporate officials to emphasize to persons from less developed and less democratic nations both the mutual relationships they hope to establish with prospective foreign firms and the autonomy those trading partners will continue to enjoy.

[b]   Currency

American firms negotiating international business deals must consider currency questions (Salcuse, 2003, at 165–77; Brett, 2001, at 188–91; Salacuse, 1991, at 131–46). How stable is the relevant foreign currency compared to the U.S. dollar? U.S. firms may wish to avoid the risk of unexpected monetary fluctuations by specifying contract prices in U.S. dollars. Firms that have confidence in the strength of the other company's national currency may decide to specify prices in that currency. Business partners may jointly share the risk of currency changes by relying on the currency of a neutral country. To minimize the impact of currency fluctuations, the parties may use a market-basket unit, such as the Euro created by the European Union. A few parties avoid currency issues through bartering contracts that provide for one side's goods or services to be exchanged for specific amounts of the other party's goods or services.

[c]   Decision-Making Process

U.S. business representatives must also determine how foreign firms operate. Do top executives make final decisions alone or must they consult with board members or subordinate groups? Do several people have to be convinced before deals become final or must a substantial number of individuals give their approval? (Brett, 2001, at 15). If many persons must be consulted, who are they and how may they be contacted by the American negotiators? When group decision-making is involved, it will usually take longer for consensus to be achieved. U.S. bargainers who ignore this factor and attempt to expedite the approval process are likely to generate suspicion and undermine the entire deal.

[d]   Different Employment Philosophies

American business people must appreciate differences involving the treatment of employees by companies in different countries. In the United States, private employers may usually terminate or lay off workers for good cause, bad cause, or no cause under the employment-at-will doctrine. In most other industrial nations, firms cannot terminate or lay off employees without cause. In countries like Japan, many corporations feel a moral obligation to retain employees except when confronted with dire circumstances. They are shocked at the short-term perspectives of American executives and their willingness to lay off workers as soon as sufficient profits are realized. Japanese executives tend to have a long-term perspective, and try to avoid arrangements that may necessitate the premature termination of employees. When U.S. advocates attempt to negotiate joint ventures with Japanese firms, they must take these differences into account when describing the partnerships they are seeking.

[e]   Government Regulation of Business

The government in the United States generally takes a laissez faire approach with respect to the regulation of private business deals. As long as those arrangements do not raise questions under applicable statutes, such as antitrust laws, they do not require government approval. In other countries, however, government bureaucracies may not only have to give final approval to the deals, but may also participate directly in the inter-firm negotiations (Brett, 2001, at 192–94; Salacuse, 1991, at 84–102). When such governmental participation is anticipated, the U.S. negotiators must determine the interests that have to be satisfied before governmental approval can be achieved. The regulatory agencies in question may not focus entirely or even primarily on business considerations. They may be more interested in broader social, political, or environmental issues. It is generally helpful to retain local counsel who are familiar with applicable legal doctrines and relevant administrative procedures. They also tend to know the administrative officials to contact when questions arise. If these areas are ignored, beneficial business accords may be thwarted. American negotiators must also prepare themselves and their firms for the months that may elapse during the governmental review process.

[f]   Importance of Giving Gifts

In some countries (*e.g.*, China), gifts or gratuities may be expected by government administrators to encourage the expeditious processing of contract approval requests. These are generally not "bribes." They are almost always "facilitation fees" that are not intended to corruptly influence the recipients, but rather to generate faster service. Such facilitation payments are outside the scope of the Foreign Corrupt Practices Act (Acuff, 1997, at 104). It is normally preferable to have these payments made by local agents who know the government officials involved and understand how such payments are to be made.

[g]   Host Country's Focus on Continuing Relationships vs. Contractual Obligations

When U.S. firms interact with other companies, they generally try to negotiate binding contractual relationships that are subject to judicial or arbitral enforcement. Each relevant term is explored and defined. Corporations from different cultures, particularly Asian nations, tend to be more relationship-oriented. They hope to create long-term business relationships that are based more on mutual trust and respect than on contractual obligations (Salacuse, 2003, at 96–97, 103–04; Thayer & Weiss, 1987, at 56–57). As a result, they take longer during their preliminary discussions to get to know each other, and they define their new partnerships in relatively general terms. If one side becomes too specific, they demonstrate a lack of trust that offends the other party. They know that when future questions arise, they will work together to resolve those issues. As the interaction develops, patience is important, because cross-cultural encounters tend to take longer than talks between people from the same culture (Acuff, 1997, at 89). American business leaders do not feel comfortable with this approach. They fear that general contractual undertakings may not receive judicial acceptance.

[6] Using the Preliminary Stage to Establish Beneficial Relationships

When individuals from different cultures interact, it can be helpful for them to employ a prolonged Preliminary Stage to get to know each other and to establish positive relationships (Adler, 2002, at 225–27). They should take the time to explore their respective national cultures, and to begin to understand each side's idiosyncrasies. During this exploratory period, they should avoid real substantive discussions, focusing instead upon interpersonal considerations. Americans find this part of the process distasteful, because they like to get down to business quickly. Negotiators who patiently establish affirmative relationships based upon mutual respect for each side's different approach to bargaining interactions enhance the likelihood of achieving beneficial, long-term partnerships. Although impatient negotiators may dislike the time it takes to get to know the opposing side, persons who do not do so may either fail to achieve agreements or negotiate terms that are less efficient than those they may have obtained had both sides initially established mutual respect and trust.

[7] Using Attitudinal Bargaining

When representatives from these different cultures interact, they need to use attitudinal bargaining to develop a mutual respect for each side's cultural and legal interests. U.S. negotiators must respectfully explain their need for certain specificity — and they must appreciate the lack of trust indicated by demands for total specificity. They must decide what terms must truly be covered in detail and which may be generally described. This accommodation should enhance the likelihood of beneficial long-term relations. The inclusion of dispute resolution clauses providing for resort to negotiation, mediation, and ultimately arbitration to resolve future disagreements can minimize the fear of judicial intervention.

[8] Overcoming Language Difficulties

[a] Culture-Specific Interpretation of Verbal and Nonverbal Signals

When negotiators from different cultures interact, language difficulties may arise (Rubinstein, 2003, at 32–36; Salacuse, 2003, at 94–96; Salacuse, 1991, at 28–36). Even though most international transactions involving American firms are conducted wholly or at least partially in English, misunderstandings may develop. Foreign representatives may interpret verbal statements and nonverbal signals differently from their American counterparts (Adler, 2002, at 95–96; Acuff, 1997, at 46–48; Cohen, 1991, at 105–130). Some cultures process information in a highly "rational" linear manner, while others do so in an indirect and more emotional nonlinear fashion (Rubinstein, 2003, at 34–35). Representatives should speak clearly and more deliberately than they might at home to be certain their message is heard. They should avoid the use of slang expressions that may not be understood by individuals who have not lived in the United States for prolonged periods. They should be especially attuned to any signs of confusion emanating from their opponents. Do they have puzzling looks on their faces or are they asking questions that suggest they have not fully understood what the speakers intended to convey? Rather than losing patience with opponents who are experiencing these difficulties, American negotiators must work more diligently to make themselves understood.

[b] Using Interpreters

On some occasions, international business negotiations must be conducted through interpreters (Hendon, Hendon & Herbig, 1996, at 58–60). Even if the foreign corporation provides translators, it is helpful for the U.S. group to have its own language specialist. It is particularly beneficial to have a negotiating team member who is fluent in the foreign language. This helps to diminish the risk of avoidable misunderstandings. U.S. representatives who are not truly fluent in a foreign language should not try to negotiate in that language. While it would certainly be appropriate for them to greet their foreign counterparts in their own language, their efforts to converse in that language during the serious negotiations may create needless problems.

[c] Choosing Language for Contract

Once transnational accords are achieved, the parties must decide whether the official contract will be expressed in English, the language of the other country, or a neutral third language. This decision may be critical when future disagreements arise, because language differences may be outcome determinative. In some cases, the parties may have official texts in both languages and specify that mediators and arbitrators who may subsequently be employed to help the parties resolve contractual disputes must be fluent in both languages.

[d] Seeking Provisions to Apply Own Laws

Most corporate leaders do not like to subject their firms to foreign laws or the jurisdiction of foreign tribunals. They are concerned that local biases will work to their detriment. They also fear that application of foreign laws will put them at a disadvantage. It is thus common for negotiators from both sides to seek provisions requiring application of their own laws when contract disputes arise. If one party is unable to convince the other to accept its entreaties in this regard, the resulting agreement may not require application of the laws of either nation. It may merely state that legal doctrines generally applied to international business transactions will be employed, leaving it to the ultimate adjudicators to determine which principles should be applied.

[9] Using Independent Mediation

Since neither firm is likely to consent to the jurisdiction of courts in the other party's country, international business contracts frequently establish their own dispute resolution procedures (Salacuse, 2003, at 68–71). It is beneficial to require the disputing parties to initially use the negotiation process to resolve their conflicts. In many cases, they can reach understandings without the need for third-party intervention. When negotiation efforts are not successful, mediation may be appropriate. They can either list the names of mutually acceptable neutrals or specify an entity that will provide proficient intervenors.

[10] Arbitration Selection Process

[a] Choosing Individuals or Groups to Intercede

When negotiation and mediation efforts are unsuccessful, the parties may have to resort to arbitration (Salacuse, 1991, at 128–30). They must specify the arbitrator selection process. Will each name a person and have those two agree upon the neutral chair or will the disputants try to select a single adjudicator? Will they name a particular individual in their agreement or list an agency — *e.g.*, International Chamber of Commerce, London Court of Arbitration, or the American Arbitration Association — from which they will obtain the names of qualified neutrals? If the latter course is employed, the parties usually strike names alternately from the list until one remains.

[b] Defining the Procedural Rules

Parties that agree to use arbitration to resolve their disputes must specify the procedural rules to be followed. How much pre-arbitration discovery is to be permitted? It must be sufficient to allow the parties to prepare adequately for trial. What trial procedures and evidentiary rules are to be used? While they can expect professional arbitrators to conduct orderly hearings, they should establish the procedural rules they wish to govern their adjudications.

§ 15.06 NATION-SPECIFIC NEGOTIATING STYLES

[1] Limits of Applicability of Behavioral Generalizations

When negotiators study the cultural backgrounds of foreign — and even domestic — opponents, they must be careful not to assume that all persons from a specific nation or culture think and act alike (Katz, 2008, at 9–10; Kahane, 2003, at 13; Sebenius, 2002, at 123–26). They only have to consider the different traits and personalities associated with attorneys from their own geographic region to realize how diverse individuals are within the same nation. Even siblings from the same household display diverse personal traits. When lawyers have to interact with other advocates, they must endeavor to determine the relevant personal characteristics indigenous to those individuals. Nonetheless, when they initially encounter persons from different cultures, it may be helpful to consider the behavioral generalizations attributed to people from the pertinent cultural backgrounds. This may provide them with a good point to begin their evaluation of their individual opponents, and it may enable them to avoid cultural taboos that could adversely affect their interactions (Gelfand & Dyer, 2000; Salacuse, 1993, at 199–208; Jonsson, 1991, at 232–42).

[2] Importance of Cultural Considerations Despite Universal Bargaining Culture

Professor William Zartman has suggested that national cultural differences have become less important over the past several decades due to the development of an international negotiation culture that is an amalgam of the diverse styles of the regular participants (Zartman, 1993, at 17–21). While it is certainly true that State Department officials who represent their respective governments in the international arena, persons who operate within the structures of formal organizations like the United Nations, the Eurpoean Union, and the World Trade Organization, and individuals who repeatedly negotiate private transnational business deals have all been influenced by an international or institutional bargaining culture (Faure, 2003, at 397, 412), it is difficult for most people to entirely shed the subtle and even overt influences of their own cultures (Watkins & Rosegrant, 2001, at 73–79). Our fundamental beliefs, customs, value systems, and verbal and nonverbal interpretations continue to be affected by our formative environments and our current surroundings (Brett & Gelfand, 2006; Lee, 2005, at 388–390; Lang, 1993, at 38–46; Cohen, 1991, at 16–18; see generally LeBaron, 2003). Our cultural backgrounds significantly affect whether we think we can control our destinies or believe they are predetermined. Our cultures determine how we attempt to resolve problems — deductively, inductively, or in some other manner (Faure, 2002, at 405). Nonverbal signals vary greatly from nation to nation (Morris, 1994). The identical English words have different meanings in the United States and in England. International negotiators who ignore these differences are likely to encounter both communicational and inter-personal problems.

[3]   Distinction of Cultural Context

[a]   High

Sociologists distinguish between *"high context"* and *"low context"* cultures (Gold, 2005, at 298–99; Tan & Lim, 2004, at 30–32; LeBaron, 2003, at 34–35; Rubinstein, 2003, at 34–35; Brett, 2001, at 20–21; Acuff, 1997, at 44–48; Cohen, 1991, at 25–27). High context cultures tend to be group-oriented. They value the establishment and preservation of lasting relationships and the perpetuation of group norms. They use face-saving techniques to avoid embarrassing overt capitulations (Cohen, 1991, at 56–61). Individuals from high context cultures often dislike auction bargaining, because of the repeated concessions associated with that process. They communicate more indirectly to avoid placing others in awkward positions. They usually favor emotional appeals enhancing long-term relationships over rational appeals based primarily on objective logic (Brett & Gelfand, 2006, at 178–79). You often have to consider the setting to understand the precise meaning of particular words or phrases (Katz, 2008, at 51–54). They are willing to accept ambiguous contractual language that enhances the inter-party relationships involved. They tend to be patient negotiators who prefer to become well acquainted with opponents before they agree to formal contractual arrangements.

[b]   Low

Low context cultures tend to be individualistic and goal-oriented. Low context negotiators are primarily interested in the attainment of legally enforceable contracts (Cohen, 1991, at 50–51). They feel comfortable with auction bargaining, believing that compromise leads to common ground. They prefer direct communication that indicates exactly what they want. They are rule-oriented individuals who want to obtain agreements that carefully define all of the relevant terms. They fear that ambiguous language may create future interpretive difficulties.

[c]   Impact on Negotiation Comfort Level

Individuals feel most comfortable when they interact with persons from same-context cultures. When people from low context cultures interact with others from high context cultures, cross-cultural conflicts may arise (Brett, 2001, at 6–23). The high context participants may feel their low context opponents are being too direct, while the low context persons may think their adversaries are unwilling to address the real issues that must be resolved. The low context negotiators cannot understand why their opponents are hesitant to match their concessions, while the high context participants cannot comprehend why their adversaries wish to openly embarrass them. If the participants are unable to accommodate each other's cultural needs, the likelihood of agreement will be slight.

[4]   Maximizing Joint Gains Through Exploration of Shared Values

It tends to be more difficult to achieve mutually efficient agreements during inter-cultural interactions than during intra-cultural encounters (Gelfand & Dyer, 2000, at 79). Nonetheless, negotiators from different cultures can maximize their joint gains if certain common values are present (Brett, et al., 1998, at 78–79). First, a belief in the value of information sharing which enables the parties to appreciate each other's needs and interests. Second, the ability to deal with multiple issues simultaneously, to permit the participants to generate trades that are mutually beneficial. Third, a desire to improve on their present agreement, causing the bargainers to continue to look for ways in which to generate further joint gains. Cultures that do not share these beliefs are less likely to achieve efficient accords.

I will explore the negotiation styles associated with individuals from important American trading partners that have been the subject of scholarly examination. We will begin with a review of the United States style, to permit readers to understand how foreigners view our approach to bargaining. We will then cover countries from Eastern and Western Europe, Asia, Africa, and Latin America. While the nations included are illustrative, they provide negotiators with issues they should evaluate when planning interactions with people from other countries (see generally Llamazares, 2008; Morrison & Conaway, 2006). Readers should recognize that the generalizations described do not reflect the behavior of all persons from the same nation.

§ 15.07   NEGOTIATION STYLES OF UNITED STATES AND COMMON TRADING PARTNERS

[1]   United States

[a]   Context

The United States is considered a highly individualistic, low context culture. We are viewed as goal-oriented and impatient (Gelfand & Dyer, 2000, at 66; Cohen, 1991, at 63–64). Most U.S. business leaders think in terms of months or calendar quarters, rather than on a long-term basis (Adler, 2002, at 219–220; Acuff, 1993, at 56). State Department officials are under pressure from political leaders who think in two or four year time frames. It is rare to hear American negotiators speak about the next century — unless it is on the immediate horizon — and we never talk about the future of our grandchildren or our great grandchildren. Americans speak fewer foreign languages than persons in other countries, and they tend to be less interested in foreign cultures (Adler, 2002, at 12).

[b]   Level of Formality

[i]   Our Reputation

Americans are considered by many foreigners to be too informal. We get on a first name basis soon after we meet someone. For people from cultures in which first names are reserved for close acquaintances, our behavior in this regard is considered disrespectful. Despite our reputation for informality, we are also viewed as impersonal advocates who are primarily interested in the deal we are negotiating. We only want to interact with our foreign adversaries to the extent necessary to obtain the terms we desire. This tendency causes foreigners to think of us as arrogant and even patronizing. We appear to be disinterested in them personally and in their clients professionally. We do not seem to be concerned about the establishment of long-term business relationships.

United States negotiators tend to feel comfortable with auction bargaining (Cohen, 1991, at 85–86). We often make quick concessions to demonstrate our willingness to compromise. While we think of this as an admirable trait, others frequently view it as a sign of over-anxious weakness. We tend to disclose important information more quickly than individuals from high context cultures who wish to establish more personal relationships before they address substantive matters. Our approach may place us at a disadvantage, because of the excessive information we are divulging. We need to learn to be more patient — especially at the beginning of transnational interactions. We should plan to engage in a prolonged Preliminary Stage to give the participants the opportunity to get to know each other. These exchanges would help us to learn about our opponents, their negotiating styles, and their underlying needs and interests. We should be careful to avoid substantive discussions until our opponents are prepared to address these issues. We should particularly avoid one-sided disclosures from us to more taciturn adversaries.

[ii]   Formality in Name Usage

When Americans interact with individuals from other countries, they should err on the side of formality. They should address people by their last names, including any relevant titles. Even when asked to use the other person's first name, Americans should continue to use that person's last name. This formality shows respect for the other participant's own culture and will be appreciated. If they really do wish to be addressed on a first name basis, they will insist upon this treatment.

[iii]   Reasons for Patience Based on Reputation

Most foreign negotiators describe Americans as competitive, win-lose bargainers (Acuff, 1993, at 56). They think we are only interested in what we can obtain for our own clients, rather than how we might structure mutually beneficial arrangements. When opposing negotiators do not move with sufficient alacrity, American representatives tend to give them "final" concessions which must be quickly reciprocated if the interaction is to continue. This seemingly "take-it-or-leave-it" approach causes many U.S. advocates to be labeled Boulwareistic (Cohen, 1991, at 88–89). It would be helpful if we were more patient. We should not rush the process when it appears that our opponents cannot move as expeditiously. We should be reluctant to present others with "final" offers, unless we have reasonably concluded that no mutual accords are likely to be achieved. Doubts should be resolved in favor of continued discussions that may enable both sides to reach common ground. When we are uncertain, we should recess talks to give both sides the opportunity to reconsider their underlying needs and interests — rather than terminating the exchanges.

[c] Explaining Our Legal System

The United States is an extremely legalistic society, with more lawyers per capita than any other country. Our legal representatives are taught to negotiate agreements that are all-encompassing and unambiguous (Acuff, 1993, at 48–49). We attempt to anticipate every possibility and have clauses covering every contingency. This desire to achieve definitive accords causes many foreign negotiators to think we do not trust them or their clients, and they resent this apparent lack of respect. We should explain our legal system to them and indicate why we are required to be so thorough. If they appreciate our underlying needs in this regard, they are likely to be more accommodating. On the other hand, we need to recognize when we are being overly legalistic and accept the need to leave certain terms unaddressed or defined in general terms. If we can create beneficial relationships, we should have confidence in our mutual ability to resolve future questions in a professional manner.

[2] Canada

When foreigners interact with Canadians, they frequently assume that they are interacting with persons who are just like individuals from the United States. They fail to appreciate the subtle and not-so-subtle differences between U.S. and Canadian bargainers (Adler & Graham, 1987; Adler, Graham & Gehrke, 1987). Despite the fact that Canada is the major trading partner of the U.S., Americans know little about the Canadian culture and few studies have attempted to document the differences between the residents of these contiguous nations.

[a] Context

Canada consists of two major, but quite different, cultures. French Canadians — "Francophones" — make up one-quarter of the population, while English Canadians — "Anglophones" — make up most of the remaining three-quarters (Adler, Graham & Gehrke, 1987, at 412). Both groups constitute low context cultures in which they tend to explicitly say what they mean. Francophones are located primarily in Quebec, the French speaking province. They prefer to speak French, even when they are fluent in both French and English. Anglophones usually speak English, even when they are bilingual. Foreigners negotiating with Francophones should always include individuals on their bargaining teams who are fluent in French.

[b] Cultural Diversity

Francophones differ significantly from Anglophones (Adler & Graham, 1987). Francophones reflect their French heritage, while Anglophones reflect their British heritage. Francophones place great emphasis on the need for security, happiness, and self-esteem, while Anglophones respect individual accomplishments and personal autonomy (Adler & Graham, 1987, at 215). Francophones value being courageous and being independent less than Anglophones, but value being intellectual more (Adler & Graham, 1987, at 222). They like to spend time debating the substantive issues that have to be negotiated. Francophones tend to exhibit a "Catholic ethic" which emphasizes family and deemphasizes work, while Anglophones tend to exhibit a "Protestant ethic" which emphasizes personal achievement and hard work (Adler, Graham & Gehrke, 1987, at 414). Although Anglophones seem similar to Americans, they tend to be more progressive on such issues as national health care, worker rights, and gay marriage. Americans interacting with Anglophones during business negotiations should thus be careful to appreciate the different business philosophies involved.

[c] Bargaining Styles

Francophones tend to employ more competitive negotiating tactics than Anglophones (Adler & Graham, 1987, at 221–22, 229–30; Adler, Graham & Gehrke, 1987, at 421). Their behavior in this regard produces higher individual returns, but lower levels of client satisfaction (Adler & Graham, 1987, at 229). Anglophones tend to employ more cooperative bargaining tactics (Adler & Graham, 1987, at 221–22; Adler, Graham & Gehrke, 1987, at 425). If Americans and Anglophones behave too openly and cooperatively with Francophones who are less open and use more competitive tactics, they may achieve less beneficial results for their own sides.

[3] Mexico

[a] Context

The establishment of the North American Free Trade Zone has greatly increased the already substantial interaction between Mexican and American business firms. Mexico is a high context culture in which close friendships are valued. Although Mexico has a long and distinguished history, it has been significantly affected by foreign domination — 300 years by the Spanish and French and many years by the United States during the mid-1800s (Grayson, 1987, at 125–27). It still feels understandably aggrieved by the seizure of what is now southern California and the annexation of Texas. Many U.S. negotiators make the mistake of treating Mexican advocates as Spanish-speaking North Americans, ignoring their strong Latin culture (Grayson, 1987, at 144). Mexican negotiators appreciate respect shown for their country's history and culture, and for their country's recent economic gains (Acuff, 1997, at 218–19).

[b] Background Sentiments

Mexico is a nation undergoing rapid economic expansion, and it hopes to use business deals with U.S. firms to advance its economic interests. Nonetheless, it continues to feel dominated by its northern neighbor (Cohen, 1991, at 43–44). It believes that the United States government does not give it the respect it deserves, and it thinks that American business firms are always trying to obtain one-sided deals that only minimally satisfy Mexican interests. They do not like to make overt concessions to U.S. opponents (Cohen, 1991, at 136–37). U.S.-Mexican relations continue to be strained by efforts by American officials to limit Mexican immigration. Mexican leaders resent the fact the United States shows more respect to other countries. While the inclusion of Mexico in NAFTA has helped to improve relations with the U.S., most Mexicans still feel they are treated as second-class trading partners.

[c] Government Structure

Although most foreigners think that Mexico has a strong central government, the President does not possess the authority to impose his will on the entrenched bureaucracies (Grayson, 1987, at 136). Many government agencies are inefficient and suspicious of change. It is thus difficult to get approval for new business deals. When bureaucrats feel that their respective jurisdictions are being threatened by proposed arrangements, they tend to resist them fiercely. In addition, administrative corruption

— generated by low compensation levels — causes many bureaucrats to demand "processing fees" to facilitate requests for agency action (Grayson, 1987, at 136). People who refuse to accept this reality often encounter approval problems.

[d] Negotiation Techniques

[i] Integrity and Dislike of Manipulation

Despite the market-place trader image Mexicans have among many Americans, most Mexican business leaders are highly principled negotiators who pride themselves on their integrity. They generally present a united bargaining front that is difficult for opponents to exploit. If they are treated with respect, they tend to use a direct style that does not include manipulative tactics. On the other hand, foreigners who treat them dishonorably are likely to engender hostility and a lack of receptivity. Mexican negotiators occasionally use press "leaks" attributing the lack of bargaining progress to their foreign counterparts to embarrass those people (Grayson, 1987, at 141–42).

[ii] Ritualistic Bluffing

Mexico is a relatively macho society in which some males attempt to demonstrate their masculine prowess through ritualistic bluffing. When such efforts are encountered, it is especially important to avoid responsive behavior that may be perceived as disrespectful. Once these rituals are concluded, it is generally beneficial to conduct private negotiating sessions in which concessions can be made with a minimal loss of face. Most bargaining progress tends to be made during these closed discussions.

[e] Reasons for Patience

When Mexicans participate in transnational bargaining, they try to establish good personal relationships with their foreign adversaries (Cohen, 1991, at 53–55; Grayson, 1987, at 133–35). They frequently use informal social events to create positive rapport. They expect their hospitality to be reciprocated and are particularly sensitive to treatment they consider patronizing. They are often offended by impatient American negotiators who seem to consider the preliminary social exchanges a waste of time. Instead of trying to move too quickly toward substantive discussions, American representatives should take the time to get to know their Mexican counterparts. This will facilitate subsequent business discussions and create positive relationships that may continue for many years.

[4] Japan

[a] Context

During the past several decades, Japanese and American business firms have become major trading partners. It is likely that these interactions will increase. It is thus beneficial for legal representatives of multinational American enterprises to understand some of the critical cultural aspects of Japanese society (Blaker, Giarra & Vogel, 2002; Hodgson, Sano & Graham, 2000; Graham & Sano, 1989; March, 1988; Moran, 1984). Japan is a high context culture that greatly values long-term relationships and the avoidance of open conflict (Thayer & Weiss, 1987, at 45). The Japanese are proud of their distinguished history and culture, and expect foreigners to respect these factors.

[b]   Level of Formality

Personal introductions are highly regarded by Japanese business leaders and government officials. The initial intervention of respected intermediaries can significantly enhance the likelihood of cordial and productive interactions. It is thus helpful to locate appropriate parties — such as old college friends — who can bring the parties together and establish cooperative environments and trusting relationships (Hodgson, Sano & Graham, 2000, at 3–5, 12–13, 36–37; Hahn, 1982, at 57). It is usually beneficial to have business cards printed that are in English on one side and Japanese on the other, since the exchange of such status information is expected (Hodgson, Sano & Graham, 2000, at 19). When business cards are exchanged, they should be examined carefully and respectfully, and not simply placed in one's briefcase or pocket. They are a formal culture who only use first names with close friends.

Americans tend to have upper level executives conduct their serious negotiations, but Japanese firms tend to use the opposite approach. When top executives attend early bargaining sessions, they are usually there to perform a ceremonial function (Hodgson, Sano & Graham, 2000, at 99–102). They do not expect discussions of a substantive nature, preferring to leave those talks to lower level managers. Japanese firms expect their lower level executives to focus on the specific terms that must be subsequently approved by higher level company representatives through a consensus-building process. Foreign agents who ignore this cultural approach and attempt to negotiate specific terms with upper Japanese executives are likely to depart without accords.

[c]   Language Considerations

The Japanese language is rather imprecise compared to English. Similar words have very different meanings. "Information comes not through the words but from the social context in which the words are uttered, from an understanding of what the speaker should be saying in contrast to what he is actually saying." (Thayer & Weiss, 1987, at 58.) For example, while the word "hai" means "yes" in some contexts, it means only "I understand" — not "I agree" — during bargaining encounters (Hendon, Hendon & Herbig, 1996, at 35). It is thus necessary to engage experienced interpreters who can precisely communicate what each party is saying, and who can read between the lines and comprehend what is really intended.

Japanese negotiators often speak English, but use translators to interpret what their English-speaking counterparts have said. This gives them an advantage, because they first hear the English comments and then have time to plan their responses while the interpreters are translating the English statements into Japanese (Hodgson, Sano & Graham, 2000, at 419). Rarely are American business negotiators fluent in Japanese. Having such persons participate on behalf of U.S. firms is both a communication advantage and a way to demonstrate to Japanese company representatives how sincerely U.S. firms wish to establish long-term relationships with Japanese businesses.

Japanese facial expressions can convey various meanings depending upon the particular circumstances involved. "The Japanese smile can be perceived as a mask of politeness, an opaque wall behind which one observes the other. It can express cooperation or denial, joy or anger, certainty or total ignorance, trust or distrust, pleasure or embarrassment. Only some knowledge of the Japanese culture and the reference to the current context of the smile may enable one to get access to its real meaning." (Faure, 2002, at 407).

The high context nature of the Japanese culture may explain why Japanese business people prefer to conduct serious negotiations through face-to-face contact (Hodgson, Sano & Graham, 2000, at 92—93). While it may be acceptable to exchange some preliminary information though telephone calls or e-mail communications, foreign representatives should appreciate the importance of personal interactions. They should either travel to Japan or invite their Japanese counterparts to their own countries.

[d]   Reasons for Patience

[i]   Thoughtful Silence of Japanese

When a Japanese negotiator is contemplating a reply to another party's new proposal, he or she often remains silent for a prolonged period (Calero, 2005, at 107–08; Hendon, Hendon & Herbig, 1996, at 63). They have an ancient proverb that "he who knows does not speak, and he who speaks does not know" (Hendon, Hendon & Herbig, 1996, at 63–64). They thus prefer silence while they determine the appropriate response. Foreign negotiators should not speak during these periods, but should quietly and patiently await their opponent's reply. They should be especially careful not to bid against themselves by making unreciprocated concessions generated by the other side's silence (Hodgson, Sano & Graham, 2000, at 107).

[ii]   Perspective on Time and Negotiations

Japanese businesspeople tend to have long-term outlooks (Tan & Lim, 2004, at 89). They think in terms of generations, not calendar quarters. They also tend to be less profit oriented. As a result, they exude an inner patience that is based on their belief that, even if they are presently unable to consummate a particular business venture, their successor may be able to accomplish that objective. It is this attitude that many American bargainers find frustrating. These Americans try to complete a proposed transaction within an inordinately curtailed period of time. This sense of time urgency inures to the benefit of their less hurried Japanese opponents (Hodgson, Sano & Graham, 2000, at 10–12).

[iii]   Focus on Group Concerns

The Japanese people tend to be group oriented. They thrive on collective decisions that are achieved through a consensus process known as "ringi." (Hendon, Hendon & Herbig, 1996, at 232–33; Watts, 1982, at 606; Van Zandt, 1970, at 47–48). It thus takes more time for them to achieve internally acceptable agreements. Many business transactions must also be approved by appropriate government officials — usually from the Ministry of International Trade and Industry (MITI) when transnational arrangements are involved (Thayer & Weiss, 1987, at 50–51). During some interactions, government representatives directly participate, while in others they merely have to approve the final accords achieved. This tripartite aspect of Japanese business deals is a time-consuming process (Cohen, 1991, at 102). Those who attempt to expedite these traditional procedures or endeavor to circumvent them through end runs to higher corporate or government officials are likely to find themselves without business accords.

[iv]   Harmonious Relationships Come First

Americans who negotiate with Japanese business agents must be patient, conciliatory, and respectful. They must take the time to establish trusting and cooperative relationships (Tan & Lim, 2004, at 115). During these preliminary social occasions, substantive discussions are considered inappropriate and should be avoided (Hodgson, Sano & Graham, 2000, at 20). Direct confrontations should be carefully avoided. They must recognize that, once harmonious relationships have been created, they should be able to achieve lasting agreements that will benefit both sides. American agents who ignore these important cultural considerations will find themselves unable to consummate the types of advantageous business transactions they may otherwise have attained through the development of appropriate intercultural rapport.

[e]   Cultural Dislike of Overt Conflict

[i]   Impact on Negotiation Initiation

Japanese are taught from birth that social conflict must be avoided whenever possible (Tan & Lim, 2004, at 90; Thayer & Weiss, 1987, at 54–55). They have created detailed rituals that are designed to permit them to conduct business dealings through the development of non-confrontational relationships (Jones, 1995, at 142–43; Thayer & Weiss, 1987, at 54–56). They do not like the auction process which creates the need for overt position changes. They ask many questions at the beginning of interactions to ascertain the true needs of their opponents, and they are usually willing to share their own interests (Brett, et al., 1998, at 73, 77; Cohen, 1991, at 64–65, 91–92). Adversaries who openly respond to these inquiries and who fail to elicit similar information from their Japanese opponents put themselves at a disadvantage. They frequently conduct serious talks in private to prevent the need for public position changes. Once Japanese negotiators think they have the information they need to assess the situation, they prefer to make initial offers that are realistic and efficient (Brett, et al., 1998, at 76; Hendon, Hendon & Herbig, 1996, at 35). They are especially resentful of opponents who disrupt the bargaining process with extreme opening positions. The Japanese participants may even "leak" information regarding their planned opening offers prior to or during the preliminary discussions to avoid embarrassing misunderstandings.

[ii]   Indirect Negative Communication

Traditional Japanese hosts feel that it is inappropriate to openly reject proposals suggested by visitors. They generally believe that such overt repudiations cause their guests to suffer a serious loss of face (Tan & Lim, 2004, at 87; Cohen, 1991, at 103). To avoid such unseemly confrontations, the Japanese often: (1) delay final decisions regarding the matters in question; (2) indirectly discuss the deficiencies associated with the proposals; (3) suggest preferable alternatives; or (4) simply ignore the issues (Cohen, 1991, at 112–13; Watts, 1982, at 606). In some cases they may provide mildly affirmative responses they hope will be understood as polite rejections (Thayer & Weiss, 1987, at 57–59; Van Zandt, 1970, at 49). For example, they may indicate a willingness "to seriously consider" or to "do their best" with respect to disfavored topics. While this may give them time to reevaluate the items, they are unlikely to yield on these issues. If they say that something "will be difficult" or they audibly breathe through clenched teeth, they usually mean "definitely not." When foreign visitors do not understand that seemingly affirmative responses are actually indented as polite rejections, they may create problems by directly or indirectly accusing their hosts of deceptive behavior. Proficient interpreters should understand these cultural nuances and provide the visitors with the information they need to avoid communication problems.

[f]   Necessity of Maintaining Noncombative, Harmonious Business Relations

It is vital for American business representatives to maintain a noncombative, harmonious tone during their dealings with Japanese agents. Anger and indignation should not be openly displayed, due to the loss of face associated with these expressions

(Hahn, 1982, at 22; Van Zandt, 1970, at 47). Overt threats rarely work and generally exacerbate bargaining relationships. Americans should not attempt to negotiate ironclad contracts that specifically cover every possible contingency that may arise. This approach is likely to be perceived as an indication that they doubt the sincere intent of their Japanese counterparts to honor their agreements. The Japanese view business contracts very differently from American businesspeople:

> [T]he Japanese envision such a business transaction as an ongoing, harmonious relationship between parties committed to creating and maintaining a mutually beneficial business relationship . . . . [T]he Japanese do not really negotiate contracts but rather business relationships themselves (Hahn, 1982, at 22).

Written agreements are thus expected to be somewhat vague and amorphous (Watts, 1982, at 604). Japanese business agents do not fear noncompliance, since "a person who owes the duty to another is under a strict moral obligation to fulfill it." (Watts, 1982, at 604) Any questions regarding the meaning and application of indefinite contractual terms are to be resolved amicably through mutual consultations.

[g] Business Interactions with Female Counterparts

American lawyers must recognize that some older Japanese businessmen are not accustomed to interacting with women in business environments. As a result, female representatives may initially find it difficult to establish traditional business relationships with their male Japanese counterparts (Hahn, 1982, at 57). As Japanese businessmen have increasingly interacted with foreign businesswomen, they have become more flexible with respect to this issue, despite the continuation of the traditional male-female distinctions within their own society.

[5] China

[a] Context

The Chinese, like the Japanese, are a high context culture (March & Wu, 2007, at 81). They are also particularly proud of their extraordinary history and expect others to respect their past accomplishments (Solomon, 1987, at 1–2). They are a relatively entrepreneurial people who enjoy the opportunity to establish economically beneficial business relationships. As in Japan, governmental ministries may become directly or indirectly involved with transnational business negotiations (see generally Solomon, 1999).

[b] Blend of Negotiating Techniques

[i] Bureaucrat, Gentleman, and Strategist

An observer has noted that "the Chinese negotiator is a blend of Maoist bureaucrat, Confucian gentleman, and Sun Tzu-like strategist." (March & Wu, 2007, at 45; Fang, 1999, at 272) The bureaucrat is cautious and tries to follow established government policy. The Confucian seeks to create mutual trust and cooperative dealings. The Sun Tzu strategist employs manipulative tactics for their own gain. In many negotiations with Chinese representatives, all three influences may be seen at different times during the same interaction (see generally Goh, 1996). They tend to distrust strangers, thus it is important for foreigners to develop close relationships before they try to negotiate business deals (March & Wu, 2007, at 192; Tan & Lim, 2004, at 46). Chinese negotiators like to use an expanded Preliminary Stage to get to know their opponents before substantive issues are discussed (Tan & Lim, 2004, at 79).

[ii] Manipulation of Sentiments

Chinese negotiators frequently try to remind opponents how much those parties need Chinese participation. They attempt to develop feelings of friendship in their opponents, and they manipulate those feelings to their own advantage (Hendon, Hendon & Herbig, 1996, at 37, 51–52; Solomon, 1987, at 3–4). They also try to create feelings of guilt in adversaries by reminding them of previous transgressions. They like to play opponents off against one another, as they did the United States and the Soviet Union for many years.

[iii] Negotiation Proficiency

Chinese negotiators are usually thoroughly prepared for bargaining encounters (Hendon, Hendon & Herbig, 1996, at 232). During preliminary bargaining discussions, Chinese participants often work to obtain the commitment of opposing parties to general principles that are favorable to them. They use those basic tenets to generate the results they prefer (Solomon, 1987, at 4–5). Chinese negotiators also like to employ protracted talks to induce less patient participants to make unreciprocated concessions (March & Wu, 2007, at 20, 56; Cohen, 1991, at 101).

[iv] Opposition to Auction Process

Chinese negotiators find the auction process distasteful, viewing repeated position changes as a sign of weakness (Cohen, 1991, at 93–95). Once they think they have extracted sufficient information and as many preliminary concessions as possible from opponents, they tend to develop firm positions they do not plan to alter significantly (Hendon, Hendon & Herbig, 1996, at 86–87; Cohen, 1991, at 66–67, 85). They announce their offers sternly and move quickly toward closure. Their uncompromising attitudes and expeditious movement toward agreement may catch unsuspecting opponents off guard. Once opponents appreciate their unwillingness to make further concessions, they must either accept or reject the proposed terms.

[v] Nibble Technique

Once business deals have been arranged, they usually require the approval of government bureaucrats. This can be a time-consuming process that may be facilitated through "gifts" to the requisite ministry representatives. After agency consent is obtained, the foreign participants think the negotiation is finished. They are surprised when the Chinese representatives discover "ambiguities" in the applicable agreements that enable them to reopen bargaining over seemingly closed issues (March & Wu, 2007, at 81; Tan & Lim, 2004, at 55, 65; Hendon, Hendon & Herbig, 1996, at 37; Cohen, 1991, at 79; Solomon, 1987, at 14–15). Adroit Chinese negotiators frequently employ this "Nibble" technique to extract additional concessions from naive and unprepared adversaries who are afraid to walk away if that becomes necessary. People who encounter this tactic should remember to demand reciprocal concessions from their Chinese partners.

[6] India

India is rapidly becoming a significant economic power. A Goldman-Sachs study recently predicted that by 2035, the Indian economy will be the third largest in the world, surpassed by only the economies of the United States and China (Kumar, 2005, at 1). More than one-third of the Fortune 500 companies have outsourced some of their software requirements to Indian firms, and more businesses are expected to negotiate similar arrangements (Tan & Lim, 2004, at 122). Despite the recent economic developments, however, India continues to be a relatively poor country, with a per capita GDP of $2200.

[a]   Context

Indian negotiators exhibit a high context communication style (Tan & Lim, 2004, at 151–52). They do not like to reject proposals as overtly as their American counterparts, and frequently use ambiguous language to avoid this necessity. Foreigners interacting with Indian negotiators should recognize the need to appreciate the surrounding circumstances and nonverbal signals to understand the verbal message actually being conveyed. Individuals who try to interpret Indian presentations literally will find it difficult to comprehend what has actually been said. Nonverbal signals may have different meanings. For example, Indians often shake their heads from side-to-side when they mean "yes," which causes many Americans to misinterpret the actual message being communicated (Calero, 2005, at 115).

[b]   Culturally Diverse Country

India is a vast and culturally diverse nation (Tan & Lim, 2004, at 123–26). Each state has its own cultural norms and value system. Although 80 percent of Indians are Hindu, there are 105 million Muslims, making India one of the largest Islamic countries in the world. There are also 22 million Christians. Religious beliefs influence social, economic, and political activities throughout the country.

India is also a linguistically diverse nation. Although Hindi, the national language, is spoken by 20 percent of the Indian people, there are eighteen official languages and 1600 secondary languages and dialects (Tan & Lim, 2004, at 125–26). Nonetheless, English is the language most often used in business dealings involving people from other nations.

Persons living in South India tend to be quite different from individuals residing in North India. South Indians tend to value punctuality and efficiency, while North Indians tend to be more casual regarding these factors. South Indians tend to be more straightforward when they negotiate than North Indians. South Indians tend to focus more on basic objectives than their North Indian counterparts, with the latter more likely to focus on the development of relationships rather than mere contracts. North Indians like to use bargaining interactions to develop long-term relationships. This is why it often takes longer to negotiate with North Indians than with South Indians. The Preliminary Stage should be carefully employed in North Indian territories to develop good working relationships before the serious discussions begin. Food and drinks are likely to be provided to advance this process.

Indians consider it very inappropriate for persons to touch something of value with their feet or shoes. It is thus improper for someone to sit with their feet on their desk or table. It is similarly unsuitable to touch a briefcase or book with one's feet. As in the Middle East, the bottom of one's feet should not be displayed to others, since this is thought to demonstrate a serious lack of respect.

[c]   Impact of Caste System

India has historically had a caste system that was reinforced by over 250 years of British rule (Kumar, 2005, at 2; Tan & Lim, 2004, at 126). The Indian people tend to believe that their positions in life have been irreversibly determined by the fortuity of birth which is reflective of their prior lives and reincarnations. They think their personalities and socio-economic circumstances cannot be altered during their lifetimes. This perspective tends to make them fatalistic, based upon the assumption that they cannot move from their caste of birth.

There are four main castes in India. The Brahmins, comprised of priests and intellectuals, are at the top, followed by the Kshatriyas, comprised of warriers, rulers, and statesmen (Tan & Lim, 2004, at 127). Traders, merchants, and artisans are Vaishyas, with laborers in the lowest Shudras caste.

[d]   Hierarchical and Collective Society

Indians tend to follow a hierarchical system in their business dealings, with senior managers being respected and obeyed by less senior personnel (Tan & Lim, 2004, at 128). When firm or departmental decisions are being made, the most senior persons are expected to speak. Less senior individuals tend to remain silent, especially if they do not agree with what has been said. When foreign representatives negotiate with Indian business groups, they should carefully work to understand the concerns of silent subordinates who will have to effectuate the terms finally agreed upon since they may passively fail to do what is expected of them (Tan & Lim, 2004, at 151).

India tends to be a collectivistic, rather than an individualistic, culture similar to Japan and China (Tan & Lim, 2004, at 150). Group interests and long-term relationships tend to take precedence over individual considerations. On the other hand, Indians can be more openly competitive than their Japanese or Chinese counterparts (Kumar, 2005, at 2). In this regard, their behavior may seem more like the individualistic style of people from countries like the U.S. or Germany. Indian negotiators like to decide what is good for their organizations, then use positional bargaining to achieve optimal results for their own side (Tan & Lim, 2004, 151). This approach may seem schizophrenic to opponents who cannot understand the overtly competitive behavior by seemingly relationship-oriented people.

[e]   Initial Agreements Merely Beginning of Bargaining
Process

Indians consider bargaining interactions as part of a long-term process which must be developed deliberately (Tan & Lim, 2004, at 125, 142). They like to obtain detailed information and carefully analyze those data before they address substantive issues (Kumar, 2005, at 4). They work to create good relationships with their business partners, and view the initial agreement as the end of the Preliminary Stage. They often rely upon ambiguous contractual language to allow them to reopen negotiations on seemingly final provisions to enable them to enhance their own returns. It is this passive-aggressive style that causes foreign negotiators to become frustrated by Indians who appear to have said "yes," but who then fail to carry out what appears to have been agreed upon. (See § 10.02[13] dealing with the "Nibble Technique" and § 10.02[30] dealing with the "Passive-Aggressive Style" for ways to counter this approach.) As a developing nation, Indians especially think that advanced countries like the U.S. should provide them with more generous terms simply to offset the economic imbalance involved, and they frequently employ this factor to extract greater concessions from representatives from such nations (Kumar, 2005, at 5).

People negotiating business deals with Indian firms should use prolonged Preliminary Stages to create beneficial professional and personal relationships before the substantive issues are addressed, especially when dealing with North Indians. When the actual contract terms are discussed, they should appreciate the high context Indian culture and not expect precise responses. They should also recognize that the provisions initially agreed upon are not final. As the business deal unfolds, the Indian representatives will work to renegotiate ambiguous provisions to their advantage.

[f] Impact of Government Involvement

Indian government officials are likely to become involved in international business negotiations (Kumar, 2005, at 1; Tan & Lim, 2004, at 132–38). Certain business arrangements must be approved by administrative agencies, and the approval process may be time consuming. Foreign firms must be patient and allow this process to evolve. If they try to expedite or circumvent this stage, the entire deal may be lost.

Indians have historically been expected to make payments to government officials to enhance the approval process. Many outsiders consider these payments to constitute "bribes" designed to corrupt the administrative process. In recent years, Indian leaders have worked diligently to eliminate this practice, and foreigners should refuse to make payments that are clearly improper.

[7] Russia

[a] Context

Despite long periods of domination by Czars and Communist leaders who attempted to impose diverse concepts of social order, Russia is a low context culture. As a result of centuries of government censorship, Russians have a penchant for secrecy, valuing individuals who possess confidential information (Sloss & Davis, 1987, at 19–20). To circumvent strong, undemocratic leaders, they developed deceptive means of achieving their objectives. They continue to respect people who use indirect — i.e., passive-aggressive — techniques to attain their goals, even when more direct measures would be effective (see generally Schecter, 1998; Smith, 1989).

[b] Background Sentiments

[i] Suspicion

Russians continue to be suspicious of outsiders, probably because of both their traditional geographical isolation and the number of times their country has been invaded by foreign powers (Sloss & Davis, 1987, at 18–19). Throughout the 1960s, 1970s, and 1980s, World War II documentaries were regularly shown on Russian television, to remind citizens of the millions of casualties suffered during those hostilities. Just as many Americans were concerned throughout the Cold War of possible Russian invasion, Russians shared similar fears vis-a-vis the United States. With the collapse of the former Soviet Union and the demise of traditional Communism, Russians are experimenting with free market economic ideas. Westerners must realize that Russians now fear capitalist invasion from Western European and North American powers. Corporate leaders interested in joint ventures with Russian business firms must move slowly to create feelings of trust in host participants who are afraid their authority may be supplanted by foreign domination.

[ii]   Lack of Ambition

As a result of centuries of strict government market regulation, most Russians have not developed any significant entrepreneurial spirit (Acuff, 1997, at 82–84). While most are relatively competitive people who still see life as a class struggle — previously between Communists and others and now between capitalists and others — the majority are not overly ambitious. Years of what Chinese have referred to as the "Communist or iron rice bowl" chilled their belief in individual accomplishment. Instead of trying to emulate the successes of others, many prefer to thwart such advances. For example, if their neighbor were to get two cows and they were asked what they would like to see, many would respond — not with a desire for their own cows — but rather with a wish for the death of their neighbor's animals.

[iii]   Desire for Respect

Russians have historically had an oligarchical decision-making system in which small groups of leaders made most fundamental decisions (Sloss & Davis, 1987, at 20–23). Most Russian negotiators still possess minimal authority and must obtain final approval of proposed agreements from higher government or firm officials (Brett, et al., 1998, at 77–78). This protracted approval process often frustrates impatient foreign negotiators. With the demise of the Communist system, Russians fear being viewed as a second-class power. They very much want to be respected for their economic and military capabilities.

[c]   Level of Patience Required

Russians have traditionally considered open compromise as a sign of weakness, and they admire individuals who can employ confrontational tactics to generate opponent concessions (Sloss & Davis, 1987, at 32). They frequently use intransigence and protracted bargaining sessions to induce careless opponents to make unilateral concessions (Hendon, Hendon & Herbig, 1996, at 41). No matter how slowly progress is being made, they like to continue interactions with expectations of future gains (Cohen, 1991, at 146; Sloss & Davis, 1987, at 29–30). Opposing parties must be especially patient to wait for the serious negotiations to begin. People who attempt to rush matters are likely to make unreciprocated concessions that will inure to the benefit of their more patient Russian adversaries (Sloss & Davis, 1987, at 32–36). Once the real exchanges commence, Russian negotiators tend to make concessions in small increments because of their distaste for overt capitulation. Opponents must either move slowly with them, or they will find themselves bidding against themselves in a losing endeavor.

[d]   Nibble Technique

Once common ground is achieved, Russians tend to prefer general language, rather than specific provisions. This allows them to reopen negotiations later as "ambiguities" are discovered (Sloss & Davis, 1987, at 25). Whenever possible, it is beneficial to include language that expressly defines the basic terms involved. When this cannot be accomplished and Russian bargainers subsequently attempt to claim an item for themselves — the "Nibble" technique — opponents should remember to demand appropriate reciprocal concessions from their Russian counterparts.

[8] France

[a] Context

France is a high context, legalistic culture, but not as high context as countries like China and Japan (Cogan, 2003, at 125–27). The French people are especially proud of their great cultures and diplomatic accomplishments and find it hard to accept their reduced stature in the international community (Cogan, 2003, at 104–05; Harrison, 1987, at 76–77). They can be especially difficult when dealing with Americans, because they do not wish to acknowledge the superior economic and political power possessed by the U.S. today (Cogan, 2003, at 130–31). They appreciate efforts by foreign visitors to partake of their extraordinary museums and their historical achievements. During the Preliminary Stage, foreign negotiators should take the time to establish beneficial working relationship with their French counterparts, since the French appreciate such personal efforts (Cogan, 2003, at 246–47). Nationalistic considerations often cause French citizens who are fluent in English to refuse to converse in that language with foreigners from the United States, Canada, or England. They insist that French be spoken, through interpreters if necessary (see generally Cogan, 2003).

[b] Negotiation Style

The French, tend to be individualistic people (Harrison, 1987, at 80–81), but to a lesser extent than Americans (Cogan, 2003, at 44–45). They dislike overt compromise, and are well known for bargaining stalemates that continue for years due to the unwillingness of either side to make new offers (Cogan, 2003, at 135–37). They would prefer no agreement to one that may cause a loss of face or status. The French are highly analytical people who try to use unemotional logic to determine the appropriate results (Cogan, 2003, at 11, 48–51; Hendon, Hendon & Herbig, 1996, at 30). They appreciate presentations based on abstract principles more than displays of economic or political power. They like to initially agree upon general principles that will guide the subsequent focus on specific issues (Salacuse, 2004, at 4). They frequently endeavor to wear down impatient opponents through shear intransigence. They do not view bargaining as a process involving a series of distinct stages, but tend to see such interactions as a battle of wills (Cogan, 2003, at 107–108). They dislike compromise, and often make concessions at the last minute when agreement seems impossible to achieve (Cogan, 2003, at 152–53).

[c] Reasons for Patience

French advocates tend to be positional, rather than interest, bargainers who become enamored with their stated positions (Cogan, 2003, at 11–12, 120–21; Harrison, 1987, at 81–82). They are often accused of Boulwareistic negotiating because of the fact they begin with offers they are reluctant to modify (Harrison, 1987, at 88–89). Their frequent failure to plan fall-back positions makes it difficult for them to gracefully modify their stated bargaining positions. They are usually accepting of the status quo and work diligently to avoid significant changes in their current situations. Opposing negotiators must be extremely patient when interacting with French representatives. If they display signs of time urgency, their French counterparts are likely to take advantage of the temporal imbalance.

[d]   Decision-Making Structure

French administrators are highly legalistic. They exercise their authority in an abstract and impersonal manner, maintaining a safe distance from those being affected by their decisions (Harrison, 1987, at 80–81). French institutions rely on elaborate rules to govern their business relationships. In this regard, they are similar to stereotypical American government bureaucrats who like to rely on agency regulations to guide their actions (Cogan, 2003, at 111–115).

[9]   Germany

[a]   Context

Contemporary Germany is an economically and industrially advanced nation (Hendon, Hendon & Herbig, 1996, at 148). Although the German language is rather precise, most foreign negotiators lack the fluency to negotiate in that language. Since most German business leaders are fluent in English, international business negotiations tend to take place in English. German industrial officials tend to be technologically advanced, yet pragmatic (Hendon, Hendon, & Herbig, 1996, at 154). Germany is a low context culture (Hendon, Hendon & Herbig, 1996, at 31, 66). Germans are direct in their approach to interpersonal dealings, and tend to state explicitly what they are thinking. German agents thoroughly prepare for bargaining encounters, and often surprise foreign visitors by the knowledge they possess about the company being represented by the United States representatives (Smyser, 2003, at 58–59). They expect their foreign counterparts to be equally prepared, and to be familiar with their German firms.

German negotiators like to develop a comprehensive rationale to support their bargaining positions (*Gesamtkonzept*) which they use to explain the issues being addressed (Smyser, 2003, at 60). During their opening statements, they use the *Gesamtkonzept* to provide a detailed philosophical basis for the points they articulate (Smyser, 2003 at 72–73). Their initial positions usually reflect not only their own interests, but also those of opposing parties which they have explored during their thorough preparation. This part of the encounter can be drawn out, as the speakers exhaustively explain why they deserve what they are requesting. Individuals negotiating with Germans should be thoroughly prepared, and develop logical explanations to support the positions they take (Smyser, 2003, at 200–202). As interactions develop, they should listen carefully for verbal leaks, as the Germans often use subtle signals to indicate their receptiveness to possible position changes (Smyser, 2003, at 205).

German negotiators tend to be quite formal, preferring the use of last names, instead of first names, and the use of formal titles — Herr for men and Frau for women including younger, unmarried females (Smyser, 2003, at 107). Foreigners speaking German should be careful to always use the formal pronoun *sie* instead of the informal pronoun *du*. Even though younger German business negotiators feel more comfortable with the use of first names, they continue to be more formal than Americans and do not like the use of nicknames (Smyser, 2003, at 150). Germans are serious negotiators who do not appreciate the use of humor by others. They are very direct when they articulate their positions, and do not like emotional arguments (Smyser, 2003, at 82–83). As the bargaining process develops, they recognize the need to make concessions, but work to maintain positions that are consistent with the underlying *Gesamtkonzept* (Smyser,

2003, at 85–86). They thus provide highly principled explanations for their position changes, and they appreciate opponents who provide overarching rationales to support their own positions. They tend to negotiate deliberately to be certain they do not make inappropriate position changes (Smyser, 2003, at 112). They can be gracious hosts during social events, but they do not like to conduct bargaining discussions during such occasions (Smyser, 2003, at 117–19).

[b]   Decision-Making Structure

Decision-making in German companies tends to be hierarchal and centralized (Smyser, 2003, at 121–22; Hendon, Hendon & Herbig, 1996, at 156). It is thus important for foreign negotiators to develop contacts with top level officials while inter-firm negotiations are being conducted. Once tentative agreements are achieved, they will be scrutinized by higher executives who must give their approval before they become final. If appropriate relationships have already been established, this process should go smoothly. Germans are precise people who prefer legalistic and detailed contracts (Hendon, Hendon & Herbig, 1996, at 113).

[c]   Internal Relations

German firms are substantially unionized and have codetermination laws which require larger companies to consult with worker representatives both at the corporate board level and at the plant level with respect to matters of interest to employees (Hendon, Hendon & Herbig, 1996, at 157). Workers are rarely laid off except for proper business reasons. Foreign investors who wish to establish joint ventures with German corporations must consider these factors before they decide to enter into commitments that will necessarily create long-range obligations.

[d]   Competitive Bargaining Nature

Germans tend to be tough bargainers (Hendon, Hendon & Herbig, 1996, at 155–56). They focus on specific terms and attempt to obtain agreements that favor their companies. Foreign representatives must be prepared for competitive interactions, and individuals who fail to heed this admonition are likely to leave with inferior agreements.

[10]   Saudi Arabia

[a]   Context

Saudi Arabia is an important nation because it possesses the world's largest oil reserves and it produces more oil than any other members of the Organization of Petroleum Exporting Countries (OPEC) (Hendon, Hendon & Herbig, 1996, at 165). It is a high context culture in which people try to avoid open confrontations. As a result, they are not always open about their actual thoughts (Hendon, Hendon & Herbig, 1996, at 175). The place a premium on appearances and the maintenance of a favorable social image. They are formal people who prefer to address individuals by their titles (Acuff, 1997, at 287). They are expansive people who often speak in loud voices accompanied by animated facial expressions and grand hand and arm movements (Acuff, 1997, at 288).

[b] Family Influence

Saudi Arabians are greatly influenced by family ties, their Islamic religion, and the House of Saud (Hendon, Hendon & Herbig, 1996, at 167–70). They maintain close family relationships, and often conduct business through various relatives. It is important for foreign negotiators to take the time to establish beneficial relationships that will continue for many years (Alon & Brett, 2007, at 60–61). It is helpful to obtain introductions from local agents with close ties to the families with whom you wish to do business. Since it is considered extremely rude to display the bottom of one's foot to another in Saudi Arabia, foreigners should never sit with the soles of their shoes exposed to others (Acuff, 1997, at 288; Morris, 1994, at 77).

[c] Influence of Religion

The Saudis believe that their Muslim religion provides them with a comprehensive guide to govern their personal and business lives. The words of the Prophet Muhammad are set forth in the Koran, and they consult this document for guidance on most important questions (Hendon, Hendon & Herbig, 1996, at 168). Most Muslims pray five times per day, and businesses are closed during these periods. Persons wishing to conduct business with Saudi business and government leaders should be careful not to propose anything that would be contrary to Islamic principles.

Muslim cultures frequently use the past as the standard to guide present decisions (Alon & Brett, 2007, at 64). They tend not to function on "clock time" as do most Western negotiators (Alon & Brett, 2007, at 58). They do not consider it rude to show up late for appointments, and they do not like to rush the decision-making process. It is thus critical for foreign negotiators to be patient. They should not berate Egyptian negotiators who show up late for meetings, nor should they seek to generate expeditious decisions. The more significant the issues to be resolved, the more protracted the discussions tend to be. Egyptians recognize the impatience in many Western negotiators, and they often use delaying tactics to obtain unreciprocated concessions from such individuals.

Muslims believe that future events are within the hands of Allah. It is thus beneficial not to indicate that future occurrences are controlled by the negotiating parties themselves. Muslims regularly use the phrase "in sha'a Allah" [God willing] when they talk about what might happen in the future to show respect for Allah's control over such occurrences (Alon & Brett, 2007, at 66–67). They thus appreciate it when foreign negotiators respect their Muslim heritage and suggest that future developments will take place "God willing."

One other factor that causes consternation among Western negotiators is the fact that Egyptians following the ancient teachings of Muhammad believe that it is contrary to Islamic law to conduct business on credit (Alon & Brett, 2007, at 65). They often characterize sales transactions in different terms to avoid the appearance of credit, even though credit is effectively being extended. It behooves foreign negotiators to accept these formulations if they wish to consummate the deals being discussed.

[d] Decision-Making Structure

[i] House of Saud

The House of Saud has ruled Saudi Arabia for many decades (Hendon, Hendon & Herbig, 1996, at 169). Family members occupy positions throughout government agencies. Since Saudi Arabia has a centralized decision-making process, House of Saud members tend to exercise influence over most significant business transactions. It is important for foreigners to establish personal relationships with House of Saud members, whenever possible. These family members respect personal integrity, and place great faith in their own impressions of others.

[ii] Bargaining Method

Bargaining with Saudi Arabians generally commences with inflated demands, followed by a series of ritualistic concessions (Acuff, 1997, at 289). Patience is especially important, because it takes time for the negotiation process to unfold. Apparent deadlines are frequently ignored (Acuff, 1997, at 289). Since Saudis have historically maintained an open door policy for family members and close friends, they are often visited by outsiders while conducting significant business negotiations with others (Hendon, Hendon & Herbig, 1996, at 175). Foreign negotiators should not perceive these interruptions as rude, but should instead be willing to continue their discussions in front of complete strangers. It is not unusual for Saudis to conduct independent negotiations with different parties simultaneously.

[iii] Method of Agreement

Once Saudi Arabians reach agreement, they confirm it orally or with a handshake (Hendon, Hendon & Herbig, 1996, at 173). They do not like lengthy and detailed contracts, which they view as a sign of distrust. As a result, their accords tend to contain general language that does not precisely define the actual terms agreed upon. They generally expect international accords to be expressed in both English and Arabic.

[iv] Government Trade Requirements

The Saudi Arabian government requires foreign firms to either have partnership relationships with Saudi companies or be represented by local commercial agents (Hendon, Hendon & Herbig, 1996, at 176). Many transnational arrangements have to receive government approval. It is quite common for "facilitation fees" to be paid to expedite the processing of government approval requests. While United States corporate leaders may fear that these payments would contravene the Foreign Corrupt Practices Act, there is little evidence to suggest that these payments are intended as corrupting bribes (Hendon, Hendon & Herbig, 1996, at 179). As mere facilitation payments, they are outside the scope of the FCPA.

[11] Egypt

[a] Context

Egyptians are part of a high context culture. They are understandably proud of their great history and culture, viewing themselves as the cradle of civilization (Quandt, 1987, at 105). Egyptians value personal and national honor, with these concepts being important in their interpersonal dealings. Egyptians consider themselves an economically advanced people, and resent being treated as citizens from another third-world Arab country.

[b]   Decision-Making Process

[i]   Independence of Nation

Egypt has been an independent Arab nation that has demonstrated a willingness to break with Arab unity to advance its own national interests (Quandt, 1987, at 106–107). On the other hand, it considers itself to be an important part of the Arab world, with a predominantly Muslim population. Egypt has a pharaonic tradition of strong leaders who are empowered to act without consultation with others. If others can convince Egyptian officials that certain agreements would be in their nation's interest, it is often easy to obtain binding commitments pertaining to future relations.

[ii]   Bureaucracies

Egypt has a history of entrenched and overlapping bureaucracies that must be satisfied before certain actions can be approved (Cohen, 1991, at 100; Quandt, 1987, at 107–08). The administrative approval process is complicated and protracted. Even Egyptian leaders find it difficult to gain bureaucratic consent to proposed action that requires administrative acceptance. Foreigners frequently use back channel contacts with governmental leaders to circumvent foreign ministry delays. The assistance of presidential aides can be especially helpful in this regard. Private intermediaries may also be employed to facilitate the approval process.

[c]   Political Climate

Egypt is greatly affected by problems associated with over-population, decreasing natural resources, and an aging and deteriorating infrastructure (Quandt, 1987, at 109–110). Although it has often been dependent on assistance from foreign powers, it still remembers the British colonialism that limited Egyptian freedom throughout the first half of the twentieth century. Egyptian leaders are thus careful to avoid international entanglements that may infringe on their country's national sovereignty.

[d]   Tribal Tradition

Egyptian negotiators continue to be influenced by tribal traditions that encourage preliminary posturing, ritualistic confrontation, and lofty rhetoric (Quandt, 1987, at 118–19). These stages are then followed by face-saving arrangements that are designed to preserve the honor of all participants. They tend to begin bargaining interactions with elaborate ritual — formal coffee and tea — intended to permit the establishment of personal relationships (Cohen, 1991, at 86–87). It is important for foreign negotiators to graciously accept this generous hospitality to create a beneficial atmosphere of trust and cooperation. Egyptians resent the rudeness and impatience exhibited by many foreign bargainers, especially those from the United States.

[e]   Need for Patience

Egyptian advocates usually begin with extreme positions and anticipate prolonged haggling as the parties attempt to ascertain each other's true needs and interests (Quandt, 1987, at 119–120). They like to rely on seemingly neutral principles to support their claims. Impatient opponents frequently pay a high price for their unwillingness to permit the process to develop in a deliberate manner. They are unable to discern the true interests of their Egyptian adversaries, and often make unnecessarily large concessions in an effort to achieve expeditious accords. When progress is not being made, Egyptian negotiators may request assistance from respected intermediaries (Quandt, 1987, at 120).

[f] Focus on Specificity of Language in Accords

Final deals are usually expressed in general terms. This allows Egyptian representatives to make subsequent demands for additional concessions as the parties are forced to clarity "ambiguities" that are discovered in their agreements. This device can be minimized through the negotiation of specific contractual provisions. When this technique does not prevent post-contract renegotiating, foreign advocates should be sure to request reciprocal concessions from Egyptian representatives as prerequisites to acceptance of their demands for changed conditions.

Summary

1. As communications and transportation systems have created a global political and economic world, the extent and importance of private and public international negotiations have increased.

2. Although national and transnational bargaining interactions have many similarities, language and cultural differences become important, and stereotypical impressions may influence interactions.

3. Inter-governmental negotiations ("Track I Diplomacy") may be conducted through formal channels or through informal back channels, and may involve bilateral or multilateral interactions.

4. Multilateral interactions tend to be conducted under the auspices of existing international organizations (*e.g.*, the United Nations) — which may define the issues and specify the procedures to be followed — and voting blocs may be used by weaker nations to enhance their bargaining power.

5. Private individuals and non-governmental institutions are becoming increasingly involved in foreign political controversies, with such "Track II Diplomacy" being employed where formal governmental participation may not be acceptable to the affected parties.

6. With the development of a global economic system, the frequency of transnational business negotiating has greatly increased, forcing American firm representatives to become better acquainted with foreign cultures and foreign negotiating styles.

7. Even though individual negotiating styles vary greatly even among people from the same background, it is beneficial when first interacting with foreign opponents to study their national cultures and their traditional negotiating styles.

Chapter 16

MEDIATION/ASSISTED NEGOTIATION

§ 16.01 RECENT INCREASE IN POPULARITY

[1] Among Lawyers and Clients

In recent years, legal practitioners and their clients have begun to recognize that mediation efforts constitute an important part of the dispute resolution process (Wissler, 2004). Attorneys have also begun to acknowledge the need to inform new clients of the availability of alternative dispute resolution procedures at the beginning of their professional relationships (Cochran, 2001, at 897; Kovach, 2004, at 128; *see generally* Schneider, 2000). This practice increases client receptivity to ADR assistance when the time is propitious, and it enhances the probability of successful neutral intervention. It also acknowledges the fact that clients — and their attorneys — must ultimately decide whether to seek ADR options (Cochran, 2001, at 901–04, citing Model Rule 1.2(a) which exhorts lawyers to consult with their clients with respect to the means by which their legal representation is to be carried out).

[2] Among Experts

Experts have articulated the benefits that *advocates* may derive from their own use of mediative problem-solving techniques during bargaining interactions (Fisher & Ury, 1981; Menkel-Meadow, 1984). Negotiators who are familiar with mediative approaches can often employ similar problem-solving tactics during their own bargaining transactions to further client interests and enhance the likelihood of efficient agreements (Slaikeu, 1996). Attorneys regularly use mediator skills to convince recalcitrant clients of the reasonableness of offers being advanced by opposing parties.

[3] Importance of Familiarity with Role

Advocates should also understand the role of neutral facilitators, so they can properly prepare themselves and their clients for mediation sessions and maximize the benefits to be derived from third-party intervention. Practitioners who occasionally or regularly act as mediators must also familiarize themselves with the techniques employed by successful conciliators. Their experience as neutral intervenors should increase their knowledge of the negotiation process and enhance their ability to function as effective negotiators when they represent future clients.

[4] Establishment of Mediation Programs

Most state courts have established mediation programs to assist litigants to settle cases they have been unable to resolve themselves (McAdoo & Hinshaw, 2002, at 475; Nolan-Haley, 1996). The Alternative Dispute Resolution Act of 1998 (29 U.S.C. § 651) requires all federal district courts to adopt local rules authorizing the use of mediation. Should litigants be *required* to participate in mediation sessions in all cases? If so, would the truly consensual nature of mediation be undermined? Should courts be empowered to impose sanctions on parties they think have failed to participate sufficiently in mediation sessions? (See generally Carter, 2002) (See also Pearlstein, 2007 (arguing that alternative dispute resolution systems function most effectively when they are developed by the parties themselves, instead of being imposed by Courts or legislatures on a top-down basis)).

[5]   Cyber Mediation Programs

The substantial expansion of cyber commerce has created a need for efficient ways to resolve disputes that arise between electronic purchasers and sellers of goods and services who may be located in different states or countries (Cole & Blankley, 2006; Katsh, 2005; Gibbons, Kennedy & Gibbs, 2002). Many e-business sites have adopted cyber mediation programs that use neutral facilitators and e-mail exchanges to resolve conflicts. The parties describe their difficulties through e-mail communications, and they are assisted by conciliators who participate in their exchanges. When cyber mediators think that over-reliance upon e-mail channels is creating negotiation difficulties, they should use one-on-one and conference telephone calls to reestablish rapport and diminish the mistrust that may have developed because of the impersonal means of communication being employed. When cyber mediation efforts are unsuccessful, many e-commerce companies require customers to resort to private arbitral procedures that may be conducted electronically or in person.

Attorneys representing e-business firms should consider the efficiency of cyber mediation systems. These programs should be specifically described in the home pages of the firms involved to apprise prospective purchasers of their obligation to resort to cyber mediation procedures before they seek further redress — either through private arbitral procedures or external legal channels. When prospective e-customers register on Internet cites, they expressly agree to use the dispute resolution procedures described to them. Lawyers assisting clients with e-business disputes should initially contact opposing parties through telephone calls to establish some rapport and to see if direct oral communications may expeditiously resolve the underlying issues. If not, they may wish to use e-mail exchanges to define the problem and search for possible solutions. Cyber mediation participants should appreciate the impersonal nature of e-mail communications and the fact that people are far more likely to flame other persons through e-mail than they would in person or via the telephone (Nadler, 2001, at 338). They are also more likely to be suspicious of the motives and trustworthiness of other e-mail communicators. Resort to occasional telephone calls can often correct these communication difficulties. The use of cyber mediation may also provide the neutral facilitators with more control over inter-party communications than they would have with in-person mediation (Larson, 2006, at 234–35).

Computer programs can also assist disputing parties achieve efficient resolutions of their underlying conflicts (Lodder & Zeleznikow, 2005). Negotiators can be asked a series of questions that are designed to determine the issues that must be addressed. When larger issues are involved, the program can elicit additional information that will help divide expansive terms into subissues. The parties are then asked to assign point values to the various subissues, with each side given a total of 100 or 200 points to be allotted. The computer program then explores ways to maximize and equalize the relative values to be given to each side. For example, a family dispute could be subdivided into issues pertaining to primary child custody and visitation rights, child support and possible alimony payments, distribution of marital property, rights to future pension payouts, and so forth. Each spouse is then directed to assign points to the different items to be exchanged. If each is given 100 points to allot, one might think they would each obtain approximately 50. The computer program, however, explores the different ways in which the parties have valued the various terms and endeavors to maximize the joint returns achieved. By assigning the different items to the spouse expressing the greater interest in those terms, the program may enable each party to end up with 70 or 75 points.

These Online Dispute Resolution (ODR) programs can be especially useful when highly emotional conflicts are involved, because they can induce the disputants to explore the underlying issues in a detached and rational manner. As the program induces the parties to define and value the different issues to be addressed, the impact of the emotional components can be minimized. The disputants can deal with themselves entirely through the Internet, with the final solution generating the most efficient terms that could be achieved through rational decision-making. On the other hand, when highly emotional controversies are present, the use of ODR programs can make it difficult for the disputing parties to communicate their feelings effectively with each other in a manner that would promote inter-party empathy and understanding (Cole & Blankley, 2006, at 202–04).

§ 16.02 MEDIATION AS INTERMEDIARY STEP BETWEEN SETTLEMENT AND LITIGATION

[1] Failing to Envision the Possibility of Mediated Negotiation

The vast majority of law suits are resolved through negotiated settlements (Birke & Fox, 1999, at 1; Williams, 1996, at 8–9). In fact, fewer than two percent of civil complaints filed in federal courts culminate in bench or jury trials. The other 98 percent are withdrawn, dismissed, or settled. Most private sector business arrangements are similarly achieved through inter-party negotiations, as are most inter-government and government-private party transactions. When direct negotiations do not generate mutual accords, many parties give up and accept their nonsettlement options. They engage in financially and emotionally costly litigation or forego what might have been mutually beneficial business deals. The substantial effort participants made toward joint agreements indicates that both sides would have preferred overall accords to their respective nonsettlement alternatives.

[2] Problems that Mediation Could Solve

The inability of advocates to achieve mutual accommodations of their competing interests does not ipso facto mean that they are better off with no agreements. Inexperienced participants may have failed to initiate the negotiation process. Each side could have simply been waiting for the other to broach the subject. One or both parties may have employed disingenuous tactics that discouraged opponents. One or both may have over- or under-stated what they required to attain mutual accords. The participants may have reached unyielding positions that neither could modify without appearing weak and losing face. Communication channels may have been disrupted because of the intense pressure on the participants. This disruption could have caused parties to ignore areas of potential overlap. Cultural differences may have generated personal misunderstandings due to different communication approaches, different value systems, different group orientations, and other similar factors (see generally LeBaron, 2003). If their bargaining deficiencies could be alleviated, the participants might realize that negotiated arrangements would still be preferable to nonsettlements.

[3]   Unfounded Fears

When adversaries are unable to achieve their own agreements, they may frequently benefit from the assistance of proficient mediators who can assist them to regenerate stalled negotiations. A number of advocates are hesitant to participate in mediation sessions, because they think those meetings will be time-consuming and/or result in the imposition of disadvantageous terms. Both of these fears are unfounded. The effective use of conciliation techniques can be highly cost effective. Litigants may avoid the substantial monetary, temporal, and psychological costs associated with formal adjudications, and post-trial appeals, while transactional negotiators may avoid the need to begin new discussions with different parties. Even though the employment of mediative efforts involves some time commitment, the return through the avoidance of litigation or the attainment of business deals more than compensates for it.

[4]   Recognizing Ultimate Authority of Parties Involved

Parties afraid that conciliators may impose unwanted terms on them do not understand the mediation process. Mediators lack the authority to dictate agreements. They are merely empowered to *assist* parties with *their own* negotiations (Bush & Folger, 1994, at 2–3; Bush & Folger, 2005, at 8). While neutral intervenors may enhance communication and help advocates develop innovative alternatives not previously considered, the final authority always rests with the parties. They must consent to any proposed arrangements. No matter how diligently mediators seek to encourage agreements, clients always control their own final destinies (Ackerman, 2002, at 75–78; Erickson & McKnight, 2001, at 205, 216–17).

[5]   Mediation as Assisted Negotiation

Advocates should recognize that mediation is essentially *assisted negotiation* (Abramson, 2004, at 67; Williams, 1996, at 10). Conciliators effectively employ bargaining skills to facilitate inter-party negotiating and encourage the attainment of mutual accords (Kovach, 2004, at 26–27; Singer, 1994, at 79–80). The negotiation stages and techniques remain the same, but the interaction becomes more complex due to the participation of neutral intervenors. As depicted in Figure 3, the legal representatives must negotiate with the mediator, through the mediator with each other, directly with each other, and with their own clients — who may decide to interact directly with each other or with the mediator. Nonetheless, the parties continue to exchange ideas and proposals, as they were previously doing alone, and the advocates retain control over any final terms agreed upon.

Figure 3

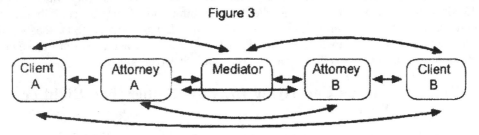

[6] Benefits

[a] Psychological

Successful conciliation efforts can significantly enhance the psychological well being of negotiating parties. Mutually beneficial agreements avoid the anxiety, trauma, and uncertainty of contested litigation and the premature breakdown of transactional discussions. More importantly, mediated solutions enable the disputing parties to participate directly in the formulation of their own final arrangements (see generally Ackerman, 2002). Mutually developed results are generally preferable to terms imposed on people through external factors such as adjudications or market constraints. "If the parties make their own agreement they are more likely to abide by it, and it will have greater legitimacy than a solution imposed from without" (Menkel-Meadow, 1985, at 502; see also Bingham, 2002, at 110; Resnik, 2002, at 155).

An additional psychological factor concerns the degree to which parties believe that conciliation procedures have been fair. The more the participants feel their voices have been heard and valued, and their underlying interests have been fairly considered, the more pleased they tend to be with the overall process and the final accords that are achieved (Allred, 2005, at 90–92). It is thus crucial for neutral facilitators to treat all parties with respect and dignity, and to make sure everyone feels they had the opportunity to fully express their viewpoints and to be heard. Even at the conclusion of the discussions, it can be beneficial to ask the participants if there is anything else they would like to say. They usually have nothing to add, but seemed pleased to have been asked.

[b] Time and Money

It has generally been assumed that effective mediation programs provide significant time and monetary savings (Bannink, 2007, at 164; Cole, 2000, at 1199–1200 and authorities cited therein). The parties are able to resolve their disputes without the need for protracted and expensive litigation. Nonetheless, as non-adjudicative dispute resolution procedures have become more formal and legalistic, some have questioned whether these alternative settlement techniques actually do save parties significant time and money (Hensler, 2002). This is especially true if agreements are not achieved until the completion of full discovery and on the eve of trial. If mediation procedures are carefully established and regularly monitored to ensure that they do not become overly technical and unduly extended, their use should save parties and courts both time and money as the vast majority of claims are resolved without the need for formal adjudications (Phillips, 2002, at 149). Recent studies of court-mandated ADR programs in Minnesota and Missouri found that most attorneys believe that the availability of effective mediation programs saves clients both time and money by contributing to more expeditious settlements of civil cases (Mc Adoo & Hinshaw, 2002, at 495–96; Mc Adoo, 2002, at 431). Even when mediated settlements are not achieved until the eve of trials, the parties are spared protracted trials and post-trial appeals.

[c] Focus on Underlying Interests Rather than Right or Wrong

The mediation process does not focus primarily on which party is "right" or "wrong" or which side should "win" or "lose," as do judicial or arbitral proceedings. It instead considers what terms the participants need to satisfy their underlying interests

(Bannink, 2007, at 165–67; Scanlon, 1999; Goodpaster, 1997, at 213–15). While litigation tends to be a retroactive-oriented "win-lose" endeavor, conciliation involves a future-oriented "win-win" process (Folberg & Taylor, 1984, at 10). Disputing parties are more satisfied with and are more likely to honor solutions they help to formulate, and this factor inures to the benefit of everyone concerned. This can be true even when the only issue involved concerns money (Freund, 1994).

[d]　High Success Rate

Even though most attorneys diligently attempt to settle their cases before trial, and 90 to 95 percent of all suits are mutually resolved through these efforts, various factors operate to impede settlement of many of the remaining 5 to 10 percent of cases that might be disposed of through effective third-party intervention. Professors Stephen Goldberg and Jeanne Brett have been able to use pre-arbitration mediation to resolve approximately 85 percent of grievance disputes that were otherwise destined for arbitral adjudication under the applicable collective bargaining agreements (Goldberg & Brett, 1983). Despite the fact that labor and management representatives had unsuccessfully sought to reach mutual accommodations through formal contractual grievance procedures requiring repeated negotiation sessions, the disputants were able to achieve mutual accords in most instances with the assistance of proficient mediators.

[e]　Assistance in Reevaluating "Principled" Positions

Disputing parties often lock themselves into unyielding "principled" positions and refuse to consider objectively the proposals being propounded by opponents. Adept conciliators can frequently induce these individuals to reconsider their own underlying needs and interests and to more realistically evaluate the proposals being suggested by their opponents (Watkins & Rosegrant, 2001, at 91–92). This phenomenon significantly enhances the likelihood of negotiated solutions.

[f]　Switch Focus from Areas of Disagreement to Areas of Agreement

Corporate officers discussing possible business transactions often terminate their interactions prematurely. If their articulated positions are far apart, they begin to think that agreement is unlikely and they look for other opportunities. They focus so intently on their areas of disagreement, that they fail to discern areas of possible joint gain (Bannink, 2007, at 167). With the assistance of skilled mediators, they may begin to appreciate the areas of positional overlap and how their areas of conflict may be transformed into mutually beneficial arrangements (Ladd, 2005, at 18–19). It should not take long for effective conciliators to induce seemingly deadlocked transactional negotiators to explore their joint interests. In many instances, these efforts will enable pessimistic participants to achieve beneficial business arrangements they never thought possible. Mediation efforts can also assist business partners who have decided to dissolve their relationships (Freund, 1997).

§ 16.03 MEDIATOR STYLES

[1]   Common Mediator Characteristics

Proficient mediators tend to possess common characteristics no matter what styles they employ (Ordover & Doneff, 2002, at 54–55; Erickson & McKnight, 2001, at 144–45, 198–201; Slaikeu, 1996, at 18–19) (see generally Boulle, Colatrella & Picchioni, 2008). They are objective individuals who are cognizant of their own biases. They have excellent communication skills — *i.e.*, they are both good, empathetic listeners and assertive speakers. They are adept readers of nonverbal signals. They have good interpersonal skills that enable them to interact well with people from diverse backgrounds and different personalities (see generally Krivis, 2006). They understand the negotiation process and the way in which conciliators can enhance that process. They can even modify their usual styles when particular dispute circumstances suggest the need for a different approach (Golann, 2000). The introduction of an individual with these skills to an otherwise stalemated negotiation can be of great benefit.

[2]   Awareness of Influence and Types

[a]   Influence

Both neutrals and advocates must recognize that mediator personalities directly influence intervenor behavior. Since mediators lack the authority to impose final terms on disputants, they must rely upon their powers of persuasion and their reputations for impartiality and fairness to encourage mutual accords (Rubin & Brown, 1975, at 62). Neutral intervenors should not merely emulate the styles employed by other people. If they copy the behavior used by individuals with different personalities, they are likely to experience discomfort and ineffectiveness. Naturally aggressive individuals tend to feel most comfortable with relatively assertive mediation techniques, while laid back people tend to prefer low key approaches. Neutrals must candidly evaluate the manner in which others have traditionally responded to them and develop mediative styles consistent with those assessments. Once they find an approach they feel comfortable using, mediators should try to maintain a consistent style that parties can anticipate when they retain their services. Neutrals who exhibit erratic behavior are unlikely to generate client confidence.

[b]   Types

Mediators tend to employ one of three diverse styles (Bush & Folger, 2005; Ladd, 2005, at 30–31; Golann, 1996, at 17–20; Bush & Folger, 1994; Moore, 2003, at 43–81). Most mediators are facilitative/elicitive. They seek to reopen blocked communication channels and to encourage direct inter-party negotiations that will enable the parties to formulate their own final terms. Other neutral facilitators focus primarily on the substantive terms being discussed. They try to determine the provisions they think the parties will jointly accept and work to induce the participants to agree to the packages they have formulated. An innovative group of conciliators are relationship-oriented. They endeavor to empower the participants and generate mutual respect that will enhance the ability of disputants to solve their own problems.

[3] Facilitative/Elicitive

[a] Approach

Facilitative/elicitive mediators attempt to regenerate party-to-party discussions to enable the participants to structure their own deals. They believe that temporary impasses are the result of communication breakdowns and/or unrealistic expectations. They work to reopen communication channels and to induce advocates to reevaluate the reasonableness of their respective positions. They use questions in an elicitive manner to generate position reconsiderations and to induce parties to explore new areas. Once facilitative/elicitive intervenors generate meaningful bargaining exchanges, they let the advocates determine what is best for themselves. They like to use joint meetings during which the parties engage in face-to-face bargaining. Separate sessions are reserved for crisis intervention when the disputants are unable to talk directly to one another (Kolb, 1983, at 46–47). These conciliators function like orchestra leaders.

[b] Nature of Interactions

Communication between facilitative/elicitive mediators and advocates is designed to reestablish inter-party discussions. The following dialogue is typical of the exchanges one might observe during separate caucus sessions:

MEDIATOR (to Negotiator A): You appear to be making significant progress. Both sides appear to be favorably disposed toward Items P and Q. How do you feel about these developments?

NEGOTIATOR A: While we could live with Items P and Q, we would prefer to obtain Item X or Y.

MEDIATOR: Would you be willing to give up Item P or Q if you could get X or Y?

NEGOTIATOR A: We certainly would.

MEDIATOR: Would you be willing to reconsider your prior refusal to move with respect to Items R and S if necessary to obtain Item X or Y?

NEGOTIATOR A: If we had to. We would prefer to exchange Item P or Q for X or Y, but would reassess our position on Items R and S if need be.

* * *

MEDIATOR (to Negotiator B): We appear to have agreement with respect to Items P and Q. How do you feel about this?

NEGOTIATOR B: Okay, but we would prefer to explore Items R and S more thoroughly before we finalize any agreement.

MEDIATOR: Would you be willing to trade Item P or Q for Item R or S?

NEGOTIATOR B: Yes.

MEDIATOR: I'm not sure whether Side A would be amenable to any reconsideration of Items R and S — unless you would be willing to reassess your view regarding Items X and Y. Would you do so if necessary to get movement on Items R and S?

NEGOTIATOR B: We should probably stay with Items P and Q, and contemplate mutual exchanges involving Items R and/or S for Items X and/or Y.

[c]   Level of Influence

Facilitative/elicitive mediators are especially appreciated by proficient negotiators who want minimal bargaining assistance and wish to control their own bargaining outcomes (*see* federal labor mediator styles discussed in Kolb, 1983).

[4]   Evaluative/Directive Mediators

[a]   Approach

Evaluative/directive mediators are typically used to interacting with relatively inexperienced negotiators who have difficulty achieving their own agreements. They tend to encounter advocates who either do not know how to initiate meaningful negotiations or are unable to explore the different issues in a manner likely to generate mutual accords. As a result, evaluative/directive neutrals feel the need to control the bargaining interactions they encounter. During the 1960s and 1970s, following the enactment of various public sector labor relations statutes giving government employees the right to engage in collective bargaining, it was common to encounter evaluative/directive mediators who thought they had to direct the negotiations being conducted by inexperienced advocates.

[b]   Nature of Interactions

Transactions conducted by evaluative/directive mediators tend to resemble parent-child interactions (Berne, 1964). The "parent"-like neutrals attempt to ascertain the needs and interests of the "child"-like participants so they can tell those individuals what they *should* accept. These mediators determine the substantive terms they believe would best resolve the underlying controversy and use a directive style to persuade the parties to accept their proposed provisions. When parties object to their suggestions, evaluative/directive mediators try to convince the parties that the proposed terms are the best they can achieve. They consider themselves "deal makers" who must decide what is best for the parties. They prefer to use separate sessions during which they probe underlying party needs and work to convince the participants to accept the terms they have formulated (*see* state labor mediator styles discussed in Kolb, 1983).

Most of the communication between evaluative/directive mediators and negotiators is one-sided — carefully controlled by the neutral intervenors. Typical exchanges during separate caucus sessions conducted during the latter stages of interactions may be seen in the following dialogues:

> MEDIATOR (to Negotiator A): I have been able to determine what is acceptable to both sides. I think Side B can live with Items P and Q, but definitely not with Items X or Y.

> NEGOTIATOR A: We were hoping to obtain Item X or Y, even if we had to give up Item P or Q or reconsider our prior rejection of Items R and S.

> MEDIATOR: I understand your concerns, but must emphasize the need for you to recognize the realities of the situation. You are fortunate that I have been able to get you Items P and Q. That was not easily accomplished. If you insist on Item X or Y, I'm certain the whole deal will unravel. Would you prefer to lose everything at this point?

> NEGOTIATOR A: If I could meet with Negotiator B and directly raise these concerns, perhaps I could convince him/her of our significant interest in Items

X and Y.

MEDIATOR: Don't you understand how diligently I have worked to explore these issues with Negotiator B? If these items were available, I would certainly have sought to get them for you. If you seek joint negotiations pertaining to Items X and Y, the great progress we have made will be lost.

* * *

MEDIATOR (to Negotiator B): After lengthy discussions with both sides, I have come to the conclusion that the parties can jointly agree upon Items P and Q. Any effort to modify these terms would be likely to destroy everything.

NEGOTIATOR B: During our earlier discussions, I got the impression that Side A might be amenable to an exchange that would give us either Item R or S. We might even be willing to reevaluate our position regarding Items X and Y if necessary. Don't you think we should explore these possibilities further?

MEDIATOR: I do not. It was an arduous process to find the common ground with respect to Items P and Q. If you insist on further talks involving Items R and S — and X and Y — I think the negotiations will stalemate. Please remember how hard I have worked to protect your interests. Do you want to risk a nonsettlement at this crucial point?

NEGOTIATOR B: I wish we could explore these other issues more fully, but I appreciate your concern. I guess we'll have to live with what you've been able to get for us.

Empirical studies have found that disputants who settle controversies with the assistance of evaluative/directive mediators often feel they have been denied "procedural justice" even if the substantive terms are fair (Welsh, 2001, at 851–53). They have not had the opportunity to express their underlying feelings and be heard by the mediator and their opponents. They also feel disrespected by the undignified process imposed upon them.

[c]   Level of Influence

Parties that are uncertain regarding the appropriate way in which to achieve negotiated agreements and who desire substantive guidance from experienced intervenors may appreciate the assistance provided by evaluative/directive conciliators. They should carefully select substantive experts who are likely to understand their particular interests. In the end, these mediators are going to directly influence the actual terms agreed upon. Individuals who prefer to control their own destinies do not usually feel comfortable with such evaluative/directive intervention (Welsh, 2004c, at 427).

[5]   Relationship-Oriented/Transformative Mediators

[a]   Approach

In their thoughtful book, Robert Baruch Bush and Joseph Folger discuss a novel approach to mediation (Bush & Folger, 1994)(*see also* Bush & Folger, 2005; Della Noce, 1999). They reject evaluative/directive and facilitative/elicitive intervention in favor of a relationship-oriented/transformative approach that is designed to transform disputants into relatively self-sufficient problem solvers. They believe that mediators should strive to empower weaker parties by demonstrating the rights and options available to the participants through settlement and nonsettlement options, and to generate mutual respect among the competing parties (McGuigan & Popp, 2007). They contend that empowered participants who truly appreciate the interests and viewpoints of their opponents can optimally work to achieve their own mutually acceptable solutions. Even when immediate agreements are not attained during relationship-oriented intervention, Bush and Folger maintain that empowered parties will be better able to handle future bargaining interactions due to their new found problem-solving skills (Bush & Folger, 2005, at 22–39; Bush & Folger, 1994, at 200–01).

Unlike evaluative/directive and facilitative/elicitive mediators who are particularly interested in resolution of the underlying disputes, relationship-oriented/transformative conciliators are primarily interested in future party relationships. While they are pleased when their efforts generate current agreements, they prefer to help disputants understand how they can effectively resolve their own future controversies. To accomplish this objective, relationship-oriented/transformative intervenors focus on two basic issues — party *empowerment* and inter-party *recognition* (Bush & Folger, 2005, at 13–15; Bush & Folger, 1994, at 20–21). They endeavor to show each side that it possesses the power to order its future relationships. They simultaneously attempt to generate inter-party empathy by inducing each side to appreciate the feelings and perspectives of their adversaries (*see community mediator* style discussed in Kolb, 1994, at 239–77).

[b]   Nature of Interactions

Exchanges between relationship-oriented/transformative mediators and advocates are quite different from those involving facilitative/elicitive and evaluative/directive neutrals. Instead of focusing primarily on the bargaining process, as do facilitative/elicitive neutrals, or substantive issues, as do evaluative/directive mediators, these innovative intervenors focus on the disputants themselves. They attempt to encourage participant deliberations and decision-making. They try to demonstrate to emotionally drained and dispirited parties that they have options they can pursue if negotiations do not prove fruitful. Typical empowerment and recognition exchanges involving relationship-oriented/transformative mediators might include:

MEDIATOR (to Negotiator A): We've discussed how the parties might resolve the underlying dispute. You do not appear to be entirely satisfied with the proposals suggested by Side B. What other issues would you like to have addressed? How would you like to have them resolved?

NEGOTIATOR A: I feel as if I must reach an agreement with Side B or else. I don't believe Side B is being fair to me. They seem to think they can force me to accept anything they offer. They don't care about my feelings regarding this matter.

MEDIATOR: Side B cannot force you to accept anything. You always have the right to walk away from these talks if you do not like the way they are progressing. If you are unable to reach an agreement with Side B, what other options would be available to you? What could you do on your own to limit the impact of the current controversy?

                              *   *   *

MEDIATOR (to Negotiator A): Why do you think Side B has behaved the way it has? What do you think are Side B's concerns here? If you were in Side B's shoes, what would you be trying to achieve through these negotiations?

* * *

MEDIATOR (to Negotiator B): Side A is not satisfied with the way these talks are progressing. Why do you think Side A is upset? What are their concerns? If you were in Side A's situation, what would you expect to achieve from these negotiations?

[c]   Level of Influence

Many facilitative/elicitive mediators believe that they work to preserve inter-party relationships when they perform their usual conciliation functions. As they attempt to enhance the negotiation process and create optimal problem-solving environments, they simultaneously endeavor to respect party empowerment. They truly wish to assist parties to structure their own agreements, and this objective can most effectively be accomplished if the participants believe they possess the power to influence the final terms agreed upon. Parties that feel impotent lack the capacity to negotiate meaningfully, and they feel they are being forced to accept the provisions proposed by their opponents or recommended by the mediators. This result would not please facilitative/elicitive neutrals who hope to encourage joint problem-solving.

Facilitative/elicitive mediators recognize that most negotiated agreements require future party interaction as the participants effectuate the terms of their arrangements. If the parties do not have sufficient mutual trust and respect, problems are likely to arise. Dissatisfied individuals may attempt to undermine the terms agreed upon. People who feel a lack of opponent respect may attempt to evade contractual obligations in an effort to retaliate against their disrespectful adversaries.

Facilitative/elicitive mediators differ from Bush/Folger relationship-oriented/transformative neutrals in one critical respect. They prefer to generate final agreements than to preserve inter-party relationships. While relationship-oriented/transformative intervenors would rather forego agreements if necessary to enhance party empowerment and recognition, facilitative/elicitive mediators would place final accords ahead of empowerment and respect. This is why Bush and Folger maintain that mediators cannot function as facilitative/elicitive and relationship-oriented/transformative intervenors simultaneously (Bush & Folger, 2005, at 228–29; Bush & Folger, 1994, at 278–79).

§ 16.04   INITIATION OF MEDIATION PROCESS

The mediation process may be initiated by: (1) one or more of the parties involved in the dispute; (2) by referrals from secondary parties; (3) by direct mediator intervention; or (4) by appointment by a recognized authority (Moore, 2003, at 85).

[1]   Direct Party Initiation

The most common way for mediation involvement to begin involves an invitation from one or more of the parties involved in the dispute (Moore, 2003, at 85–86). Individual parties are often reluctant to suggest mediation, because they fear that the other party or parties will view such a unilateral request as a sign of weakness. The parties are probably at or near an impasse, with neither immediately willing to move toward the other. If one proposes mediator intervention, it will signal a flexibility in its current position. In addition, a one-sided request for mediation may cause suspicion on the part of the other party or parties, who may suspect that the moving party plans to employ mediation for its own gain. Such suspicions can be best negated if the party invoking mediation seeks the participation of a highly respected neutral whose integrity is unlikely to be questioned by the other party or parties. The requesting party may directly contact such a person or ask for assistance from a respected mediation service.

Despite the possible misinterpretations that may arise from a unilateral proposal for mediator assistance, a party should not hesitate to raise this issue with the other party or parties if it thinks that neutral facilitation may advance the negotiations. Litigating parties should recognize that the vast majority of such disputes will be resolved through negotiations rather than through adjudications. As a result, if their own bargaining interactions have not proved fruitful, one should not be reluctant to suggest mediator assistance. If this issue is raised in an appropriate manner, the initiating party may induce acceptance by the other party or parties and convert the situation into a joint mediation request. Even if the other parties do not readily consent to mediation, the initiating party may be able to initiate mediator participation and allow the neutral intervenor to convene a joint session at which he or she formally commences the process. This diminishes the onus on the party that unilaterally invoked the process.

The optimal situation involves a joint request from the negotiating parties for neutral assistance. This approach avoids any negative implications associated with a one-sided request for mediation, and it indicates that the relevant parties are all committed to the mediation process. This approach also enables the parties to negotiate about the neutral facilitator to be selected or the mediation service to be asked to participate. This makes it more likely that the bargaining participants will have confidence in the neutrality of the mediator selected.

[2]   Referrals by Secondary Parties

In some conflict situations, the assistance of a neutral intervenor is not requested by one of the negotiating parties, but is proposed by someone else. For example, when several workers or lower level managers are involved in an employment controversy, a non-involved manager may propose mediator assistance, which may be provided by another respected firm official or an outside specialist. A family counselor may recommend neutral facilitation to spouses who appear to be headed towards a divorce but who have been unable to resolve the underlying issues amicably.

When a disinterested third party proposes mediator assistance, the reactive devaluation that might be associated with the unilateral suggestion by one of the disputing parties is avoided. Neither party is likely to think that the other plans to use mediation simply to further its own interests as might be the case if that party were the mediation initiator. The disputants can accept the third party's suggestion without fear of exuding weakness, and with the hope that both will become committed to the mediation process.

[3]   Direct Mediator Initiation

On rare occasions, outside neutrals endeavor to initiate the mediation process. For example, a local official may seek to facilitate discussions among community groups involved in a public dispute. In the international arena, a neutral government may try to interject itself in a dispute involving other nations. Both President Jimmy Carter and President William Clinton used this approach with respect to the conflict between the Israelis and the Palestinians. The public personae of such intervenors may be sufficient to generate party acceptance of their involvement and allow the mediation process to move forward.

When wholly private disputes are involved, it may be difficult for outside parties to inject themselves into controversies without encountering party reluctance. The disputants may find it presumptuous for such seeming interlopers to become involved with their conflicts. In such cases, it would usually take a highly respected neutral to intervene successfully.

[4]   Initiation by Recognized Authority

In some instances, negotiating parties have mediation assistance imposed upon them by external agencies (Moore, 2003, at 90). This is quite common with respect to labor disputes in which state or federal mediation agencies intervene without party invitation. Neutral facilitation may similarly be imposed upon disputing spouses by family service agencies. Such government intervention is likely to occur because of the significant public interest associated with the particular disputes involved. The labor mediation services seek to minimize production and service interruptions associated with work stoppages, while the family service agencies seek to protect the interests of children affected by parental conflicts. Local court rules frequently authorize judges to appoint mediators who will assist litigants with settlement discussions.

When government agencies with reputations for providing professional mediation services enter disputes, their facilitators are usually accepted by the disputing parties. The intervenors may initially encounter some party reluctance, especially in the family dispute area, but such party resistance is likely to diminish as the neutral facilitators demonstrate their impartial and professional capabilities. The disputants recognize the fact that they must ultimately resolve their differences, and most are likely to appreciate the assistance being provided. Litigants are also likely to acknowledge the benefits of mutual settlements over win-lose adjudications and accept the intervention of court-appointed facilitators.

§ 16.05   TIMING OF INITIAL MEDIATION INTERVENTION

[1]   Time Required to Reach Conciliatory State

The timing of initial mediation efforts can be crucial with respect to both litigation settlement discussions and transactional talks. If neutral intervention occurs prematurely, the parties may be unreceptive. They may not even be sufficiently prepared to participate meaningfully in mediation sessions. On the other hand, if conciliatory attempts begin in a belated manner, the parties may be locked into unyielding positions that are difficult to alter (Golann, 2002, at 325).

On many occasions, plaintiffs are unreceptive to settlement discussions at the outset of litigation. They are angry and want to obtain retribution for the wrongs committed against them. At this point, they view their legal representatives at gladiators who have been retained to vanquish their evil adversaries. Defendants feel wrongly accused and demand complete vindication. When parties have this mind-set, negotiations — even when mediator assisted — are unlikely to produce beneficial results. Legal advocates and prospective conciliators must wait until these persons have begun to recognize the monetary and psychological costs associated with continued warfare before they can effectively encourage transition from the gladiator mode to a conciliatory state.

Premature neutral intervention is unlikely to be fruitful.

[2]   Early Stages of Litigation

Once plaintiff and defendant attorneys have become knowledgeable regarding the factual and legal issues involved and have apprised their respective clients of the costs and risks associated with contemporary litigation, the time is ripe for settlement discussions. During the early stages of the litigation process, the parties often contemplate settlement possibilities with relatively open minds. They have not yet convinced themselves of the seeming invincibility of their respective positions. At this point, gentle but persistent encouragement by neutral intervenors should be sufficient to ensure continued settlement discussions.

[a]   Judicial Involvement

[i]   Settlement Suggestion

In some cases, litigants are unable to commence settlement talks on their own — usually because the parties naively believe that whoever initiates settlement efforts exudes weakness (McEwen & Wissler, 2002, at 134–35). They feel that this weakness may be exploited by their opponents. Trial judges who encounter such circumstances should permit the parties to save face by initiating the negotiation process for them (Rubin & Brown, 1975, at 47, 58). Judges should casually broach the topic of settlement and encourage the litigants to explore the operative circumstances by themselves. These judicial officials should simultaneously indicate a willingness to participate more actively at any time either or both parties request assistance. They should also advise the parties of the benefits they may derive from outside mediative intervention.

[ii]   Pressure

It is the immediacy of impending trial dates that induces most attorneys and their clients to seriously consider settlement. Awareness of increasing financial and emotional pressures apply a great deal of pressure toward this end. Settlement pressure is effectively enhanced by judges who work diligently during pretrial stages to keep cases moving inexorably toward trial. Unnecessary delays should be avoided whenever possible.

[b]   Immediacy of Trial

Shortly before scheduled trial dates, the litigants are anxious to avoid the need for formal adjudications. The parties are psychologically exhausted. If a real impasse is going to develop, it will usually occur at this stage of the proceedings. At this moment, the litigants are most amenable to conciliative assistance. Either or both parties may indicate a receptiveness to mediator intervention. If they fail to do so, judges should encourage neutral involvement by a judicial official or an outside individual.

[3]   During Trial

Judges and mediators should conversely understand that once trials have commenced, the parties become temporarily disinterested in on-going settlement discussions. By this point, the economies associated with mutual resolutions have significantly diminished, and the parties are wholly prepared for adjudication. Each side is psychologically convinced that it will achieve beneficial results. (Regarding "optimistic overconfidence" *see* Kahneman & Tversky, 1995, at 46–49) As the adjudication process unfolds, however, unanticipated developments may induce one or both parties to reconsider the benefits that may be derived from further settlement discussions. Mediators who felt ineffective at the outset of the trial may now encounter greater party receptivity.

[4]   Transactional Negotiations

The timing of initial intervention is also likely to be critical with respect to transactional negotiations. Business parties must initially assess the economic benefits they can derive from contemplated transactions and appropriately plan their opening positions. Unlike many litigants, business parties usually have no difficulty initiating discussions. If talks are progressing well, there may be no need for mediative assistance. Nonetheless, if problems are encountered, the parties should acknowledge the benefits that may be derived from neutral intervention. Too often, business firms that are unable to achieve mutual accords on their own give up and walk away. If they continue to believe that mutually beneficial deals could be structured, they should not hesitate to request mediative assistance.

What functions could transactional mediators perform? (Peppet, 2004). They could assist parties to reopen blocked communication channels. They could obtain confidential information the parties would not be willing to share directly with each other, enabling the neutral facilitators to look for ways to optimize joint gains. To avoid the impact of "reactive devaluation" when proposals are advanced by interested participants, mediators could suggest terms they think might be mutually beneficial. When emotional conflicts arise, the neutral persons could reframe difficult issues to neutralize their impact and help the parties preserve their relationships.

When transactional discussions are not fruitful, the parties should not wait until a complete cessation of talks before they ask for neutral intervention. Once unyielding final positions are reached, the parties are likely to give up on the current negotiations and contemplate discussions with other business partners. It thus behooves business negotiators to seek mediative help *before* they become wholly unreceptive to further discussions.

§ 16.06 MEDIATOR SELECTION

[1]   Mediation Style Desired

[a]   Greater Participant Control

When negotiating parties seek the assistance of neutral intervenors, they should carefully evaluate the type of mediation assistance they desire (Abramson, 2004, at 129–43). Do they want the help of a facilitative/elicitive neutral, an evaluative/directive neutral, or a relationship-oriented/transformative neutral? Advocates who wish to control their own interactions — but who feel a strong need to achieve agreements — would probably prefer a facilitative/elicitive style that provides bargaining assistance but permits the parties to determine their own final terms (Goldfien & Robbennolt, 2007, at 300–01). These parties do not want mediators who try to dictate terms. They instead wish to obtain the assistance of individuals who merely enhance the bargaining process through an elicitive approach.

[b]   More Directive Intervention

Advocates who are inexperienced negotiators and have difficulty with the give-and-take inherent in the bargaining process may appreciate the assistance of evaluative/directive mediators (Goldfien & Robbennolt, 2007, at 302–03). These neutrals can take charge of the interactions and steer the discussions in the appropriate direction. If directive neutrals are to be used, it is imperative that the parties have complete faith in the judgment and integrity of those intervenors. Only then will the advocates be willing to accept their recommendations with confidence.

[c]   Enhanced Participant Empowerment

Individuals who feel a lack of control over their personal destinies may benefit from the help of relationship-oriented/transformative intervenors. This type of intervention is especially appropriate with respect to truly personal controversies generating strong emotional feelings. Disputes involving family members, business partners, employer-employee relationships, and neighbors frequently fall within this category — particularly when unequal financial or emotional relationships are present. These people would most likely resent attempts by evaluative/directive mediators to control their bargaining outcomes. They might also fear that facilitative/elicitive neutrals are insufficiently attuned to the unequal relationships involved. They would thus benefit from the attention to empowerment and recognition issues they would expect to receive from relationship-oriented/transformative intervenors.

[2]   Number of Mediators

[a]   Function

Once parties determine the type of mediation assistance they prefer, they must decide how many mediators they need. In the vast majority of negotiation situations, one proficient neutral is sufficient. As long as that individual has the respect of both parties, they should be capable of providing the requisite help. In some cases, however, multiple mediators may be beneficial. If unusually technical issues are involved, the parties may want neutral intervenors who are both substantive experts and process experts. Since they may not be able to find both qualities in the same person, they may wish to use two or three neutrals who may each provide different expertise.

When family disputes are involved, pairs of mediators are often employed. One is usually familiar with the legal issues and the negotiation process, while the other is a social worker or counselor. The former tries to enhance the bargaining interaction, and the latter works to diminish the psychological impact of the dispute on the spouses and their children.

[b]   Distrust and/or Cultural Differences

Multiple neutrals may also be required in cases in which mutual distrust or significant cultural differences would preclude the selection of a single mediator. In these instances, the parties may each name a preferred neutral and have those two individuals select a third person who would be relatively acceptable to both sides. For example, international business controversies may concern firms from diverse areas of the world that do not trust neutrals from the opposing company's culture. Each firm could select a neutral from its own culture, and authorize those two to select the third from a neutral nation.

Empirical research indicates that men and women often behave differently during mediation, especially when they are clients involved in divorce proceedings (Pines, Gat & Tal, 2002). Males tend to suppress their emotions during marital conflicts, while females tend to openly express their feelings of pain and insult. Evidence suggests that the female voice may be less heard during dispute resolution sessions than male expressions. The female tendency to be more cooperative may place them at a disadvantage when they interact with male opponents who are likely to behave more competitively, causing the women to obtain less advantageous divorce settlements (Pines, Gat & Tal, 2002, at 24–25). Mediators in general — and divorce mediators in particular — should be especially attuned to these possible gender-based differences, to ensure that women are not adversely affected by cultural differences that may favor males in settings involving male and female antagonists.

[3]   Conciliation Services

[a]   Resources

In some cases, parties can readily agree upon the designation of a mutually respected mediator. In many cases, however, the lack of inter-party trust and conflict-related animosity may preclude joint agreement on this vital issue. Parties unable to agree upon a single neutral may request assistance from private or public conciliation services. Private entities such as the American Arbitration Association, the International Chamber of Commerce, the Lawyers Mediation Service, or J.A.M.S. may provide lists of qualified mediators. In some instances, local courts or government agencies may provide the names of potential intervenors.

If particular expertise would be helpful, the parties can request the names of individuals who possess the requisite knowledge. After the parties receive a list of qualified neutrals, they should evaluate the backgrounds of those people to ensure their impartiality and acceptability. If they have previously acted as advocates, which sides did they represent? If prior mediation clients are listed, the parties may telephone them to determine their views of the mediators. Some parties even telephone the candidates themselves to ascertain their levels of professional experience, mediation philosophies, and fee schedules.

[b]   Process of Elimination

Once the parties have reviewed the list of qualified neutrals, they can select the most acceptable candidate. If they are unable to agree upon a single person, they may agree to strike names alternately until one remains. That individual then becomes their intervenor. In rare instances in which the parties are not satisfied with any of the names on the provided list, they may request an additional list of candidates. Since party confidence in the designated neutral is critical to that individual's capacity to provide effective mediation assistance, the disputants should take the time to select someone with whom they are likely to feel comfortable.

§ 16.07 PARTY AND MEDIATOR PREPARATION

[1]   Recognizing Importance

Parties frequently fail to appreciate the fact that mediation is *assisted negotiation*. As a result, they go to conciliation sessions unprepared. This lack of planning causes many advocates to be less forceful than they could have been. It also undermines the capacity of neutral intervenors to perform their functions effectively.

[2]   Lawyer

[a]   Understanding Mediation as Negotiation

Parties should prepare for mediation as they would for any negotiation (Abramson, 2005; Abramson, 2004, at 153–217; Kovach, 2004, at 151–54). They must be thoroughly familiar with the operative facts and relevant legal doctrines. They should also review the previous bargaining sessions with their opponents, to comprehend how their transaction has developed and why they may have been unable to achieve mutually acceptable terms on their own. They must appreciate the underlying needs and interests of their own client and those of the other side. They must remember the negotiating styles of their opponents. Advocates must realize the need to be prepared *to negotiate* during the impending mediation sessions — with the neutral intervenor, through that person with their adversaries, and directly with their opponents.

[b]   Careful Review of Positions and Nonsettlement Options

Negotiators should formulate principled opening positions that can be divided into components and be rationally defended on a component-by-component basis during their mediation sessions. They may decide to prepare formal pre-mediation position statements they can either send to the mediator ahead of time or take to the initial group session (Herman, Cary & Kennedy, 2001, at 332–33). They must reconsider their initially established goals in light of their previous negotiation exchanges with their adversaries. They should either reconfirm the propriety of their prior bargaining objectives, or develop rationales to support their modified goals. They must finally review their nonsettlement alternatives to ensure they do not make the mistake of accepting mediator-generated terms that are actually worse than what would happen if no agreement were achieved. This error occasionally happens when parties try to please the neutral participants and forget about their own needs and interests. Parties must always remember that no agreement is preferable to one that is less beneficial than their best nonsettlement option.

[c]   Familiarity with Mediator

Advocates should attempt to become familiar with the mediation style of the designated conciliator. Is that individual evaluative/directive, facilitative/elicitive, or relationship-oriented/transformative? Are they likely to be an active or a passive participant? Are they going to ask general or specific questions regarding each side's circumstances? If they have not dealt with this person before, advocates should not hesitate to ask other attorneys about the mediation style of the neutral participant.

[3]   Client

[a]   Against Intimidation and Open Speech

If clients are expected to attend the initial mediation session, the advocates must prepare their respective clients for what may be expected to occur (Abramson, 2004, at 229–37; Herman, Cary & Kennedy, 2001, at 329–31; Lawrence, 2000, at 428–29). Clients should be especially cautioned about neutral intervenors who like to directly challenge the positions and opinions of the parties. This minimizes the likelihood clients will be unduly intimidated by that kind of behavior. Clients should generally be instructed not to speak when the attorneys and the mediator are directly interacting. Instead of making open statements that may undermine their own interests, they should be told to communicate in private with their own advocate. Clients should also be cautioned about nonverbal signals, to minimize the likelihood they will inadvertently disclose confidential information to their opponents.

[b]   Clients Negotiating Directly with Mediator

Is the mediator someone who likes to interact directly with the clients themselves? If yes, each client must be prepared for this possibility. In some instances, it may be beneficial to give the client a mini-course on negotiating to enable that person to forcefully advance his or her own interests when asked to do so. This type of preparation is particularly important with respect to mediators who ask the legal representatives to leave the room so that he or she may discuss the transaction with the clients alone. If an attorney thinks that his or her client would be at an unfair disadvantage if he or she had to negotiate without the assistance of counsel, the lawyer should refuse to leave the client alone.

[4]   Mediator

[a]   Full Knowledge of Relevant Documents

Designated mediators should also prepare for scheduled sessions to the extent possible (Kovach, 2004, at 142–51). They should review any written materials given to them by the parties to familiarize themselves with the basic issues, the current party positions, and apparent party interests. Conciliators involved with litigation disputes generally receive copies of the complaint, answer, and relevant motions. These documents can provide them with important information. Even neutrals dealing with transactional controversies may be given copies of prior proposals and supporting position statements. These can be quite informative.

[b]   Familiarity with Negotiator Styles Involved

It can be beneficial for mediators to become familiar with advocate negotiating styles prior to scheduled meetings. They may ask other conciliators or other advocates they know regarding the individuals with whom they must interact. For example, when former President Carter was preparing for his Camp David meetings with Egypt's Anwar Sadat and Israel's Menachem Begin, he reviewed detailed psychological profiles on each that had been prepared for him by United States intelligence experts (Kolb, 1994, at 377). He believed that this information was particularly helpful when he was attempting to determine the appeals that would be likely to persuade the foreign leaders involved and the topics he should avoid discussing.

[c]   Plan of Action

Mediators should think about how they plan to conduct their initial session with the parties, and how they plan to conduct subsequent joint sessions (Moore, 2003, at 102–117). How do they plan to help the disputants define the relevant issues and explore their underlying needs and interests? How do they hope to use separate caucus sessions to further their problem-solving function? Table 4 sets forth a brief checklist that mediators should consider as they prepare for scheduled conciliation interactions.

TABLE 4
Mediation Preparation Form

A. OBJECTIVES DURING JOINT SESSIONS WITH PARTIES:

1. How do you plan to explain your function to the parties as a neutral, communication/problem-solving facilitator? How will you communicate the confidentiality of party-mediator discussions and the inadmissibility of settlement talks if final accords are not achieved?

2. What are the issues that must be resolved if a mutual accord is to be achieved?

3. What are the current positions of the parties with respect to each of the relevant issues?

4. Do the parties appear to understand each other's positions and underlying interests? Do they comprehend the relevant factual circumstances and operative legal doctrines? If not, how do you plan to educate them?

B. OBJECTIVES DURING SEPARATE SESSIONS WITH PARTIES:

1. What does each party hope to achieve and what are the underlying interests each is endeavoring to satisfy?

2. What information should you know that the parties have been unwilling to disclose in front of their opponents? What secret concerns do they have regarding the possible impact of this transaction on other deals?

3. What issues can be given to one party at minimal cost to the other party? What issues involve significantly conflicting interests? Try to emphasize the areas of overlap and minimize the areas of conflict.

4. What unexplored alternatives might reasonably satisfy the underlying interests of the parties? How does each think the other's underlying interests should be satisfied?

5. What overall package would optimally satisfy the underlying interests of the parties? How can you most forcefully explain the benefits to be derived by each party from the overall package being considered?

§ 16.08   PRELIMINARY MEDIATOR — PARTY CONTACT AND INITIAL SESSION

[1]   Impartiality

When parties first select a mediator, or a conciliation service or judicial official designates a neutral intervenor, the parties either contact that individual or that person contacts them. It is imperative that these contacts be handled in a manner that avoids any appearance of partiality (Moore, 2003, at 85–101). One party frequently telephones the mediator to inform them of their appointment and to schedule the first meeting. While it is appropriate for the contacting party to describe the general controversy, some mediators are hesitant to have the caller describe their own side's position. They fear that such one-sided communication at this early stage may cause the other side to suspect possible mediator bias. Similar procedures are generally followed if the mediator contacts each party separately.

Mediators with judicial or arbitral backgrounds often feel uncomfortable with ex parte discussions of a substantive nature during preliminary contacts with parties. Such ex parte conversations would be considered improper if conducted with actual adjudicators to prevent possible undue influence over the decision-making process without the knowledge of the other side. Experienced neutrals recognize, however, that different considerations apply to mediation interactions. The parties understand that neutral facilitators lack the authority to impose terms on non-consenting participants, and they realize that most mediation encounters involve the use of separate caucus sessions that permit ex parte discussions between the parties and the conciliators. These mediators thus accept the propriety of detailed ex parte discussions from the beginning that enable the neutral facilitators to commence the learning process.

When mediators contact client attorneys, they should request the attendance at the initial session by the client, or, if a corporation or organization is involved, a person with authority to speak on behalf of that entity (Golann, 1996, at 176–77). Having such individuals participate in the first mediation session is important for two reasons. Mediators wish to be sure the clients are fully aware of the relevant issues involved and the interests of the other side. In addition, it is difficult to move toward final settlement agreements when the people who have to approve the basic elements are not present (Golann, 1996, at 176–79).

[2]   Simultaneous Communications

To avoid possible misunderstandings, parties often arrange conference calls that permit them to speak to the neutral intervenor together. Mediators who must initially telephone the parties frequently use this same technique to communicate with both sides simultaneously. Nonetheless, some neutrals consider these precautions unnecessary. They do not hesitate to call the parties separately or to accept ex parte communications and to discuss particular party positions during these exchanges. They assume that both sides recognize that they are doing this and will not allow these contacts to compromise their impartiality.

[3]   Discernment of Important Topics

During their preliminary communications with the parties, mediators generally provide a brief summary of their view of the conciliation process (Kovach, 2004, at 160–62). They emphasize their impartial function and the fact they do not plan to support the positions of either side. They remind the participants that they lack the authority to impose any terms the parties do not find mutually acceptable. They may note that while adjudications focus primarily on past events as courts or arbitrators try to determine who was right or wrong, mediation is a forward-looking process designed to help the parties reach agreements that will solve their problems and enable them to move ahead. Most neutrals note that all mediation discussions will remain confidential and may not be used in subsequent judicial or arbitral proceedings. If voluntary mediation is involved, mediators should be certain the parties have knowingly agreed to participate in the conciliation process. This is especially important when parties are not represented by legal counsel (Nolan-Haley, 1999, at 832–33).

[4]   Initial Meeting Space Considerations

[a]   Location

Most mediators prefer to conduct the initial meeting at a neutral location — the mediator's office or another non-party site (Golann, 1996, at 96–97; Slaikeu, 1996, at 65–66). They reasonably fear that if they meet at the offices of one of the parties, the other side may feel intimidated or disrespected. Nonetheless, when the parties themselves express a desire to meet at one side's place of business, neutrals normally honor that request.

[b]   Room

An ideal meeting room has enough space to accommodate all of the participants, is sufficiently private to preclude unwanted interruptions, and has external space that may be used for separate caucus sessions by the parties alone or with mediator involvement. The furniture should be arranged in a nonconfrontational configuration (Moore, 2003, at 154–56). When bargaining adversaries who have been unable to achieve mutual accords interact, they tend to sit directly across from one another in highly combative positions. They often sit with their arms folded across their chests and with their legs crossed — highly unreceptive postures. Neutral intervenors should endeavor to create more conciliatory atmospheres (Kagel & Kelly, 1989, at 109). Appropriate seating arrangements can also diminish the impact of power imbalances that may exist (Wiseman & Poitras, 2002, at 56–57).

[5]   Initiating Non-Adversarial Communications

Mediators should make sure the disputants initially shake hands and take seats that are not directly across from one another. A round table may be used with the mediator on one side and the parties situated relatively close to each other along the same portion of the table. If a square or rectangular table is used, the parties should be positioned along adjoining sides in an "L" configuration or adjacent to one another along the same side. Whenever possible, the participants should be encouraged to address each other on a first name basis to reinforce the informal and personal nature of the interaction. It is generally easier for people to disagree with impersonal opponents than personalized adversaries. In addition, the creation of positive moods in the disputants increases the likelihood of cooperative behavior and decreases the probability of competitive conduct (Shapiro, 2002, at 69–70).

[6]   Establishing Leadership Role

Mediators should assume control over the sessions (Slaikeu, 1996, at 75–76; Golann, 1996, at 26–27). Someone must determine how the discussions are going to proceed, and the neutral participants are in the best position to do this. If they fail to assume a leadership role, the negotiations may deteriorate into unproductive adversarial exchanges. The establishment of mediator control also enhances the ultimate capacity of the neutral intervenors to generate discussions that are likely to produce beneficial results. Mediators should assume an optimistic demeanor that encourages the disputants to think of settlement as a mutually beneficial outcome (Golann, 1996, at 77).

[7]   Explaining Conciliation Process

As soon as the parties are comfortable, the mediator should explain the conciliation process (Boulle, Colatrella & Picchioni, 2008, at 61–75; Oberman, 2005, at 793–94; Ordover & Doneff, 2002, at 61–62; Golann, 1996, at 98–99; Slaikeu, 1996, at 77–80; Moore, 2003, at 212–220; Kovach, 2004, at 158–62). This is especially important when inexperienced advocates or clients are present. The neutral intervenors should emphasize their impartiality and the fact they lack the authority to impose settlement terms. This is especially important, because many disputants who participate in mediated discussions feel that they lack control over the outcomes that may be agreed upon (Welsh, 2002, at 183–84). Mediation is not a win-lose adjudication, but a win-win form of assisted negotiation. The mediators are merely present to encourage inter-party bargaining and facilitate the consideration of alternative proposals. The parties will have the final say with respect to any terms that may be agreed upon. The mediator should explain the use of joint sessions and the possible use of separate caucus sessions to promote the mediation process. When necessary, the mediator may articulate behavioral guidelines designed to ensure full party participation in an orderly and nondisruptive manner (Moore, 2003, at 219–20).

Individuals who participate in mediated settlement discussions judge the fairness of those procedures not only by the substantive terms agreed upon, but also by their perception of the procedural fairness involved (Welsh, 2002, at 184–85; Welsh, 2001, at 791–92, 817–830). "The presence of four particular process elements result in heightened perceptions of procedural justice: the opportunity for disputants to express their 'voice,' assurance that a third party considered what they said, and treatment that is both even-handed and dignified." (Welsh, 2002, at 185) Mediators should always emphasize the fact that the disputants will have the chance to express their concerns fully in circumstances that guarantee careful consideration by both the other disputants and the neutral facilitators. They should also make it clear that the mediation process will be completely even-handed and conducted in a dignified and impartial manner. By articulating these critical safeguards at the outset, mediators can begin to enhance disputant perceptions of procedural justice.

[8]   Importance of Confidentiality

[a]   Reminding Litigants

Confidentiality is a crucial aspect of the mediation process. It is also important for mediators to establish trust — both in themselves and the mediation process (Deason, 2006, at 1393–94). These factors encourage the participants to speak openly about their interests, concerns, and desires. If they thought that their candid disclosures could be used against them in subsequent proceedings, few participants would be forthcoming and little progress could be made. Most mediators specifically remind litigants that evidentiary rules generally preclude the admission of settlement discussions in subsequent arbitral or judicial proceedings (Fed. Rule of Evidence 408; Erickson & McKnight, 2001, at 201–05; Kovach, 2004, at 269–70; Kirtley, 1995). Some experts believe that mediators should ask the disputants for permission to take notes, promising to use those notes solely to further the mediation process (Moore, 2003, at 219). Despite oral and even written confidentiality agreements, parties occasionally seek to introduce mediation statements in subsequent judicial proceedings (Cole, 2006, at 1424–25). Courts should refuse to admit such evidence, and should sanction parties who deliberately violate confidentiality provisions.

[b]   During Separate Caucus Sessions

Confidentiality is especially important with respect to disclosures made during separate caucus sessions conducted by the mediator with each side. Neutral intervenors must emphasize the fact that all information disclosed during separate caucuses will remain confidential — unless the interested party authorizes the mediator to convey that knowledge to the other side or disclosure is required under a special statute pertaining to the particular circumstances involved (Kirtley, 1995). Mediators frequently remind the participants that they may not be compelled by either party to divulge conciliation session disclosures in any other forum. Some mediators express these ground rules in written form and give copies to the participants, while others rely upon their oral representations (Golann, 1996, at 106–10).

[9]   Receiving Uninterrupted Views and Positions

[a]   Asking Litigants to Summarize

Once the fundamental guidelines have been established, mediators generally ask the parties to summarize their respective positions (Boulle, Colatrella & Picchioni, 2008, at 75–82; Kovach, 2004, at 162–67). Each side is given the opportunity to accomplish this objective free from opponent interruptions (Moore, 2003, at 221–31; Taylor, 2002, at 134–36; Gulliver, 1979, at 221–25). Whenever one side objects to something contained in the other side's presentation, they are gently but firmly told they will have the chance to express their views once this party has finished speaking. During these summaries, mediators usually take brief notes, and they occasionally ask questions to clarify uncertain points. They want to be certain they fully comprehend the underlying issues and interests (Sinclair & Stewart, 2007, at 204–07). They also want to be certain each side has heard the other's perspective. Mediators should carefully listen for allusions to hidden agendas that are not being openly discussed by the disputants, but will have to be addressed before mutual accords can be achieved (Folberg & Taylor, 1984, at 42–43).

Mediators should recognize the different types of interests being expressed (Boulle, Colatrella & Picchioni, 2008, at 86). Some will be the type of *substantive* issues negotiating parties openly discuss. These may involve money or the way in which a contractual provision is to be applied. Mediator assisted negotiation should enable the parties to address these matters in an objective and detached manner. Some may concern *procedural* issues which pertain to the way in which the dispute has been handled by one or both parties. The mediation process should diminish the impact of these concerns by providing both parties with a fair and open interactive process. Others may relate to *psychological* issues that concern emotional needs, such as a desire fro respect or sympathy. These matters may be addressed during cathartic expressions that enable each side to indicate how they feel regarding the way in which they have been treated.

Litigants often confuse the mediation function with the adjudication process, and they make opening statements that would be more appropriate in court room settings (Herman, Cary & Kennedy, 2001, at 334; Lawrence, 2000, at 426–28). They forget the fact that conciliators lack the authority to impose terms on the disputants. Instead of making legal arguments designed to generate favorable mediator rulings, they should discuss the underlying issues in a manner designed both to educate the opposing side and to precipitate joint problem-solving efforts (Abramson, 2004, at 195–204; Taylor, 2002, at 134–36). They must make statements that will induce the opposing party to begin a collaborative process that should lead toward mutually acceptable settlement terms.

[b]   Active Listening

Full party disclosure may be enhanced through "active listening." (Boulle, Colatrella & Picchioni, 2008, at 142–26; Ladd, 2005, at 125; Kovach, 2004, at 52–53; Golann, 1996, at 75–76). Nonjudgmental but empathetic interjections such as "I understand," "I see," "I understand how you feel," "um hum," etc. can be used to encourage participant openness (Moore, 2003, at 175–77, 197–98; Slaikeu, 1996, at 227–29; Kovach, 2004, at 52–55). Warm eye contact and an open face can also be beneficial. This approach encourages both sides to thoroughly express their underlying feelings and beliefs in a relatively sympathetic atmosphere (Della Noce, 1999, at 283–86). The mediator is actively listening to their circumstances, and each party feels that the opposing side is finally being forced to appreciate their side of the controversy. After the parties have summarized their respective positions, it is generally beneficial for the neutral to restate those positions to demonstrate a basic comprehension of the relevant information and to reflect the apparent feelings of the parties (Folberg & Taylor, 1984, at 112–14). This lets the participants know that they have been heard and their feelings have been validated.

[10]   Controlled Cathartic Venting

When emotionally-charged controversies and relationships are involved, cathartic "venting" may permit the dissipation of strong feelings that may preclude the realistic consideration of possible solutions. The mediator should allow the requisite venting in an environment that is likely to minimize the creation of unproductive animosity (Ladd, 2005, at 35–60; Golann, 2004, at 549–50; Moore, 2003, at 172–77; Golann, 2002, at 309–10; Kovach, 2004, at 64–69). While candid feelings may be expressed, intemperate personal attacks must not be tolerated. Extreme statements can be adroitly reframed to make them more palatable to the other side (Ladd, 2005, at 35–37; Slaikeu, 1996, at 232–33). For example, "I don't think that referring to X as a 'total jerk' or an 'asshole' is likely to induce X to consider your position with an open mind. Let's focus instead on the specific issues that are bothering you." Once both sides have been allowed to participate fully in the cathartic process, they may be able to put their emotional baggage behind them and get on with more productive discussions (Sinclair & Stewart, 2007, at 200–01; Evans & Evans, 2002, at 88). This phenomenon explains why mediators must be attuned to emotional intelligence that eneables them to deal with disputant emotional feelings (Ladd, 2005; Schreier, 2002).

To enhance the cathartic process, it is important for clients to attend initial mediation sessions (Welsh, 2001, at 845, 852–55). Even if opening statements are made on their behalf by their legal representatives, the clients should be asked if they wish to speak. They will often disclose personal feelings that must be heard and addressed before they will be ready to seek closure of their disputes through settlement agreements. If their need for cathartic venting is not recognized, they may feel dissatisfied with the final terms agreed upon even when those terms are substantively fair. In some cases, if their attorneys have done a good job of expressing their feelings, the clients will decline the opportunity to speak for themselves and be perfectly satisfied with the procedural fairness of the mediation process.

One way to enhance the healing process involves the use of a sincere apology at the conclusion of the cathartic process (see generally Pavlick, 2003). This does not require one party to admit culpability. They may merely indicate how sorry they are that the other side has suffered a loss, recognizing the financial or emotional trauma sustained. They may alternatively state how sorry they are the opponent feels the way he or she does, acknowledging that party's feelings. On some occasions, a full admission of responsibility and a forthright apology may be necessary to enable the disputants to get beyond their current controversy. This may be especially true with respect to parties with on-going relationships that have been negatively affected by the existing dispute.

[11] Assisting Mutual Understanding and Neutral Reformulation of Underlying Issues

During their frequently protracted one-on-one negotiations, parties that have been unable to achieve mutual accommodations of their competing interests often lock themselves into unalterable "principled" positions. They reach the point at which they are merely reiterating their respective positions in a nonconciliatory manner. They are so intent on the advancement of their own interests that they fail to listen meaningfully to the representations and suggestions being articulated by their opponents (Matz, 1999).

When mediators become involved in the negotiation process, they must initially endeavor to reestablish meaningful communication between the parties (Moore, 2003, at 196–200; Lawrence, 2000, at 436–37). If conciliation efforts are to have a beneficial impact, the participants must be induced to listen carefully to one another and to the neutral intervenor. They must be persuaded to appreciate the underlying interests and fundamental objectives of each other. During the initial joint session, the mediator must assist the parties to reopen blocked communication channels. If the parties cannot agree upon the precise issues to be resolved and if each prefers its own often value-laden formulations, the neutral should reframe the underlying problems in a way that is acceptable to both sides (Moore, 2003, at 236–42; Kovach, 2004, at 180–81). This neutral reformulation of the underlying issues can induce the participants to begin to view the disputed items in a more dispassionate manner.

The presence of individual clients or corporate officers with decision-making authority is normally required at the first formal mediation conference to ensure their comprehension of the exact status of their particular negotiations. It is beneficial to have both parties articulate their respective positions in environments in which each is compelled to listen to the underlying reasoning and objectives of the other. This procedure may induce previously recalcitrant opponents to acquire a greater appreciation for rationales that have been summarily rejected in a pro forma manner during prior discussions. This technique also allows neutral intervenors to obtain and demonstrate an unbiased familiarity with the operative facts and applicable legal doctrines. This enhances their credibility and the acceptability of settlement proposals they subsequently suggest.

[12] Role-Reversal

When it appears that one or both advocates are not seriously listening to the positions being articulated by opposing counsel, it may be beneficial to employ a different approach. Each participant may be asked to summarize the views of the other side until it is apparent that he or she actually understands the other party's situation. This *role-reversal technique* generally enhances each party's respect for the other side's interests and positions. It can also diminish the impact of the "attribution bias" (Korobkin, 2006, at 598–300) which causes people to blame others for negative consequences they suffer — and blame external factors beyond their own control for negative results they may have contributed to.

[13]   Recognizing Roadblocks

Neutral intervenors must recognize the factors that are likely to impede an objective exploration of the pertinent factual and legal issues by the parties during initial settlement conferences. The frustrations that have been generated during the previous unsuccessful negotiations may have made it difficult for the disputants to evaluate the relevant circumstances in an objective manner. Their myopic focus on their unyielding positions may have made them unable to imagine alternative formulations. These alternatives may beneficially accommodate their competing interests. Proficient mediators can effectively reopen blocked communication channels and induce recalcitrant participants to interact on a more open and professional basis.

[14]   Enlightening Without Embarrassing

Communication problems occasionally arise from unrealistic client expectations. Mediators should be cognizant of direct or indirect indications that lawyers are having difficulty moderating excessive client aspirations. For example, although legal practitioners may acknowledge the reasonableness of opposing counsel's positions, they may suggest that their client is unwilling to consider those terms. Other lawyers may merely express client opposition to settlement proposals without providing any support for the client intransigence. When it becomes apparent that clients do not appreciate the legal, factual, and/or economic realities involved, neutral intervenors should attempt to enlighten those people in a fashion that does not embarrass them or their legal representatives (Golann, 1996, at 50–53). An objective but candid discussion of the way in which similar cases or transactions have recently been adjudicated or resolved can be particularly persuasive. The parties can then be asked why they think their circumstances are so different from these prior situations (Ordover & Doneff, 2002, at 71–73).

[15]   Alleviating Client Distrust of Own Counsel

Mediators must appreciate the fact that some clients do not entirely trust their own legal counsel. This is especially true with respect to plaintiffs who are being represented on a contingent fee basis. These claimants may fear that their attorneys are more interested in expeditious settlements than protracted adjudications, especially when the settlements may enable them to obtain their fee more quickly. When such client suspicions are detected and it appears that counsel are actually providing accurate legal advice, mediators should not hesitate to indicate how proficiently their attorneys are advancing their interests.

[16]   Low-Profile Mediation

During some introductory conciliation meetings, the parties begin to negotiate meaningfully with one another. If they appear to be making actual progress, it is a propitious moment for the neutral participant to engage in passive mediation. The intervenor should smile benignly at the person speaking, until they are finished. If the mediator then turns toward the other party for a response, they are likely to generate further discussion. As long as the parties continue to exchange information and ideas, the mediator should maintain a low profile and permit the advocates to conduct their own talks. When inter-party communication begins to lag, the conciliator may interject questions designed to stimulate further negotiation progress or suggest alternatives the participants may not have contemplated.

[17]   Appraisal of Real Distance Between Litigants

At the conclusion of initial mediation sessions, particularly those pertaining to law suits, some mediators ask the advocates to confidentially indicate on separate sheets of paper the minimum settlement terms they would be willing to accept. This information is not to be divulged to opposing counsel, but is intended to apprise the mediator of the real distance remaining between the litigants. In some situations, conciliators discover that the parties are much closer together than their publicly stated positions otherwise indicated.

§ 16.09   SUBSEQUENT SESSIONS

[1]   With Lawyers Alone

Although clients should normally be required to attend initial conciliation conferences to allow mediators to ascertain their expectations and to permit their enlightenment when necessary, it is frequently preferable to conduct subsequent settlement discussions with the lawyers alone. This is especially likely when commercial or employment disputes are involved. Those professionals tend to have a better understanding of the mediation function. Furthermore, when clients are present, legal advocates feel the need to engage in more posturing and to openly support the positions of their clients (Neale & Bazerman, 1991, at 6). In the absence of clients, they are usually more forthcoming regarding the strengths and weaknesses of their positions. If the lawyers can be convinced that certain proposals are reasonable, they can normally be expected to recommend those terms to their clients. If it appears that attorneys will encounter unrealistic client resistance, mediators can agree to meet with them and their clients to provide additional support for the recommended provisions.

[2]   Direct Client Involvement

In some cases, such as divorce or neighborhood mediation, it is neither possible nor desirable to preclude direct client involvement (Abramson, 2004, at 186–92). Their presence is necessary both to defuse emotional difficulties and to begin the healing process that is especially important when future child custody or neighbor interactions will be prescribed (*see generally* Taylor, 2002). Similar concerns may militate in favor of client presence with respect to the mediation of other emotionally charged conflicts (*see generally* Relis, 2007). When these situations are involved, the neutral intervenors must establish guidelines that permit meaningful client participation during the cathartic process and encourage beneficial settlement discussions (Erickson & McKnight, 2001, at 23–35). Disputants who directly participate in facilitated settlement discussions are more likely to view the mediation process favorably than those who do not personally participate (Resnik, 2002, at 155; Bingham, 2002, at 109–110; Mc Ewen & Wissler, 2002, at 140–41).

When clients attend mediation sessions, their degree of personal animosity toward each other may occasionally become an impediment to fruitful discussions. When this happens, mediators may decide to ask the clients to skip the next session or two to permit the conciliator and the attorneys to explore settlement options in a less confrontational atmosphere (Herman, Cary & Kennedy, 2001, at 344). The lawyers can keep their clients informed of developments, and can articulate client interests during the session they do not attend. Once the clients have had time to calm down and appreciate the progress being made, they can be invited to rejoin the discussions.

§ 16.10   EXPLORING INNOVATIVE SETTLEMENT ALTERNATIVES

[1]   Enhancing the Process

[a]   Encouraging Further Exploration

Advocates who have reached an impasse during their own negotiations frequently focus exclusively on their own stated positions causing them to ignore other possible options. Neither party is willing to suggest new alternatives, lest they be perceived as weak. Neutral intervenors can significantly enhance the bargaining process by encouraging the parties to explore other formulations in a non-threatening manner under circumstances that do not require either advocate to make overt concessions (Moore, 2003, at 252–68; Erickson & McKnight, 2001, at 64; Lawrence, 2000, at 432–33; Folberg & Taylor, 1984, at 49–53). If the way in which particular issues are phrased appears to impede open discussions, the mediator can either reframe them in a manner both parties find palatable or divide those issues into manageable subparts (Moore, 2003, at 236–42; Kovach, 2004, at 236–38).

[b]   Scheduling Special Meetings

A special meeting may be scheduled for the express purpose of permitting the exploration of alternative settlement options (Moore, 2003, at 252–59; Fisher & Ury, 1981, at 58–83). The conciliator should encourage the parties to explain their needs, interests, and objectives (Welsh, 2001, at 855–56; Matz, 1999). The advocates should be prompted by careful, gentle probing to discuss these critical issues (Bannink, 2007, at 168–72). What does each side really hope to achieve? What do the parties fear might occur if they do not attain their goals or if they accede to certain proposals being suggested by their opponent? If the participants can be induced to express themselves in a candid fashion, this substantially enhances the likelihood of negotiated resolutions (Fisher & Ury, 1981, at 41–57). Whenever possible, the mediator should introduce objective standards the parties can use to guide their evaluations and exchanges (Folberg & Taylor, 1984, at 57).

[c]   Interests and Needs Analysis

An effective needs and interests analysis stimulates the disclosure of information not previously divulged (Kagel & Kelly, 1989, at 123–24). Communication channels are usually reopened, and stalled negotiations are revitalized in a way that does not cause either party to suffer a loss of face (Folberg & Taylor, 1984, at 53–57). Mediator patience is crucial during this phase, because it takes time for the advocates to move from the adversarial mode to the cooperative mode. If the neutral facilitator attempts to rush things, the problem-solving process is likely to break down. Once relatively cooperative communication has been reestablished, conciliator silence, accompanied by supportive smiles and gestures, may be sufficient to encourage the parties to engage in meaningful bargaining. When necessary, the interjection of nonthreatening inquiries and suggested options may be employed to maintain a positive negotiating environment.

[d]   Detrimental Nature of Competitive Interactions

The parties must be encouraged to explore bargaining alternatives that have not been previously considered due to the competitive nature of their interaction. Law suit disputants must recognize their capacity to formulate solutions that could not be achieved through the adjudication process. For example, an individual suing a neighbor who cut down a beautiful tree on the complaining party's side of their property line may prefer a sincere apology and a replacement tree over protracted litigation and a permanently strained relationship. A plaintiff involved in a defamation action may prefer an immediate public retraction to the possibility of future monetary relief. Divorcing spouses may consider special child-care arrangements that a judge would be reluctant to order. A severely injured plaintiff may prefer a structured settlement that will guarantee lifetime care to a substantial present verdict that may be exhausted prematurely.

[2]   Transactional Negotiations

[a]   Circumstances Warranting Exploration

Even transactional negotiators should be encouraged to examine unarticulated alternatives (Peppet, 2004). If parties discussing an international business arrangement cannot agree whether to specify contractual payment in the currency of the seller or the purchaser, they may consider the use of a market-basket currency such as that of the European Union. Parties disagreeing on the official language to govern their relationship may agree upon a dual language approach or the use of a neutral third language. Parties negotiating the sale of business assets may disagree about the one to assume the risk of unknown liability. The buyer typically wants to exclude responsibility for unknown liabilities, while the seller wants the buyer to assume these risks. These firms can resolve their controversy by establishing an escrow account funded by the buyer. This account would cover unknown liabilities for a specified period of time. The excess escrow funds would be returned to the buyer at the expiration of that time period.

[b]   Encouraging Consideration of Mutually Beneficial Options

Reasonable substitutes for articulated demands should be sought during these brainstorming sessions. The participants should be encouraged to think of options that would beneficially satisfy the underlying needs and interests of both sides (Lang & Taylor, 2000, at 27–28; Folberg & Taylor, 1984, at 49–53). They need to engage in cooperative problem-solving that is designed to generate "win-win" results (Hartje, 1984, at 173–74). Significant issues must be distinguished from less important matters, and the parties must be induced to focus primarily on those topics that have to be resolved if a final accord is to be achieved. How might the critical needs of each client be satisfied or protected by different options? Which alternatives acceptable to one side would least trammel the interests of the other party?

[c] Role Reversal

It is occasionally helpful to have the advocates engage in role reversal. Once the underlying needs and interests of the parties have been discerned, each legal representative can be asked to indicate the ways in which his or her opponent's rights may be optimally protected (Hartje, 1984, at 161). This technique may generate options that have been previously ignored. It should simultaneously induce each side to develop a greater appreciation for the needs of the other side.

[d] Face-Saving Party Movement

Mediators should try not to place disputants in positions in which they would be required to make overt capitulations. A face-saving means of compromise should be provided whenever possible. For example, a significant concession may be counterbalanced by a seemingly reciprocal relinquishment to preserve the aura of mutuality. Lawyers should be provided with rationales they can use to convince their clients of the reasonableness of settlement proposals their principals might otherwise be reluctant to accept.

[e] Passive-Aggressive Individuals

[i] Danger

Conciliators should be particularly wary of passive-aggressive individuals who do not directly reject suggested solutions advanced during mediation discussions. They indirectly undermine the negotiation process either by obliquely undercutting apparently reasonable offers ("*Yes*, that is a generous proposal, *but* it does not sufficiently advance the interests of my particular client because . . . ") or by employing procrastination or tardiness to subvert settlement talks. These people usually find negotiations and the concomitant auction process distasteful, but are unable to express these fellings overtly.

[ii] Eliciting Definitive Party Objectives

It is frequently beneficial to ask passive-aggressive negotiators to articulate the specific objectives of their respective clients, to compel them to state definitive positions that may provide the basis for further discussions. These individuals must be forced to participate actively in the conciliation process as formulators of alternative proposals and not merely as critics of suggestions made by others. On the other hand, if a number of participants are involved in the particular transaction, a passive-aggressive impediment to settlement may be temporarily ignored until the others have agreed upon specified terms. These conditions can then be presented to the passive-aggressive person as a fait accompli that he or she would be likely to accept due to the absence of viable alternatives.

[f] "True Believer" Personality

[i] Danger

Litigators who exhibit "true-believer," win-lose personality traits (Hoffer, 1951) may similarly challenge the patience of the most professional mediators. These people often lack the capacity to tolerate the uncertainty associated with close cases, and they minimize their internal dissonance by convincing themselves of the unassailable virtue of their positions (Kahneman & Tversky, 1995, at 46–49). By the time they have completed their pretrial preparations, they have become certain of total victory. A similar difficulty can be caused by "optimistic overconfidence" which induces plaintiffs to over-estimate the probability of their success at trial and causes defendants to similarly over-estimate their own side's likelihood of success at trial (Korobkin, 2006, at 284–88). It is particularly difficult for conciliators to deal with these people, because they fear that their acknowledgment of weakness will undermine their ability to aggressively litigate the matter if necessary. Transactional negotiators occasionally exhibit true-believer styles, as they convince themselves of their entitlement to everything they have requested from their opponents.

[ii] Inducing Exploration of Relevant Issues

Adroit mediators may induce true-believer individuals to explore the relevant issues in an abstract, hypothetical fashion that permits them to detach the conciliation evaluations from the circumstances of the actual interaction. For example: "If, for the sake of discussion, we were to assume . . . , how might this hypothetical issue by appropriately analyzed and resolved?" It is almost never productive for conciliators to directly challenge the personally held beliefs of true-believer negotiators, because they are normally able to reject those overtures in a manner that allows them to preserve their false inner confidence and prevent meaningful exploration of the underlying issues.

[g] Watching for Signs of Impasse

Joint conciliation sessions do not always move inexorably toward mutual accords. Mediators must be cognizant of those verbal and nonverbal signals that indicate that joint meetings are approaching an irreconcilable impasse (Lang & Taylor, 2000, at 25–27). The parties are continuing to place exaggerated emphasis on unyielding, legalistic positions designed more to impress their respective clients than to influence their opponents. They may have changed their seating arrangement from a cooperative setting into a more confrontational configuration — sitting directly opposite each other. The participants may be wringing their hands and/or gnashing their teeth in utter frustration regarding the lack of progress, or they have crossed their arms and legs in a wholly unreceptive manner. When these negative signs are perceived, it may be time to suggest separate mediation sessions.

§ 16.11 CONDUCTING SEPARATE MEDIATION SESSIONS

[1] Benefit

When joint meetings do not achieve fruitful results, it is frequently beneficial to propose separate caucuses that will enable neutral participants to meet individually with each side (Boulle, Colatrella & Picchioni, 2008, at 106–13; Moore, 2003, at 369–77; Herman, Cary & Kennedy, 2001, at 337–38; Moore, 1987). Since separate encounters can only be effective when undertaken with the cooperation and confidence of the parties, it is advantageous to ask the participants if they would be amenable to a bifurcated approach. If one side is really opposed to this technique, it would be unlikely that separate sessions would be productive. In most instances, the parties readily consent to separate caucuses, and their commitment to this process enhances the likelihood of success.

[2]   Confidentiality

[a]   As Guideline

Mediators who are considering the use of segregated discussions should explain at a joint session that they would like to explore the matter with each side individually. The conciliators should emphasize the fact that they do not intend to support either side as such. They merely wish to explore each party's underlying needs, interests, and objectives in an environment that may be more conducive to candor than a joint meeting. They must expressly promise to maintain the confidences shared by the participants during private discussions — except when they are specifically authorized to divulge the information in question. Once these basic guidelines are established, the disputants are ready for separate mediation sessions.

[b]   Expressing Intention to Disclose Only Authorized Information and Principles

During the separate meetings, conciliators must endeavor, in a non-judgmental manner, to ascertain the true underlying interests and beliefs of the respective participants (Slaikeu, 1996, at 91–109). Most mediators also begin to determine the minimal goals each side hopes to achieve. When they first meet with each participant, they should reaffirm the fact that all discussions will remain confidential unless they are expressly given permission to convey certain information to the other side. They should note, however, that they do plan to convey general principles that are divulged without disclosing particular details. For example, if a plaintiff in a wrongful termination case indicates a willingness to forego reinstatement in favor of an appropriate monetary arrangement, the neutral intervenor may have to indirectly disclose this objective when exploring possible resolutions with the defendant-employer. This would be accomplished without the disclosure of the monetary range being contemplated by the plaintiff.

[3]   Eliciting Higher Level of Disclosure

When separate caucus meetings commence, it is often advantageous for the neutral intervenors to ask each participant what they — as mediators — should know that they were unable to learn during the joint discussions. This inquiry acknowledges the fact that disputing parties are frequently willing to divulge information to conciliators in confidence that they would be unwilling to disclose in the presence of their adversaries. This question must be propounded in an open and wholly non-threatening manner to encourage the desired candor. At this stage, mediators should try not to put participants on the defensive by asking them to explain their behavior. Individuals who are asked *why* they have or have not done something are likely to withdraw from the conciliation process. It is more productive to ask them about their aspirations and their concerns.

Mediators can use private caucus sessions to control the flow of information between the parties. There are times when full disclosure of certain facts or thoughts can be an impediment to negotiation success (see generally Ayres & Nalebuff, 1997). While the disputants may be willing to disclose such information to a neutral facilitator in a confidential setting, they would not wish to have it communicated to their opponents. Mediators must be careful not to disclose things that might undermine settlement discussions, and to rephrase disclosures of an emotional or accusatory nature that might offend the other side.

[4]   Educating Participants About Negotiation Process

Neutral intervenors should be aware of the fact that particular representatives may not understand the negotiation process (Slaikeu, 1996, at 48). When necessary, conciliators should not hesitate to provide one or both sides with a mini-course on bargaining procedures. A brief discussion of the negotiation stages and the problem-solving approach may be helpful with respect to the uninitiated. Since personal embarrassment may result if this educational function were performed during joint sessions, it is preferable to cover this topic during separate meetings.

[5]   Using Conditional Offers to Generate Real Position Changes

There are occasions when negotiating parties are a great distance apart and neither is willing to make a unilateral concession of a meaningful nature lest this action be perceived as a sign of weakness. For example, in a civil suit the Plaintiff may have begun with a $2,000,000 demand and the Defendant with a $10,000 offer. The Plaintiff then moves to $1,990,000, and the Defendant counters with $15,000. After the Plaintiff goes to $1,980,000 and the Defendant offers $20,000, it becomes obvious that dramatic action is necessary if the parties hope to achieve a settlement within a reasonable period of time.

When this type of situation arises, John Estes, a highly respected Texas mediator, often uses "conditional offers" to get the parties moving. He generally begins by asking the Defendant, in a separate caucus session, if it would be willing to move to $100,000 *if* the Plaintiff were willing to come down to $1,700,000. He usually suggests a smaller increase in the Defendant's offer than decrease in the Plaintiff's demand, because plaintiffs can begin at any point and inexperienced negotiators often start with wholly unrealistic positions. He also raises this topic with the Defendant first, recognizing that if he can get the Defendant to make such a conditional offer it will look like a *sure gain* to the Plaintiff causing that party to become more risk averse under traditional "gain/loss framing" discussed in Section 6.02(8)(c). This makes it likely that the Plaintiff will respond favorably to the Defendant's conditional movement.

The risk to the Defendant is minimal. If the Plaintiff refuses to accept the Defendant's conditional offer and responds with a demand of $1,970,000, the Defendant can withdraw its conditional offer and counter with an offer of $25,000. This approach clearly indicates that no real movement will be forthcoming until the Plaintiff accepts the need for more significant position changes.

If the Defendant's conditional offer is accepted, either wholly or partially, the Plaintiff responds with a demand of $1,700,000 or $1,750,000, and the mediator asks the Defendant to make another conditional offer of $200,000 if the Plaintiff will counter with $1,400,000 or $1,500,000. After several rounds of such conditional offers, the parties may reach positions where the Plaintiff is demanding $1,100,000 and the Defendant is offering $350,000. Although the parties are still a ways apart, they have made great progress, and they have begun serious negotiations. The mediator should be able to continue to help them articulate meaningful reciprocal position changes that will move them toward common ground.

[6] Understanding Concerns Over Settlement Term Ramifications

[a] Explanations

During the early portion of separate sessions, it is often instructive to ask the participants to explain any concerns they may have regarding the ramifications they associate with specific settlement terms that are being considered. One or both parties may think that a negotiated agreement on the current issues may prejudice another matter involving the same participants or adversely affect some other relationship. If these concerns are well founded, they will have to be addressed before any resolution of the immediate controversy can be amicably obtained. For example, a defendant might fear that a settlement of the present case may generate law suits by other similarly situated individuals. A business firm may fear that an agreement with respect to the instant matter may affect other contracts that contain "most favored nation" (MFN) clauses requiring it to give equally advantageous terms to other contractual partners. A confidentiality clause may assuage the concerns of the defendant that fears additional law suits, while a rearrangement of the relevant terms may take care of the concerns of the corporation with MFN clauses in other contracts by avoiding the inclusion of provisions that would be affected by those MFN obligations.

[b] Assuaging Unfounded Client Fears

It is not unusual for mediators to conclude that the fears expressed in private by negotiating parties appear to be unfounded. A thoughtful and empathetic assessment of the real consequences of bargained results may help to alleviate the anxiety that is preventing a mutual resolution of the current problems. This must be done with sensitivity to the feelings of the concerned participants and in a manner designed to induce those parties to recognize the fact that their fears are unreasonable. The following example may be instructive:

> SIDE A NEGOTIATOR: If we enter into a ten year lease with Side B, we may lose out on a better deal that may arise in the coming years. Yet Side B is unwilling to enter into a lease of shorter duration, and this is the building we would really like to lease.

> MEDIATOR: Haven't you been looking for new space for several years now?

> SIDE A NEGOT.: Yes, we have.

> MEDIATOR: Have you noticed a lowering of rents over that period of time?

> SIDE A NEGOT.: As a matter of fact, we haven't. Rents have actually been rising at the rate of two to three percent per year.

> MEDIATOR: Do you really think Side B will be giving other parties lower rents in the next several years?

> SIDE A NEGOT.: Now that you mention it, I doubt that will happen.

If the concerns expressed by Side A regarding possible future rent reductions were valid, then the mediator would have to explore options that might assuage those fears:

> MEDIATOR: I can understand why you would not like to lock your firm into a ten year rent commitment. Would you be willing to do so if Side B agreed to include a clause promising to give your firm the benefit of any future rent reductions given to other companies? What if Side B agreed to a clause providing for the reopening of the rent issue after the first five years of the lease?

[7] Looking Out for Impediments

While meeting separately with the participants, mediators should look for possible intra-group difficulties that may impede settlement talks (Slaikeu, 1996, at 24–25, 56–57). What constituencies must be satisfied before any accord can be approved? What are their underlying interests and how may they be addressed? Are all interested constituencies currently represented at the negotiation table? If not, how might that objective be accomplished? Advocates who are ignoring constituent conflicts must be convinced of the need for full intra-group participation if the assisted discussions are to be successful.

[8] Understanding Plausibility of Positions

[a] Probing Questions

During some separate sessions, parties continue to assert wholly unrealistic positions. If mediators were to directly challenge those views, the parties would probably become defensive and more intransigent. It is more productive to explore these positions in a nonthreatening manner. This can be accomplished through the use of probing questions (Erickson & McKnight, 2001, at 64). The conciliator takes out a writing pad and explains how helpful it would be for them to fully comprehend the way in which that particular party has calculated its current position. The mediator wants to induce that side to break its overall demand/offer into components that must be valued on an individualized basis.

[b] Breaking Demand/Offer Into Components

The probing questions initially pertain to the more finite aspects of the party's position to leave minimal room for puffing. How has that side valued the real property or the destroyed automobile? If the response is realistic, the neutral intervenor writes it down and goes on to the value of the building and equipment or the lost earnings. If it is unreasonable, the conciliator may cite a recent property appraisal or blue book car valuation that is substantially different from the one being offered, followed by a seemingly innocent question regarding the way in which the participant determined its valuation. In most cases, the party will feel embarrassed and be induced to provide a more realistic figure.

Most advocates advancing unreasonable positions are unprepared for component-by-component evaluations. When they are forced to provide explanations for each aspect of their overall positions, they tend to give more defensible numbers. Once this questioning process is finished, the final figure is often one-fourth or one-fifth of what was being demanded or four or five times what was being offered. This technique can greatly narrow the distance between the disputants.

[9]   Non-Oppositional Issues

[a]   Minimizing Conflict Through Emphasis On Less Controverted Issues

When negotiators reach impasses, they are usually focusing almost entirely on their areas of disagreement. As a result, they frequently fail to consider other areas where their interests may overlap. Mediators must be especially attuned to the issues in which the interests of the parties are not diametrically opposed (Golann, 1996, at 244–46). These items should be highlighted, because they may provide the basis for cooperative solutions that may simultaneously enhance the needs of both sides. Points of immediate confrontation can be minimized through the development of alternative formulations that emphasize the areas of common interest and downplay the areas of direct conflict.

[b]   Inducing Committment to Settlement

As the parties tentatively resolve the less controverted issues, they become psychologically committed to an overall settlement. Their focus on the mutually agreeable terms begins to convince them that the conflicted items are not as important as they initially thought. They do not want to permit their substantial progress on the cooperative issues to be negated through impasses on the few remaining terms. As a result, both sides become more amenable to settlement, making the mediator's job easier.

[10]   Formulating Proposals for Final Agreement

[a]   Review of Strengths and Weaknesses

Once the underlying needs and interests have been determined and possibly acceptable alternatives have been explored with the individual parties, mediators generally attempt to formulate comprehensive proposals they hope will lead to final agreements. They may first review the strengths and weaknesses of the terms being proposed by each side to demonstrate the significant risks associated with nonsettlement (Lawrence, 2000, at 438–39; Slaikeu, 1996, at 104–05). Financial and emotional transaction costs may also be noted. At this point, the parties are likely to be most receptive to mediator-generated formulations.

[b]   Single-Text Approach

[i]   Avoiding Multiple Interpretation Problems

When a number of different issues are involved, some conciliators employ the *single text approach*. When the time is ripe, the neutral intervenors draft a single document that reflects the areas of discerned commonality and appears to entail reciprocal concessions by both sides (Slaikeu, 1996, at 123–29). After the single text is prepared, the mediator shares that document with each party during separate sessions. The neutral listens carefully to each side's criticisms and suggestions, and then redrafts the appropriate provisions. Even when advocates submit their own proposed terms, the conciliator incorporates those suggestions into the single text. In this manner, the mediator retains control over the drafting process, and he or she is only required to work with a single official document. This avoids the problems that are often created when each participant attempts to work from its own written submission.

[ii]   Controversial Aspect

Some mediators disapprove of the single text approach, because they think that mediators should not write settlement agreements for disputing parties. These mediators believe that their drafting of a single text may compromise their neutrality. They also fear that their drafting of the final terms may discourage unrepresented parties from seeking their own legal representation before they accept binding commitments. As a result of these concerns, these neutrals refuse to engage directly in the writing of settlement terms, preferring to leave that task to the disputants themselves.

[iii]   Negating Suspicion

The single-text device also enables the conciliator to negate two frequent impediments to final agreements. Advocates tend to be suspicious of proposals suggested by their adversaries. They assume that opponents are attempting to obtain provisions that satisfy their own interests. (Regarding this "reactive devaluation" tendency, see Korobkin, 2006, at 316–18; Raiffa, 2003, at 282–83; Lawrence, 2000, at 440–41; Ross, 1995, at 26 ff.) The single-text format generates an overall draft formulated by the neutral intervenor who has no reason to favor one party over the other. The participants are thus more receptive to terms coming from the unbiased mediator (Mnookin & Ross, 1995, at 23).

[iv]   Offering Sure Gains

The single-text device also enables the neutral intervenor to formulate proposals that appear to provide *gains*, rather than *losses*, for both sides. Since people tend to accept a *sure gain* over a possibly greater gain but reject a *certain loss* they might possibly avoid, final proposals that seem to guarantee *sure gains* for both sides are more likely to be found acceptable by the disputants (Korobkin & Guthrie, 1994, at 129–38). Even in the litigation context, the conciliator should emphasize the gain each side will receive from the final resolution of their controversy. The plaintiff will receive the sure benefit of the settlement, while the defendant will get the certain gain of the unexpended transaction costs saved by joint agreement.

[v]   Shuttle Mediation

As the single text provisions are being explored and redrafted, the mediator engages in "shuttle mediation." That person goes back and forth between the parties refining their suggestions.

[A]   Facilitative/Elicitive

Facilitative/elicitive mediators generally use the closing phase of the resolution process to generate mutually formulated provisions. During the separate caucuses, they listen carefully to the actual desires of the parties. They then endeavor to encourage joint problem-solving. Even though these neutral intervenors are functioning as communication facilitators between the parties, they try to limit their messages to the actual intentions of the interested participants. Instead of imposing final provisions, these neutrals merely want to participate in *assisted negotiations* in which the parties continue to control their own destinies. When they think it beneficial, they even schedule joint sessions at the end to enable the parties to structure their final terms together. The continuing presence of the neutral intervenor minimizes the likelihood that these joint discussions will deteriorate into unproductive confrontations.

[B]   Evaluative/Directive

Evaluative/directive neutrals often use this stage of the mediation process to formulate the terms they believe the parties would be willing to accept. Most mediators do not feel comfortable dictating final terms to negotiating parties, and they attempt to incorporate provisions the participants appear to desire. These neutrals would only employ a more directive approach when required by the inability of inexperienced negotiators to comprehend their own needs.

[C]   Relationship-Oriented/Transformative

Relationship-oriented/transformative conciliators tend to focus less on bargaining substance and more on the underlying inter-party relationship. During the separate sessions, they attempt to accomplish two objectives. They hope to generate sufficient participant empowerment to enable them to resolve their own conflicts. They demonstrate the options available to each side, and indicate how nonsettlements are not necessarily negative. They simultaneously endeavor to induce each side to recognize the feelings, perceptions, and motives of the other. They try to get each party to place itself in the shoes of its opponent. They believe that this recognitional process enhances the parties' mutual relationship and increases their ability to interact successfully with each other and with others in the future.

[D]   Safeguarding Client Adherence

Once the parties have agreed upon the terms contained in the mediator's text, the neutral drafter should carefully review the items agreed upon to be sure that there are no misunderstandings. They should also be certain that the specified terms satisfy the critical underlying interests of both sides (Slaikeu, 1996, at 165–57). If the conciliator is concerned that a party may subsequently attempt to modify or reject some of the pertinent provisions, they can ask the participants to indicate their assent to everything by initialing each term. The mediator may also avoid future difficulties by agreeing to prepare the final settlement agreement for the parties (Folberg & Taylor, 1984, at 60–61). This function should not entail much additional work, because the accord would be based on the final text approved by the disputants. The neutral participant would merely have to clarify ambiguous language and clean up unartfully drafted provisions.

[11]   Scheduling Future Meetings at Breakdown of Current Negotiations

When separate caucus discussions begin to break down, conciliators frequently recess the talks to give the parties time to reconsider their current positions and to permit time constraints to enhance settlement pressure. To avoid future scheduling difficulties, it is generally preferable to agree now to future joint or separate meeting dates, instead of trying to do this after the present sessions have ended. In addition, parties that have been asked to supply information to the mediator or to the other side should be given specific instructions regarding the accomplishment of this task.

[12]   Importance of Patience

When mediation efforts are not moving expeditiously toward settlement, neutral intervenors must be patient. If they attempt to rush the parties, unproductive intransigence is likely to result. It takes time for combatants to reconsider the merits of established positions and reevaluate their real nonsettlement alternatives. It is unlikely that meaningful settlement discussions can again occur until the participants have had the chance to reassess their respective situations.

[13]   Moving Toward Final Agreement

Near the end of most mediations, the parties begin to realize that mutually beneficial agreements can be achieved. How should they move from their present positions toward settlement? (Moore, 2003, at 309–318) First, they can move incrementally from their current positions toward a compromise result approximately half way between their existing offers. Each side may be hesitant to make larger concessions without being certain of opponent reciprocity. By moving together in increments, they can avoid unreciprocated position changes. Although this approach may lead to final accords, the moving parties often forego the possibility of integrative bargaining that would enable them to expand the overall pie and simultaneously improve their respective situations.

A second closure technique may involve a unilateral or joint leap to a conclusion, as either one side or both sides move directly from their current positions to a mutually acceptable result. This technique is most likely to occur after extended and often difficult negotiations, when the parties begin to appreciate the obvious result that will be acceptable to both. They no longer wish to continue incremental position changes, and one or both suggest a result they are almost certain will resolve their dispute.

A third closure device relies upon objective criteria or a consensus process to achieve final accords. With mediator assistance, the parties agree upon general principles that should guide their discussions. The parties then apply these principles to their specific issues and reach final terms. They may alternatively agree upon a formula to be used to accomplish the same result.

When other impasse-breaking methods do not produce the desired results, the parties may employ a fourth approach that relies upon procedural steps. For example, they may create a definitive time line and require each side to make alternating concessions until an agreement is achieved. Parties not moving with sufficient quickness can be penalized. If a single item, such as money is involved, the negotiators may agree to split the difference between their existing positions. When multi-issue disputes are involved, the participants can agree to have each alternately choose how to resolve particular issues until they have all been settled. A third procedural approach might involve the intervention of an additional neutral third party who would be asked to suggest final terms the parties have agreed to accept.

[14]   Achieving Psychological Closure

When disputes involve parties with on-going relationships, the attainment of agreements on substantive terms may not fully resolve the controversy. One or both parties may still feel a need for psychological closure (Moore, 2003, at 332–346). Mediators should be cognizant of this phenomenon and work to achieve a complete closure that will optimally preserve the parties' relationship. The party or parties who are perceived as having acted wrongfully should be asked to go through a multi-step healing process. They must initially acknowledge what has occurred to disrupt the relationship. They must then accept responsibility for the role they played in this disruption, and affirm their interest in the maintenance of a positive and mutually beneficial relationship. They should offer a sincere apology for the harm they may have caused, and request forgiveness for their behavior. At this point, the parties should engage in a joint act of reconciliation that will allow their relationship to continue to flourish in the future.

[15]   Establishing Procedures to Guarantee Implementation of Terms Agreed Upon

In many cases, once a mediator assists litigators or business associates to reach a settlement agreement, the parties expeditiously comply with the terms of that agreement. Money or other items of value may be exchanged, and other nonmonetary conditions may be implemented. In some situations, however, the agreement cannot be fully effectuated within a short period of time. One or both parties may be required to engage in certain conduct or refrain from specified behavior over a number of months or even years. If the parties do not agree upon a monitoring mechanism to ensure continued satisfaction of the agreement terms, further disagreements may develop. The mediator should thus explore procedural steps that can be used to guarantee future party compliance (Moore, 2003, at 348–356). Performance standards and effectuation timetables can be incorporated in the parties' agreement. The mediator or another trusted person, or a joint committee, may be designated to monitor future performance. The parties may agree upon a dispute resolution mechanism to be used in case of subsequent disagreements. They may first be required to negotiate with each other, with mediator assistance if needed. If such discussions do not resolve the matter, they may agree to binding arbitration. When arbitration is specified, the parties should be encouraged either to select the person to serve as the arbitrator or to agree upon a selection process that will guarantee the appointment of a mutually acceptable neutral.

[16]   Mediators Advising Clients or Evaluating Conflicts

Mediators should never give parties legal advice, because this would be inconsistent with their neutral facilitation role. If the mediators are not members of the pertinent state bar, such advice may constitute the unauthorized practice of law (Moffitt, 2003b, at 98–102). If unrepresented persons ask for such advice, they should be encouraged to contact attorneys who could provide them with the requisite advice (Menkel-Meadow, 2001, at 984). What should mediators do if one or both parties ask them to evaluate the issues being discussed? (Golann, 1996, at 22–24). Some neutrals steadfastly refuse to express their opinions regarding the merits of disputes, fearing that this action might compromise their impartiality (*e.g.*, Love, 1997; Kovach & Love, 1996). Other mediators, however, are willing to engage in evaluative discussions (*e.g.*, Stempel, 1997). They realize that legal representatives often prefer to work with mediators who are willing to evaluate the issues in dispute (Laflin, 2000, at 486). Parties are especially likely to expect mediators to engage in some evaluative behavior when the neutral facilitators are lawyers who have been trained to analyze legal situations (see generally Guthrie, 2001). To avoid any appearance of favoritism, even evaluative/directive mediators generally attempt to avoid definitive opinions, preferring to talk in generalities that focus on the strengths and weaknesses of each side's positions (Herman, Cary & Kennedy, 2001, at 314). This approach can be especially effective when used to question unrealistic party positions (Welsh, 2004d, at 643–46). Nonetheless, to preserve party autonomy, mediators should be sure disputants are amenable to evaluative conciliation before they offer their definitive advice (Love & Cooley, 2005).

Professor Leonard Riskin has noted the difficulty parties and neutral observers may encounter when trying to distinguish between evaluative and facilitative activities. "Many mediators both evaluate and facilitate — on the same issue, on different issues, simultaneously or at different times. In addition, even if a mediator intends to facilitate, others may interpret the behavior as an evaluation." (Riskin, Winter 2003, at 23; Stempel, 2000, at 263–64) (*see also* McDermott & Obar, 2004, at 95 (finding that almost half of employment mediators employ some evaluative techniques)) In an effort to diminish the debate surrounding the propriety of "evaluative" conduct, Professor Riskin suggests the use of different terms. He prefers to employ the terms "directive" and "elicitive" to distinguish between mediator behavior that directs the parties toward or away from particular results ("directive") and mediator conduct designed to draw out party information or perspectives ("elicitive"). (Riskin, Winter 2003, at 24) Neutral facilitators who consider direct evaluations improper can often accomplish the identical result through a series of questions designed to lead the parties to the same conclusions that would have been articulated more directly by an evaluative mediator. Most neutrals would consider the elicitive approach more effective, whenever possible, because it leads the parties toward the desired ends in a manner that is more consistent with the underlying philosophy of party self-determination. (See also Riskin, 2003).

§ 16.12   NEUTRAL EVALUATIONS, MINI-TRIALS, AND SUMMARY JURY TRIALS

[1]   Renewing Bargaining Efforts with Neutral Evaluators

In those instances in which separate and joint mediation sessions are not progressing satisfactorily toward final accords, conciliators may recommend alternative procedures in an effort to regenerate meaningful negotiations. They may ask an experienced attorney to provide a "neutral evaluation" of the parties' respective positions (Ordover & Doneff, 2002, at 49–52; Kovach, 2004, at 10–12). Each side is given the opportunity to summarize and support its current proposals. When this process is finished, the evaluator indicates which side they believe has the better claim with respect to each issue in dispute. When litigants are involved, the neutral individual states how they think a court would be likely to resolve the dispute. If the evaluator is an experienced and respected neutral, the parties would probably find that person's assessment persuasive. By carefully pointing out the strengths and weaknesses of each party's case, the appraiser may be able to generate searching party reappraisals and renewed bargaining efforts.

When transactional negotiations are involved, a respected neutral can still provide an independent evaluation of the strengths and weaknesses of each proposal. Whether the participants are attempting to structure a domestic or international business deal, resolve a collective bargaining dispute, or agree upon a rezoning arrangement, the perspective of a neutral professional can be beneficial. The neutral can suggest the way in which he or she thinks each item should be allocated, and hope that this device induces the interested parties to reconsider their existing bargaining positions.

[2]   Mini-Trial Procedure

[a]   Assessing Nonsettlement Options

The neutral intervenor may attempt to educate the recalcitrant participants concerning the realities of the situation through the use of a mini-trial procedure. Litigants who have been unable to achieve a negotiated resolution of their controversy may be ignoring the real consequences of nonsettlement. One or both sides may be entertaining delusions of grandeur regarding the likely outcome of the adjudication process. As long as these unrealistic expectations continue, it would be virtually impossible for a conciliator to generate a mutual accord. During these moments, a mini-trial procedure can be of great assistance.

[b]   Process of Mini-Trial

The mediator functions as the presiding official. If the parties have complete faith in that individual, they may present their case before that person alone. In most instances, however, the presiding neutral employs the services of an advisory panel comprised of two or three officials from the plaintiff and the defendant business entities (Cooley, 2000, at 253–55; Trachte-Huber & Huber, 1998, at 508–21; Goodpaster, 1997, at 232–33; Nolan-Haley, 1992, at 191–98). The attorneys then present abbreviated cases before the presiding neutral and the advisory panel. The advocates briefly summarize the operative factual circumstances. Key witnesses may be called to testify briefly regarding the more salient matters. Once the advisory panel members have gained an appreciation for the strengths and weaknesses of each side's positions, they are encouraged to consult with their respective legal representatives. The parties are then asked to reestablish negotiations with the assistance of the mediator. In appropriate situations, the presiding neutral may be asked to provide an advisory assessment that is intended to generate more realistic inter-party settlement talks.

[c]   Lloyd's of London Approach

Judge Hubert Will developed a modified mini-trial approach, described as his "Lloyds of London" technique (Will, Merhige & Rubin, 1977, at 206–10). Neutrals using this approach ask the disputants to analyze their controversy from the perspective of an insurance company representative. After both sides have summarized their respective positions, each is instructed to objectively assess the likely trial result if the case were adjudicated. What is the probability the plaintiff would prevail? If the plaintiff were to obtain a favorable determination, what would be the anticipated monetary judgment? The presiding neutral then multiplies each side's probability estimate times that side's predicted award if the plaintiff were to win.

[d]   Optimism of Plaintiffs/Pessimism of Defendants

In most cases, plaintiff attorneys predict a greater likelihood of success than defendant lawyers, and plaintiff advocates generally forecast higher verdicts than defense counsel (Raiffa, 2003, at 146–47; Birke & Fox, 1999, at 14–15). For example, the plaintiff-attorney may predict an 80 percent probability of trial success and a $200,000 judgment if he or she were to prevail, while the defendant-lawyer may anticipate a 50 percent probability of plaintiff success with a likely $150,000 result. From the plaintiff's perspective the case appears to be worth $160,000 (0.8 x $200,000), while the defense would seem to value the case at $75,000 (0.5 x $150,000). Each party is then asked how much it believes it would cost to try the case. The plaintiff may suggest an overall cost of $30,000, with the defendant projecting a $50,000 cost.

The difference between the parties' projected $160,000 and $75,000 valuations may seem insurmountable. Nonetheless, once the transaction costs are factored in, the picture dramatically changes. The plaintiff must *subtract* the expected $30,000 cost from its anticipated $160,000 verdict, because it would have to expend that amount of time and resources, while the defendant must *add* the anticipated $50,000 cost to its predicted $75,000 award for the same reason. With a plaintiff value of $130,000 ($160.000-$30,000) and a defendant value of $125,000 ($75,000 + $50,000), a more manageable $5,000 gap remains. A proficient mediator should be able to convince the litigants that a settlement in the $125,000 to $130,000 range would be preferable to the risks and emotional costs associated with trial.

[3]   Summary Jury Trial

When the mini-trial approach is either inappropriate (*e.g.*, where individual litigants rather than business firms are involved) or unsuccessful, the parties may employ a summary jury trial procedure (Kovach, 2004, at 12–13; Cooley, 2000, 251–53). The litigants select a six-person jury from the local jury pool. As in a mini-trial, the legal representatives summarize the relevant evidence, and key witnesses may give abbreviated testimony. The presiding neutral then instructs the jury panel on the pertinent legal principles that should govern their deliberations. Some presiding officials inform jurors at the outset that their decision will only be advisory. Others do not, hoping that jurors will take proceedings more seriously if they do not know that their determinations are not binding.

The jurors are asked to render their verdict. It is frequently helpful for presiding officials to ask advisory juries for special verdicts that require them to address each pertinent issue separately to apprise the parties of their view with respect to each controverted matter. This approach provides the litigants with crucial information regarding the strengths and weaknesses of each of their positions. These advisory verdicts often form the basis for regenerated settlement discussions.

§ 16.13   REGULATION NEGOTIATION/MEDIATION

[1]   Background

When large federal, state, and municipal agencies oversee particular areas, the regulation adoption/amendment process may be protracted, contentious, and expensive. Administrative procedure statutes require the publication of proposed regulations, the holding of public hearings, and documented agency deliberations. Once this process is finished and new regulations are issued, adversely affected parties frequently request judicial intervention. The resulting court proceedings may continue for several years. If agency reconsideration is ultimately directed, five or more years may elapse before rules become final.

When highly contentious issues are involved, the regulatory process is usually lengthy. This is almost always guaranteed when controversial environmental changes are involved or visible zoning modifications are considered. Some government officials have begun to recognize that it may be advantageous to use the negotiation process prior to the regulation adoption stage to avoid subsequent administrative and judicial proceedings. Instead of merely publishing proposed regulations, agencies initially determine the interest groups most likely to be affected by the contemplated rules. Representatives of these different groups are then asked to participate in what has become known as a "regulation-negotiation proceeding" — a "reg.-neg. proceeding" for short. [Similar negotiation-mediation procedures may be used by courts to seek solutions for complex public interest law suits that may significantly affect the rights of many diverse groups (O'Brien, 2003).]

[2]   Solicitation of All Groups

Despite the reg.-neg. characterization, most regulation-negotiation proceedings are really "regulation-negotiation-mediation" proceedings, due to the participation of neutral facilitators. Respected neutral experts are asked to solicit the participation of the relevant interest groups, ranging from business organizations and administrative officials to public interest spokespeople. The process can only function effectively if all interest groups are adequately represented. It is thus better to err on the side of inclusion, rather than exclusion (O'Brien, 2003, at 429–31).

[3]   Selection of Issues and Experts

Once the diverse participant groups are selected, neutral facilitators attempt to elicit the information they need to determine and define the issues that must be addressed. When technical, scientific, environmental, and/or economic issues are involved, respected experts may be asked to provide their insights. The individuals selected must be viewed as unbiased and enjoy general acceptability among the different groups if their opinions are to be persuasive.

[4]   Appointment of Subcommittees

When substantial questions must be overcome, it is often beneficial to appoint subcommittees comprised of representatives from each group. These subcommittees focus on specific issues or groups of issues. They try to agree upon the precise problems that must be addressed and look for alternatives that may prove mutually acceptable. It is especially important for the participants to explore options that minimize the adverse impact on any group. Even if the final terms are not considered perfect by any constituency, the fact that these provisions are generally acceptable to everyone may prove to be more important to the overall success of the reg.-neg. process.

[5]   Ensuring Consideration of All Parties Involved

The neutral facilitators must ensure that each group's interests receive thoughtful consideration. This helps to generate mutual respect among the different participants and is conducive to the development of amicable solutions. If diverse participants can be induced to appreciate the concerns of opposing parties, this can significantly reduce distrust and enhance the dispute resolution process. Use of the single-text approach can be especially beneficial during reg.-neg. discussions, to minimize problems that might otherwise result from the presence of diverse participants and contentious issues.

[6]   Decision by Consensus

After the participants have had the opportunity to define the relevant issues and evaluate the options available to them, they must begin to look for common ground. Whenever possible, decisions should be made by consensus, rather than by majority vote. Even when most participants support a particular proposal, if a group is unalterably opposed to that suggestion, it may be able to prevent the adoption of that provision or delay effectuation of that term through protracted litigation. It thus behooves the parties to respect the rights and interests of all representative groups.

[7]   Governing Agency Approval

When mutually acceptable regulations are drafted, they are recommended to the governing agency for final approval. Even when no overall agreement can be achieved, the reg.-neg. process may narrow the pertinent issues and induce the different groups to agree upon numerous factual matters. If these ideas are carefully considered by the agency during the formal rule-making process, it decreases the likelihood of subsequent legal challenges by parties dissatisfied with the promulgated regulations. Furthermore, even if litigation were to occur, a prior narrowing of the factual and legal issues should make the resulting legal proceedings more efficient. The enactment of the Negotiated Rulemaking Act of 1990 encouraged federal agencies to make greater use of the reg.-neg. process (Singer, 1994, at 148). The basic provisions of that temporary statute were permanently codified in the Administrative Dispute Resolution Act of 1996.

§ 16.14   USE OF ADJUDICATOR AS PRETRIAL MEDIATOR

[1]   Not Scheduled to Preside

Most governmental and private arbitration procedures recognize that pretrial settlement discussions should preferably be conducted under the guidance of neutrals who will not preside over the subsequent adjudications should no mutual accords be achieved. This practice permits the conciliators to ask pointed questions that might expose latent case weaknesses. They can also offer forthright assessments concerning the persuasiveness of particular arguments without the parties fearing prejudicial consequences if their disputes are ultimately tried. They know that their candid settlement disclosures will not be admissible during the succeeding judicial or arbitral proceedings, and they are confident that different individuals will preside at those adjudications. Nonetheless, not all jurisdictions are able or willing to guarantee that settlement conference judges will not be assigned to try the cases they are unable to mediate successfully. Furthermore, arbitrators who have been selected to determine particular disputes may occasionally perform conciliative functions prior to or even during their arbitral proceedings.

[2]   Scheduled to Preside

[a]   Importance of Neutral Demeanor

In some cases, judges or arbitrators who are scheduled to conduct the actual adjudications actively participate in pretrial settlement discussions (Brunet, 2003, at 243–45). When this happens, the parties may understandably fear the possibility of prejudicial trial rulings if they are unable to resolve their controversies amicably. This concern is especially real when nonjury adjudications are anticipated, as is true with respect to arbitral cases. Under these circumstances, the conciliators should diligently strive to maintain professionally neutral demeanors throughout the settlement stage. The neutral participants should emphasize from the outset that no settlement discussion disclosures would be considered during subsequent trial proceedings. The parties should further be advised that no one would be disadvantaged because it refused to assent to settlement proposals.

When judges are exposed to settlement demands and offers during pre-trial settlement sessions that fail to generate final accords, they may be influenced by the impact of anchoring (Wistrich, Guthrie & Rachlinski, 2005, at 1286–93). If they subsequently have to decide how much to award prevailing plaintiffs, they are likely to award greater sums to claimants who demanded more during the settlement discussions than to claimants who articulated more modest demands (*id.* at 1289–91). Advocates who appreciate the impact of this psychological phenomenon would be wise to engage in strategic behavior during settlement discussions overseen by presiding judges or arbitrators, with plaintiffs demanding excessive amounts and with defendants offering minimal sums. This type of behavior would greatly decrease the likelihood the settlement conferences would have the desired result of producing final accords. The only way to effectively prevent the impact of this anchoring effect would be either to prohibit the parties from stating specific demands and offers or to require the presiding neutrals to recuse themselves should the settlement discussions fail to produce agreements.

[b]   Encouraging Litigants to Autonomously Explore Options

Designated adjudicators who conduct settlement conferences frequently feel most comfortable when they merely encourage the litigants to explore settlement options themselves. They explain the obvious benefits to be derived from mutual accommodations of the litigants' competing interests and hope that this admonition will be sufficient to generate meaningful inter-party negotiations. Through this non-intrusive technique, the conciliators are able to avoid the perceived prejudice that might arise if they were to obtain more detailed knowledge of the parties' confidential settlement exchanges.

Even presiding judges are increasingly becoming directly involved in settlement discussions. Many do not hesitate to suggest how they think cases would be resolved if not settled (Brunet, 2003). These highly evaluative judicial mediators may cause litigants to question their impartiality when nonsettled cases must be tried before the people who have already suggested how the case should be decided (Brunet, 2003, at 241–48). Judges who offer case evaluations during settlement conferences should be careful not to be so definitive that parties think they have completely prejudged the outcome. They should also remind the litigants that they will not consider confidential information disclosed during settlement discussions if they must subsequently preside over trials necessitated by nonsettlements.

[c]   Requesting Other Court Official to Take More Active Role

When scheduled adjudicators conclude that more participatory conciliation efforts would be beneficial, they may ask other court officials (*e.g.*, magistrates) or other neutrals to become involved. Those individuals can then engage in active conciliation under circumstances in which they can guarantee that confidential disclosures will not be divulged to the presiding officials. This procedure should be employed in any situations in which designated adjudicators determine that more active mediation would be required to generate mutual accords.

[d]   Withdrawal from Potential Nonsettlements

On some occasions, scheduled adjudicators become convinced that settlement agreements can be achieved if they become more active participants in the negotiation process. After they become more directly involved, they begin to realize that the parties may be unable to reach accords. If they fear that their involvement in these settlement discussions has gone beyond the bounds of propriety for the persons scheduled to preside at the subsequent adjudications, they should not hesitate to withdraw and have the cases assigned to other neutrals for final resolution (Wistrich, Guthrie & Rachlinski, 2005, at 1292–93). If this option were explained to the disputants during the critical stages of the mediation discussions, it might induce greater cooperation from the parties. They would no longer be afraid of the possible prejudice that might result if they were unduly forthright in front of the persons who will try their cases. They might even be more receptive to settlement proposals formulated by the neutral intervenors.

[3]   Merely Asking About Distance Between Party Offers

Some neutral intervenors like to ask about the monetary distance that remains between the disputants' most recent offers without inquiring about the specific positions involved. Since these mediators do not obtain any information regarding the actual proposals being advanced by the parties, it is impossible for them to determine which side should be encouraged to reassess its particular circumstances. This approach thus limits meaningful mediation assistance.

[4]   Encouraging Enhanced Party Participation

[a]   Scheduled Adjudicator Mediation

Although it is occasionally awkward for designated adjudicators to participate actively in settlement discussions, there is one direct benefit to be derived from this procedure. It tends to encourage the participants to be more conciliatory, because neither side wants to appear obstinate in front of the individual who will preside at any resulting adjudication. They are more hesitant to unduly exaggerate the strength of their claims or to engage in outright mendacity, in recognition of the fact that either approach would become apparent at trial. They also do not wish to develop reputations for uncooperative behavior that could adversely affect their representational efforts in future cases.

[b]   Unscheduled Adjudicator Mediation

It is possible to encourage similar settlement candor even in instances in which the conciliators will not adjudicate unresolved disputes. Conciliators may employ a case-evaluation or mini-trial approach that requires the litigants to summarize their respective positions in writing during the final phase of the mediation process. These summaries could then be given — with the litigants' complete knowledge — to the designated adjudicators prior to the commencement of the trial procedures. The participants would thus be reluctant to exaggerate excessively or engage in overt prevarication during their settlement talks, since these tactics would be discovered by the ultimate adjudicators.

[5] Propriety of Mediation by Adjudicator

During private conversations, judges and arbitrators occasionally indicate that they are reluctant to participate actively in settlement discussions with respect to controversies they are scheduled to try. This view is particularly prevalent among less experienced adjudicators. A number of experienced adjudicators have begun to realize that many parties would actually like to rekindle previously unproductive settlement discussions, but they do not know how to accomplish this objective without appearing weak. When presiding neutrals ask these disputants whether they think additional talks may be beneficial, they frequently respond affirmatively. Most presiding individuals then offer to leave the room if the parties prefer to conduct their negotiations alone. When litigants permit adjudicators to remain and actively participate in their settlement talks, the neutral intervenors carefully assure those parties that nothing they disclose during their settlement exchanges will be considered should they ultimately have to determine the underlying issues.

[6] Further Benefits

Many adjudicators who have decided to become more actively involved in settlement discussions have begun to appreciate the benefits that may be derived from their efforts. Even advocates who initially responded negatively to settlement overtures from presiding neutrals have succumbed to subsequent settlement blandishments on numerous occasions. This is especially likely where the two sides have locked themselves into uncompromising positions that neither is able to reconsider without the face-saving assistance of the neutral intervenor. Once the basic issues have been identified and thoughtfully explored, the parties often discern reasonable solutions they previously failed to appreciate during their own adversarial interactions.

§ 16.15 REGULATION OF MEDIATOR CONDUCT

[1] Historically Loose

For many years, the conduct of most private mediators was virtually unregulated. Attorney-mediators were minimally affected by the Code of Professional Responsibility or the more recent Model Rules of Professional Conduct (Morgan & Rotunda, 2008; Menkel-Meadow, 2002; Folberg & Taylor, 1984, at 252–55). Neutral intervenors from other disciplines were governed by their own ethical codes (Folberg & Taylor, 1984, at 250–51). Judicial mediators were subject to minimal due process constraints. It was generally acknowledged that while mediators might emphasize different aspects of proposed settlements to each side to induce them to focus on the terms most beneficial to each, overt deception would never be appropriate (Cooley, 1997; Benjamin, 1995). Although mediators may reframe offers received during separate caucus sessions to make them more palatable to the other side, they may not misrepresent the true nature of such offers to deceive the offer recipients into believing the offers are more generous than they really are (Kovach, 2005, at 134). Deliberate deceit would destroy the integrity a mediator requires to function effectively as a neutral facilitator, and it would undermine party respect for the mediation process.

States did not prescribe detailed standards that had to be satisfied by individuals who wished to function as neutral intervenors (For arguments in favor of mediator certification, *see* Harges, 1997; Weckstein, 1996). As long as a particular person was acceptable to disputants, they could act as a conciliator. Even states with minimal prerequisites only required a limited amount of training. Although public and private appointing agencies generally listed only persons with neutral experience, it was not difficult for most applicants to qualify. (Regarding state laws regulating mediation, *see* Chantilis, 1996). Lawsuits by dissatisfied parties against mediators have been extremely rare and courts have not been receptive to the few suits filed (Moffitt, 2003a). This trend is unlikely to change unless mediators violate generally accepted standards regarding neutral facilitator behavior (Young, 2006b; Moffitt, 2003b).

[2] Appreciation of Need

By the early 1990s, the laissez-faire approach to mediator regulation had begun to change. ADR neutrals increasingly considered themselves part of a distinct profession, and they began to appreciate the need for separate professional standards (Moore, 2003, at 447–50; Symposium, 1995, at 95). Nonetheless, they were uncertain regarding the appropriate way in which to promulgate generally applicable behavioral rules and they were concerned about the extent of regulation that should be imposed (see generally Bush, 2004; Della Noce, Antes & Saul, 2004; Lang & Taylor, 2000).

[3] Summary of "Standards of Conduct for Mediators"

[a] Party Self-Determination and Mediator Impartiality

Finally, in 1994, the American Arbitration Association (AAA), the American Bar Association (ABA), and the Society of Professionals in Dispute Resolution (SPIDR) adopted "The Standards of Conduct for Mediators" (Symposium, 1995, in Appendix). In 2005, these three organizations completed a three-year review process that generated some changes in the precise language of the different sections of these standards of conduct (Young, 2006a). It is hoped that these regulations will not only guide the conduct of AAA, ABA, and SPIDR (now Association for Conflict Resolution) mediators, but also establish guidelines for state regulators and other private organizations that wish to promulgate their own restrictions. Standard I recognizes the principle of party self-determination, not only with respect to the actual outcomes but also regarding mediator selection and process design based on the belief that party acceptance of neutrals is essential for effective conciliation. Standard II requires conciliators to "conduct the mediation[s] in an impartial manner" This exhortation acknowledges the fact that "[t]he concept of mediator impartiality is central to the mediation process."

[b] Complete Disclosure of Potential Mediator Conflicts of Interest

Covered neutrals are obliged by Standard III "to make a reasonable inquiry to determine whether there are any facts that a reasonable individual would consider likely to create a potential or actual conflict of interest" and "to disclose . . . all actual and potential conflicts of interest that are reasonably known to the mediator" that could raise a question about their impartiality. This provision notes that neutrals "shall avoid the appearance of conflict . . . both during and after a mediation." Individuals being considered for neutral appointment should inform the prospective participants about any financial stake they may have in any interested party, and indicate any past or present relationships with parties or advocate firms that may be perceived as sources of possible bias. Conciliators should always resolve doubts with respect to possible conflicts in favor of complete disclosure. If revealed information does not affect party confidence in the ability of the individual to perform mediation functions in an impartial manner, the disputants are perfectly free to select that person.

[c]   Statement of Competence

Standard IV, the section on conciliator competence, is understandably vague. It merely provides that "[a] mediator shall mediate only when the mediator has the necessary competence to satisfy the reasonable expectations of the parties." It goes on to note that "[a]ny person may be selected as a mediator, provided that the parties are satisfied with the mediator's competence and qualifications." No minimal educational or experiential prerequisites are included, in deference to party self-determination and in recognition of the fact that neither educational training nor neutral experience can guarantee mediator competence.

[d]   Confidentiality

Standard V requires mediators to "maintain the confidentiality of all information obtained by the mediator . . . , unless otherwise agreed to by the parties or required by applicable law." It states that "[a] mediator who meets with any persons in private session during a mediation shall not convey directly or indirectly to any other person any information that was obtained during that private session without the consent of the disclosing person." Conciliators are encouraged to discuss confidentiality expectations with the participants to avoid misunderstandings. When private caucus sessions are contemplated, mediators should expressly discuss the need for confidentiality prior to the separate meetings. The confidentiality obligation requires neutral intervenors to maintain party confidences both during and after mediation sessions.

[e]   Preserving Quality of Mediation Process

Standard VI provides that "[a] mediator shall conduct a mediation . . . in a manner that promotes diligence, timeless, safety, presence of the appropriate participants, party participation, procedural fairness, party competency and mutual respect among all participants." This provision is designed to guarantee procedurally fair conciliation efforts. Under the 1994 version, conciliators were told to "refrain from providing professional advice," and instructed, where pertinent, to suggest that parties seek their own outside professional assistance. This admonition was designed to avoid the difficulties that may be encountered when neutrals offer gratuitous advice to parties regarding the legal ramifications of terms they are contemplating. Although this language is no longer contained in the revised Standards, the admonition is implicit in both the self-determination and impartiality Standards.

Standard VI(A)(4) provides that "[a] mediator should promote honesty and candor between and among all participants, and a mediator shall not knowingly misrepresent any material fact or circumstance in the course of a mediation." Could a mediator ethically state a party's offer as his or her own proposal to avoid the reactive devaluation that might occur if the offer came directly from one of the disputants? (*See* Kovach, 2005, at 134).

Throughout both unassisted and assisted negotiations, the disputants must determine their own legal rights through appropriate channels. Mediators should thus refrain from providing legal advice to particular parties. Nonetheless, it must be recognized that some neutral intervenors are willing to give their opinion with respect to controverted legal or factual issues. So long as they perform this function as neutral evaluators, and not as legal advisors to specific parties, this behavior would not contravene the Standards. (In 2002, the ABA adopted Model Rule 2.4(b) which requires attorney-mediators to explain their neutral role to disputants and indicate that they do not represent either party (Morgan & Rotunda, 2008, at 76).)

The overall commitment to party self determination might be read by some as a repudiation of the evaluative/directive approach in which mediators employ more directive techniques to generate party agreements. Evaluative/directive conciliators would undoubtedly disagree with this interpretation, emphasizing the fact that they only become more directive *after* they have determined the needs and objectives of the participants. To the extent that evaluative/directive mediators do endeavor to generate settlements that are consistent with party desires, their efforts should not be considered contrary to the self determination mandate.

Mediators should not permit the self determination principle to sanction the acceptance of settlement terms they believe to be truly unconscionable. Negotiations occasionally involve parties with significant power imbalances due to extreme financial or emotional inequalities. This phenomenon is especially likely with respect to certain family disputes between spouses or parents and children (see Kolb, 1994, at 17–58, 191–237; Singer, 1994, at 31–54; Folberg & Taylor, 1984, at 147–86). It may also arise in controversies involving landlords and tenants or employers and individual employees who are not represented by labor organizations or legal counsel.

When conciliators fear that party power imbalances would be likely to generate unfairly one-sided agreements, they should not hesitate to advise the weaker participants to obtain legal assistance. If financial constraints would preclude the retention of paid counsel, the individuals could be referred to legal aid organizations or appropriate public interest groups. If these suggestions were ignored and the neutral intervenors feared they would be used by the stronger party to obtain unconscionable terms, they could exercise their right to withdraw from the negotiations. In most instances, the participation of conciliators should act as a moderating influence that should discourage the negotiation of wholly one-sided agreements (Honoroff & Opotow, 2007, at 162–63; Folberg & Taylor, 1984, at 245–49).

[f]   Advertising

The Standards of Conduct expressly limit conciliator advertising and business solicitation. Standard VII directs neutrals to be truthful with respect to their advertising and other efforts to generate business. Mediators should only refer to professional certification by public or private entities if those organizations have specific procedures for qualifying neutrals and they have been accorded the requisite certification. When in doubt, individuals should consult the agencies they are thinking of citing.

[g]   Fee Disclosure

Standard VIII concerns mediator fees. It requires conciliators to fully disclose and explain the basis for any fees charged to parties. Neutral intervenors are encouraged to inform disputants regarding their fees at the beginning of the mediation process. Once conciliation services have been completed, mediators should provide parties with sufficiently detailed billing information to apprise them of the manner in which the final statement was calculated. Should mediators ever be permitted to work on a contingent fee basis under which they only get paid if the parties reach an agreement or under which they are paid a percentage of the monetary sum agreed upon? (See Peppet, 2003). Standard VIII(B)(2) now provides that such arrangements should not be employed.

[4]   Generality of Rules and Applicability of Outside Ethical Guidelines

[a]   AAA, ABA, and ACR Standards of Conduct

It is apparent that the AAA, ABA, and ACR Standards of Conduct do not provide an exhaustive set of professional guidelines. They only include general prescriptions. (Similar mediation standards are set forth in the AAA's "Consumer Due Process Protocol" (1998).) Individuals who function as mediators should also acknowledge the applicability of other ethical obligations that arise from the authority associated with their special positions. For example, neutral intervenors should recognize that it is never appropriate to employ deliberately deceptive tactics to take advantage of unsuspecting parties. While mediators frequently focus on different aspects of proposed terms when they meet with the different parties — emphasizing the aspects that benefit each side — they may not misrepresent the provisions involved.

Circumspection is particularly required in those situations in which disputants or their legal counsel accord undue deference to mediator authority. When it appears that the participants are effectively providing conciliators with unusually expansive discretion to formulate final settlement packages, the neutrals should be especially careful not to abuse the trust granted to them. It is imperative that mediators always avoid behavior that could undermine party or public confidence in the mediation process. The short-term benefits that might be derived from the use of questionable conciliation techniques would not outweigh the resulting loss of respect for neutral intervention.

[b]   Proposed CPR Institute/Georgetown Law Center Model Rule of Professional Mediator Conduct

A joint effort between the CPR Institute for Dispute Resolution and the Georgetown University Law Center has produced a "Proposed Model Rule of Professional Conduct for the Lawyer as Third Party Neutral" (Plapinger & Menkel-Meadow, 1999)(*see also* Menkel-Meadow, 1997). The Proposed Rule covers six areas: (1) neutral diligence and competence; (2) participant confidentiality; (3) neutral impartiality; (4) avoidance of neutral conflicts of interest; (5) appropriateness of mediator fees; and (6) the fairness and integrity of the process. The drafters hope this Proposed Rule will provide attorney-neutrals with more definitive guidance than is presently available through either the Model Rules or the AAA/ABA/SPIDR Standards of Conduct for Mediators. These two entities have also prepared a proposed set of guidelines that would regulate the conduct of ADR provider organizations (18 Alternatives 109 (2000)).

[c]   Uniform Mediation Act

In 2001, the National Conference of Commissioners on Uniform State Laws approved the Uniform Mediation Act (Uniform Mediation Act, 2002; see generally Uniform Mediation Act Symposium, 2003; Reuben, 2003). In the coming years, state legislatures will have to decide whether to adopt, in whole or in part, the provisions contained in that Uniform Act (Comment, 2000; Reuben & Rogers, 1999). The Commissioners believe that mediation has reached a sufficiently mature stage to warrant consideration of uniform statutes that would guide parties that participate in mediation programs throughout the United States.

Section 2 defines the relevant terms. Section 3, which denotes the scope of the Uniform Act, indicates that it applies to judicially and legislatively mandated mediation programs, and to voluntarily undertaken mediation. Section 3(b) states that the Uniform Act does not apply to collective bargaining interactions, that are regulated under other statutes, or to mediation conducted by a judge who might make a ruling on the case being discussed. Section 4 explains the privileged nature of mediation communications, and states that such confidential exchanges shall not be discoverable or admissible in adjudicative proceedings, unless the privilege is expressly waived by the relevant participants pursuant to Section 5 or required by other statutory provisions. Section 4(b) provides that the privilege extends to parties participating in mediation, to the mediators, and to non-party participants (*e.g.*, experts, friends, and supporters) who are all authorized to prevent the disclosure of confidential information by any participant in their mediation sessions. In Section 4(c), the Uniform Act notes that information otherwise discoverable or admissible is not rendered non-discoverable or inadmissable solely by reason of its disclosure in mediation.

Section 6 sets forth the various exceptions to the confidentiality provided by Section 4. For example, the privilege does not apply to threats to inflict bodily harm or to commit crimes of violence, to efforts to conceal crimes or to further on-going criminal activity, to claims of misconduct or malpractice filed against mediators, mediation parties, non-party participants, or to party representatives, or to proceedings involving claims of abuse, neglect, abandonment, or exploitation in which a child or adult protective services agency is involved. Under Section 6(b), a court, administrative agency, or arbitrator may, following an in camera hearing, order the disclosure of mediation communications not otherwise available if it finds that the need for disclosure substantially outweighs the interest in protecting confidentiality in a criminal proceeding or in a proceeding to prove a claim, to rescind or reform a settlement agreement, or to avoid liability on a contract arising out of mediation. Section 6(c) indicates that a mediator may not be compelled to testify with respect to a proceeding to prove a claim, to rescind or reform an agreement, or to avoid liability on a contract resulting from mediation.

Under Section 7, a mediator shall not make a report, assessment, evaluation, or finding pertaining to mediation sessions to a court or administrative agency, except to the extent of reporting that mediation occurred, or to report abuse, neglect, abandonment, or exploitation to a public agency responsible for protecting children or adults against such mistreatment (see Izumi & La Rue, 2003). Section 8 provides that mediation communications shall remain confidential beyond adjudicative proceedings to the extent agreed upon by the parties and to the extent set forth in applicable statutory provisions.

Section 9 requires prospective mediators to disclose all potential conflicts of interest that might affect their impartiality before they accept mediation assignments. Section 10 states that attorneys or other non-lawyer representatives may accompany parties to mediation sessions and participate in those proceedings.

The most controversial part of the Uniform Mediation Act concerns the scope of confidentiality and the parties authorized to assert that privilege (*compare* Hughes, 2001, and Hughes, 1998, with Deason, 2001; *see also* Reuben, 2003; Reich, 2001). Do you think the Uniform Act is over or under protective of participant confidentiality? Should mediators have the right to assert the confidentiality privilege, or should only parties be able to do so? Are the Act's confidentiality exceptions too expansive or too narrow? State legislatures considering adoption of Uniform Act provisions will have to determine where to draw lines with respect to these difficult issues.

[5]   Need to Focus More on Contextual Factors and Party Relationships

Honoroff and Opotow argue that most of the existing ethical codes governing mediators focus too much on what mediators should do from an abstract and detached perspective, and not enough on what they should do in the particular circumstances in which mediators actually operate (Honoroff & Opotow, 2007). They suggest that mediation practices that might be appropriate for business and commercial disputes, in which the parties are generally represented by legal counsel and have no affirmative duties to disclose confidential information, would not be appropriate for most family and divorce disputes, in which the parties are minimally assisted by attorneys and where significant economic and/or emotional imbalances may exist. They assert that ethical rules should recognize these situation-specific concerns and apply different rules to different settings. While it might be appropriate for mediators to ignore full disclosure in business and commercial conflicts, they should be obliged to promote full disclosure in family and divorce conflicts (Honoroff & Opotow, 2007, at 159–60). Mediators may feel free to employ separate caucus sessions to further discussions in business and commercial disputes, but should generally encourage joint sessions with respect to family and divorce disputes to allow the parties to deal directly with each other when they determine future family matters.

§ 16.16   SOME CRITICISM AND RESPONSE

[1]   Mediated Settlements and Observance of Legal Rights

Some experts have suggested that law suit mediation should be sparingly used, to prevent settlement accommodations that may seriously undermine fundamental legal rights (Fiss, 1984) (*see also* Hensler, 1995, discussing the pros and cons of using ADR procedures to resolve mass tort cases). These observers ignore the fact that most civil cases involve fact-specific disputes that are unlikely to have much precedential value with respect to other litigants. These controversies are especially suited to neutral intervention. If the parties can be induced to view the operative factual circumstances in a detached manner, they should be able to formulate mutually acceptable resolutions.

[2]   Significant Constitutional or Statutory Questions

Law suits occasionally concern significant legal issues that transcend the interests of the particular parties. They may raise constitutional or statutory questions that are likely to affect many people. These are cases that are likely to receive thorough judicial consideration. As a result, conciliators should be hesitant to encourage expedient compromises that may not fully protect the rights of these and other parties. Nonetheless, if the immediate litigants indicate a desire for mediation assistance with respect to these disputes, neutrals should not refuse to provide the requested help. They should, however, be careful to avoid settlements that contravene applicable legal principles or fundamental public policies.

Even when landmark cases are being litigated, neutral intervention may be beneficial. The litigants may be induced to narrow the scope of the legal issues involved, and may agree upon uncontroverted factual matters. They may be encouraged to develop efficient discovery procedures that will expedite the litigation process (Sabatino, 1998, at 1310–16). These efforts should actually enhance the likelihood the parties will obtain definitive judicial resolutions of the underlying legal principles.

[3]   Domestic Violence Cases

Many people have questioned the appropriateness of mediation intervention with respect to domestic violence cases, believing that the battered victims frequently lack the personal empowerment needed for meaningful participation (Zylstra, 2001; see also Taylor, 2002, at 201 (regarding difficulties involved with mediation of child abuse cases)). Despite the weighty concerns of these individuals, it is interesting to note that the Navajo Tribe has historically used respected tribal leaders to seek peaceful resolutions of domestic violence cases (Coker, 1999). While the Navajo Peacemakers have had some real success in this area, the use of mediation procedures in domestic violence cases should be carefully controlled to be sure that victim rights are not unfairly sacrificed. Similar mediation problems may be encountered when dealing with other extreme power imbalances between the negotiating parties (Gewurz, 2001, at 136–37).

Summary

1. When law suit settlement discussions or transactional negotiations break down, it is frequently beneficial to ask mediators to facilitate the bargaining process.

2. Mediators may be primarily facilitative/elicitive, evaluative/directive, or relationship-oriented/transformative. Disputing parties should initially decide which form of neutral intervention they would prefer.

3. Parties should prepare for mediation sessions as thoroughly as they would for negotiation meetings, knowing that they will negotiate with the neutral participants, as well as through mediators, and directly with opponents.

4. Mediators should also prepare for scheduled interactions by reviewing available party documents and by determining the optimal way to proceed with settlement discussions.

5. Most mediators initially schedule joint sessions to explain their facilitative function, their impartiality and lack of capacity to impose terms, and the confidential nature of participant communications.

6. When joint sessions do not produce accords, mediators generally schedule separate caucuses that enable them to explore underlying needs and interests confidentially with each party.

7. During both joint and separate sessions, mediators look for areas of joint interest and encourage the generation of alternative formulations that may be mutually beneficial.

8. Neutral case evaluations, mini-trials, or summary jury trials may be employed to apprize litigants of likely adjudication results.

9. Regulation-negotiation procedures can be used by government agencies to facilitate the drafting and approval of controversial regulations.

Chapter 17

NEGOTIATION ETHICS

§ 17.01 HONESTY

[1] Deception Inherent in Negotiation

It is easy to exhort legal practitioners to behave in an exemplary manner when they participate in the negotiation process:

[T]he lawyer is not free to do anything his client might do in the same circumstances . . . . [T]he lawyer must be at least as candid and honest as his client would be required to be . . . . Beyond that, the profession should embrace an affirmative ethical standard for attorneys' professional relationships with courts, other lawyers and the public: *The lawyer must act honestly and in good faith.* Another lawyer . . . should not need to exercise the same degree of caution that he would if trading for reputedly antique copper jugs in an oriental bazaar . . . . [S]urely the professional standards must ultimately impose upon him a duty not to accept an unconscionable deal. While some difficulty in line-drawing is inevitable when such a distinction is sought to be made, there must be a point at which the lawyer cannot ethically accept an arrangement that is completely unfair to the other side. . . . (Rubin, 1975, at 589, 591) (emphasis in original) (*See also* Bordone, 2005 (asserting that the *Getting to Yes* interest-based, joint-gain maximizing approach is so clearly established as the proper way to negotiate that the ABA should promulgate a set of ethical standards to regulate attorney bargaining interactions that would discipline lawyers who engage in "bluffing, puffing [or] deception" of any kind designed to advance their own side's interests at the expense of the other side)).

Despite the nobility of such pronouncements, others maintain that "[p]ious and generalized assertions that the negotiator must be 'honest' or that the lawyer must use 'candor' are not helpful." (White, 1980, at 929) They recognize that negotiation interactions involve a deceptive process in which a certain amount of "puffing" and "embellishment" is expected, as the participants attempt to convince their opponents that they must obtain better terms than they must actually achieve (Krivis & Zadeh, 2006; Korobkin, 2005, at 257–260; Friedman & Shapiro, 1995, at 245–47; Steele, 1986, at 1391–95).

Observers also note that trustworthiness is a relative concept.

[T]rustworthiness and its outward manifestation — truth telling — are not absolute values. For example, no one tells the truth all of the time, nor is perpetual truth telling expected in most circumstances. To tell the truth in some social situations would be a rude convention. Consequently, when one speaks of the essential nature of trustworthiness and truth telling, one actually is talking about a certain circumstance or situation in which convention calls for trustworthiness or truth telling. Thus, a person considered trustworthy and a truth teller actually is a person who tells the truth at the right or necessary time. (Steele, 1986, at 1388)(*see also* DePaulo, et al., 1996; Bok, 1978 (indicating degree to which most people employ "social lies" on a regular basis) (see generally Meadow-Menkel & Wheeler, 2004).

[2] Appropriate and Inappropriate Misrepresentations

It would not be particularly useful to engage in a pious and hypocritical discussion of negotiation ethics. If I were to suggest that all mendacity should be proscribed, even generally accepted "puffing" and "embellishment" would be precluded. Questions about authorized limits or minimum settlement objectives could no longer be answered with the usual dissembling or outright prevarication. Almost all professional bargainers who have been asked about these ethical issues have indicated that deceptive replies are not inappropriate in these circumstances. They believe that advocates who ask these questions have no right to expect forthright replies. The inquiries pertain to confidential lawyer-client matters that concern excluded client values or settlement intentions. As a result, most attorneys suggest that questions relating to these areas need not be candidly answered during the negotiation process.

I frequently surprise law students by telling them that while I have rarely participated in legal negotiations in which both participants did not lie, I have encountered few dishonest practitioners. I suggest that the fundamental question is not whether legal negotiators may lie, but when and about what they may permissibly dissemble. Students initially find it difficult to accept the notion that disingenuous "puffing" and deliberate mendacity do not always constitute reprehensible conduct.

It is ironic to note that deceptive tactics are usually employed at the outset of bargaining transactions. Side A, which is willing to pay 2 X informs Side B that it cannot pay more than X. Side B, which is willing to accept 1 1/2 X, states that it must obtain at least 2 1/2 X if a deal is to be achieved. Both participants are pleased that their interaction has begun successfully, even though both have begun with intentionally misleading statements. Some lawyers attempt to circumvent this moral dilemma by formulating opening positions that do not directly misstate their actual intentions. For example, Side A may indicate that it "doesn't *wish* to pay more than X," or Side B may say that it "would not be *inclined* to accept less than 2 1/2 X." While these preliminary statements may be technically true, the italicized verbal leaks ("wish to"/"inclined to") would inform attentive opponents that these speakers do not really mean what they appear to be communicating.

When students or practicing attorneys are asked whether they expect opposing counsel to candidly disclose their true authorized limits or their actual bottom lines at the beginning of bargaining interactions, most exhibit discernible discomfort. They recall the numerous times they have commenced negotiations with exaggerated position statements they did not expect their adversaries to take literally. Thus, they begin to understand the dilemma confronted regularly by all legal negotiators.

> On the one hand the negotiator must be fair and truthful; on the other he must mislead his opponent. Like the poker player, a negotiator hopes that his opponent will overestimate the value of his hand. Like the poker player, in a variety of ways he must facilitate his opponent's inaccurate assessment. The critical difference between those who are successful negotiators and those who are not lies in this capacity both to mislead and not to be misled. . . . [A] careful examination of the behavior of even the most forthright, honest, and trustworthy negotiators will show them actively engaged in misleading their opponents about their true position . . . . To conceal one's true position, to mislead an opponent about one's true settling point is the essence of negotiation (White, 1980, at 927–28).

Some writers criticize the use of deceptive negotiating tactics to further client interests (*e.g.*, Alfini, 1999). They maintain that these devices diminish the likelihood of Pareto optimal results, because "deception tends to shift wealth from the risk-averse to the risk-tolerant" (Peters, 1987, at 7; *see* Norton, 1989, at 537–38). While this observation is undoubtedly true, it is unlikely to discourage the pervasive use of ethically permissible tactics designed to deceive risk-averse opponents into believing they must accept less beneficial terms than they need actually accept. It is thus unproductive to discuss a utopian negotiation world in which complete disclosure is the norm. The real question concerns the types of deceptive tactics that may ethically be employed to enhance bargaining interests (Norton, 1989). Attorneys who believe that no prevarication is ever proper during bargaining encounters place themselves and their clients at a disadvantage. They permit their less candid opponents to obtain settlements that transcend the terms to which they are objectively entitled (Wetlaufer, 1990, at 1230).

[3]   Material Fact vs. Settlement Intentions and Values

The rather schizophrenic character of the ethical conundrum encountered by legal negotiators is apparent in the ABA Model Rules of Professional Conduct, which were adopted by the House of Delegates in August of 1983. Rule 4.1(a), which corresponds to EC 7-102(A)(5) under the ABA Code of Professional Responsibility, states that "a lawyer shall not knowingly make a false statement of material fact or law to a third person" (Morgan & Rotunda, 2008, at 92). This seemingly unequivocal principle is intended to apply to both litigation and negotiation settings (Rotunda, 1995, at 167). An explanatory Comment under this Rule reiterates the fact that "[a] Lawyer is required to be truthful when dealing with others on a client's behalf . . . ." (See also Rule 8.4(c) which states that it is "professional misconduct for a lawyer to . . . (c) engage in conduct involving dishonesty, fraud, deceit or misrepresentation (Morgan & Rotunda, 2008, at 128)). Nonetheless, Comment 2 acknowledges the difficulty of defining "truthfulness" in the unique context of the negotiation process:

> Whether a particular statement should be regarded as one of fact can depend on the circumstances. Under generally accepted conventions in negotiation, certain types of statements ordinarily are not taken as statements of material fact. Estimates of price or value placed on the subject of a transaction and a party's intentions as to an acceptable settlement of a claim are in this category . . . . [Morgan & Rotunda, 2008, at 93]

Even state bars that have not appended this Comment to their version of Rule 4.1 have appropriately recognized the ethical distinctions drawn in that Comment.

Although the ABA Model Rules unambiguously proscribe all lawyer prevarication, they reasonably, but confusingly, exclude mere "puffing" and dissembling regarding one's true minimum objectives (Rotunda, 1995, at 167–68; Lowenthal, 1982, at 101). These important exceptions appropriately recognize that disingenuous behavior is indigenous to most legal negotiations and could not realistically be prevented due to the nonpublic nature of bargaining interactions.

> If one negotiator lies to another, only by happenstance will the other discover the lie. If the settlement is concluded by negotiation, there will be no trial, no public testimony by conflicting witnesses, and thus no opportunity to examine the truthfulness of assertions made during the negotiation. Consequently, in negotiation, more than in other contexts, ethical norms can probably be violated with greater confidence that there will be no discovery and punishment. (White, 1980, at 926) [*But cf.* Monroe v. State Bar, 10 Cal. Rptr. 257, 261, 358 P.2d 529, 533 (1961) (sustaining a nine-month suspension of a practitioner, since "[i]ntentionally deceiving opposing counsel is ground for disciplinary action."]

One of the inherent conflicts with regard to this area concerns the fact that what people label acceptable "puffing" when they make value-based representations during legal negotiations may be considered improper mendacity when uttered by opposing counsel. When material facts are involved, attorneys may not deliberately misrepresent the actual circumstances. They may employ blocking techniques to avoid answering opponent questions, but they may not provide false or misleading answers. If they decide to respond to inquiries pertaining to material facts, they must do so honestly. They must also be careful not to issue partially correct statements they know will be misinterpreted by their opponents. This was recognized by the Eighth Circuit in *NLRB v. Waymouth Farms*, 172 F.3d 598 (8th Cir. 1999), wherein the court held that an employer that had misrepresented its true intentions during negotiation talks with the representative labor union concerning the firm's decision to relocate its business committed an unfair labor practice, because the duty to bargain requires the negotiating parties to provide each other with truthful information. (*See also* Crane v. State Bar Assn., 30 Cal.3d 117, 635 P.2d 163 (1981) (sustaining discipline of attorney who deliberately deleted language from trust deed without notifying affected party)).

Professor Scott Peppet has argued that the existing Model Rules assume adversarial interactions in which disputing parties endeavor to advance the interests of their own clients at the expense of bargaining efficiency (Peppet, 2005). He believes that negotiating lawyers should be allowed to establish their own rules of conduct requiring a greater degree of candor and openness, and a good faith commitment to cooperative bargaining. They might, for example, prohibit even puffing and embellishment, and require a cooperative/problem-solving approach designed to generate mutually efficient agreements. Parties who violate such specific rules would be subject to bar discipline. Given the relatively private nature of bargaining interactions and the difficulty in determining whether a negotiator has actually misrepresented material law or fact, how effectively could a bar committee determine if someone has misstated their bottom line or over or under stated the value of particular items being exchanged for strategic purposes? (Gilson & Mnookin, 1994, at 519–20).

The Litigation Section of the ABA drafted Ethical Guidelines for Settlement Negotiations that were approved by the House of Delegates in 2002. These Guidelines are only advisory — not mandatory — and they reflect the standards of conduct set forth in the applicable provisions of the Model Rules (Haussmann, 2004).

[4]   Risk of Dishonesty

Even though advocate prevarication during legal negotiations rarely results in bar disciplinary action, practitioners must recognize that other risks are created by truly dishonest bargaining behavior. Attorneys who deliberately deceive opponents or who withhold information they are legally obliged to disclose may be guilty of fraud. Contracts procured through fraudulent acts of commission or omission are voidable, and the responsible advocates and their clients may be held liable for monetary damages (Steele, 1986, at 1395–96; Perschbacher, 1985, at 86–94, 126–30; Rubin, 1975, at 587). It would be particularly embarrassing for lawyers to make misrepresentations that could cause their clients additional legal problems transcending those the attorneys were endeavoring to resolve. Since the adversely affected clients might thereafter sue their culpable former counsel for legal malpractice, the ultimate injury to the reputations and practices of the deceptive attorneys could be momentous (Perschbacher, 1985, at 81–86, 107–12). Legal representatives who employ clearly improper bargaining tactics may even subject themselves to judicial sanctions (*e.g.*, Eash v. Riggins Trucking, Inc., 757 F.2d 557 (3d Cir. 1985)).

Most legal representatives always conduct their negotiations with appropriate candor, because they are moral individuals and/or believe that such professional behavior is mandated by the applicable ethical standards. A few others, however, do not feel so constrained. These persons should consider the practical risks associated with disreputable bargaining conduct. Even if their deceitful action is not reported to the state bar and never results in personal liability for fraud or legal malpractice, their aberrational behavior is likely to be discovered eventually by their fellow practitioners. As other attorneys learn that particular lawyers are not trustworthy, future interactions become more difficult for those people (Herman, Cary & Kennedy, 2001, at 175–76; Murnighan, 1992, at 230–31; Watson, 1985, at 299). Factual and legal representations are no longer accepted without time-consuming and expensive verification. Oral agreements on the telephone and handshake arrangements are no longer acceptable. Executed written documents are required for even rudimentary transactions. Attorneys who contemplate the employment of unacceptable deception to further present client interests should always be cognizant of the fact that such conduct may seriously jeopardize their future effectiveness (Deason, 2006, at 1410). No short-term gain achieved through deviant behavior should ever be permitted to outweigh the likely long-term consequences of those improper actions.

When lawyers negotiate, they must constantly decide whether they are going to divulge relevant legal and/or factual information to opposing counsel. If they decide to disclose some pertinent information, may they do so partially or is complete disclosure required? They must also determine the areas they may permissibly misrepresent and the areas they may not distort.

[5] Overt Misrepresentation of Factual Information

[a] Vs. Legal Doctrine

When lawyers are asked if negotiators may overtly misrepresent legal or factual matters, most provide immediate negative replies. Many cite Model Rule 4.1 and suggest that this prohibition covers all intentional misrepresentations. While they are correct with respect to deliberate misstatements concerning material legal doctrines, they are not entirely correct with respect to factual issues. Almost all negotiators expect opponents to engage in "puffing" and "embellishment." Advocates who hope to obtain $50,000 settlements may initially indicate that it will take $150,000 or even $250,000 to resolve the dispute. They may also embellish the pain experienced by their client, so long as their exaggerations do not transcend the bounds of expected propriety. Individuals involved in a corporate buy out may initially over or under value the real property, the building and equipment, the inventory, the accounts receivable, the patent rights and trademarks, and the good will.

[b] Estimated Value of Items

It is clear that lawyers may not intentionally misrepresent *material facts*, but it is not always apparent what facts are *"material."* The previously noted Comment to Rule 4.1 explicitly acknowledges that "estimates of price or value placed on the subject of a transaction and a party's intentions as to an acceptable settlement of a claim" do not constitute "material" facts under that provision. It is thus ethical for legal negotiators to misrepresent the value their client places on particular items. For example, attorneys representing one spouse involved in a marital dissolution may indicate that their client wants joint custody of the children, when he or she does not. Lawyers representing a party attempting to purchase a particular company may understate their client's belief regarding the value of the good will associated with the target firm. So long as the statement conveys their side's belief — and does not falsely indicate the view of an outside expert, such as an accountant — no Rule 4.1 violation would occur.

James v. Lifeline Mobile Medics, 341 Ill.App.3d 451, 792 N.E.2d 461 (2003), involved a person who claimed to have been wrongfully terminated. She obtained a verdict awarding her $243,969.64. While this verdict was being appealed, the parties discussed settlement options. The attorney for the defendant sent a letter to plaintiff's counsel stating that the defendant's "financial picture is dire if not desperate" and indicating that if the full judgment amount had to be paid, bankruptcy would be the only alternative. The parties thereafter negotiated an agreement calling for an initial payment of $200,000 and a final payment of $25,000. After the defendant submitted an insufficiently funded check to the plaintiff, the court ordered the defendant to tender a cashier's check covering the full $225,000 plus interest, which was done. The plaintiff thereafter learned that the defendant actually had a net worth of $1,400,000, $400,000 of which was in cash. She moved to set aside the settlement agreement and recover the remaining unpaid portion of the original judgment. While the appellate court acknowledged that "erroneous statements as to matters of opinion, such as representations of the value of property, do not amount to fraud . . . , a misrepresentation [that] relates to a specific extrinsic fact materially affecting the value of matters at issue . . . [that] is peculiarly within the knowledge of the speaker, and . . . made with knowledge of its falsity" may constitute actionable fraud. The court found that the defendant counsel's deliberate misrepresentations concerning his client's financial situation for the purpose of inducing the plaintiff to accept a lower settlement amount were sufficiently material to provide the basis for a fraud claim. The court concluded that the defense lawyer's statements concerning his client's financial circumstances and bankruptcy intentions constituted "misrepresentations that [went] beyond the usual hyperbole of accepted negotiation techniques." The dissenting judge, however, would have rejected the fraud claim, because he thought the representations in question were mere hyperbole that the plaintiff's counsel should have independently verified. Given the specificity of the financial misrepresentations involved and the confidential nature of the information being disclosed, I would find it difficult to suggest that this involved the type of "puffing" expected during negotiation discussions. The statements were knowingly false and designed to mislead the plaintiff's attorney. They also pertained to information highly material to the settlement talks.

Suppose the seller of real property or a business is negotiating with a prospective buyer. Could the seller indicate that other parties may also be interested in the property or business in question? Most people would consider this to be mere puffing. Could the seller state that someone has made a specific offer for the property or business when no one has made such an offer? This is entirely different from the initial statement that others may be interested, because this involves a specific factual representation known only to the seller, and it is certainly material to the transaction being discussed with the prospective buyer.

Suppose the seller hopes to obtain $2.5 million for the property or business, but would accept $2.35 million if necessary. Could the seller state that the prospective purchaser would have to pay $2.5 million if they hope to obtain the property or business? Most lawyers would find such a statement to be mere puffing, excluded from Model Rule 4.1 coverage by the comment excepting statements pertaining to settlement intentions. Suppose the seller has an offer from another party for $2.4 million, could the seller state that they have an offer of $2.5 million? Since this misrepresentation pertains to a highly relevant factual matter which the prospective buyer has the right to rely upon, it would appear to contravene both Rule 4.1 and expose the seller to tort liability for fraudulent misrepresentation. (*See, e.g.,* *Kabatchnick v. Hanover-Elm Building Corp.*, 328 Mass. 341, 103 N.E.2d 692 (1952) (statements from landlord to current renter that he had offer from another party for specific amount when he had no such offer found actionable misrepresentation which renter had the right to rely upon).) Could the seller simply state that they have another offer and indicate that it will cost the prospective buyer $2.5 million to purchase their property or business? So long as they do not indicate that the other offer is for more than it actually is, such a statement would probably be regarded as acceptable puffing concerning the amount the seller hopes to obtain. The prospective purchaser should ask the seller the exact amount of the offer they have received, and if the seller refuses to provide a specific answer realize that some puffing is most likely involved.

[c]   Settlement Intentions

It is important to emphasize that the Rule 4.1 exception for puffing does not wholly excuse all misstatements regarding client settlement intentions. During the early stages of bargaining interactions, most practitioners do not expect opponents to disclose exact client desires. As negotiators approach final agreements, however, they anticipate a greater degree of candor. If negotiators were to deliberately deceive adversaries about this issue during the Closing Stage or the Cooperative/Integrative Stage, most attorneys would consider them dishonest, even though the Rule 4.1 proscription would remain inapplicable.

[d]   Misrepresentations Made to Neutral Facilitators

When lawyers representing clients interact with judicial settlement facilitators or private mediators, may they puff and embellish as they can with opposing attorneys pursuant to Comment 2 to Rule 4.1? *ABA Formal Opin.* 93-370 (1993) indicated that knowing misrepresentations to judicial mediators regarding client settlement intentions and subjective values would be impermissible, based upon the view that the Comment 2 exception only applies to bargaining interactions with *opposing counsel.* Since such misstatements to judicial officials would not be confined to adversarial communications, they would contravene Rule 4.1. (*See* Kovach, 2001; Alfini, 1999, Meyerson, 1997 (arguing for greater degree of lawyer candor when advocates are communicating with mediators).)

In *ABA Formal Opin.* 06-439 (2006), the ABA had to decide whether the logic of *Formal Opin.* 93-370 (1993) barred puffing and embellishment to nonjudicial mediators. If it followed the reasoning of the 1993 Opinion, lawyers could not misrepresent client settlement intentions and values to all neutral parties, but it felt uncomfortable with such an expansive prohibition. As a result, it decided to limit the coverage of the prior Opinion to judicial officers, and it held that such conversations with judicial settlement facilitators are governed by Model Rule 3.3(a)(1) which forbids lawyers from knowingly making false statements of material fact to tribunals. As a result, it held that Comment 2 to Rule 4.1 would still apply to communications between advocates and nonjudicial mediators in separate caucus sessions, allowing the use of traditional puffing and embellishment.

[e]   Lawyer Opinion

A crucial distinction is drawn between statements of lawyer opinion and statements of material fact. When attorneys merely express their opinions — *e.g.,* "I think the defendant had consumed too much alcohol"; "I believe the plaintiff will encounter future medical difficulties" — they are not constrained by Rule 4.1. Opposing counsel know that these recitations only concern the personal views of the speakers. These statements are critically different from lawyer statements indicating that they have witnesses who can testify to these matters. If representations regarding witness information is knowingly false, the misstatements would clearly contravene Rule 4.1.

[6]   Partial Disclosure of Information

[a]   Prevalence

Negotiators regularly use selective disclosures to enhance their positions. They divulge the legal doctrines and factual information beneficial to their claims and withhold the circumstances that are not helpful. In most instances, these selective disclosures are expected by opponents and are considered an inherent aspect of bargaining interactions. When attorneys emphasize their strengths, opposing counsel must attempt to ascertain their hidden weaknesses. They should carefully listen for verbal leaks and look for nonverbal signals that may indicate the existence of possible opponent problems. Probing questions may be used to elicit some negative information, and external research may be employed to gather other relevant data. These efforts are particularly important when opponents limit their disclosures to circumstances favoring their clients, since their partial disclosures may cause listeners to make erroneous assumptions.

[b]   Correcting Opponents' Factual or Legal Misunderstandings

When I discuss negotiating ethics with legal practitioners, I often ask if lawyers are under a duty to disclose information to correct erroneous factual or legal assumptions made by opposing counsel. Most respondents perceive no obligation to correct legal or factual misunderstandings generated solely by the carelessness of opposing attorneys. Respondents only hesitate when opponent misunderstandings may have resulted from misinterpretations of seemingly honest statements made by them. For example, when a plaintiff attorney embellishes the pain being experienced by a client with a severely sprained ankle, the defense lawyer may indicate how painful *broken ankles* can be. If the plaintiff representative has said nothing to create this false impression, should they be obliged to correct the obvious defense counsel error? Although a respectable minority of respondents believe that an affirmative duty to correct the misunderstanding may exist here — due to the fact that plaintiff embellishments may have inadvertently contributed to the misunderstanding — most respondents feel no such obligation. As long as they have not directly generated the erroneous belief, it is not their duty to correct it. They could not, however, include their opponent's misunderstanding in their own statements, since this would cause them to issue knowing falsehoods.

When opponent misunderstandings concern legal doctrines, almost no respondents perceive a duty to correct those misconceptions. They indicate that each side is obliged to conduct its own legal research. If opposing counsel make incorrect assumptions or carelessly fail to locate applicable statutes or cases, those advocates do not have the right to expect their adversaries to provide them with legal assistance. The more knowledgeable advocates may even continue to rely on precedents supporting their claims, so long as they do not distort the decisions supporting their positions.

Under some circumstances, partial answers may mislead opposing counsel as effectively as direct misrepresentations (see Comment 1 to Model Rule 4.1, Morgan & Rotunda, 2008, at 93). For example, the plaintiff in *Spaulding v. Zimmerman*, 263 Minn. 346, 116 N.W.2d 704 (1962), sustained cracked ribs and fractured clavicles in an automobile accident. After the ribs and clavicles had healed, the defense lawyers had the plaintiff examined by their own medical expert who detected an aorta aneurysm that plaintiff attorneys did not know about. While defense counsel were probably under no ethical obligation to voluntarily disclose existence of the aneurysm and could use blocking techniques to avoid answering opponent inquiries regarding the plaintiff's condition, they could not overtly misrepresent their physician's findings. Could defense attorneys respond to plaintiff counsel questions by indicating that "the ribs and the clavicles have healed nicely?" Would this partial disclosure constitute a deliberate misrepresentation of material fact, because the defendant lawyers realize that plaintiff counsel are interpreting this statement in a more expansive manner? Most practitioners have indicated that they would refuse to provide partial responses that would mislead plaintiff counsel into believing the plaintiff had completely recovered (see Herman, Cary & Kennedy, 2001, at 176–77). Recipients of answers limited to such specific conditions should become suspicious and ask follow-up inquiries about other problems that may have been discovered.

[7]   Nondisclosure of Information

[a]   Obligation to Disclose

[i]   Attorney Responsibility to Conduct Own Research

Even though Model Rule 4.1(a) states that attorneys must be truthful when they make statements concerning material law or fact Comment 1 expressly indicates that lawyers have "no affirmative duty to inform an opposing party of relevant facts." (Morgan & Rotunda, 2008, at 93) In the absence of special relationships or express contractual or statutory duties, practitioners are normally not obliged to divulge relevant legal or factual information to their adversaries (Korobkin, 2005, at 260–63; McKay, 1990, at 19). This doctrine is premised upon the duty of representatives to conduct their own legal research and factual investigations. Under our adversary system, attorneys do not have the right to expect their opponents to assist them in this regard. It is only when cases reach tribunals that Model Rule 3.3(a)(2) imposes an affirmative obligation on advocates "to disclose to the tribunal legal authority in the controlling jurisdiction known to the lawyer to be directly adverse to the position of the client and not disclosed by opposing counsel." (Morgan & Rotunda, 2008, at 79) No such duty is imposed, however, with respect to pertinent factual circumstances that are not discovered by opposing counsel.

Stare v. Tate, 21 Cal.App.3d 432, 98 Cal. Rptr. 264 (1971), involved divorce negotiations designed to divide the spouses' community property on an equal basis. When valuing certain property, Ms. Stare's attorney made a mathematical error that understated the actual value by $100,000. Although Mr. Tate and his lawyer were aware of this miscalculation, they said nothing and agreed to settlement terms that deprived Ms. Stare of $50,000. Since Mr. Tate and his lawyer were fully aware of Ms. Stare's miscalculation and sought to take advantage of it, the court reformed the property settlement to provide Ms. Stare with the additional $50,000 she deserved.

Brown v. County of Genesee, 872 F.2d 169 (6th Cir. 1989), concerned a county attorney who was negotiating the settlement of a Rehabilitation Act claim with the lawyer representing a diabetic employee. The claimant's attorney made a proposal to place the employee at a certain salary level which they believed to be the highest she could attain, when she could actually have been placed at a higher level. The court found that the county attorney had no legal or ethical duty to correct their erroneous belief in this regard, since the mistake by the claimant and her counsel was due to their failure to examine or to understand the public records available to everyone, and her counsel could have requested this information. The court thus refused to modify the claimant's settlement agreement to allow her to receive the higher salary, because the mistaken belief was unilateral, rather than mutual. Should the county attorney, as a public officer, have been under an affirmative duty to correct the claimant's obvious misunderstanding?

[ii] Client's State of Health

Suppose attorneys representing a severely injured plaintiff learn, during the critical stages of settlement talks, that their client has died due to unrelated factors. Would they be under any ethical duty to disclose this fact to defense counsel who are clearly assuming continuing pain and medical care for the plaintiff? Although one court held that "plaintiff's attorney clearly had a duty to disclose the death of his client both to the Court and to opposing counsel prior to negotiating the [settlement] agreement" (*Virzi v. Grand Trunk Warehouse & Cold Storage Co.*, 571 F. Supp. 507, 512 (E.D. Mich. 1983)), this conclusion is not required by the Comment to Rule 4.1 pertaining to negotiation discussions. Nonetheless, since the death of the plaintiff would presumably have necessitated the substitution of plaintiff's estate executor, plaintiff counsel may have been under a duty to notify defense attorneys of this development before concluding any agreement that would have affected the estate. (*see also* Kentucky Bar Assn. v Geisler, 938 S.W.2d 578 (Ky. Sup. Ct. 1997) (sustaining public reprimand for plaintiff attorney who failed to notify defense counsel that plaintiff had died during their negotiations)).

A similar issue would arise if plaintiff lawyers learned that their client had miraculously recovered from the serious condition that provides the basis of the current law suit. If plaintiff attorneys had previously answered interrogatories concerning the health of the plaintiff, they would probably be obliged under *Fed. Rule of Civ. Pro.* 26(e)(2) to supplement their previous responses.

> A party is under a duty seasonably to amend a prior response to an interrogatory, request for production, or request for admission if the party learns that the response is in some material respect incomplete or incorrect and if the additional or corrective information has not otherwise been made known to the other parties during the discovery process or in writing.

Suppose the party possessing the relevant information regarding the plaintiff is not the plaintiff's attorney, but rather defense counsel? This issue was confronted by the Minnesota Supreme Court in *Spaulding v. Zimmerman*, 263 Minn. 346, 116 N.W.2d 704 (1962) (discussed in section 6[b], *supra*). Plaintiff Spaulding was injured in an automobile accident when Defendant Ledermann's car, in which the plaintiff was riding, collided with Defendant Zimmerman's vehicle. He suffered multiple rib fractures, bilateral fractures of the clavicles, and a severe cerebral concussion. Several doctors who treated the plaintiff concluded that his injuries had completely healed. As the trial date approached, the defense attorneys had Spaulding examined by a neurologist who was expected to provide expert testimony for the defense. That physician agreed that the ribs and clavicles had healed, but he discovered a life-threatening aneurysm on Spaulding's aorta. Defense counsel were never asked by plaintiff counsel about the results of this examination, and defense lawyers did not volunteer any information about it.

A settlement agreement was achieved, which had to be approved by the trial court since Spaulding was a minor. After the case was settled, Spaulding discovered the aneurysm, which was surgically repaired, and he sued to set aside the prior settlement. The trial court vacated the settlement, and this decision was sustained by the Minnesota Supreme Curt. Despite the fact that most people would undoubtedly regard an affirmative duty to disclose the crucial information as the morally appropriate approach, the Minnesota Supreme Court correctly determined that the defense attorneys were under no ethical duty to volunteer the new medical information to plaintiff counsel. In fact, without client consent, the confidentiality preservation obligation then imposed by Model Rule 1.6 precluded volitional disclosure by defense counsel under these circumstances (Morgan & Rotunda, 2004, at 179–80). Comment 5 explicitly stated that "[t]he confidentiality rule applies not merely to matters communicated in confidence by the client but also to all information relating to the representation, whatever its source." (Morgan & Rotunda, 2004, at 180–81).

The *Spaulding Court* circumvented the Rule 1.6 prohibition by holding that as officers of the court, defense counsel had an affirmative duty to disclose the newly discovered medical information to the trial court prior to its approval of the settlement agreement. Had Spaulding not been a minor, the Court may have had to enforce the original accord, because of the absence of any trial court involvement in the settlement process. If courts are unwilling to impose affirmative disclosure obligations on advocates who possess such critical information pertaining to opposing clients, they should sustain the resulting settlement agreements despite the lack of disclosure. This would at least permit defense lawyers to divulge the negative information as soon as the settlement terms have been satisfied. By voiding such agreements after plaintiffs learn of the withheld information, courts effectively require defense attorneys to remain silent even after the law suits have been finally resolved.

The Restatement (3rd) of the Law Governing Lawyers attempts to protect defense attorneys who decide to divulge medical information in *Spaulding*-type situations. Section 66 states that lawyers who voluntarily disclose information concerning a condition posing a risk of death or serious bodily injury to their opponents should not be found in violation of Rule 1.6 nor be subject to legal malpractice liability to their own clients. In 2002, the ABA House of Delegates amended Model Rule 1.6 to comport with Section 66 of the Restatement. Amended Rule 1.6(b)(1) permits — but does not require — attorneys to disclose otherwise confidential information when necessary "to prevent reasonably certain death or substantial bodily harm." (Morgan & Rotunda, 2008, at 22). States with Model Rules will most likely accept this ABA amendment or reinterpret traditional Rule 1.6 to allow such disclosures.

In 2003, the ABA House of Delegates further amended Model Rule 1.6 to permit — but not require — a lawyer to reveal confidential client information "to prevent the client from committing a crime or fraud that is reasonably certain to result in substantial injury to the financial interests or property of another and in furtherance of which the client has used or is using the lawyer's services." (Rule 1.6(b)(2), Morgan & Rotunda, 2008, at 22) New Rule 1.6(b)(3) similarly permits a lawyer to disclose confidential client information to prevent or mitigate substantial injury to the financial interests or property of another that has or is reasonably certain to result from previous client criminal action or fraud in furtherance of which the client has used the lawyers services (Morgan & Rotunda, 2008, at 22–23). This exception does not apply where an attorney has been retained to represent the client with respect to the criminal or fraudulent acts in question (Comment 8 to Rule 1.6, Morgan & Rotunda, 2008, at 25).

[iii] Fact-Finding Questions

Attorneys can easily avoid these disclosure problems by remembering to ask the appropriate questions concerning uncertain areas before they enter into settlement agreements. Defense lawyers can directly ask if the plaintiff's condition has changed in any way. Plaintiff representatives could not ethically misrepresent the material condition of their client. If they were to use blocking techniques to avoid direct responses, defense lawyers should restate their inquiries and demand specific answers. If plaintiff attorneys know that defense counsel have had the plaintiff examined by a medical expert, they should always ask about the results of that examination. They should also request a copy of the resulting medical report, since they are entitled to that information in exchange for the right of defense counsel to have the plaintiff examined. While defense counsel may merely confirm what plaintiff lawyers already know, it is possible that plaintiff attorneys will obtain new information that will affect settlement discussions.

[iv]   Laws or Judicial Decisions

Suppose plaintiff or defense lawyers are on the verge of a law suit settlement based upon a line of State Supreme Court cases favoring their client. The morning of the day they are going to conclude their transaction, the State Supreme Court issues an opinion overturning those beneficial decisions and indicating that the new rule applies to all pending cases. Would knowledgeable attorneys whose position has been undermined by these legal changes be obligated to inform their unsuspecting opponents about these critical judicial developments? Almost all practitioners asked this question respond in the negative, based on their belief that opposing counsel are obliged to conduct their own legal research. Sagacious lawyers would recognize, however, that they could no longer rely upon the overturned decisions to support their afternoon discussions, because these legal misstatements would contravene Rule 4.1. On the other hand, they could probably ask their unsuspecting adversaries if they could cite a single case supporting their position!

Suppose settlement talks have continued while a defense motion for summary judgment has been pending before the trial court. One morning, the plaintiff lawyer receives a court order in the mail granting the defendant summary judgment. If the plaintiff attorney phones the defense counsel and realizes that they have not yet received notice of their summary judgment victory, could plaintiff counsel try to settle the case without disclosing this fact? No Model Rule appears to answer this question, and a few attorneys have indicated no hesitancy to seek a settlement without disclosure. Most lawyers, however, believe that as officers of the court they would have an affirmative duty to notify defense counsel of the court's communication, since receipt by one side is expected to reach the other side simultaneously. A number of judges I have asked have unanimously agreed with the latter view, stating that they would vacate any settlement achieved by plaintiff counsel without disclosure.

[8]   Authorized Limits

A frequently debated area concerns representations about one's authorized limits. Many attorneys refuse to answer "unfair" questions concerning their authorized limits, because these inquiries pertain to confidential attorney-client communications. If negotiators decide to respond to these queries, must they do so honestly? Some lawyers believe that truthful responses are required, since they concern material facts. Other practitioners assert that responses about client authorizations merely reflect client valuations and settlement intentions and are thus excluded from the scope of Rule 4.1 by the drafter's Comment. As a result, they think that attorneys may distort these matters (Rubin, 1995, at 453–54).

Negotiators who know they cannot avoid the impact of questions concerning their authorized limits by labeling them "unfair" and who find it difficult to provide knowingly false responses can employ an alternative approach. If the plaintiff counsel who is demanding $150,000 asks the defendant attorney who is presently offering $75,000 whether they are authorized to provide $100,000, the recipient may treat the $100,000 figure as a new plaintiff proposal. That individual can reply that the $100,000 sum suggested by plaintiff counsel is more realistic but still excessive. The plaintiff attorney may become preoccupied with the need to clarify the fact that they did not intend to suggest any reduction in their outstanding $150,000 demand. That person would probably forego further attempts to ascertain the authorized limits possessed by the defendant attorney!

§ 17.02   UNCONSCIONABLE TACTICS AND AGREEMENTS

[1]   Offensiveness

In recent years, a number of legal representatives — especially in large urban areas — have decided to employ highly offensive tactics to advance client interests. They may be rude, sarcastic, or nasty. These individuals erroneously equate discourteous actions with effective advocacy. They use these techniques as a substitute for lawyering skill. Proficient practitioners recognize that impolite behavior is the antithesis of competent representation.

Model Rule 1.3 provides that "[a] lawyer shall act with reasonable diligence and promptness in representing a client," and Comment 1 indicates that "[a] lawyer must . . . act with commitment and dedication to the interests of the client and with zeal in advocacy upon the client's behalf" (Morgan & Rotunda, 2008, at 15). Nonetheless, Comment 1 further states that "[t]he lawyer's duty to act with reasonable diligence does not require the use of offensive tactics or preclude the treating of all persons involved in the legal process with courtesy and respect."

Legal representatives should eschew tactics that are merely designed to humiliate or harass opponents. ABA Model Rule 4.4 expressly states that "a lawyer shall not use means that have no substantial purpose other than to embarrass, delay, or burden a third person . . . ." (Morgan & Rotunda, 2008, at 96; Herman, Cary & Kennedy, 2001, at 178; Lowenthal, 1982, at 102) Demented win-lose negotiators may endeavor to achieve total annihilation of adversaries through the cruel and unnecessary degradation of opposing counsel. Not only is such behavior morally reprehensible, but it needlessly exposes the offensive perpetrators to future recriminations that could easily be avoided through common courtesy. In litigation situations, it may expose the inappropriate actors to judicial sanctions. (*See, e.g., Lee v. American Eagle Airlines,* 2000 U.S. Dist. LEXIS 4198 (S.D. Fla. 2000) (unruly behavior by plaintiff lawyers warranted significant reduction in attorney fees they earned on behalf of prevailing plaintiff)). This approach also guarantees the offensive actors far more nonsettltments than are experienced by their more cooperative cohorts.

[2]   Secretly Taping Telephone Negotiations

Lawyers negotiate regularly on the telephone. In the near future, most people will use video phones via Internet connections. Since most people do not hear many words communicated during these discussions — and would undoubtedly miss many nonverbal signals being emitted during video phone exchanges — they may be tempted to secretly tape their bargaining conversations to enable them to review these interactions carefully once they have been concluded. Would such conduct be unethical? Although federal law does not prohibit the secret taping of telephone calls by one of the participants without the other party's knowledge, some states make such conduct illegal. In those jurisdictions, it would obviously be improper for lawyers to contravene these statutory prohibitions. What if such secret taping is not illegal? Some State Bar Associations have indicated that where secret taping is not proscribed by law, attorneys do not behave unethically when they engage in such behavior (Pitulla, 1994, at 102). Other State Bar Associations, however, have reached the opposite conclusion, believing that attorneys conducting telephone conversations with other lawyers have the right to expect those discussions to remain untaped without the knowledge and consent of both parties.

[3]   Accepting One-Sided Arrangements

Rule 4.3 of the 1980 Discussion Draft of the ABA Model Rules would have instructed attorneys not to conclude any agreement "the lawyer knows or reasonably should know . . . would be held to be unconscionable as a matter of law." (Lowenthal, 1982, at 103) This provision would have codified the admonition of Judge Rubin against the negotiation of "unconscionable deals" (Rubin, 1975, at 591). Nonetheless, this proposal was omitted from the final draft, most likely because of its superfluous nature. If negotiated contracts are "unconscionable as a matter of law," they would be subject to legal challenges that may vitiate the entire transactions. It thus behooves legal advocates to avoid the consummation of truly unconscionable accords (Adler & Silverstein, 2000, at 42–48).

What about seemingly one-sided arrangements that have not been procured through improper means and do not constitute legally unconscionable agreements? Should it be considered unethical or morally reprehensible for attorneys to negotiate such contracts? This concept would place the responsible advocates in a tenuous position. If courts would be unlikely to find the proposed agreements illegal and the opposing parties were perfectly willing to consummate the apparently skewed transactions, should the prevailing legal representatives refuse to conclude the deals merely because they believe the transactions may unreasonably disadvantage their opponents? Why should the subjective personal judgments of these lawyers take precedence over the willingness of their opponents and their attorneys to conclude the proposed exchanges? These individuals may not know — and may never know — why their opponents considered these deals "fair." Their adversaries may have been aware of factual or legal circumstances that either undermined their own positions or bolstered those of the other side.

Some lawyers might reasonably feel compelled to mention the apparently one-sided aspect of suggested transactions to their own clients. A few might even feel the need to explore this concern at least obliquely with opposing counsel. Would it be appropriate for them to refuse to consummate the agreements even when the other participants still favor their execution? If they continued to sanctimoniously oppose the proposed deals, should they be subject to bar discipline for failing to represent their client with appropriate zeal or to liability for legal malpractice? Attorneys who are positioned to conclude lawful arrangements that would substantially benefit their clients should be hesitant to vitiate the transactions based solely on their own personal conviction that the proffered terms are "unfair" to their opponents. How many lawyers in these circumstances would inform their clients that they were unwilling to recommend offers tendered by opposing parties in response to wholly proper bargaining tactics, merely because they thought the proposed terms were too generous?

[4]   Inaccurate Document Preparation

Once settlement agreements are achieved, attorneys are obliged to prepare documents that reflect the actual intentions of the negotiating parties. If a lawyer were to deliberately change a term or delete something that was agreed upon, the client may be held liable for fraud and the attorney would be subject to discipline (*e.g., Crane v.*

State Bar, 30 Cal.3d 117, 635 P.2d 163 (1981)). If one side has prepared the settlement agreement and the other side realizes that the drafter has inadvertently omitted an important provision, while no specific Model Rule directly addresses this situation, *ABA Formal Open.* 86-1518 (1986) indicated that the party aware of the omission should contact the drafting attorney to correct the error.

What should attorneys do if they receive confidential attorney-client information from opposing counsel that was sent by mail, fax, or e-mail by mistake? In 1992, the ABA issued Formal Opinion 92-368 which indicated that lawyers who receive documents containing confidential information they know or should reasonably know were inadvertently sent to them by opposing counsel should refrain from examining those materials further, promptly notify the senders of their inadvertent mistake, and abide by the senders' instructions regarding the disposition of the materials. In 2002, however, the ABA amended the Model Rules of Professional Conduct and narrowed the obligation of attorneys who receive confidential information inadvertently sent by opposing counsel.

Model Rule 4.4(b) states that "A lawyer who receives a document relating to the representation of the lawyer's client and knows or reasonably should know that the document was inadvertently sent shall promptly notify the sender" (Morgan & Rotunda, 2008, at 96). The new Rule does not require the receiving lawyer to refrain from examining the materials or to abide by the corrective instructions from the sending attorney. Comment 2 indicates that "[w]hether the lawyer is required to take additional steps, such as returning the original document, is a matter of law beyond the scope of these Rules, as is the question of whether the privileged status of a document has been waived." Comment 3 specifically acknowledges the dilemma faced by lawyers in this situation.

> Some lawyers may choose to return a document unread, for example, when the lawyer learns before receiving the document that it was inadvertently sent to the wrong address. Where a lawyer is not required by applicable law to do so, the decision to voluntarily return such a document is a matter of professional judgment ordinarily reserved to the lawyer.

As a result of the new Model Rule 4.4(b) language, the ABA issued Formal Opinion 05-437 recognizing that the protective approach set forth in Formal Opinion 92-368 was no longer operative.

Given the sanctity of the attorney-client privilege and the importance of protecting the communications between lawyers and their clients, it is surprising that the ABA has abandoned the more protective approach taken in Formal Opinion 92-368. This is especially true in the twenty-first century world in which confidential information can easily be transmitted electronically by attorneys who do not intend to disclose the information contained in electronic files sent to opposing counsel. The failure of the ABA to deal with this matter more specifically is especially troubling given the ability of e-mail file recipients to mine the metadata contained in those files to discover word changes made in those documents before they were made final and to, in some cases, discern the editorial comments made by opposing lawyers and even their clients as the sent drafts were being finalized.

[5]   E-mail and Cell Phone Negotiations

In recent years, it has become common for attorneys to conduct settlement discussions through e-mail exchanges. Information of a highly confidential nature may be included in such communications. Since it is possible for computer hackers to gain access to such information, must the communicating attorneys employ an encryption system designed to minimize the risk? *ABA Formal Open.* 99-413 (1999) reasonably recognized that the risk associated with e-mail transmissions is not that different from telephone calls (especially from cellular phones) and fax transmissions. It thus indicated that it would not be unreasonable for lawyers to use unencrypted e-mail to convey confidential information to other attorneys.

When parties send documents to others in electronic form, they often inadvertently include critical information that is not obvious on the face of those documents — and which they do not intend to share with the document recipients. Parties who know how to "mine" electronic files for hidden information may be able to determine exactly how documents were prepared and edited, and even uncover editorial comments made by persons who reviewed earlier drafts. Lawyers should use "reasonable care" when transmitting electronic documents to prevent the disclosure of metadata containing client confidences.

May attorneys who receive electronic files ethically mine those files for hidden metadata that will provide them with information the file senders clearly did not intend them to find? American Bar Association Formal Op. 06-442 (2006) indicated that lawyers have no ethical obligation to refrain from mining metadata embedded in electronic files received through e-mail from adverse parties. This decision should be contrasted with Model Rule 4.4(b) which provides that "[a] lawyer who receives a document relating to the representation of the lawyer's client and knows or reasonably should know that the document was inadvertently sent shall promptly notify the sender." (Morgan & Rotunda, 2008, at 96) Should lawyers be under a similar obligation when they receive electronic files containing accessible metadata they know the senders did not intend to include? A similar conclusion was reached by the Maryland Bar Ethics Committee [Op. 2007-09], but the Maryland Committee emphasized the fact that the Maryland Bar had not adopted Model Rule 4.4(b).

Both the New York Bar [N.Y. State Ethics Op. 749 (2001)] and the Alabama Bar [Ala. State Bar Disciplinary Commission Op. 2007-02 (2007)] have indicated that such mining of metadata in electronic files contravenes Model Rule 8.4, which provides that it constitutes "professional misconduct" for a lawyer to "engage in conduct involving dishonesty, fraud, deceit, or misrepresentation [or] . . . conduct that is prejudicial to the administration of justice." The Alabama Bar stated that the "mining of metadata constitutes a knowing and deliberate attempt by the recipient attorney to acquire confidential and privileged information in order to obtain an unfair advantage against an opposing party." The District of Columbia Bar has taken an intermittent position by indicating that it is unethical to mine metadata contained in electronic documents received from opposing counsel if the receiving attorney has *actual knowledge* that the metadata were inadvertently sent [D.C. Legal Ethics Comm. Op. 341 (2007)]. The D.C. Bar further indicated that lawyers have an ethical duty to use available means to remove such metadata before they send files electronically to other attorneys.

Attorneys frequently use cellular telephones to conduct negotiations. If they communicate confidential client information during these calls, may they be found to have impermissibly compromised the Model Rule 1.6 rights of their clients? State Bar

Associations have divided over this issue, with some indicating that confidential information should not be discussed over cellular telephones that can be overheard by eavesdroppers, and with others finding such communications sufficiently private to preclude violations. (see U.S. Law Week (1/1/02) at 2382–2383). With the ubiquitous use of cellular phones and federal and state restrictions on eavesdropping, I would expect the ABA and most State Bar Associations to ultimately find that the use of this communication mode to discuss confidential client information does not contravene Rule 1.6.

[6]   Threat of Criminal Prosecution

Practitioners and law students occasionally ask whether lawyers who represent clients in civil actions arising out of arguably criminal conduct may suggest the possibility of criminal prosecution if the civil suit negotiations are not completed successfully. DR 7-105(A) of the ABA Code of Professional Responsibility, that is still followed by some jurisdictions, states that lawyers shall not "threaten to present criminal charges solely to obtain an advantage in a civil matter" (Morgan & Rotunda, 2008, at 420). This provision might be read to preclude the mention of possible criminal action to advance civil suit discussions. Courts have appropriately acknowledged, however, that neither DR 7-105(A) nor extortion or compounding of felony prohibitions should be interpreted to prevent civil litigants from mentioning the availability of criminal action if related civil claims are not resolved or to preclude clients from agreeing to forego the filing of criminal charges in exchange for money paid to resolve their civil suits (*Committee on Legal Ethics v. Printz*, 187 W.Va. 182, 416 S.E.2d 720 (1992)). Nonetheless, legal representatives must be careful not to use the threat of criminal prosecution to obtain *more* than is owed or have their clients agree not to testify at future criminal trials. "Seeking payment beyond restitution in exchange for foregoing criminal prosecution or seeking any payments in exchange for not testifying at a criminal trial . . . are still clearly prohibited." (416 S.E.2d at 727) In a similar case, the Oregon Supreme Court, held that it was unethical for an attorney to threaten the possibility of criminal charges *solely* to obtain an advantage regarding negotiations pertaining to a related civil matter (*In re* Charles, 290 Or. 127, 618 P.2d 1281 (1980)). A threat to invoke criminal proceedings to enhance one's bargaining position in an *unrelated* civil dispute would almost certainly be improper, because of the extortionate nature of the threat (*Bluestein v. State Bar*, 13 Cal.3d 162, 529 P.2d 599 (1974)).

The Model Rules do not contain any provision analogous to DR 7-105(A), and it is clear that the drafters deliberately chose not to prohibit the threat of criminal action to advance civil suit settlement talks pertaining to the same operative circumstances (Pitulla, 1992, at 106). As a result, the ABA Standing Committee on Ethics and Professional Responsibility indicated in *Formal Opinion* 92-363 (1992), that it is not unethical under the Model Rules for attorneys to mention the possibility of criminal charges during civil suit negotiations, as long as they do "not attempt to exert or suggest improper influence over the criminal process." (Pitulla, 1992, at 106) Nevertheless, legal representatives must still not demand excessive compensation that may contravene applicable extortion provisions or promise that their clients will not testify at future criminal trials, since such a commitment would contravene public policy.

§ 17.03   POTENTIAL ATTORNEY-CLIENT CONFLICTS OF INTEREST

Clients obtain the services of attorneys to benefit from the legal expertise provided by such specialists and to obtain the advice of detached professionals. In most cases, attorneys provide clients with unbiased advice and work diligently to further client interests. In some instances, however, the interests of the clients and their lawyers may diverge (Korobkin, 2002, at 310–12). For example, individuals who claim to have been wrongfully discharged from employment may prefer reinstatement to their former positions over generous back pay agreements. Their attorneys, who are probably being compensated on a contingent fee basis, cannot get one-third or forty percent of their reinstatement. As a result, their legal representatives may encourage them to forego reinstatement in favor of greater monetary relief. A victim of sexual or racial harassment may prefer an apology to monetary compensation. Their contingent fee counsel may prefer more tangible relief, and fail to seek the relief the client really wants to obtain.

Lawyers must always recognize the unfailing duty they owe to their clients. Under Model Rule 1.2(a), attorneys "shall abide by a client's decisions concerning the objectives of representation" and "shall abide by a client's decision whether to settle a matter." (Morgan & Rotunda, 2008, at 12). While attorneys may attempt to influence the objectives they think clients should seek, once clients have decided what they want to obtain from the legal representation, their lawyers must work diligently to satisfy those client objectives. Even when attorneys do not like offers made by opposing parties, they must acknowledge their ethical obligation under Model Rule 1.4(a) to keep their clients reasonably informed about the status of matters (Morgan & Rotunda, 2008, at 16). Lawyers may only reject offers of settlement without client consultation where the clients have already made it clear that such proposals would be unacceptable. (see Comment 2 to Model Rule 1.4 in Morgan & Rotunda, 2008, at 17).

§ 17.04   CONCLUDING ADMONITIONS

Despite the contrary impression of some members of the general public, I have generally found attorneys to be conscientious and honorable people. I have encountered few instances of questionable behavior. I would thus like to conclude with the admonitions I impart to my Legal Negotiating students as they prepare to enter the legal profession. Lawyers must remember that they have to live with their own consciences, and not those of their clients or their partners. They must employ tactics they are comfortable using, even in those situations in which other people encourage them to employ less reputable behavior. If they adopt techniques they do not consider appropriate, not only will they experience personal discomfort, but they will also fail to achieve their intended objective due to the fact they will not appear credible when using those tactics. Attorneys must also acknowledge that they are members of a special profession and owe certain duties to the public that transcend those that may be owed by people engaged in other businesses (Condlin, 1992, at 77). Even though ABA Model Rule 1.3 states that "[a] lawyer shall act with reasonable diligence," Comment 1 expressly recognizes that "a lawyer is not bound . . . to press for every advantage that might be realized for a client. . . . [A] lawyer may have authority to exercise professional discretion in determining the means by which a matter should be pursued." (Morgan & Rotunda, 2008, at 15).

Popular negotiation books occasionally recount the successful use of questionable techniques to obtain short-term benefits. The authors glibly describe the way they have employed highly aggressive, deliberately deceptive, or equally opprobrious bargaining tactics to achieve their objectives. They usually conclude these stories with parenthetical admissions that their bilked adversaries would probably be reluctant to interact with them in the future. When negotiators engage in such questionable behavior that they would find it difficult, if not impossible, to transact future business with their adversaries, they have usually transcended the bounds of propriety. No legal representatives should be willing to jeopardize long-term professional relationships for the narrow interests of particular clients. Zealous representation should never be thought to require the employment of personally compromising techniques.

Lawyers must acknowledge that they are not guarantors — they are only legal advocates. They are not supposed to guarantee client victory no matter who disreputably they must act to do so. They should never countenance witness perjury or the withholding of subpoenaed documents. While they should zealously endeavor to advance client interests, they should recognize their moral obligation to follow the ethical rules applicable to all attorneys.

Untrustworthy advocates encounter substantial difficulty when they negotiate with others. Their oral representations have to be verified and reduced to writing, and many opponents even distrust their written documents. Negotiations are especially problematic and cumbersome. If nothing else moves practitioners to behave in an ethical and dignified manner, their hope for long and successful legal careers should induce them to avoid conduct that may undermine their future effectiveness.

Attorneys should diligently strive to advance client objectives while simultaneously maintaining their personal integrity. This philosophy will enable them to optimally serve the interests of both their clients and society (Cohen, 2001). Legal practitioners who are asked about their insistence on ethical behavior may take refuge in an aphorism of Mark Twain: "Always do right. This will gratify some people, and astonish the rest!"

Summary

1. Although most participants regularly misstate some things during legal negotiations, few engage in unethical behavior.

2. Model Rule 4.1 prohibits intentional misrepresentation of material law or fact, but it excludes statements regarding client valuations and settlement intentions.

3. Attorneys are generally under no obligation to volunteer information to opponents, but they may not make knowingly false statements concerning material facts or law, or provide partial information they know would be likely to mislead others.

4. Model Rule 4.4 proscribes conduct that is merely designed to humiliate or harass opponents, and attorneys should avoid offensive behavior that would undermine their long-term bargaining effectiveness.

5. Neither the Code of Professional Responsibility nor the Model Rules prevent legal representatives from mentioning the possibility of criminal charges to advance civil suit negotiations arising from the same circumstances, but they must not demand extortionate compensation nor promise that their clients will not testify at future criminal trials.

6. Lawyers must live with their own consciences and not those of their clients or partners. They must employ tactics they are comfortable using both to preserve their own integrity and to guarantee their future effectiveness.

APPENDIX

NEGOTIATION EXERCISES

Rules and Objectives

Several simulation exercises have been included for the benefit of those readers who would like to practice the concepts discussed in this book. It is occasionally beneficial for participants to function in teams of two. The disagreements that usually arise between partners regarding bargaining goals and strategies reminds advocates of the fact they must often work as diligently to convince their clients to approve particular settlements as they must to induce opposing counsel to accept proposed terms.

All of the participants should receive copies of the General Information sheets. The attorneys for each side should also be provided with copies of the Confidential Information sheets pertaining to their client. Neither side may show their Confidential Information sheet to the opponents during the negotiation process. They may only disclose the information contained on that form orally. If they are unable to convince their opponents of the veracity of their factual representations, they must determine how they can enhance their credibility.

Participants may never disclose the *specific aspects* of their *scoring system*. While they may indicate that one item is worth twice as much as another term, they may not divulge that one is worth 10 points and the other is worth 20 points. Everyone should conduct their interactions as they would if they were involved with real client transactions.

A specific time limit should be provided for each exercise. The participants may either be given several days or weeks to meet whenever they wish or be instructed to meet for one or two hours at a set time to conclude their entire transaction. I prefer to establish a one or two week time frame that permits the actors to meet whenever and as frequently as they wish.

It is beneficial to have various groups negotiate the same exercise simultaneously. When they are finished, their diverse results and different experiences can be compared. This provides the participants with fairly objective feedback concerning the comparative value of their respective agreements. The advocates should be encouraged to be candid with each other regarding the factors that most influenced their interactions. This is the type of information negotiators rarely obtain from real-life opponents. What did opposing counsel do that enhanced or undermined their situations? Were they credible speakers? Did they appear to emit unintended verbal leaks or nonverbal signals? What induced the parties to reach their mutual agreement or terminal impasse? What might each side have done differently to more effectively advance their interests? Were any ethical questions raised?

* * *

The PERSONAL INJURY EXERCISE is provided due to the familiarity most attorneys have with basic tort law concepts. It is a classic constant sum problem, with each dollar obtained by the plaintiff constituting an equal debit for the defendant. If participants allow the tentative client views stated in their respective Confidential Information sheets to govern their preliminary bargaining conduct, the side making the first real offer is likely to be at a disadvantage. Plaintiff representatives would have their client's $250,000 objective in mind, while defendant lawyers would be thinking of their client's $2,000,000 bottom line. Thousands of practicing attorneys have negotiated this problem at continuing legal education programs around the country, and I continue to be amazed by the divergent results achieved. The settlements usually range from $250,000–300,000 to $1,900,000–2,000,000! I occasionally get settlements in the $2,500,000–3,000,000 range, despite the $2,000,000 nonsettlement option available to defendants.

The SEXUAL HARASSMENT EXERCISE is included for several reasons. It involves some interesting and novel legal issues, and it is difficult to quantify the student-plaintiff's monetary damages. There is room for cooperative bargaining. The student-plaintiff can achieve many points for an "A-" grade and for a personal apology from the professor-defendant accompanied by his promise to obtain psychiatric counseling, yet neither of these terms costs him anything. Both parties gain from a mutual commitment to keep the terms of their accord confidential. It is important for the negotiators to attempt to determine these mutually beneficial areas during the Information Stage of their interaction. Individuals representing the professor-defendant must frequently decide whether they may ethically indicate, expressly or implicitly, that their agreement to the above terms is costly for their side.

The RODRIGUEZ v. DOUGLAS CHEMICAL CO. EXERCISE permits participants to negotiate an interesting "wrongful termination" claim. Plaintiff attorneys must recognize that their claim is invalid if they are unable to convince the State Supreme Court to adopt the "public policy" exception to the traditional "employment-at-will" doctrine, while defense counsel must acknowledge the egregious nature of this case and the possibility of substantial company exposure if the "public policy" exception were adopted. The most efficient agreements should include (1) McTavish recommendations, (2) "To Whom It May Concern" recommendations, (3) promises that Douglas Chemical will provide no other reference information to prospective employers, (4) a confidentiality provision, and (5) a plaintiff willingness to forego reinstatement with Douglas Chemical. The most competitive bargaining will concern the amount of compensation to be given to the plaintiff.

The CHINESE JOINT VENTURE EXERCISE exposes students to an international business negotiation, and the Confidential Information pages do not contain specific point values for the different items to be negotiated. Only general client interests are described. This requires negotiators to determine the relative values of the various items from general statements provided by their respective clients.

The MODIFIED NASA DECISION MAKING EXERCISE is intended to be instructive regarding the manner in which group decisions are made and the way in which competitive tendencies frequently influence what appear to be purely cooperative interactions. This Exercise is especially instructive for corporate or agency counsel who must regularly interact with other departments within their own organizations. Since the stranded moon explorers must attempt to survive together, there is no reason for either detail or its members to view the other detail or its members as competitors. Nonetheless, when this Exercise is conducted, counterproductive competitive behavior is usually discernible. During the initial phase, each participant should be given five to ten minutes to individually rank the fifteen items in order of perceived importance.

During the second phase of this Exercise, details of from eight to fifteen persons must be formed. Each detail must then engage in an intra-detail negotiation that is designed to achieve a group consensus with respect to their ranking of the fifteen items. I usually provide each detail with ten to fifteen minutes for this purpose, to make them experience some degree of time urgency. It is interesting to watch for "leaders" to emerge. They tend to be implicitly selected by their detail because of their physical location in the group (*e.g.*, at the head of the table), their age and/or sex, their professional status, their appearance, or their personal inclination to lead their group. Participants should observe the way in which the leaders and others attempt to minimize group conflict and to maximize group harmony. How do the leaders work (mediate) to resolve disputes regarding particular items? How do they function to defuse competitive tendencies that develop?

The third phase of this Exercise involves inter-detail negotiations. Pairs of details are given from fifteen to twenty minutes to resolve two basic issues: (1) which detail will remain behind and which will attempt to rendezvous with the parent ship; and (2) which supplies will be assigned to each of the details. By having details of eight to fifteen members, the group members must initially decide whether they should all participate in the inter-detail negotiations or select one or two representatives to speak for them. (Groups consisting of less than eight members can normally all participate in such intergroup transactions, while groups of over fifteen members must necessarily bargain through chosen representatives.) Individuals who do not readily trust other people are particularly hesitant to permit the adoption of a representational scheme — unless they are to be the designated spokespersons. Details generally argue about which group should try to rendezvous with the parent ship, with both expressing the desire to be assigned this task. Once this issue is resolved, the details tend to fight over the distribution of the undamaged items. They normally exhibit highly competitive tendencies. What if one group were to be asked to divide the items between the detail that should go and the detail that should remain, with the other group being thereafter allowed to decide whether it would prefer to go or to remain? Does this Exercise remind participants of the manner in which many law firm or business firm decisions are made?

PERSONAL INJURY EXERCISE

General Information

At approximately 11:30 p.m. on a rainy and dark Friday evening last November, accountant Jim Denver was driving his Continental up Powell Street in San Francisco. He had just completed a long and acrimonious dinner meeting with a difficult, but important, client. Although he had consumed three or four Martinis during the course of his lengthy discussions, he felt in complete control of his faculties when he concluded the meeting.

As a result of the emergency session with his client, Denver was forced to miss a prestigious social event that his wife had been eagerly anticipating. He realized she would be very angry over the situation, and he was in a great hurry to return home to assuage her feelings. As Denver was heading up a particularly steep portion of Powell Street, he swerved toward the middle of the road to avoid a double-parked car, and he drove precariously close to an oncoming cable car on which Norma Peterson was riding.

Denver's mind was on both the problems with his client and his wife's ire, and he did not see Peterson, who was clumsily dismounting from the cable car in front of him. Peterson slipped on the wet pavement into the path of Denver's automobile, and she was directly struck before Denver could even apply his brakes.

Peterson suffered a broken back resulting in paralysis from the waist down. She was 40 years old at the time of the mishap. Peterson, who was a successful patent attorney at the time of the accident with Denver, has adapted herself well to her present condition and she is currently able to conduct her business as effectively as ever. However, one month ago, her husband instituted marital dissolution proceedings. She contends that this was brought on by her paralyzed condition.

Peterson has sued Denver for $5,000,000. Her medical expenses and lost earnings total about $250,000. The State of California is a comparative negligence jurisdiction. Any settlement figure agreed upon must be paid to Peterson immediately.

Plaintiff's Confidential Information

You are aware that on the night of the accident, Peterson had been drinking heavily at a bar with a favorite male associate from her office. She had not intended to leave the cable car where she did, but, in her intoxicated state, had fallen off the car and slipped on the wet pavement into the path of Denver's automobile. Nevertheless, you have located an apparently reliable witness who is positive that Denver was speeding and swerving sharply at the moment he struck Peterson. You have suspicions that Denver may have consumed several drinks too many before he commenced his drive home, but you have not been able to substantiate this fact.

You have been informed that Mr. Peterson had been planning to dissolve his marriage prior to the accident due to his wife's extra-marital affairs, and you know that her injury did not precipitate this action. In fact, Peterson's disability may have precluded his filing for dissolution at an earlier time.

Peterson, who is reputed to be a solid citizen, is terrified of the adverse consequences that might be caused to her lucrative practice should her clients learn of her drinking and "dating" proclivities. She has thus decided *not* to press her suit against Denver to trial. She would like to recover at least $250,000 to cover her medical expenses and lost earnings, and would be pleased to recover any amount above that figure. She is presently earning $375,000 per year.

Since Peterson does not wish to take this case to trial, you will automatically be placed at the *bottom* of Plaintiff groups if you fail to reach any agreement. If you achieve a settlement, your group placement will be determined by the amount of money Peterson is to receive.

Defendant's Confidential Information

You know that your client had been drinking on the night in question, but you doubt that this adversely influenced his driving ability. However, you suspect that he was driving too fast for such a damp and dark night on busy Powell Street. You also realize that Denver's mind was on his client and wife at the moment it should have been concentrating on the traffic, and you believe that a jury could conclude that he had driven negligently.

You have learned of the excellent reputation which Peterson has in the community, and you have been led to believe that her paralysis has caused her husband to sue for dissolution after fifteen years of apparently blissful marriage. You have discovered from investigation that Peterson had visited a bar with one of her male associates prior to the time she had boarded the cable car on Powell Street, but she has stated that she had only stopped off after work to help him celebrate his birthday. She has denied any heavy drinking. Although you believe that she had been out quite late to have merely been engaged in a friendly birthday celebration, you have no hard evidence to refute Peterson's story.

Your client is worried about the effect any adverse publicity could have on his business, and he would like to settle the case as soon as possible. Denver has a $1,000,000 automobile insurance policy, and has the personal assets to cover an additional $1,000,000. The insurance carrier has authorized you to pay the entire $1,000,000 policy limit, and Denver has said that he is willing to provide an additional $1,000,000 cash, if necessary. He is hoping, however, that you will be able to settle this matter within the scope of his insurance coverage.

If you reach a settlement, your group placement will be determined by the amount of money you agree to pay to Peterson. If you do not achieve any settlement, you will be treated as if you lost a $2,000,000 judgment, with that $2,000,000 figure being used to determine your group placement.

SEXUAL HARASSMENT EXERCISE

General Information

Last year, Jane Doe was a first year law student at the Yalebridge Law School, which is part of Yalebridge University, a private, non-sectarian institution. Ms. Doe was a student in Professor Alexander Palsgraf's Tort Law class.

During the first semester, Professor Palsgraf made sexually suggestive comments to Ms. Doe on several occasions. These comments were always made outside of the classroom and when no other individuals were present. Ms. Doe unequivocally indicated her personal revulsion toward Professor Palsgraf's remarks and informed him that they were entirely improper and unappreciated.

During the latter part of the second semester, Professor Palsgraf suggested to Ms. Doe in his private office that she have sexual relations with him. Ms. Doe immediately rejected his suggestion and told Professor Palsgraf that he was "a degenerate and disgusting old man who was a disgrace to the teaching profession."

Last June, Ms. Doe received her first year law school grades. She received one "A", two "A-", one "B+", and one "D", the latter grade pertaining to her Tort Law class. She immediately went to see Professor Palsgraf to ask him about her low grade. He said that he was sorry about her "D", but indicated that the result might have been different had she acquiesced in his previous request for sexual favors.

Ms. Doe then had Professor Irving Prosser, who also teaches Tort Law at Yalebridge, review her exam. He said that it was a "most respectable paper" that should certainly have earned her an "A-" or "B+", and possibly even an "A".

Ms. Doe has sued Professor Palsgraf in state court for $250,000 based upon three separate causes of action: (1) sexual harassment in violation of Title IX of the Education Amendments of 1972; (2) intentional infliction of emotional distress; and (3) fraud. Professor Palsgraf has a net worth of $450,000, including the equity in his $350,000 house and a $50,000 library of ancient Gilbert's outlines.

It is now early August, and Ms. Doe will begin her second year of law school in several weeks.

Confidential Information — Jane Doe

Your client wants to obtain several forms of relief from Professor Palsgraf: (1) a grade of "A" or "A-" in Tort Law; (2) the resignation of Professor Palsgraf from the Yalebridge Law School; and (3) a sufficiently large sum of money to deter such offensive conduct by other professors in the future.

Score *plus* 35 points if Professor Palsgraf agrees to change Ms. Doe's Tort Law grade to "A-", and *plus* 50 points if he agrees to change her grade to "A".

Score *plus* 200 points if Professor Palsgraf agrees to resign from the Yalebridge Law School faculty. If Professor Palsgraf does not resign, but agrees to take a one-year leave of absence or a one-year sabbatical leave from the Law School during the *coming* academic year (*i.e.*, Ms. Doe's second year), score *plus* 50 points. If Professor Palsgraf agrees to take a leave of absence and/or a sabbatical leave during the coming year *and* the following year (*i.e.*, Ms. Doe's final two years of law school), score *plus* 75 points.

If Professor Palsgraf does not resign, but does agree to seek psychiatric counseling *and* personally apologize to Ms. Doe, score *plus* 50 points.

Score *plus* 2 points for each $1,000, or part thereof, Professor Palsgraf agrees to immediately pay Ms. Doe in settlement of her suit.

Ms. Doe is concerned about the publicity surrounding this matter and the impact that publicity may have on her future employment opportunities. Score *plus* 50 points for a clause guaranteeing the confidentiality of any settlement reached with Professor Palsgraf.

Since Ms. Doe wishes to have this matter resolved now so that she may concentrate fully on her legal education, you will automatically be placed at the *bottom* of your group if no settlement agreement is achieved.

Confidential Information — Professor Palsgraf

Your client realizes that his conduct was entirely inappropriate, and he is deeply sorry for the difficulty he has caused Ms. Doe. He would thus be willing to submit to psychiatric counseling and to personally apologize to Ms. Doe. Should you agree to either or both of these requirements, you lose *no points*.

Professor Palsgraf fears that Ms. Doe may ask for his resignation from the Yalebridge Law School, and he would rather lose everything before he would forfeit his Yalebridge position. Should you agree to have Professor Palsgraf resign his Yalebridge professorship, you must *deduct* 500 points.

Your client recognizes that he will have to provide Ms. Doe with the grade she should have received. He is readily willing to change her grade to "A-", and you lose *no points* for agreeing to an "A-." Professor Palsgraf does not think that Ms. Doe's exam performance was really worthy of an "A". You thus *lose* 50 points if you agree to have Ms. Doe's Tort Law grade changed to an "A".

Professor Palsgraf is currently eligible for a one-year, paid "sabbatical leave." He has been saving this leave to enable him to go to Cambridge University in two years. If you agree to have Professor Palsgraf take that "sabbatical leave" during either of the next two academic years, you *lose* 25 points. Should you agree to have him take a "leave of absence" during either of the next two academic years, which, unlike a "sabbatical leave," would not involve a continuation of his salary, you *lose* 100 points. (If you agree to both a one-year "sabbatical" *and* a one-year unpaid "leave of absence," you *lose* a total of 125 points.)

Professor Palsgraf will almost certainly have to provide Ms. Doe with monetary compensation for the wrong he committed. You *lose* 3 points for each $1,000, or part thereof, you agree to pay Ms. Doe. Any agreement regarding the payment of money must be operative immediately — no form of future compensation may be included.

Professor Palsgraf is concerned about the publicity surrounding this tragic affair. Score *plus* 50 points for a clause guaranteeing the confidentiality of any settlement reached.

Since Professor Palsgraf believes that the continuation of this law suit may ruin his outstanding legal career, you will automatically be placed at the *bottom* of your group if no settlement is achieved.

RODRIGUEZ v. DOUGLAS CHEMICAL CO. EXERCISE

General Information

The Douglas Chemical Company ("Douglas Chemical") produces various chemical products at its East Dakota facility. Several of its manufacturing processes involve the use of highly toxic substances regulated by the East Dakota Environmental Protection Act. The East Dakota Environmental Protection Agency requires chemical companies to detoxify hazardous substances before releasing such substances into rivers or ground waters. Substances which cannot be sufficiently detoxified must be removed by licensed toxic waste firms.

Alicia Rodriguez is a physical chemist. After she received her Ph.D. from the University of East Dakota fifteen years ago, she accepted a position with Douglas Chemical. Until last year, she worked in the Research and Development Department. Last December 1st, she was promoted to Director of the Environment Protection Department. Her salary was increased to $75,000 per year.

When Dr. Rodriguez took over the Environmental Protection Department, she discovered that her predecessor had been falsifying Company records to permit the release of highly toxic substances into the Green River which flows past the Douglas Chemical facility. Dr. Rodriguez found that her predecessor had been filing false reports with the East Dakota Environmental Protection Agency. Those reports indicated that only detoxified substances were being released into the Green River.

Dr. Rodriguez immediately informed Ezra Douglas, the Company President, of her discovery. Mr. Douglas indicated that the East Dakota Environmental Protection regulations were overly strict. He said that the Company was not releasing an excessive amount of toxic substances into the Green River, and he suggested that no real harm was being caused by the Company's action. He told Dr. Rodriguez that she would have to be more of a "team player" if she wished to remain at Douglas Chemical. Dr. Rodriguez stated that she would not falsify Company records to permit the unlawful release of toxic substances into the Green River. Mr. Douglas informed her that any disclosure of Company practices to the East Dakota Environmental Protection Agency would result in her termination.

Last December 15, Dr. Rodriguez met with Peter Connolly, Director of the East Dakota Environmental Protection Agency. She informed Dr. Connolly of the existing Douglas Chemical toxic substance release practice and provided copies of both the correct and the falsified Douglas Chemical records. On December 16, Dr. Connolly had water samples taken from areas of the Green River adjacent to the Douglas Chemical facility and discovered excessive levels of toxic substances. Samples taken from the Douglas Chemical release pipes were found to contain unusually high levels of toxic substances. On December 17, the East Dakota Environmental Protection Agency issued a citation against Douglas Chemical, and on December 20, it obtained a temporary restraining order prohibiting the further release of toxic substances by Douglas Chemical.

On December 21, Mr. Douglas called Dr. Rodriguez into his office. He informed her that she was not working out in her new position. He said that he was unwilling to have a disloyal individual in his employ. Mr. Douglas then informed Dr. Rodriguez that she was being terminated.

On January 5, Mr. Douglas was contacted by Ed Barrett, a vice president of the Jacobs Petroleum Company. Mr. Barrett told Mr. Douglas that Jacobs Petroleum was planning to ask Dr. Rodriguez to become Director of Chemical Processing, a position which would have paid her $80,000 per year. Mr. Douglas told Mr. Barrett that Dr. Rodriguez had recently been discharged by Douglas Chemical because of her "poor attitude." He said that Dr. Rodriguez had been a wholly uncooperative manager. On January 6, Mr. Barrett told Dr. Rodriguez that Jacobs Patroleum would be unable to offer her the Chemical Processing position, because of her "past difficulties" at Douglas Chemical.

Last February 1, Dr. Rodriguez filed a civil action in the East Dakota Circuit Court alleging: (1) that her termination based upon her unwillingness to falsify toxic chemical records contravened public policy; and (2) that Mr. Douglas' statements to Mr. Barrett constituted defamation. She sought actual damages of $500,000 and punitive damages of $1,000,000.

No East Dakota statute or regulation expressly protects individuals who are terminated because of their unwillingness to participate in practices violating the State Environmental Protection Act. Although the East Dakota Supreme Court has traditionally followed the "employment-at-will" doctrine, under which an employer may discharge an employee for "good cause, bad cause, or no cause at all," three of its seven Justices indicated in a recent decision that they might adopt a "public policy" exception if particularly egregious circumstances were involced. The East Dakota Civil Code specifically provides "qualified immunity" against defamation liability for employers who provide reference information in response to requests for such information from other business entities.

Any monetary sum that Douglas Chemical agrees to pay to Dr. Rodriguez must be *payable immediately*. It may *not be payable* in future installments.

Confidential Information — Rodriguez Attorneys

Dr. Rodriguez is particularly concerned about her professional reputation. Although this law suit has not yet generated significant public interest, she is afraid that a public trial might cause other companies to regard her as a trouble-maker. If you fail to achieve a settlement agreement resolving this case, you will automatically be placed at the *bottom of your group.*

Dr. Rodriguez has been discussing employment opportunities with the McTavish Chemical Company. McTavish Vice President Susan Travis has told Dr. Rodriguez that she will be offered a position as Director of Research, at $78,000 per year, if she can resolve her suit against Douglas Chemical expeditiously and quietly.

Dr. Rodriguez does not wish to return to Douglas Chemical — unless she is unable to obtain employment with another company. She is thus willing to forego any offer of reinstatement, so long as she obtains the other terms she desires.

Although Dr. Rodriguez has not yet sustained any substantial monetary loss, she has suffered extreme emotional discomfort. She is outraged at the manner in which Douglas Chemical treated her, and believes that she deserves some meaningful monetary compensation. Score *plus* 2 points for each $1,000, or part thereof, in compensation you obtain from Douglas Chemical.

Dr. Rodriguez would like to obtain: (1) a favorable reference from Douglas Chemical to McTavish Chemical; (2) a "To Whom It May Concern" letter of reference for future use; and (3) a promise that Douglas Chemical will provide no other reference information to prospective employers in the future. Score *plus* 50 points for a favorable recommendation letter from Douglas Chemical to McTavish Chemical; *plus* 50 points for a favorable "To Whom It May Concern" letter to be given to Dr. Rodriguez on Douglas Chemical stationery; and *plus* 50 points for a clause providing that Douglas Chemical will not provide any other reference information concerning Dr. Rodriguez to other prospective employers.

If Douglas Chemical is unwilling to provide Dr. Rodriguez with a favorable reference to McTavish Chemical, she may be forced, at least in the short run, to seek reemployment with Douglas Chemical. If you are unable to obtain a favorable reference to McTavish Chemical *but* obtain an offer of reinstatement to Dr. Rodriguez's former position in the Research and Development Department, score *plus* 25 points.

Dr. Rodriguez would like to ensure that the details surrounding this unfortunate situation will remain private. Score *plus* 50 points for a provision stating that the circumstances indigenous to this dispute *and* the terms of the settlement agreement will remain confidential.

Confidential Information — Douglas Chemical Attorneys

The Douglas Chemical Company is particularly concened about the negative publicity already associated with this dispute. It fears that a public trial will further exacerbate this problem. You have thus been instructed to achieve a settlement agreement, if at all possible, and will be placed at the *bottom of your group* if you fail to do so.

It is obvious that Dr. Rodriguez was terminated because of her disclosures to the East Dakota Environmental Protection Agency. Although that Agency does not have any specific regulation protecting such "whistle-blowers" and the East Dakota courts have traditionally followed the "employment-at- will" doctrine, you fear that this is the type of case which might induce the East Dakota Supreme Court to reconsider the issue. If it were to adopt a "public policy" exception, Dr. Rodriguez would be able to seek monetary damages for lost earnings and emotional distress. She might even be awarded punitive damages. You also fear that the "qualified immunity" provision might not protect Douglas Chemical against liability for the negative statements previously made to Mr. Barrett of Jacobs Petroleum. If a jury became sufficiently outraged regarding Dr. Rodriguez's termination and the statements made to Mr. Barrett, its monetary award could be substantial.

You realize that Dr. Rodriguez is a highly skilled professional who should be able to obtain employment with another company in the near future, thus minimizing her lost earnings. You recognize, however, that she is entitled to some compensation for the unconscionable way in which she has been treated by Douglas Chemical. Score *minus* 1 point for each $1,000, or part thereof, of compensation you agree to provide, *up to* $100,000. Score *minus* 3 points for each $1,000, or part thereof, of compensation you agree to provide *over* $100,000.

Douglas Chemical does not wish to reemploy Dr. Rodriguez. It believes that her reinstatement might cause further difficulties. If you are able to achieve a settlement agreement that does *not* provide for any offer of reinstatement, score *plus* 50 points. You believe that Dr. Rodriguez will request a favorable reference letter to enhance her future employment opportunities. Since she was a satisfactory employee prior to her contact with the East Dakota Environmental Protection Agency, Douglas Chemical is willing to provide such a letter to enable her to locate a new position. You have learned that McTavish Chemical is considering Dr. Rodriguez for a possible position. You lose *no points* for an agreement to provide a favorable reference to McTavish Chemical, since her employment by that business entity would eliminate any reinstatement issue. If, however, you agree to provide a more general "To Whom It May Concern" reference that could be used by Dr. Rodriguez in future years, you *lose* 25 points.

Douglas Chemical is concerned about the publicity associated with this controversy. Score *plus* 50 points for a provision specifying that the circumstances surrounding this dispute *and* the terms of the settlement agreement will remain confidential.

GENERAL INFORMATION — CHINESE JOINT VENTURE

The Eastern Electric Light Company, a Delaware Corporation, has been manufacturing light bulbs and small electrical appliances since 1923. Eastern Electric has been doing well financially in recent years, with gross revenues for the last fiscal year of $350,000,000. It has been thinking of entering the expanding market in the People's Republic of China ("China"), but is unwilling to enter that market alone. It would thus like to develop a joint venture with a Chinese firm. It was recently contacted by Mu Electronics, a three-year old limited liability company headquartered in Beijing. Mu Electronics also manufactures light bulbs and small electrical appliances, but its factory consists of an antiquated facility that was formerly owned and operated by the Chinese Government. Despite the inefficiencies associated with such an old plant, Mu Electronics has been doing remarkably well for a newly-formed company. Last year, it had gross sales of $10,000,000. The Mu Electronics managers think that they could generate much greater revenues if they could obtain an infusion of foreign funds, modernize their existing facility, and develop a national sales campaign.

Representatives of Eastern Electric and Mu Electronics are endeavoring to negotiate the terms of a mutually acceptable joint venture. They must agree upon the financial support to be provided by Eastern Electric, the percentage of Mu Electronics stock Eastern Electric is to acquire, the collateral Eastern Electric is to be given in case the joint venture fails or the Chinese Government decides to nationalize Mu Electronics, the official language to be used in the official joint venture documents, the applicable law to govern future contractual disputes, the dispute resolution procedures to be used to resolve any such controversies, and any other matters the representatives consider important.

CONFIDENTIAL INFORMATION — EASTERN ELECTRIC

Mu Electronics provides Eastern Electric with the exact target of opportunity it has been seeking. It is a new, but already successful, firm with outstanding managers and a well-trained labor force. Eastern Electric believes that the infusion of new capital should enable a modernized Mu Electronics to greatly expand its currently limited production. You have thus been instructed to reach a joint venture agreement with Mu Electronics if at all possible.

Eastern Electric realizes that Mu Electronics will require an initial infusion of approximately $25,000,000 to modernize the production facility and will probably require about $10,000,000 per year for the next few years to develop a national sales campaign. If these goals are achieved, it is believed that Mu Electronics could increase its current $10,000,000 gross revenues to the $50-75 million range. You have thus been authorized to agree to the $25,000,000 initial outlay and to $10,000,000 per year thereafter for the following four years. You should be extremely reluctant to promise financial support above these figures over the first five years, and should refuse to make any definitive commitments beyond the first five years of this joint venture — unless absolutely necessary. If the projected joint venture revenue figures are not met during this time frame, Eastern Electric would be hesitant to contribute further financial support.

Chinese law does not permit foreign firms to hold majority ownership in Chinese corporations. If possible, Eastern Electric would like to obtain a fifty percent share that would give it the same power possessed by Mu Electronics. It would also like to have the name of the joint venture firm changed to "Mu-Eastern Electronics." If you are unable to achieve a 50-50 share division, you must at least obtain a promise that Eastern Electric will be given one-quarter of Mu Electronics shares by the end of the first year and one-third of Mu Electronics shares by the end of the initial five year period. Eastern Electric would also like to be guaranteed the right to immediately name one-quarter of the Mu Electronics Corporate Board members and to name one-third of the Board by the end of the initial five-year period. It would also like to be able to immediately name one Executive Vice President of Mu Electronics and to be able to name a second Executive Vice President within the next five years. (Mu Electronics currently has seven Executive Vice Presidents.)

Eastern Electric would like to be guaranteed fifty percent of Mu Electronics profits. If it is unable to achieve this profit division, it would like to be promised a profit split in proportion to its share of Mu Electronics shares.

Eastern Electric is concerned about the uncertain fate of the free market system in China in the coming years. If Communist hard-liners regain control, they may outlaw private firms and nationalize existing businesses. To protect Eastern Electric interests, you have been instructed to seek a provision giving Eastern Electric a secured interest in the building, equipment, and real property of Mu Electronics. It would also like to obtain the right to petition the Chinese Government for just compensation for any Mu Electronics property that is nationalized.

You must agree with Mu Electronics whether English, Chinese, or some third language is to be the official contract language. Although you would prefer English to govern, you recognize that Mu Electronics will probably reject this option. If you are unable to obtain English as the official language, you would prefer to have English and Chinese texts govern jointly. If compelled, however, you may reluctantly agree to Chinese as the official language.

You must also agree upon the legal doctrines to govern the interpretation and application of your joint venture agreement. Eastern Electric would prefer to have United States law and the Delaware Corporate Code govern and is unalterably opposed to reliance on Chinese law due to the uncertainty surrounding the evolving Chinese law regulating private business arrangements. If you cannot obtain an agreement to apply United States law, you would like to get Mu Electronics to agree to the application of European Union doctrines. If this proposal is unacceptable to Mu Electronics, you would then prefer language merely stating that the terms of your joint venture agreement will be interpreted according to business doctrines that are generally applied by the international community when resolving transnational business controversies.

Since Mu Electronics is unlikely to submit itself to jurisdiction of United States courts and Eastern Electric is unwilling to subject itself to the jurisdiction of Chinese judicial tribunals, you must agree upon a mutually acceptable procedure to resolve contractual disputes that may arise. You would like to specify that the Presidents, or their designates, of Eastern Electric and Mu Electronics will initially endeavor to negotiate an acceptable resolution of any disagreement regarding the interpretation and application of the joint venture agreement. In case these efforts are not successful, you would like to specify a list of three or four respected international conciliators who would be used on a rotating basis to mediate any disputes. In case conciliation efforts are unsuccessful, you would like to use binding arbitration procedures to resolve the matter. You would prefer a tripartite system under which Eastern Electric and Mu Electronics representatives would each appoint their own arbitrator, with these two individuals attempting to agree upon a third neutral arbitrator. Should the designated arbitrators be unable to agree upon the neutral arbitrator, you would like to require the parties to follow the appointment procedure used by the International Chamber of Commerce. You would like a requirement that all designated mediators and arbitrators be fluent in both English and Chinese.

CONFIDENTIAL INFORMATION — MU ELECTRONICS

Mu Electronics desperately requires external financial support. Although it has experienced great financial success during its first three years of existence, it needs millions of dollars to modernize its antiquated manufacturing facility. With new financial support, Mu Electronics could probably expand sales throughout China and increase gross annual revenues from the current $10,000,000 to the $75,000,000 or even $100,000,000 range. Since no other firms have expressed an interest in a joint venture with Mu Electronics, it is imperative that you achieve a mutually acceptable arrangement with Eastern Electric.

Mu Electronics has estimated that it will take an initial investment of at least $15,000,000 to modernize its existing production plant. To provide some leeway, you have been instructed to seek as much over this $15,000,000 initial investment figure as possible. After the first year plant changes, Mu Electronics believes that it will take a minimum of $5,000,000 per year to generate a national sales campaign. If you could obtain commitments in excess of this $5,000,000 per year figure, this would greatly enhance the future prospects of Mu Electronics. You would like to obtain such an annual commitment for nine years following the plant modernization year, but would be willing to accept a shorter commitment if necessary. If you cannot get a full nine-year commitment, you would like to obtain a general promise that Eastern Electric will endeavor to continue this annual support so long as annual revenues are increasing.

Chinese corporate law prohibits majority ownership of Chinese firms by foreign interests. It would thus be unlawful for Eastern Electric to hold over fifty percent of the Mu Electronics shares. While Eastern Electric may seek a fifty percent share interest, this would be wholly unacceptable to Mu Electronics which insists on maintaining majority interest. You may grant a thirty percent interest to Eastern Electric as soon as the joint venture is agreed upon. Assuming Eastern Electric continues to provide annual financial support of at least $5,000,000, you may also agree to grant that firm a forty percent interest by the end of the fifth year of the new relationship. You should only exceed forty percent with great reluctance, and you may not grant more than a forty-five percent share under any circumstances. Since your firm is named after Mr. Mu, the founder of the business, you would like to retain the Mu Electronics name in future years.

It is likely that Eastern Electric will demand the right to select several members of the Mu Electronics Board of Directors. Since that firm will hold at least a quarter of Mu Electronics shares, you would be perfectly willing to let Eastern Electric name one-quarter of the Corporate Board members. By the end of the initial five-year period, you may even permit Eastern Electric to name up to forty percent of the Corporate Board. You may not, however, allow that company to name over forty percent.

Mu Electronics currently has seven Executive Vice Presidents. It assumes that Eastern Electric will insist on the right to name one, two, or possibly even three Executive Vice Presidents to protect its economic interest in Mu Electronics. Since such a request is common in joint ventures, you are authorized to agree to Eastern Electric control over one or even two Executive Vice Presidencies. Since Mu Electronics has been planning to expand the number of Executive Vice Presidents from seven to ten, you may agree to let Eastern Electric name three Executive Vice Presidents, so long as this is only done after the total number is expanded to ten.

You anticipate that Eastern Electric will demand the right to half of the profits generated by Mu Electronics following the joint venture. Your firm considers this an excessive figure, and will not accept any deal that gives Eastern Electric more than forty percent of Mu Electronics profits. You have been authorized to give Eastern Electric a profit share equal to the percent of Mu Electronics shares held by that firm — i.e., up to thirty percent at the outset and up to forty percent by the end of the initial five year period.

Mu Electronics recognizes that Eastern Electric is concerned about the uncertain future of the free market in China and fears nationalization of private firms if Communist hard-liners regain control. You suspect that Eastern Electric will ask for a secured interest in the building, equipment, and real property of Mu Electronics. Since such an interest would be unenforceable if the government decided to nationalize the entire firm, you are perfectly willing to agree to such a provision. You are merely concerned about the moral obligation to inform Eastern Electric that such a secured interest would most likely be unenforceable if Mu Electronics was ultimately nationalized. What you may either additionally or alternatively do is grant Eastern Electric the right to petition the Chinese Government for just compensation for any Mu Electronics property nationalized.

Mu Electronics would like to have the Chinese draft of the joint venture contract constitute the official draft and will not permit the English draft to govern. If you are unable to obtain an agreement specifying that the Chinese draft is controlling, you would be willing to allow the English and Chinese texts to govern jointly.

The parties must agree upon the legal doctrines that will govern the interpretation and application of their joint venture agreement. Mu Electronics would like to have Chinese law apply, but realizes the hesitancy of foreign firms to agree to such an arrangement due to the evolving nature of Chinese private venture legal doctrines. Mu Electronics is unalterably opposed to the application of United States law to contractual matters, because it fears the law will favor U.S. companies. You have been authorized to agree to the application of European Union doctrines, and if this is unacceptable, to a provision merely stating that the terms of the joint venture agreement will be interpreted according to business doctrines generally applicable by the international community when resolving transactional business disputes.

Mu Electronics is unwilling to submit itself to jurisdiction of United States courts and assumes that Eastern Electric would be unwilling to submit to Chinese judicial jurisdiction. As a result, the parties must agree upon a mutually acceptable dispute resolution procedure. You are willing to allow the assistance of internationally respected mediators, and would even be willing to submit unresolved controversies to an international arbitral panel. You are flexible regarding the exact arbitrator selection procedures, so long as the procedures would guarantee the selection of qualified neutrals who are fluent in Chinese.

MODIFIED NASA DECISION MAKING EXERCISE*

Department of Education and Training

American Arbitration Association

INSTRUCTIONS: You are a member of one of two space details assigned to the mission ship "Galaxy," which was originally scheduled to rendezvous with the parent ship "Angel" on the lighted surface of the moon. Due to mechanical difficulties, however, the Galaxy was forced to land on the dark side of the moon some 200 miles from the rendezvous point. During piloting and landing, some of the crew and both Detail A and Detail B captains died. Much of the equipment aboard was damaged. No one knows for sure how long the ship's life support systems will last because all gauges were broken. Detail A piloted the mission and Detail B was to explore the surface before returning to the parent ship. *Survival of both Details is crucial.* Below are listed the 15 items left intact and undamaged after landing. Your task is to *individually rank* them in order of their importance to the survival of the remaining crew of the mission ship, Galaxy. Place the number 1 by the most important item, the number 2 by the second most important, and so on through number 15, the least important.

MODIFIED NASA EXERCISE
Inventory of Undamaged Material

— Ten Blankets

— 100 Cartons of Food Concentrate (20-day Ration for Each Crew Member)

— 150 Feet of Nylon Rope

— Parachute Silk From 3 Parachutes

— One Portable Heating Unit that is Self Lighting

— Two .45 Caliber Loaded Pistols

— One Case Dehydrated Milk

— Three 100 lb. Tanks of Oxygen (Each Tank Holds 20-Day Supply for Each Crew Member)

— One Stellar Map of the Moon's Constellation

— One Life Raft

— One Magnetic Compass that Functions on the Moon

— 5 Gallons of Water (Normally a 10-Day Ration for Each Member of the Crew)

— Five Light Flares Containing Their Own Oxidizing Agent

— First Aid Kit Containing Injection Needles

— Solar-Powered FM Receiver-Transmitter

MODIFIED NASA EXERCISE
Decision by Consensus

INSTRUCTIONS: This is an exercise in group decision-making. Your Detail is to use the method of group consensus in reaching its decision. This means that the ranking for each of the 15 survival items *must* be agreed on by each Detail member before it becomes a part of the group decision. Consensus is difficult to reach. Therefore, not every ranking will meet with everyone's complete approval. Try, as a Detail, to make each ranking one with which all group members can at least partially agree. Here are some guides to use in reaching consensus:

1. Avoid arguing for your own individual judgments. Approach the task on the basis of logic.

2. Avoid changing your mind merely to reach agreement and avoid conflict. Only support solutions with which you at least partially agree.

3. Avoid "conflict-reducing" techniques such as majority vote, averaging, or trading in reaching decisions.

4. View differences of opinion as helpful rather than as hindrances in decision-making.

On the Modified NASA Consensus Form place the individual rankings made earlier by each group member.

MODIFIED NASA EXERCISE — CONSENSUS FORM

MODIFIED NASA EXERCISE — CONSENSUS FORM

ITEMS	A	B	C	D	E	F	G	H	AGRT.
Ten Blankets									
100 Cartons of Food Concentrate									
150 Feet of Nylon Rope									
Parachute Silk From Three Parachutes									
One Portable Heating Unit									
Two .45 Caliber Loaded Pistols									
One Case of Dehydrated Milk									
Three 100 lb. Tanks of Oxygen									
One Stellar Map of Moon Constellation									
One Life Raft									
One Magnetic Compass									
5 Gallons of Water									
Five Light Flares									
First Aid Kit									
Solar Powered FM Receiver-Transmitter									

MODIFIED NASA — CONSENSUS FORM
MODIFIED NASA EXERCISE
Decision by Negotiation

INSTRUCTIONS: Detail A will attempt to *survive* while *waiting for help* from the parent ship "Angel."

Detail B will attempt to *survive* and *make* the rendezvous with the parent ship "Angel."

This is an exercise in group decision-making. Your Detail is to use the method of group negotiations in reaching its decision. Both groups must decide which Detail will remain with the disabled mission ship "Galaxy" (*i.e.*, which group will be designated "Detail A") and which group will endeavor to rendezvous with the parent ship "Angel" (*i.e.*, which group will be designated "Detail B"). Both groups must also agree upon the division of the inventoried items between Details A and B (*i.e.*, which items will remain with Detail A and which will be taken with Detail B).

Modified NASA Negotiated Agreement Form is provided to list the terms of your negotiated agreement.

MODIFIED NASA — NEGOTIATED AGREEMENT FORM

ITEMS	GROUP A	GROUP B
Ten Blankets		
100 Cartons of Food Concentrate		
150 Feet of Nylon Rope		
Parachute Silk From Three Parachutes		
One Portable Heating Unit		
Two .45 Caliber Loaded Pistols		
One Case of Dehydrated Milk		
Three 100 lb. Tanks of Oxygen		
One Stellar Map of Moon Constellation		
One Life Raft		
One Magnetic Compass		
5 Gallons of Water		
Five Light Flares		
First Aid Kit		
Solar Powered FM Receiver-Transmitter		

BIBLIOGRAPHY

Aarow, K., Mnookin, R., Ross, L., Tversky, A. & Wilson, R., *Barriers to Conflict Resolution* (W.W. Norton 1995).

Abramson, H., *Mediation Representation* (NITA 2004).

Abramson, H., "Problem-Solving Advocacy in Mediations: A Model of Client Representation," 10 *Harvard Negotiation Law Review* 103 (2005).

Ackerman, R., "Disputing Together: Conflict Resolution and the Search for Community," 18 *Ohio State Journal on Dispute Resolution* 27 (2002).

Acuff, F., *How to Negotiate Anything with Anyone Anywhere Around the World* (American Management Assn. 1993).

Acuff, F., *How to Negotiate Anything with Anyone Anywhere Around the World* (American Management Assn. Expanded Edition 1997).

Acuff & Villere, "Games Negotiators Play," *Business Horizons* 70 (February 1976).

Adair, W. & Brett, J., "Culture and Negotiation Process" in *The Handbook of Negotiation and Culture* 158 (Gelfand, M. & Brett, J., eds.) (Stanford Bus. Books 2004).

Adler, N., *International Dimensions of Organizational Behavior* (South-Western 4th ed. 2002).

Adler, N., Brahm, R. & Graham, J., "Strategy Implementation: A Comparison of Face-to-Face Negotiations in the People's Republic of China and the United States," 13 *Strategic Management Journal* 449 (1992).

Adler, N., Doktor, R. & Redding, S.G., "From the Atlantic to the Pacific Century: Cross-Cultural Management Reviewed," 12 *Journal of Management* 295 (1986).

Adler, N. & Graham, J., "Business Negotiations: Canadians Are Not Just Like Americans," 4 *Canadian Journal of Administrative Sciences* 211 (1987).

Adler, N. & Graham, J., "Cross-Cultural Interaction: The International Comparison Fallacy?" 20 *Journal of International Business Studies* 515 (1989).

Adler, N., Graham, J. & Gehrke, T., "Business Negotiations in Canada, Mexico, and the United States," 15 *Journal of Business Research* 411 (1987).

Adler, R., "Flawed Thinking: Addressing Decision Biases in Negotiation," 20 *Ohio State Journal on Dispute Resolution* 683 (2005).

Adler, R. & Silverstein, E., "When David Meets Goliath: Dealing With Power Differentials in Negotiations," 5 *Harvard Negotiation Law Review* 1 (2000).

Alfini, "Settlement Ethics and Lawyering in ADR Proceedings: A Proposal to Revise Rule 4.1," 19 *Northern Illinois University Law Review* 255 (1999).

Allred, K., "Distinguishing Best and Strategic Practices: A Framework for Managing the Dilemma Between Creating and Claiming Value," 16 *Negotiation Journal* 387 (2000).

Allred, K., "Relationship Dynamics in Disputes" in *The Handbook of Dispute Resolution* 83 (Moffitt, M. & Bordone, R., eds.) (Jossey-Bass 2005).

Alon, I. & Brett, J., "Perceptions of Time and Their Impact on Negotiations in the Arabic-Speaking Islamic World," 23 *Negotiation Journal* 55 (2007).

Amanatullah, E., Morris, M. & Curhan, J., "Negotiators Who Give Too Much: Unmitigated Communion, Relational Anxieties, and Economic Costs in Distributive and Integrative Bargaining," 95 *Journal of Personality and Social Psychology* 723 (2008).

American Arbitration Assn., *Consumer Due Process Protocol* (1998)

Andersen, P., *The Complete Idiot's Guide to Body Language* (Alpha 2004).

Anderson, D., *Dispute Resolution: Bridging the Settlement Gap* (JAI Press 1996).

Arrow, K., Mnookin, R., Ross, L., Tversky, A. & Wilson, R., *Barriers to Conflict Resolution* (W.W. Norton 1995).

Axelrod, R., *The Evolution of Cooperation* (Basic Books 1984).

Ayres, I., "Fair Driving: Gender and Race Discrimination in Retail Car Negotiations," 104 *Harvard Law Review 817* (1991).

Ayres, I., "Further Evidence of Discrimination in New Car Negotiations and Estimates of Its Cause," 94 *Michigan Law Review 109* (1995).

Ayres, I. & Nalebuff, B., "Common Knowledge as a Barrier to Negotiation," 44 *U.C.L.A. Law Review* 1631 (1997).

Babcock, L. & Laschever, S., *Ask For It* (Bantam (2008).

Babcock, L. & Laschever, S., *Women Don't Ask* (Princeton Univ. Press 2003).

Bacharach, S. & Lawler, E., *Bargaining: Power, Tactics and Outcomes* (Jossey-Bass 1981).

Baer, J., *How to Be an Assertive (Not Aggressive) Woman in Life, Love, and on the Job* (Signet 1976).

Balachandra, L., Bordone, R., Menkel-Meadow, C., Ringstrom, P. & Sarath, E., "Improvisation and Negotiation: Expecting the Unexpected," 221 *Negotiation Journal* 415 (2005).

Bannink, F., "Solution-Focused Mediation: The Future With a Difference," 25 *Conflict Resolution Quarterly* 163 (2007).

Barkai, J., "Teaching Negotiation and ADR: The Savvy Samurai Meets the Devil," 75 *University of Nebraska Law Review 704* (1996).

Barry, B., Fulmer, I. & Van Kleef, G., "I Laughed, I Cried, I Settled: The Role of Emotion in Negotiation" in *The Handbook of Negotiation and Culture* 71 (Gelfand, M. & Brett, J., eds.) (Stanford Business Books 2004).

Barsness, Z. & Bhappu, A. "At the Crossroads of Culture and Technology: Social Influence and Information-Sharing Processes During Negotiation" in *The Handbook of Negotiation and Culture* 350 (Gelfand, M. & Brett, J., eds.) (Stanford Business Books 2004).

Bartos, O., *Process and Outcome of Negotiations* (Columbia Univ. Press 1974).

Bartos, O., "Simple Model of Negotiation: A Sociological Point of View," in *The Negotiation Process: Theories and Applications 13* (I.W. Zartman, ed.) (Sage 1978).

Bastress, R. & Harbaugh, J., *Interviewing, Counseling, and Negotiating* (Little, Brown 1990).

Bazerman, M., "Creating Value, Weighing Values," 8 *Negotiation* 9 (2005).

Bazerman, M., Curhan, J. & Moore, D., "The Death and Rebirth of the Social Psychology of Negotiation" in *Blackwell Handbook of Social Psychology: Interpersonal Processes* 196 (Fletcher, G. & Clark, M., eds., Blackwell 2001).

Bazerman, M. & Neale, M., *Negotiating Rationally* (Free Press 1992).

Bazerman, M. & Shonk, K., "The Decision Perspective to Negotiation" in *The Handbook of Dispute Resolution* 52 (Moffitt, M. & Bordone, R., eds.) (Jossey-Bass 2005).

Beck, C. & Frost, L., "Competence as an Element of Mediation Readiness," 25 *Conflict Resolution Quarterly* 255 (2007).

Beier, E. & Valens, E., *People Reading* (Warner 1975).

Bellow, G. & Moulton, B., *Negotiation* (Foundation Press 1981).

Bendahmane, D. & McDonald, J., *International Negotiation* (Foreign Service Institute, U.S. Department of State 1984).

Bendahmane, D. & McDonald, J., *Perspectives on Negotiation* (Foreign Service Institute, U.S. Department of State 1986).

Benjamin, R., "The Constructive Uses of Deception: Skills, Strategies, and Techniques of the Folkloric Trickster Figure and Their Application by Mediators," 13 *Mediation Quarterly 3* (1995).

Bernard, P. & Garth, B., *Dispute Resolution Ethics* (ABA Sec. of Dispute Resolution 2002).

Berne, E., *Games People Play* (Grove Press 1964).

Bingham, L., "Why Suppose? Let's Find Out: A Public Policy Research Program on Dispute Resolution," 2002 *Journal of Dispute Resolution* 101 (2002).

Binnendijk, H., *National Negotiating Styles* (Foreign Service Institute, U.S. Department of State 1987).

Birke, R. & Fox, C., "Psychological Principles in Negotiating Civil Settlements," 4 *Harvard Negotiation Law Review 1* (1999).

Blaker, M., Giarra, P. & Vogel, E., *Case Studies in Japanese Negotiating Behavior* (U.S. Instit. of Peace Press 2002).

Blount, S., "Whoever Said that Markets Were Fair?" 16 *Negotiation Journal* 237 (2000).

Bok, S., *Lying: Moral Choice in Public and Private Life* (Pantheon 1978).

Bolling, L., "Strengths and Weaknesses of Track Two: A Personal Account" in *Conflict Resolution: Track Two Diplomacy 53* (J. McDonald & D. Bendahmane, eds.) (Foreign Service Institute, U.S. Department of State 1987).

Bordone, R., "Fitting the Ethics to the Forum: A Proposal for Process-Enabling Ethical Codes," 21 *Ohio State Journal on Dispute Resolution* 1 (2005).

Borg, J., *Persuasion: The Art of Influencing People* (Pearson 2004).

Bordone, R., "Teaching Interpersonal Skills for Negotiation and for Life," *Negotiation Journal* 377 (Oct. 2000).

Boulle, L., Colatrella, M. & Picchioni, A., *Mediation: Skills and Techniques* (LexisNexis 2008).

Bowles, H., Babcock, L. & McGinn, K., "Constraints and Triggers: Situational Mechanics of Gender in Negotiation," 89 *Journal of Personality and Social Psychology* 951 (2005).

Brach, D., "A Logic for the Magic of Mindful Negotiation," 24 *Negotiation Journal* 25 (2008).

Brams, S., Doherty, A., & Weidner, M., "Game Theory: Focusing on the Players, Decisions, and Agreements" in *International Multilateral Negotiation 95* (I.W. Zartman, ed.) (Jossey-Bass 1994).

Brand, N., *How ADR Works* (BNA Books 2002).

Brazil, W., "Hosting Mediations as a Representative of the System of Civil Justice," 22 *Ohio State Journal on Dispute Resolution* 227 (2007).

Brazil, W., "Settling Civil Cases: What Lawyers Want From Judges," 23 *Judges Journal 14* (1984).

Brazil, W., "Should Court-Sponsored ADR Survive?" 21 *Ohio State Journal on Dispute Resolution* 241 (2006).

Brett, J., *Negotiating Globally* (Jossey-Bass 2001).

Brett, J., Adair, W., Lempereur, A., Okumura, T., Skikhirev, P., Tinsley, C. & Lytle, A., "Culture and Joint Gains in Negotiation," 14 *Negotiation Journal 61* (1998).

Brett, J. & Gelfand, M., "A Cultural Analysis of the Underlying Assumptions of Negotiation Theory" in *Negotiation Theory and Research* (L. Thompson, ed.) (Psychology Press 2006).

Brockner, J. & Rubin, J., *Entrapment in Escalating Conflicts: A Social Psychological Analysis* (Springer-Verlag 1985).

Brodt, S. & Thompson, L., "Negotiating Teams: A Levels of Analysis Approach," 5 *Group Dynamics: Theory, Research, and Practice* 208 (2001).

Brown, J., "Creativity and Problem-Solving," 87 *Marquette Law Review* 697 (2004a).

Brown, J., "The Role of Apology in Negotiation," 87 *Marquette Law Review* 665 (2004b).

Brown, J., "The Role of Hope in Negotiation," 44 *U.C.L.A. Law Review 1661* (1997).

Brunet, E., "Judicial Mediation and Signaling," 3 *Nevada Law Journal* 232 (2003).

Burgoon, J., Buller, D. & Woodall, W., *Nonverbal Communication: The Unspoken Dialogue* (McGraw-Hill 1996).

Burgoon, J., Dillard, J.P., & Doran, N., "Friendly or Unfriendly Persuasion: The Effects of Violations of Expectations by Males and Females," 10 *Human Communication Research 283* (1983).

Burrell, Donohue & Allen, "Gender-Based Perceptual Biases in Mediation," 15 *Communication Research 447* (1988).

Burton, Farmer, Gee, Johnson & Williams, "Feminist Theory, Professional Ethics, and Gender-Related Distinctions in Attorney Negotiation Styles," 1991 *Journal of Dispute Resolution 199* (1991).

Bush, R., "One Size Does Not Fit All: A Pluralistic Approach to Mediator Performance Testing and Quality Assurance," 19 *Ohio State Journal on Dispute Resolution* 965 (2004).

Bush, R. & Folger, J., *The Promise of Mediation* (Jossey- Bass 1994).

Bush, R. & Folger, J., *The Promise of Mediation* (Jossey-Bass Revised Edition 2005).

Calero, H., *The Power of Nonverbal Communication* (Silver Lake Pub. 2005).

Cameron, N., *Collaborative Process: Deepening the Dialogue* (C.L.E. Society of British Columbia 2004).

Camp, J., *Start With No* (Crown Bus. 2002).

Campbell, M. & Docherty, J., "What's in a Frame? (That Which We Call a Rose by Any Other Name Would Smell as Sweet)," 87 *Marquette Law Review* 769 (2004).

Carli, L., "Gender and Social Influence," 57 *Journal of Social Issues* 725 (2001).

Carter, R., "Oh, Ye of Little [Good] Faith: Questions, Concerns and Commentary on Efforts to Regulate Participant Conduct in Mediations," 2002 *Journal of Dispute Resolution* 367 (2002).

Cash, T. & Janda, L., "The Eye of the Beholder," *Psychology Today 46* (December 1984).

Chantilis, P., "Mediation U.S.A.," 26 *University of Memphis Law Review 1031* (1996).

Chinkin, C., "Gender, Human Rights, and Peace Agreements," 18 *Ohio State Journal on Dispute Resolution* 867 (2003).

Cialdini, R., *Influence: The Psychology of Persuasion* (William Morrow 1993).

Ciarrochi, J., Forgas, J. & Mayer, J., *Emotional Intelligence in Everyday Life* (Psychology Press 2006).

Cochran, R., "Professional Rules and ADR: Control of Alternative Dispute Resolution Under the ADA Ethics 2000 Commission Proposal and Other Professional Responsibility Standards," 29 *Fordham Urban Law Journal* 895 (2001).

Cogan, C., *French Negotiating Behavior* (U.S. Instit. of Peace Press 2003).

Cohen, A., "Negotiation, Meeet New Governance: Interests, Skills, and Selves," 33 *Law & Social Inquiry* 503 (2008).

Cohen, H., *Negotiate This* (Warner Bus. Books 2003).

Cohen, H., *You Can Negotiate Anything* (Lyle Stuart 1980).

Cohen, J., "When People Are the Means: Negotiating with Respect," 14 *Georgetown Journal of Legal Ethics* 739 (2001).

Cohen, R., *Negotiating Across Cultures* (U.S. Institute of Peace Press 1991).

Coker, D., "Enhancing Autonomy for Battered Women: Lessons from Navajo Peacemaking," 47 *U.C.L.A. Law Review 1* (1999).

Cole, S., "Managerial Litigants? The Overlooked Problem of Party Autonomy in Dispute Resolution," 51 *Hastings Law Journal 1199 (2000)*.

Cole, S., *"Protecting Confidentiality in Mediation: A Promise Unfulfilled,"* 54 *Kansas Law Review* 1419 (2006).

Cole, S. & Blankley, K., "Online Mediation: Where We Have Been, Where We Are Now, and Where We Should Be," 38 *University of Toledo Law Review* 193 (2006).

Colosi, T., *On and Off the Record: Colosi on Negotiation* (Amer. Arb. Assn. 2nd ed. 2001).

Comment, "The Concern Over Confidentiality in Mediation — An In-Depth Look at the Protection Provided by the Proposed Uniform Mediation Act," 2000 *Journal of Dispute Resolution 113* (2000).

Condlin, R., "Bargaining in the Dark: The Normative Incoherence of Lawyer Dispute Bargaining Role," 51 *Maryland Law Review 1* (1992).

Condlin, R., "Bargaining With a Hugger: The Weaknesses and Limitations of a Communitarian Conception of Legal Dispute Bargaining, or Why We Can't All Just Get Along," 9 *Cardozo Journal of Conflict Resolution* 1 (2007).

Condlin, R., "'Cases on Both Sides': Patterns of Argument in Legal Dispute-Negotiation," 44 *Maryland Law Review 65* (1985).

Condlin, R., "'Every Day and in Every Way We Are All Becoming *Meta* and *Meta*,' or How Communitarian Bargaining Theory Conquered the World (of Bargaining Theory)," 23 *Ohio State Journal on Dispute Resolution* 231 (2008).

Condlin, R., "'What's Love Got To Do With It?' 'It's Not Like They're Your Friends For Christ's Sake': The Complicated Relationship Between Lawyer and Client," 82 *Nebraska Law Review* 211 (2004).

Cooley, J., *The Mediator's Handbook* (NITA 2000).

Cooley, J., "Mediation Magic: Its Use and Abuse," 29 *Loyola University Chicago Law Journal 1* (1997).

Craver, C., "Clinical Negotiating Achievement as a Function of Traditional Law School Success and as a Predictor of Future Negotiating Performance," 1986 *Missouri Journal of Dispute Resolution 63* (1986).

Craver, C., "Don't Forget Your Problem Solving Function," 69 *American Bar Association Journal 254* (1983).

Craver, C., "The Impact of Gender on Clinical Negotiating Achievement," 6 *Ohio State Journal on Dispute Resolution 1* (1990).

Craver, C., "The Impact of a Pass/Fail Option on Negotiation Course Performance," 48 *Journal of Legal Education 176* (1998).

Craver, C., "The Impact of Student GPAs and a Pass/Fail Option on Clinical Negotiation Course Performance," 15 *Ohio State Journal on Dispute Resolution 373* (2000).

Craver, C., "Mediation: A Trial Lawyer's Guide," *Trial 37* (June 1999).

Craver, C., "Negotiation as a Distinct Area of Specialization," 9 *American Journal of Trial Advocacy 377* (1986).

Craver, C., "Negotiation Ethics: How to be Deceptive Without Being Dishonest/How to be Assertive Without Being Offensive," 38 *South Texas Law Review 713* (1997).

Craver, C., "The Negotiation Process," 27 *American Journal of Trial Advocacy* 271 (2003).

Craver, C., "Negotiation Styles: The Impact on Bargaining Transactions," *Dispute Resolution Journal* 48 (Feb.–Apr. 2003).

Craver, C., "Negotiation Techniques," 24 *Trial* 65 (June 1988).

Craver, C., "Race and Negotiation Performance," *Dispute Resolution Magazine* 22 (Fall 2001).

Craver, C., *Skills & Values: Legal Negotiation* (Lexis 2009).

Craver, C., "When Parties Can't Settle," *Judges Journal* 4 (Winter 1987).

Craver, C. & Barnes, D., "Gender, Risk Taking, and Negotiation Performance," 5 *Michigan Journal of Gender & Law 299* (1999).

Crosby, P., *The Art of Getting Your Own Sweet Way* (McGraw-Hill 1981).

Cross, J., "A Theory of the Bargaining Process," in *Bargaining: Formal Theories of Negotiation 191* (O. Young, ed.) (Univ. of Illinois Press 1975).

Crowley, T., *Settle It Out of Court* (John Wiley & Sons 1994).

Crump, L., "A Temporal Model of Negotiation Linkage Dynamics," 23 *Negotiation Journal* 117 (2007).

Curhan, J., Elfenbein, H. & Xu, H., "What Do People Value When They Negotiate? Mapping the Domain of Subjective Value in Negotiation," 91 *Journal of Personality and Social Psychology* 493 (2006).

Davidson, M.N. & Greenhalgh, L., "The Role of Emotion in Negotiation: The Impact of Anger and Race," 7 *Research on Negotiation in Organizations* 3 (1999).

Dawson, R., *Roger Dawson's Secrets of Power Negotiating* (Career Press 2d ed. 2001).

Dawson, R., *You Can Get Anything You Want* (Simon & Schuster 1985).

Deason, E., "Enforcing Mediated Settlement Agreements: Contract Law Collides with Confidentiality," 35 *U.C. Davis Law Review* 33 (2001).

Deason, E., "The Need for Trust as a Justification for Confidentiality in Mediation: A Cross-Disciplinary Approach," 54 *Kansas Law Review* 1387 (2006).

Deason, E., "Predictable Mediation in the U.S. Federal System," 17 *Ohio State Journal on Dispute Resolution* 239 (2002).

Deason, E., "The Quest for Uniformity in Mediation Confidentiality: Foolish Consistency or Crucial Predictability?" 85 *Marquette Law Review* 79 (2001).

Deaux, K., *The Behavior of Women and Men* (Brooks/Cole Publishing 1976).

De Dreu, C., Beersma, B., Stroebe, K. & Euwema, M., "Motivated Information Processing, Strategic Choice, and the Quality of Negotiated Agreement," 90 *Journal of Personality and Social Psychology* 927 (2006).

Della Noce, D., "Seeing Theory in Practice: An Analysis of Empathy in Mediation," 15 *Negotiation Journal 271* (1999).

Della Noce, D., Antes, J., Bush, R. & Saul, J., "Signposts and Crossroads: A Model for Live Action Mediator Assessment," 23 *Ohio State Journal on Dispute Resolution* 197 (2008).

Della Noce, D., Antes, J. & Saul, J., "Identifying Practice Competence in Transformative Mediators: An Interactive Rating Scale Assessment Model," 19 *Ohio State Journal on Dispute Resolution* 1005 (2004).

DePaulo, B. & Kashy, D., "Everyday Lies in Close and Casual Relationships," 74 *Journal of Personality and Social Psychology 63* (1998).

DePaulo, B., Kashy, D., Kirkendol, S., Wyer M. & Epstein, J., "Lying in Everyday Life," 70 *Journal of Personality and Social Psychology 979* (1996).

Dietmeyer, B. & Kaplan, R., *Strategic Negotiation* (Dearborn Trade Pub. 2004).

Dimitrius, J.-E. & Mazzarella, M., *Reading People* (Random House 1998).

Docherty, J., "Culture and Negotiation: Symmetrical Anthropology for Negotiators," 87 *Marquette Law Review* 711 (2004).

Donaldson, M., *Fearless Negotiating* (McGraw-Hill 2007).

Donohue, W. & Taylor, P., "Role Effects in Negotiation: The One-Down Phenomenon," 23 *Negotiation Journal* 307 (2007).

Druckman, D., "Departures in Negotiation: Extensions and New Directions," 20 *Negotiation Journal* 185 (April 2004).

Druckman, D., *Negotiations: Social Psychological Perspectives* (Sage 1977).

Druckman, D., Rozelle, R. & Baxter, J., *Nonverbal Communication* (Sage 1982).

Dupont, C., "Coalition Theory: Using Power to Build Cooperation" in *International Multilateral Negotiation 148* (I.W. Zartman, ed.) (Jossey-Bass 1994).

Dupont, C., "International Business Negotiations" in *International Negotiation* (V. Kremenyuk, ed.) (Jossey-Bass 1991).

"Draft Principles for ADR Provider Organizations," 18 *Alternatives 109* (2000).

Eckel, C., de Oliveira, C.M., & Grossman, P., "Gender and Negotiation in the Small: Are Women (Perceived to Be) More Cooperative Than Men?" 24 *Negotiation Journal* 429 (2008)

Edwards, H. & White, J., *The Lawyer as a Negotiator* (West 1977).

Eisenberg, M., "Private Ordering Through Negotiation: Dispute- Settlement and Rulemaking," 89 *Harvard Law Review 637* (1976).

Ekman, P., *Telling Lies* (Norton 1992).

Ekman, P. & Friesen, W., *Unmasking the Face* (Prentice-Hall 1975).

Ekman, P., O'Sullivan, M. & Frank, M., "A Few Can Catch a Liar," 10 *Psychological Science 263* (May, 1999)

Ekman, P., O'Sullivan, M., Friesen, W. & Scherer, K., "Invited Article: Face, Voice, and Body in Detecting Deceit," 15 *Journal of Nonverbal Behavior 125* (Summer 1991)

Elgin, S., *The Gentle Art of Verbal Self-Defense* (Prentice- Hall 1980).

Elster, J., "Strategic Uses of Argument" in *Barriers to Conflict Resolution 236* (K. Arrow, R. Mnookin, L. Ross, A. Tversky & R. Wilson, eds.) (W.W. Norton 1995).

Epstein, L., "Cyber E-Mail Negotiation vs. Traditional Negotiation: Will Cyber Technology Supplant Traditional Means of Settling Litigation?" 36 *Tulsa Law Journal* 839 (2001).

Enderlin, C., *Shattered Dreams*(Other Press 2002).

English, C., "Mediator Immunity," 63 *George Washington Law Review 759* (1995).

Erickson, S. & McKnight, M., *The Practitioner's Guide to Mediation* (John Wiley & Sons 2001).

Evans, G., *Play Like a Man, Win Like a Woman* (Broadway Books 2000).

Evans, M. & Tyler-Evans, M., "Aspects of Grief in Conflict: Re-Visioning Response to Dispute," 20 *Conflict Resolution Quarterly* 83 (2002).

Fairman, C., "A Proposed Model Rule for Collaborative Law," 21 *Ohio State Journal on Dispute Resolution* 73 (2005).

Fairman, C., "Why We Still Need a Model Rule for Collaborative Law: A Reply to Professor Lande," 22 *Ohio State Journal on Dispute Resolution* 707 (2007).

Fang, T., *Chinese Business Negotiating Style* (Sage 1999).

Fassina, N., "Constraining a Principal's Choice: Outcome Versus Behavior Contingent Agency Contracts in Representative Negotiations," 20 *Negotiation Journal* 435 (2004).

Fast, J., *Body Language* (Pocket Books 1970).

Faure, G., "International Negotiation: The Cultural Dimension" in *International Negotiation* 392 (V. Kremenyuk, ed.) (Jossey-Bass 2d ed. 2002).

Faure, G. & Rubin, J., *Culture and Negotiation* (Sage Publications 1993).

Faure, G. & Sjustedt, G., "Culture and Negotiation: An Introduction" in *Culture and Negotiation 1* (G. Faure & J. Rubin, eds.) (Sage Publications 1993).

Fay, "Settlement Approaches," *Seminars for Newly Appointed United States District Judges 67* (1973–1975).

Felder, R., *Bare-Knuckle Negotiation* (John Wiley & Sons 2004).

Feldman, R., Forrest, J. & Happ, B., "Self-Promotion and Verbal Deception: Do Self-Presenters Lie More?" 24 *Basic and Applied Social Psychology* 163 (2002).

Firth, A., *The Discourse of Negotiation* (Pergamon 1995).

Fisher, R., "What About Negotiation as a Specialty?," 69 *American Bar Association Journal 1221* (1983).

Fisher, R., Kopelman, E. & Schneider, A., *Beyond Machiavelli* (Harvard Univ. Press 1994).

Fisher, R. & Shapiro, D., *Beyond Reason* (Viking 2005).

Fisher, R. & Ury, W., *Getting to Yes* (Houghton Mifflin 1981).

Fiss, O., "Against Settlement," 93 *Yale Law Journal 1073* (1984).

Folberg, J. & Golann, D., *Lawyer Negotiation Theory, Practice, and Law* (Aspen 2006).

Folberg, J. & Milne, A. & Salem, P., *Divorce and Family Mediation: Models, Techniques, and Applications* (Guilford 2004).

Folberg, J. & Taylor, A., *Mediation* (Jossey-Bass 1984).

Ford. C., *Lies! Lies!! Lies!!! The Psychology of Deceit* (American Psychiatric Press 1996).

Forester, J., "Responding to Critical Moments with Humor, Recognition, and Hope," 20 *Negotiation Journal* 221 (April 2004).

Forgas, J., "On Feeling Good and Getting Your way: Mood Effects on Negotiator Cognition and Bargaining Strategies," 74 *Journal of Personality and Social Psychology* 565 (1998).

Frank, M. & Ekman, P., "The Ability to Detect Deceit Generalizes Across Different Types of High-Stake Lies," 72 *Journal of Personality & Social Psychology* 1429 (1997).

Freeman, M., *Renegotiate with Integrity* (Freeman Bus. Books 2006).

Frenkel, D. & Stark, J., *The Practice of Mediation* (Wolters Kluwer 2008)

Freshman, C., Hayes, A. & Feldman, G., "The Lawyer-Negotiator as Mood Scientist: What We Know and Don't Know About How Mood Relates to Successful Negotiation," 2002 *Journal of Dispute Resolution* 13 (2002).

Freund, J., *The Acquisition Mating Dance and Other Essays on Negotiating* (Prentice Hall Law & Business 1987).

Freund, J., "Anatomy of a Split-Up: Mediating the Business Divorce," 52 *The Business Lawyer* 479 (1997).

Freund, J., *The Neutral Negotiator: Why and How Mediation Can Work to Resolve Dollar Disputes* (Prentice Hall Law & Bus. 1994).

Freund, J., *Smart Negotiating* (Simon & Schuster 1992).

Friedman, R. & Shapiro, D., "Deception and Mutual Gains Bargaining: Are They Mutually Exclusive?" 11 *Negotiation Journal* 243 (1995).

Fry, P. & Coe, K., "Achievement Performance of Internally and Externally Oriented Black and White High School Students Under Conditions of Competition and Cooperation Expectancies," 50 *British Journal of Educational Psychology 162* (1980).

Fuchs-Burnett, T., "Mass Public Corporate Apology," 57 *Dispute Resolution Journal* 27 (May–June 2002).

Galanter, M., "A World Without Trials?" 2006 *Journal of Dispute Resolution* 7 (2006).

Galinsky, A. & Mussweiler, T., "First Offers as Anchors: The Role of Perspective-Taking and Negotiator Focus," 81 *Journal of Personality and Social Psychology* 657 (2001).

Gelfand, M. & Brett, J., *The Handbook of Negotiation and Culture* (Stanford Bus. Books 2004).

Gelfand, M. & Dyer, "A Cultural Perspective on Negotiation: Progress, Pitfalls, and Prospects," 49 *Applied Psychology 62* (2000).

Gewurz, I., "(Re)Designing Mediation to Address the Nuances of Power Imbalance," 19 *Conflict Resolution Quarterly* 135 (2001).

Gibbons, L., Kennedy, R. & Gibbs, J., "Cyber-Mediation: Computer-Mediated Communications Medium Massaging the Message," 32 *New Mexico Law Review* 27 (2002).

Gifford, D., "A Context-Based Theory of Strategy Selection in Legal Negotiation," 46 *Ohio State Law Journal* 41 (1985).

Gifford, D., *Legal Negotiation: Theory and Applications* (West 2d ed. 2007).

Gifford, D., "The Synthesis of Legal Counseling and Negotiation Models: Preserving Client-Centered Advocacy in the Negotiation Context," 34 *U.C.L.A. Law Review* 811 (1987).

Gillespie, J., Thompson, L., Loewenstein, J. & Gentner, D., "Lessons from Analogical Reasoning in the Teaching of Negotiation," 15 *Negotiation Journal 363* (1999).

Gilligan, C., *In a Different Voice* (Harvard Univ. Press 1982).

Gilson, R. & Mnookin, R., "Disputing Through Agents: Cooperation and Conflict Between Lawyers in Litigation," 94 *Columbia Law Review* 509 (1994).

Goh, B.C., *Negotiating with the Chinese* (Dartmouth Pub. 1996).

Golann, D., "Death of a Claim: The Impact of Loss Reactions on Bargaining," 20 *Negotiation Journal* 539 (2004).

Golann, D., "Is Legal Mediation a Process of Repair — or Separation? An Empirical Study and Its Implications," 7 *Harvard Negotiation Law Review* 301 (2002).

Golann, D., *Mediating Legal Disputes* (Aspen Law & Bus. 1996).

Golann, D., "Variations in Mediation: How — and Why — Legal Mediators Change Styles in the Course of a Case," 2000 *Journal of Dispute Resolution 41* (2000).

Gold, J., "ADR Through a Cultural Lens: How Cultural Values Shape Our Disputing Processes," 2 *Journal of Dispute Resolution* 289 (2005).

Goldberg, S. & Brett, J., "An Experiment in the Mediation of Grievances," 106 *Monthly Labor Review No. 3, 23* (March 1983).

Golden, J., Moy, H.A. & Lyons, A., "The Negotiation Counsel Model: An Empathetic Model for Settling Catastrophic Personal Injury Cases," 13 *Harvard Negotiation Law Review* 211 (2008).

Goldfien, J. & Robbennolt, J., "What If the Lawyers Have Their Way? An Empirical Assessment of Conflict Strategies and Attitudes Toward Mediation Styles," 22 *Ohio State Journal on Dispute Resolution* 277 (2007).

Goldman, A., *Settling for More* (B.N.A. 1991).

Goldman, B., *The Science of Settlement* (ALI-ABA 2008).

Goldstein, C. & Weber, S., "The Art of Negotiating," 37 *New York Law School Law Review 325* (1992).

Goleman, D., *Emotional Intelligence* (Bantam 1995).

Goleman, D., *Social Intelligence* (Bantam 2006).

Goleman, D., *Working with Emotional Intelligence* (Bantam 1998).

Goodpaster, G., *A Guide to Negotiation and Mediation* (Transnational 1997).

Goodpaster, G., "A Primer on Competitive Bargaining," 1996 *Journal of Dispute Resolution 325* (1996).

Graham, J. & Sano, Y., *Smart Bargaining: Doing Business with the Japanese* (Harper Business 1989).

Gray, B., "Negotiating with Your Nemesis," 19 *Negotiation Journal* 299 (2003).

Grayson, G., "Mexico: A Love-Hate Relationship with North America" in *National Negotiating Styles 125* (H. Binnendijk, ed.) (Foreign Service Institute, U.S. Department of State 1987).

Greenhalgh, L., "The Case Against Winning in Negotiations," 3 *Negotiation Journal* 167 (1987).

Greig, F., "Propensity to Negotiate and Career Advancement: Evidence From an Investment Bank that Women Are on a 'Slow Elevator'," 24 *Negotiation Journal* 495 (2008).

Gross, S. & Syverud, K., "Getting to No: A Study of Settlement Negotiations and the Selection of Cases for Trial," 90 *Michigan Law Review* 319 (1991).

Guernsey, T., *A Practical Guide to Negotiation* (NITA 1996).

Guinier, L., Fine, M., & Balin, J., "Becoming Gentlemen: Women's Experiences at One Ivy League Law School," 143 *University of Pennsylvania Law Review 1* (1994).

Gulliver, P., *Disputes and Negotiations: A Cross-Cultural Perspective* (Academic Press 1979).

Guthrie, C., "Better Settle than Sorry: The Regret Aversion Theory of Litigation Behavior," 1999 *University of Illinois Law Review* 43 (1999).

Guthrie, C., "Framing Frivolous Litigation: A Psychological Theory," 67 *University of Chicago Law Review 163* (2000).

Guthrie, C., "The Lawyer's Philosophical Map and the Disputant's Perceptual Map: Impediments to Facilitative Mediation and Lawyering," 6 *Harvard Negotiation Law Review* 145 (2001).

Guthrie, C., "Panacea or Pandora's Box? The Costs of Options in Negotiation," 88 *Iowa Law Review* 601 (2003).

Guthrie, C., "Principles of Influence in Negotiation," 87 *Marquette Law Review* 829 (2004).

Guthrie, C., "Prospect Theory, Risk Preference, and the Law," 97 *Northwestern University Law Review* 1115 (2003).

Guthrie, C., Rachlinski, J. & Wistrich, A., "Inside the Judicial Mind," 86 *Cornell Law Review* 777 (2001).

Guthrie, C. & Saly, D., "The Impact of the Impact Bias on Negotiation," 87 *Marquette Law Review* 817 (2004).

Gutterman, S., *Collaborative Law: A New Model for Dispute Resolution* (Bradford Pub. 2004).

Hagberg, J., *Real Power* (Winston Press 1984).

Hahn, "Negotiating with the Japanese," *California Lawyer 21* (March 1982).

Hall, E., *The Hidden Dimension* (Anchor 1966).

Hall, E., *The Silent Language* (Anchor 1973).

Hall, J., *Nonverbal Sex Differences* (Johns Hopkins Univ. Press 1984).

Halpern, R., "Negotiation Blunders: Allowing Yourself to be Double-Bracketed," *Negotiator Magazine* (Oct. 2003) (http://www.negotiatormagazine.com).

Hammond, J., Keeney, R. & Raiffa, H., *Smart Choices* (Harvard Business School Press 1999).

Hamner, W. & Yukl, G., "The Effectiveness of Different Offer Strategies in Bargaining," in *Negotiations: Social Psychological Perspectives 137* (D. Druckman, ed.) (Sage 1977).

Hansen, M., "The New Rule Models," *ABA Journal* 50 (Jan. 2001)

Harges, B., "Mediator Qualifications: The Trend Toward Professionalization," 1997 *Brigham Young University Law Review 687* (1997).

Harper, R., Weins, A. & Matarazzo, J., *Nonverbal Communication: The State of the Art* (Wiley-Interscience 1978).

Harragan, B., *Games Mother Never Taught You* (Warner Books 1977).

Harrison, M., "France: The Diplomacy of a Self-Assured Middle Power" in *National Negotiating Styles 75* (H. Binnendijk, ed.) (Foreign Service Institute, U.S. Department of State 1987).

Harsanyi, J., "Bargaining and Conflict Situations in Light of a New Approach to Game Theory," in *Bargaining: Formal Theories of Negotiation 74* (O. Young, ed.) (Univ. of Illinois Press 1975).

Hartje, "Lawyer's Skills in Negotiations: Justice in Unseen Hands," 1984 *Missouri Journal of Dispute Resolution 119* (1984).

Hartwell, S., "Understanding and Dealing With Deception in Legal Negotiation," 6 *Ohio State Journal on Dispute Resolution*, 171 (1991).

Harvard Business Essentials, *Negotiation* (Harvard Bus. School Press 2003).

Hatta, T., Ohbuchi, K. & Fukuno, M., "An Experimental Study on the Effects of Exitability and Correctability on Electronic Negotiation," 23 *Negotiation Journal* 283 (2007).

Haussmann, B., "The ABA Ethical Guidelines for Settlement Negotiations: Exceeding the Limits of the Adversarial Ethic," 89 *Cornell Law Review* 1218 (2004).

Henden, D., Henden, R. & Herbig, P., *Cross-Cultural Business Negotiations* (Quorum 1996).

Henley, N., *Body Politics: Power, Sex, and Nonverbal Communication* (Prentice-Hall 1977).

Hensler, D., "A Glass Half Full, a Glass Half Empty: The Use of Alternative Dispute Resolution in Mass Personal Injury Litigation," 73 *Texas Law Review 1587* (1995).

Hensler, D., "Suppose It's Not True: Challenging Mediation Ideology," 2002 *Journal of Dispute Resolution* 81 (2002).

Hermann, G.N., *Plea Bargaining* (Lexis Nexis 2d ed. 2004).

Hermann, G.N., Cary, J. & Kennedy, J., *Legal Counseling and Negotiating: A Practical Approach* (Lexis Nexis 2001).

Hermann, P., *Better Settlements Through Leverage* (Aqueduct 1965).

Herman, M. & Kogan, N., "Effects of Negotiators' Personalities on Negotiating Behavior," in *Negotiations: Social Psychological Perspectives 247* (D. Druckman, ed.) (Sage 1977).

Heumann, M. & Hyman, J., "Negotiation Methods and Litigation Settlement Methods in New Jersey: 'You Can't Always Get What You Want'," 12 *Ohio State Journal on Dispute Resolution* 253 (1997).

Hodgson, J., Sano, Y. & Graham, J., *Doing Business with the New Japan* (Rowman & Littlefield 2000).

Hoffer, E., *The True Believer* (Harper & Row 1951).

Hogan, K., *The Psychology of Persuasion* (Pelican Pub. 1996).

Hogan, K. & Speakman, J., *Covert Persuasion* (John Wiley & Sons 2006).

Hollander-Blumoff, R. & Tyler, T., "Procedural Justice in Negotiation: Procedural Fairness, Outcome Acceptance, and Integrative Potential," 33 *Law & Social Inquiry* 473 (2008).

Honoroff, B. & Opotow, S., "Mediation Ethics: A Grounded Approach," 23 *Negotiation Journal* 155 (2007).

Hopmann & Walcott, "The Impact of External Stresses and Tensions on Negotiations," in *Negotiations: Social Psychological Perspectives 301* (D. Druckman, ed.) (Sage 1977).

Houston, & Sunstein, "Risk Assessment, Resource Allocation, and Fairness: Evidence from Law Students," 48 *Journal of Legal Education 496* (1998).

Hughes, S., "A Closer Look — The Case for a Mediation Confidentiality Privilege Still Has Not Been Made," 5 *Dispute Resolution Magazine* 14 (Winter 1998).

Hughes, S., "The Uniform Mediation Act: To the Spoiled Go the Privileges," 85 *Marquette Law Review* 9 (2001).

Hurder, A., "The Lawyer's Dilemma: To Be or Not To Be a Problem-Solving Negotiator," 14 *Clinical Law Review* 253 (2007).

Hyman, J., "Trial Advocacy and Methods of Negotiation: Can Good Trial Advocates Be Wise Negotiators?" 34 *U.C.L.A. Law Review* 863 (1987).

Ikle, F., *How Nations Negotiate* (Harper & Row 1964).

Ilich, J., *Dealbreakers and Breakthroughs* (John Wiley & Sons 1992).

Ilich, J., *Power Negotiating* (Addison-Wesley 1980).

Ilich, J., *The Art and Skill of Successful Negotiation* (Prentice Hall 1973).

Izumi, C. & La Rue, H., "Prohibiting 'Good Faith' Reports Under the Uniform Mediation Act: Keeping the Adjudication Camel Out of the Mediation Tent," 2003 *Journal of Dispute Resolution* 67 (2003).

Jandt, F., *Win-Win Negotiating: Turning Conflict into Agreement* (Wiley 1985).

Johnston, J. & Waldfogel, J., "Does Repeat Play Elicit Cooperation? Evidence From Federal Civil Litigation," 31 *Journal of Legal Studies* 39 (2002).

Jones, "E., Evidentiary Concepts in Labor Arbitration: Some Modern Variations on Ancient Legal Themes," 13 *U.C.L.A. Law Review 1241* (1966).

Jonsson, C., "Cognitive Theory" in *International Negotiation 229* (V. Kremenyuk, ed.) (Jossey-Bass 1991).

Kagel, S. & Kelly, K., *The Anatomy of Mediation* (B.N.A. 1989).

Kahane, D., "Dispute Resolution and the Politics of Cultural Generalization," *Negotiation Journal* 5 (Jan. 2003).

Kahneman, E., "New Challenges to the Rationality Assumption," 3 *Legal Theory* 105 (1997).

Kahneman, D., Knetsch & Thaler, "Experimental Tests of the Endowment Effect and the Coase Theorem," 98 *Journal of Political Economics* 1325 (1990).

Kahneman, D. & Tversky, A., "Conflict Resolution: A Cognitive Perspective" in *Barriers to Conflict Resolution 45* (K. Arrow, R. Mnookin, L. Ross, A. Tversky & R. Wilson eds.) (W.W. Norton 1995).

Kahneman, D. & Tversky, A., "Prospect Theory: An Analysis of Decision Under Risk," 47 *Econometrica 263* (1979).

Kaplow, L. & Shavell, S., *Decision Analysis, Game Theory, and Information* (Foundation Press 2004).

Karrass, C., *Give and Take* (Crowell 1974).

Karrass, C., *The Negotiating Game* (Crowell 1970).

Karrass, G., *Negotiate to Close* (Simon & Schuster 1985).

Kashy, D. & DePaulo, B., "Who Lies?" 70 *Journal of Personality and Social Psychology 1037* (1996).

Katsh, E., "Online Dispute Resolution" in *The Handbook of Dispute Resolution* 425 (Moffitt, M. & Bordone, R., eds.) (Jossey-Bass 2005).

Katsh, E. & Rifkin, J., *Online Dispute Resolution* (Jossey-Bass 2001).

Katz, L., *Principles of Negotiating International Business* (2008).

Kelley, T., *The Art of Innovation* (Doubleday 2001).

Kennedy, G., *Essential Negotiation* (The Economist 2004).

Kennedy, G., *Kennedy on Negotiation* (Gower 1998).

Kheel, T., *The Keys to Conflict Resolution* (Four Walls Eight Windows 1999).

Kirtley, A., "The Mediation Privilege's Transition from Theory to Implementation: Designing a Mediation Privilege Standard to Protect Mediation Participants, the Process and the Public Interest," 1995 *Journal of Dispute Resolution 1* (1995).

Kiser, R., Asher, M. & McShane, B., "Let's Not Make a Deal: An Empirical Study of Decision Making in Unsuccessful Settlement Negotiations," 5 *Journal of Empirical Legal Studies* 551 (2008).

Kochan, T. & Lipsky, D., *Negotiations and Change* (ILR Press 2003).

Kohn, A., *No Contest* (Houghton Mifflin 1986).

Kolb, D., *The Mediators* (MIT Press 1983).

Kolb, D., "More than Just a Footnote: Constructing a Theoretical Framework for Teaching About Gender in Negotiation," 16 *Negotiation Journal 347* (2000).

Kolb, D. & Associates, *When Talk Works: Profiles of Mediators* (Jossey-Bass 1994).

Kolb, D. & Putnam, L., "Negotiation Through a Gender Lens" in *The Handbook of Dispute Resolution* 135 (Moffitt, M. & Bordone, R., eds.) (Jossey-Bass 2005).

Kolb, D. & Williams, J., *Everyday Negotiation* (Jossey-Bass 2003).

Kolb, D. & Williams, J., *The Shadow Negotiation* (Simon & Schuster 2000).

Kolb, D. & Faure, G., "Organization Theory: The Interface of Structure, Culture, Procedures, and Negotiation Processes" in *International Multilateral Negotiation 113* (I.W. Zartman, ed.) (Jossey-Bass 1994).

Korda, M., *Male Chauvinism: How It Works* (Berkeley 1972).

Korda, M., *Power: How to Get It, How to Use It* (Random House 1975).

Korobkin, R.., "A Positive Theory of Legal Negotiation." 88 *Georgetown Law Journal 1789* (2000).

Korobkin, R., "Aspirations and Settlement," 88 *Cornell Law Review* 1 (2002).

Korobkin, R., "The Endowment Effect and Legal Analysis," 97 *Northwestern University Law Review* 1227 (2003).

Korobkin, R., *Negotiation Theory and Strategy* (Aspen Law & Bus. 2002).

Korobkin, R., "Psychological Impediments to Mediation Success: Theory and Practice," 21 *Ohio State Journal on Dispute Resolution* 281 (2006).

Korobkin, R., "The Role of Law in Settlement" in *The Handbook of Dispute Resolution* 254 (Moffitt, M. & Bordone, R., eds.) (Jossey-Bass 2005).

Korobkin, R. & Guthrie, C., "Heuristics and Biases at the Bargaining Table," 87 *Marquette Law Review* 795 (2004).

Korobkin, R. & Guthrie, C., "The Law of Bargaining," 87 *Marquette Law Review* 839 (2004).

Korobkin, R. & Guthrie, C., "Opening Offers and Out of Court Settlement: A Little Moderation Might Not Go a Long Way," 10 *Ohio State Journal on Dispute Resolution* 1 (1994).

Korobkin, R. & Guthrie, C., "Psychological Barriers to Litigation Settlement: An Experimental Approach," 93 *Michigan Law Review 107* (1994).

Korobkin, R. & Guthrie, C., "Psychology, Economics, and Settlement: A New Look at the Role of the Lawyer," 76 *Texas Law Review* 77 (1997).

Kovach, K., *Mediation: Principles and Practice* (West 3d ed. 2004).

Kovach, K., *Mediation: Principles and Practice* (West 2nd ed. 2000).

Kovach, K., "Musings on Idea(l)s in the Ethical Regulation of Mediators: Honesty, Enforcement, and Education," 21 *Ohio State Journal on Dispute Resolution* 123 (2005).

Kovach, K., "New Wine Requires New Wineskins: Transforming Lawyer Ethics for Effective Representation in a Non-Adversarial Approach to Problem-Solving: Mediation," 28 *Fordham Urban Law Journal* 935 (2001).

Kovach, K. & Love, L., "Evaluative Mediation is an Oxymoron," 14 *Alternatives to the High Cost of Litigation* 31 (1996).

Kramer, H., *Game, Set, Match: Winning the Negotiations Game* (ALM Pub. 2001).

Kray, L. & Babcock, L., "Gender in Negotiations: A Motivated Social Cognitive Analysis" in *Negotiation Theory and Research* 203 (L. Thompson, ed.) (Psychology Press 2006).

Kray, L. & Locke, C., "To Flirt or Not to Flirt? Sexual Power at the Bargaining Table," 24 *Negotiation Journal* 483 (2008).

Kray, L., Thompson, L. & Galinsky, A., "Battle of the Sexes: Gender, Stereotype Confirmation and Reactance in Negotiations," 80 *Journal of Personality and Social Psychology* 942 (2001).

Kremenyuk, V., *International Negotiation* (Jossey-Bass 1991).

Kremenyuk, V., *International Negotiation* (Jossey-Bass 2d ed. 2002).

Krieger, S., Neumann, R., McManus, K. & Jamar, S., *Essential Lawyering Skills* (Aspen Law & Bus. 1999).

Kritek, P., *Negotiating at an Uneven Table* (Jossey-Bass 1994).

Kritzer, H., *Let's Make a Deal* (Univ. of Wisconsin Press 1991).

Krivis, J., *Improvisational Negotiation* (Jossey-Bass 2006).

Krivis, J. & Zadeh, M., "Back to Deception: 'Winning' Mediation By Understanding Body Language," 24 *Alternatives to the High Cost of Litigation* 113 (2006).

Krohnke, D., "ADR Ethics Rules to be Added to Rules of Professional Conduct," 18 *Alternatives 108* (2000).

Kumar, R., "Negotiating With the Complex, Imaginative Indian," *Ivey Business Journal* 1 (March/April 2005).

Kurtzberg & Medvec, "Can We Negotiate and Still be Friends?" 15 *Negotiation Journal 355* (1999).

Ladd, P., *Mediation, Conciliation and Emotions* (Univ. Press of America 2005).

Laflin, M., "Preserving the Integrity of Mediation Through the Adoption of Ethical Rules for Lawyer-Mediators," 14 *Notre Dame Journal of Law, Ethics & Public Policy*

479 (2000).

Lande, J., "Possibilities for Collaborative Law: Ethics and Practice of Lawyer Disqualification and Process Control in a New Model of Lawyering," 64 *Ohio State Law Journal* 1315 (2003).

Lande, J., "Practical Insights From an Empirical Study of Cooperative Lawyers in Wisconsin," 2008 *Journal of Dispute Resolution* 203 (2008).

Lande, J., "Principles for Policymaking About Collaborative Law and Other ADR Processes," 22 *Ohio State Journal on Dispute Resolution* 619 (2007).

Lang, M. & Taylor, A., *The Making of a Mediator* (Jossey-Bass 2000).

Lang, W., "A Professional's View" in *Culture and Negotiation 38* (G. Faure & J. Rubin, eds.) (Sage Publications 1993).

Larrick, R. & Wu, G., "Claiming a Large Slice of a Small Pie: Asymmetric Disconfirmation in Negotiation," 93 *Journal of Personality and Social Psychology* 212 (2007).

Larson, D., "Technology Mediated Dispute Resolution (TMDR): A New Paradigm for ADR," 21 *Ohio State Journal on Dispute Resolution* 629 (2006a).

Larson, D., "Technology Mediated Dispute Resolution (TMDR): Opportunities and Dangers," 38 *University of Toledo Law Review* 213 (2006b).

Latz, M., *Gain the Edge: Negotiating to Get What You Want* (St. Martin's Press 2004).

Lawrence, J., "Mediation Advocacy: Partnering with the Mediator," 15 *Ohio State Journal on Dispute Resolution* 425 (2000).

Lax, D. & Sebenius, J., *The Manager as Negotiator: Bargaining for Cooperation and Competitive Gain* (Free Press 1986).

Lax, D. & Sebenius, J., *3-D Negotiation* (Harvard Bus. School Press 2006).

Lax, D. & Sebenius, J., "Three Ethical Issues in Negotiation," 2 *Negotiation Journal* 363 (1986).

Le Baron, M., *Bridging Cultural Conflicts* (Jossey-Bass 2003).

Le Baron, M., "Culture-Based Negotiation Styles" (2004) at http://www.beyondintractability.org/m/culture_negotiation.jsp

Lebow, R., *The Art of Bargaining* (Johns Hopkins University Press (1996).

Lee, I., "In Re Culture: The Cross-Cultural Negotiations Course in the Law School Curriculum," 20 *Ohio State Journal on Dispute Resolution* 375 (2005).

Le Poole, S., *Never Take No For an Answer* (Kogan Page 1991).

Levi, D., "The Role of Apology in Mediation," 72 *New York University law Review* 1165 (1997).

Levin, E., *Negotiating Tactics* (Fawcett 1980).

Levine, H., "Mediating the War of Olives and Pines: Consensus-Based Land-Use Planning in a Multicultural Setting," 21 *Negotiation Journal* 29 (2005).

Levinson, J., Smith, M. & Wilson, O., *Guerilla Negotiating* (Wiley 1999).

Lewicki, R. & Hiam. A., *Mastering Business Negotiation* (Jossey-Bass 2006).

Lewicki, R. & Litterer, J., Minton, J. & Saunders, D., *Negotiation* (Irwin 1994).

Lewicki, R., Litterer, J., Saunders, D. & Minton, J., *Negotiation: Readings, Exercises and Cases* (Irwin 1993).

Lewicki, R., Saunders, D. & Minton, J., *Negotiation: Readings, Exercises, and Cases* (Irwin McGraw-Hill 3rd ed. 1999).

Lewis, D., *Power Negotiating Tactics and Techniques* (Prentice-Hall 1981).

Lieberman, D., *Never Be Lied to Again* (St. Martins Griffin 1998).

Lisnek, P., *A Lawyer's Guide to Effective Negotiation and Mediation* (West 1993).

Llamazares, O., *How to Negotiate Successfully in 50 Countries* (Global Marketing 2008).

Lodder, A. & Zeleznikow, J., "Developing an Online Dispute Resolution Environment: Dialogue Tools and Negotiation Support Systems in a Three-Step Model," 10 *Harvard Negotiation Law Review* 287 (2005).

Love, L., "The Top Ten Reasons Why Mediators Should Not Evaluate," 24 *Florida State University Law Review* 937 (1997).

Love, L. & Cooley, J., "The Intersection of Evaluation by Mediators and Informed Consent: Warning the Unwary," 21 *Ohio State Journal on Dispute Resolution* 45 (2005).

Lowenthal, G., "A General Theory of Negotiation Process, Strategy, and Behavior," 31 *Kansas Law Review 69* (1982).

Lytle, A., Brett, J. & Shapiro, D., "The Strategic Use of Interests, Rights, and Power to Resolve Disputes," 15 *Negotiation Journal* 31 (1999).

Maccoby, E. & Jacklin, C., *The Psychology of Sex Differences* (Stanford Univ. Press 1974).

Macduff, I., "Your Place or Mine? Culture, Time, and Negotiation," 22 *Negotiation Journal* 31 (2006).

Macfarlane, J., "The Emerging Phenomenon of Collaborative Family Law (CFL): A Qualitative Study of CFL Cases (2005) http://www.justice.gc.ca/en/ps/pad/reports/2005-FCY-1.pdf

Mandonik, B., *I Hear What You Say, But What Are You Telling Me?* (Jossey-Bass 2001).

Maggiolo, W., *Techniques of Mediation in Labor Disputes* (Oceana 1972).

Malhotra, D. & Bazerman, M., *Negotiation Genius* (Bantam 2007).

Maoz, I., "Evaluating the Communication Between Groups in Dispute: Equality in Contact Interventions Between Jews and Arabs in Israel," 21 *Negotiation Journal* 131 (2005).

March, R., *The Japanese Negotiator: Subtlety and Strategy Beyond Western Logic* (Kodansha Intl. 1988).

March, R. & Wu, S.-H., *The Chinese Negotiator* (Kodansha Intl. 2007).

Marone, N., *Women and Risk* (St. Martins Press 1992).

Matz, D., "Ignorance of Interests," 4 *Harvard Negotiation Law Review 59* (1999).

Maxwell, D., "Gender Differences in Mediation Style and Their Impact on Mediator Effectiveness," 9 *Mediation Quarterly 353* (1992).

Mayer, B., *Beyond Neutrality* (Jossey-Bass 2004).

Mayer, B., *The Dynamics of Conflict Resolution: A Practitioner's Guide* (Jossey-Bass 2000).

Mayer, R., *How to Win Any Negotiation* (Career Press 2006).

Mayer, R., *Power Plays* (Times Bus. 1996).

Maynard, D., *Inside Plea Bargaining* (Plenum 1984).

Mayo, C. & Henley, N., *Gender and Nonverbal Behavior* (Springer-Verlag 1981).

Mc Adoo, B., "All Rise, the Court is in Session: What Judges Say About Court-Connected Mediation," 22 *Ohio State Journal on Dispute Resolution* 377 (2007).

Mc Adoo, B., "A Report to the Minnesota Supreme Court: The Impact of Rule 114 on Civil Litigation Practice in Minnesota," 25 *Hamline Law Review* 401 (2002).

Mc Adoo, B. & Hinshaw, A., "The Challenge of Institutionalizing Alternative Dispute Resolution: Attorney Perspectives on the Effect of Rule 17 on Civil Litigation in Missouri," 67 *Missouri Law Review* 473 (2002).

McCormack, M., *On Negotiating* (Dove Books 1995).

McCormack, M., *What They Don't Teach You at Harvard Business School* (Bantam 1984).

McDermott, E.P. & Obar, R., "'What's Going On' in Mediation: An Empirical Analysis of the Influence of a Mediator's Style on Party Satisfaction and Monetary Benefit," 9 *Harvard Negotiation Law Review* 75 (2004).

McDonald, J. & Bendahmane, D., *Conflict Resolution: Track Two Diplomacy* (Foreign Service Institute, U.S. Department of State 1987).

McEwen, C. & Wissler, R., "Finding Out If It Is True: Comparing Mediation and Negotiation Through Research," 2002 *Journal of Dispute Resolution* 131 (2002).

McGinn, K. & Croson, R., "What Do Communication Media Mean For Negotiators? A Question of Social Awareness" in *The Handbook of Negotiation and Culture* 334 (Gelfand, M. & Brett, J., eds.) (Stanford Business Books 2004).

McGuigan, R. & Popp, N., "The Self in Conflict: The Evolution of Mediation," 25 *Conflict Resolution Quarterly* 221 (2007).

McIntosh, P., "Feeling Like a Fraud," (Wellesley College 1985) (Paper Published by Stone Center for Developmental Services and Studies Works in Progress Series).

McKay, R., "Ethical Considerations in Alternative Dispute Resolution," 45 *Arbitration Journal 15* (Mar. 1990).

Medvec, V. & Galinsky, A., "Putting More on the Table: How Making Multiple Offers Can Increase the Final Value of the Deal," 8 *Negotiation* 4 (2005).

Mendelsohn, G, "Lawyers as Negotiators," 1 *Harvard Negotiation Law Review* 139 (1996). Menkel-Meadow, C., "Aha? Is Creativity in Legal Problem Solving and Teachable in Legal Education?" 6 *Harvard Negotiation Law Review* 97 (2001).

Menkel-Meadow, C., "The Art and Science of Problem-Solving Negotiation," *Trial 48* (June 1999).

Menkel-Meadow, C., "Ethics in ADR: The Many 'Cs' of Professional Responsibility and Dispute Resolution," 28 *Fordham Urban Law Journal* 979 (2001).

Menkel-Meadow, C., "For and Against Settlement: Uses and Abuses of the Mandatory Settlement Conference," 33 *U.C.L.A. Law Review 485* (1985).

Menkel-Meadow, C, "The Lawyer as Consensus Builder: Ethics for a New Practice," 70 *Tennessee Law Review* 63 (2002).

Menkel-Meadow, C.,"The Silences of the Restatement of the Law Governing Lawyers: Lawyering as Only Adversary Practice," 10 *Georgetown Journal of Legal Ethics 631* (1997).

Menkel-Meadow, C., "Teaching About Gender and Negotiation: Sex, Truths, and Videotape, " 16 Negotiation Journal 357 (2000).

Menkel-Meadow, C., "Toward Another View of Legal Negotiation: The Structure of Problem Solving," 31 *U.C.L.A. Law Review 754* (1984).

Menkel-Meadow, C., "Why Hasn't the World Gotten to Yes? An Appreciation and Some Reflections," 22 *Negotiation Journal* 485 (2006).

Menkel-Meadow, C. & Wheeler, M., *What's Fair: Ethics for Negotiators* (Jossey-Bass 2004).

Merrills, J., *International Dispute Settlement (Cambridge Univ. Press 1998)*.

Meyer, A., "Function of the Mediator in Collective Bargaining," 13 *Industrial & Labor Relations Review 159* (1960).

Miller, L. & Miller, J., *A Woman's Guide to Successful Negotiating* (McGraw-Hill 2002).

Mnookin, R., "Strategic Barriers to Dispute Resolution: A Comparison of Bilateral and Multilateral Negotiations," 8 *Harvard Negotiation Law Review* 1 (2003).

Mnookin, R., Peppet, S. & Tulumello, A., *Beyond Winning: Negotiating to Create Value in Deals and Disputes* (Harvard Univ. Press/Belknap 2000).

Mnookin, R., Peppett, S. & Tulumello, A., "The Tension Between Empathy and Assertiveness," 12 *Negotiation Journal* 217 (1996).

Mnookin, R. & Ross, L., "Introduction" in *Barriers to Conflict Resolution 2* (K. Arrow, R. Mnookin, L. Ross, A. Tversky & R. Wilson, eds.) (W.W. Norton 1995).

Moffitt, M., "Contingent Agreements: Agreeing to Disagree About the Future," 87 *Marquette Law Review* 691 (2004).

Moffitt, M., "Pleadings in the Age of Settlement," 80 *Indiana Law Journal* 727 (2005).

Moffitt, M., "Suing Mediators," 83 *Boston University Law Review* 147 (2003a).

Moffitt, M., "Ten Ways to Get Sued: A Guide for Mediators," 8 *Harvard Negotiation Law Review* 81 (2003b).

Moffitt, M. & Bordone, R., *The Handbook of Dispute Resolution* (Jossey-Bass 2005).

Montville, J., "The Arrow and the Olive Branch: A Case for Track Two Diplomacy" in *Conflict Resolution: Track Two Diplomacy 5* (J. McDonald & D. Bendahmane, eds.) (Foreign Service Institute, U.S. Department of State 1987).

Mookherjee, S.N., *Effective Negotiation* (Icfai Univ. Press 2007).

Moore, C., *The Mediation Process* (Jossey-Bass 3d ed. 2003).

Moran, R., *Getting Your Yen's Worth: How to Negotiate with Japan, Inc.* (Gulf 1984).

Morgan, T. & Rotunda, R., *Model Code of Professional Responsibility, Model Rules of Professional Conduct, and Other Selected Standards on Professional Responsibility* (Foundation Press 2008).

Morris, D., *Bodytalk* (Crown 1994).

Morris, M., Nadler, J., Kurtzberg, T. & Thompson, L., "Schmooze or Lose: Social Friction and Lubrication in E-Mail Negotiations," 6 *Group Dynamics: Theory, Research, and Practice* 89 (2002).

Morrison, T. & Conaway, W., *Kiss, Bow, or Shake Hands* (Adams Media 2006).

Mosten, F., "Collaborative Law Practice: An Unbundled Approach to Informed Client Decision Making," 2008 *Journal of Dispute Resolution* 163 (2008).

Movius, H., "The Effectiveness of Negotiation Training," 24 *Negotiation Journal* 509 (2008).

Murnighan, J.K., *Bargaining Games* (William Morrow 1992).

Musashi, M., *The Book of Five Rings* (T. Cleary, ed.) (Shambhala 1993).

Nadler, J., "Distributing Adventitious Resources: The Effects of Relationship and Grouping," 12 *Social Justice Research* 131 (1999).

Nadler, J., "Electronically-Mediated Dispute Resolution and E-Commerce," *Negotiation Journal* 333 (Oct. 2001).

Nadler, J., "Rapport in Negotiation and Conflict Resolution," 87 *Marquette Law Review* 875 (2004a).

Nadler, J., "Rapport in Legal Negotiation: How Small Talk Can Facilitate E-Mail Dealmaking," 9 *Harvard Negotiation Law Review* 223 (2004b).

Nadler, J. & Shestowsky, D., "Negotiation, Information Technology, and the Problem of the Faceless Other" in *Negotiation Theory and Research* 145 (L. Thompson, ed.) (Psychology Press 2006).

Neale, M. & Bazerman, M., *Cognition and Rationality in Negotiation* (Free Press 1991).

Neale, M. & Fragale, A., "Social Cognition, Attribution, and Perception in Negotiation: The Role of Uncertainty in Shaping Negotiation Processes and Outcomes" in *Negotiation Theory and Research* 27 (L. Thompson, ed.) (Psychology Press 2006).

Nelken, M., *Negotiation: Theory and Practice* (LexisNexis 2007).

Nelken, M., *Understanding Negotiation* (Anderson 2001).

Niederle, M. & Vesterlund, L., "Do Women Shy Away From Competition? Do Men Compete Too Much?" (2005) http://www.nber.org/papers/w11474

Niederle, M. & Vesterlund, L., "Gender Differences in Competition," 24 *Negotiation Journal* 447 (2008).

Nierenberg, G., *The Art of Negotiating* (Cornerstone 1968).

Nierenberg, G., *The Complete Negotiator* (Barnes & Noble 1996).

Nierenberg, G., *Fundamentals of Negotiating* (Cornerstone 1973).

Nierenberg, G. & Calero, H., *How to Read a Person Like a Book* (Cornerstone 1971).

Nierenberg, G. & Calero, H., *Meta-Talk* (Cornerstone 1981).

Nierenberg, J. & Ross, I., *Women and the Art of Negotiating* (Simon & Schuster 1985).

Nolan-Haley, J., *Alternative Dispute Resolution in a Nutshell* (West 1992).

Nolan-Haley, J., "Court Mediation and the Search for Justice Through Law," 74 *Washington University Law Quarterly* 47 (1996).

Nolan-Haley, J., "Informed Consent in Mediation: A Guiding Principle for Truly Educated Decisionmaking," 74 *Notre Dame Law Review* 775 (1999).

Norton, E., "Bargaining and the Ethic of Process," 64 *New York University Law Review* 493 (1989).

Novey, P. & Novey, T., "Don't Make Daddy Mad or Teaching Women How to Negotiate with Men," 13 *Transactional Analysis Journal* 97 (1983).

Oberman, S., "Mediation Theory vs. Practice: What Are We Really Doing? Re-Solving a Professional Conundrum," 20 *Ohio State Journal on Dispute Resolution* 775 (2005).

O'Brien, M., "At the Intersection of Public Policy and Private process: Court-Ordered Mediation and the Remedial Process in School Funding Litigation," 18 *Ohio State Journal on Dispute Resolution* 391 (2003).

O'Hara, E. & Yarn, D., "On Apology and Conscience," 77 *Washington Law Review* 1121 (2002).

O'Quin, K. & Aronoff, J., "Humor as a Technique of Social Influence," 44 *Social Psychology Quarterly* 349 (1981).

Ordover, A. & Doneff, A., *Alternatives to Litigation* (NITA 2002).

Orr, D. & Guthrie, C., "Anchoring, Information, Expertise, and Negotiation: New Insights from Meta-Analysis," 21 *Ohio State Journal on Dispute Resolution* 597 (2006).

Paplinger, E. & Menkel-Meadow, C., "ADR Ethics," *Dispute Resolution Magazine* 20 (Summer 1999).

Pavlick, D., "Apology and Mediation: The Horse and the Carriage of the Twenty-First Century," 18 *Ohio State Journal on Dispute Resolution* 829 (2003).

Pearlstein, A., "The Justice Bazaar: Dispute Resolution Through Emergent Private Ordering as a Superior Alternative to Authoritarian Court Bureaucracy," 22 *Ohio State Journal on Dispute Resolution* 739 (2007).

Pease, A. & Pease, B., *The Definitive Book of Body Language* (Bantam 2006).

Peck, C., *Cases and Materials on Negotiation* (B.N.A. 1980).

Peck, C. & Fletcher, R., "A Course on the Subject of Negotiation," 21 *Journal of Legal Education 196* (1968).

Peppet, S., "Lawyers' Bargaining Ethics, Contract, and Collaboration: The End of the Legal Profession and the Beginning of Professional Pluralism," 90 *Iowa Law Review* 475 (2005).

Peppet, S., "Contract Formation in Imperfect Markets: Should We Use Mediators in Deals?" 19 *Ohio State Journal on Dispute Resolution* 283 (2004).

Peppet, S., "Contractarian Economics and Mediation Ethics: The Case for Customizing Neutrality Through Contingent Fee Mediation," 82 *Texas Law Review* 227 (2003).

Peppet, S., "The Ethics of Collaborative Law," 2008 *Journal of Dispute Resolution* 131 (2008).

Peppet, S., "Lawyers' Bargaining Ethics, Contract, and Collaboration: The End of the Legal Profession and the Beginning of Professional Pluralism," 90 *Iowa Law Review* 475 (2005).

Perkins, A., "Negotiations: Are Two Heads Better Than One?" 71 *Harvard Business Review* 13 (Nov.–Dec. 1993).

Perschbacher, R., "Regulating Lawyers' Negotiations," 27 *Arizona Law Review 75* (1985).

Peters, G., "The Use of Lies in Negotiation," 48 *Ohio State Law Journal 1* (1987).

Phillips, B., *Finding Common Ground: A Field Guide to Mediation* (Hells Canyon Publishing 1994).

Phillips & Piazza, "Using Mediation to Resolve Disputes," *California Lawyer 11* (October 1983).

Phillips, J., "Mediation as One Step in Adversarial Litigation: One Country Lawyer's Experience," 2002 *Journal of Dispute Resolution* 143 (2002).

Phillips, B. & Piazza, A., "How to Use Mediation," 10 *Litigation* 31 (Spr. 1984).

Phillips, B. & Piazza, A., "Using Mediation to Resolve Disputes," *California Lawyer* 11 (Oct. 2002).

Pines, A., Gat, H. & Tal, Y., "Gender Differences in Content and Style of Argument Between Couples During Divorce Mediation," 20 *Conflict Resolution Quarterly* 23 (Fall 2002).

Pinkley, R. & Northcraft, G., *Get Paid What You're Worth* (St. Martins 2000).

Pitulla, J., "The Ethics of Secretly Taping Phone Conversations," *ABA Journal* 102 (Feb. 1994).

Pitulla, J., "Using the Ultimate Threat Against an Opposing Party," 78 *American Bar Association Journal 106* (Oct. 1992).

Posin, D., "Mediating International Business Disputes," 9 *Fordham journal of Corporate and Financial Law* 449 (2004).

Pratkanis, A. & Aronson, E., *Age of Propaganda* (W.H. Freeman 1991).

Prestia, P., "Decision Tree: Good Tool for Analysis," *Le Nouvelles 60* (March 1994).

Pruitt, D., *Negotiation Behavior* (Academic Press 1981).

Pruitt, D. & Rubin, J., *Social Conflict* (Random House 1986).

Putnam, L., "Transformations and Critical Moments in Negotiations," 20 *Negotiation Journal* 275 (2004).

Quandt, W., "Egypt: A Strong Sense of National Identity" in *National Negotiating Styles 105* (H. Binnendijk, ed.) (Foreign Service Institute, U.S. Department of State 1987).

Quilliam, S., *Body Language* (Firefly Books 2004).

Rachlinski, J., "Gains, Losses, and the Psychology of Litigation," 70 *Southern California Law Review* 113 (1996).

Rachlinski, J., "The Uncertain Psychological Case for Paternalism," 97 *Northwestern University Law Review* 1165 (2003).

Raiffa, H., *The Art and Science of Negotiation* (Belknap/ Harvard 1982).

Raiffa, H. (with J. Richardson & D. Metcalfe), *Negotiation Analysis* (Belknap/ Harvard Univ. Press. 2003).

Rapoport, A., *Strategy and Conscience* (Harper & Row 1964).

Rapoport, A., *Two-Person Game Theory* (Univ. of Michigan Press 1966).

Reardon, K., *The Skilled Negotiator* (Jossey-Bass 2004). Reich, J., "A Call for Intellectual Honesty: A Response to the Uniform Mediation Act's Privilege Against Disclosure," 2001 *Journal of Dispute Resolution* 197 (2001).

Reilly, P., "Teaching Law Students How to Feel: Using Negotiations Training to Increase Emotional Intelligence," 21 *Negotiation Journal* 301 (2005).

Relis, T., "Consequences of Power," 12 *Harvard Negotiation Law Review* 445 (2007).

Resnik, J., "Mediating Preferences: Litigant Preferences for Process and Judicial Preferences for Settlement," 2002 *Journal of Dispute Resolution* 155 (2002).

Reuben, R., "The Sound of Dust Settling: A Response to Criticisms of the UMA," 2003 *Journal of Dispute Resolution* 99 (2003).

Reubin, R. & Rogers, N., "Major Step Forward: Proposed Uniform Mediation Act Goes Public for Comments," *Dispute Resolution Magazine 18* (Summer 1999).

Rich, A., *Interracial Communication* (Harper & Row 1974).

Richardson, J., "How Negotiators Choose Standards of Fairness: A Look at the Empirical Evidence and Some Steps Toward a Process Model," 12 *Harvard Negotiation Law Review* 415 (2007).

Ringer, R., *To Be or Not to Be Intimidated?* (M. Evans & Co. 2004).

Ringer, R., *Winning Through Intimidation* (Fawcett 1973).

Riskin, L., "The Contemplative Lawyer: On the Potential Contributions of Mindfulness Meditation to Law Students, Lawyers, and Their Clients," 7 *Harvard Negotiation*

Law Review 601 (2002)

Riskin, L., "Decisionmaking in Mediation: The New Old Grid and the New New Grid System," 79 *Notre Dame Law Review* 1 (2003).

Riskin, L., "Who Decides What?" *Dispute Resolution Magazine* 22 (Winter 2003).

Robbennolt, J., "Apologies and Legal Settlement: An Empirical Examination," 102 *Michigan Law Review* 460 (2003).

Rogers, N., & McEwen, C., *Mediation: Law, Policy, Practice* (Lawyers Coop. & Clark Boardman Callaghan 2nd ed. 1994).

Rooney, G., "The Use of Intuition in Mediation," 25 *Conflict Resolution Quarterly* 239 (2007).

Ross, G., *Trump-Style Negotiation* (John Wiley & Sons 2006).

Ross, L., "Reactive Devaluation in Negotiation and Conflict Resolution" in *Barriers to Conflict Resolution 26* (K. Arrow, R. Mnookin, L. Ross, A. Tversky & R. Wilson, eds.) (W.W. Norton 1995).

Ross, L. & Stillinger, C., "Barriers to Conflict Resolution," 7 *Negotiation Journal* 389 (1991).

Rotunda, R., *Professional Responsibility* (West 1995).

Royce, T., "The Negotiator and the Bomber: Analyzing the Critical Role of Active Listening in Crisis Negotiations," 21 *Negotiation Journal* 5 (2005).

Rubin, A., "A Causerie on Lawyers' Ethics in Negotiation," 35 *Louisiana Law Review 577* (1975).

Rubin, A. & Will, H., "Some Suggestions Concerning the Judge's Role in Stimulating Settlement Negotiations," 75 *Federal Rules Decisions 227* (1977).

Rubin, J., "Psychological Traps," *Psychology Today 52* (March 1981).

Rubin, J. & Brown, B., *The Social Psychology of Bargaining and Negotiation* (Academic Press 1975).

Rubin, J. & Swap, W., "Small Group Theory: Forming Consensus Through Group Processes" in *International Multilateral Negotiation 132* (I.W. Zartman, ed.) (Jossey-Bass 1994).

Rubin, M., "The Ethics of Negotiations: Are There Any?" 56 *Louisiana Law Review 447* (1995).

Rubinson, R., "Client Counseling, Mediation, and Alternative Narratives of Dispute Resolution," 10 *Clinical Law Review* 833 (2004).

Rubinstein, R., "Cross-Cultural Considerations in Complex Peace Operations," *Negotiation Journal* 29 (Jan. 2003).

Ryan, E., "The Discourse Beneath: Emotional Epistemology in Legal Deliberation and Negotiation," 10 *Harvard Negotiation Law Review* 231 (2005).

Sabatino, J., "ADR as Litigation Lite': Procedural and Evidentiary Norms Embedded within Alternative Dispute Resolution," 47 *Emory Law Journal 1289* (1998).

Said, "The Mediator's Dilemma: The Legal Requirements Exception to Confidentiality Under the Texas ADR Statute," 36 *South Texas Law Review 579* (1995).

Salacuse, J., *The Global Negotiator* (Palgrave 2003).

Salacuse, J., "Implications for Practitioners" in *Culture and Negotiation 199* (G. Faure & J. Rubin, eds.) (Sage Publications 1993).

Salacuse, J., "Lessons for Practice" in *Power and Negotiation* 255 (Zartman, I.W. & Rubin, J., eds.) (University of Michigan Press 2002).

Salacuse, J., *Making Global Deals* (Houghton Mifflin 1991).

Salacuse, J., "Negotiating: The Top Ten Ways That Culture Can Affect Your Negotiation," *Ivey Business Journal* 1 (Sept./Oct. 2004).

Salacuse, J., "Your Place or Mine: Deciding Where to Negotiate," 8 *Negotiation* 7 (2005).

Samborn, H., "The Vanishing Trial," *ABA Journal* 24 (Oct. 2002).

Sammataro, J., "Business and Brotherhood, Can They Coincide? A Search Into Why Black Athletes Do Not Hire Black Agents," 42 *Howard Law Journal 535* (1999).

Savir, U., *The Process* (Random House 1998).

Sax, L., *Why Gender Matters* (Doubleday 2005).

Scali, J., "Backstage Mediation in the Cuban Missile Crisis" in *Conflict Resolution: Track Two Diplomacy 73* (J. McDonald & D. Bendahmane, eds.) (Foreign Service Institute, U.S. Department of State 1987).

Scanlon, K., *Mediator's Deskbook* (CPR Institute for Dispute Resolution 1999).

Schatzki, M., *Negotiation* (Signet 1981).

Schecter, J., *Russian Negotiating Behavior* (U.S. Instit. of Peace Press 1998).

Scheflen, A., *Body Language and the Social Order* (Prentice- Hall 1972).

Schelling, T., "An Essay on Bargaining," XLVI *The American Economic Review No. 3, 281* (June 1956).

Schelling, T. "An Essay on Bargaining," in *Bargaining: Formal Theories of Negotiation 319* (O. Young, ed.) (Univ. of Illinois Press 1975).

Schelling, T., *The Strategy of Conflict* (Oxford Univ. Press 1960).

Schneider, A., "Aspirations in Negotiation," 87 *Marquette Law Review* 675 (2004).

Schneider, A., "Building a Pedagogy of Problem-Solving: Learning to Choose Among ADR Processes," 5 *Harvard Negotiation Law Review* 113 (2000).

Schneider, A., "Effective Responses to Offensive Comments," 10 *Negotiation Journal 107* (1994).

Schneider, A., "Not Quite a World Without Trials: Why International Dispute Resolution is Increasingly Judicialized," 2006 *Journal of Dispute Resolution* 119 (2006).

Schneider, A., "Perception, Reputation and Reality," *Dispute Resolution Magazine* 24 (Summer 2000).

Schneider, A., "Shattering Negotiation Myths: Empirical Evidence on the Effectiveness of Negotiation Style," 7 *Harvard Negotiation Law Review* 143 (2002).

Schneider, A. & Honeyman, C., *The Negotiator's Fieldbook* (A.B.A. Sect. of Disp. Res. 2006).

Schneider, A. & Mills, N., "What Family Lawyers Are *Really* Doing When They Negotiate," 44 *Family Court Review* 612 (2006).

Schoonmaker, A., *Negotiate to Win* (Prentice Hall 1989).

Schreier, L., "Emotional Intelligence and Mediation Training," 20 *Conflict Resolution Quarterly* 99 (2002).

Schwartz, B., *The Paradox of Choice* (Harper Collins 2004).

Schweitzer, M. & Croson, R., "Curtailing Deception: The Impact of Direct Questions on Lies and Omissions," 10 *International Journal of Conflict Management* 225 (1999).

Schweitzer, S., *Winning With Deception and Bluff* (Prentice- Hall 1979).

Scott, B., *Negotiating* (Paradigm 1988).

Scott, B., *The Skills of Negotiating* (Wildwood House 1981).

Sebenius, J., "Caveats for Cross-Border Negotiators," 18 *Negotiation Journal* 121 (2002).

Senger, J., "Decision Analysis in Negotiation," 87 *Marquette Law Review* 723 (2004).

Shapiro, D., "Negotiating Emotions," 20 *Conflict Resolution Quarterly* 67 (2002).

Shapiro, D. & Bies, R., "Threats, Bluffs, and Disclaimers in Negotiations," 60 *Organizational Behavior and Human Decision Processes* 14 (1994).

Shapiro, R., *Dare to Prepare* (Crown Bus. 2008).

Shapiro. R. & Jankowski, M., *Bullies, Tyrants, and Impossible People* (Crown Bus. 2005).

Shapiro, R. & Jankowski, M., *The Power of Nice* (John Wiley & Sons 2001).

Shavell, S. *Economic Analysis of Law* (2004).

Shell, G.R., *Bargaining for Advantage* (Viking 1999).

Sher, B., *Wishcraft: How to Get What You Really Want* (Ballantine 1979).

Siegel, S. & Fouraker, L., *Bargaining and Group Decision Making* (McGraw-Hill 1976).

Sinclair, L. & Stuart, W., "Reciprocal-Influence Mediation Model: A Guide for Practice and Research," 25 *Conflict Resolution Quarterly* 185 (2007).

Singer, L., *Settling Disputes* (Westview Press 2nd ed. 1994).

Sjöstedt, G., "Asymmetry in Multilateral Negotiation Between North and South at UNCED" in *Power and Negotiation* 177 (Zartman, I.W. & Rubin, J., eds.) (University of Michigan Press 2002).

Sjöstedt, G., *Professional Cultures in International Negotiation* (Lexington Books 2003).

Skopec, E. & Kiely, L., *Everything's Negotiable* (Amacom 1994).

Slaikeu, K., *When Push Comes to Shove: A Practical Guide to Mediating Disputes* (Jossey-Bass 1996).

Sloss, L. & Davis, M., "The Soviet Union: The Pursuit of Power and Influence Through Negotiation" in *National Negotiating Styles 17* (H. Binnendijk, ed.) (Foreign Service Institute, U.S. Department of State 1987).

Small, D., Gelfand, M., Babcock, L. & Gettman, H., "Who Goes to the Bargaining Table? The Influence of Gender and Framing on the Invitation to Negotiate," 93 *Journal of Personality and Social Psychology* 600 (2007).

Smeltzer & Watson, "Gender Differences in Verbal Communication During Negotiations," 3 *Communication Research Reports* 74(1986).

Smith, M., *When I Say No, I Feel Guilty* (Bantam 1975).

Smith, R.F, *Negotiating With the Soviets* (Indiana Univ. Press 1989).

Smyser, W.R., *How Germans Negotiate* (U.S. Instit. of Peace Press 2003).

Solomon, R., *Chinese Negotiating Behavior* (U.S. Instit. of Peace Press 1999).

Solomon, R., "China: Friendship and Obligation in Chinese Negotiating Style" in *National Negotiating Styles 1* (H. Binnendijk, ed.) (Foreign Service Institute, U.S. Department of State 1987).

Stamato, L., "Voice, Place, and Process: Research on Gender, Negotiation, and Conflict Resolution," 9 *Mediation Quarterly 375* (1992).

Stanovich, K. & West, R., "On the Relative Independence of Thinking Biases and Cognitive Ability," 94 *Journal of Personality and Social Psychology* 672 (2008).

Stark, P. & Flaherty, J., *The Only Negotiating Guide You'll Ever Need* (Broadway Books 2003).

Steele, W., "Deceptive Negotiating and High-Toned Morality," 39 *Vanderbilt Law Review 1387* (1986).

Steinberg, L., *Winning with Integrity* (Random House 1999).

Stempel, J., "Beyond Formalism and False Dichotomies: The Need for Institutionalizing a Flexible Concept of the Mediator's Role," 24 *Florida State University Law Review 949* (1997).

Stempel, J., "The Inevitability of the Eclectic: Liberating ADR from Ideology," 2000 *Journal of Dispute Resolution* 247 (2000).

Sternlight, J. & Robbennolt, J., "Good Lawyers Should Be Good Psychologists: Insights for Interviewing and Counseling Clients," 23 *Ohio St. Journal on Dispute Resolution* 437 (2008).

Stiver, "Work Inhibitions in Women," (Wellesley College 1983) (Paper Published by Stone Center for Developmental Services and Studies Works in Progress Series).

Stone, D., Patton, B. & Heen, S., *Difficult Conversations* (Viking 1999).

Thorpe, W. & Yates, S., "An Overview of the Revised Model Standards of Conduct for Mediators," 12 *Dispute Resolution Magazine* 30 (2006).

Strauss, A., *Negotiations: Varieties, Contexts, Processes, and Social Order* (Jossey-Bass 1978).

Student Project, "Recent Developments: The Uniform Arbitration Act," 1999 *Journal of Dispute Resolution* 219 (1999).

Stuhlmacher, A. & Walters, A., "Gender Differences in Negotiation Outcome: A Meta-Analysis," 52 *Personnel Psychology 653* (1999).

Sullivan, B., O.Connor, K. & Burris, E., "Negotiator Confidence: The Impact of Self-Efficacy on Tactics and Outcomes," 42 *Journal of Experimental Social Psychology* 567 (2006).

Sun Tzu, *The Art of War* (J. Clavell, ed.) (Delta 1983).

Susskind, L., "Handle With Care: Negotiating Strategic Alliances," 8 *Negotiation* 1 (2005).

Symposium, "Standards of Professional Conduct in Alternative Dispute Resolution," 1995 *Journal of Dispute Resolution 95* (1995).

Taft, L., "Apology Subverted: The Commodification of Apology," 109 *Yale Law Journal 1135* (2000).

Tan, J.S. & Lim, E., *Strategies for Effective Cross-Cultural Negotiation* (McGraw Hill 2004).

Tannen, D., *Talking From 9 to 5* (William Morrow 1994).

Tannen, D., *That's Not What I Meant* (William Morrow 1986).

Tannen, D., *You Just Don't Understand* (William Morrow 1990).

Taylor, A., *The Handbook of Family Dispute Resolution* (Jossey-Bass 2002).

Temkin, B., "Misrepresentation by Omission in Settlement Negotiations: Should There Be a Silent Safe Harbor?" 18 *Georgetown Journal on Legal Ethics* 179 (2004).

Teply, L., *Legal Negotiation in a Nutshell* (West 2d ed. 2005).

Tesler, P., *Collaborative Law: Achieving Effective Resolution in Divorce Without Litigation* (A.B.A. Sect. of Family Law 2001).

Thayer, N. & Weiss, S., "Japan: The Changing Logic of a Former Minor Power," in *National Negotiating Styles 45* (H. Binnendijk, ed.) (Center for Study of Foreign Affairs, U.S. Department of State 1987).

Thomas, J., *Negotiate to Win* (Collins 2005).

Thompson, L., *The Mind and Heart of the Negotiator* (Prentice Hall 3d ed. 2005).

Thompson, L. & DeHarpport, "Social Judgment, Feedback, and Interpersonal Learning in Negotiation," 58 *Organizational Behavior and Human Decision Processes* 327 (1994).

Thompson, L., Levine, J. & Messick, D., *Shared Cognition in Organizations* (Lawrence Erlbaum Assoc. 1999).

Thompson, L. & Nadler, J., "Negotiating Via Information Technology: Theory and Application," 58 *Journal of Social Issues* 109 (2002).

Thompson, L., Nadler, J. & Kim, P., "Some Like It Hot: The Case For the Emotional Negotiator" in *Shared Cognition in Organizations: The Management of Knowledge* 139 (Thompson. L., Levine, J. & Messick, D., eds.) (Lawrence Erlbaum 1999).

Thompson, L., Neale, M. & Sinaceur, M., "The Evolution of Cognition and Biases in Negotiation Research: An Examination of Cognition, Social Perception, Motivation, and Emotion" in *The Handbook of Negotiation and Culture* 7 (Gelfand, M. & Brett, J., eds.) (Stanford Bus. Books 2004).

Tinsley, C., O'Connor, K. & Sullivan, B., "Tough Guys Finish Last: The Perils of a Distributive Reputation," 88 *Organizational Behavior and Human Decision Processes* 621 (2002).

Tone, "The Role of the Judge in the Settlement Process," *Seminars for Newly Appointed United States District Judges 57* (1973–1975).

Tonn, J., *Mary P. Follett* (Yale Univ. Press 2003).

Tornquist, L., "The Active Judge in Pretrial Settlement: Inherent Authority Gone Awry," 25 *Willamette Law Review 743* (1989).

Trachte-Huber, E.W. & Huber, S., *Mediation and Negotiation* (Anderson 1998).

Tversky, A. & Kahneman, D., "The Framing of Decisions and the Psychology of Choice," 211 *Science 453* (1981).

"The Uniform Mediation Act," 22 *Northern Illinois University Law Review* 165 (2002).

"Uniform Mediation Act Symposium," 2003 *Journal of Dispute Resolution* 1 (2003).

Ury, W., *Getting to Peace* (Viking 1999).

Ury, W., *Getting Past No* (Bantam Books 1991).

Ury, W., *The Power of a Positive No* (Bantam 2007).

Ury, W., Brett, J. & Goldberg, S., *Getting Disputes Resolved* (Harvard Program on Negotiation 1993).

Van Boven, L., Gilovich, T. & Medvec, V., "The Illusion of Transparency in Negotiations," 19 *Negotiation Journal* 117 (2003).

Van Kleef, G., De Dreu, C. & Manstead, A., "The Interpersonal Effects of Anger and Happiness in Negotiations," 86 *Journal of Personality and Social Psychology* 57 (2004).

Van Zandt, H., "How to Negotiate in Japan," *Harvard Business Review 45* (November-December 1970).

Volkema, R., *Leverage* (Amacom 2006).

Volkema, R., *The Negotiation Toolkit* (Amacom 1999).

Von Neumann, J. & Morgenstern, O., *Theory of Games and Economic Behavior* (Princeton Univ. Press 1944, 1972).

Vrij, A., *Detecting Lies and Deceit* (John Wiley & Sons 2000).

Vrij, A., Edward, K., Roberts, K. & Bull, R., "Detecting Deceit Via Analysis of Verbal and Nonverbal Behavior," 24 *Journal of Nonverbal Behavior* 239 (2000).

Vuorela, T., "Laughing Matters: A Case Study of Humor in Multicultural Business Negotiations," 21 *Negotiation Journal* 105 (2005).

Wall, Rude & Schiller, "Judicial Participation in Settlement," 1984 *Missouri Journal of Dispute Resolution 25* (1984).

Walton, R. & McKersie, R., *A Behavioral Theory of Labor Negotiations* (McGraw-Hill 1965).

Wanis-St. John, A., "Back-Channel Negotiation: International Bargaining in the Shadows," 22 *Negotiation Journal* 119 (2006).

Warren, R., "American Friends Service Committee Mediation Efforts in Germany and Korea" in *Conflict Resolution: Track Two Diplomacy 27* (J. McDonald & D. Bendahmane, eds.) (Foreign Service Institute, U.S. Department of State 1987).

Warschaw, T., *Winning By Negotiation* (McGraw-Hill 1980).

Watkins, M., "Principles of Persuasion," 17 *Negotiation Journal* 115 (April. 2001).

Watkins, M., *Shaping the Game* (Harvard Bus. School Press 2006).

Watkins, M. & Rosegrant, S., *Breakthrough in International Negotiation* (Jossey-Bass 2001).

Watson, A., "Mediation and Negotiation: Learning to Deal with Psychological Responses," 18 *University of Michigan Journal of Law Reform* 293 (1985).

Watts, "Briefing the American Negotiator in Japan," 16 *International Lawyer 597* (1982).

Webb, S. & Ousky, R., *The Collaborative Way to Divorce: The Revolutionary Method That Results in Less Stress, Lower Costs, and Happier Kids — Without Going to Court* (Hudson Street Press 2006).

Weckstein, D., "Mediator Certification: Why and How," 30 *University of San Francisco Law Review 757* (1996).

Welsh, N., "Disputants' Decision Control in Court-Connected Mediation: A Hollow Promise Without Procedural Justice," 2002 *Journal of Dispute Resolution* 179 (2002).

Welsh, N., "Making Deals in Court-Connected Mediation: What's Justice Got to Do With It?" 79 *Washington University Law Quarterly* 787 (2001).

Welsh, N., "The Place of Court-Connected Mediation in a Democratic Justice System," 5 *Cardozo Journal of Conflict Resolution* 117 (2004a).

Welsh, N., "Perspectives of Fairness in Negotiation," 87 *Marquette Law Review* 753 (2004b).

Welsh, N., "Reconciling Self-Determination, Coercion, and Settlement in Court-Connected Mediation" in *Divorce and Family Mediation: Models, Techniques, and Applications* 420 (Folberg, J., Milne, A. & Salem, P., eds.) (Guilford 2004c).

Welsh, N., "Stepping Back Through the Looking Glass: Real Conversations with Real Disputants About Institutionalized Mediation and Its Value," 19 *Ohio State Journal on Dispute Resolution* 573 (2004d).

Wenke, R., *The Art of Negotiation for Lawyers* (Richter 1985).

Wetlaufer, G., "The Ethics of Lying in Negotiations," 75 *Iowa Law Review 1219* (1990).

Wetlaufer, G., "The Limits of Integrative Bargaining," 85 *Georgetown Law Review 369* (1996).

White, J., "The Lawyer as a Negotiator: An Adventure in Understanding and Teaching the Art of Negotiation," 19 *Journal of Legal Education 337* (1967).

White, J., "Machiavelli and the Bar: Ethical Limitations on Lying in Negotiation," 1980 *American Bar Foundation Research Journal 926* (1980).

White, S. & Neale, M., "The Role of Negotiator Aspirations and Settlement Expectations in Bargaining Outcomes," 57 *Organizational Behavior and Human Decision Processes 303* (1994).

Will, H., Merhige, R. & Rubin, A., *The Role of the Judge in the Settlement Process* (1983).

Will, H. Merhige, R. & Rubin, A., "The Role of the Judge in the Settlement Process," 75 *Federal Rules Decisions 203* (1977).

Williams, G., *A Lawyer's Handbook for Effective Negotiation and Settlement* (4th ed. 1992).

Williams, G., *Legal Negotiation and Settlement* (West 1983).

Williams, G., "Negotiation as a Healing Process," 1996 *Journal of Dispute Resolution 1* (1996).

Williams, G. & Craver, C., *Legal Negotiating* (Thomson/West 2007).

Wilson. T. & Gilbert, D., "Affective Forecasting," 35 *Advances in Social Psychology* 345 (2003).

Winkler, J., *Bargaining for Results* (Facts on File 1984).

Wiseman, V. & Poitras, J., "Mediation Within a Hierarchical Structure: How Can It Be Done Successfully?" 20 *Conflict Resolution Quarterly* 51 (2002).

Wissler, R., "Barriers to Attorneys' Discussion and Use of ADR," 19 *Ohio State Journal on Dispute Resolution* 459 (2004).

Wistrich, A., Guthrie, C. & Rachlinski, J., "Can Judges Ignore Inadmissible Information? The Difficulty of Deliberately Disregarding," 153 *University of Pennsylvania Law Review* 1251 (2005).

Wittes, T., *How Israelis and Palestinians Negotiate* (U.S. Instit. of Peace Press 2005).

Woolf, B., *Friendly Persuasion* (G.P. Putnam's Sons 1990).

Young, K., *Negotiating with the Chinese Communists: The United States Experience, 1953–1967* (McGraw-Hill 1968).

Young, M., "Sharks, Saints, and Samurai: The Power of Ethics in Negotiations," 24 *Negotiation Journal* 145 (2008).

Young, O., *Bargaining: Formal Theories of Negotiation* (Univ. of Illinois Press 1975).

Young, O., "Strategic Interaction and Bargaining," in *Bargaining: Formal Theories of Negotiation 3* (O. Young, ed.) (Univ. of Illinois Press 1975).

Young, P., "Rejoice! Rejoice! Rejoice, Give Thanks, and Sing: ABA, ACR, and AAA Adopt Revised Model Standards of Conduct for Mediators," 5 *Appalachian Journal of Law*, 195 (2006a).

Young, P., "Take It or Leave It. Lump It or Grieve It: Designing Mediator Complaint Systems that Protect Mediators, Unhappy Parties, Attorneys, Courts, the Process, and the Field," 21 *Ohio State Journal on Dispute Resolution* 721 (2006b).

Zartman, I.W., *The Fifty Percent Solution* (Doubleday 1976).

Zartman, I.W., *International Multilateral Negotiation* (Jossey-Bass 1994).

Zartman, I.W., "Introduction: Two's Company and More's a Crowd: The Complexities of Multilateral Negotiation" in *International Multilateral Negotiation 1* (I.W. Zartman, ed.) (Jossey-Bass 1994).

Zartman, I.W., *The Negotiation Process: Theories and Applications* (Sage 1978).

Zartman, I.W., *Power and Negotiation* (Univ. of Michigan Press 2002).

Zartman, I.W., "A Skeptic's View" in *Culture and Negotiation 17* (G. Gaure & J. Rubin, eds.) (Sage Publications 1993).

Zartman, I.W. & Berman, M., *The Practical Negotiator* (Yale Univ. Press 1982).

Zwier, P. & Guernsey, T., *Advanced Negotiation and Mediation Theory and Practice* (N.I.T.A. 2005).

Zylstra, A., "Mediation and Domestic Violence: A Practical Screening Method for Mediators and Mediation Program Administrators," 2001 *Journal of Dispute Resolution* 253 (2001).

INDEX

[References are to section numbers.]

A

AAA STANDARDS
Mediation/assisted negotiation (See
MEDIATION/ASSISTED NEGOTIATION, subhead:
Standards of Conduct for Mediators)

ABA STANDARDS
Mediation/assisted negotiation (See
MEDIATION/ASSISTED NEGOTIATION, subhead:
Standards of Conduct for Mediators)

ADJUDICATOR AS PRETRIAL MEDIATOR
Mediation/assisted negotiation (See
MEDIATION/ASSISTED NEGOTIATION)

ADMINISTRATIVE AGENCIES (See REGULA-
TION NEGOTIATION/MEDIATION)

ADVERSARIAL METHODOLOGY (See
COMPETITIVE/ADVERSARIAL STYLE)

ADVERSITY, DEALING WITH
Abrasive tactics, professional response to . . . 7.03[3]
Contingent agreements for future uncertainties, use of
. . . 7.03[10]
Difficult personalities
    Attitudinal bargaining . . . 12.06[2]
    Inevitability of dealing with . . . 12.06[1]
    Setting good example and other strategies
        . . . 12.06[3]
Directed questions inducing problem-solving mindset
. . . 7.03[5]
Envisioning oneself in adversary's position
    Active listening . . . 7.03[9][a]
    Contentious topics, resting . . . 7.03[9][b]
    Participants in negotiation, changing
        . . . 7.03[9][c]
    Recessing temporarily . . . 7.03[9][d]
Focus of discussions, changing . . . 7.03[7]
Future uncertainties, contingent agreements for dealing
with . . . 7.03[10]
Impasse, risk of . . . 7.03[6]
Nonsettlement options . . . 7.03[1], [2]
Problem-solving mindset, directed questions inducing
. . . 7.03[5]
Professional response to abrasive tactics . . . 7.03[3]
Questioning skills, trust elicited through . . . 7.03[4]
Setting, changing . . . 7.03[8]
Trust elicited through questioning skills . . . 7.03[4]

AGENDA, CONTROL OF
Power bargaining (See POWER BARGAINING)

AGGRESSIVE BEHAVIOR
Anger (See ANGER)
Beneficial impact . . . 10.02[16][a]
Defense . . . 10.02[16][c]
Gender differences . . . 10.02[16][d]

AGGRESSIVE BEHAVIOR—Cont.
Gladiator personalities . . . 12.18[3][c]
Japanese dislike of overt conflict . . . 15.07[4][e][i]
Passive-aggression (See PASSIVE-AGGRESSION)
Responses of opponent, monitoring . . . 10.02[16][b]

ALTERNATIVE DISPUTE RESOLUTION
Mediation/assisted negotiation (See
MEDIATION/ASSISTED NEGOTIATION)

AMBIGUITY, CONSTRUCTIVE
Power bargaining . . . 7.04[2][m]

ANGER
Defense . . . 10.02[15][d]
Feigned anger, care in usage of . . . 10.02[15][c]
Purpose . . . 10.02[15][a]
Real anger, danger of . . . 10.02[15][b]

ANXIETY
Closing stage . . . 8.01[2]
Humor to relieve, use of . . . 7.04[2][d][iii][B]

APOLOGY
Benefits of . . . 5.03[5]

ARBITRATION
Procedure . . . 15.05[10][b]
Selection of arbitrator . . . 15.05[10][a]

ARGUMENT
Power bargaining (See POWER BARGAINING)

ASSISTED NEGOTIATION (See
MEDIATION/ASSISTED NEGOTIATION)

ATTITUDINAL BARGAINING
Benefits of . . . 5.03[4]
Difficult personalities, dealing with . . . 12.06[2]
Transnational business negotiations . . . 15.05[7]

ATTORNEYS
Authority (See AUTHORITY TO BARGAIN)
Client, continuation of interactions with . . . 6.01[2][i]
Conflict of interest, attorney-client . . . 17.03
Misrepresentations (See DECEPTION)
Needs of . . . 2.01[2]
Negotiation counsel model
    Early investigation and expeditious assistance
        . . . 12.19[1]
    Exploitation by adversarial opponent, avoiding
        . . . 12.19[2]
Opinions of counsel vs. statement of material fact
. . . 17.01[5][e]
Opposing counsel (See OPPOSING COUNSEL)
Perspectives, influence on client choices of attorney
. . . 3.01[12]
Preparing to negotiate (See PREPARATION)

ATTRIBUTION BIAS
Generally . . . 3.01[10]

[References are to section numbers.]

[References are to section numbers.]

[References are to section numbers.]

[References are to section numbers.]

[References are to section numbers.]

[References are to section numbers.]

[References are to section numbers.]

[References are to section numbers.]

[References are to section numbers.]

[References are to section numbers.]

[References are to section numbers.]

[References are to section numbers.]

T

[References are to section numbers.]